Modern Real Estate Practice In New York

FOR SALESPERSONS AND BROKERS

SIXTH EDITION

EDITH LANK with
JUDITH DEICKLER, Consulting Editor

Review Board:
Joseph A. Sullivan, William Jay Lipman

Real Estate Education Company®
a division of Dearborn Financial Publishing, Inc.

This publication is designed to provide accurate and authoritative information in regard to the subject matter covered. It is sold with the understanding that the publisher is not engaged in rendering legal, accounting, or other professional service. If legal advice or other expert assistance is required, the services of a competent professional person should be sought.

Publisher: Carol L. Luitjens
Senior Acquisitions Editor: Diana Faulhaber
Managing Editor: Ronald J. Liszkowski
Art Manager: Lucy Jenkins

Published by Real Estate Education Company®,
a division of Dearborn Publishing, Inc.®
155 North Wacker Drive
Chicago, Illinois 60606-1719
(312) 836-4400
http://www.real-estate-ed.com

Printed in the United States of America.

98 99 10 9 8 7 6 5 4 3

Library of Congress Cataloging-in-Publication Data

Lank, Edith.
    Modern real estate practice in New York : for salespersons and
brokers / Edith Lank with Judith Deickler. — 6th ed.
        p.   cm.
    Includes index.
    ISBN 0-7931-2414-X
    1. Vendors and purchasers—New York (State)   2. Real estate
business—Law and Legislation—New York (State)   3. Real estate
development—Law and Legislation—New York (State)   I. Deickler,
Judith. II. Title.
KFN5166.L36   1997   97-3695
346.74704'37—dc21   CIP

Contents

Preface

The sixth edition of *Modern Real Estate Practice in New York* is dedicated to hundreds of thousands of real estate students and instructors whose enthusiastic acceptance has made it the best-selling real estate textbook in the Empire State. Once again, many valuable suggestions for the new edition have come from those who use the book.

Those suggestions have always played a great part in the evolution of the text. For the Sixth Edition, we paid particular attention to your classroom needs with our revised table of contents. We also made every effort to make this textbook learning-friendly, using classroom-tested features such as highlighted key terms and concepts and margin notes. Of course, all state–mandated topics for both the sales and the brokers course are included in the text.

The author would like to thank Judith J. Deckler, GRI, her Consulting Editor, for the many hours devoted to making this the best edition yet of *Modern Real Estate Practice in New York*. For the Sixth Edition, we were also very ably assisted by an experienced, talented review board comprised of Joseph A. Sullivan, Noreast Real Estate Group and William Jay Lipman, New York University Real Estate Institute.

The author is particularly grateful to Arthur Elfenbein, New York University Real Estate Institute, for his unflagging support and assistance on this and previous editions of the text and to Babette Yuhas.

Special thanks also go to Eileen F. Taus, Westchester County Board of REALTORS®; Frank Langone, Joseph Sabella, and Anthony Agelire, RETC of Greater New York; Jane A. Wilson, EA, The American Real Estate School and Mary Manfred, Real Estate Learning Center, Inc.

The author would also like to thank the following instructors for their assistance with this edition: Peter A. Karl, III, SUNY Institute of Technology, Anthony J. DiChiara, GRI, ME, MS, Niagara University; Wendy A. Tilton, New York University; Uri Shamir, Queens College; James V. Pugliese, CRB, GRI, Coldwell Banker Prime Properties; Richard J. Sobelsohn, The Sobelsohn School; Samuel J. Irlander, New York University Real Estate Institute; D. J. Sperano, Fingerlakes Community College/Corning Community College; Anna Y. Tam, American Real Estate School; Michael K. Brady, IFA, RAM, State University of New York; James R. Trevitt, Broome County Board of REALTORS®; Michael D. Jesmer, Syracuse Real Estate, Inc.; and Richard Levin, Don Milton, and David M. Alexander, all of the Greater Rochester Association of REALTORS®.

Special contributions to earlier editions came from George M. Vaughn, GRI, CRB, CRS, LTG, Anthony Agelire, Paul Desseault, Thomas E. DeCelle, Rolando Santiago, Charles E. Davis, Beverly L. Deickler, Esq.; Peter Karl III; Leon Katzen, Esq.; William Lang, Jr.; George Lasch; John Mataraza; James Myers, Esq.; Thomas Thomassian; Dorothy Tymon and Chris E. Wittstruck, Esq.

Assistance and encouragement has also been gratefully received from Gail Bates, Mary Anne Moore, William Stavola, Willard Roff and Joseph Amello of the New York Department of State; Charles M. Staro, Georgianne Bailey and Mark Morano of the New York State Association of REALTORS®, Bonnie May and Thomas R. Viola of the State Division of Housing and Community Renewal; Liz Duncan and Jeff Lubar with the National Association of REALTORS®, P. Gilbert Mercurio of the Westchester County Board of REALTORS®, John Piper and Sandra Kleps of the Greater Rochester Association of REALTORS®; bankers Rose Bernstein and Gaye Greene; and Real Estate Education Company's Robert Kyle and Anita Constant, who first sponsored this book. Carol Luitjens, Ruth Curran, Ron Liszkowski and Diana Faulhaber helped this sixth edition through the editorial process.

Valuable help has also come from attorneys Michael Wallender, counsel to the New York State Association of REALTORS®, Paul Anderson, Abraham Berkowitz, Demetrios Coritsidis, Donald Friedman, Harold Geringer, David Henehan, Benjamin Henszey, Ezra Katzen, James Loeb, Robert Mendohlson, Joseph M. O'Donnell, Louis Ryen, Karen Schafer, Sally Smith, Christine Van Benschoten and Garrett Lacara.

Among REALTORS® who offered suggestions and assistance are Ronald Baroody, Thomas Carozza, John Cyr, Barry Deickler, Ruth De Roo, Thomas Galvin, Harold Kahn, Norman Lank, William Lester, Robert Michaels, John Sobeck, Michael Stucchio, John Tyo, Thomas Wills III, Rex Vail, Jeff Wolk and Rita Scharg.

Thanks are due also to instructors John Alberts, Professor Kenneth Beckerink, Cindy Faire, Jim Foley, John Keaton, Eli Kimels, Nicholas Morabito, Joseph O'Donnell, Edween Reagh, Alvin Schwartz, Professor U. Shamir, Marcia Spada, Larry Rockefeller, Jonathan Easterling, Marie Esposito, Richard Fuchs, Irving Levine, Stephen Mendolla, Selwyn Price, Professor Patrick Falci and Dominic Telesco.

Instructors are encouraged to write to the publisher on school letterheads for the complimentary instructor's manual that accompanies this textbook. The author would also like to recommend to them the National Real Estate Educators Association, 11 South LaSalle Street, Suite 1400, Chicago, IL 60603-1210. The association offers workshops, publications and conferences and has a chapter in New York State.

Part of the fascination of the real estate field is the way it changes and adapts to new economic and social conditions. The author always enjoys discussing new information, suggestions and criticism with students and instructors who write:

Edith Lank
240 Hemingway Drive
Rochester, NY 14620

About the Author

Edith Lank has been a licensed broker in New York for more than 25 years and has taught real estate at St. John Fisher College. Her award-winning weekly column on real estate, distributed by the Los Angeles Times Syndicate, has appeared in newspapers in Buffalo, Rochester, Syracuse, Schenectady, Amsterdam, Elmira, Brooklyn, Binghamton, Kingston, Ithaca, Middletown, Westchester and Rockland counties and Long Island, as well as in 100 other newspapers around the country.

She has hosted her own television and radio shows, and is a frequent speaker at Associations of REALTORS® functions. Ms. Lank has published eight books on real estate including *The 201 Questions Every Homebuyer and Homeseller Must Ask, The Homebuyer's Kit, The Homeseller's Kit* and *Your Home as a Tax Shelter*, all available from Dearborn Financial Publishing, Inc.® Her work has been honored by the Monroe County Bar Association, Women in Communications, local and national associations of REALTORS®, the National Association of Real Estate Editors, the Real Estate Educators Association and Governor Mario Cuomo. A graduate of Penn Yan Academy and Syracuse University, she is a member of Phi Beta Kappa.

License Law

Joan wants to earn money at home. Neighbor Shanice suggests Joan do telemarketing, phoning homeowners to see if anyone is interested in selling. Shanice, who has a real estate license, will give Joan $25 for every lead that results in a listing. Joan has no real estate license, but Shanice says this is not illegal because Joan won't do any actual listing or selling. Is there a problem here?

Like every other state, New York has enacted real estate license laws to protect the public from incompetent or dishonest brokers and salespersons, to set standards and qualifications for licensees and to maintain high standards in the real estate industry. The licensee who is not familiar with the law's requirements could face fines, loss of license and, theoretically, even imprisonment.

Purpose of Real Estate License Laws

The New York **Department of State,** Division of Licensing Services, has the power to issue licenses and enforce the **real estate license law.** The law is enforced through fines; reprimands; and the **denial, suspension or revocation of licenses.**

State Board of Real Estate. The Division of Licensing Services shares regulatory duties with New York's State Board of Real Estate, which has 15 members. At least five are real estate brokers, the remainder are members of the public, and the Secretary of State serves as chairperson. The board has the power to promulgate **rules and regulations** in some legal areas that affect real estate licensees and also examines applicants, approves real estate schools and helps enforce the real estate laws.

Violation of the license law is a misdemeanor punishable by up to a year in jail and a fine of up to $1,000.

The New York Real Property Law, **Article 12-A,** which went into effect in 1922, is the main source of law for real estate licenses in New York. Copies of the law and regulations or a license application may be obtained by writing to

New York Department of State
Division of Licensing Services
84 Holland Avenue
Albany, NY 12208

or to a local office listed in Table 1.1. The Licensing Division maintains a consumer assistance phone line in Albany at 518-474-4664. (The Secretary of State is in charge of the Department of State.)

Table 1.1   Offices of the Department of State, Division of Licensing Services

Albany	84 Holland Ave., Albany, NY 12208 518-474-4429
Binghamton	State Annex Bldg., Binghamton, NY 13901 607-773-7722
Buffalo	65 Court St., Buffalo, NY 14202 716-847-7110
Hauppauge	NYS Office Bldg., Veterans Hwy., Hauppauge, NY 11787 516-360-6579
New York City	270 Broadway, New York, NY 10007 212-417-5747
Syracuse	Hughes State Office Bldg., Syracuse, NY 13202 315-428-4258
Utica	State Office Bldg., Utica, NY 13501 315-793-2533

▼ Who Must Be Licensed?

Any person who *for another and for a fee* performs any of the activities described in the license law must hold a real estate license unless specifically exempted. Table 1.2 shows a breakdown of licenses by county.

Broker. A real estate **broker** is any person, firm, partnership or corporation that for another and for a fee (or the expectation of a fee) performs any of the following services:

1. Negotiates any form of real estate transaction
2. Lists or attempts to list real property for sale
3. Negotiates a loan secured by a mortgage
4. Negotiates or makes a lease
5. Collects rents
6. Sells a lot or parcel of land by auction
7. Negotiates a lot relating to the sale of subdivided land
8. Exchanges real property
9. Relocates commercial or residential tenants
10. Engages in the sale of condominiums and cooperatives
11. Sells a business that has more than half its value in real estate

Soliciting, processing, placing and negotiating mortgage loans on one- to four-family dwellings for a fee also requires registration with the state banking department as a mortgage broker.

Salesperson. A real estate **salesperson** is one who assists in any of the services performed by a broker. A broker is authorized to operate his or her own real estate business; a salesperson can work only in the name of and under the supervision of a licensed broker. The salesperson may never accept a commission from anyone except his or her supervising or principal broker.

Associate broker. A license as **associate broker** is available for the broker who chooses to work as a salesperson under the name and supervision of another broker. The associate broker must meet all the qualifications for a broker's license and pass the broker's examination, but transacts business in the name of the sponsoring broker, exactly as a salesperson would.

Table 1.2   Real Estate Licenses by County

County	Brokers	Salespersons	County	Brokers	Salespersons
Albany	933	1,016	Oneida	345	353
Allegany	41	56	Onondaga	1,044	1,112
Bronx	1,143	1,779	Ontario	197	228
Broome	335	349	Orange	830	1,017
Cattaraugus	104	198	Orleans	33	83
Cayuga	92	117	Oswego	102	139
Chautauqua	206	417	Otsego	129	150
Chemung	114	153	Putnam	307	387
Chenango	31	87	Queens	4,290	7,344
Clinton	59	90	Rensselaer	237	242
Columbia	219	164	Richmond	842	1,751
Cortland	72	58	Rockland	941	1,604
Delaware	160	170	St. Lawrence	120	164
Dutchess	776	1,140	Saratoga	644	1041
Erie	1,710	2,899	Schenectady	218	170
Essex	107	160	Schoharie	77	92
Franklin	62	103	Schuyler	22	17
Fulton	80	39	Seneca	47	49
Genesee	81	127	Steuben	113	178
Greene	157	188	Suffolk	4,433	6,370
Hamilton	30	36	Sullivan	255	316
Herkimer	95	174	Tioga	37	29
Jefferson	126	213	Tompkins	203	132
Kings	3,077	5,589	Ulster	499	393
Lewis	13	27	Warren	224	262
Livingston	91	188	Washington	76	91
Madison	93	110	Wayne	118	163
Monroe	1,778	2,285	Westchester	3,856	4,612
Montgomery	81	88	Wyoming	51	65
Nassau	5,259	7,099	Yates	48	45
New York	9,701	9,012	Outside NYS	1,769	490
Niagara	276	452	State Total	49,314	64,172

Source: New York State, Department of State, Division of Licensing Services.

Exceptions. The provisions of the license law requiring licensure do not apply to the following:

- Public officers while they are performing their official duties.
- Persons acting under order of a court (executors, guardians, referees, receivers, administrators).
- Attorneys licensed in New York. (An attorney who employs real estate salespersons, however, must obtain a real estate broker's license.) Attorneys are not required to take the licensing examination.

- A resident manager employed by one owner to manage rental property when the leasing of units or the collection of rents is part of the manager's regular duties.
- Certain authorized tenant organizations and not-for-profit corporations enforcing the housing code of the City of New York.

Qualifications for Licensure

A licensed salesperson must

- be 18 or older;
- have never been convicted of a felony (Some exceptions are made for an executive pardon, a certificate of good conduct from a parole board or a certificate of relief from disabilities);
- be either a citizen or a legal permanent resident of the United States;
- successfully complete a 45-hour prelicensing course approved by the Department of State;
- pass the state's licensing examination; and
- have a sponsoring broker prior to obtaining the license.

A licensed broker or an associate broker must meet the same requirements, except that the minimum age is 19, the required courses of study total 90 hours and a sponsoring broker is no longer needed. Instead, the prospective broker must submit proof of one full year's experience as a licensed salesperson or two years' equivalent experience, subject to approval by the Department of State, in some other aspect of real estate or proof of a license from a state with which New York has a reciprocity agreement (see Table 1.4). The experience requirement is based on a point system, which is discussed later in this chapter.

Table 1.3 shows the requirements for salesperson's and broker's licenses.

▼ Education Requirements

The Department of State certifies certain educational institutions to offer two *qualifying education* courses. One **qualifying course** covers the necessary *45 hours' instruction for a salesperson's license; the second 45-hour qualifying course completes the 90-hour prelicensing requirement for a broker.* The courses must be taken in order. Topics to be covered and the time devoted to each are set by law. Successful completion requires 80 percent attendance and the passing of a final examination.

License Examinations

Walk-in examinations are open to any interested person, either before or after completion of the 45-hour qualifying course. Applicants should arrive at least 15 minutes before the scheduled times. Space is available on a first-come, first-served basis.

Same Day License Status. Candidates who participate in real estate salesperson walk-in examinations at the *Albany* and *New York City* test centers in accordance with posted schedules may receive the results of the examination and obtain licensed status on the same day. A pass or fail grade will be distributed to each applicant who wishes to receive immediate notification. Individuals who pass can apply for licensure on the day of the test. To do so, he or she must bring a *fully completed* real estate salesperson application, application fee and exam fee to the examination center. If the application is acceptable, a certificate

Table 1.3   Requirements for Licensing in New York

Salesperson:	Broker:
At least 18	At least 19
No felony*	No felony*
Permanent resident U.S.	Permanent resident U.S.
Sponsoring broker	Full year's experience*
45-hour course	90 hours' study
Pass state exam ($15)	Pass state exam ($15)
$50 (two years) license fee	$150 (two years)

*Some exceptions possible

of licensure will be issued that will allow individuals to begin their real estate salesperson careers immediately. This certificate is valid until a permanent license is issued.

Other locations for salespersons and brokers licensing examinations are as follows. (For examination dates, times and locations, call the Division of Licensing Services at 518-474-4429.)

Albany
84 Holland Avenue
Basement A Wing

Binghamton
New York State Annex
164 Hawley Street
Room 303, 3rd Floor

Buffalo
State Office Bldg.
65 Court Street
Hearing Room Part 5
Main Floor

Hauppauge
State Office Bldg.
Veterans Highway
2nd Floor
Room 2B-43

Newburgh
New York State Armory
355 South William Street

V.F.W. Hall
68 Lincoln Road
Franklin Square
Basement

New York City
State Office Bldg.
270 Broadway
Sixth Floor

Plattsburgh
Clinton County Community College
Lake Shore Drive
Route 9 South

Rochester
State Office Bldg. Annex
Monroe Development Center
620 Westfall Road

Syracuse
Postal Workers Union
407 East Taft Road
North Syracuse

Utica
State Office Bldg.
207 Genesee Street
7th Floor

Watertown
State Office Bldg.
317 Washington Street
Dept. of State Office

The examinations cover material from the prelicensing courses. One hour is allowed for the salespersons' test, two and one-half hours for the brokers'.

Examinees should bring to the examination a photo ID, two number-two pencils and a check or money order for $15 (no cash is accepted). An identifying thumbprint will be taken. Scrap paper is furnished and must be turned in before the applicant leaves the room. Calculators are allowed but must be noiseless and hand-held with no tape printout. Passing grade is 70.

In a typical recent year the Department of State administered 20,780 salesperson's examinations, with 12,300, or two out of three, passing. Broker's examinations were taken by 4,488, of whom 3,020, about three out of four, passed.

Notice of success or failure is mailed to the applicant's home address promptly. If the slip is marked "Passed," it is good for no more than two years toward a license application. If two years elapse without a license application, the state examination must be repeated.

Unlimited retakes are allowed, each with a $15 fee.

Licensing Procedure

The salesperson's license application (see Figure 1.1) is provided by the school where the 45-hour course was successfully completed and is signed by the broker who will supervise the new licensee and be responsible for his or her actions. It is accompanied by a $50 license fee and proof that the applicant has passed the state licensing exam.

The broker's application includes details of all past transactions during the apprenticeship period as a salesperson. Figure 1.2 shows part of the broker's application, detailing transactions during the required year's full-time activity as a licensed salesperson. At least 1,750 points must be offered as evidence of experience. Those applying with two years' equivalent experience in general real estate must show at least 3,500 points.

The applicant for an associate broker's license not only lists past transactions but also includes the signature of the principal broker with whose firm the new associate broker will be working.

Both applications include a child support statement, certifying whether applicants have any obligation to pay child support and, if so, whether they are four months or more in arrears. Applicants must have this statement notarized. Applicants who fail to have the statement notarized will have the application returned to them.

▼ Fees

The Department of State charges the following application fees:

- Broker, original license and renewal: $150
- Associate broker, original license and renewal: $150
- Salesperson, original license and renewal: $50
- Branch office, original and renewal: $150
- Apartment information vendor's license: $400
- License examination: $15

▼ Issuing the License

Each license is good for two years, except for the apartment information vendor's license, which is good for one year. Each licensee is issued a license and pocket card from the Department of State. For a more professional identification when dealing with the public, picture identification cards are now available.

Figure 1.1   Real Estate Salesperson License Application

Application for license as:

• **Real Estate Salesperson**

NYS Department Of State
Division of Licensing Services
84 Holland Avenue
Albany NY 12208

Please read all instructions carefully, as incomplete applications will be returned.

- A **nonrefundable $50 fee** and your **original examination admission slip** marked **"PASSED" must accompany** this application. The fee should be in the form of a check or money order made payable to the Department of State. **Do not send cash**. Mail to the above address.

- *Background data: Print or type All Responses in Ink; One Character for Each Space Provided.*

- *Sign in the appropriate places and have the Child Support Statement notarized.*

Important Information

Any person who is four months or more in arrears in child support may be subject to having their business, professional and driver's licenses suspended.

The intentional submission of a false written statement for the purpose of frustrating or defeating the lawful enforcement of support obligations is punishable pursuant to Section 175.35 of the Penal Law which makes it a class E felony to offer a false instrument for filing with the State or local government with intent to defraud.

Eligibility

- You are not eligible to file this application if you are either a member of the partnership, or are an officer or own voting stock in the corporation that is the sponsoring broker.

- If you intend to be associated with any Real Estate Broker(s) other than the one named in this application, you must file separate applications and fees for each such association.

Privacy Notification

The Department of State's Division of Licensing Services is required to collect the federal Social Security and Employer Identification numbers of all licensees. The authority to request and maintain such personal information is found in section 5 of the Tax Law. Disclosure by you is mandatory. The information is collected to enable the Department of Taxation and Finance to identify individuals, businesses and others who have been delinquent in filing tax returns or may have understated their tax liabilities and to generally identify persons affected by the taxes administered by the Commissioner of Taxation and Finance. It will be used for tax administration purposes and any other purpose authorized by the Tax Law, but will not be available to the public. A written explanation is required where no numbers are provided. This information will be maintained in the Licensing Information System by the Director of Administration at 162 Washington Avenue, Albany, NY 12231.

Figure 1.1 (continued)

| FOR OFFICE USE ONLY | CLASS 4 | KEY | REGISTRATION NUMBER | CASH NUMBER | FEE $50 |

E W S ☐☐☐☐☐/☐☐   B ☐☐☐☐☐/☐☐

Background Data

1. Applicant's Name:
   Last
   ☐☐☐☐☐☐☐☐☐☐☐☐☐☐☐☐☐☐☐☐☐☐☐☐☐☐☐☐☐☐☐☐☐

   First ☐☐☐☐☐☐☐☐☐☐☐☐☐☐☐☐☐☐☐☐   M.I. ☐

2. Home Address: Number and Street (PO Box may be added for assured delivery)
   ☐☐☐☐☐☐☐☐☐☐☐☐☐☐☐☐☐☐☐☐☐☐☐☐☐☐☐☐☐☐☐☐☐☐☐☐

   City ☐☐☐☐☐☐☐☐☐☐☐☐☐☐☐☐☐☐☐☐☐   State ☐☐   ZIP + 4 ☐☐☐☐☐☐☐☐☐

   County ☐☐☐☐☐☐☐☐☐☐☐☐☐☐☐☐☐☐☐☐   Social Security Number (If Applicable) ☐☐☐☐☐☐☐☐☐

3. Sponsoring Broker or Firm Name (Exactly as it appears on the broker's license)
   ☐☐☐☐☐☐☐☐☐☐☐☐☐☐☐☐☐☐☐☐☐☐☐☐☐☐☐☐☐☐☐☐☐☐☐☐

4. Office address at which applicant will be permanently stationed (Number and Street)
   ☐☐☐☐☐☐☐☐☐☐☐☐☐☐☐☐☐☐☐☐☐☐☐☐☐☐☐☐☐☐☐☐☐☐☐☐

   City ☐☐☐☐☐☐☐☐☐☐☐☐☐☐☐☐☐☐☐☐   State ☐☐   ZIP + 4 ☐☐☐☐☐☐☐☐☐

   County ☐☐☐☐☐☐☐☐☐☐☐☐☐☐☐☐☐☐☐   Federal Taxpayer ID (If Applicable) ☐☐☐☐☐☐☐☐☐☐

5. Are you 18 years of age or older? .... ☐ Yes ☐ No

6. Have you ever been convicted of a crime or offense (not a minor traffic violation) or has any license, commission or registration ever been denied, suspended or revoked in this state or elsewhere?
   If Yes, attach a statement of details. .... ☐ Yes ☐ No

7. Have you ever applied for or been issued a real estate broker's or salesperson's license in this state?
   If Yes, in what year: _____ *Under what name:* _____ ☐ Yes ☐ No

Child Support Statement

State: _____   County: _____

I, _____ certify that I (am) (am not) under obligation to pay child support.
If I have child-support obligations, I further certify that I (do) (do not) meet one of the following requirements:
   (a)   I am not four months or more in arrears in the payment of child support; or
   (b)   I am making child-support payments (i) by income execution or (ii) by court approved payment plan or (iii) by a plan agreed to by the parties; or
   (c)   My child-support obligation is the subject of pending court proceeding; or
   (d)   I am receiving public assistance or supplemental social security income.

_____
Signature

Sworn to this _____ day of _____, 19_____

_____
Notary Public

Figure 1.2   Partial Broker Application

Real Estate Broker/Associate Broker Application Instructions.

== **Education & Experience**

Education:

If you are applying for a real estate broker license based on education and experience, you must submit the original school certificates bearing the raised seal for both the qualifying salesperson and broker courses.

If you are currently licensed as a real estate salesperson in New York and your salesperson qualifying course certificate is on file with the Department of State, you need only submit a school certificate for the broker qualifying course.

If you have completed non-approved coursework which may be **equivalent**, you may apply for a waiver of the qualifying course requirement. This must be done prior to submitting this application. To apply for a waiver, submit a school transcript showing completion of the course(s) you feel may be applicable. Also, submit a course description that details the contents of the course(s) you completed. Both the description and the transcript should be available from the school where you took the course(s). Send these, along with a letter requesting a waiver of the qualifying education requirement to:

Department of State
Division of Licensing
Bureau of Educational Standards
84 Holland Avenue
Albany NY 12208-3490

Experience:

You must meet one of the following experience requirements to be eligible for licensure as a real estate broker. To assure consistency and fairness in evaluating your qualifying experience, the Department of State will utilize a point system which takes into consideration the amount and type of qualifying activities performed and assigns a weighted value to each function. Determine which type of experience you will be claiming from the chart below and fill out the corresponding experience supplement (A, B or C).

If You Are Using:	STANDARD 1 - LICENSED REAL ESTATE SALESPERSON - At least one year of full time, active participation as a licensed real estate salesperson under the supervision of a licensed real estate broker. Full time is defined as 35 hours per week for 50 weeks.	STANDARD 2 - EQUIVALENT EXPERIENCE - At least two years of full time active participation in the general real estate business (activity that does not require licensure as a real estate salesperson). Two years full time is defined as 35 hours per week for 100 weeks.	STANDARD 3 - COMBINED EXPERIENCE - At least two years of full time activity that is a combination of standards one and two. Two years full time activity is defined as 35 hours per week for 100 weeks.
You must accumulate a minimum of:	**1750 POINTS**	**3500 POINTS**	**3500 POINTS**
Use Experience Supplement:	**A**	**B**	**C**

Privacy Notification:

The Department of State's Division of Licensing Services is required to collect the Federal Social Security and Employer Identification numbers of all licensees. The authority to request and maintain such personal information is found in section 5 of the Tax Law. Disclosure by you is mandatory. The information is collected to enable the Department of Taxation and Finance to identify individuals, businesses and others who have been delinquent in filing tax returns or may have understated their tax liabilities and to generally identify persons affected by the taxes administered by the Commissioner of Taxation and Finance. It will be used for tax administration purposes and any other purpose authorized by the Tax Law, but will not be available to the public. A written explanation is required where no numbers are provided. This information will be maintained in the Licensing Information System by the Director of Administration at 162 Washington Avenue, Albany, NY 12231.

Figure 1.2 (continued)

Applicant Name (Last, First, M.I., Suffix)	Experience **Supplement A** Licensed Salesperson Activity Only	Registration Number

Instructions for completing Supplement A

You must accumulate a minimum of <u>1750</u> points* to qualify for a broker's license based on experience as a <u>real estate salesperson</u>. Applicants must also be licensed as a real estate salesperson for a minimum period of one year*.

1. In the Number of Transactions Performed column, enter the amount of your activity for each category.
2. Multiply the number of transactions performed by the point value indicated to arrive at the points earned for that category.
3. Add the points earned for each category to arrive at your total points.
4. Enter the total figure in the Total Qualifying Points Box. This is your final qualifying points earned.
   * Except those using combined experience.

You must also complete the experience report on the other side of this page to report your qualifying experience. Points earned for that experience must be calculated below.

Category	Point Value X	Number of Transactions Performed =	Total Points Earned
Residential Sales:			
1. Single Family, condo, co-op unit, multi family (2 to 8 unit), farm (with residence, under 100 acres)	250 X	_____ =	_____
2. Exclusive listings	10 X	_____ =	_____
3. Open listings	1 X	_____ =	_____
4. Binders effected	25 X	_____ =	_____
5. Co-op unit transaction approved by seller and buyer that fails to win Board of Directors approval	100 X	_____ =	_____
Residential Rentals:			
6. Rentals or subleases effected	25 X	_____ =	_____
7. Exclusive Listings	5 X	_____ =	_____
8. Open Listings	1 X	_____ =	_____
9. Property Management -Lease renewal	2 X	_____ =	_____
-Rent collections per tenant/per year	1 X	_____ =	_____
Commercial Sales:			
10. Taxpayer/ Storefront	400 X	_____ =	_____
11. Office Building	400 X	_____ =	_____
12. Apartment Building (9 units or more)	400 X	_____ =	_____
13. Shopping Center	400 X	_____ =	_____
14. Factory/Industrial warehouse	400 X	_____ =	_____
15. Hotel/Motel	400 X	_____ =	_____
16. Transient garage/parking lot	400 X	_____ =	_____
17. Multi-unit commercial condominium	400 X	_____ =	_____
18. Urban commercial development site	400 X	_____ =	_____
19. Alternative sale type transaction	400 X	_____ =	_____
20. Single-tenant commercial condo	250 X	_____ =	_____
21. Listings	10 X	_____ =	_____
Commercial Leasing:			
22. New Lease - aggregate rental $1 to $200,000	150 X	_____ =	_____
23. New Lease - aggregate rental $200,000 to $1 million	250 X	_____ =	_____
24. New Lease - aggregate rental over $1 million	400 X	_____ =	_____
25. Renewal - aggregate rental $1 to $200,000	75 X	_____ =	_____
26. Renewal - aggregate rental $200,000 to $1 million	125 X	_____ =	_____
27. Renewal - aggregate rental over $1 million	200 X	_____ =	_____
28. Listings	10 X	_____ =	_____
Commercial Financing (includes residential properties of more than four units):			
29. $1 to $500,000	200 X	_____ =	_____
30. $500,000 to $5,000,000	300 X	_____ =	_____
31. Over $5,000,000	400 X	_____ =	_____
Miscellaneous:			
32. Sale vacant lots, land (under 100 acres)	50 X	_____ =	_____
33. Sale vacant land (more than 100 acres)	150 X	_____ =	_____
34. Other, must be fully explained	____ X	_____ =	_____

Total Qualifying Points ▸ [   ]

A salesperson's principal broker keeps the salesperson's license; the pocket card must be carried by the salesperson. The broker's license must be prominently displayed in the place of business.

Licensing corporations, partnerships and other legal entities. A license issued to a corporation entitles a designated officer to act as a broker, but that person also must secure a license personally. One officer may act as the real estate broker under the corporate or business license. Every other officer or partner who wishes to act as a broker must secure another license, which will expire on the same day as the corporate or business license. An officer or partner of a licensed corporation or other legal entity may not be licensed as a real estate salesperson or associate broker.

Maintaining a License

Various license laws and regulations affect a licensee's business practices.

Change of business address, status or name. All licensees must notify the department in writing of any change in their business address. A filing fee of $10 must accompany all such notifications. Failure to notify the department of a change is grounds for suspension of a license. When a broker moves his or her office to a different address, the broker must cross out the former address on the license and pocket card of each licensee and replace it with the new address. The broker also must complete a change of address form and send it to the DOS with the appropriate fee. Each individual licensee affiliated with that broker also must complete a change of address form and send it to the DOS.

Any license status change (such as from associate broker to broker), change of employment or name change also must be relayed to the DOS by filling out the appropriate form and paying a fee.

Display of licenses. The broker's license must be displayed prominently at the place of business. Salespersons' licenses need not be displayed, but they may be displayed if the broker chooses to do so.

Commissions. No individual may legally accept a commission or other compensation for performing any of the activities regulated by the license law unless he or she holds a valid New York real estate license at the time the activity is performed. A salesperson may not accept a commission from anyone other than his or her supervising broker. Brokers may not receive compensation from more than one party to a transaction without the knowledge and consent of all parties involved (dual compensation). Brokers may share commissions only with their own salespersons and associate brokers or with other licensed brokers. Note that a broker may compensate a salesperson or employee of another real estate broker for services rendered if that other broker knows about the compensation.

Disclosure of interest. Licensees may not buy or acquire an interest in property listed with them for their own account without first making their true position known to the owners involved. Similarly, licensees may not act as brokers or salespersons in the sale of property in which they have an interest without revealing the interest to all parties to the transaction.

Offers to purchase. All offers to purchase property must be presented promptly to the owner of the property.

Termination or Changes in Association

When a salesperson or associate broker terminates an association with a broker, the supervising broker must notify the Department of State, submit a $10 fee and return the license to the licensee. The license may be endorsed to a new sponsoring broker by establishing a new record of association with the DOS. The fee for filing a record of association is $10.

Revocation or suspension of a broker's license automatically causes the licenses of those affiliated with the broker to be suspended, pending a change of association.

A real estate salesperson who terminates his or her association with a broker must turn over to the broker any and all listing information obtained during the association. This is required whether the information was originally given to the salesperson by the broker or acquired by the salesperson during the association.

Renewal and Continuing Education

Real estate licenses must be renewed every two years. A licensee who does not renew within two years of expiration must retake the licensing examination.

Continuing education. To renew a license, a licensee must complete 22.5 hours of **continuing education.** Active licensed brokers who have been continuously licensed and active as full-time salespersons and/or brokers for the preceding 15 years and attorneys licensed to practice in New York State are exempt from the continuing education requirement.

Brokerage Management in Accordance with License Laws

Brokers must follow a variety of laws and regulations as they operate their brokerage businesses.

Place of business. Every New York real estate broker must maintain a principal place of business within the state (with the rare exception of some nonresident brokers).

Business name and sign. Any business name used by a New York real estate broker must be approved by the Department of State. A sign readable from the sidewalk must be posted conspicuously on the outside of the building. If the office is located in an apartment building, office building or hotel, the broker's name and the words *Licensed Real Estate Broker* must be posted in the space that lists the names of the building's occupants.

Branch offices. A broker may maintain a *branch office* or offices; a separate license must be maintained for each. The principal broker must pay expenses for the branch office and supervise it closely.

Maintaining documents. Every real estate broker must maintain a file of all agency disclosure forms, listings, offers, closing statements and certain other documents for a period of three years. (Most brokers keep all records indefinitely as a matter of good business practice.)

These records must contain the names and addresses of the sellers, buyers and mortgagees; the sales prices; the amount of deposit paid on contract; the commissions charged; and the expenses of procuring a mortgage loan or, if the broker has purchased for resale, the net profit and expenses that relate to the transaction. Brokers must keep copies of statements showing all payments made by them. Brokers also must keep filed with each transaction the disclosure of agency statements and any other required disclosure documents signed by buyers and sellers. All these records must be made available to the Department of State on request.

Delivery of documents. A real estate broker must immediately deliver to all parties signing the document duplicate originals of any document relating to a real estate transaction prepared by the broker or one of his or her salespeople.

Care and handling of funds. A real estate broker must not commingle money or other properties belonging to others with his or her own funds. The broker who holds other people's money must maintain a separate, federally insured *New York bank* account to be used exclusively for the deposit of these monies and must deposit them immediately. Within a reasonable time period the broker must render an account of the funds to the client and remit any funds collected. Interest earned, if any, does not belong to the broker. It belongs to the client.

▼ Obligations to Other Parties and Other Brokers

The license law expressly prohibits a broker from interfering with or trying to frustrate other parties' existing contracts.

No broker may accept the services of any other broker's associates without that broker's knowledge, and brokers cannot pay other broker's associates directly without that broker's knowledge. Brokers are prohibited from negotiating the sale, lease or exchange of any property directly with an owner who has an existing written contract that grants exclusive authority to another broker. This means that brokers may not interfere with another broker's exclusive listing agreement.

Other Licenses or Registrations Involving Real Estate

An apartment information vendor's license is available to anyone over the age of 18 who is trustworthy and able to maintain a $5,000 interest-bearing escrow account. The license is renewable annually for a $400 fee. **Apartment information vendors** engage in the business of furnishing information concerning the location and availability of residential rental property, including apartments. They must provide prospective tenants with a contract or receipt with specific information regarding the services they offer. They also must display a sign in all offices bearing the same information, post their license in all offices and notify the Department of State of any changes in name or address.

Certification or licensing of *appraisers* is not required for all appraisal work but is necessary for most appraisals related to mortgage loans. New York State licenses and certifies appraisers at different levels, depending on the applicants' experience, education and examinations. Requirements are detailed in Chapter 23.

Mortgage banking companies. Mortgage bankers are not thrift institutions and offer neither checking nor savings accounts. Because they do not use depositors' money, they are subject to considerably less regulation than thrift institutions. They make real estate loans that may later be sold to investors (with the mortgage company receiving a fee if it continues servicing the loans). Mortgage bankers originate a large percentage of all home loans. They are *not mortgage brokers.* Mortgage bankers must file a $50,000 surety bond with the Superintendent of Banks, or establish a trust fund in the same amount, that can be used to reimburse customers if it is determined that the mortgage banker has charged improper fees.

Mortgage brokers. **Mortgage brokers** are registered with the state Banking Department to bring borrowers and lenders together. They charge a fee, often of the borrower, for their services. The Superintendent of Banks may require a mortgage broker to obtain a surety bond or establish a trust fund in the amount of $25,000.

Any person, firm, association or corporation engaged in the business of *buying and selling securities* must file a Registration Statement with the New York State Department of Law. This requirement applies to the sale of condominiums, shares of cooperative apartment corporations or commercial cooperative corporations, interests in homeowners' associations or interests in time-share projects. Each registration is valid for a period of four years. There is an important exception to this rule. Those with real estate licenses who sell condominiums, cooperative shares, interests in homeowners' associations or interests in time-share projects (and not other types of securities) do not have to register with the Department of Law.

▼ **Licensing Nonresidents**

Nonresidents of New York may be licensed as New York real estate brokers or salespersons by conforming to all the provisions of the license law except maintaining a place of business within the state.

The department will recognize the license issued to a real estate broker or salesperson by another state if the laws of his or her home state permit licenses to be issued to New York licensees without requiring them to take that state's licensing examination (see Table 1.4). If a particular state's laws do not include these provisions, the nonresident applicant must pass the licensing examination.

Every nonresident applicant must file an irrevocable consent form, which allows the nonresident to be sued in New York State.

Advertisements

Advertising must not be misleading in any way. All real estate advertisements must contain the name of the broker's firm and must clearly indicate that the party who placed the ad is a real estate broker. *Blind ads* which contain only a telephone number, are prohibited.

All advertisements that state that a property is in the vicinity of a geographic area or territorial subdivision must include as part of the advertisement the name of the geographic area or territorial subdivision in which the property is actually located.

For Sale signs. A broker must obtain an owner's consent to place a For Sale sign on the owner's property.

Table 1.4 States Offering Reciprocity with New York Licenses

Arkansas	Broker and Sales two years' licensure and current. (Business and residence must be in Arkansas.)
Connecticut	Broker and Sales—current licensure only. (Business and residence must be in Connecticut.)
Delaware	Broker and Sales—two years' licensure and current. (Business and residence must be in Delaware.)
Massachusetts	Broker only—two years' licensure and current. (Business and residence must be in Massachusetts.)
Nebraska	Broker and Sales—two years' licensure and current. (Business and residence must be in Nebraska.)
Oklahoma	Broker only—two years' licensure and current. (Business and residence must be in Oklahoma.)
West Virginia	Broker and Sales—current licensure only. (Business and residence must be in West Virginia.)

All need *current* certification (dated within six [6] months, from the real estate commission where license was obtained), completed application, irrevocable consent form and the appropriate fee.

Applicants seeking a reciprocal real estate salesperson's license must be sponsored by a broker holding a current New York State broker's license.

Suspension and Revocation of Licenses

The Division of Licensing Services may hear complaints and/or initiate investigations into any alleged violations of the license law or its rules and regulations. Anyone found guilty of untrustworthiness or incompetence may have his or her license suspended or revoked or may be fined or reprimanded. **Untrustworthiness or incompetence may include any of the following acts:**

- Making any substantial misrepresentation
- Making any false promise likely to influence, persuade or induce
- Making a false statement or misrepresentation through agents, salespersons, advertising or otherwise
- Accepting, if a salesperson, a commission or valuable consideration for any real estate service from any person except the licensed broker with whom the salesperson is associated
- Acting for or receiving compensation from more than one party in a transaction without the knowledge of all parties involved (dual agency)
- Failing within a reasonable amount of time to account for or remit any monies belonging to others that come into his or her possession
- Being untrustworthy or incompetent to act as a real estate licensee
- Paying a commission or valuable consideration to any person for services performed in violation of the law
- Obtaining a license falsely or fraudulently or making a material misstatement in the license application
- Negotiating with an owner or a landlord with knowledge that the owner or landlord has an exclusive written contract with another broker
- Offering a property for sale or lease without the authorization of the owner
- Accepting the services of any salesperson who is employed by another broker
- Giving legal opinions or performing title examinations
- Entering into a net listing contract (when a seller authorizes a broker to procure a specified amount of money for the property and allows the broker to keep any money above the specified amount obtained from the sale)

- Discriminating because of race, creed, color, national origin, age, sex, disability or marital status in the sale, rental or advertisement of housing or commercial space
- Failing to provide definitions of exclusive-right-to-sell and exclusive-agency listings
- Failing to provide a list of multiple-listing service members
- Engaging in improper, fraudulent or dishonest dealing
- Committing any violation of license law

Note that **misrepresentation** is a false statement or the concealing of a material fact made in an attempt to induce another party to take an action, whether this occurs maliciously, ignorantly or carelessly.

Investigation of complaint and hearing. If the department feels that a complaint warrants further investigation, it will send an investigator to interview the alleged violator about the charge. In some cases the investigation is preceded by a formal letter of complaint from the department. If the investigation results in sufficient evidence, the department will conduct a hearing. Individuals accused of violation of the law may defend themselves or be represented by an attorney. The department investigates roughly 2,500 complaints annually, with about 1,000 resulting in disciplinary action.

Penalties. An offender who has received any sum of money as commission, compensation or profit in connection with a license law violation may be held liable for up to four times that amount in damages in addition to having his or her license suspended or revoked. If a license is revoked, one year must pass before a new license application is made.

The Department of State also may impose a fine not to exceed $1,000. Violation of the license law also constitutes a misdemeanor, and a licensee may be tried in criminal court in addition to the DOS hearing. Criminal actions can be prosecuted by the attorney general of the State of New York. A misdemeanor is punishable by a fine of not more than $1,000 and/or imprisonment for not more than one year.

Appeal. The action of the Department of State is subject to review. Any determination in granting or renewing a license, revoking or suspending a license, or imposing a fine or reprimand may be appealed.

Revocation of broker's license. Revocation of a broker's license automatically suspends the licenses of all salespeople affiliated with that broker until they find another supervising broker and their licenses are reissued.

When a salesperson is accused of violating the license law, the supervising broker is also held accountable if the broker knew or should have known of the violation or, having found out about the problem, retained any fees or commissions arising from the transaction.

Unlicensed Real Estate Assistants

In today's real estate market, many real estate agents find that using unlicensed assistants is very useful. These assistants can do a fair amount of paperwork and legwork, leaving the agents free to use their time finding clients and negotiating transactions. However, it is imperative that unlicensed assistants refrain from performing any real estate activities for which a license is required. According

to the Department of State, an unlicensed assistant may safely engage in the following activities:

- Answer the phone, forward calls and take messages
- Arrange appointments, by telephone, for the licensee
- Follow up on loan commitments after a contract has been negotiated and generally secure status reports on the loan progress
- Assemble documents for closing
- Write ads for the approval of the broker and place approved classified advertising
- Type contract forms for the approval of the broker
- Compute commission checks
- Place signs on or remove them from properties
- Order items of repair as directed by the broker
- Prepare flyers and promotional information for approval by the broker
- Schedule appointments for licensees to show listed property
- Gather information for a comparative market analysis
- Gather information for an appraisal
- Monitor licenses and personnel files
- Perform secretarial and clerical duties such as typing letters and filing

Key Terms

apartment information vendor	Department of State
Article 12-A	misrepresentation
associate broker	qualifying course
broker	real estate license law
commingling	rules and regulations
continuing education	salesperson
denial, suspension or revocation of license	

Summary

In New York, licensees must be permanent residents of the United States, must never have been convicted of a felony and must pass state examinations before licensure. A salesperson must have completed a prescribed 45-hour qualifying course, be at least 18 years old and be sponsored by a licensed broker. A broker must be at least 19 years old, with an additional 45 hours of approved study and one full year's experience as a licensed salesperson. Some exceptions to these requirements are possible.

The real estate license, which covers a two-year period, costs $50 for a salesperson and $150 for a broker. An associate broker license designates a fully qualified broker who chooses to remain in a salesperson's capacity under a supervising broker. Those exempt from licensing requirements include New York State attorneys, public officials while performing their public duties, persons acting under court order and resident managers employed by one owner to collect rents and manage property and certain tenant organizations in New York City.

Every resident broker must have a principal place of business within the state, post a sign readable from the sidewalk or in the lobby of an office building, obtain a separate license for each branch office and display the principal broker's license prominently. Brokers who handle other people's money must maintain a separate escrow account for those funds. The broker must immediately deliver duplicate originals of all documents to the persons signing them and must keep a file of all documents relating to real estate transactions for at least three years.

Commissions may be collected only by the supervising broker and may be shared only with other brokers and the broker's own associates. Advertisements must contain the name of the broker's firm.

Laws, rules and regulations governing licensees are administered by the New York Department of State, which may, after hearings, suspend or revoke licenses. Violations of these laws, rules and regulations is also a misdemeanor.

CHAPTER

1

Questions

1. Joan, who has no real estate license, canvasses homeowners by phone to see if they are interested in selling their homes. Shanice, who is licensed, gives Joan $25 for every lead she turns up. Does this violate license law?
   a. No, because the gift is not more than $25.
   b. No, because Joan does not actually list or sell property.
   c. Yes, because Shanice is paying compensation for services that require licensure.
   d. Yes, because Joan is using a home telephone with no broker's sign outside her house.

2. Real estate license laws were instituted to
   a. raise revenue through license fees.
   b. limit the number of brokers and salespersons.
   c. match the federal government's requirements.
   d. protect the public and maintain high standards.

3. In New York, real estate licenses are under the supervision of the
   a. Real Estate Commission.
   b. Board of REALTORS®.
   c. Department of State.
   d. Department of Education.

4. A New York resident does *not* need a real estate license to perform which of the following actions?
   a. Sell his cousin's house in return for a television set
   b. Offer tenants in a torn-down building a list of new rental spaces for a fee
   c. Write a lease for a tenant in a building he owns
   d. Buy lots on behalf of a developer for a fee

5. Which of the following does *not* require a license in New York?
   a. Selling condominiums
   b. Selling mobile homes
   c. Selling land at auction
   d. Selling shopping plazas

6. A duly licensed salesperson may accept a bonus from
   a. a grateful seller.
   b. a grateful buyer.
   c. another salesperson.
   d. None of the above

7. A fully qualified broker who chooses to remain as a salesperson under another broker's sponsorship is licensed as a(n)
   a. adjunct salesperson.
   b. sales associate.
   c. associate broker.
   d. principal broker.

8. To obtain a broker's license, one must reach the age of
   a. 18.   c. 20.
   b. 19.   d. 21.

9. A broker must have completed how many hours of prescribed study?
   a. 15   c. 45
   b. 30   d. 90

10. Which of the following meets a requirement for a broker's license in New York State?
    a. Completion of 50 hours in real estate courses
    b. Age of at least 18
    c. One year's experience as a licensed salesperson
    d. Membership in the New York State Association of REALTORS®

11. Generally, real estate licenses are good for a period of
    a. one year.
    b. two years.
    c. three years.
    d. four years.

12. A nonresident broker seeking a New York license must
    a. post a bond of $5,000.
    b. be a citizen of the United States.
    c. find a New York attorney to act as a sponsor.
    d. allow himself or herself to be sued in New York State.

13. In the office a broker must display
    a. all brokers' licenses.
    b. all salespersons' licenses.
    c. no licenses.
    d. only salespersons' licenses.

14. Salesperson Jackson told the telephone company to print the following ad under Real Estate in the Yellow Pages: Alissia Jackson, Licensed Salesperson, Residential Property a Specialty, 473-4973. She should have included her
    a. area code.
    b. broker's name.
    c. office address.
    d. home phone number.

15. An infraction of the license law is legally classified as a(n)
    a. violation.
    b. offense.
    c. misdemeanor.
    d. felony.

16. The Department of State has revoked Ted Toller's license for fraud. Which of the following is true?
    a. Toller may appeal the revocation.
    b. His salespersons may continue in business for 90 days, because they were not found guilty.
    c. Toller may continue his business for 90 days if he posts a bond with the DOS.
    d. Toller may have his license reinstated if he signs an irrevocable consent form.

17. If a principal broker loses her license, her associated salespersons must immediately
    a. appoint one of their number to serve as supervisor.
    b. stop listing and selling.
    c. obtain broker's licenses.
    d. move the office to another location.

18. A broker need *not* be
    a. licensed by the state.
    b. at least 19 years old.
    c. a REALTOR®.
    d. already experienced in real estate.

19. Don Houseknecht lists his house with Bob Broker. Don offers a bonus commission of $500 to the agent who brings a good buyer before Thanksgiving. Sally Salesperson, who is associated with the cooperating firm of Orville Otherbroker, effects the sale on November 1. Sally may collect that bonus from
    a. Don.
    b. Orville.
    c. Bob.
    d. no one.

20. A broker must post a sign at the place of business
    a. inside the broker's office.
    b. on the outside door of the office.
    c. above each salesperson's desk.
    d. visible from the sidewalk or in a lobby.

21. A real estate broker must keep all documents pertaining to a real estate transaction on file for how long?
    a. Two years
    b. Three years
    c. Seven years
    d. Indefinitely

22. The term *commingling* pertains to
    a. mixing the broker's funds with escrow deposits.
    b. soliciting the services of another broker's salespersons.
    c. failing to deliver duplicate originals of contracts.
    d. promoting business at social gatherings.

2 ► The Law of Agency

Bob Broker listed the Bensons' attractive house for sale, decided he'd like to live there himself, and offered to pay the full asking price. When the sale closed, Bob collected the commission originally agreed on. Was there a conflict of interest?

The real estate practitioner needs a thorough knowledge of the law of agency to avoid violations of fiduciary duty.

Overview of Agency Discussion

In this and the following chapter, the **law of agency** and its impact on the real estate industry are reviewed. In this chapter, the basic law of agency is covered, with emphasis on the duties of agents to their clients and to their customers.

In Chapter 3 ("Types of Agency"), the various types of possible agency relationships and the need for brokers to develop policies for disclosure of representation are discussed. Problems caused by possible conflicts of interest, such as those arising from dual agency (when one agent represents two clients in the same transaction) and self-dealing (when an agent buys property on his or her own behalf), are analyzed. In Chapter 4 (The Business of Real Estate Brokerage), the impact of government regulation is reviewed. The critical influence of antitrust legislation is covered, and such matters as restraint of trade, group boycotts, broker liability and employee and independent contractor status are discussed.

What Is an Agent?

Real estate brokers and salespersons are commonly referred to as *agents.* Legally, however, the term refers to strictly defined legal relationships. In the case of real estate, it is a relationship between licensees and buyers and sellers (or between licensees and landlords and tenants). In the law of agency (the body of law that governs these relationships), the following terms have specific definitions:

- **Agent**—the individual who is authorized to and consents to represent the interests of another person. In the real estate business the broker firm is the agent of the seller, buyer, landlord or tenant. The salesperson is the agent of the broker.
- **Principal**—the individual who hires and delegates to the agent the responsibility of representing his or her interests. In the real estate business this is the buyer or seller or the landlord or tenant.
- **Agency**—the fiduciary relationship between the principal and the agent.
- **Fiduciary**—the relationship of trust and confidence to the principal between the agent and the principal.
- **Client**—the principal.

- **Customer**—the third party with whom the agent deals on behalf of the principal.

The principal-agent relationship evolved from the master-servant relationship under English common law. The servant owed absolute loyalty to the master. This loyalty superseded the servant's personal interest as well as any loyalty the servant might owe to others. The agent owes the principal similar loyalty. As masters used the services of servants to accomplish what they could not or did not want to do for themselves, the principal uses the services of the agent. The agent is regarded as an expert on whom the principal can rely for specialized professional advice.

There is a distinction between the duties owed by the agent to a client and the duties owed to a customer. The *client* is the principal to whom the agent gives *advice* and *counsel* and whose interest must be put above the interest of all others. The agent is entrusted with certain *confidential information* and has *fiduciary responsibilities* (discussed in greater detail later) to the principal. In contrast, the *customer* is entitled to factual information and fair and honest dealings as a consumer but does not receive advice and counsel or confidential information about the principal. The agent works *for* the principal and *with* the customer. Essentially, the agent is an advocate for the principal.

The relationship between the principal and agent must be *consensual:* the principal *delegates* authority; the agent *consents* to act. The parties must mutually agree to form the relationship.

▼ **Types of Agents**

An agent may be classified as a universal agent, general agent or special agent. A **universal agent** has authority to represent the principal in *all matters that can be delegated.* The universal agent can enter into any contract on behalf of the principal without prior permission. He or she can act for the principal in a broad range of areas in many facets of the principal's life.

A **general agent** is empowered to represent the principal in a *specific range of matters.* The general agent may bind the principal to any contract within the scope of the agent's authority. This type of authority can be created by a general power of attorney, which makes the agent an attorney-in-fact.

A **special agent** is authorized to represent the principal in *one specific transaction or business activity under detailed instructions.* A real estate broker is usually a special agent. If hired by a seller, the broker's duty is limited to finding a ready, willing and able buyer for the property. If hired by the buyer, the broker's duty is limited to finding a suitable property for the buyer. As a special agent, the broker is not authorized to bind the principal to any contract. The principals must bind themselves to the terms of contracts.

An **agency coupled with an interest** is a relationship in which the agent has some interest in the property being sold. Such an agency *cannot be revoked by the principal, nor can it be terminated upon the principal's death.* For example, a broker might supply the financing for a condominium development, provided the developer agrees to give the broker the exclusive right to sell the completed condo units. Because this agent has a special interest in the transaction, the developer may not revoke the listing agreement after the broker provides the financing.

Creation of Agency

Agents are employed for their expertise. Simply providing services does not in itself create an agency relationship, however, because in addition to services, an agency involves representation. Therefore, no agency exists without mutual consent between the principal and the agent. The agent consents to undertake certain duties on behalf of the principal, subject to the principal's control. The principal authorizes the agent to perform these acts when dealing with others.

There are no specific formalities required to create an agency relationship. An agency relationship can be created by either an oral or a written agency agreement between the principal and the agent. It can also be implied from words or conduct. Of course, to ensure that all parties have a clear understanding of the agency relationship, it is in everyone's best interest to create an agency relationship with a written agreement.

The most common way of creating an agency relationship is through an *express agreement* (an agreement that is expressed in words, either spoken or written). A written agreement that creates an agency relationship between a seller and a broker is called a **listing agreement.** A listing agreement authorizes the broker to find a buyer or tenant for the owner's property. A written agreement that creates an agency relationship between a buyer and a broker is called a *buyer agency agreement.* A buyer agency agreement describes the activities and responsibilities the buyer expects from the broker in finding the appropriate property for the buyer to purchase.

An agency also could be created with an *implied agreement.* This occurs when both the principal and the agent act as if an agency exists, even though they have not expressly entered into an agreement. Providing services that are accepted by the principal can create an implied agency relationship. For instance, a broker advises a seller on a fair listing price, gives helpful hints on how the seller can make the house more marketable, shows the property to several buyers and continually refers to himself or herself as the *seller's agent.* The seller sets the listing price according to the broker's advice, makes the recommended repairs to the house and agrees to numerous showings. In this case, there may be an implied agency relationship. Note, however, that an implied agency relationship is not established simply by virtue of custom and practice. There must be sufficient evidence to show that the seller authorized the broker to produce a buyer under circumstances in which a reasonable seller would be expected to compensate the broker for the services. The fact that a seller simply allows a broker to show the property is not sufficient to create an implied agency agreement.

The requirement for agency disclosure (discussed in Chapter 3) reduces the incidence of implied agency in a residential transaction. However, it is often difficult for customers to understand the complexities of the law of agency. Buyers easily can assume that when they contact a salesperson to show them property, the salesperson becomes "their agent." An implied agency with the buyer can result if the words and conduct of the salesperson do not dispel this assumption. In the end it is a *person's actions that control the creation of an agency relationship, not just his or her words.*

When someone claims to be an agent but there is no agreement, the principal can establish an agency by **ratification**—in other words, by accepting (ratifying) the conduct of the agent as that of an agent.

An agency relationship also may be created by *estoppel.* This occurs when someone states incorrectly that another person is his or her agent and a third person relies on that representation. The principal cannot later deny the existence of an agency. Estoppel is essentially a process of representation and reliance.

Compensation. It is commonly assumed that a person is the agent of the one who pays the compensation. However, this assumption is inaccurate. The *source of compensation does not determine agency;* the agent does not necessarily represent the person who pays the commission. In fact, agency can exist even if there is no fee involved (a gratuitous agency). Buyers, sellers and brokers can make any agreement they choose about compensating the broker, regardless of which one is the agent's principal. For example, the seller could agree to pay a commission to a broker who is the buyer's agent. Written agency agreements should always state how the agent is to be compensated.

Agency and Brokerage

The business of bringing buyers and sellers or landlords and tenants together in the marketplace is known as **brokerage.** In the real estate business a *broker* is one who is licensed to assist others in real estate transactions and to *charge a fee for services.* The real estate *salesperson* works on behalf of and is licensed to represent *one specific supervising broker.*

The *principal* who employs the broker may be a seller, a prospective buyer, an owner who wishes to lease property or someone seeking property to rent. The broker acts as the *agent* of the principal, who usually compensates the broker with a **commission** or fee for having successfully performed the service for which the broker was employed. **Generally, that service is to procure a prospective purchaser, seller, lessor or lessee who is ready, willing and able to enter into a contract.** The principal is also known as the *client.*

▼ Seller as Principal

If a seller contracts with a broker to market the seller's real estate, the broker becomes an *agent* of the seller; the seller is the *principal,* the broker's *client.* A buyer who contacts the broker to review properties listed with the broker's firm is the broker's customer, **unless the buyer enters into an agreement for agency representation.** Though obligated to deal honestly with all parties to a transaction and to comply with all aspects of the license law, the broker is strictly *accountable only to the principal*—in this case the seller.

The listing contract for residential properties usually authorizes the broker to use licensees employed by the broker as well as the services of other, cooperating brokers in marketing the seller's real estate. Cooperating brokers assist the broker (agent) as *subagents* in some areas, however, it is more common to act as agents for the purchaser. The relationship of a salesperson or an associate broker to an employing broker is also an agency. These licensees are thus agents of the broker in addition to being subagents of the principal.

▼ Buyer as Principal

The practice of buyers hiring brokers to find real estate with certain characteristics or usable for specific purposes is becoming more common. In this situation the broker and the buyer usually draw up an agreement that details the nature of the property desired, the amount of the broker's compensation and how it is to be paid. The buyer becomes the *principal,* the broker's *client.* In this case the broker, as agent, is the **buyer's broker** and is strictly accountable to the buyer. The seller is the *customer.*

▼ **Broker/ Salesperson Relationships**

A person licensed to perform any real estate activities on behalf of a licensed real estate broker is known as a *real estate salesperson* (or *associate broker*). The salesperson is responsible to the broker under whom he or she is licensed. A salesperson can carry out only those responsibilities assigned by that broker.

A broker is licensed to act as the principal's agent and thus can collect a commission for performing his or her assigned duties. A salesperson or associate broker, on the other hand, has no authority to make contracts or receive compensation directly from a principal. All of a salesperson's activities must be performed in the name of his or her supervising broker. The broker is fully responsible for the real estate actions of all salespeople licensed under him or her. This is known as *vicarious liability*.

The salesperson functions as an *agent* of the broker and a **subagent** of the principal (the buyer or the seller). Thus, both the broker and the broker's salespersons and associate brokers have a fiduciary relationship with the principal. Cooperating brokers also may be broker's agents, acting as agents of the listing broker, not as subagents. As an agent for the listing broker, there is vicarious liability for the listing broker, not for the seller.

▼ **Importance of Agency Law to Licensees**

Agency law has become an increasingly vital topic for all real estate agents. While most of the legal principles of agency law have remained unchanged for decades, the practical application of those laws to real estate agents has dramatically changed the face of the real estate business in the past decade.

As mentioned earlier, real estate agents are *fiduciaries*—they are held to the same legal standards of loyalty, trust and confidence as attorneys. No other sales profession has higher professional standards. However, the significance of a real estate licensee's fiduciary responsibilities was not really emphasized until the mid-1980s.

At that point, state regulatory bodies across the nation began to recognize problems caused by the real estate agent's close, ongoing contact with the real estate buyer. An agent owes his or her fiduciary loyalty only to the client, which at that time was nearly always the seller. However, because of the working relationship that developed between the agent and the buyer (who was known as the *customer*), all the parties involved, including the broker, became confused about whom the agent was really working for and whom the agent had to be loyal to.

As a response to this confusion, states began to initiate statutory **disclosure** laws, which required that real estate licensees clearly disclose whom they were really working for. As a result of these legal changes, the real estate industry has experienced a kind of revolution in the area of agency law.

Whom does the agent represent? The problem of conflicting agent loyalty was a natural outgrowth of the development of multiple-listing services (MLSs). In the 1960s and 1970s the real estate business boomed, and cooperation between brokers became common. These brokers began to form MLSs—organizations of brokers formed to share listing information. It became quite common for one broker to take a listing and another broker to find a buyer for that listing. In fact, by the late 1970s, nearly two-thirds of all transactions involved two different brokers (a listing broker and a selling broker).

For the most part, the selling agents involved in these cooperative sales considered themselves "facilitators," working for the good of both parties. But by the 1970s, the industry had defined the selling agent's role as that of the listing broker's *subagent,* which meant that both listing and selling agents worked only for the seller. Many of these so-called subagents were completely unaware of the conflicts of interest inherent in the role they played.

In the early 1980s the Federal Trade Commission, after an exhaustive survey of consumers, revealed that the public was totally confused about whom a real estate agent was working for. When buyers involved in cooperative transactions were asked whom they thought the selling agent was working for, more than 70 percent said they believed the selling agent was working for them. The reality was that in the vast majority of these transactions, the agent was legally bound to represent and work for the best interests of the seller.

The Association of License Law Officials (ARELLO) is a professional organization of real estate regulators from all 50 states. ARELLO published its Report on Subagency in 1985. In the report, the regulators emphasized certain conclusions that were a preamble to change. These conclusions included the following:

- There is confusion in the industry (and among the public) as to whom a real estate agent represents.
- As a starting point, agents should begin disclosing to consumers whom they are working for.
- There are no contractual barriers that require that an agent represent the seller in all transactions. Buyers as well as sellers may be legally represented.

Throughout the late 1980s, many states began drafting legislation that would require agents to disclose whom they represented to all the parties involved. In 1991, New York enacted a disclosure law that, in the opinion of many, was a model for the nation. At this time, nearly all states have such disclosure regulations. (Agency disclosure also is discussed in Chapter 3.)

Fiduciary Responsibilities

A broker has the right to reject agency contracts that in his or her judgment violate the law, ethics or high standards of the office. After a brokerage relationship has been established, however, the broker owes the principal the duty to exercise care, skill and integrity in carrying out instructions.

An agent's **fiduciary relationship** with his or her principal is a relationship of trust and confidence. (Other types of fiduciaries include trustees, executors and guardians.) In part, this trust and confidence is based on the fact that the fiduciary (in this case, the real estate agent) has special skills and expertise that give him or her an advantage over the principal. If the agent were not expected to act with special care and skill, it would be difficult for a principal to confide in and trust the agent. And if the principal could not count on the agent to act in the principal's best interest, the agency relationship itself would be meaningless.

▼ Basic Agency Relationships

Before we discuss the fiduciary responsibilities owed to principals by their agents, it is important to take a quick look at the types of agency relationships that may exist in a given transaction. The first agency relationship is between the seller and the listing broker. The broker agrees to perform diligently to find a ready, willing and able buyer. The seller is the principal, the broker is the agent.

The broker typically has licensed salespeople to help list and market property. Legally, the salesperson is the agent of the broker. Because the listing broker is the seller's agent, so are his or her affiliated salespeople. As mentioned earlier, the salespeople are the agents of the broker and the subagents of the seller. Both the listing broker and the affiliated salespeople owe their fiduciary duties to the seller (unless otherwise agreed).

The listing broker and cooperating brokers (other members of the MLS) will begin to market the listed property. As they do so, they work with various prospective buyers. Both the listing broker and the cooperating brokers (and their affiliated salespeople) usually represent the seller. The buyers are their customers. Cooperating brokers and salespeople who choose to represent the seller owe their fiduciary duties to the seller, not the buyer.

However, some cooperating brokers may be working under a buyer-agency agreement and represent the buyer. Thus, they no longer represent the seller. They owe their fiduciary duties to the buyer, not the seller.

▼ **Fiduciary Duties to the Principal**

The confidential relationship created by agency carries with it certain duties that the broker must fulfill: the duties of care, confidentiality, loyalty, obedience, accounting and disclosure, which can be memorized as CC-LOAD. (See Figure 2.1.)

Care. The broker must exercise a reasonable degree of care while transacting business entrusted to him or her by the principal. The degree of care that must be exercised is based not on the care a reasonable layperson would exercise but on the care that a reasonable real estate broker would exercise. **Remember, real estate brokers are expected to have special skills and expertise in the real estate field. They must be knowledgeable about real property laws, land-use issues, financing, transfer of title and so on.**

Brokers should be skilled in the following areas:

- Valuing property (to determine a reasonable listing price and a reasonable purchase price)
- Clarifying the principal's needs regarding the transaction
- Discovering pertinent facts about the neighborhood, the property and the parties to the transaction and disclosing this information to the principal
- Filling in and explaining in very simple terms the purpose and effect of the contract forms involved (the listing agreement or buyer agency agreement and the purchase contract)
- Recommending that the principal seek expert advisers (such as attorneys, accountants or inspectors) when appropriate
- Making reasonable efforts to sell or find the property
- Explaining different financing options available from local lenders
- Negotiating offers and counteroffers
- Meeting contract deadlines

If a broker represents the seller, care and skill include helping the seller arrive at an appropriate and realistic listing price, discovering facts that affect the seller and disclosing them and properly presenting the contracts that the seller signs. It also means making reasonable efforts to market the property, such as advertising, holding open houses and helping the seller evaluate the terms and conditions of offers to purchase.

Figure 2.1 Agent's Responsibilities

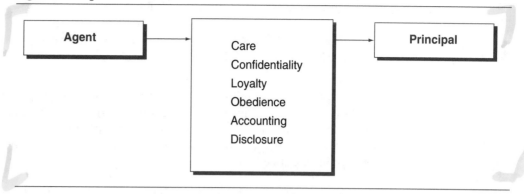

For example, suppose a broker sells a home a few days after the listing agreement is signed. While the seller is initially pleased with the quick sale, she later realizes that the broker set the listing price too low. The seller also discovers that plans for a nearby shopping center were approved a few months ago. When the shopping center is completed in eight months, her property will be worth even more. The broker, who claimed to be an expert on her neighborhood, had no idea about the new shopping center. There were also several clauses in the sales contract that the seller didn't understand. When she asked the broker about them, he shrugged off her concern. Now she realizes that the clauses were important and were not to her advantage. If she had understood their effect, she would have consulted an attorney. The broker breached his duty to exercise reasonable care and skill when fulfilling the terms of the agency contract. He should have had a basic knowledge about property values, new developments in the neighborhood, and the importance of contract terms.

A broker who represents the buyer will be expected to help the buyer locate suitable property and evaluate property values, neighborhood and property conditions; discover financing alternatives; and handle offers and counteroffers with the buyer's interest in mind.

A broker who does not make a reasonable effort to properly represent the interests of the principal could possibly be found negligent. The broker is liable to the principal for any loss resulting from the broker's negligence or carelessness.

Confidentiality. An agent cannot disclose any confidential information learned from or about the principal. For example, if the agent is representing the seller, information about the principal's financial condition cannot be disclosed to potential buyers, including the fact that the principal will accept a price lower than the listing price. The same rule applies to any confidential facts that might harm the principal's bargaining position, such as the fact that the seller must quickly move out of the area. Similarly, a buyer's broker would not reveal the buyer's readiness to pay more if necessary.

This duty of confidentiality is related to the duty of loyalty (discussed below). Confidential information never can be revealed, even if it would mean a larger commission or quicker closing date for the agent. Even after the agency relationship has terminated—for instance, after the sale has closed—confidential information should be kept confidential.

The duty of confidentiality may be curtailed by other legal responsibilities. A broker may not maintain confidentiality if the information is something he or she is obligated to disclose because of the duty to deal honestly with a customer. For example, if the broker knows about a hazardous condition on the property, it must be disclosed to the buyer.

Loyalty. An agent must always place the principal's interests above those of other persons, including the agent's own interests. The seller's agent, for example, must try to obtain the highest possible price, the buyer's agent to obtain the lowest. The agent must never take advantage of a chance to profit at the principal's expense.

Of course, other factors besides purchase price must be considered. The agent must try to get the best offer in terms of the overall benefits to the principal. For example, an offer with a lower purchase price may be in the seller's best interest because of the financing terms, closing date or other concessions. The agent must try his or her best to negotiate such an offer, even though it may mean a smaller commission for the agent.

For example, one buyer has offered $175,000 for the seller's property. The buyer is willing to make a 10 percent downpayment and wants the seller to pay all the closing costs. Buyer number two has offered $170,000 for the property. This buyer is willing to make a 20 percent downpayment, pay his normal share of the closing costs, and let the seller live in the house for an extra two weeks while she finds a new house to purchase. As far as the seller is concerned, the second offer is better. The broker must not try to encourage the seller to accept the first offer, just because it will mean a larger commission.

Note that New York laws forbid brokers or salespeople to buy property listed with them for their own accounts or for accounts in which they have a personal interest without first disclosing that interest and receiving the principal's consent. Likewise, by law neither brokers nor salespeople may sell property in which they have a personal interest without informing the purchaser of that interest.

Obedience. The fiduciary relationship obligates the broker to act in good faith at all times, obeying the principal's instructions in accordance with the contract. That obedience is not absolute, however. The broker may not obey any instructions that are unlawful or unethical. For example, the broker may not follow instructions to make the property unavailable to members of a minority group or to conceal a defect in the property. Because illegal acts do not serve the principal's best interest, obeying such instructions violates the broker's duty of loyalty. On the other hand, a broker who exceeds the authority assigned in the contract will be liable for any losses that the principal suffers as a result.

If a broker knows or has reason to suspect that the client will ask him or her to do something unlawful or unethical, the broker should either refuse to accept the listing or should terminate the listing if it already exists.

Accounting. Brokers must be able to report the status of all funds entrusted to them. Real estate license laws require that brokers give duplicate originals of all documents to all parties affected by such documents and keep copies of them on file for three years. In addition, brokers must immediately deposit all funds entrusted to them in special trust, or escrow, accounts. It is illegal for brokers to commingle (mix) such monies with personal funds or to retain any interest such monies earn.

Disclosure. It is the broker's duty to pass on to the principal all facts or information the broker obtains that could affect the principal's decisions. The duty of disclosure includes relevant information or *material facts* that the agent knows or should have known. (A material fact is any fact that is relevant to a person making a decision.) The agent is obligated to discover facts that a reasonable person would feel are important in choosing a course of action, regardless of whether they are favorable or unfavorable to the principal's position.

The underlying rationale here is that in the course of a transaction, principals must make critical decisions. Agents must supply their clients with all the material facts, so that the principals may make informed choices and give their informed consent to the acts of their agents.

The broker must volunteer pertinent information whether or not the client knows enough to ask for it. For example, a broker has presented an offer to her principal, the seller. The offer involves seller financing (the buyer will make a small downpayment, and the seller will finance the difference between the downpayment and the purchase price). The broker knows that the buyer has a history of defaulting on his obligations. Even though the seller does not ask the broker whether she knows the buyer's credit history, the broker must express a concern about the financial status of the buyer and perhaps recommend that the seller require that the buyer obtain a preapproved mortgage. In many cases, a broker may be held liable for damages for failure to disclose material facts.

Some of the types of information it is imperative to disclose include

- the relationship between an agent and other parties to the transaction. For instance, if the agent is representing the seller and the buyer is a relative of the agent, the agent must disclose that fact to the seller. Because the principal relies on the broker's loyal advice and counsel, it is important for the principal to know if the broker has any interest in the buyer's decision. Other relationships that must be disclosed include close friends and close business associates. For example, suppose the broker and the buyer have agreed that as soon as the buyer has purchased the property, she will subdivide it and relist it with the broker. This is a relationship that the seller-principal has a right to know about. It would be even better for the agent to sever his or her agency relationship with the seller and represent the friend, business associate or relative in the transaction as a buyer's broker.
  If the agent is acting for himself or herself, that also must be disclosed. New York forbids brokers and salespersons to buy or sell property in which they have a personal interest without informing the seller or purchaser of that interest. For instance, if the agent owns shares in a corporation that is offering to purchase the property, that fact must be disclosed to the seller-principal. It is prudent to make such a disclosure in writing as part of the purchase contract before it is signed.
  If a buyer's broker has a similar type of relationship with the property seller, that relationship must be fully disclosed to the buyer.
- the existence of other offers. All offers should be immediately submitted to the principal until the sale is closed, even though they may be disadvantageous to the agent or even to the principal. The seller's agent must remember

that it is up to the principal to reject or accept an offer; it is not the seller's agent's job to evaluate the offers and submit only the most favorable. Failing to submit all offers immediately is a violation of the license law.

- the status or form of the earnest money deposit. For example, the seller's agent always must inform the principal if the earnest money is in the form of a promissory note or a postdated check. If the broker fails to do so and the seller cannot collect on the note or check, the broker may be liable to the seller for the amount of the deposit.
- the buyer's financial condition. The seller's agent should always encourage a seller to independently investigate the financial strength of any buyer. It is dangerous for the broker to advise the seller on the buyer's financial condition. If the seller's broker knows of any negative information about the buyer, however, he or she must inform the seller at once. For example, if the broker knows that the buyer will find it virtually impossible to come up with the required down payment, this information must be relayed to the seller. Naturally, the buyer's broker must keep the buyer's financial condition confidential, unless to do so would breach the agent's duty to treat the seller fairly.
- the value of the property. One of the reasons sellers use real estate brokers to market their properties and buyers use brokers to help them purchase properties is that brokers have expertise in the area of property values. Brokers must always give their true opinions of a property's value, and should never inflate that value to obtain a listing or complete a sale. The broker would be wise to disclose the sale prices of pertinent comparable properties, including all those the broker should know about if he or she had studied the marketplace.
- any commission split. The listing broker should disclose to the seller any fee-sharing arrangement with a cooperating broker. The exact amount of the split does not have to be revealed, just the fact of its existence. This means that the listing broker must describe to the seller the general company policy regarding cooperating with subagents, cooperating agents and buyer agents.
- contract provisions. The broker must explain to his or her client the important provisions of any contract the client is going to sign. If the client requires anything more than a simple explanation, the broker must advise the client to seek competent legal advice.
- property deficiencies. If a broker represents a buyer, he or she must disclose the deficiencies of a property as well as contract or financing issues that are not to the buyer's benefit. The buyer's broker should also suggest the lowest price the buyer should pay based on comparable values, regardless of the listing price, and how long a property has been listed or why the seller is selling.

▼ Breach of Fiduciary Duties

If agents breach their fiduciary duties, they may be subject to a variety of penalties. Note that some of these penalties can be imposed regardless of whether the agent's breach of duties caused the principal any actual harm. Penalties for breaching fiduciary duties include

- loss of the commission,
- loss of the agent's license or other disciplinary action by the state,
- adverse judgment in a civil suit and
- rescission of the transaction by court order.

▼ Scope of Authority

While agents must fulfill their fiduciary responsibilities, they must also act within the scope of their authority. Agents may complete only those activities authorized, or permitted, by their principals. Real estate agents, who are almost always special agents, have only the authority granted to them by their listing or buyer broker agreements. For example, the listing broker is authorized to find a ready, willing and able buyer, but generally has no authority to sign contracts for the seller, initial changes to an offer, receive the full purchase price on behalf of the seller or permit early occupancy.

The authority granted to a listing broker should be stated expressly in the listing agreement. In a typical listing contract, the seller specifically authorizes the broker to place a sign on the property, advertise, show property, cooperate with other brokers, use the services of the local MLS and accept earnest money deposits. Usually, the broker is not given the right to sign contracts, although in exceptional cases, the broker may be appointed as attorney-in-fact under a separately granted power of attorney. The power of attorney must be recorded before the attorney-in-fact can sell or purchase property on behalf of the principal.

A buyer's broker is generally given the authority to seek out appropriate property. The broker is not given the right to sign a purchase contract on behalf of the buyer without a recorded power of attorney.

In addition to express authority, the broker is often granted that authority which is customary or incidental to accomplish the stated purposes of the agency. For a seller's agent, this may include the use of his or her salespeople to "sit" at an open house.

▼ **Agent's Responsibilities to Other Parties in the Transaction**

Even though an agent's primary responsibility is to the principal, the agent also has duties to third parties. The duties to the third party or customer include

- reasonable care and skill in performance,
- honest and fair dealing and
- disclosure of material facts that the licensee knows or should know that affect the desirability or value of the property and that are not discoverable by the buyer on reasonable inspection.

Opinion versus fact. Whatever the specific topic, brokers, salespeople and other staff members must be careful about the statements they make to third parties. They must be sure that the customer understands whether the statement is an *opinion* or a *fact*. Statements of opinion are only permissible as long as they are offered as opinions and without any *intention to deceive*.

For instance, a broker is showing a house to a buyer and says, "This house has the best view in the neighborhood." This statement is obviously a statement of opinion, and because the buyer can look out the window and judge the view for himself, the statement is not made with an intent to deceive.

Statements that are an exaggeration of a property's benefits are called **puffing**. If the broker said in the previous example, "This house has the best view in the whole county—no, the whole state!" her statement would be considered puffing. It is an obvious exaggeration. Puffing is considered a sales tactic and is legal, at least in part because most buyers expect real estate agents to make these kinds of "salesmanship" statements in their presentation. However, real estate agents must be careful to make sure that their "puffing" is not accepted by buyers as a fact. For instance, telling a prospective buyer that a home "will appreciate at least 50 percent in the next five years" may be an exaggeration, but it is also a misleading statement that a buyer could easily accept as a fact. Licensees must be sure that none of their statements can be interpreted as *fraudulent*. **Fraud** is the *intentional misrepresentation of a material fact in such a way as to harm or take advantage of another person.* Misrepresentation is discussed in more detail below.

Environmental concerns. Disclosure of environmental health hazards, which can render properties unsalable, also may be required. Frequently the buyer or the buyer's mortgage lender will request inspections or tests to determine the presence or level of risk. Licensees are urged to obtain advice from state and local authorities responsible for environmental regulation whenever toxic waste dumping; contaminated soil or water; nearby chemical or nuclear facilities; or health hazards such as radon, asbestos or lead paint may be present.

Latent defects. Brokers and salespersons should be aware that some courts have ruled that a seller is responsible for revealing to a buyer any **latent defects** in a building. A latent (or hidden) defect is one that is not discoverable by ordinary inspection. Regardless of whether the agent represents the buyer or the seller, the broker likewise is responsible for disclosing known hidden defects to the buyer. Buyers have been able either to rescind the sales contract or to receive damages when latent defects are not revealed. Examples of such hidden defects include a leaking underground oil storage tank, a buried drain tile that causes water to accumulate and a driveway built partly on adjoining property.

New York courts are continuing to rule on the duties of real estate agents toward their customers. While the traditional principle of caveat emptor (let the buyer beware) is still the law, it has been modified to require that both the seller and the broker disclose known material facts. To protect himself or herself from liability in this area, a broker should ask the seller for all the pertinent facts about the physical condition of the property and should, in turn, reveal those facts to potential purchasers. The broker does not have to complete a detailed physical inspection; asking the seller for all pertinent facts should be sufficient. Although a seller may be understandably reluctant to discuss such facts, the broker can assure the seller that such disclosure will protect the seller from potential liability, protect the broker from potential liability and enable the broker to market the property in the most effective way possible.

According to the Department of State Division of Licensing Services, it is not the broker's duty to verify all of the seller's representations, unless the broker uses such representations in marketing the property. However, if the broker knows or has reason to know that the seller has indeed made a misrepresentation or failed to disclose material facts, the broker is required to make a full disclosure. In fact, many brokers use a Property Condition Disclosure Statement form, which helps the broker ask the seller all the right questions. The information gathered through the use of such a form should be promptly disclosed to prospective purchasers.

A 1995 amendment to the New York State Real Property Law (Section 443-a) provides that the failure of an owner or occupant, or his or her agent, to disclose that the property for sale or lease was at any time occupied by someone who was HIV positive or diagnosed with AIDS or any other disease which is highly unlikely to be transmitted through occupancy, or that the property may have been the site of a homicide, suicide, or other death or any other felony will not give the buyer any right of legal action or be grounds for disciplinary action against the broker. A buyer may submit written inquiry for the information; the seller may choose whether or not to respond.

According to a New York Supreme Court Appellate Division case, *Stambovsky v. Akley* (the so-called haunted house case), this duty of disclosure does not apply to psychic phenomena. When deciding whether to reveal that a property is haunted, a broker evidently is free to follow the property owner's directions.

The 1995 amendment to the New York State Real Property Law (Section 443-a) provides that the failure of an owner, occupant or the agent of an owner or occupant to disclose certain types of information will not give the buyer any right of legal action or be grounds for disciplinary action against the broker. For instance, the fact that the property is or is suspected to be the site of a homicide, suicide, other death or any other felony crime does not have to be disclosed.

Furthermore, the fact that the property was ever owned or occupied by someone who had or was suspected to have HIV or AIDS or any other disease that is highly unlikely to be transmitted through occupancy of a dwelling does not have to be disclosed either. (In fact, discussing the previous owner's or occupant's condition in reference to AIDS or HIV infection may constitute discrimination against the handicapped, according to the 1988 amendments to the federal Fair Housing Act.) To gain information about the possibility that crimes have been committed on the property, a prospective purchaser may submit a written inquiry; and the seller or the seller's agent may choose whether to respond to the inquiry.

Misrepresentations. One of the most common complaints against real estate agents is that of misrepresentation. Misrepresentations violate the broker's duty of honesty and fair dealing and the duty to disclose material facts to third parties.

To successfully sue a real estate agent for misrepresentation, the plaintiff (the one bringing the suit) must be able to prove that

- the broker made a misstatement (oral or written) to the buyer or failed to disclose a material fact to the buyer,
- the broker either knew or should have known that the statement was not accurate or that the information should have been disclosed,
- the buyer reasonably relied on such statement and
- the buyer was damaged as a result of that reliance.

Misrepresentation can be an affirmative statement, such as "A new roof was put on this house three years ago" when the broker knows the roof is 12 years old. It can also be a failure to disclose a material fact such as a latent defect (discussed earlier). For instance, if the broker knows the basement regularly floods but does not disclose that fact to the buyer, the broker is guilty of misrepresentation. Note that while misrepresentations are often oral or written statements, they can be actions as well, such as a nod of the head.

The misstatement does not have to be intentional to be misrepresentation. A real estate agent can be liable for misrepresentation if he or she knew or should have known about the falsity of the statement.

Brokers around the country have been held liable for misrepresentations in the following types of cases:

- Water seepage. The broker should have known that the property's basement had water seepage problems because the broker was aware of the neighboring property's water drainage problems.
- Operating expenses and income. The broker showed the buyer falsified operating statements to sell a restaurant.
- Termite infestation. The broker, acting for the seller, plastered over termite damage.
- Free of liens and encumbrances. The broker mistakenly told the buyer that the seller owned the property free and clear of all encumbrances.
- Filled land. The broker made an unauthorized statement to the buyer that the property was not a "filled lot." (The house later sank when the fill settled.)
- Property condition. The salesperson stated the heater was in good working condition. The seller had concealed the problem with the heater, but the salesperson spoke as if he knew about the working condition of the heater, when in fact he did not.
- Easements. When a buyer asked a broker about easements on a property, the broker said not to worry. Three months later, the city used the easement to lay water pipes.
- Zoning. The broker negligently misrepresented the property's zoning.

If a contract to purchase real estate is obtained as a result of misstatements made by a broker or salesperson, the contract may be disaffirmed or renounced by the purchaser. In such a case the broker will lose a commission. If either party suffers loss because of misrepresentations, the broker can be held liable for damages.

Dual agency. Sometimes a broker may have the opportunity to receive compensation from both the buyer and the seller in a transaction. An agent cannot, however, give undivided loyalty to two or more principals in the same transaction. Thus, real estate license laws prohibit a broker from representing and collecting compensation from both parties to a transaction without their prior knowledge and written consent. More difficult to handle is the situation in which a seller's broker, for example, emotionally adopts a buyer and unconsciously begins to work for the buyer's best interest, so that an unintended and illegal **dual agency** results.

A common complaint against agents is that of *undisclosed dual agency,* which occurs when an agent acts in the best interests of one party to a transaction while legally representing the other. This situation can occur if an agent deals with those with whom he or she has a close business or personal relationship while acting as the fiduciary of another. An example might be when a buyer's agent sells a close relative's property to a client without the informed consent of that client.

Self-dealing. Problems can also occur when brokers list property, then decide to buy it themselves and collect the agreed-on commission. This is referred to as **self-dealing.** At that point those brokers represent themselves but continue to act as the sellers' agents as well. Agents in this position may decide to give up the listing, collect no commission and just represent themselves as buyers.

The Broker's Compensation

The broker's compensation is specified in the listing agreement, management agreement or other contract with the principal and is subject to negotiation between the parties. Compensation usually is computed as a percentage of the total amount of money involved, but it could be a flat fee or other consideration. It usually is considered to be earned when the broker has accomplished the work for which he or she was hired after a seller accepts an offer from a ready, willing and able buyer. A **ready, willing and able buyer** is one who is *prepared to buy on the seller's terms, is financially capable and is ready to take positive steps toward consummation of the transaction.*

Many listing agreements contain a preclusive agreement (an "as, if and when" clause), providing that the broker will not collect the commission unless and until the sale has actually closed. The broker, however, is usually entitled to a commission if the transaction is not consummated for any of the following reasons:

- The owner changes his or her mind and refuses to sell.
- There are defects in the owner's title that the owner has not corrected.
- The owner commits fraud with respect to the transaction.
- The owner is unable to deliver possession within a reasonable time.
- The owner insists on terms not in the listing (for example, the right to restrict the use of the property).
- The owner and the buyer agree to cancel the transaction.

In other words, *a broker generally is due a commission if a sale is not consummated because of the seller's default.* In rare situations the commission may still be due even when it is the buyer who defaults.

The broker is entitled to a fee if he or she is the **procuring cause of sale;** produces a ready, willing and able buyer; or brings about a **meeting of the minds.** If several brokers disagree as to which one brought about a sale, the one with the best claim to be the procuring cause is that broker who brought the parties into agreement, as evidenced by the sales contract. A meeting of the minds is said to have taken place when the parties are in agreement on price, down payment, financing method and other essential terms.

New York allows a broker who fears avoidance of commission to file an affidavit of entitlement—or, in some cases, a lien (financial claim)—against property. An affidavit of entitlement is not a lien and does not affect the closing.

New York's Real Property Law makes it illegal for a broker to share a commission with unlicensed people. This regulation forbids any form of gift or compensation such as giving a TV set to a friend for providing a valuable lead or paying finder's fees and portions of the commission. **Kickbacks,** the return of part of the commission as gifts or money to buyers or sellers, are also prohibited.

▼ **Salesperson's Compensation**

The compensation of a salesperson is set by agreement between broker and salesperson. A broker may pay a salary to a salesperson or, more commonly, a share of the commissions from transactions originated by a salesperson (the commission "split"). *The salesperson may never accept compensation from any buyer or seller, and may not accept compensation from any broker except the one broker with whom he or she is associated, except with the full knowledge of his or her broker.* (Article 175.B).

Note that a salesperson can accept compensation from a former broker for fees earned while still associated with that broker. For example, a salesperson may be entitled to a commission for the sale of a listed property that closed after the salesperson associated with a new broker. In that case, accepting compensation from the former broker is permissible.

Termination of Agency

Because the agency relationship involves so many responsibilities, it is important to know both how agencies are created and how they are terminated. An agency relationship may be terminated at any time (except when coupled with an interest) for any of the following reasons:

- Death or incompetence of either party (Since an amendment to New York State law in 1975, agency need not automatically terminate on the incompetence of the principal; a power-of-attorney document may contain wording that makes it survive incompetence.)
- Destruction or condemnation of the property
- Expiration of the terms of the agency
- Mutual agreement to terminate the agency
- Renunciation by the agent or revocation by the principal (In New York the principal acting in good faith always has the power to cancel a listing at any time. The principal may, however, be required to reimburse the broker for expenses if the principal cancels before the agency's expiration. Damages could be awarded to the agent if the principal acted in bad faith.)
- Bankruptcy of either party
- Completion or fulfillment of the purpose for which the agency was created

> **AN AGENCY MAY BE TERMINATED BY**
>
> - death or incompetence of either party,
> - destruction or condemnation of the property,
> - expiration of the terms,
> - mutual agreement,
> - renunciation by agent,
> - revocation by principal,
> - bankruptcy or
> - completion of the purpose

The question of when an agency relationship ends can be important. For example, suppose agent John listed and sold Margaret's property. Three weeks after closing, Margaret shows up at one of John's open houses. Is Margaret still John's client? Probably not, but John must clarify this with Margaret. Because it is often difficult to treat a former client as a customer, some firms will obtain a written dual agency consent agreement from both parties or enter into a buyer agency relationship with the former client.

Remember that the broker may not disclose to a new client information obtained in confidence from a former client during the agency relationship. Even though the agency relationship may have terminated, the duty of confidentiality has not.

▼ Duncan and Hill Decision

In a court decision, *Duncan and Hill v. the Department of State,* involving a Rochester real estate firm, the court considered the question, "To what extent can a real estate agent participate in the preparation of a real estate offer and counteroffer?" After the broker refused to return a $200 deposit to the prospective purchaser, the charge was made that the broker, not being an attorney, illegally prepared legal documents: an offer, a counteroffer and an acceptance. The court ruled that by inserting detailed terms of the mortgage into the offer the broker was indeed engaged in the *unauthorized practice of law.*

The court cautioned brokers not to insert any provision that requires legal expertise and to confine themselves to a general description of the property, price to be paid and mortgaging to be secured. The court also said brokers may readily protect themselves by inserting in the document a clause that states that the contract is subject to the approval of the attorneys for the parties.

Key Terms

agency	latent defects
agency coupled with an interest	law of agency
agent	listing agreement
brokerage	meeting of the minds
buyer's broker	misrepresentation
client	principal
commission	procuring cause of sale
customer	puffing
disclosure	ratification
dual agency	ready, willing and able buyer
fiduciary	self-dealing
fiduciary relationship	special agent
fraud	subagent
general agent	universal agent
kickbacks	

Summary

Real estate brokerage is the bringing together, for a fee or commission, of people who wish to buy, sell, exchange or lease real estate.

Real estate brokerage is governed by the law of agency. A real estate broker is the agent, hired by either a buyer or a seller of real estate to sell or find a particular parcel of real estate. The person who hires the broker is the principal or client. The principal and the agent have a fiduciary relationship under which the agent owes the principal the duties of care, confidentiality, loyalty, obedience, accounting and disclosure.

The broker's compensation in a real estate sale generally takes the form of a commission, which is often a percentage of the real estate's selling price. The broker is considered to have earned a commission when he or she procures a ready, willing and able buyer for a seller or brings about a meeting of the minds.

A broker may use salespeople to assist in this work. The salesperson works as a subagent on the broker's behalf as either an employee or an independent contractor. The salesperson is the broker's agent and the seller's subagent (or, if specifically retained as such, the buyer's agent).

CHAPTER 2 Questions

1. The relationship between broker and seller is generally a(n)

    a. special agency.
    b. general agency.
    c. ostensible agency.
    d. universal agency.

2. A broker hired by an owner to sell a parcel of real estate must comply with

    a. any instructions of the owner.
    b. the law of agency.
    c. the concept of caveat emptor.
    d. all instructions of the buyer.

3. A buyer's broker is told by the buyer that he had filed for bankruptcy the year before. What responsibility does the broker have to the seller when conveying an offer to purchase? The buyer's broker

    a. should discuss with the buyer her duty to reveal the bankruptcy to the MLS.
    b. has a duty of fair dealing toward the seller and must discuss the buyer's finances with the seller honestly.
    c. can politely refuse to provide any answers that would violate her duty of confidentiality to the buyer.
    d. has no responsibility to the seller, because she is the buyer's agent.

4. A listing may be terminated when either broker or principal

    a. gets married.
    b. goes bankrupt.
    c. overfinances other property.
    d. becomes 21 years of age.

5. When retained by the buyer, the broker owes a prospective seller

    a. obedience to lawful instructions.
    b. confidentiality about the seller's financial situation.
    c. honest, straightforward treatment.
    d. undivided loyalty.

6. The salesperson who sincerely tries to represent both buyer and seller is in danger of falling into

    a. fraud.   c. dual agency.
    b. puffing.   d. general agency.

7. A seller who wishes to cancel a listing agreement in New York

    a. must cite a legally acceptable reason.
    b. may not cancel without the agent's consent.
    c. may be held liable for money and time expended by the broker.
    d. may not sell the property for six months afterward.

8. A broker is entitled to collect a commission from both the seller and the buyer when

    a. the broker holds a state license.
    b. the buyer and the seller are related.
    c. both parties know about and agree to such a transaction.
    d. both parties have attorneys.

9. A house was purchased in 1950 for $4,500. The seller knows properties have appreciated and asks the broker to try to sell it for $100,000. The broker knows the value could be more than $200,000. The broker should
   a. take the listing as offered and sell it quickly.
   b. purchase the house himself for the full $100,000, including in the contract that he is a licensed broker.
   c. buy the house through his aunt, who has a different last name.
   d. tell the seller that the house is worth much more.

10. An example of a latent defect would be a
    a. large crack in the dining room ceiling.
    b. roof with warped shingles.
    c. used-car lot next door.
    d. malfunctioning septic tank.

11. Commissions usually are earned when
    a. the buyer makes a purchase offer.
    b. the seller accepts the buyer's offer without conditions.
    c. a new mortgage has been promised by the lender.
    d. the title to the property is searched.

12. Even if a proposed transaction does not go through, the broker sometimes may collect a commission if the
    a. buyer turns out to be financially unable.
    b. seller refuses to do repairs required by the lender.
    c. seller simply backs out.
    d. lender does not appraise the house for the sales price.

13. A meeting of the minds occurs when the
    a. seller signs a listing agreement.
    b. buyer is introduced to the seller.
    c. buyer and seller agree on the price and terms of the sale.
    d. final closing (settlement) of the transaction takes place.

14. George signed a 120-day listing with Bay Realty. After 60 days George decided not to sell. He instructed Bay Realty not to show the house and to take the property off the market. When is the agency of Bay Realty terminated?
    a. On the 121st day
    b. After a reasonable time
    c. On the 61st day
    d. When the listing expires

15. The *Duncan and Hill* decision warned real estate licensees against
    a. drawing up legal documents.
    b. entering into dual agency.
    c. committing fraud.
    d. puffing.

16. Bob Broker buys a property listed with his firm and collects the agreed-upon commission. In this transaction, Bob
    a. may have a conflict of interest.
    b. represents both the buyer and seller.
    c. may be considered to be self-dealing.
    d. All of the above

Types of Agency and the Real Estate Brokerage Business

The Murphys have approached broker Susan to help them in their search for a new house, explaining that they need help in finding the right property and negotiating the best deal with the seller. After some discussion, Susan realizes that one of her listed properties would be perfect for their needs. Can Susan adequately represent the Murphys without violating her duties as an agent of the seller?

Traditionally, real estate agents represented the sellers in real estate transactions, but it has become increasingly common for agents to represent buyers as well. Regardless of whom the agent represents, the potential for conflicts of interest cannot be overlooked. Real estate agents must be prepared to act in the best interest of their clients, while dealing honestly with other parties.

Agency Alternatives

An agent is someone who *represents a principal in a transaction.* The agent owes the principal the duties of *reasonable care, confidentiality, loyalty, obedience, accounting* and *disclosure of any facts* that might affect the principal's decisions. In real estate agencies, the agent is the broker and the principal is the broker's client. Agency relationships between a broker and a seller are usually created through *listing agreements,* in which a broker agrees to act as the agent of a seller. Agency relationships between a broker and a buyer are usually created through *buyer agency agreements.*

Real estate brokers frequently enlist the help of other brokers to market their listed properties. A common example is a *multiple listing service* (MLS) for residential properties, in which participating brokers agree to share commissions between the **listing broker** and the **selling broker** (the one who finds the buyer). This arrangement may create a **subagency**—in which the selling broker is acting as a subagent of the seller—or the selling broker may be acting as the **broker's agent.**

Because a real estate transaction involves two parties—the buyer and the seller—it is possible for an agent to represent either one or both. In a **single agency,** the agent represents only one party. A single agency can be a traditional **seller agency,** in which the agent represents the seller, or a **buyer agency,** in which the agent represents the buyer. In a **dual agency,** the agent represents both parties in the same transaction. Note that the New York Department of State regards the exercise of dual agency with great suspicion. (Dual agency without full written disclosure to and approval of all parties is illegal.)

Subagency

When a broker accepts a listing from a seller, the agency relationship is clear: the broker becomes the seller's agent. By extension, any salespersons who work for the broker become subagents of the seller, because the salespersons are agents of the broker. The situation is less clear, however, in the case of another broker who procures a buyer for the property. Is the other broker acting as a subagent of the seller, an agent of the buyer or an agent of the listing broker? The answer to this question is critical in determining the obligations and responsibilities of brokers and their principals.

▼ **Creating a Subagency**

A subagency is created by the acts or agreements of the parties involved. The seller must consent to the subagency explicitly by agreement. Other cooperating brokers must accept or reject subagency, whereas the listing broker's own agents are implied subagents. The subagent (selling broker) also must consent to subagency and is free to reject an offer of subagency in favor of acting as the buyer's agent or in favor of acting as the listing broker's agent.

Blanket offer of subagency. Traditionally, one of the most common ways that a subagency was created was through participation in an MLS. By agreeing to submit a listing to the MLS, the seller agreed to a **blanket unilateral offer of subagency** to all participating brokers. However, the seller now chooses whether to offer subagency or to have the listing broker act as a cooperating broker or cooperate with a buyer's broker.

An *offer* of subagency, by itself, does not create a subagency relationship. The offer must be accepted by the subagent. In the case of blanket offers of subagency through an MLS, acceptance is usually *implicit*. When a selling broker shows the property to a potential buyer or procures an offer, it is implied that the broker has *accepted the blanket offer of subagency*. However, because there is no explicit written acceptance of the subagency, it is not always clear when, or even if, the acceptance has been made. The selling broker may be acting as a buyer's agent or as a broker's agent. If the selling agent is working as a buyer's agent, that would have to be disclosed to the seller or the seller's agent immediately. If the selling agent is acting as a broker's agent it would be the listing agent's responsibility to inform the seller of that situation.

Another problem with blanket offers of subagency concerns selling brokers who may show the property to several different clients. For example, a broker who accepts the offer of subagency when he or she shows a property to customer *A* may then choose to act as a buyer's broker for client *B*, who is also shown the property. The selling broker in this situation potentially is acting as a dual agent. Even if he or she formally terminates the initial subagency relationship, there may be a conflict of interest regarding confidential information obtained from the seller or the listing broker during the course of the subagency relationship. If the broker feels compromised in this situation, it would be wise to disclose the conflict to both the buyer-client and the seller-customer and get the **informed consent** of both to proceed.

Selective offer of subagency. Not all properties are submitted to an MLS. For instance, nonresidential properties often are listed exclusively with only one broker. Sometimes a listing broker wants to work cooperatively with only a few select brokers to find a buyer. Although these arrangements are usually informal—they typically are little more than an oral agreement to a commission split—they may result in the **implied creation of a subagency.** As a result, the cooperating broker would have fiduciary responsibilities toward the seller, and the seller would be liable for the acts of the cooperating broker.

To avoid potential conflicts, these cooperation agreements should be put in writing, with the responsibilities of all parties clearly defined. In addition, the listing broker must disclose such relationships to the seller and obtain the seller's *informed consent* for the creation of subagencies.

Rejecting the blanket offer of subagency. A cooperating broker in an MLS transaction is considered a subagent of the seller unless they declare themselves to be an agent of the buyer. Cooperating brokers are free to act as buyer's agents if they so choose. Because acceptance of a blanket offer of subagency is often implicit, however, a broker who wishes to work as a buyer's broker or broker's agent should explicitly reject the offer of subagency at the earliest opportunity. This can be done by informing the seller or the listing agent orally or in writing that the broker will be working as the agent of either the buyer or the listing broker in the transaction.

▼ **The Principal-Subagent Relationship**

To decide whether to act as a subagent, a broker must understand the consequences of the subagency relationship. A selling broker who is a subagent of the seller has the same fiduciary duties to the seller as does the listing agent, including *loyalty, confidentiality* and *disclosure.* On the other hand, a selling broker who is acting as the buyer's agent owes the seller only the obligation of fair and honest business dealing.

Brokerage without subagency. Some sellers do not wish to offer subagency to all the members of an MLS. As the principal, the seller is liable for the actions of a subagent, just as he or she is liable for the actions of the listing broker. This potentially enormous liability is a good reason for not wanting to offer subagency. Furthermore, sellers often believe that selling brokers are likely to favor the interests of the buyer over those of the sellers, regardless of the subagency relationship. Sellers know that agents who work closely with buyers often begin to feel protective of the buyers' interests.

If a seller does not wish to offer subagency to MLS members but still wants to gain exposure through an MLS, he or she can make a **blanket unilateral offer of cooperation.** With this offer the seller agrees to a commission split with the selling broker but does not offer or consent to any subagency relationship. In other words, a seller agrees to pay the selling broker part of the commission for finding a buyer but does not risk being held liable for any statements or actions on the part of the selling broker.

For example, a seller makes a blanket unilateral offer of cooperation and her listing is entered into the MLS. The selling broker finds a buyer for her property but, unknown to the seller, makes fraudulent statements about the property to the buyers. The seller would not be liable for those fraudulent statements, because the selling broker was not the seller's agent.

The *blanket offer of cooperation* is a relatively new phenomenon. In the past, most MLSs required that sellers make a *blanket offer of subagency.* Now sellers can choose to offer either subagency or cooperation *without subagency, or both.* The only requirement is that the seller provide for the selling broker's compensation. When an MLS listing includes only a blanket offer of cooperation, the selling broker often acts as the buyer's agent. However, the existence of an agency relationship between the selling broker and the buyer is not automatic or mandatory. The selling broker may simply be acting as the agent of the listing broker.

Disclosure to seller. A broker who acts as a subagent also has a higher standard of *disclosure with respect to the seller*. In particular, a subagent is obligated to inform the seller of the possible negative consequences of any offer made by the buyer, even though such information may tend to make the seller more hesitant to accept the offer. Some selling brokers are not comfortable with this aspect of subagency because it tends to dampen the working relationship between the selling broker and the buyer.

Disclosure to other parties. The relationship between a subagent (selling broker) and a principal (seller) in a real estate transaction is not clearly understood by many buyers. Buyers who use a selling broker's services to find a property often believe that that broker is working on their behalf when, in fact, the broker has a fiduciary duty to act in the best interest of the seller.

For example, Jameson is looking for a house. She contacts Mendez, a broker, who shows her many houses over the course of several weeks. Jameson tells Mendez the kind of house she is looking for and gives him information about her ability to buy and her time frame for buying. By the time Jameson finds a house she is interested in, she feels very comfortable with Mendez and begins to think of Mendez as *her* real estate agent. In fact, Mendez is a subagent of the seller. Jameson makes an offer on the house, telling Mendez that she is willing to pay up to $8,000 more than her initial offer. Mendez has a duty to relay this information to the seller, who immediately counteroffers with a higher selling price. Because she wrongly believed Mendez to be acting on her behalf, Jameson will end up paying more for the house than she otherwise might have.

This potential for confusion has led to stringent disclosure laws that require all types of agents to adequately disclose their agency relationships to all parties in a real estate transaction.

Dual (Double) Agency

In a **dual agency,** the broker represents *both buyer and seller in the same transaction*. Because the buyer and seller have competing goals, dual agency represents an inherent conflict of interest for the broker. It is often impossible for a dual agent to fully satisfy the fiduciary requirements of confidentiality and full disclosure with respect to both parties in a transaction. Consequently, dual agency by its nature may involve something less than full representation of each client and is typically something that should be avoided.

▼ Informed Consent

Dual agency is legal, however, with the informed consent of both parties. To ensure informed consent, a *written document* should be drafted and signed by both principals. This document should indicate that the principals consent to the dual agency and understand that

- the agent may not provide undivided loyalty to either principal;
- the principals' confidential information regarding pricing strategy will be protected, as well as any other information agreed to by the principals;
- the agent may be paid fees as specified, either by one or by both principals;
- dual agency does involve potential conflicts of interest because one principal may feel compromised unfairly or that one might be favored over the other;
- if either principal is uncomfortable with the dual agency process, he or she should not proceed; and
- the principals should have received approval from their attorneys before proceeding in a dual agency situation.

When dual agency exists but is not fully disclosed in writing to the parties, the broker faces serious consequences. These include loss of license or other disciplinary action, loss of commission on the sale and liability for damages if the sale is rescinded. Because of these risks, brokers must be constantly aware of the potential for undisclosed dual agency situations.

▼ **Undisclosed Dual Agency**

A broker does not have to embark intentionally on a dual agency situation to suffer the consequences of undisclosed dual agency. In fact, **undisclosed dual agency** *is often unintentional.* Although the buyer and seller may specifically request that a broker act as a dual agent, a dual agency situation may arise without the broker's realizing it. Examples of such situations include in-house sales and sales by cooperating brokers who are acting as buyers' agents.

In-house sales. Whenever a broker takes a listing, the broker and all salespeople who work for the broker become agents or subagents of the seller. This is true for all salespeople in all offices of the brokerage. Any time that a salesperson or broker acts as a buyer agent (either explicitly or implicitly) with respect to any of the firm's in-house listings, dual agency exists, and appropriate steps must be taken to avoid liability.

Cooperating buyer agents. *Cooperating brokers* may be deemed to be subagents of the seller. When the seller offers subagency in the listing contract and the cooperating broker (or his or her salesperson) does not disclaim seller subagency, a dual agency may exist.

There are two ways for a broker to avoid liability arising from undisclosed dual agency. One is to simply avoid any situation that calls for or implies representation of both parties. Often this is not possible; for example, in cases where dual agency arises unintentionally without the broker's prior knowledge. The second way to handle dual agency is to make a full disclosure of facts to both buyer and seller, as discussed above, and to obtain their informed consent for the broker to act as dual agent. If such consent cannot be obtained, one or the other of the agency relationships must be terminated immediately.

The requirement for informed consent of both parties generally precludes any sort of blanket consent to dual agency. Consent should be obtained from each party on a case-by-case basis.

▼ **Problems with Consensual Dual Agency**

Consent is necessary for dual agency because, by its very nature, dual agency is a limited form of representation. All parties must agree regarding both the types of services the broker will provide and the limits that will apply to the customary duties of an agent to a principal. For example, limits must be placed on either the duty of confidentiality or the duty to disclose all information. Or it may be agreed that the buyer will be represented by one salesperson from the broker's firm and the seller by another. The broker must make the office policies clearly understood by all affiliated licensees.

Company policy. The possibility of dual agency should be discussed with clients at the time the agency agreement (listing or buyer agency) is entered. Clients should be informed of the possibility of in-house sales and of the policy of the broker's office regarding such sales. The broker also should determine the client's attitude toward possible in-house sales before entering the agency relationship, to ensure that both client and broker are in general agreement as to how the matter will be handled. For example, a listing broker and the seller may agree that the property can be shown to the broker's buyer clients, but that no negotiations will take place until the issue of dual agency has been resolved. As noted above, dual agency should be entered into only on a case-by-case basis, between a broker and a particular buyer and seller.

Dual agency is inherently risky for the broker. It is the broker's responsibility to ensure that all parties fully understand the precise nature of the relationship and agree to the terms of the dual agency arrangement. This is easier said than done. In addition, to be meaningful and protect the broker from liability, disclosures and consents must be made at an early stage in the representation. The risks of dual agency practice are one reason why many brokers choose to adopt a policy of providing single agency services only.

Single Agency

In a single agency, the broker represents only one of the parties in a transaction, either the buyer or the seller. The party represented by the broker is the *broker's client,* and other parties or their agents are treated as customers by the broker. If the broker's client is the seller, the broker deals with buyers or their agents as customers only. If the buyer is the broker's client, sellers and listing agents are treated as customers.

A single agency broker may choose to represent only sellers (seller agency) or only buyers (buyer agency), but also may choose to represent both. This can lead to potential conflicts, as in the case where a buyer client (principal) is interested in a property listed by a seller client (also a principal). When such situations arise, the single agency broker may formally terminate the agency relationship with the buyer. If this occurs, the broker also should inform the seller of the previous agency relationship with the buyer, although he or she may not disclose confidential information that was obtained during the time the buyer was a client. For example, the broker may not disclose to the seller that the buyers are willing to pay *x* number of dollars for a property they really like because this is information the broker learned while representing those buyers.

Seller Agency

Seller agency has traditionally been the most common form of real estate agency. In a seller-agency relationship, the broker acts as the agent of the seller, who is the broker's client. All buyers are treated as customers. Seller agency usually is established when the broker enters a written listing agreement with a seller, although written or oral agreements are not strictly necessary to create an agency relationship.

When a broker accepts a listing and becomes a seller's agent, all of the broker's salespeople automatically become subagents of the seller because the real estate license law treats all salespeople as agents of the broker for whom they work. If a salesperson attempts to represent a buyer as a client in a transaction with a seller who has listed property with the salesperson's broker, the result is a dual agency.

For example, Tilson, a real estate broker, obtains a listing agreement with Johnston. All of Tilson's salespeople, including Hernandez, automatically become subagents of Johnston. If Hernandez agrees to represent a buyer, Aroika, who is interested in Johnston's property, Hernandez will find himself in a dual agency situation.

It is important to remember that a salesperson is a subagent with respect to all of the listings of the brokerage, even those listings that were obtained by a different salesperson or a different office of the brokerage.

▼ Handling In-House Sales

A substantial part of many brokerage businesses consists of *sales of in-house listings* (listings generated by that same broker or the broker's licensees). As agents of the broker and subagents of the seller, all salespersons in the brokerage have an obligation to use their best efforts to find a buyer for properties that are listed with the brokerage. In-house sales also avoid the need to split the commission with another brokerage.

In-house sales are perfectly legal, as long as the buyer is informed that the salesperson is acting as an agent of the seller, and the salesperson does not do anything to imply that he or she is representing the buyer. Complications can and do arise, however, especially in the case where a buyer (customer) has a current or previous agency (client) relationship with the broker. In these cases, an *undisclosed dual agency may be the result.*

For example, Jane lists her home for sale with ABC Realty, and she also asks ABC to help her find a new home. She decides to make an offer on Fred's property, which is also listed with ABC. Because ABC is the agent of both Jane and Fred (as sellers), this situation gives rise to a dual agency. ABC cannot act as the selling broker in Jane's purchase from Fred without the informed consent of both parties.

▼ Handling Cooperative Sales

Cooperation among brokers, either selectively or through an MLS, is common practice in the real estate industry. When a property is sold through a broker who is not the listing broker, it is important to clarify the agency relationships among all of the people involved. The cooperating or selling broker (or his or her salesperson) must inform the listing agent whether he or she is acting as a subagent of the seller, as an agent of the buyer or simply as a broker's agent with no agency relationship with either buyer or seller.

When an MLS listing includes a blanket offer of subagency, the selling broker or salesperson will normally be considered to be a subagent of the seller, unless this relationship is specifically disavowed. If the selling broker is, in fact, acting as an agent of the buyer, the potential for dual agency exists.

Disclosure of seller agency. A seller agent should discuss the nature of the agency relationship with the seller at the time the listing agreement is entered. If the property will be submitted to an MLS, the agent also should discuss whether there will be a blanket offer of subagency and vicarious liability. With regard to buyers, the agent must disclose the nature of the client relationship with the seller at the earliest practical opportunity to avoid any possibility that the buyer will misunderstand whom the agent represents.

Buyer Agency

Although real estate agents have traditionally represented sellers, buyer agency has become increasingly popular. In a buyer-agency relationship, the broker represents the buyer as a *client*, rather than treating the buyer as merely a *customer*. Buyer agency allows the broker to provide services to buyers that might otherwise be inappropriate, such as assistance in negotiating the terms of the contract to the buyer's best advantage.

▼ **Benefits of Buyer Agency: Who Needs an Agent?**

Many buyers prefer to have their own agency representation. Buyer agency can have advantages for both the buyer and the broker.

Benefits for the buyer. A buyer-agency relationship has several benefits for the buyer, including

- *access to a larger marketplace.* Traditional brokers often limit their sample of properties to those that guarantee a commission. In other words, they limit their property search to those listed in-house or in the MLS. However, a buyer's broker, whose commission is protected by a buyer-agency agreement, is motivated to show the buyer all available properties that meet the buyer's requirements, including open listing properties, for-sale-by-owner properties, foreclosure and probate sales, sales by trusts and pension plans and properties that are not yet on the market.
- *stronger negotiating strategy.* A buyer's broker views a transaction from the buyer's perspective. A buyer's broker's only loyalty is to the buyer. Thus, the buyer is in a stronger negotiating position. The broker can use his or her expert knowledge of the marketplace and negotiating skills to help the buyer purchase a home on the most favorable terms possible.
- *fiduciary responsibilities of the broker.* A buyer's broker is held to a higher standard of skill and care in dealing with the buyer (the broker's client) than is a subagent of the seller or the seller's listing agent, both of whom owe fiduciary duties to the seller. Buyer's brokers have an affirmative duty to their clients to thoroughly investigate and completely disclose all facts that bear on a buyer's decision to buy. Buyer's brokers are held to the same standard of performance in dealing with the buyer that the listing broker is held to in dealing with the seller. On the other hand, buyer's brokers have a duty to be honest and deal fairly with sellers, but owe no duty to advise and counsel sellers.
- *confidentiality.* A buyer's broker must not disclose confidential information about the buyer to the seller. For example, the amount of money the buyer is willing to pay for a property may not be disclosed to the seller. Even the buyer's identity—should the buyer wish to remain anonymous—cannot be disclosed without the buyer's permission.
- *counseling instead of selling pressure.* Brokers who represent sellers use their best efforts to persuade a buyer to purchase the seller's property. On the other hand, a buyer's agent gives the buyer expert advice, counseling and information about a prospective purchase. The buyer's broker helps the buyer evaluate different properties and different courses of action and then helps the buyer get the best possible deal once the buyer decides to make an offer. For instance, a buyer's broker may suggest that the buyer visit a home at different times during the day or week to check noise levels, traffic and exposure to other nuisances. A buyer's broker may also advise the buyer to chat with neighbors to get a feel for the neighborhood. A buyer's broker will check various sources to discover as much information about the house and neighborhood as possible and will review the proposed contract for unfavorable terms. All these services are in marked contrast to what is provided to a buyer by a seller's agent or subagent, whose main goal is finding a buyer for a property.

Benefits for the broker. There are also benefits for the broker who represents a buyer, including

- *greater client loyalty.* A seller's agent or subagent often spends considerable time showing various properties to a buyer, only to have that buyer buy a property through another agent. Buyer's brokers have greater control over whether a commission is earned and little fear of losing the buyer to another broker.

- *avoiding conflicts of loyalty.* A broker who represents the buyer avoids the problem of conflicting loyalties. Brokers who act as the seller's subagents often spend many hours with buyers and may never meet the seller at all. They may begin to feel a sense of loyalty toward the buyer they know so well and forget about the duty of loyalty they owe to the seller. It is sometimes difficult for these brokers to tell the seller just how much the buyer is willing to pay for the property or to refrain from telling the buyer just how anxious the seller is to sell (even though both are required by agency law). But buyer's brokers are free to keep the buyer's plans, needs and desires confidential. They are free to act in accordance with the loyalty they naturally feel toward the buyer they are working with.

- *no liability for the acts of the listing agent.* A buyer's broker has no agency relationship with either the seller or the listing agent. Thus, a buyer's broker cannot be vicariously liable for the actions of either the seller or the listing agent. A buyer's broker is less likely to be sued for things that are not the broker's fault.

▼ Buyer-Agency Agreements

To avoid misunderstandings, a buyer-agency agreement should be in writing and should specify the types of services that the broker will provide and the means of compensation for the broker. The agreement should indicate whether the buyer must work exclusively with that broker or is allowed to work with other brokers as well. This is a significant issue when the broker's compensation is a contingent fee. If the buyer is allowed to work with other brokers, the buyer's broker risks losing his or her fee. The most common form of agreement is an exclusive right to represent.

A buyer-agency agreement also should address potential conflicts of interest, such as a case where the buyer wants to purchase a property that is listed with the broker. For example, the agreement may provide that such transactions are not covered by the buyer-agency arrangement. Another potential conflict arises when a broker locates a property that is suitable for two or more buyer clients. This situation can be covered in the buyer-agency agreement by stating that the property will be offered to the buyers on a first-come, first-served basis. Buyer-agency agreements are discussed in more detail later in this chapter.

▼ Compensating Buyer Agents

An agency relationship does not depend on the source of the agent's compensation. Buyer agents may be compensated by either the buyer or the seller. Naturally, the way in which fees are to be paid should be stated in writing and clearly understood well in advance to avoid potential conflict between the buyer and the broker.

Seller-paid fee. There is no legal or ethical barrier that prohibits the seller from paying the buyer's broker fee or authorizing the listing broker to share fees with the buyer's broker. Either way is a matter of contract and may be handled in advance by appropriate language in both the seller's listing agreement and the buyer's representation agreement. In fact, this is probably the most common method of compensation today. Remember, the payment of fees does not determine whom an agent represents. As long as the agency relationship is clear and explicit, it does not matter legally whether the buyer or the seller pays the fee.

The seller may pay the buyer's broker's fee through a commission split or by crediting the buyer a specific amount out of the sales proceeds at closing. The most common method is the commission split, where the listing broker has written authorization to split the commission with the buyer's broker. (As part of their standard language, many standard listing agreements provide that the listing broker is authorized to do so. See Figure 3.2 later in this chapter.)

A buyer's broker who is planning on a traditional commission split should ask the listing broker whether the listing broker is authorized and willing to split the commission with the buyer's broker. If the listing broker is not authorized to split the commission, the buyer's broker should advise the buyer of that fact. The buyer then may decide to reduce the offering price to a net amount that reflects that the buyer is to pay his or her broker's fee. The seller and the listing broker will have to reach their own agreement on whether to reduce the listing broker's commission.

Now that most MLSs accept listings in which sellers can offer cooperation regarding commission instead of subagency, there is likely to be more acceptance by sellers, buyers and brokers of such a commission-splitting arrangement.

Note that with a commission split, the end financial result for the seller is the same as if the selling broker were a subagent and the commission were split between the listing broker and the selling broker. In this case, the selling broker just happens to represent the buyer. For the most part, the fact that buyers have their own agents has no significant impact on the overall compensation paid to the agents in a transaction. Whether the cooperating agent is a subagent or a buyer's agent, the fees are substantially the same.

Buyer-paid fee. Buyer-agent compensation also can be paid directly by the buyer. This arrangement has the advantage of avoiding any appearance that the buyer's agent is acting as a subagent of the seller and also gives the buyer's agent greater control over getting paid. The compensation may take the form of an hourly rate, a flat fee or a percentage commission.

- Hourly rate. Under an hourly rate arrangement, the broker is actually acting as a consultant. The hourly fee is payable whether or not the buyer actually purchases a property.
- Percentage fee. A percentage fee is based on the sales price of the home the buyer purchases. The primary benefit of this arrangement is that real estate agents and their clients are accustomed to a percentage arrangement. The obvious disadvantage is that it is in the broker's interest to find the buyer a more expensive house, because the higher the price, the higher the fee.
- Flat fee. Under this arrangement, the buyer's broker is paid a flat fee if the buyer purchases a house located through the broker. The amount of the fee is based on the broker's estimate of the work and skills involved.

Some buyer's agent agreements provide that the buyer is obligated to pay the fee but is entitled to a credit for any amount the seller agrees to pay. Thus, the buyer would not pay the buyer's broker fee in a typical MLS sale, where the buyer's broker will get a split of the listing broker's commission. However, the buyer would be obligated to pay the fee if the property purchased were unlisted.

▼ **Working Relationships with Buyers**

Buyers as customers. Not every buyer wants to be represented by an agent. Some buyers like working with several different brokers. Some buyers, especially experienced buyers, are happy with the services provided by a seller's agent: help in finding a suitable property, information about property values, help in preparing and presenting their offer and aid in securing financing. All of these services can be provided to a customer by an agent representing a seller.

Buyers as clients. Other buyers, however, want more than customer services. They need and want advice, something the seller's broker cannot provide them with. These are the buyers who will benefit most by buyer agency.

▼ **Buyer-Agent Disclosures**

A buyer agent should discuss the nature of the agency relationship with his or her client when the buyer-agency agreement is established. The fact of buyer agency must be disclosed immediately to any listing agent or seller with whom the buyer agent is dealing on behalf of the buyer, and the buyer agent should explicitly reject any offer of seller subagency.

Agency Forms

The majority of agency relationships of any type are created by written agreement between the agent and the principal. In the case of real estate agency, the relationship between the seller and the listing agent is defined by the *listing agreement*. The relationship between the buyer and the agent is defined by the *buyer-agency agreement*.

▼ **Listing Agreements**

The three common types of listings are the *exclusive-right-to-sell-listing*, the *exclusive-agency listing* and the *open listing*. The primary difference between these types of listings relates to the conditions under which the broker will have earned a commission. Their similarities and differences are examined in Table 3.1.

THREE COMMON TYPES OF LISTING AGREEMENTS
1. Exclusive right to sell
2. Exclusive agency
3. Open listing

Exclusive-right-to-sell listing. The **exclusive-right-to-sell listing** provides the greatest protection for the broker. The broker under this arrangement has earned a commission if the property is sold during the listing term, regardless of who procures the buyer.

Exclusive-agency listing. By comparison, an **exclusive-agency listing** entitles the broker to a commission if the property is sold during the listing term, unless the seller acting alone (i.e., not through another broker) is the one who procures the buyer. If the seller procures the buyer without involving a broker, no commission is due.

Open listing. The **open listing** is the least restrictive of the three types. In an open listing the seller may employ any number of brokers and need pay a commission only to that broker who successfully produces a ready, willing and able buyer. A seller who personally sells the property without the aid of any of the brokers is not obligated to pay any of them a commission. A listing contract generally creates an open listing unless the wording specifically provides otherwise.

When a broker represents a landlord in procuring tenants for a property, the most common agreement is the exclusive right to rent, which is similar in

Table 3.1   Listing Agreements

	Listing Agent Entitled to Commission if Sold by:		
Type of Listing	Seller	Agent	Other Broker
Open Listing		x	
Exclusive-Agency Listing		x	x
Exclusive-Right-to-Sell Listing	x	x	x

effect to the exclusive right to sell. The broker earns a commission if the property is leased during the term of the agreement, regardless of who procures the tenant.

Net listing.   With a net listing the broker is free to offer the property for sale at any price. If the property is sold, the broker pays the seller only the net amount previously agreed on and keeps the rest. This type of listing is *illegal* in New York. It lends itself to fraud and is seldom in the seller's best interest.

Multiple listing.   Not a type of listing, an MLS is organized within a geographic area by a group of brokers who agree to distribute and share listing information.

The multiple-listing agreement, while not actually a separate form of listing, is in effect an exclusive-right-to-sell or exclusive-agency agreement with an additional authority to distribute the listing to other brokers who belong to the MLS. The obligations among member brokers of a multiple-listing organization vary widely. Most provide that on sale of the property the commission will be divided between the listing broker and the selling broker. Terms for division of the commission vary by individual arrangement among brokers.

Under most multiple-listing contracts the broker who secures the listing is not only authorized but obligated to turn the listing over to the MLS within a definite period of time so that it can be distributed to other member brokers.

Termination of listings.   A listing, like any agency relationship, may be ended for any of the following reasons:

- Performance of the object (sale of the property)
- Expiration of the time period stated in the agreement
- Abandonment by a broker who spends no time on the listing
- Revocation by the owner (although the owner may be liable for the broker's expenses)
- Cancellation by the broker or by mutual consent
- Bankruptcy, death or insanity of either party
- Destruction of the property
- A change in property use by outside forces (such as a change in zoning)

All listings should specify a definite period of time during which the broker is to be employed. The use of automatic extensions of time in exclusive listings is *illegal* in New York.

Figure 3.1 Disclosure of Lead-Based Paint and Lead-Based Paint Hazards

LEAD-BASED PAINT OR LEAD-BASED PAINT HAZARD ADDENDUM

It is a condition of this contract that, until midnight of _____ , Buyer shall have the right to obtain a risk assessment or inspection of the Property for the presence of lead-based paint and/or lead-based paint hazards* at Buyer's expense. This contingency will terminate at that time unless Buyer or Buyer's agent delivers to the Seller or Seller's agent a written inspection and/or risk assessment report listing the specific existing deficiencies and corrections needed, if any. If any corrections are necessary, Seller shall have the option of (i) completing them, (ii) providing for their completion, or (iii) refusing to complete them. If Seller elects not to complete or provide for completion of the corrections, then Buyer shall have the option of (iv) accepting the Property in its present condition, or (v) terminating this contract, in which case all earnest monies shall be refunded to Buyer. Buyer may waive the right to obtain a risk assessment or inspection of the Property for the presence of lead-based paint and/or lead based paint hazards at any time without cause.

*Intact lead-based paint that is in good condition is not necessarily a hazard. See EPA pamphlet "Protect Your Family From Lead in Your Home" for more information.

Disclosure of Information on Lead-Based Paint and Lead-Based Paint Hazards

Lead Warning Statement

Every Buyer of any interest in residential real property on which a residential dwelling was built prior to 1978 is notified that such property may present exposure to lead from lead-based paint that may place young children at risk of developing lead poisoning. Lead poisoning in young children may produce permanent neurological damage, including learning disabilities, reduced intelligence quotient, behavioral problems, and impaired memory. Lead poisoning also poses a particular risk to pregnant women. The Seller of any interest in residential real property is required to provide the Buyer with any information on lead-based paint hazards from risk assessments or inspections in the Seller's possession and notify the Buyer of any known lead-based paint hazards. A risk assessment or inspection for possible lead-based paint hazards is recommended prior to purchase.

Seller's Disclosure (initial)

_____ (a) Presence of lead-based paint and/or lead-based paint hazards (check one below):

❑ Known lead-based paint and/or lead-based paint hazards are present in the housing (explain).

_____

_____

❑ Seller has no knowledge of lead-based paint and/or lead-based paint hazards in the housing.

_____ (b) Records and reports available to the Seller (check one below):

❑ Seller has provided the Buyer with all available records and reports pertaining to lead-based paint and/or lead-based paint hazards in the housing (list documents below).

_____

_____

❑ Seller has no reports or records pertaining to lead-based paint and/or lead-based paint hazards in the housing.

Buyer's Acknowledgment (initial)

_____ (c) Buyer has received copies of all information listed above.

_____ (d) Buyer has received the pamphlet *Protect Your Family from Lead in Your Home.*

_____ (e) Buyer has (check one below):

❑ Received a 10-day opportunity (or mutually agreed upon period) to conduct a risk assessment or inspection for the presence of lead-based paint and/or lead-based paint hazards; or

❑ Waived the opportunity to conduct a risk assessment or inspection for the presence of lead-based paint and/or lead-based paint hazards.

Agent's Acknowledgment (initial)

_____ (f) Agent has informed the Seller of the Seller's obligations under 42 U.S.C. 4582(d) and is aware of his/her responsibility to ensure compliance.

Certification of Accuracy

The following parties have reviewed the information above and certify, to the best of their knowledge, that the information provided by the signatory is true and accurate.

Buyer: _____ (SEAL) Date _____

Buyer: _____ (SEAL) Date _____

Agent: _____ Date _____

Seller: _____ (SEAL) Date _____

Seller: _____ (SEAL) Date _____

Agent: _____ Date _____

Obtaining listings. All legal owners of the property or their authorized agents as well as the listing salesperson and/or broker should sign the listing agreement. The listing salesperson can sign the contract in the broker's name if authorized by the broker.

Information needed for listing agreements. When taking a listing, the broker must obtain as much information as possible on the parcel of real estate. This ensures that all possible contingencies can be anticipated, particularly when the listing will be shared in a multiple-listing arrangement. Some of the information accompanies the actual listing contract; some is furnished to prospective buyers on separate information sheets. It includes the following (where appropriate):

- Names and addresses of owners
- Adequate description of the property
- Size of lot (frontage and depth)
- Number and size of rooms and total square footage
- Construction and age of the building
- Information relative to the neighborhood (schools, transportation)
- Current taxes
- Amount of existing financing
- Utilities and average payments
- Appliances to be included in the transaction
- Date of occupancy or possession
- Possibility of seller financing
- Zoning classification (especially important for vacant land)
- Detailed list of exactly what personal property and fixtures will or will not be included in the sales price

The agent should search the public records for information on zoning, lot size and yearly taxes. The true tax figure should be used, disregarding any present veteran's, aged or religious exemption or any addition for unpaid water bills.

Seller disclosures. A real estate broker, as an agent of the seller, is responsible for disclosing any material information regarding the property. Getting as much initial information from the seller as possible, even if it requires asking penetrating and possibly embarrassing questions, will pay off in the long run by saving both principal and agent from potential legal difficulties. Following are some items that must be disclosed.

- If a property lies in an agricultural district, this fact must be disclosed.
- The lack of available utilities also must be disclosed. If there is a surcharge for utility services, notice must include the type and amount of the surcharge. Sellers must furnish, on request, information on utility bills and must sign a statement that there is a smoke alarm.
- All sellers and lessors of housing built before 1978 and their agents must disclose the presence of known lead-based paint or lead-related hazards to prospective buyers or renters, pursuant to federal law implemented by a rule promulgated jointly by the Environmental Protection Agency (EPA) and the Department of Housing and Urban Development (HUD). Sellers and lessors also must provide to prospective buyers and renters (a) any reports or records pertaining to the presence of lead-based paint hazards and (b) a HUD/EPA booklet called "Protect Your Family from Lead in Your Home." Buyers must be allowed a 10-day period to have an inspection or risk assessment performed at their option and expense. Contracts of sale and leases

must, where appropriate, contain a lead warning statement and an acknowledgment statement by the buyer or tenants. Sample disclosure and acknowledgment statements appear in Figure 3.1. Copies must be retained by seller or landlord and agent for three years from completion of the transaction. Sublets are covered by the rule. The rule does not require testing, removal or abatement of lead-based paint and does not invalidate leases or sales contracts. Violation of the rule may result in civil and criminal penalties and potential triple damages.

Environmental hazards. When property is listed, questions should be raised about the possible presence of environmental hazards. The real estate broker must not assume expertise in these matters. It is enough to be alert for situations that might raise a red flag and to recommend, where it seems indicated, that the seller consult a licensed engineer. In some situations an environmental audit may be indicated. As always, troublesome questions can be taken to an attorney. Environmental hazards are of increasing importance, not only because buyers may suffer damage to their health but also because in some cases purchasers have been held responsible for cleanup of existing problems.

Rental property. In the sale of multifamily dwellings and other income-producing properties, the seller should be ready to present a statement of rents and expenses, preferably prepared by an accountant. Prospective buyers want statements about leases and security deposits. The listing agent should verify zoning and the legality of existing use. The seller should be informed of the necessity for a certificate of occupancy at transfer. Arranging with tenants to show the property at reasonable times also is important.

Truth-in-Heating Law. New York's Truth-in-Heating Law requires the seller to furnish, on written request, two past years' heating and cooling bills to any prospective buyer of a one- or two-family home. Sellers also must furnish a statement of the extent and type of insulation they have installed together with any information they may have about insulation installed by previous owners.

If HUD has determined that the property is in a flood-prone area, a buyer may need to obtain flood insurance before placing certain kinds of mortgages. The listing agent can anticipate this by consulting a flood area map at the time of listing. Maps may be ordered from the Federal Emergency Management Agency, Flood Map Distribution Center, 6930 (A-F) San Tomas Road, Baltimore, MD 21227-6227, or by calling toll-free 1-800-333-1363.

Some municipalities may have restrictive ordinances regarding aquifer protection zones, wetlands protection or steep slopes. Listing agents should keep current with all potential restrictions on use of land.

New York State requirements. The New York Real Property Law requires that the broker have attached to or printed on the reverse side of an exclusive agreement for a one- to three-family dwelling a separately signed statement to the following effect:

An exclusive-right-to-sell listing means that if you, the property owner, find a buyer for your house or if another broker finds a buyer, you must pay the agreed-on commission to the present broker.

Figure 3.2 Listing Agreement

Form A
4/25/94

(1) **EXCLUSIVE RIGHT TO SELL AGREEMENT**

THIS AGREEMENT is effective (2) _____ ,19___, and confirms that (3) _____ has (have) appointed
(4) _____ to act as Agent for the sale of property known as _____ , **New**
York.

(5) In return for the Agent's agreement to use Agent's best efforts to sell the above property, the Owner(s) agree(s) to grant the Agent the exclusive right to sell this property under the following terms and conditions:

PERIOD OF AGREEMENT

1.   This agreement shall be effective from the above date and shall expire at midnight on (6) _____ , 19__.

PRICE AT WHICH PROPERTY WILL BE OFFERED AND AUTHORITY

2.   The property will be offered for sale at a list price of (7) _____ and shall be sold, subject to negotiation, at such price and upon such terms to which Owner(s) may agree. The word Owner refers to each and <u>ALL</u> parties who have ownership interest in the property and the undersigned represent(s) they are the sole and exclusive owners and are fully authorized to enter into this agreement.

(8) **COMMISSION TO BE PAID TO AGENT**

3.   The Agent shall be entitled to and Owner shall pay to Agent one commission of _____ of the selling price. Both the Owner(s) and the Agent acknowledge that the above commission rate was not suggested nor influenced by anyone other than the parties to this Agreement. Owner(s) hereby authorizes Agent to make an offer of cooperation to any other licensed real estate broker with whom Agent wishes to cooperate. Any commission due for a sale brought about by a Sub-Agent (another broker who is authorized by Agent to assist in the sale of Owner(s) property) or to an authorized Buyer(s) Agent shall be paid by the Agent from the commission received by the Agent pursuant to this Paragraph.

The commission offered by Agent to Sub-Agents shall be _____ of the gross selling price. The commission offered by Agent to Buyer(s) Agents shall be _____ of the gross selling price.

In the event that Owner(s) authorizes Agent to compensate a Buyer('s) Agent, Owner(s) acknowledges Owner's(s') understanding that such Buyer's Agent is not representing Owner(s) as Sub-Agent and that the Buyer's Agent will be representing only the interests of the prospective purchaser.

(9) **OWNER(S) OBLIGATIONS AFTER THE EXPIRATION OF THIS AGREEMENT**

4.   Owner(s) understands and agrees to pay the commission referred to in paragraph 3, if this property is sold or transferred or is the subject of a contract of sale within _____ months after the expiration date of this agreement involving a person with whom the Agent or a Cooperating Broker or the Owner(s) negotiated or to whom the property is offered, quoted or shown during the period of this listing agreement. Owner(s) will not, however, be obligated to pay such commission if Owner(s) enters into a valid Exclusive Listing Agreement with another New York State licensed real estate broker after the expiration of this agreement.

(10) **WHO MAY NEGOTIATE FOR OWNER(S)**

5.   Owner(s) agree(s) to direct all inquiries to the Agent. Owner(s) elect(s) to have all offers submitted through Agent ___ or Cooperating Agent ___.

(11) **SUBMISSION OF LISTING TO MULTIPLE LISTING SERVICE**

6.   Both Owner(s) and Agent agree that the Agent immediately is to submit this listing agreement to the Westchester Multiple Listing Service, Inc. ("WMLS"), for dissemination to its Participants. No provision of this agreement is intended to nor shall be understood to establish or imply any contractual relationship between the Owner(s) and WMLS nor has WMLS in any way participated in any of the terms of this agreement, including the commission to be paid. Owner(s) acknowledge(s) that the Agent's ability to submit this listing to WMLS or to maintain such listing amongst those included in any compilation of listing information made available by WMLS, is subject to Agent's continued status as a member in good standing of the Westchester County Board of REALTORS, Inc., and Agent's status as a Participant in good standing of WMLS.

(12) **FAIR HOUSING**

7.   Agent and Owner agree to comply fully with local, state and federal fair housing laws against discrimination on the basis of race, color, religion, sex, national origin, handicap, age, marital status and/or familial status, children or other prohibited factors.

Source: Model form developed by Westchester County Board of REALTORS® for optional use by its members.

Figure 3.2   (continued)

⑬ AUTHORIZATION FOR "FOR SALE" SIGN AND OTHER SERVICES

8.   Agent __ is (__ is not) authorized to place a "For Sale" sign on the property. Owner acknowledges that Agent has fully explained to Owner(s) the services and marketing activities which Agent has agreed to provide.

⑭ REQUIREMENTS FOR PUBLICATION IN WMLS COMPILATION

9.   This listing agreement is not acceptable for publication by WMLS unless and until the Owner(s) has duly signed this agreement and an acknowledgement reflecting receipt of the definitions of "Exclusive Right to Sell" and "Exclusive Agency" required by the New York State Department of State - Division of Licensing Services.

⑮ RENTAL OF PROPERTY

10.   Should the Owner(s) desire to rent the property during the period of this agreement, Agent is hereby granted the sole and exclusive right to rent the property, exclusive "FOR RENT" sign privilege and the Owner(s) agrees to pay Agent a rental commission of _____. The applicable commission for the lease term is due and will be paid __ upon the execution of the lease __ upon the date of occupancy. The commission for each and any subsequent renewal thereof, is due and will be paid upon the commencement of each renewal term.

⑯ TERMINATION

11.   Owner(s) understands that if Owner(s) terminates the Agent's authority prior to the expiration of its term, Agent shall retain its contract rights (including but not limited to recovery of its commission, advertising expenses and/or any other damages) incurred by reason of an early termination of this agreement.

⑰ ADDITIONAL POINTS

12.   Additional Points of Agreement, if any:_____
_____

⑱ IN-HOUSE SALES

13.   If the Broker has an agency relationship with the buyer ["buyer's broker"], and that buyer expresses interest in property owned by a seller who also has an agency relationship with the Broker ["seller's broker"], a conflict has arisen.

The Broker shall immediately advise both the buyer client and the seller client of the pertinent facts including the fact that a dual agency situation has arisen, and that the **following options are available:**

[a] **The Broker and buyer could dissolve their Agency relationship.** The buyer may then seek to retain another broker, and/or an attorney, or may represent (her)himself. This would release the buyer from any Broker employment contract which was entered into with the Broker. Broker may continue to act as agent for the seller.

[b] **The Broker and the seller could dissolve their Agency relationship. The** seller may then seek to retain another broker, and/or an attorney, or may represent (her)himself. This would release the seller from any listing agreement which was entered into with Broker. The Broker may continue to act as Agent for the buyer.

[c] **With fully informed consent, the buyer and seller may elect to continue with the brokerage firm serving as a consensual dual agent, which is the exception to the general rule that agents serve one principal.** As a dual agent, the firm and its licensee agents have a duty of fairness to both principals. By mutual agreement the buyer and seller may identify who will negotiate for each principal. For example: [a] the licensee who signed the buyer as a principal of the brokerage firm may negotiate on behalf of the buyer principal and [b] the licensee who signed the seller as a principal of the firm may negotiate on behalf of the seller principal.

In either case, the brokerage commission will be paid by the seller in accordance with the listing agreement with the seller, unless different arrangements have been negotiated.

As a dual agent, the firm and its agents cannot furnish undivided loyalty to either party.

As a dual agent, the firm and its licensee agents have a duty not to disclose confidential information given by one principal to the other principal, such as the price one is willing to pay or accept. Such information may already be known to the firm and its agents. If the information is of such a nature that the agent cannot fairly give advice without disclosing it, the agent cannot properly continue to act as an agent.

The buyer, seller and broker shall memorialize the option of their mutual choice by executing a statutory disclosure notice. If there is no mutual agreement, the proposed transaction between buyer and seller shall not be pursued.

Figure 3.2   (continued)

(19) ALL MODIFICATIONS TO BE MADE IN WRITING

14.   Owner(s) and Agent agree that no change, amendment, modification or termination of this agreement shall be binding on any party unless the same shall be in writing and signed by the parties.

_____   _____
(OWNER)   (DATE)   (AGENT)

_____   By: _____
(OWNER)   (DATE)   (Authorized Representative)   (DATE)

Owner's Mailing Address:_____   Agent's Address: _____
_____   _____
_____   _____

Owner's Telephone: _____   Agent's Telephone: _____

(20) DEFINITIONS

         In accordance with the requirements of the New York State Department of State the undersigned Owner(s) does (do) hereby acknowledge receipt of the following:

         1.   Explanation of "Exclusive Right to Sell" listing;
         2.   Explanation of "Exclusive Agency" listing;
         3.   A list of Participants of Westchester Multiple Listing Service, Inc.

EXPLANATION OF EXCLUSIVE RIGHT TO SELL: (As worded verbatim by the Department of State)

         An "exclusive right to sell" listing means that if you, the owner of the property find a buyer for your house, or if another broker finds a buyer, you must pay the agreed commission to the present broker.

EXPLANATION OF EXCLUSIVE AGENCY: (As worded verbatim by the Department of State)

         An "exclusive agency" listing means that if you, the owner of the property find a buyer, you will not have to pay a commission to the broker. However, if another broker finds a buyer, you will owe a commission to both the selling broker and your present broker.

(21) "THE FAIR HOUSING ACT"

         The Civil Rights Act of 1968 known as the Federal Fair Housing Law makes illegal any discrimination based on race, color, religion, sex or national origin in connection with the sale or rental of housing. The 1988 amendment to this Act (The Fair Housing Amendments Act of 1988) expands the coverage of this law to handicapped persons and families with children. Agent and Owner agree to comply fully with State and local statutes and Federal Fair Housing laws.

Article X of the REALTOR Code of Ethics states:
         "REALTORS shall not deny equal professional services to any person for reasons of race, color, religion, sex, handicap, familial status or national origin. REALTORS shall not be parties to any plan or agreement to discriminate against a person or persons on the basis of race, color, religion, sex, handicap, familial status or national origin."

(22) _____ _____
                                                      Owner

                              _____
                                                      Owner

An exclusive-agency listing means that if you, the property owner, find a buyer, you will not have to pay a commission to the broker. However, if another broker finds a buyer, you will owe a commission to both the selling broker and your present broker.

If an exclusive listing of residential property is obtained by a broker who is a member of an MLS, (1) the broker must give the homeowner a list of the names and addresses of all member brokers and (2) the listing agreement must allow the seller to choose whether all negotiated offers to purchase will be submitted through the listing broker or through the selling broker.

When the broker begins discussions with a potential seller, the broker must disclose for which party he or she will be working, and the seller should sign an acknowledgment that disclosure of agency was received.

Sample listing agreement. The individual specifics of a listing may vary from area to area. Following is a section-by-section analysis of a sample agreement; the numbered items in the list refer to the specific provisions of the contract (see Figure 3.2) used by the Westchester Putnam Multiple Listing Service.

1. *Exclusive right to sell.* The title specifies that this document is an "exclusive right to sell" the property.
2. *Date.* The date of the listing contract is the date it is executed (signed); this may not always be the date the contract becomes effective.
3. *Names.* The names of all persons having an interest in the property should be specified.
4. *Broker or firm.* The name of the broker or firm entering into the listing must be clearly stated in the agreement.
5. *Contract.* This section establishes the document as a bilateral contract and states the promises by both parties that create and bind the agreement.
6. *Termination of agreement.* Both the exact time and the date should be stated to avoid misunderstandings.
7. *Listing price.* Many brokers prefer not to refer to this as the *asking price*.
8. *Commission rate.* This important paragraph establishes the broker's rate of commission. Each brokerage firm is free to set its own fee schedule and to negotiate commission rates if it wishes to. The paragraph also makes an offer of subagency to other members of the MLS and states whether the seller will allow the listing agent to offer part of the commission to a buyer's broker.
9. *Extension clause.* This section, permitted in New York, protects the broker if, after the listing expires, the owner sells the property to someone with whom the original broker had dealt during the listing period. This extension clause does not apply if the owner has relisted the property with another agent.
10. *Negotiation.* The owner agrees to refer all inquiries to the agent and chooses to have any offers submitted by either the listing agent or the selling agent, who may belong to a different firm.
11. *Multiple-listing service.* The agent will circulate information on the listing to all members of the MLS immediately. In some other areas the listing office may have one, two or three days of "office exclusive" before the listing is submitted to the MLS.
12. *Fair housing.* Both parties agree to comply with local, state and federal fair housing laws.
13. *For Sale sign.* The agent may not place a sign on the property without authorization.

14. *Requirements.* The owner(s) must sign this agreement before it is acceptable for publication.
15. *Rental.* If the owner wishes to rent the property during the life of the agreement, the agent has sole and exclusive right to act as the rental agent. The owner will pay the agent a commission for this service.
16. *Termination.* The agent is entitled to payment for advertising expenses, damages and commission if the owner terminates the agreement before it expires.
17. *Additional points.* Anything not illegal may be agreed on by seller and agent. For example, an understanding that "no commission will be due if seller's brother purchases within 30 days" would go here.
18. *In-house sales.* A broker must notify the seller and the buyer that a dual agency situation exists and that both the seller and buyer can dissolve their agency agreement with the broker or with informed consent continue with the broker serving as a consensual dual agent.
19. *Signatures.* The contract should be signed by all owners. The sales associate signs on behalf of the broker or firm; the contract is not made with the individual salesperson.
20. *Definitions.* The seller must receive an explanation of types of listings and a list of all MLS participants, as required by the Department of State.
21. *Civil rights legislation.* This clause serves to alert the owner that both federal and state legislation protect against discrimination.
22. *Owner's acknowledgment.* The seller acknowledges notification of listing definitions.

▼ Buyer Agency Agreements

Agreements between buyers and buyer agents are sometimes referred to as *buyer listings, buyer representation agreements,* or *buyer-agency agreements.* Like a listing agreement, a buyer-agency agreement is also an employment contract. In this case, however, the broker is employed as the buyer's agent. The principal is the buyer, rather than the seller. The purpose of the agreement is to find a suitable property. An agency agreement gives the buyer a degree of representation that is possible only in a fiduciary relationship.

Types of buyer agency agreements. There are three basic types of buyer-agency agreements:

1. *Exclusive buyer agency agreement.* This is a completely exclusive-agency agreement. The buyer is legally bound to compensate the agent whenever he or she purchases a property of the type described in the contract. The broker is entitled to payment regardless of who located the property. Even if the buyer finds the property independently, the agent is entitled to payment.
2. *Exclusive agency buyer agency agreement.* Like an exclusive buyer agency agreement, this is an exclusive contract between the buyer and the agent. However, this agreement limits the broker's right to payment. The broker is entitled to payment only if he or she locates the property that the buyer ultimately purchases. The buyer is free to find a suitable property without being obligated to pay the agent.
3. *Open buyer agency agreement.* This agreement is a non–exclusive agency contract between a broker and a buyer. It permits the buyer to enter into similar agreements with an unlimited number of brokers. The buyer is obligated to compensate only the broker who locates the property ultimately purchased by the buyer.

A broker also may wish to represent a buyer with respect to a single property only. This is similar to obtaining a single-party listing from a seller for the sale of an otherwise unlisted property to a specific buyer. In this kind of arrangement, the buyer agrees to pay the broker a fee if the buyer purchases a specific property. The broker does not reveal the exact location of the property until the agreement is signed.

In any buyer agency agreement, the buyer's broker should clarify the types of services to be offered to the buyer client (in addition to the traditional services rendered by real estate licensees to buyers as customers). These could include such tasks as the structuring of the transaction, investment analysis, assistance in development, assistance in financing and negotiating the sale. Naturally, a buyer's broker must advise the buyer to seek professional legal, tax or other experts should the need arise.

Some of the central issues of a buyer agency agreement include exclusivity, termination date and conflicts of interest.

- *Exclusivity.* An exclusive representation agreement offers the most protection for the broker. It provides a better means for the broker to protect his or her investment of time, energy and skill. If the agency agreement is nonexclusive, the buyer can buy a property through any agent, and the broker has little chance of earning a commission. Open buyer agency agreements also lead to disputes between brokers about who found the property the buyer purchased and who is entitled to the commission.
- *Termination date.* As with a listing agreement, the time and date of termination should be specified to prevent later conflicts. Naturally, the contract period is fully negotiable between the parties. If the broker wants to be reimbursed for a sale that takes place on a certain property after the buyer agency agreement terminates, the broker should insert an extension clause like that found in most listing agreements. Of course, buyer agency agreements can be terminated by mutual consent.
- *Conflicts of interest.* Sometimes a buyer may want to purchase a property listed by the buyer's broker. In this case, the buyer's broker would be put in the position of acting as a dual agent. Another type of conflict would arise if the broker were showing more than one buyer client the same property. The buyer agency should address these types of conflicts and resolve them one way or another. For instance, some agreements provide that the broker will represent the buyer in all cases except in-house listings. Many agreements include an acknowledgment by the buyer that the broker may represent more than one buyer and that if more than one buyer is interested in the same property, it will not be considered a conflict of interest.

An example of a buyer agency agreement appears in Figure 3.3.

Because the agency contract employs the agent to represent the buyer and locate a suitable property, the licensee needs to obtain detailed financial information from the buyer. In addition, the buyer's agent will need specific information about the buyer's specific requirements for a suitable property.

New York Agency Disclosure Requirements

Disclosure of agency relationships in residential transactions is governed by Real Property Law section 443 (RPL 443). This law requires that brokers and salespersons give prospective sellers and buyers (or landlords and tenants) a disclosure statement that describes the roles of sellers' agents, buyers' agents,

Figure 3.3   Exclusive Buyer Agency Agreement

EXCLUSIVE BUYER AGENCY AGREEMENT

COMMISSIONS OR FEES FOR REAL ESTATE SERVICES TO BE PROVIDED ARE NEGOTIABLE BETWEEN REALTOR AND CLIENT. THIS IS A LEGALLY BINDING AGREEMENT. YOU MAY WISH TO CONSULT AN ATTORNEY BEFORE SIGNING IT. FOR THE PURPOSES OF THIS AGREEMENT THE TERM "BUYER" SHALL BE USED TO DESCRIBE PROSPECTIVE PURCHASER(S) OR TENANT(S).

1. APPOINTMENT OF BROKER

By this agreement,_____("Buyer") appoints

_____ ("REALTOR")

as Buyer's exclusive agent, subject to the terms and conditions stated in this Agreement.

By appointing REALTOR as Buyer's exclusive agent, Buyer agrees to conduct all negotiations for the types of property described in Section 2 below through REALTOR and to refer to REALTOR all contact made with Buyer about such properties from other brokers, salespersons, sellers and others during the term of this Agreement.

2. PURPOSE OF AGENCY

Buyer desires to purchase / lease real property (which may include items of personal property) described as follows:
Type: ( ) Residential   ( ) Commercial   ( ) Residential Income   ( ) Industrial   ( ) Vacant Land   ( ) Other
General Description:

_____

_____

Approximate Price Range: $ _____ to $ _____

General Location:_____

_____

Preferred Terms:_____

_____

Other:_____

_____

3. TERM OF AGENCY: REALTOR's authority to act as Buyer's exclusive agent under this Agreement shall begin _____and shall end at midnight _____.

4. REALTOR'S REPRESENTATIONS AND SERVICES: REALTOR represents that REALTOR is duly licensed under the laws of the State of New York as a real estate broker. REALTOR will assist Buyer in locating property of the type described in Section 2 of this Agreement and to negotiate for Buyer any offer by Buyer to purchase or lease such property. During the term of this Agreement, REALTOR will give Buyer information describing and identifying properties which appear to REALTOR to substantially meet the terms set forth in Section 2.

5. COMPENSATION OF REALTOR: In consideration of the services performed by REALTOR under the terms of this Agreement, Buyer agrees to pay REALTOR the following fee(s): (Initial all applicable sections).

_____a. Non-Refundable Retainer: Buyer shall pay REALTOR a Non-Refundable Retainer of $ _____ to be paid to REALTOR herewith whether or not Buyer purchases or leases any property.
_____ This Retainer shall be credited against the Hourly Fee described in subsection (b) below or the Transaction Fee described in subsection (c) below.
_____b. Hourly Fee: Buyer will pay REALTOR at the rate of $ _____per hour for all services performed by REALTOR under the terms of this Agreement, to be billed _____and to be paid within five (5) days after Buyer receives a bill for such services from REALTOR.

Figure 3.3   (continued)

_____ This Hourly Fee shall be credited against the Transaction Fee described in subsection (c) below and shall be kept by REALTOR whether or not a Transaction Fee is earned.

_____c. **Transaction Fee:** Buyer shall pay REALTOR a Transaction Fee which is the lesser of $ _____ or_____% of the purchase or total lease price (and renewals and/or expansions, if applicable) of any property purchased or leased by Buyer. This Transaction Fee shall be due and payable upon closing of the Purchase and Sale Contract or Lease providing, however, if such Contract or Lease fails to close due to default by the Buyer this Transaction Fee shall become immediately due and payable to REALTOR. REALTOR is authorized to attempt to obtain payment of the Transaction Fee from the Seller or Lessor of the property , but Buyer shall have the obligation to pay REALTOR the Transaction Fee set forth in this Agreement if REALTOR cannot obtain payment of such fee from the Seller or Lessor of the property. If within_____ days after the expiration of this Agreement, Buyer purchases or leases any property which REALTOR has submitted to Buyer during the term of this Agreement, Buyer will pay REALTOR the Transaction Fee stated above.

_____d. **Other:** _____

_____

6. OTHER POTENTIAL BUYERS: Buyer understands that other potential buyers have entered or may enter into similar agency contracts with REALTOR which may involve the purchase or lease, through REALTOR, of the same or similar property or properties as Buyer is attempting to purchase or lease. Buyer consents to REALTOR'S representation of such other buyers.

7. CONFLICTING INTERESTS: If REALTOR has an ownership interest in or is an agent for any owner in the sale or lease of any property in which Buyer expresses an interest (e.g. a "company listing"), REALTOR shall immediately notify Buyer of such facts. In such event, if Buyer decides to purchase or lease such property, Buyer will acknowledge the ownership interest of REALTOR or REALTOR'S contractual relationship with that owner and will allow REALTOR to act as dual agent for Buyer and owner. While acting in a dual agency capacity, REALTOR may not, without the express permission of the respective party, disclose to the other party that owner will accept a price less than the listing price or that Buyer will pay a price greater than the price offered. Furthermore, REALTOR'S position as dual agent shall be neutral with respect to both parties, and REALTOR shall act effectively as a mediator between the parties. Buyer is encouraged to refer to New York State DISCLOSURE REGARDING REAL ESTATE AGENCY RELATIONSHIPS, a copy of which is delivered herewith.

8. NONDISCRIMINATION: REALTOR and Buyer agree that all actions carried out under this Agreement shall be in full compliance with local, state and federal fair housing laws against discrimination on the basis of race, creed, color, religion, national origin, sex, familial status, marital status, age or disabilities.

9. PROFESSIONAL COUNSEL: REALTOR hereby recommends that Buyer seek legal, tax, property financing, property inspection, appraisal, environmental engineering and other professional advice (if appropriate) relating to any proposed transaction. Buyer agrees that Buyer will not rely on REALTOR for such professional advice nor rely on REALTOR for payment for such services.

10. OTHER _____

_____

11. ENTIRE AGREEMENT AND ASSIGNABILITY: This Agreement constitutes the complete agreement between REALTOR and Buyer relating to the exclusive agency of REALTOR for Buyer. No modification of any terms of this Agreement shall be valid or binding unless such modification is in writing and signed by Buyer and REALTOR. This agreement is not assignable without written approval of Buyer and REALTOR.

Date:_____   _____**BUYER**

                                             _____**BUYER**

REALTOR: _____   **BY:** _____

Figure 3.4   Agency Disclosure Form

Disclosure Regarding Real Estate Agency Relationships

Before you enter into a discussion with a real estate agent regarding a real estate transaction, you should understand what type of agency relationship you wish to have with that agent.

New York State law requires real estate licensees who are acting as agents of buyers or sellers of property to advise the potential buyers or sellers with whom they work of the nature of their agency relationship and the rights and obligations it creates.

Seller's or Landlord's Agent

If you are interested in selling or leasing real property, you can engage a real estate agent as a seller's agent. A seller's agent, including a listing agent under a listing agreement with the seller, acts solely on behalf of the seller. You can authorize a seller's or landlord's agent to do other things including hire subagents, broker's agents or work with other agents such as buyer's agents on a cooperative basis. A subagent, is one who has agreed to work with the seller's agent, often through a multiple listing service. A subagent may work in a different real estate office.

A seller's agent has, without limitation, the following fiduciary duties to the seller: reasonable care, undivided loyalty, confidentiality, full disclosure, obedience and a duty to account.

The obligations of a seller's agent are also subject to any specific provisions set forth in an agreement between the agent and the seller.

In dealings with the buyer, a seller's agent should (a) exercise reasonable skill and care in performance of the agent's duties; (b) deal honestly, fairly and in good faith; and (c) disclose all facts known to the agent materially affecting the value or desirability of property, except as otherwise provided by law.

Buyer's or Tenant's Agent

If you are interested in buying or leasing real property, you can engage a real estate agent as a buyer's or tenant's agent. A buyer's agent acts solely on behalf of the buyer. You can authorize a buyer's agent to do other things including hire subagents, broker's agents or work with other agents such as seller's agents on a cooperative basis.

A buyer's agent has, without limitation, the following fiduciary duties to the buyer: reasonable care, undivided loyalty, confidentiality, full disclosure, obedience and a duty to account.

The obligations of a buyer's agent are also subject to any specific provisions set forth in an agreement between the agent and the buyer.

In dealings with the seller, a buyer's agent should (a) exercise reasonable skill and care in performance of the agent's duties; (b) deal honestly, fairly and in good faith; and (c) disclose all facts known to the agent materially affecting the buyer's ability and/or willingness to perform a contract to acquire seller's property that are not inconsistent with the agent's fiduciary duties to the buyer.

Broker's Agents

As part of your negotiations with a real estate agent, you may authorize your agent to engage other agents whether you are a buyer/tenant or seller/landlord. As a general rule, those agents owe fiduciary duties to your agent and to you. You are not vicariously liable for their conduct.

Agent Representing Both Seller and Buyer

A real estate agent acting directly or through an associated licensee, can be the agent of both the seller/landlord and the buyer/tenant in a transaction, but only with the knowledge and informed consent, in writing, of both the seller/landlord and the buyer/tenant.

In such a dual agency situation, the agent will not be able to provide the full range of fiduciary duties to the buyer/tenant and seller/landlord.

Figure 3.4   (continued)

The obligations of an agent are also subject to any specific provisions set forth in an agreement between the agent and the buyer/tenant and seller/landlord.

An agent acting as a dual agent must explain carefully to both the buyer/tenant and seller/landlord that the agent is acting for the other party as well. The agent should also explain the possible effects of dual representation, including that by consenting to the dual agency relationship the buyer/tenant and seller/landlord are giving up their right to undivided loyalty.

A BUYER/TENANT OR SELLER/LANDLORD SHOULD CAREFULLY CONSIDER THE POSSIBLE CONSEQUENCES OF A DUAL AGENCY RELATIONSHIP BEFORE AGREEING TO SUCH REPRESENTATION.

General Considerations

You should carefully read all agreements to ensure that they adequately express your understanding of the transaction. A real estate agent is a person qualified to advise about real estate. If legal, tax or other advice is desired, consult a competent professional in that field.

Throughout the transaction you may receive more than one disclosure form. The law requires that each agent assisting in the transaction to present you with this disclosure form. You should read its contents each time it is presented to you, considering the relationship between you and the real estate agent in your specific transaction.

Acknowledgment of Prospective Buyer/Tenant

(1) I have received and read this disclosure notice.

(2) I understand that a seller's/landlord's agent, including a listing agent, is the agent of the seller/landlord exclusively, unless the seller/landlord and buyer/tenant otherwise agree.

(3) I understand that subagents, including subagents participating in a multiple listing service, are agents of the seller/landlord exclusively.

(4) I understand that I may engage my own agent to be my buyer's/tenant's broker.

(5) I understand that the agent presenting this form to me,

_____ of
(name of licensee)

_____ is
(name of firm)

(check applicable relationship)
_____ an agent of the seller/landlord
_____ my agent as a buyer's/tenant's agent

Dated:
Buyer/Tenant:

Dated:
Buyer/Tenant:

Acknowledgment of Prospective Seller/Landlord

(1) I have received and read this disclosure notice.

(2) I understand that a seller's/landlord's agent, including a listing agent, is the agent of the seller/landlord exclusively, unless the seller/landlord and buyer/tenant otherwise agree.

(3) I understand that subagents, including subagents participating in a multiple listing service, are agents of the seller/landlord exclusively.

(4) I understand that a buyer's/tenant's agent is the agent of the buyer/tenant exclusively.

(5) I understand that the agent presenting this form to me,

_____ of
(name of licensee)

_____ is
(name of firm)

(check applicable relationship)
_____ my agent as a seller's/landlord's agent
_____ an agent of the buyer/tenant

Dated:
Seller/Landlord:

Dated:
Seller/Landlord:

Figure 3.4   (continued)

Acknowledgment of Prospective Buyer/Tenant and Seller/Landlord to Dual Agency

(1) I have received and read this disclosure notice.

(2) I understand that a dual agent will be working for both the seller/landlord and buyer/tenant.

(3) I understand that I may engage my own agent as a seller's/landlord's agent or a buyer's/tenant's agent.

(4) I understand that I am giving up my right to the agent's undivided loyalty.

(5) I have carefully considered the possible consequences of a dual agency relationship.

(6) I understand that the agent presenting this form to me,

_____ of

(name of licensee)

_____ is

(name of firm)

a dual agent working for both the buyer/tenant and seller/landlord, acting as such with the consent of both the buyer/tenant and seller/landlord and following full disclosure to the buyer/tenant and seller/landlord.

Dated: Dated:
Buyer/Tenant: Seller/Landlord:

Dated: Dated:
Buyer/Tenant: Seller/Landlord:

Acknowledgment of the Parties to the Contract

(1) I have received, read and understand this disclosure notice.

(2) I understand that _____ of

(name of real estate licensee)

_____ is

(name of firm)

(Check applicable relationship)   _____   an agent of the seller/landlord

_____   an agent of the buyer/tenant

_____   a dual agent working for both the buyer/tenant and seller/landlord, acting as such with the consent of both buyer/tenant and seller/landlord and following full disclosure to the buyer/tenant and seller/landlord.

I also understand that _____ of

(name of real estate licensee)

_____ is

(name of firm)

(Check applicable relationship)   _____   an agent of the seller/landlord

_____   an agent of the buyer/tenant

_____   a dual agent working for both the buyer/tenant and seller/landlord, acting as such with the consent of both buyer/tenant and seller/landlord and following full disclosure to the buyer/tenant and seller/landlord.

Dated: Dated:
Buyer/Tenant: Seller/Landlord:

Dated: Dated:
Buyer/Tenant: Seller/Landlord:

listing brokers' agents and dual agents (see Figure 3.4). The buyer or seller must sign an acknowledgment that certifies that he or she has read the disclosure form and understands the role of the particular agent in the transaction.

RPL 443 applies to residential transactions involving the sale or lease of one- to four-unit residential property. A listing agent must obtain the seller's signed acknowledgment before entering a listing agreement. A buyer agent must obtain the buyer's signed acknowledgment before entering an agreement to represent the buyer.

Signed acknowledgments. Agents in a transaction must obtain signed acknowledgments of disclosure from all parties with whom they interact in the transaction. For example, a seller agent (listing broker, listing broker's salesperson or seller subagent cooperating broker or salesperson) must provide the disclosure and obtain the acknowledgment from all prospective buyers or their buyer agents at the time of the **first substantive contact** between the agent and the prospective buyer or buyer agent. (An example of a first substantive contact with a buyer is when the buyer walks into the agent's office and begins discussing his or her real estate needs or financial situation.) Similarly, buyer agents must obtain this acknowledgment from the seller or the seller's agent at the time of first substantive contact. (The first substantive contact with a seller may occur when the seller begins explaining his or her reasons for selling.)

RPL 443 provides a special form of acknowledgment for consensual dual agency transactions. This acknowledgment is essential for such transactions, but the broker also should have the parties sign a more specific consent to dual agency that spells out the precise nature of the relationship of the parties in the particular transaction.

Finally, if a purchase agreement is entered into between a buyer and seller, both must sign an acknowledgment regarding the role of any agent who is a party to the transaction, unless both parties are represented by attorneys who arrange for and prepare the contract.

Copies of the agency disclosure forms obtained in the course of a broker's business must be maintained for three years. If any buyer or seller refuses to sign the forms, the agent may make a written affirmation that the disclosure form was provided to that party (see Figure 3.5). This statement should be maintained in the broker's file in lieu of the signed acknowledgment.

RPL 443 also provides for *broker's agents.* In theory, a broker's agent is a cooperating broker who is an agent of the listing broker but not strictly a subagent of the seller. A broker's agent has fiduciary duties to the seller, but the seller is not liable for acts of the broker's agent unless the seller specifically authorizes those acts. Although this concept came directly from the Department of State, it remains to be seen whether this limited liability will be upheld by the courts.

A second disclosure requirement is found in DOS (Department of State) Regulation 175.7, which states "A real estate broker shall make it clear for which party he is acting and he shall not receive compensation from more than one party except with the full knowledge and consent of all parties." This requirement applies to all types of transactions, not just residential.

Figure 3.5 Disclosure Affirmation

DECLARATION PURSUANT TO SECTION 443 (3) (F) OF THE REAL PROPERTY LAW

State of New York)

) ss.:

_____ (name), being duly sworn, deposes and says:

1. I am the principal broker/associate broker/licensed salesperson affiliated with _____ (name of agency).

2. I make this Affidavit in compliance with Section 443 (3) (F) of the New York State Real Property Law.

3. On the _____ day of _____ _____ , 199_____ , I presented to _____ (name of buyer or seller) the disclosure forms required pursuant to Section 443 of the Real Property Law. The form of the Disclosure Form as presented is attached to this statement.

4. The above named buyer/seller refused to execute an acknowledgment of the receipt of this disclosure form despite my request that it be executed.

5. A copy of this statement and additional copies of the Disclosure Form are being mailed to the person(s) named in paragraph 3, contemporaneously with the execution of this Affidavit.

_____

(Name)

Brokers must be careful to observe the requirement of DOS 175.7 regarding compensation from more than one party. This rule is not strictly limited to compensation related to the sale itself (commission or buyer agent fee); *it applies to any compensation that is in any way related to the transaction.* Thus a selling agent who accepts compensation for arranging the buyer's loan (mortgage broker's commission), in addition to sharing in the commission split for the sale, is in violation of DOS 175.7.

Note that the effectiveness of state-mandated disclosure statements has come under question recently. In a well-publicized Minnesota case (*Edina Realty*), a court ruled that a real estate company failed to disclose a dual agency situation adequately, even though the real estate licensees involved complied with the requirements of the state disclosure statute. While Minnesota has since revised its law to clarify its disclosure requirements, this case was an important reminder that complete, full disclosure is always vital and that in some cases, merely complying with statutory requirements may not be enough.

Key Terms

blanket unilateral offer of cooperation	first substantive contact
blanket unilateral offer of subagency	implied creation of a subagency
	informed consent
broker's agent	listing agent
buyer agency	open listing
cooperating broker	seller agency
dual agency	selling agent
exclusive-agency listing	single agency
exclusive right to represent	subagency
exclusive-right-to-sell listing	undisclosed dual agency

Summary

Real estate agents may act in a variety of capacities. Agency relationships exist between a broker and client, between a broker and his or her salespersons and between cooperating brokers. It is vital that agents understand their relationships to the parties in a transaction and act accordingly.

Single agents represent only one party in a transaction, the buyer or the seller. Buyer agents represent buyers, although their compensation may be provided by the seller. Seller agents represent the seller. Unless a cooperating agent (selling agent) specifically rejects an agency relationship with a seller, he or she will normally be deemed a subagent of the seller in the transaction. Listing agents should always obtain the informed consent of the seller before entering cooperative agreements that create subagencies.

A dual agent represents both the buyer and the seller in the same transaction. Unless both parties have given their informed written consent to this form of representation, dual agency is strictly forbidden and can result in severe penalties. Dual agency can arise or be implied in many situations, often without conscious action by the agent. In-house sales, cooperating brokers who are buyer agents, and broker or salesperson self-dealing are all situations of potential dual agency.

Disclosure of agency relationships is required by law. Brokers and salespersons must disclose the nature of their representation to all parties whom they represent as agents and to all parties with whom they have substantive contact in the course of representing a client.

1. Cooperating brokers would not be
   a. subagents.
   b. brokers' agents.
   c. buyers' agents.
   d. sellers' agents.

2. Broker John Brown owes customer Susie Smith
   a. loyalty.
   b. fairness and honesty.
   c. confidentiality.
   d. accounting.

3. The Agency Disclosure form must be presented, explained and signed
   a. when the customer makes an offer.
   b. when the seller accepts an offer.
   c. at the first substantive contact.
   d. when the seller and buyer first meet.

4. The acknowledgment to the contract need not be signed when
   a. attorneys represent both parties and prepare the contract.
   b. the closing is delayed.
   c. there is no earnest money deposit.
   d. the closing is in escrow.

5. In a single agency agreement in which a broker represents a seller
   a. the buyer is the client.
   b. the seller is the client.
   c. the seller is the customer.
   d. the buyer is a subagent.

6. On the sale of an "in-house" listing to buyer client Murphy, broker Susan
   a. can terminate the buyer-agency agreement.
   b. can get the informed consent of both parties.
   c. may be acting as a dual agent.
   d. Any of the above

7. Cooperating brokers must inform the listing agent whether they are acting as
   a. subagents of the seller.
   b. buyers' agents.
   c. brokers' agents.
   d. All of the above

8. A buyer's agent owes the seller
   a. loyalty.
   b. confidentiality.
   c. honest and fair business dealing.
   d. accounting.

9. An agency relationship is determined by
   a. the source of compensation.
   b. how well the parties know each other.
   c. agreement between the principal and the agent.
   d. first substantive contact.

10. Undisclosed dual agency may result in Broker Joan Jones
    a. losing her license.
    b. losing the commission.
    c. being liable for damages.
    d. All of the above

11. When Broker Tony Thomas purchases a property through an MLS, the potential is high for

    a. a conflict of interest.
    b. his not collecting a fee.
    c. a dual agency.
    d. All of the above

12. Real Property Law section 443 disclosure requirements apply only to

    a. sale or lease of one- to four-unit residential properties.
    b. all types of real estate transactions.
    c. mortgage financing arrangements.
    d. commercial properties.

13. When listing a property, ABC Realty best protects its chances of earning a commission if the listing is a(n)

    a. exclusive-right-to-sell listing.
    b. for sale by owner.
    c. exclusive-agency listing.
    d. open listing.

14. Broker Susan represents Murphy as a buyer's agent. She wants to show Murphy a property she has listed. If broker Susan shows Murphy the property, she

    a. will have done nothing wrong.
    b. must disclose to the seller that she is also representing the buyer.
    c. must first get the informed, written consent of both the buyer and the seller to her acting as a dual agent in the transaction.
    d. must first notify the Secretary of State that she intends to represent both the buyer and the seller.

The Business of Real Estate Brokerage

John, the broker for North End Realty, is having a conversation over lunch with Mary, who is the broker for Valley Realty. When the discussion turns to one of John's new listings, an impressive home in one of the town's finer neighborhoods, he casually mentions that the owner has agreed to pay the usual 7 percent commission, and offers Mary a 50/50 commission split if she can find a buyer for the property. Is there anything wrong with this conversation?

Federal and state laws have important consequences for the operation of real estate businesses. Some of the more important of such laws relate to antitrust restrictions, operation of multiple listing services (MLSs) and the employment status of agents who work for a broker.

Vicarious Liability

Liability that is created not because of a person's actions but because of the relationship between the liable person and other parties is called **vicarious liability.** Subagency creates circumstances or situations that result in vicarious liability. For example, suppose that the sellers explain to the listing agent that the roof leaks and needs repairs. The sellers want to be sure that potential buyers know about the problem roof, and the listing agent assures the sellers that she will tell all prospective buyers. Another member of the MLS, who is acting as a subagent of the sellers, intentionally keeps the roof problems a secret from the purchaser. When the purchaser discovers the problem, he sues the selling broker, the listing broker and the sellers. Even though the sellers did nothing wrong themselves, they can be held liable for the actions of the subagent through the principle of vicarious liability. Vicarious liability is an important principle to bear in mind when deciding which form of agency is most desirable. For example, by choosing to represent the buyer rather than be a subagent of the seller, a licensee may lessen the potential for vicarious liability. (The benefits of buyer agency and seller agency are discussed in Chapter 3.)

> **ANTITRUST LAWS PROHIBIT**
>
> - price fixing,
> - group boycotting,
> - market allocation and
> - tie-in arrangements.

Antitrust Laws

Antitrust laws are designed to prevent the unreasonable **restraint of trade** (business) as a result of the cooperation or conspiracy of various members of the trade. One of the most important antitrust acts is the Sherman Antitrust Act. The Sherman Act prohibits any kind of contract, combination or conspiracy in the restraint of trade. A *conspiracy* is defined as *two or more separate business entities participating in a common scheme or plan, the effect of which is the restraint of trade.* Antitrust laws prohibit practices such as

- **price-fixing:** an agreement between members of a trade to artificially maintain prices at a set level;

- **group boycotting:** an agreement between members of a trade to exclude other members from fair participation in the activities of the trade;
- **market allocation:** an agreement between members of a trade to refrain from competition in specific market areas; and
- **tie-in arrangements:** arrangements by which provision of certain products or services is made contingent on the purchase of other unrelated products or services.

In 1950, in the case of *United States v. National Association of Real Estate Boards,* the Supreme Court recognized that *trade,* as used in the Sherman Act, included the real estate brokerage business. Therefore, the real estate business is subject to the restraints of antitrust laws. In this case, the mandatory fee schedules that were set and enforced by real estate boards were held to violate the Sherman Act. In the 1970s several more real estate boards and associations were prosecuted under antitrust laws for unfair restraint of trade. The result of those cases is that real estate agents and professional real estate associations must exercise extreme care to avoid any appearance of price-fixing in regard to real estate commissions.

Violation of the Sherman Act is a felony, and penalties can be as high as $350,000 for an individual and $10 million for corporations. A jail term of up to three years is also possible.

The Clayton Antitrust Act supplements the Sherman Act. Under the Clayton Act private parties are allowed to sue antitrust violators, and if successful, they can recover three times the damages incurred plus court costs and attorneys' fees.

The Federal Trade Commission (FTC) has the power to declare trade practices unfair and to enforce compliance with the Sherman Act and some sections of the Clayton Act, but it cannot impose penal sanctions. The Department of Justice also has the power to fine antitrust law violators.

Most states, including New York, have laws against monopolies, restraints of trade, and unfair trade practices.

▼ **Commissions**

Any conversation between two brokers from different brokerages regarding commission rates charged to clients is strictly off-limits. The only permissible discussion of commissions between two competing brokers would be a discussion of the commission split between a listing broker and a selling broker in a cooperative sale. Brokers may discuss client commission rates with their salespeople as a matter of office policy, but they may never discuss such rates with brokers from other offices.

In *United States v. Foley,* a conspiracy to fix commission rates was found when a member of a board of REALTORS® announced at a board function that he was raising his gross commission rate, and that he did not care what others did. The court viewed the announcement as an invitation to conspire, and the subsequent actions of the other board members were viewed as an acceptance of this invitation. This case is important, because it illustrates the fact that alleged conspirators do not actually have to consult with each other to be judged guilty of conspiring to fix commission rates.

The prohibition against discussion of commission rates among independent brokers extends to publication as well as conversation. Many years ago, certain real estate associations maintained mandatory commission rates for their members, but today an association would be in trouble if it attempted to publish recommended rates or a even a survey of going rates. For the same reason, MLSs do not publish the commission rates that are charged to owners, only the amount of commission offered to cooperating brokers.

▼ Group Boycotts

The object of a **group boycott** is to hurt or destroy a competitor; it takes only two brokers to form a group that can be found guilty of a group boycott. For example, if two brokers agree to refuse to cooperate with a third broker or agree to cooperate with that third broker but on less-favorable terms, that action is an automatic violation of the antitrust act.

Two independent brokers should never engage in negative conversation regarding the business practices of a third broker, because such a conversation could be construed as an attempt at a group boycott of the third broker. A broker who questions the ethics or practices of another broker may freely choose not to do business with such a broker but may not convey his or her feelings to other brokers in any manner that might lead them to take similar action.

▼ Market Allocation

Agreements between brokers to divide their markets or customers and refrain from competing with each other's business violate antitrust laws. *These agreements could be about geographic territories, price ranges, or types of properties, sociological divisions of business or the refusal to deal with a competitor.*

▼ Tie-in Agreements

A **tie-in,** or tying, **agreement** is defined as an agreement to sell one product only on the condition that the buyer purchase another product as well. An example of a real estate tying agreement would be a so-called list-back clause. For example, a subdivision developer may sell a lot to a builder on the condition that the builder agree to list (or list back) the improved property with the developer for resale to a home buyer. A property management agreement that requires that the owner list the managed property with the manager should the owner decide to sell it is another example of a tying agreement. Tie-in agreements are violations of the antitrust laws.

▼ Enforcement

The Sherman Act is enforced by the U.S. Attorney General through the Antitrust Division of the Department of Justice. Both civil and criminal actions can be brought against those who violate antitrust laws. A corporation found guilty of violating the Sherman Act can be fined up to $10 million; an individual may be fined up to $350,000 and/or be sentenced to three years in prison.

▼ Risk Reduction

Brokers are liable both for their own actions and the actions of their licensees; therefore, it is imperative that brokers educate themselves on antitrust issues. Brokers also should train their licensees to be aware of what may constitute an antitrust law violation. Brokers never should use forms that contain preprinted commission rates, listing periods or protection periods. Each of these provisions should include a blank that will be filled in after negotiation between the parties.

Brokers always should take care to establish their fees and other listing terms independently, without consulting any competing firms. Each business judgment and negotiated term should be documented in the form of a confidential memo. Brokers also must avoid discussing business plans with competitors.

Multiple Listing Services

Multiple listing services (MLSs) play an important role in the marketing of property, especially residential property. The ability to participate in an MLS greatly enhances the exposure of a property in the market, providing advantages not only to the seller but to the participating listing broker as well. The importance of MLSs in the real estate industry has been recognized in a number of court cases that have imposed obligations on these services to provide open access on a nondiscriminatory basis.

▼ Access to MLS

An MLS must permit access by any licensed real estate broker who can satisfy the requirements of the MLS. These requirements must be reasonable, and they may not be discriminatory in nature or effect. The charge for membership in the MLS must be equivalent to the cost involved in setting up the new member, and fees must be reasonable and nondiscriminatory.

MLS regulations may not unreasonably restrict the operations of its members. Participating brokers may not be prohibited from membership in another MLS or from cooperating with non-MLS brokers. The MLS may not regulate a broker's office hours, and it may not restrict the types of properties that can be advertised through the MLS.

A court decision from the 11th Circuit Federal Court of Appeals (which includes Florida, Georgia and Alabama) has held that a REALTOR® MLS may not exclude non-REALTORS® from membership. The implications of this case may well lead to elimination of such restrictions on a nationwide basis. In New York, MLSs are considering this provision on a voluntary basis.

Salesperson Employment Status

All licensed salespeople are required by law to work for a broker in their real estate activities. In doing so, the salesperson may be employed either as an **employee** or as an **independent contractor.** The distinction between an employee and an independent contractor is an important one, with significant tax consequences as well as important effects on the ability of a broker to control the activities of his or her salespeople.

▼ Employee Status

The employer-employee relationship allows a broker to exercise certain controls over salespeople. The broker can require that an employee adhere to regulations affecting working hours, office routine and dress standards. As an employer a broker is required by the federal government to withhold Social Security tax and income tax from the compensation paid to employees. An employee is covered by unemployment insurance and workers' compensation. A broker may provide employees with fringe benefits, such as health insurance, Social Security contributions, pension plans, sick leave and paid vacations. Such benefits are variously estimated to add 25 percent to 50 percent to the cost of an employee's base salary. A broker who chooses to regard salespersons as employees must take such costs into consideration when working out commission schedules.

▼ Independent Contractor Status

Most salespersons act as independent contractors. A survey by the National Association of REALTORS® found that nine out of ten real estate firms treated their sales associates as independent contractors. Brokers traditionally have maintained this relationship to avoid the bookkeeping problems of withholding taxes, Social Security payments, unemployment insurance and other such items that become complex when based not on a regular salary but on unpredictable commissions.

Errors and omissions insurance. A broker may carry errors and omissions insurance on all salespeople, regardless of their status as employees or independent contractors. The cost may be borne by the broker or by the salesperson.

▼ **Tests of Employment**

The broker who chooses independent contractor status for associates should keep on file agreements signed by the associates with wording that has been reviewed by the broker's attorney. Recent safe-harbor guidelines provide that the IRS will not challenge independent contractor status where the associate (1) is licensed as a real estate broker or salesperson, (2) has income based on sales output and subject to fluctuation and (3) performs services pursuant to a written contract specifying independent contractor status.

In 1986, New York State adopted similar guidelines on independent contractor status for real estate licensees, whose situation had been unclear with regard to state programs such as unemployment insurance and workers' compensation insurance. The New York Department of Labor, in evaluating associates' status with regard to unemployment insurance, also stresses the importance of a current, written contract between broker and salesperson. A sample contract that meets the Department of Labor requirements, suggested by the New York State Association of REALTORS®, is shown in Figure 4.1.

The requirements for independent contractor status under New York State law are as follows:

1. Substantially all of the licensee's compensation (whether or not paid in cash) for services performed on behalf of the broker must be directly related to sales or other output, rather than to the number of hours worked.
2. There must be a written contract for services between the broker and the licensee, *executed within the past fifteen months,* that indicates that the licensee is employed as an independent contractor.
3. The written contract between the broker and licensee must not have been executed under duress (i.e., the broker cannot force the licensee to sign the agreement, although the broker could choose not to maintain the licensee's license if he or she refuses to sign).
4. The written contract must contain the following provisions:
   - That the licensee will be treated for all purposes by the broker as an independent contractor
   - That the licensee will be paid a commission directly related to gross sales or other output without deduction for taxes
   - That the licensee will not receive any compensation related to the number of hours worked
   - That the licensee will not be treated as an employee for federal or state tax purposes
   - That the licensee may work any hours he or she chooses
   - That the licensee may work out of his or her home as well as out of the broker's office
   - That the licensee is free to engage in outside employment

Figure 4.1 Sample Independent Contractor Agreement

AGREEMENT

THIS AGREEMENT, (hereinafter "Agreement") made and entered into this day of _____ 199 , by and between _____ (hereinafter "Sales Associate") and _____ (hereinafter "Broker").

WHEREAS, the Sales Associate and the Broker are both duly licensed pursuant to Article 12-A of the Real Property Law of the State of New York; and

WHEREAS, the Sales Associate and the Broker wish to enter into this Agreement in order to define their respective rights, duties and obligations.

NOW THEREFORE, in consideration of the terms, covenants, conditions and mutual promises contained herein, and other good and valuable consideration, it is hereby stipulated and agreed as follows:

1. The Sales Associate is engaged as an independent contractor associated with the Broker pursuant to Article 12-A of the Real Property Law and shall be treated as such for all purposes, including but not limited to Federal and State taxation, withholding, unemployment insurance and workers' compensation; and

2. The Sales Associate (a) shall be paid a commission on his or her gross sales, if any, without deduction for taxes, which commission shall be directly related to sales or other output; (b) shall not receive any remuneration related to the number of hours worked; and (c) shall not be treated as an employee with respect to such services for Federal and State tax purposes; and

3. The Sales Associate shall be permitted to work any hours he or she chooses; and

4. The Sales Associate shall be permitted to work out of his or her own home or the office of the Broker; and

5. The Sales Associate shall be free to engage in outside employment; and

6. The Broker may provide office facilities and supplies for the use of the Sales Associate, but the Sales Associate shall otherwise bear his or her own expenses, including but not limited to automobile, travel and entertainment expenses; and

7. The Broker and Sales Associate shall comply with the requirements of Article 12-A of the Real Property Law and the regulations pertaining thereto, but such compliance shall not affect the Sales Associate's status as an independent contractor nor would it be construed as an indication that the Sales Associate is an employee of the Broker for any purposes whatsoever; and

8. This contract and the association created hereby may be terminated by either party hereto at any time upon notice given to the other; and

9. This Agreement is deemed to have been entered into in, and will be construed and interpreted in accordance with the laws of the State of New York; and

10. BY SIGNING BELOW THE UNDERSIGNED STIPULATE AND AGREE THAT THEY HAVE COMPLETELY READ THIS AGREEMENT, THAT THE TERMS HEREOF ARE FULLY UNDERSTOOD AND VOLUNTARILY ACCEPTED BY THEM AND THAT THIS AGREEMENT IS NOT SIGNED UNDER DURESS.

IN WITNESS WHEREOF, the parties hereto have executed this Agreement as of the day and year first above written.

_____
SALES ASSOCIATE

_____
BROKER

PREPARED BY THE NEW YORK STATE
ASSOCIATION OF REALTORS®, INC.

Source: Reprinted with permission of the New York State Association of REALTORS®, Inc.

- That the broker may provide office facilities and supplies for use by the licensee, but the licensee will otherwise bear his or her own expenses, including automobile, travel and entertainment expenses
- That the licensee and broker will act in accordance with the terms of the Real Property Law and Department of State real estate regulations
- That either the licensee or the broker may terminate the agreement at any time on notice to the other

The existence of a written agreement is clearly an important aspect of maintaining an independent contractor relationship between the broker and the salesperson. However, the written agreement will not prevent employee status from being implied as a result of the conduct of the broker and salesperson. For example, if the broker requires that the salesperson attend staff meetings or includes the salesperson in a company pension plan, this may be seen as evidence that the relationship between them is actually that of employer and employee. The consequences of such a determination can be drastic for both the broker and the salesperson.

The employment contract between the broker and the salesperson or associate broker should be renewed each year. The contract should include provisions for the termination of employment.

For the broker, the determination that a salesperson is actually an employee will result in liability for state and federal unemployment insurance premiums; workers' compensation and disability insurance coverages; and federal and state withholding taxes, including the employer's share of Social Security taxes. For the salesperson, the result will be the inability to claim self-employment expense deductions on IRS Form 1040 Schedule C, as well as the fact that the salesperson's commission payments will be subjected to withholding for all applicable state and federal taxes.

The dilemma for brokers who want to maintain independent contractor status for their associates is that this limits the ability of the brokers to control the activity of their salespeople. Too much control often leads to the conclusion that the salesperson is an employee. On the other hand, brokers are legally liable for the actions of their salespeople, and have an obligation under the Real Property Law and Department of State regulations to supervise their salespeople's activities. The New York State law regarding independent contractor status for real estate licensees recognizes part of this dilemma and specifically states that compliance with the Real Property Law and Department of State real estate regulations will not be construed as an indication of employee status (see Figure 4.2).

Exemption from business taxation. The New York City Department of Finance has issued a Statement of Audit Procedure that will exempt salespersons and associate brokers from the New York City Unincorporated Business Tax if the following 11 requirements are met:

1. The individual must hold only one license as a salesperson or associate broker.
2. The individual must be affiliated with only one real estate brokerage firm at a time, and that firm must hold the individual's license and be named on such license.

Figure 4.2   Unemployment Insurance Notice for Real Estate Salespersons

**NEW YORK STATE,
DEPARTMENT OF LABOR,
UNEMPLOYMENT INSURANCE DIVISION
NOTICE TO EMPLOYERS**

Persons Engaged in Real Estate Sales

Effective October 1, 1986, services performed by a licensed real estate broker or sales associate are excluded from coverage if it can be proven that all of the following conditions are met:

(A) substantially all of the remuneration (whether or not paid in cash) for the services performed by such broker or sales associate is directly related to sales or other output (including the performance of services) rather than to the number of hours worked;

and

(B) the services performed by the broker or sales associate are performed pursuant to a written contract executed between such broker or sales associate and the person for whom the services are performed within the past twelve to fifteen months;

and

(C) such contract was not executed under duress and contains the following provisions:

1. that the broker or sales associate is engaged as an independent contractor associated with the person for whom services are performed pursuant to Article 12-A of the Real Property Law and shall be treated as such for all purposes;

2. that they (a) shall be paid a commission directly related to their gross sales or other output without deduction for taxes; (b) shall not receive any remuneration related to the number of hours worked; and (c) shall not be treated as employees with respect to such services for federal and state tax purposes;

3. that they shall be permitted to work any hours they choose;

4. that they shall be permitted to work out of their own homes or the office of the person for whom services are performed;

5. that they shall be free to engage in outside employment;

6. that the person for whom the services are performed may provide office facilities and supplies for the use of the broker or sales associate, but that they shall otherwise bear their own expenses, including but not limited to automobile, travel, and entertainment expenses;

7. that the person for whom the services are performed and the broker or sales associate shall comply with the requirements of Article 12-A of the Real Property Law and the regulations pertaining thereto, but such compliance shall not affect their status as independent contractors nor should it be construed as an indication that they are employees of such person for any purpose whatsoever;

8. that the contract and the association may be terminated by either party at any time upon notice to the other.

3. All printed material used by the individual must display the name of the real estate brokerage firm with which the individual is affiliated.
4. The brokerage firm must provide the individual with office facilities, that is, a desk, telephone, supplies, etc., at the office of the brokerage firm at no cost to the individual.
5. All listings produced by the individual must be subject to approval by a supervising employee of the brokerage firm. The individual must not have any legal authority to bind the brokerage firm in any agreements.
6. The individual must qualify for nonemployee status under the Internal Revenue Code.
7. The individual may not have any employees. If the individual claims a deduction on Form 1040 Schedule C for commissions or other compensation paid, this requirement is not met.
8. The individual may not take a deduction on Form 1040 Schedule C for a home office. Separate deductions for telephone, automobile, entertainment, travel or postage, or contributions to a Keogh plan are permitted.
9. The individual may not engage in purchases or sales of real estate as a dealer.
10. The individual may not engage in any other regular trade or business activities related to real estate.
11. The individual may not, in his or her own name, and as a salesperson or associate broker, receive checks for commissions or other payments from

any person other than the brokerage firm with which he or she is affiliated, be a party to a brokerage or cobrokerage agreement, or advertise a property for sale or lease.

In addition, an individual must meet at least three of the following five requirements:

1. The individual must be subject to minimum office hours or performance goals in terms of commissions earned or listings obtained by the brokerage firm with which the individual is affiliated.
2. The individual must be subject to standards of behavior or to direction or training as to real estate sales techniques or be required to attend periodic meetings of sales staff.
3. The individual may not claim a deduction on Form 1040 Schedule C for advertising expenses.
4. The individual must be subject to periodic written performance evaluation.
5. If the brokerage firm with which the individual is affiliated carries errors and omissions insurance, the individual must be covered at no additional cost to the individual.

The Broker's Responsibility To Manage and Supervise

A broker has many special responsibilities. A broker must be an effective real estate sales agent, a business manager, a financial analyst, a marketer, a personnel manager and a leader. A broker should also be familiar with basic real estate law. Here we will focus on some of the basic tasks that must be accomplished before a real estate brokerage can operate effectively and within the parameters of the license law.

▼ Organization of the Brokerage Company

Naturally, one of the first steps a broker takes when starting a brokerage business is deciding what *form of ownership* the company will take. The form of ownership is essentially the framework for the brokerage business. The way a business is organized will determine the broker's legal obligations for the company's debts, his or her tax obligations and his or her decision-making powers. Because the form of ownership has so many legal and tax implications, brokers should always consult an attorney and an accountant before making a decision.

There are various forms of ownership that can accommodate sole ownership or joint ownership. These include the sole proprietorship, corporation, S corporation, general partnership, limited partnership and limited liability company (but the limited liability company is not yet permitted to be a real estate licensee).

Sole proprietorship. The broker is the sole owner of a sole proprietorship. The broker bears all the responsibility for the company and is solely responsible for all debts and other liabilities; the broker also can claim all the earnings and profits of the company.

Many small businesses are sole proprietorships because they are relatively simple to create and the legal paperwork is minimal. However, the existence of a sole proprietorship depends largely on the broker. If the broker dies or becomes incapacitated, the company may not survive.

Corporation. A corporation is a separate legal entity (often referred to as a *legal fiction* or an *artificial person*) created under state laws. A corporation consists of an association of one or more individuals or other corporations (shareholders) but has an existence that is separate from those shareholders. A corporation has the legal capacity to enter into contracts and own property.

There are several advantages to the corporate form of business ownership. The owners (or shareholders) of a corporation are *not liable for the debts of the corporation* (other than employee wages) unless they have signed a personal guarantee of the corporation's obligations. In other words, the debts, judgments or bankruptcies of the corporation will not affect the individual shareholders. All the shareholders risk is their original investment in the corporation.

A corporation has a perpetual existence—it does not die. Therefore, if a managing broker dies or becomes incapacitated, the brokerage can continue to operate (as long as another broker is found to carry on the business). The ownership of the corporation can be easily transferred to another person simply by selling the corporate stock. In addition, a corporation may have an unlimited number of owners and may earn an unlimited amount of income.

A major disadvantage of corporate ownership is the phenomenon known as *double taxation.* The corporation's profits are taxed once at the corporate level, and then, when those profits are distributed to the shareholders, the profits are taxed again at the individual level. Also, individual owners cannot take advantage of corporate losses; losses may be applied only against the corporation's future profits.

S corporation. An S corporation has nearly all of the advantages of a regular corporation. An added benefit is that the profits and losses of the business are passed on directly to the shareholders. There is no double taxation. The shareholders pay the taxes on the corporate profits or deduct corporate losses on their individual tax returns.

There can be no more than 75 shareholders in an S corporation, and no more than 20 percent of the income may come from passive investments (such as investment property rentals). There are also strict rules on when the corporation can declare S corporation status. If any of these rules are violated, the corporation will be deemed a regular corporation.

General partnership. *A partnership is a business in which two or more co-owners engage in a business for profit.* All owners can have an equal say in management and can share equally in the profits or losses of the business. The partnership is not a taxable entity like the corporation, so the individual partners pay the taxes on the earnings. A partnership may dissolve on the death, bankruptcy or disability of one of the partners, unless the partnership agreement provides otherwise.

Limited partnership. A limited partnership must have at least one general partner (who manages the company and is liable for all partnership obligations) and one or more limited partners (who are merely investors and are responsible for neither the partnership management nor the partnership's financial liabilities).

Limited liability companies. New York allows limited liability companies and limited liability partnerships to be formed. These companies enjoy the limited liability of corporate shareholders and the tax advantages of partnerships. These companies are similar in effect to S corporations, but have fewer restrictions on their formation and income sources.

Recruiting Licensees. Once a brokerage company is formed, the broker must find salespeople to recruit. Recruiting is an important part of any broker's job. Not only must the broker choose the best associates available, the broker also must be careful not to violate any antidiscrimination laws.

Before taking on associates, the owner must consider the company's overall goals, public image and available space. Whether the firm wants part-time salespersons or only full-timers should be decided beforehand. Recruiting must be coordinated with training. The small office that offers informal one-on-one training may recruit on a continuing basis. The large firm may prefer a single recruitment campaign followed by a number of classroom training sessions. Advertising, career nights and trial training sessions are often used for recruitment. Classified or small display ads in newspapers are common.

The broker who takes on anyone who walks in the door risks a loss in office morale, the financial drain of an unproductive associate and legal problems arising from unethical associates. Common methods of selection include application forms, aptitude tests and personal interviews.

Among topics explored during an interview may be the applicant's attitude toward number of hours worked, weekend and evening work and the amount of income anticipated from commissions. Other jobs presently held should be discussed. The prospective associate's attitudes toward ethics and civil rights should be explored. The manager often cautions the applicant that no income may be forthcoming for three to six months and explains that a regular draw against future commissions is inconsistent with independent contractor status. In explaining the nature of real estate brokerage, the manager can stress the necessity for a salesperson to handle stress, face disappointments and accept occasional rejection. The decision to take on a particular salesperson should consider not only the profit potential but also whether the individual fits the company image and will contribute to office harmony.

While going through the recruiting process, the broker must keep **fair employment laws** in mind. The broker must be sure that recruiting tools such as classified ads do not run afoul of these laws. These employment laws include Title VII of the Civil Rights Act of 1964, the Civil Rights Act of 1866, the Age Discrimination in Employment Act and the Americans with Disabilities Act. Naturally, state laws also apply. The U.S. Department of Housing and Urban Development (HUD) has stated that *employee* as used in the act also refers to independent contractor.

Fair employment laws are designed to prevent employers from basing hiring and firing decisions on factors that are unrelated to job performance. When recruiting new licensees (as well as hiring office staff and unlicensed assistants), a broker should avoid asking questions regarding *marital status, children or plans to have children, age, origin or nationality, religion* and *physical and mental condition*. Any applications that are used should comply with all fair employment laws. Advertisements should include such phrases as *equal opportunity employer*. All recruiting and interviewing activities should remain consistent, no matter who is applying for the job.

All managerial decisions, not just hiring decisions, should be based on job performance rather than on protected characteristics. Other types of management decisions include those regarding advancement, salary or compensation increases, fringe benefits and firing.

▼ Training

A good company training program aids in recruitment and builds reputation. The well-trained associate requires less attention during early transactions and is eager to try out the techniques taught. An educated salesperson is more likely to succeed and to remain with the company. The broker is legally responsible for training (and supervising) his or her affiliated salespeople.

Even a small office can usually offer excellent one-on-one, on-the-job training, with the newcomer led step by step through the first few transactions. The sales meeting technique is often used in medium-sized offices. Periodic training sessions are integrated into sales meetings. Full coverage of the material requires a number of months with this method. Organized classrooms are most often run by multiple-office companies or franchise operations. They offer efficient instruction and are one of the main inducements for franchise affiliation. Occasionally several small independent firms combine to operate an organized classroom.

It is important to include various legal issues in training sessions. Information *on licensing laws, agency duties and liabilities, discrimination laws* and *antitrust laws* should be included in training sessions.

▼ Policy and Procedures Guide

A written **policy and procedures guide** contributes to the smooth running of the company, heads off misunderstandings, serves as a reference for settling disputes and can be an excellent tool for recruiting and training associates. A loose-leaf format makes revisions simple. Care must be taken not to violate a salesperson's independent contractor status through inappropriate wording. *Suggested Procedures Guide* is a suitable title. Except where legal and ethical considerations are under discussion, the word *must* is inappropriate. "Sales meetings are held each Monday morning at 9:30" is better than "Associates are required to attend each Monday. . . ." The guide should be as concise as possible. It should say nothing, for example, about how to secure a listing; instead, it can detail procedures to follow after the listing is obtained.

Company policy. A typical guide starts with a sketch of the company's history and goals. Background information on the owner and manager is appropriate, with names and responsibilities of personnel. A job description for the associates follows. Independent contractor status is briefly reviewed, with a list of items provided by the company and another list of those to be provided by the associate. A concise treatment of ethical and legal considerations is appropriate: civil rights guidelines to be followed both within the office and in listing and selling (see Chapter 16), a review of the fiduciary duty to clients, policy on buyers' brokers, the theory of hidden defects, nonsolicitation orders that may be in effect in the area and local sign restrictions or regulations. Company policy regarding the termination of a salesperson is also discussed.

The associate needs to know the procedures followed in relationships with attorneys, the franchise or MLS to which the office belongs and cooperating offices. The guide may suggest (but not dictate) appropriate goals for an associate in terms of number of listings and sales, hours of floor duty and attendance at sales meetings, and it may discuss the desk cost per associate.

Paperwork should be described in detail: what forms are available; what reports are to be turned in with listings, contracts or deposits, and to whom. A sample of each form and sales aid used in the office should be included. Supplies, signs, lockboxes, business cards and use of equipment such as the copier, fax machine or computer terminal are discussed. Housekeeping information includes rules on desk use, lights, heat, ashtrays, coffee or kitchen equipment, parking and office hours.

Sales meetings, caravan tours, open houses and floor duty (opportunity time, office time) should be covered in the guide. The responsibilities and opportunities of the associate on floor duty are spelled out in detail to prevent misunderstandings. Advertising policy includes a discussion of frequency and size of ads, discrimination consideration, paperwork procedures, deadlines, individual budgets and follow-up reports to be turned in. A section on telephones describes the answering service used, specifies policy on long-distance calls and entries in a long-distance log, briefly discusses standard telephone-answering techniques and sets standards for customer rotation and the channeling of calls.

▼ The Supervision Requirement

The New York real estate law requires that real estate brokers manage and supervise their affiliated licensees. The broker must ensure that all licensees comply with the license laws and the duties imposed by agency law. According to Regulation 175.21, a broker's supervision must consist of *"regular, frequent and consistent personal guidance, instruction, oversight and superintendence by the real estate broker with respect to the general real estate brokerage business conducted by the broker, and all matters relating thereto."*

By law, brokers are responsible for the actions of their salespeople. In fact, in many cases, if an affiliated licensee violates the license law, the broker may be subject to disciplinary action along with the affiliated licensee. According to Section 442-c of the Real Property Law, a violation of the license law by a real estate salesperson or employee of the broker is cause for a reprimand. It is also a cause for revocation or suspension of the broker's license if the broker (1) had actual knowledge of the violation or (2) retained the benefits, profits or proceeds of a transaction wrongfully negotiated by the salesperson or employee after notice of the salesperson's or employee's misconduct.

Furthermore, both the broker and any affiliated salesperson must keep written records of all the real estate listings obtained by the salesperson and of all sales and other transactions effected by the salesperson during the period of his or her affiliation with that broker. If that salesperson later decides to apply for a broker's license, these records must be submitted to the Department of State with the application for a broker's license.

Professional Organizations

Years ago real estate brokers realized the need for an organization to help improve their business abilities and to educate the public to the value of qualified ethical brokers. The National Association of REALTORS® (NAR) was organized in 1908 to meet this need. This association is the parent organization of most local real estate boards and associations that operate throughout the United States, and the professional activities of all REALTORS®—active members of local boards that are affiliated with the national association—are governed by the association's **Code of Ethics.** (See Appendix B.)

The term REALTORS® is a registered trademark. A similar organization, The National Association of Real Estate Brokers (Realtists), was founded in 1947. Members subscribe to a code of ethics that sets professional standards for all Realtists.

These are trade associations. Licensed brokers and salespersons are not required to join.

▼ **New York State Association of REALTORS®**

The New York State Association of REALTORS® is a member board of the National Association of REALTORS®, which represents more than 32,000 REALTORS® and REALTOR®-ASSOCIATES in New York State. The staff consists of an executive director; an administrator; and directors of education, legislation, communications and membership services. The New York State Society of Real Estate Appraisers is a division of the state association. The former Commercial Investment Division is now known as the New York State Commercial Association of REALTORS®, Inc.

Educational services. The National Association of REALTORS® and The New York REALTORS® Institute administer a structured educational program. The course of study leads to the designation Graduate, REALTORS® Institute **(GRI).** To earn the GRI designation, the candidate must successfully complete six modules that cover business skills, law, finance, investment, construction and valuation. All are approved by the state for continuing education credit. GRI courses are offered during the year at various locations around the state.

▼ **Designations**

Designations, like college degrees, are awarded by various real estate organizations after study, examinations and experience. Various real estate bodies award these designations. Some are associated with the National Association of REALTORS®, and some are independent organizations. Among the more well-known designations are

- American Society of Appraisers: ASA;
- American Society of Real Estate Counselors: CRE, Counselor of Real Estate;
- Appraisal Institute: MAI, Member of the Appraisal Institute; SRA, Senior Residential Appraiser;
- Commercial Investment Real Estate Institute: CCIM, Certified Commercial-Investment Member;
- Institute of Real Estate Management: CPM, Certified Property Manager; ARM, Accredited Residential Manager; AMO, Accredited Management Organization;
- International Real Estate Federation (FIABCI): CIPS, Certified International Property Specialist;
- National Council of Exchangors: EMS, Equity Marketing Specialist;
- Real Estate Educators Association: DREI, Designated Real Estate Instructor;
- Real Estate Securities and Syndication Institute: SRS, Specialist in Real Estate Securities;
- REALTORS® Land Institute: ALC, Accredited Land Consultant;
- REALTORS® National Marketing Institute: CRB, Certified Real Estate Brokerage Manager; CRS, Certified Residential Specialist;
- REALTORS® Real Estate Buyer's Agent Council: ABR, Accredited Buyer's Representative;

- Society of Industrial and Office REALTORS®: SIOR; PRE, Professional Real Estate; and
- Women's Council of REALTORS®: LTG, Leadership Training Graduate; RRC, Referral and Relocation Certification.

Key Terms

antitrust laws	multiple-listing service
designations	policy and procedures guide
employee	price-fixing
fair employment laws	restraint of trade
group boycott	tie-in arrangement
independent contractor	vicarious liability
market allocation	

Summary

Vicarious liability is created not because of a person's actions but because of the relationship between the liable person and other parties. Subagency often creates circumstances or situations that result in vicarious liability.

Antitrust laws prohibit competing brokers from discussing commission rates charged to clients and also the publication of such rates. Brokers also must refrain from negative discussions about other brokers to avoid the appearance of a group boycott.

MLSs must operate in such a manner as not to deny reasonable access to any interested party. Membership requirements must be reasonable, and the charge for membership must be related to the costs involved. Discriminatory policies are forbidden.

An MLS may not impose restrictions on the operations of its members, such as prohibiting membership in other MLS organizations or cooperation with non-members. Attempts by an MLS to regulate the business hours of its members or to restrict the types of properties advertised through the MLS also are forbidden.

Whether a salesperson is employed as an employee or an independent contractor has serious implications for both the salesperson and the broker. Employees are subject to tax withholding and may not file schedule C to deduct business expenses for federal income tax purposes. Brokers must withhold income and Social Security taxes from employees, but not from independent contractors. Employees are covered by programs such as unemployment insurance and workers' compensation, and the employer is responsible for the premiums and taxes associated with these programs.

The classification of a licensee as an employee or an independent contractor depends on the conduct of the licensee and the broker. A written agreement is important under federal and state law to show independent contractor status, but other factors are of equal or greater significance. The compensation of an independent contractor must be related to performance and not to hours worked, and the broker is limited in the degree of control that may be exerted over an independent contractor's behavior. Participation in benefits such as pension plans or sick pay may indicate that the licensee is an employee.

While recruiting and training licensees, brokers must pay attention to more than selecting effective, successful salespeople. Brokers must also keep fair employment laws in mind. Office policies and procedure guides should emphasize the broker's commitment to the principles of fair employment, fair housing and full compliance with licensing regulations.

Designations are awarded after study, examinations and experience by various organizations. The New York State Association of REALTORS® awards the GRI designation to graduates of the REALTORS® Institute.

1. XYZ Realty and MLN Real Estate decide that they will not cooperate with the new broker in town, Homes Bought Realty. This would be an antitrust violation called

   a. market allocation.
   b. tie-in arrangement.
   c. price-fixing.
   d. group boycotting.

2. When the market was depressed in New Town, New York, the brokers association decided to lower commission rates to have a better chance to list properties. This would be an antitrust violation called

   a. market allocation.
   b. tie-in arrangement.
   c. price-fixing.
   d. group boycotting.

3. Town House Realty offered new condominiums for sale. Buyers were told they must make their selections for appliances from Town House Realty's catalog. No other appliances would be permitted. Appliances were furnished through a distributor owned by Town House Realty. This would be an antitrust violation called

   a. market allocation.
   b. tie-in arrangement.
   c. price-fixing.
   d. group boycotting.

4. Broker Margo Marz and broker Nate National decided each could make more money if Margo took the east side of town and Nate took the west side of town. This would be an antitrust violation called

   a. market allocation.
   b. tie-in arrangement.
   c. price-fixing.
   d. group boycotting.

5. An MLS may

   a. regulate a broker's office hours.
   b. prohibit membership in another MLS.
   c. set reasonable and nondiscriminatory membership fees.
   d. restrict the types of property advertised through the MLS.

6. A broker may require a salesperson who is an independent contractor to

   a. work established hours.
   b. comply with Article 12-A of Real Property Law.
   c. accept a regular salary.
   d. have an oral contract.

7. Safe-harbor IRS guidelines for independent contractor status do not include

   a. being licensed as a real estate broker or salesperson.
   b. having fluctuating income based on sales output.
   c. Social Security contributions by the broker.
   d. performing services according to a written independent contractor agreement.

8. If a salesperson is an employee, he or she is entitled to

   a. unemployment insurance.
   b. workers' compensation.
   c. federal and state withholding.
   d. All of the above

9. New salesperson Ann Apple wants to be able to claim self-employment expense deductions on IRS Form 1040 Schedule C. She should
   a. have an independent contractor agreement with her broker in writing.
   b. keep a detailed record of her expenses.
   c. pay her own state and federal taxes and Social Security.
   d. All of the above

10. In an independent contractor agreement with Ann Apple, the broker should include
    a. that she will be compensated only by commissions directly based on sales.
    b. the days and hours that she will work.
    c. that she may not work outside the office.
    d. that she will be paid both a salary and commissions.

11. At a booth in the neighborhood coffee shop, Bob Broker is seated with his friendly rival, Olive Otherbroker. Olive says, "Did you hear about that firm that's charging a flat fee for selling property? Do you think they'll make it?" Bob's proper response is to
    a. explain to Olive that flat fees are allowed by law, just as commissions are.
    b. assure Olive that his commission rates are not going to change.
    c. caution Olive about the dangers of discussing commission rates with competing firms.
    d. say "good-bye" immediately and walk out.

12. A broker for North End Realty tells a broker from Valley Realty that a house has been listed "at the usual 7 percent commission, and we will be glad to cooperate with you and give you half, if your company sells it." There may be an antitrust violation in
    a. the offer to cooperate in marketing the property.
    b. the promise of a 50/50 split.
    c. the phrase "the usual 7 percent commission."
    d. There is no antitrust problem here.

13. An independent contractor is generally
    a. paid a regular salary, with commissions as a bonus.
    b. reimbursed for all business expenses.
    c. paid commissions on sales.
    d. given two weeks of paid vacation each year.

14. Commission rates are set by
    a. state law.
    b. local custom.
    c. the broker.
    d. agreement between the client and broker.

CHAPTER 5

Estates and Interests

After the Foxes moved into a rented house, they installed an ornate wrought-iron handrail for steps leading from their lawn to the sidewalk. The landlord refused to reimburse them for money spent on the handrail, which angered Tom Fox so much that he decided to remove it. Does he have the right to?

The real estate professional needs to understand the nature of real estate and how it differs from personal property.

Real Estate Transactions

The purchase or rental of real estate is quite different from dealings in personal property like automobiles, groceries or television sets. Even the simplest of real estate transactions brings into play a body of complex laws.

> **RIGHTS OF OWNERSHIP INCLUDE**
>
> - possession,
> - control of property,
> - enjoyment,
> - exclusion and
> - disposition.

Real property has often been described as a **bundle of legal rights.** A person who purchases real estate is actually buying the rights previously held by the seller. These *rights of ownership* include the right to *possession*, the right to *control the property* within the framework of the law, the right of *enjoyment* (to use the property in any legal manner), the right of *exclusion* (to keep others from entering or occupying the property) and the right of *disposition* (to be able to sell or otherwise transfer the property) (see Figure 5.1). Within these ownership rights are included further rights to devise (leave by will), mortgage, encumber, cultivate, explore, lease, license, dedicate, give away, abandon, share, trade or exchange the property.

Land, Real Estate and Real Property

The words *land, real estate* and *real property* often are used to describe the same thing. There are, however, important differences.

▼ Land

The term *land* refers to more than just the surface of the earth; it includes things permanently attached to the land by nature only, such as trees and water. Land ownership also includes minerals and substances below the earth's surface together with the air above up to infinity.

Thus **land** is defined as the *earth's surface extending downward to the center of the earth and upward to infinity, including things permanently attached by nature only* (see Figure 5.2).

Figure 5.1   The Bundle of Legal Rights

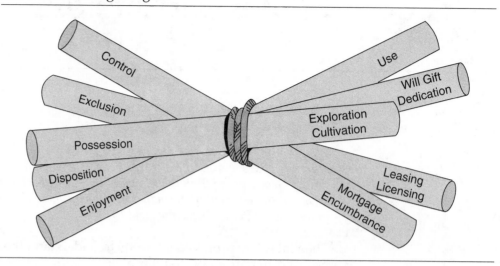

A specific tract of land is commonly referred to as a **parcel,** which has specific boundaries.

▼ **Real Estate**

The term *real estate* is broader than the term land and includes all permanent **improvements**—buildings on the land as well as streets, utilities, sewers and other *man-made additions* to the property.

Real estate is defined as the *earth's surface extending downward to the center of the earth and upward into space, including all things permanently attached to it by nature and by people* (see Figure 5.2).

▼ **Real Property**

The term *real property* is broader still and includes the *bundle of legal rights of ownership.*

Thus **real property** is defined as the *earth's surface extending downward to the center of the earth and upward into space, including all things permanently attached to it by nature and by people, as well as the interests, benefits and rights included in ownership* (see Figure 5.3).

In everyday usage, the term *real estate* or realty is commonly used for *real property.*

Subsurface rights, the rights to the natural resources lying below the earth's surface, may be owned separately.

A landowner, for example, may sell to an oil company the rights to any oil and gas found in the land. The landowner could then sell the land to a purchaser and in the sale reserve the rights to all coal that may be found in the land. After these sales, three parties have ownership interests in this real estate: (1) the oil company owns all oil and gas, (2) the seller owns all coal and (3) the new landowner owns the rights to the remaining real estate.

Mineral rights also may be leased. Much of the farmland in southwestern New York State is subject to oil and gas leases.

Figure 5.2   Land and Real Estate

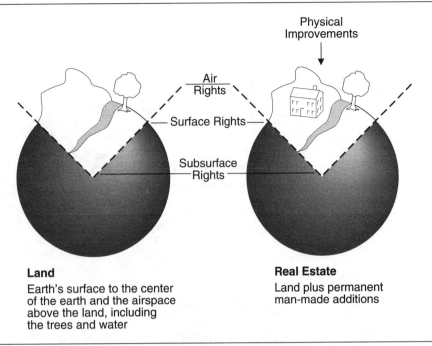

Land
Earth's surface to the center
of the earth and the airspace
above the land, including
the trees and water

Real Estate
Land plus permanent
man-made additions

The rights to use the airspace above the land may be sold or leased independently of the land itself. Such air rights are an increasingly important part of real estate, particularly in large cities, where air rights over railroads have been purchased to construct huge office buildings like the Met-Life Building in New York City. For the construction of such a building, the developer must purchase not only the air rights above the land but also numerous small portions of the actual land to construct the building's foundation supports.

Until the development of airplanes, air rights were considered to be unlimited. Today, however, the courts permit reasonable interference with these rights by aircraft, as long as the owner's right to use and occupy the land is not interfered with. Governments and airport authorities often purchase air rights next to an airport to provide glide patterns for aircraft.

With the continuing development of solar power, courts may consider tall buildings that block sunlight from smaller buildings to be interfering with the smaller buildings' rights to solar energy.

The rights in one parcel of real property could therefore be owned by many people: (1) an owner of the **surface rights,** (2) an owner of subsurface mineral rights, (3) an owner of subsurface gas and oil rights and (4) an owner of the air rights.

Riparian rights are the owner's rights in land bordering a river or stream. In New York, persons owning land bordering nonnavigable streams own the property to the midpoint of the stream. Those whose land borders navigable streams own the property to the high-water mark (the limit of the rise of medium tides); the riverbed belongs to the state (see Figure 5.4).

Figure 5.3   Real Property

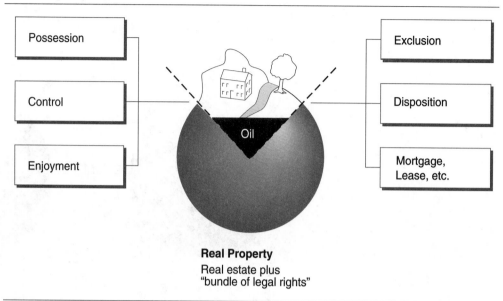

Real Property
Real estate plus
"bundle of legal rights"

Closely related to riparian rights are the **littoral rights** of owners whose land borders large lakes, bays and oceans. They may enjoy unrestricted use of the water but own the land only up to the high-water mark (see Figure 5.5). All land below this point is owned by the government.

Riparian and littoral rights cannot be sold separately or kept when the land is sold.

Where land adjoins streams, an owner is entitled to all *accretions,* increases resulting from the deposit of soil by the action of the water or wind. An owner may also lose land through gradual *erosion* or through *avulsion,* due to a change in the channel of a stream.

Real Property Versus Personal Property

Nearly everything that can be owned may be classified as either real or personal property.

Personal property is *all property that does not fit the definition of real estate.* Personal property is *movable,* or mobile. Items of personal property, also referred to as **chattels,** include possessions like refrigerators, drapes, clothing, money, bonds and bank accounts (see Figure 5.6).

It is possible to change an item of real estate to personal property. A growing tree is real estate, but if the owner cuts down the tree and thereby severs it from the earth, it becomes personal property. The process is known as *severance.*

The reverse situation is also possible. Personal property can be changed to real estate. If an owner buys cement, stones and sand and constructs a concrete walk, materials that were originally personal property are changed into real estate because they have become a permanent improvement on the land.

Trees and crops are generally considered in two classes. Trees, perennial bushes and grasses that do not require yearly cultivation are considered real estate.

Figure 5.4   Riparian Rights

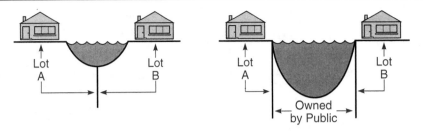

Annual crops of wheat, corn, vegetables and fruit, known as **emblements,** are generally considered personal property. A mobile home is usually considered personal property unless it is permanently attached to the land by a foundation.

▼ **Fixtures**

An article of personal property that has been permanently attached to land or a building is known as a fixture and becomes part of the real estate.

Examples of fixtures are furnaces, elevator equipment, kitchen cabinets, light fixtures and sinks. Almost any item that has been added as *a permanent part* of a building is considered a fixture.

Trade fixtures. An article owned by a tenant and attached to a rented space for use in conducting a business is a **trade fixture.** Examples of trade fixtures are bowling alley equipment, store shelves and restaurant equipment. Agricultural fixtures such as chicken coops and toolsheds also are included in this definition (see Figure 5.6).

Trade fixtures remain the personal property of the tenant and may be removed on or before the last day the property is rented. The tenant must, however, restore the property to its original condition, repairing holes left by bolts, for example. Those not removed become the property of the landlord.

FOUR LEGAL TESTS OF A FIXTURE:

1. The adaptation of the article to the real estate
2. The method of annexation of the item
3. The intention and relationship of the parties
4. The existence of an agreement

Legal tests of a fixture. Courts apply four basic tests to determine whether an article is a fixture (and therefore a part of the real estate) or removable personal property. These tests are based on (1) the adaptation of the article to the real estate, (2) the method of annexation (attachment) of the item, (3) the intention and relationship of the parties and (4) the existence of an agreement.

Although these tests seem simple, court decisions do not always agree on whether something is a fixture. Annexation alone is not a final test. The front door key, for example, is not attached, but it is clearly a fixture that belongs with the house.

The distinction between personal and real property is of great importance in the sale of real estate. When a contract for the sale of property is being negotiated, buyers and sellers must be guided by clear written agreements about what "goes with" the real estate being sold.

▼ **Uses of Real Estate**

Real estate brokers deal with many different types of real property (see Figure 5.7). Real estate generally can be classified in these categories:

Figure 5.5   Littoral Rights

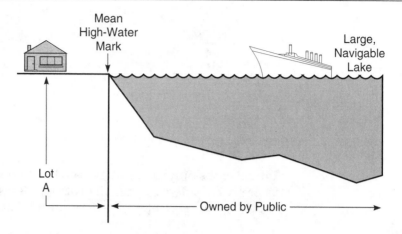

<table>
<tr><td>Mean
High-Water
Mark</td></tr>
</table>

Large, Navigable Lake

Lot A

Owned by Public

FIVE BASIC CATEGORIES OF REAL PROPERTY:

1. Residental
2. Commercial
3. Industrial
4. Agricultural
5. Special-purpose

- **Residential**—all property used for housing, from acreage to small city lots, both single-family and multifamily, in urban, suburban and rural areas
- **Commercial**—business property, including offices, shopping malls, theaters, hotels and parking facilities
- **Industrial**—warehouses, factories, land in industrial districts and research facilities (Industrial property is sometimes referred to as manufacturing property in New York City.)
- **Agricultural**—farms, timberland, pastureland and orchards
- **Special-purpose**—religious institutions, schools, cemeteries, hospitals and government-held lands

Estates (Ownership) In Land

A buyer's choice of ownership type will affect the owner's legal right to sell without the consent of others and also the right to leave the property to chosen heirs. The real estate practitioner needs to understand various forms of ownership so that buyers, sellers, tenants and landlords can be alerted to the need for legal input to avoid future problems. This chapter will discuss various interests in real estate and the basic forms of real estate ownership.

The amount and kind of **interest** (ownership) that a person has in real property is an **estate in land.** Estates in land are either freehold estates or leasehold estates (those involving rentals).

Freehold estates exist for a lifetime or forever. The freehold estates recognized in New York are (1) fee simple, (2) qualified (determinable) fee, (3) fee on condition and (4) life estates.

The first three of these estates continue for an indefinite period and can be inherited after the owner's death. A life estate ends at the death of the person on whose life it is based.

Leasehold estates are estates for a specific period of time. They are classified as:

Estate for years: Commonly established by a lease, written or (if for a period of less than one year) oral. An estate for years gives the tenant possession of the property for a fixed time.

Figure 5.6 Real versus Personal Property

Real Estate	**Personal Property**	**Fixture**	**Trade Fixture**
Land and anything permanently attached to it	Movable items not attached to real estate; items severed from real estate	Item of personal property converted to real estate by attaching it to the real estate with the intention that it become permanently a part thereof	Item of personal property attached to real estate that is owned by a tenant and is used in a business; legally removable by tenant

Periodic estate, estate at will, estate at sufferance: These leasehold estates are covered at length in Chapter 8. Each lasts for an indefinite length of time.

▼ Fee Simple Estate

An estate in **fee simple** is the *most complete type of ownership in real estate*. A fee simple estate is one in which the owner is entitled to all rights in the property. There is no time limit—it is said to run forever. On the death of its owner the estate passes to the owner's heirs. The terms *fee, fee simple* and *fee simple absolute* are basically the same. New York law provides that a **grant** (sale or gift) of real property automatically **conveys** (transfers) fee simple ownership unless the terms of the grant show a clear intention to convey a lesser estate.

▼ Qualified Fee Estate

Sometimes a gift or sale provides that the real property must be used for a specific purpose. The deed that transfers the property might state Smith gives the land "to the Jones Foundation so long as it is used for a wildlife preserve." If the Jones Foundation later built a corporate headquarters on the land, ownership would *automatically* revert to Smith (or Smith's heirs). The Jones Foundation owned only a *qualified fee.*

▼ Fee on Condition

A *fee on condition* is slightly different. The deed transferring ownership to the Jones Foundation might have been worded so that if the land were ever used for any purpose except a wildlife preserve, the land would *not automatically revert* back to Smith. Smith or Smith's heirs would, however, have the right to file suit in court to recover the property.

Real estate brokers and salespersons need to know just enough about qualified fee and fee on condition to alert sellers and buyers to the need for legal counsel if such a situation occurs.

▼ Life Estates

A **life estate** is *limited to the life of some specific person*. The owner does not have the right to pass ownership to heirs, because the life estate ends with the death of the owner or a third party. Life estates may be *ordinary* or *pur autre vie.*

Figure 5.7   Uses of Real Property

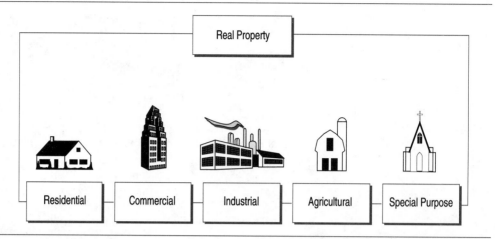

- An *ordinary* life estate lasts as long as the owner, the life tenant, is alive. *A* may leave a life estate to *B*, who will have all the incidents of ownership for the rest of his or her life. *B* does not, however, have the right to leave the property to anyone at death.
- A life estate *pur autre vie* (for another life) lasts as long as a particular third party, named by the original owner, is alive. Mrs. *A* might, for example, leave her home to son *B*, to be owned by *B* "as long as my brother, Felix, is alive and living in the home." *B* (or *B*'s heirs) would be complete owner of the property, but only until Mrs. *A*'s brother's death.

Remainder and reversion. The person who sets up the life estate provides for the future ownership of the property. After the death of the life tenant the property may revert to the original owner or pass to someone else (see Figure 5.8).

- **Remainder interest:** Mr. *A* may leave the family homestead to the second Mrs. *A* for her lifetime with the provision that it pass, at her death, to the son of his first marriage, *A*, Jr. During Mrs. *A*'s lifetime, *A*, Jr., owns a *remainder interest* and is known as a *remainderman*.
- **Reversionary interest:** Mr. *A* may give his home to poor relative *B* for *B*'s lifetime with the provision that at *B*'s death ownership reverts (returns) to *A* (or, if *A* has died, to *A*'s heirs). During *B*'s lifetime Mr. *A* owns a *reversionary interest*.

A life tenant's interest in real property is true ownership. The life tenant cannot, however, permanently injure the land or property, acts known in legal terms as *waste*. A life tenant is entitled to all income and profits arising from the property. A life interest could theoretically be sold, leased, mortgaged or given away, but it always will terminate (end) on the death of the person against whose life the estate is measured.

▼ **Not Used in New York State**

A husband's life estate in the real estate of his deceased wife is called *curtesy*. *Dower* is the life estate that a wife has in the real estate of her deceased husband. New York law no longer recognizes dower and curtesy as legal life estates.

Figure 5.8 Life Estate

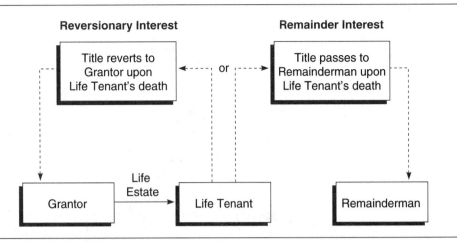

New York is not a community property state (where husband and wife are presumed to own marital property jointly—as a community) and recognizes no special community property rights in real estate.

In some states the estate known as **homestead** gives the owner special rights in property used as a family home. New York does not have any special right of homestead.

Forms of Ownership

A fee simple estate in land may be held (1) in **severalty,** where **title** is held by one owner; (2) in **co-ownership,** where title is held by two or more persons; or (3) in **trust,** where title is held by a third person for the benefit of another.

The form by which property is owned is important to the real estate broker for two reasons: (1) *the form of ownership existing when a property is sold determines who must sign the various documents involved* (listing contract, acceptance of offer to purchase, sales contract and deed) and (2) *the purchaser must determine in what form he or she wishes to take title. When questions about these forms are raised, the real estate broker should recommend that the parties seek legal advice.*

The word *tenant,* when used with various forms of ownership, does not refer to someone who is renting the property. Instead it means the person who holds ownership.

▼ Severalty

Severalty is the ownership of property by one person only. Ownership is severed or separated from any form of co-ownership and is also referred to as *sole ownership.* When the owner dies, the property passes to the owner's heirs or as otherwise provided by the owner's will.

▼ Co-Ownership

When title to one parcel of real estate is owned by two or more persons or organizations, those parties are said to be *co-owners.* New York recognizes the following forms of ownership: (1) tenancy in common, (2) joint tenancy and (3) tenancy by the entirety.

Tenancy in common. A **tenant in common** owns an **undivided interest** in the property. Although an owner may have, say, a one-half or one-third interest in

Figure 5.9   Tenancy in Common

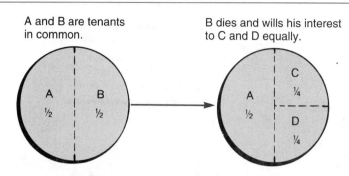

a property, it is impossible to distinguish physically which specific half or third of the property is owned. The deed creating a tenancy in common may or may not state the fractional interest held by each co-owner. If no fractions are stated, each owns an equal share. For example, if five people hold title, each would own an undivided one-fifth interest. Upon the death of a co-owner, his or her interest passes to heirs or devisees named in the owner's will (and the tenancy in common would continue) (see Figure 5.9).

A second important characteristic of a tenancy in common is that *each owner* can sell, convey, mortgage or transfer that interest *without the consent* of the other co-owners.

In New York a **conveyance** (sale or gift) to persons not married to each other automatically creates a tenancy in common unless otherwise stated in the deed. Property inherited by two or more persons is owned by them as tenants in common unless the will stated otherwise.

When an unmarried couple buys a home together, they have a decision to make. If one dies, should that person's share go to heirs named in a will or, if there is no will, to what the state calls *natural heirs:* spouse, parents, siblings, children? If so, they will take title as tenants in common. If, however, they would like the surviving partner to become complete owner automatically, their deed should make it clear they are taking title as joint tenants.

Joint tenancy. The basis of **joint tenancy** is *unity of ownership.* The property is owned by a group made up of two or more people. The death of one of the joint tenants simply means there is one fewer person in the group. The remaining joint tenants automatically receive the share owned by the deceased tenant, by **right of survivorship**, no matter what that person's will might have ordered. Only the last survivor, who becomes sole owner, may dispose of the property by will (see Figure 5.10).

Creating joint tenancies. To create a joint tenancy in New York, language in the deed must specifically state that title is taken in that form of ownership. Acquisition of property by two or more executors, trustees or guardians creates in them a joint tenancy.

Four unities are required to create a joint tenancy:

1. Unity of *time*—all joint tenants acquire their interest at the same time.

FOUR UNITIES REQUIRED TO CREATE A JOINT TENANCY:

1. Unity of Time
2. Unity of Title
3. Unity of Interest
4. Unity of Possession

Figure 5.10   Joint Tenancy with Right of Survivorship

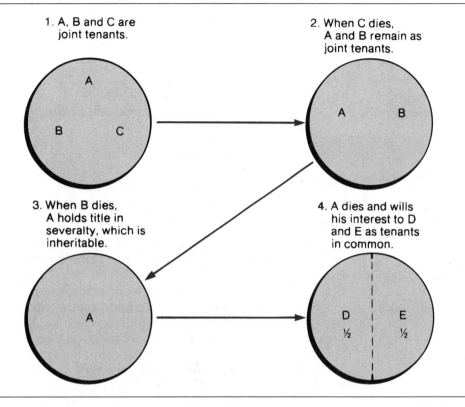

1. A, B and C are joint tenants.

2. When C dies, A and B remain as joint tenants.

3. When B dies, A holds title in severalty, which is inheritable.

4. A dies and wills his interest to D and E as tenants in common.

2. Unity of *title*—all joint tenants acquire their interest by the same deed.
3. Unity of *interest*—all joint tenants hold equal ownership interests.
4. Unity of *possession*—all joint tenants hold an undivided interest in the property.

Terminating joint tenancies. While a joint tenant is free to convey (sell or give away) his or her interest in the jointly held property, doing so will destroy the joint tenancy. For example, if *A, B* and *C* hold title as joint tenants and *A* sells her interest to *D*, then *D* will own a one-third interest as a tenant in common with *B* and *C*, who will continue to own their two-thirds interest as joint tenants (see Figure 5.11). If *D* dies, one-third interest will go to *D's* heir. If *B* dies, *C* will own two-thirds.

Joint tenancies also may be terminated by bankruptcy or foreclosure sale proceedings.

Termination of co-ownership by partition suit. Tenants in common or joint tenants may file in court a suit to **partition** the land. The right of partition is a legal way to end co-ownership when the parties do not agree. If the court determines that the land cannot be physically divided (acreage, for example), it will order the real estate sold and the proceeds divided among the co-owners. Such a forced sale, however, may not yield full market value.

Tenancy by the entirety. A **tenancy by the entirety** is a *special joint tenancy between husband and wife. (It is used in New York, but is not used in all* states.) The

Figure 5.11 Combination of Tenancies

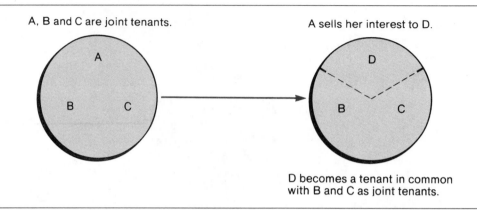

owners must be husband and wife when they receive the property. They have rights of survivorship, but there is no right to partition.

In New York a conveyance to a married couple automatically creates in them a tenancy by the entirety unless the deed specifies otherwise. A tenancy by the entirety is also automatically created with respect to a cooperative apartment by a transfer of the shares and a proprietary lease to a married couple unless the assignment specifies otherwise. Divorce breaks the tenancy by the entirety, and the ex-spouses immediately become tenants in common.

Trusts

Property owners may provide for their own financial care and/or that of others by establishing trusts. Such trusts may be created by agreement during a property owner's lifetime (inter vivos or living trust) or established by will after the owner's death (testamentary trust).

PARTIES TO A TRUST:

1. Trustor
2. Trustee
3. Beneficiary

There are three parties to a trust: the trustor, the trustee and the beneficiary(s). The individual creating a trust, the **trustor**, makes an agreement conveying assets to the **trustee** with the understanding that the trustee will assume certain duties. These duties include the care and investment of the trust assets to produce income. After payment of operating expenses and trustee's fees, this income is paid to or used for the benefit of one or more **beneficiaries.** These trusts may continue for the beneficiaries' lifetimes or until the beneficiaries reach certain ages.

Ownership of Real Estate by Business Organizations

Ownership by a business organization makes it possible for many people to hold an interest in the same parcel of real estate. Investors may be organized in various ways to finance a real estate project. Sometimes real estate is owned by the organization itself, sometimes directly by the investors. Business organizations may be categorized as partnerships, corporations, syndicates or limited liability companies. The purchase or sale of real estate by any business organization involves complex legal questions, and legal counsel is required.

All of the following types of business organizations contrast with **sole proprietorship,** a business owned by one individual.

▼ Partnerships

An association of two or more people to carry on a business as co-owners and share in the business's profits and losses is a **partnership.** Partnerships are classified as general and limited. In a **general partnership** all partners participate to some extent in the operation and management of the business and may be held personally liable for business losses and obligations. A **limited partnership** includes general partners as well as limited, or silent, partners. The business is run by the general partner or partners. The limited partners do not participate, and each can be held liable for the business's losses *only* to the extent of his or her investment. The limited partnership is a popular method of organizing investors in a real estate project. If a general partner dies, the partnership is dissolved, unless the partnership agreement provides otherwise.

▼ Corporations

A **corporation** is an artificial person or legal entity created under the laws of the state from which it receives its charter. Because the corporation is a legal person, real estate ownership by a corporation is an *ownership in severalty.* A corporation is managed and operated by its *board of directors,* which is elected by the shareholders.

As a legal entity, a corporation exists indefinitely (in perpetuity). The death of one of the shareholders, officers or directors does not affect title to property owned by the corporation.

Individuals participate, or invest, in a corporation by purchasing stock. Because stock is *personal property,* stockholders do not have a direct ownership interest in real estate owned by a corporation. Each stockholder's liability for the corporation's losses usually is limited to the amount of his or her investment.

▼ Limited Liability Company

The **limited liability company** is a hybrid entity that combines the freedom to manage the company offered by partnerships with the limited liability for all the owners and avoidance of income taxes offered by corporations. The owners pay taxes on earnings and profits received from the limited liability company.

▼ Syndicates

A **syndicate** *is a joining together of two or more people or firms to carry out one or more business projects.* It may be organized into a number of ownership forms, including co-ownership (tenancy in common, joint tenancy), partnership, trust, limited liability company or corporation.

A *joint venture* is an organization of two or more people or firms to carry out a *single project.* A joint venture lasts for a limited time and is not intended to establish a permanent relationship.

The real estate practitioner who organizes or sells a real estate venture involving investors who expect to benefit without active participation should be alert for special registration or licensing required by the state department of law for syndication activity.

Cooperative and Condominium Ownership

In this century apartment dwellers have turned to arrangements under which they own their living space. Cooperative ownership was the first to develop; condominium ownership appeared later.

▼ Cooperative Ownership

Under the usual **cooperative** arrangement, title to land and building is held by a *corporation.* Tenants buy stock in the corporation and receive proprietary leases to their apartments. As stockholders they exercise control over the administration of the building through an elected board of directors. Barring any violation of antidiscrimination laws, directors usually can approve or disapprove of prospective purchasers of the apartment leases. Tenants contribute monthly fees to cover maintenance costs, the corporation's property taxes and the overall mortgage on the building.

The corporation, however, is financially vulnerable. If other tenants cannot pay their monthly charges, the owner/occupant may lose out in the event of a forced sale of the property. Cooperative ownership is found in and around New York City more than in other parts of the state.

Although the stock in a cooperative might be considered personal property, a real estate license is needed for the sale of cooperatives. In addition, the Internal Revenue Service allows the owners of cooperative apartments to treat the units as if they were real estate for income tax purposes, provided that the corporation qualifies under Section 216 of the Internal Revenue Code.

▼ **Condominium Ownership**

The owner of each **condominium** apartment holds a *fee simple title* to his or her dwelling unit and also to a percentage of the other parts of the building and land, known as the **common elements.** The condominium owners hold the common elements as *tenants in common,* but with *no right to partition.*

The condominium form of ownership is often used for apartment buildings. These may range from freestanding highrise buildings to town house arrangements. The common elements include such items as the land, walls, hallways, elevators, stairways and roof. Lawns and recreational facilities such as swimming pools, clubhouses and golf courses also may be considered common elements.

In addition, condominium ownership is sometimes used for commercial property or office buildings. The word *condominium* could apply even to a group of single detached houses whose ownership was organized in this fashion.

The owner of a condominium unit receives a separate tax bill and may mortgage the individual living unit. Default in the payment of taxes or a mortgage loan by one unit owner may result in a foreclosure sale of that owner's unit but will not affect the ownership of the other unit owners.

Operation and administration. In New York State, the condominium property is customarily administered by an association of unit owners or a board of managers elected by the unit owners. It may manage the property on its own or engage a professional property manager. Owners pay monthly charges for maintenance expenses.

Town house ownership is a hybrid form. Town house occupants own the land directly beneath their unit and the living unit, including roof and basement, in fee simple. Sometimes a small lawn or patio is individually owned as well. Single houses on extra-small lots, in what is known as cluster housing, sometimes use this form of ownership. A town house owner becomes a member of a homeowners' association, which owns the common elements.

For tax assessment purposes, a homeowner's association is distinguished from a condominium owner's association in that units in a homeowner's association are assessed in the same manner as single-family homes (the assessments are higher). In a condominium association, the units are assessed in the same manner as rental apartment house dwellings (the assessments are lower).

Time-sharing is a variation of condominium ownership in which the buyer receives the right to use a living unit, usually in a resort area, for a specific portion of a year. The buyer might own an undivided one-twelfth interest together with a right to use the facility for one month of the year.

Key Terms

agricultural real estate	limited liability company
air rights	limited partnership
beneficiary	littoral rights
bundle of legal rights	parcel
chattels	partition
co-ownership	partnership
commercial real estate	personal property
common elements	real estate
condominium	real property
convey	remainder interest
conveyance	residential real estate
cooperative	reversionary interest
corporation	right of survivorship
devise	riparian rights
emblements	severalty
estate in land	sole proprietorship
fee simple	special-purpose real estate
fixture	subsurface rights
freehold estates	surface rights
general partnership	syndicate
grant	tenancy by the entirety
homestead	tenant in common
improvement	title
industrial real estate	trade fixture
interest	trust
joint tenancy	trustee
land	trustor
leasehold estates	undivided interest
life estate	

Summary

Even the simplest real estate transactions involve a complex body of laws. The person who buys real estate receives not only the land itself but also the legal rights to use the land in certain ways that formerly were held by the seller.

Land includes not only the earth's surface but also the mineral deposits under the earth and the air above it. The term real estate further includes man-made improvements attached to the land. Real property includes real estate plus the bundle of legal rights associated with its ownership.

The same parcel of real estate may be owned and controlled by different parties, one owning surface rights, one owning air rights and another owning the subsurface rights.

Ownership of land includes also the right to use the water on or adjacent to it. Riparian rights give the owner of land next to water that cannot be navigated by boat ownership to the middle of the stream. A river that can be navigated belongs to the landowner only up to the high-water mark; the riverbed belongs to the state. Littoral rights are held by owners of land bordering large lakes and oceans and include use of the water and ownership of the land up to the high-water mark.

All property that does not fit the definition of real estate is classified as personal property, also known as chattels. When articles of personal property are permanently attached to land, they may become fixtures and part of the real estate. Personal property installed by a tenant for a business purpose, however, is classified as a trade fixture, remains personal property and may be removed.

Real property can be classified according to its general use as residential, commercial, industrial, agricultural or special-purpose.

An estate is the amount and kind of interest a person holds in land. Freehold estates are estates of indefinite length. Leasehold estates are those for which the length can be determined accurately. They concern landlords and tenants.

Estates that can be inherited include fee simple, fee on condition and qualified fee estates. Life estates can be granted for the life of the new owner or for the life of some third party (pur autre vie). At the end of the life estate, ownership can go back to the original owner (reverter) or pass to a designated third party (remainder). Homestead in New York is not an estate and community property is not part of New York law.

Sole ownership or ownership in severalty indicates that title is held by one person or entity.

Title to real estate can be held at the same time by more than one person. It is important for purchasers to recognize the issues involved in the manner of taking title, which include their ability to will the property or transfer it without the consent of the other joint owner. Title questions should be discussed with an attorney prior to purchasing jointly owned property.

Under tenancy in common an individual owner may own an unequal share, may sell his or her interest and has the right to leave the share to any designated beneficiaries. When two or more persons not married to each other hold title to real estate, they own it as tenants in common unless their deed specifically states some other intention.

Joint tenancy involves two or more owners with the right of survivorship. Upon the death of one owner that person's share passes to the remaining co-owner(s). The intention to establish joint tenancy with right of survivorship must be stated clearly in their deed, and four unities must exist. Both tenants in common and joint tenants have the right to force a sale by partition.

Tenancy by the entirety is a special joint tenancy for property acquired by husband and wife. Unless their deed specifically states they wish to own the property in another way, they will own it by the entirety. Neither can force a sale by partition. Divorce changes their ownership to tenancy in common.

Real estate ownership also may be held in trust. Title to the property is conveyed by the trustor to a trustee, who administers it for the benefit of a beneficiary.

Various types of business organizations may own real estate. A corporation is a legal entity and holds title to real estate in severalty. A partnership or limited liability company may own real estate in its own name. A syndicate is an association of two or more persons or firms to make an investment. Many syndicates are joint ventures organized for only a single project.

With cooperative ownership, title to the property, often an apartment building, is held by a corporation that pays taxes, principal and interest on the building's mortgage, and operating expenses. The purchaser of an apartment receives shares in the corporation and a long-term lease to the living unit and pays monthly charges to cover a share of expenses.

Under condominium ownership each occupant/owner holds fee simple title to a living unit plus a share of the common elements. Each owner receives an individual tax bill and may mortgage the unit. Expenses for operating the building are collected by an owners' association through monthly assessments. In town house ownership each occupant usually owns the land directly below the unit, and a homeowners' association may own the common elements.

1. A specific tract of land is known as a
   a. devise.
   b. parcel.
   c. chattel.
   d. littoral.

2. The definition of land includes
   a. sewers, roads and streets.
   b. buildings permanently attached.
   c. the right of enjoyment.
   d. the airspace above the surface.

3. Real property is often referred to as a bundle of legal rights. Among these is the right of
   a. navigation.
   b. exclusion.
   c. avulsion.
   d. emblement.

4. Ben Jones, owner of a farm in Steuben County, may find that an oil company wants to lease his
   a. littoral rights.
   b. subsurface rights.
   c. air rights.
   d. riparian rights.

5. Man-made, permanent additions to land are called
   a. fixtures.
   b. parcels.
   c. improvements.
   d. trade fixtures.

6. When a building is to be constructed above land owned by another, the builder purchases the landowner's
   a. riparian rights.
   b. subsurface rights.
   c. air rights.
   d. littoral rights.

7. Dana Fox owns land along the Mohawk River and as the owner, has certain
   a. riparian rights.
   b. subsurface rights.
   c. air rights.
   d. littoral rights.

8. When Miriam Enton sells her farm, which of the following will not be a part of the real estate?
   a. Fences
   b. Permanent buildings
   c. Farm equipment
   d. Growing trees

9. Two months into the one-year rental period the tenant installs awnings over the front windows. Which of the following is true?
   a. Tenant must remove the awnings before the lease is up.
   b. Awnings are considered personal property due to their permanent nature.
   c. Tenant may not remove the awnings.
   d. Awnings are considered trade fixtures.

10. When Sally opened her hair salon, she installed three shampoo basins, four large plate-glass mirrors and custom work-station counters. Just before the expiration of the lease, she has the right to remove
    a. everything but the shampoo basins because they are attached to the plumbing.
    b. only the mirrors, and then only if holes in the walls are repaired.
    c. all of the items mentioned above.
    d. nothing, because all of the items became fixtures when they were attached.

11. Fred and Celia Tomkins are building a deck off their kitchen. A dealer has just unloaded a truckload of lumber onto their driveway. At this point the lumber is considered
    a. a chattel.
    b. real estate.
    c. a fixture.
    d. a trade fixture.

12. When the Tomkinses' deck is completed, the lumber will be considered
    a. a chattel.
    b. real estate.
    c. a parcel.
    d. a trade fixture.

13. The owner who signs a contract promising to sell all the real estate without listing any exceptions has no right to take his
    a. tomato plants.
    b. drapes.
    c. portable dishwasher.
    d. dining room chandelier.

14. Special-purpose real estate includes
    a. apartment houses.
    b. churches.
    c. factories.
    d. shopping malls.

15. Property that is part of the commercial market includes
    a. office buildings for lease.
    b. apartments for rent.
    c. churches.
    d. factories.

16. The most complete ownership recognized by law is a(n)
    a. life estate.
    b. fee simple estate.
    c. leasehold estate.
    d. estate at will.

17. Julia inherited her cousin's house, but it is hers only as long as the dog, Buster, is alive and well and living in the house. When Buster dies, the house is to go to her cousin's son. The cousin's son is a
    a. beneficiary.
    b. remainderman.
    c. life tenant.
    d. limited partner.

18. John and Mary Alessi owned a small apartment house by the entirety. Mary had a will leaving half her estate to John and half to her daughter Susan. After Mary was killed in an automobile accident, Susan owned how much of the apartment house?
    a. None
    b. One-quarter
    c. One-third
    d. One-half

19. Ownership of real property by one person is called ownership in
    a. trust.
    b. severalty.
    c. entirety.
    d. condominium.

20. A house was purchased by Howard Evers and Tinker Chance. Evers paid one-third of the cost, and Chance paid the balance. The seller's deed conveyed the property "to Howard Evers and Tinker Chance" without further explanation. Evers and Chance are
    a. joint tenants.
    b. tenants in common, each owning a one-half undivided interest.
    c. tenants in common, with Evers owning an undivided one-third interest.
    d. general partners in a joint venture.

21. If property is held by two or more owners as tenants in common, on the death of one owner the ownership of his or her share will pass to the
    a. remaining owner or owners.
    b. heirs or whoever is designated under the deceased owner's will.
    c. surviving owner and/or his or her heirs.
    d. deceased owner's surviving spouse.

22. In New York a deed conveying property to a married couple, such as to "Frank Peters and Marcia Peters, husband and wife," creates a
    a. joint tenancy.
    b. tenancy by the entirety.
    c. tenancy in common.
    d. periodic tenancy.

23. Which of the following statements applies equally to joint tenants and tenants by the entireties?
    a. There is no right to file a partition suit.
    b. The survivor becomes complete owner.
    c. There may be more than two owners.
    d. The deed must state the type of tenancy desired.

24. An artificial person created by legal means is known as a
    a. trust.
    b. corporation.
    c. limited partnership.
    d. joint tenancy.

25. A syndicate formed to carry out a single business project is commonly known as a
    a. joint venture.
    b. corporation.
    c. limited partnership.
    d. joint tenancy.

Liens and Easements

Eric buys a vacation cottage, and the seller tells him she has always used an easement to go across a neighbor's land to the lake. Eric worries about whether he will have that same right, or whether the neighbor might deny him lake access. Could he end up going to court to argue that he needs the right-of-way?

Real estate brokers often come up against claims by nonowners as they follow through on real estate transactions: a shared driveway, an old judgment placed against a seller's property, a neighbor's garage built six inches over the property line. Agents need a working knowledge of the concepts and vocabulary involved so they can assist attorneys in clearing up encumbrances.

Encumbrances

An **encumbrance** is a right or interest in a property held by a party who is not the owner of the property. Classifications of encumbrances are:

1. *Liens:* financial claims against the property
2. *Usage encumbrances:* restrictions, easements and encroachments.

Liens

A financial claim against real estate that provides security for a debt or obligation of the property owner is a **lien**. If the claim is not paid, the lienholder, or creditor, may ask a court to order the real estate sold for full or partial satisfaction of the debt, a process known as *foreclosure of the lien.*

A lien may be voluntary or involuntary. A **voluntary lien** is created by the owner's action, such as placing a mortgage loan. An **involuntary lien** is created by law. A real estate tax lien, for example, is an involuntary lien; it is placed on the property without any action by the property owner.

Liens may also be classified as either general or specific. As illustrated in Figure 6.1, **general liens** usually affect all the property of a debtor, both real and personal. They include judgments, estate and inheritance taxes, debts of a deceased person, corporation franchise taxes and federal and state income taxes.

Specific liens, on the other hand, are secured by a specific parcel of real estate and affect only that particular property. As illustrated in Figure 6.2, these include mechanics' liens, mortgages, real estate taxes, special assessments, liens for certain public utilities, vendors' liens, vendees' liens and surety bail bond liens.

- *Real estate taxes* (discussed further in Chapter 22) have first claim against the property.

> **ENCUMBRANCES MAY DIVIDE INTO TWO GENERAL CLASSIFICATIONS:**
>
> 1. Liens—financial claims against the property
> 2. Usage encumbrances—restrictions, easements and encroachments

Figure 6.1   General Liens

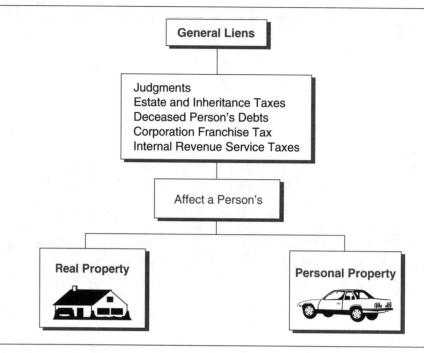

- *Judgments* are court orders to pay a debt, such as an unpaid bill. They become liens against all real property owned by an individual in that county when they are docketed (filed) in the county clerk's office. They may also be filed in other counties in New York State and against personal property.
- *Mechanics' liens* are placed against a specific property by workers or suppliers who have not been paid for labor or materials used in construction or repairs of that property.

To give immediate public notice that a legal action is pending, the outcome of which affects the title to real property, a *lis pendens* may be placed against a parcel of real estate.

Effects of Liens on Title

If the buyer agreed, an owner could sell a parcel of real estate even though it was encumbered by a lien. The lien, however, would remain with the property because liens and other encumbrances *run with the land;* that is, they will bind successive owners if steps are not taken to clear them up.

Liens attach to property, not to the property owner. Although a purchaser who buys real estate subject to a lien may not be personally responsible for payment of the debt, the property is still encumbered and the creditor could take court action to foreclose the lien.

▼ Priority of Liens

Tax liens. Real estate taxes and special assessments generally take **priority** over all other liens. If the property goes through a court-ordered sale to satisfy unpaid debts or obligations, outstanding real estate taxes and special assessments will be paid from the proceeds *first.* The remainder will be used to pay other outstanding liens in the order of their priority. For example, if the courts ordered a parcel of land sold to satisfy a judgment lien entered in the public record on February 7, 1990, subject to a first mortgage lien recorded January 22,

Figure 6.2 Specific Liens

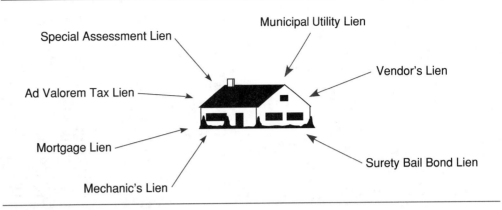

1984, and to this year's as-yet-unpaid real estate taxes, the proceeds of the sale would be distributed in the following order:

1. To the taxing bodies for this year's real estate taxes
2. To the mortgage lender for the entire amount of the mortgage loan outstanding as of the date of the sale (if proceeds remain after payments of taxes)
3. To the creditor named in the judgment lien (if any proceeds remain after paying the first two items)
4. To the foreclosed-on landowner (if any proceeds remain after paying the first three items plus costs of foreclosure).

Liens other than general taxes and special assessments take priority from the date of recording in the public records of the county where the property is located (see Figure 6.3).

Subordination agreements. Subordination agreements are written agreements between lienholders to change the priority of mortgage, judgment and other liens under certain circumstances.

Liens Other Than Real Estate Taxes

Aside from real estate tax and special assessment liens, the following types of liens may be charged against real property either voluntarily or involuntarily.

▼ Mortgage Liens

A **mortgage lien** is a voluntary lien on real estate given to a lender by a borrower as security for a loan. It becomes a lien on real property when the mortgage funds are disbursed and the mortgage document is delivered. The lender files or records the mortgage in the office of the county clerk or register of the county where the property is located. Mortgage lenders generally require a *first mortgage lien*; this means that (aside from taxes) no other liens against the property will take priority over the mortgage lien. Second mortgages and home equity loans do not, of course, have first priority. When the debt is fully paid, the lien is removed from the property by filing a satisfaction certificate signed by the lender.

▼ Mechanics Liens

A **mechanics lien** covers a situation in which an owner has not paid for work done on the property or the general contractor has been paid but has not paid

Figure 6.3   Priority of Liens

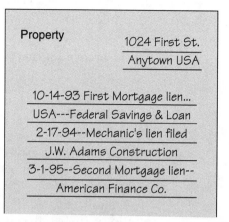

First Priority   Real Estate Taxes/Special Assessments

Next Priority
according to
order of filing
in public record

Property   1024 First St.
                            Anytown USA

10-14-93 First Mortgage lien...
USA---Federal Savings & Loan
2-17-94--Mechanic's lien filed
J.W. Adams Construction
3-1-95--Second Mortgage lien--
American Finance Co.

subcontractors or suppliers of materials. A claim for a mechanic's lien must be placed within four months of the completion of the work on a single dwelling and eight months on other buildings. A mechanic's lien is valid for one year and may be renewed.

New York's lien law allows nonresidential brokers' claims for leasing commissions to be filed as mechanics' liens. On the theory that the negotiation of a long-term lease constitutes an improvement of commercial property, a broker may enter a mechanic's lien in the public records for unpaid commissions. Such a lien may be filed only if the property is to be used for other than residential purposes, if the lease is for three years or longer and if the broker was working under a written commission agreement. The lien must be filed within eight months of the date when the commission became due.

Similarly, real property law allows a broker to file an affidavit of entitlement to commission for negotiation of a contract for the purchase or lease of any real property. Such an affidavit, although entered in the public records, *does not become a lien* against the property.

Judgments. A judgment is a decree issued by a court. When the decree provides for money to be awarded to the creditor, it is referred to as a money judgment. A judgment differs from a mortgage in that a specific parcel of real estate was never given as security for the debt.

A judgment becomes a *general involuntary lien on all real property* in the county owned by the debtor when it is docketed (filed) with the county clerk. Transcripts of the lien also may be docketed in any other county in New York if the creditor wishes.

A judgment is a lien against real property for ten years and can be renewed for ten more.

A judgment takes priority from the date the judgment is docketed in the county clerk's office. Judgments are enforced through the sale of the debtor's real or personal property by a sheriff. When the sale yields enough to satisfy the debt, the sheriff's report of sale will show that the sale yielded sufficient money to satisfy the debt and the record will be cleared of the judgment.

A judgment also can be satisfied, of course, by the debtor's payment of the debt in full. Debtors who pay such a debt and fail to record a satisfaction piece—a document that states that the debt has been paid in full—are often surprised to find the judgment still on their credit records years later.

Lis pendens. Considerable time may elapse between the filing of a lawsuit and the rendering of a judgment or other decree. When any suit is filed that affects title to a parcel of real estate (such as an action for specific performance), a lis pendens (or notice of pendency) is immediately recorded to give notice to interested parties, such as prospective purchasers and lenders, that there is a cloud on the title.

▼ **Other Liens**

Federal **estate taxes** and state *inheritance taxes* (as well as the debts of deceased persons) are *general involuntary liens* that encumber a deceased person's real and personal property. These are normally paid or cleared in probate court proceedings.

A *vendor's lien* is a *seller's claim* in cases where the seller did not receive the full agreed-on purchase price.

A vendee's lien is a buyer's claim against a seller's property in cases where the seller failed to deliver title. This may occur when property is purchased under an installment contract (contract for deed, land contract) and the seller fails to deliver title after all other terms of the contract have been satisfied.

Municipalities that furnish water or services such as refuse collection are given the right to a lien on the property of an owner who refuses to pay bills.

A real estate owner who must stand trial for a crime may choose to put up real estate instead of cash as surety for bail (or other family members may pledge their real estate). The execution and recording of such a *surety bail bond* creates a lien enforceable by the state if the accused person does not appear in court.

New York state levies a **corporation franchise tax** on corporations as a condition of allowing them to do business in the state. Such a tax is a lien on all property, real and personal, owned by the corporation. New York City also imposes a tax on corporations doing business in the city, which becomes a lien on the corporation's property.

An *environmental lien* may be levied by the federal government for costs and damages incurred in removal or remedial action under the Comprehensive Environmental Response, Compensation, and Liability Act (CERCLA), the environmental cleanup act. The lien attaches only to the property subject to the cleanup.

An *Internal Revenue Service (IRS) tax lien* results from failure to pay any portion of federal income or withholding taxes. It is a lien on all the taxpayers's real and personal property.

Other liens include those for unpaid condominium common charges in favor of the board of managers or condominium association, liens for unpaid maintenance or other charges in favor of a cooperative corporation; and liens for New York State income and transfer taxes and some Uniform Commercial Code (UCC) filings.

Deed Restrictions

Private agreements that affect the use of land are **deed restrictions** *and covenants.* They usually are placed by the owner when the property is sold, and they may be included in the deed. Deed restrictions typically would be imposed by a developer to maintain specific standards in a subdivision or to require that a property be used for a specific purpose. For example, property owners in a subdivision may not be allowed to park recreational vehicles in the street.

Easements

A right acquired by one party to use the land of another party for a special purpose is an **easement**. Easements commonly are created by written agreement between the parties. An easement may be either appurtenant or in gross.

▼ Easement Appurtenant

The permanent right to use another's land for the benefit of a neighboring parcel is an **easement appurtenant**. For example, *A* and *B* own properties in a lake resort community, but only *A*'s property borders the lake. *A* may grant *B* an easement across *A*'s property to give *B* access to the beach (see Figure 6.4). An easement appurtenant *runs with the land* (is permanent), so that if *B* sells the property to *C*, *C* acquires the same right-of-way over *A*'s land. If *A* sells to *D*, *B* still owns the easement. Easements appurtenant involve two adjoining parcels of land.

> **FOUR TYPES OF EASEMENTS:**
>
> 1. Appurtenant
> 2. In gross
> 3. By necessity
> 4. By prescription

The property that benefits is called the **dominant estate;** the one that is used is the **servient estate**. In the case of the right-of-way, *B*'s property, which can use the neighbor's land, is the dominant estate; *A*'s property, which must allow the use, is the servient estate.

▼ Easement in Gross

A mere right to use the land of another is an **easement in gross**. Such an easement does not involve any adjoining estate. Common examples are the right to run high-tension, telephone or cable TV lines. In Figure 6.4, utility lines run by right of an easement along the boundary line between the lots.

A personal easement in gross generally does not pass with the land. In the beginning of the chapter, we asked whether Eric would have the same easement right across his neighbor's land in order to reach the lake as the present owner had. If that easement were an appurtenant easement and benefited Eric's new vacation cottage, Eric would have the same easement rights as the previous owner. However, if the previous owner had an easement in gross, Eric could be denied access to the lake.

▼ Easement by Necessity

In certain cases, if the only access to a parcel is through another's property, the owner may acquire an easement by necessity to reach his or her land. In Figure 6.4, *A* owns an easement by necessity, from the road across *B*'s land.

▼ Easement by Prescription

Under specific circumstances one may acquire the permanent right to *use* another's property by doing so for a period (in New York State) of ten years, creating an **easement by prescription**. **Tacking** allows consecutive owners to

Figure 6.4 Easements

The owner of Lot A has an **easement by necessity** across Lot B to gain access to his property from the paved road. The owner of Lot B has an **easement appurtenant** across Lot A so that Lot B's owner may reach the lake. The utility company has an **easement in gross** *across both parcels of land* for its electric power lines.

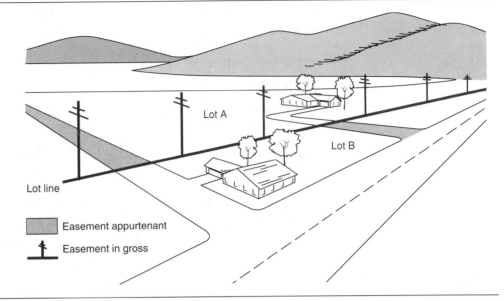

accumulate the ten years' usage. (A similar process, **adverse possession,** sometimes allows the user to acquire actual *ownership;* see Chapter 20.) Through *tacking,* a party who did not use the property for the entire required period may still claim an easement by prescription. The parties must have been *successors in interest,* such as an ancestor and heir, landlord and tenant or seller and buyer.

▼ **Party Walls**

A wall shared by two buildings and constructed on the boundary line between two owners' lots is shared by the owners. Each owns his or her side of the **party wall** and an easement right in the other half. A party wall may not be demolished without the consent of both owners. Each owner is responsible for maintaining his or her half.

▼ **Encroachments**

When a building, fence or driveway illegally extends beyond the land of its owner and covers some land of an adjoining owner or a street, an **encroachment** arises. Encroachments usually are disclosed by either a physical inspection of the property or a survey. A survey shows the location of all improvements on a property and whether any improvements extend over the lot lines. If a building encroaches on neighboring land, the neighbor may be able to recover damages or secure removal of the portion of the building that encroaches. Encroachments of ten years may give rise to ownership by adverse possession.

For encroachments of six inches or less by the wall of a building, the encroacher receives an easement by prescription unless the offended neighbor seeks removal within one year or damages within two years.

Licenses

Not classified as an encumbrance because it is not a permanent right, a privilege to enter the land of another for a specific purpose is known as a **license.** Examples of license include permission to park in a neighbor's driveway or to erect a billboard. The permission given by a license may be withdrawn.

Key Terms

adverse possession	judgment
corporation franchise tax	license
deed restrictions	lien
dominant estate	lis pendens
easement	mechanic's lien
easement appurtenant	mortgage lien
easement by necessity	notice of pendency
easement by prescription	party wall
easement in gross	priority
encroachment	servient estate
encumbrance	specific lien
estate taxes	subordination agreement
general lien	tacking
involuntary lien	voluntary lien

Summary

Encumbrances against real estate may be in the form of liens, deed restrictions, easements and encroachments.

Liens are financial claims against the real and personal property of a debtor. Liens are either general, covering all real and personal property of a debtor/owner, or specific, covering only the one parcel of real estate described in the mortgage, tax bill, building or repair contract or other document. Liens can be enforced by court-ordered foreclosure, that is, sale of the property to satisfy unpaid debt(s).

With the exception of real estate tax liens, which come first, the priority of liens is generally determined by the order in which they are placed in the public records.

Mortgage liens are given to lenders to provide security for mortgage loans. Mechanics' liens protect general contractors, subcontractors and material suppliers whose work adds value to real estate.

A judgment is a court decree obtained by a creditor, usually for a monetary award from a debtor. When docketed (filed), it becomes a lien on all the debtor's real property in the county where it was docketed, and it may be similarly docketed in any other county in New York State. Lis pendens, or notice of pendency, is a recorded notice that a lawsuit is awaiting trial in court and may result in a judgment.

Federal estate taxes and state inheritance taxes are general liens against a deceased owner's property. A vendor's lien is a seller's claim against a purchaser who has not paid the entire purchase price, and a vendee's lien is a purchaser's claim against a seller under an installment contract who has not conveyed title.

Deed restrictions are placed on land by sellers who wish to control future uses of the property.

An easement is a permanent right one has to use land owned by another. Easements appurtenant involve two neighboring tracts. The tract benefited is known as the dominant estate; the tract subject to the easement is called the servient estate. An easement in gross is a right such as that granted to utility companies to maintain poles, wires and pipelines.

An encroachment is physical intrusion of some improvement on another's land. A license is temporary permission to enter another's property for a specific purpose.

1. Which of the following is considered a lien on real estate?

   a. An easement running with the land
   b. An unpaid mortgage loan
   c. A public footpath
   d. A license to erect a billboard

2. Contractor Hammond was hired to build a room addition to the Elkins' home. Hammond completed the work several weeks ago but still has not been paid. In this situation Hammond is entitled to a mechanic's lien, which will be a

   a. general lien.   c. lis pendens.
   b. specific lien.   d. voluntary lien.

3. Which of the following liens usually would be given highest priority?

   a. A mortgage dated last year
   b. The current real estate tax
   c. A mechanic's lien for work started before the mortgage was made
   d. A judgment rendered yesterday

4. Jim Chard was not paid for roofing the Hills' ranch home. How long does he have to file a mechanic's lien?

   a. Four months   c. One year
   b. Eight months   d. Ten years

5. Jim's mechanic's lien will remain against the property for at least

   a. four months.   c. one year.
   b. eight months.   d. ten years.

6. A homeowner's neighbor plans to file a suit against the homeowner because of a boundary dispute. When the neighbor learns that the property is for sale, which of the following will she and her attorney use to protect her interest?

   a. Lis pendens
   b. Prescription
   c. Affidavit of entitlement
   d. Satisfaction piece

7. When the Cratchetts failed to pay for Tim's orthopedic surgery, Dr. Welby obtained a money judgment, which, upon docketing, becomes a lien against the Cratchetts'

   a. vacant land.   c. apartment house.
   b. home.   d. All of the above

8. Donna Majors sold David Berel a parcel of real estate; title has passed, but to date Berel has not paid the purchase price in full as originally agreed. If Majors does not receive payment, which of the following could she use to enforce the payment?

   a. Mortgage lien   c. Lis pendens
   b. Vendee's lien   d. Vendor's lien

9. When the Cratchetts pay off their doctor's judgment, they should

   a. record a satisfaction certificate.
   b. put a lis pendens on the apartment house.
   c. notify their mortgagee.
   d. grant an easement appurtenant.

10. In New York City, property may be subjected to a lien for the owner's

    a. jaywalking.   c. shoplifting.
    b. traffic tickets.   d. public disturbance.

11. A telephone company runs its poles and wires with the rights granted by an easement
    a. by necessity.
    b. appurtenant.
    c. by prescription.
    d. in gross.

12. The farmer who allowed promoters to run the Woodstock rock festival on his land granted them a(n)
    a. easement by necessity.
    b. dominant estate.
    c. voluntary lien.
    d. license.

13. To establish an easement by prescription in New York, a person must use another's property for an uninterrupted period of
    a. five years.
    b. ten years.
    c. fifteen years.
    d. twenty years.

14. Rayburn's neighbor Jones regularly uses Rayburn's driveway to reach Jones's garage on Jones's property. Jones has an easement over Rayburn's driveway. Rayburn's property is properly called
    a. the dominant estate.
    b. an estate.
    c. a leasehold.
    d. the servient estate.

15. A shared driveway agreement will probably take the form of a(n)
    a. voluntary lien.
    b. easement appurtenant.
    c. affidavit of entitlement.
    d. certificate of satisfaction.

16. A party wall
    a. straddles a boundary line.
    b. faces a main road.
    c. is located only on a servient estate.
    d. is owned by one party.

17. Eric buys a vacation cottage whose previous owner had an easement appurtenant for access to the lake across a neighbor's land. If Eric wants to reach the lake, he must
    a. renegotiate with the neighbor.
    b. apply to a court for an easement by necessity.
    c. pay a token rental to the neighbor.
    d. simply go ahead and use the crossing.

18. The lien with first claim against real estate is
    a. the property tax.
    b. a mechanic's lien.
    c. a first mortgage.
    d. whatever lien was first recorded.

19. Linda Allen owns a condominium apartment in Manhattan; a cabin on three acres in the Catskills, where she keeps a boat; and a house in Florida. If one of her creditors sues her in Manhattan and obtains a judgment, that judgment may be placed as a lien against the
    a. Manhattan apartment only.
    b. apartment and cabin.
    c. apartment, cabin and boat.
    d. apartment, cabin and Florida house.

20. Deed restrictions are created by a
    a. seller.
    b. buyer.
    c. neighborhood association.
    d. governmental agency.

21. The right to run a power line across the back of someone's property is an example of an easement
    a. in gross.
    b. by prescription.
    c. by necessity.
    d. in common.

Real Estate Instruments: Deeds

Norm and Michelle bought a farm from Michelle's parents. Recently Norm heard that a quitclaim deed offers the least protection to the propertyowner. That's all he received when they bought the farm, and he's worried. If Michelle died, could her parents take the farm back? Are there steps he should take?

A deed is a written instrument by which a property owner as "grantor" conveys and transfers to a "grantee" an ownership interest in real estate. Deeds must be understood (though never drawn up) by the real estate practitioner.

Legal Descriptions

One of the essential elements of a valid deed is an adequate description of the *land* being conveyed. (The deed does not usually describe buildings on the land.) A **legal description** is an *exact way of describing real estate that will be accepted in a court of law.*

Legal descriptions should never be changed or combined without information from a competent authority such as a surveyor or title attorney. Street address and property tax account number, although helpful for quick reference to what is being described, are not usually acceptable as legal descriptions.

Land can be described by three methods:

1. Metes and bounds
2. Government survey
3. Reference to a plat (map) filed in the county clerk's office in the county where the land is located, a tax map or a prior recorded instrument

In New York a legal description may combine different descriptive methods. Also used is reference to a previously recorded deed or mortgage.

> **LAND CAN BE DESCRIBED BY THREE METHODS:**
>
> 1. Metes and bounds
> 2. Government survey
> 3. Reference to a plat (map) filed in the county clerk's office in the county where the land is located

▼ Metes and Bounds

A **metes-and-bounds** description uses the boundaries and measurements of the land in question.

It starts at a definite point called the **point (place) of beginning** (POB) and proceeds clockwise around the boundaries of the tract by reference to measurements and directions. A metes-and-bounds description always ends at the point where it began (the POB).

In a metes-and-bounds description **monuments** are fixed objects used to establish boundaries. In the past, natural objects such as stones and large trees were

Figure 7.1 Metes-and-Bounds Tract

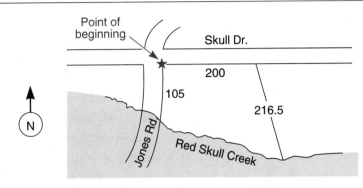

commonly used as monuments. Today man-made markers are more common because natural objects may change or be removed. An example of a metes-and-bounds description of a parcel of land (shown in Figure 7.1) appears below.

> A tract of land located in the City of Elmira, County of Chemung, State of New York, described as follows: Beginning at the intersection of the east line of Jones Road and the south line of Skull Drive; thence east along the south line of Skull Drive 200 feet; thence south 15 degrees east 216.5 feet, more or less, to the center thread of Red Skull Creek; thence northwesterly along the center line of said creek to its intersection with the east line of Jones Road; thence north 105 feet, more or less, along the east line of Jones Road to the place of beginning.

Metes-and-bounds descriptions are used everywhere, from rural undeveloped areas to Manhattan, with street intersections used as monuments.

▼ **Rectangular (Government) Survey System**

The **rectangular survey system**, sometimes called the *government survey method*, was established by Congress in 1785 as a standard method for describing western lands acquired by the government. It is seldom used in New York or any of the other 13 original states.

The rectangular survey system is based on sets of intersecting lines: principal meridians and base lines. *Principal meridians* are north and south lines; *base lines* run east and west. They are located by reference to degrees of longitude and latitude.

Townships. Using these meridians and base lines, land is surveyed into six-mile-square *townships*, each with identifying reference numbers. Each township contains 36 square miles.

Sections. A township is further divided into 36 numbered *sections*. Sections are numbered 1 through 36, as shown in Figure 7.2. Section 1 is always in the northeast, or upper right-hand, corner.

Each section contains one square mile, or *640 acres*. As illustrated in Figure 7.3, each section may be divided into smaller parcels for reference purposes. The southeast quarter is a 160-acre tract; this would be abbreviated as SE¼. Quarter

Figure 7.2   Sections in a Township

sections can be divided into quarters or halves and further divided by quarters. The SE¼ of SE¼ of SE¼ of Section 1 would be a ten-acre square in the lower right-hand corner of Section 1.

▼ **Recorded Plat of Subdivision**

The third method of land description is by *lot and map number* referring to a **plat of subdivision** filed with the clerk of the county where the land is located. The recorded plat of subdivision method is also known as the block and lot method.

The first step in subdividing land is the preparation of a *plat (map)* by a licensed surveyor or engineer, as illustrated in Figure 7.4. On this plat the land is divided into blocks and lots, and streets or access roads for public use are indicated. Lots are assigned numbers or letters. Lot sizes and street details are indicated. When properly signed and approved, the subdivision plat may be recorded in the county in which the land is located; it thereby becomes part of the legal description. In describing a lot from a recorded subdivision plat, the lot number, name or number of the subdivision plat and name of the county and state are used. For example:

THAT TRACT OR PARCEL OF LAND, situated in the Town of Brighton, County of Monroe, and State of New York, known and designated as Lot No. 8 of the Fertile Acres Tract. Said Lot is situated on Dearing Lane and is of the dimensions shown on a map of Fertile Acres filed in the Monroe County Clerk's Office in Liber 125 of Maps at page 95.

The word *liber* is Latin for *book*. Sometimes a *reel* number is used, referring to a specific reel of microfilm records.

▼ **Preparation and Use of a Survey**

A licensed surveyor is trained and authorized to locate a given parcel of land. A *survey* sets forth the legal description. A survey map shows the location and dimensions of the parcel and the location, size and shape of buildings on the lot. Surveys may be required for conveying a portion of a given tract of land, placing a mortgage loan, showing the location of new construction, locating roads and highways and determining legal descriptions.

Figure 7.3   A Section

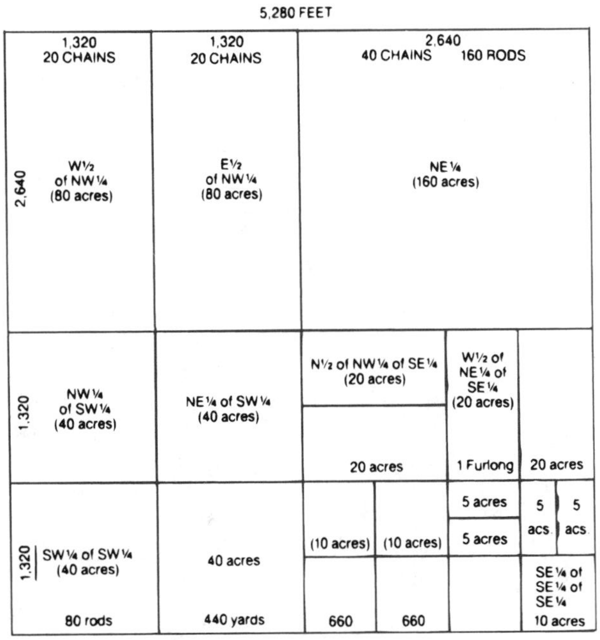

	5,280 FEET		
1,320 20 CHAINS	1,320 20 CHAINS	2,640 40 CHAINS 160 RODS	

(A section diagram divided into quarters and subdivisions:)

- W½ of NW¼ (80 acres)
- E½ of NW¼ (80 acres)
- NE¼ (160 acres)
- NW¼ of SW¼ (40 acres)
- NE¼ of SW¼ (40 acres)
- N½ of NW¼ of SE¼ (20 acres)
- W½ of NE¼ of SE¼ (20 acres)
- 20 acres — 1 Furlong — 20 acres
- SW¼ of SW¼ (40 acres)
- 40 acres
- (10 acres) (10 acres)
- 5 acres — 5 acres
- 5 acs | 5 acs
- SE¼ of SE¼ of SE¼ (10 acres)
- 80 rods — 440 yards — 660 — 660 — 10 acres

Measuring Elevations

▼ Air Lots

The owner of a parcel of land may subdivide the air above the land into *air lots.* This type of description is found in titles to tall buildings located on air rights or condominium units.

▼ Datum

A point, line or surface from which elevations are measured or indicated is a **datum,** defined by the United States Geodetic Survey as mean sea level at New York harbor. Many large cities have established a local official datum. In preparing a subdivision plat for condominium use, a surveyor describes each condominium unit by reference to the elevation of the floors and ceilings above the city datum.

Benchmarks.   To aid surveyors, permanent reference points called **benchmarks** have been established throughout the United States (see Figure 7.5).

▼ Condominium

A sufficient description of condominium property must include (1) a description of the land on which the building and improvements are located; (2) a designation of the unit conveyed as listed in the declaration, filed in accordance with the *New York Condominium Act;* and (3) a description of the common interest or the percentage of the common interest that is conveyed with the unit.

Deeds

A **deed** is a *written instrument by which an owner of real estate intentionally conveys his or her right, title or interest in a parcel of real estate.* Sometimes a deed transfers only a part of the owner's interest.

All deeds must be in writing, in accordance with the requirements of the statute of frauds. The owner, who grants (sells or gives the land) is referred to as the

Figure 7.4   Subdivision Plat Map

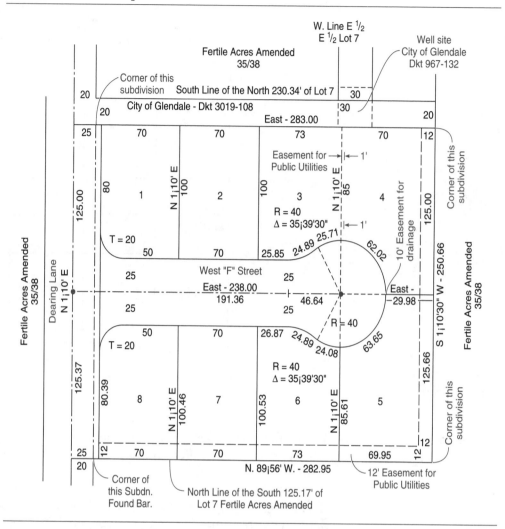

grantor, and the new owner (who receives the title) is called the **grantee.** A deed is always *executed* (signed) by the grantor (or other authorized person).

Occasionally, as in mortgage assumptions and condominium transfers, it is also signed by the grantee.

The requirements for a valid deed are a *grantor* having the legal capacity to execute (sign) the deed;

- a *grantee* named with reasonable certainty so that he or she can be easily identified;
- a recital of *consideration;*
- a *granting clause* (words of conveyance) ;
- a *habendum clause* (to define ownership);
- designation of any limitations on the conveyance of a full fee simple estate;
- an *adequate description* (a legal description) of the property conveyed;
- *exceptions and reservations* affecting the title;
- the *signature of the grantor, and (if the deed is to be recorded) acknowledgment;* and
- *delivery* of the deed and *acceptance* by the grantee to pass title.

Figure 7.5   Benchmark

Grantor. In New York a person must be of sound mind and have reached the age of 18 to effect a valid conveyance. A contract executed by an incompetent or a minor is *voidable* by the courts; that is, it may be set aside in a lawsuit conducted on behalf of the incompetent or minor. A minor may also void (or rescind) a contract upon reaching the age of 18. A minor who is married, however, may convey property used as a home as if he or she had reached the age of 18.

Grantee. To be valid a deed must name a grantee in such a way that he or she is readily identifiable. In New York both grantee and grantor must be identified by address if the deed is to be recorded.

Consideration. To be valid all deeds must contain a clause acknowledging the grantor's receipt of consideration. **Consideration** is something of value given in an exchange. Where a purchase price is not involved, "Love and affection" may be sufficient consideration, though often it is customary to recite a *nominal* consideration such as "$10.00 and other good and valuable consideration." In New York State the full dollar amount of consideration is seldom stated in the deed, except when the instrument is signed by a fiduciary such as an executor or trustee, or by an attorney-in-fact pursuant to a power of attorney.

Granting clause (words of conveyance). A deed must contain words in the *granting clause* that state the grantor's intention to transfer (convey) ownership of the property.

If more than one grantee is involved, the granting clause should cover the creation of their specific rights in the property. The clause might state, for example, that the grantees will take title as joint tenants or tenants in common. This is especially important because specific wording is necessary to create a joint tenancy.

Deeds that convey the entire fee simple interest of the grantor usually contain wording such as "to Jacqueline Smith and to her heirs and assigns forever." A deed creating a life estate would convey property "to Jacqueline Smith for the duration of her natural life."

Habendum clause. When it is necessary to define or explain the ownership to be enjoyed by the grantee, a *habendum clause* follows the granting clause. The habendum clause begins with the words "to have and to hold." Its provisions must agree with those set down in the granting clause.

Exceptions and reservations. A grantor may reserve some right in the land for his or her own use (an easement, for instance). A grantor also may place certain restrictions on a grantee's use of the property. A developer, for example, can restrict the number of houses that may be built on a one-acre lot in a subdivision. Such restrictions may be stated in the deed or contained in a previously recorded document (such as the subdivider's master deed) that is expressly mentioned in the deed.

Description of real estate. For a deed to be valid it must contain an adequate description of the real estate conveyed. Land is considered adequately described if a competent surveyor can locate the property from the description used.

Signature of grantor. A deed must be signed by *all grantors.* New York permits a grantor's signature to be signed by an **attorney-in-fact,** a person who has been given power of attorney to sign for the grantor. Usually the power of attorney must be recorded in the county where the property is located. Because the power of attorney ends on the death of the person granting the authority, evidence must be submitted that the grantor is alive at the time the attorney-in-fact signs the deed. This is typically done with a phone call placed during the closing.

An *acknowledgment* is a declaration made by a person who is signing a document before an authorized public officer. The term *acknowledgment* also refers to a document or section in a document that states that the person signing the deed or other document is known to the officer or has produced sufficient identification. It provides evidence that the signature is genuine.

Although an acknowledgment is usually made before a *notary public,* it can also be taken by a judge, justice of the peace or other qualified person.

An acknowledgment is not required to make a deed valid, but in New York all deeds, mortgages and similar documents must be acknowledged before they can be recorded (entered in the public records). In some cases they can be signed before a witness, who would then swear to the validity of the signature before an authorized public official.

From a purely practical point of view a deed that is not acknowledged is not satisfactory and could cause problems. To help ensure good title, a grantee should always require acknowledgment of the grantor's signature on a deed so that it may be recorded. Further requirements before a deed may be recorded are detailed in Chapter 20.

Delivery and acceptance. Before a transfer of title by deed can take effect, there must be an actual **delivery** of the deed by the grantor and **acceptance** by the grantee. *Title is said to pass when a deed is delivered.* (**Title** *is the right to all the bundles of rights inherent in real property ownership.*)

In England during the Middle Ages, when few people were literate, transfer of title occurred in the following manner: The seller took the buyer into the field in question, and they walked the boundaries together ("beating the bounds").

Then the seller reached down, took up a clod of earth to represent the whole field and handed it to the buyer. At the moment when the buyer seized the clod he became owner of the land. Today a document is used instead of a clod of earth, but title still transfers at the moment of delivery and acceptance, and the owner is still said to be *seized* of the property. The Middle English word **seisin** still denotes ownership and control.

▼ **Execution of Corporate Deeds**

A corporation can convey real estate only after a resolution passed by its *board of directors*. If all or a substantial portion of a corporation's real estate is being conveyed, the holders of at least two-thirds of the stock also must approve.

Rules pertaining to religious corporations and not-for-profit corporations vary widely and may require a court order authorizing the conveyance. Because the legal requirements must be followed explicitly, an attorney should be consulted for all corporate conveyances.

▼ **Types of Deeds**

The forms of deeds used in New York are

- full covenant and warranty deed,
- bargain and sale deed with covenant against grantor's acts,
- bargain and sale deed without covenant against grantor's acts,
- quitclaim deed,
- executor's deed and
- referee's deed.

COMMON FORMS OF DEEDS:

- Full covenant and warranty deed
- Bargain and sale deed with covenant against grantor's acts
- Bargain and sale deed without covenant against grantor's acts
- Quitclaim deed
- Executor's deed
- Referee's deed

Warranty deeds. For a purchaser of real estate, a **full covenant and warranty deed** provides the *greatest protection* of any deed (shown in Figure 7.6). In it the grantor makes certain **covenants,** or warranties, which are legal promises that the grantee will have unchallenged ownership. The basic warranties are

- *covenant of seisin (ownership):* The grantor warrants that he or she is the owner of the property and has the right to convey it.
- *covenant against encumbrances:* The grantor warrants that the property is free from any liens or encumbrances except those specifically stated in the deed.
- *covenant of quiet enjoyment:* The grantor guarantees that the grantee's title is good against anyone who challenges the grantee's ownership.
- *covenant of further assurance:* The grantor promises to obtain and deliver any instrument needed to make the title good.
- *covenant of warranty forever:* The grantor promises that if at any time in the future the title fails, he or she will be liable.

These covenants in a warranty deed are not limited to matters that occurred during the time the grantor owned the property; they extend back to all previous owners. The grantee is entitled to money damages if any of the warranties are ever breached.

A deed in New York must contain a *lien covenant*, stating that the seller holds the proceeds of the sale in trust against unpaid improvements to the property.

In New York State the seller need not deliver a full covenant and warranty deed unless the purchase agreement requires it. In many upstate areas the warranty deed is the one used most commonly. In other areas a bargain and sale deed with covenant is more usual.

Figure 7.6   Full Covenant and Warranty Deed

Standard N.Y. B.T.U. Form 8003 — 8-53 — Warranty Deed With Full Covenants — Individual or Corporation. (single sheet)   35-3100-021
                                                                                                                   Form 31-21

THIS INDENTURE, made the   day of   , nineteen hundred and

BETWEEN

party of the first part, and

party of the second part,

WITNESSETH, that the party of the first part, in consideration of Ten Dollars and other valuable consideration paid by the party of the second part, does hereby grant and release unto the party of the second part, the heirs or successors and assigns of the party of the second part forever,

ALL that certain plot, piece or parcel of land, with the buildings and improvements thereon erected, situate, lying and being in the

TOGETHER with all right, title and interest, if any, of the party of the first part of, in and to any streets and roads abutting the above-described premises to the center lines thereof; TOGETHER with the appurtenances and all the estate and rights of the party of the first part in and to said premises; TO HAVE AND TO HOLD the premises herein granted unto the party of the second part, the heirs or successors and assigns of the party of the second part forever.

AND the party of the first part, in compliance with Section 13 of the Lien Law, covenants that the party of the first part will receive the consideration for this conveyance and will hold the right to receive such consideration as a trust fund to be applied first for the purpose of paying the costs of the improvement and will apply the same first to the payment of the cost of the improvement before using any part of the total of the same for any other purpose.

AND the party of the first part covenants as follows: that said party of the first part is seized of the said premises in fee simple, and has good right to convey the same; that the party of the second part shall quietly enjoy the said premises; that the said premises are free from incumbrances, except as aforesaid; that the party of the first part will execute or procure any further necessary assurance of the title to said premises; and that said party of the first part will forever warrant the title to said premises.

The word "party" shall be construed as if it read "parties" whenever the sense of this indenture so requires.

IN WITNESS WHEREOF, the party of the first part has duly executed this deed the **day** and **year** first above written.

IN PRESENCE OF:

Bargain and sale deed with covenant against grantor's acts (special warranty deed). With these deeds the grantors imply that they have title to the property and add only one covenant, stating that they have done nothing to encumber the property while it was in their possession. This deed is used in most sale transactions and by fiduciaries (executors and trustees). The grantors are willing to warrant about the time they owned the property but not about previous owners.

This **bargain and sale deed with covenant** (against grantor's acts) is normally used in real estate transactions in the New York City area; the buyer may look to title insurance for protection in the event of future title problems. In most other states this deed is known as a **special warranty deed**.

Bargain and sale deed without covenant. A **bargain and sale deed** without covenant contains no warranties. It does, however, *imply* that the grantor holds title to the property. The grantee has little legal recourse if defects later appear in the title. The bargain and sale deed without covenant is also commonly used in New York City, as well as in foreclosure and tax sales and as a *referee's deed.*

Quitclaim deeds. A **quitclaim deed** provides the grantee with the least protection. It carries no covenant or warranties and conveys only whatever interest the grantor may have. If the grantor has no interest in the property, the grantee will acquire nothing and will have no claim against the grantor. A quitclaim deed can convey title as effectively as a warranty deed if the grantor has good title, but it provides no guarantees.

A quitclaim deed commonly is used for simple transfers within a family and for property transferred during divorce settlements. In our example at the beginning of the chapter, Norm was worried about the quitclaim deed he and his wife received when they bought his wife's parents' farm. He doesn't need to worry about the effectiveness of the deed—it did indeed transfer the title to the farm.

A quitclaim deed also can be used to clear a cloud on a title when persons who may or may not have some claim to property are asked to "sign off."

Executor's and referee's deeds. An **executor's deed** is a bargain and sale deed with covenant; a *referee's deed* contains no covenants or warranties although it does *imply* seisin (ownership). The *full consideration* (sales price) usually is stated in these cases so that it is a matter of public record.

Other Real Estate Instruments

Among other important instruments used in the practice of real estate are listing agreements, which were discussed in detail in Chapter 2; leases, the subject of Chapter 8; purchase and sale contracts, option agreements and land contracts, which will be treated in Chapter 9.

Key Terms

attorney-in-fact	grantee/grantor
bargain and sale deed	legal description
bargain and sale deed with	metes and bounds
covenant	monuments
benchmarks	plat of subdivision
consideration	point (place) of beginning
covenants	quitclaim deed
datum	rectangular survey system
deed	seisin
delivery and acceptance	special warranty deed
full covenant and warranty deed	warranty deed
title	

Summary

Documents affecting interests in real estate must contain a legal description that accurately identifies the property involved. Land is described by (1) metes and bounds, (2) rectangular (government) survey and (3) recorded plat of subdivision.

In a metes-and-bounds description the actual location of monuments is the most important consideration. The description always must enclose a tract of land; the boundary line must end at the point at which it started.

The rectangular survey system is not used in New York. It involves surveys based on principal meridians. Land is surveyed into squares 36 miles in area, called townships. Townships are divided into 36 sections of one square mile each. Each square mile contains 640 acres.

Land can be subdivided into lots by means of a recorded plat of subdivision. An approved map giving the size, location and designation of lots and specifying the location and size of streets is filed in the recorder's office of the county where the land is located.

A survey is the usual method of certifying the legal description of a parcel of land. Surveys often are required when a mortgage or new construction is involved.

Air lots, condominium descriptions and other measurements of vertical elevations may be computed from the Geodetic Survey datum, which is mean sea level in New York harbor. Most large cities have established local datums. The elevations from these datums are further supplemented by reference points, called benchmarks.

The voluntary transfer of an owner's title is made by a deed, executed (signed) by the owner as grantor to the purchaser or donee as grantee.

Among the most common requirements for a valid deed are a grantor with legal capacity to contract, a readily identifiable grantee, a granting clause, a legal description of the property, a recital of consideration, exceptions and reservations on the title and the signature of the grantor. In addition, the deed should be acknowledged before a notary public or other officer to provide evidence that the signature is genuine and to allow recording. Title to the property passes when the grantor delivers a deed to the grantee who accepts it.

A general warranty deed provides the greatest protection of any deed by binding the grantor to certain covenants or warranties. A bargain and sale deed with covenant warrants only that the real estate has not been encumbered by the grantor. A bargain and sale deed without covenant carries with it no warranties but implies that the grantor holds title to the property. A quitclaim deed carries no warranties whatsoever and conveys only whatever interest the grantor possesses in the property.

Figure 7.7 Plat Map of Braddock Estates

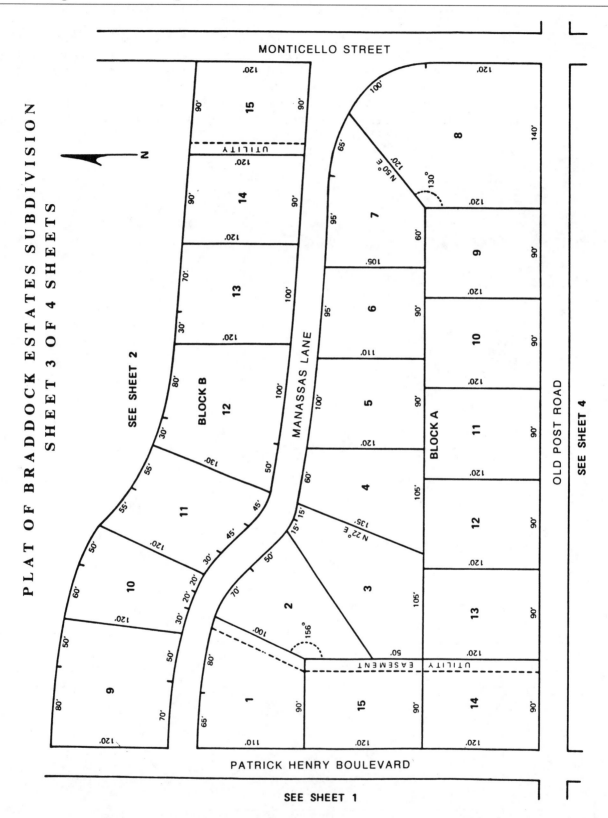

Questions

1. When Norm and his wife bought a farm from her parents, they received only a quitclaim deed. This was most likely because
   a. that's the type often used for in-family transactions.
   b. he will own the farm only during his wife's lifetime.
   c. he and his wife own as tenants by the entirety.
   d. a mortgage was involved.

2. If Tom Flock buys a new home in the Buffalo subdivision known as Vista Ridge, his land probably bears a legal description based on
   a. the rectangular survey.
   b. metes and bounds.
   c. the recorded plat.
   d. the street address.

3. According to the accompanying plat map (Figure 7.7), which of the following lots has the most frontage on Manassas Lane?
   a. Lot 10, Block B   c. Lot 8, Block A
   b. Lot 11, Block B   d. Lot 7, Block A

4. On the plat, how many lots have easements?
   a. One   c. Three
   b. Two   d. Four

5. The least acceptable legal method for identifying property is
   a. the rectangular survey.
   b. lot and block.
   c. the street address.
   d. metes and bounds.

6. It is essential that every deed be signed by the
   a. grantor.
   b. grantee.
   c. grantor and grantee.
   d. devisee.

7. Title to property transfers at the moment a deed is
   a. signed.
   b. acknowledged.
   c. delivered and accepted.
   d. recorded.

8. Consideration in a deed refers to
   a. gentle handling of the document.
   b. something of value given by each party.
   c. the habendum clause.
   d. the payment of transfer tax stamps.

9. A declaration before a notary or other official providing evidence that a signature is genuine is an
   a. affidavit.
   b. acknowledgment.
   c. affirmation.
   d. estoppel.

10. A notary's acknowledgment of the signature on a deed is necessary
    a. for the deed to be valid.
    b. for the deed to be recorded.
    c. before transfer tax can be paid.
    d. to give constructive notice of the transfer.

11. Arthur signs a deed to Michelle as grantee, has it acknowledged and receives payment from her. Arthur arranges to meet Michelle the next morning at the courthouse to give the deed to her. Michelle will own the property
    a. immediately because she has paid for it.
    b. the next morning when she receives the deed.
    c. when she records the deed.
    d. as soon as she signs the deed the next morning.

12. The grantee receives greatest protection with what type of deed?
    a. Quitclaim
    b. Warranty
    c. Bargain and sale with covenant
    d. Executor's

13. A bargain and sale deed with covenant against grantor's acts is commonly used
    a. by executors.
    b. upstate.
    c. in divorce settlements.
    d. to clear cloud from a title.

Real Estate Instruments: Leases

Connie Smith has lived comfortably in her apartment for the first two years of a three-year lease. Now she has been asked to show the premises to potential buyers of the building. She is considering refusing to let anyone in, because she doesn't want to be turned out with a month's notice by a new landlord.

Leases spell out the rights of landlords and tenants, and real estate brokers need to know the provisions that may be included in leases as well as those prohibited by law.

Leasing Real Estate

A **lease** is a contract between an owner of real estate (known as the **lessor**) and a tenant (the **lessee**) that transfers the right to possession and use of the owner's property for a specified period of time. The agreement sets forth the length of time the contract is to run, the amount to be paid by the lessee for the right to use the property and the rights and obligations of the parties.

The landlord grants the tenant the right to occupy the premises and use them for purposes stated in the lease. In return the landlord retains the right to receive payment for the use of the premises as well as a *reversionary right* to retake possession after the lease term has expired.

The **statute of frauds** requires that a *lease for a term of more than one year be in writing* to be enforceable. It also should be signed by both lessor and lessee. A lease for one year or less can be binding even if it is not written.

Leasehold Estates

A tenant's right to occupy land is called a **leasehold estate.** Just as there are several types of freehold (ownership) estates, there are various leasehold estates. The four most important are the (1) estate for years; (2) periodic estate, or estate from period to period; (3) tenancy at will; and (4) tenancy at sufferance (see Table 8.1). All are recognized in New York State.

▼ Estate for Years

A leasehold estate that continues for a *definite period of time,* whether for years, months, weeks or even days, is called an **estate for years**. It always has a specific starting and ending time. When that time expires, the lessee is required to leave. No notice is required to end the lease when the time is up. A lease for years may be terminated ahead of time by mutual consent, but otherwise neither party may terminate without showing that the other has breached the lease agreement.

An estate for years need not last for years or even for one year. The main point is that it begins and ends at a specific time.

Table 8.1   Leasehold Estates

Type of Estate	Distinguishing Characteristics
Estate for Years	For Definite Period of Time
Periodic Estate	Automatically Renews
Tenancy at Will	For Indefinite Period of Time
Tenancy at Sufferance	Without Landlord's Consent

▼ **Periodic Estate**

Periodic estates, sometimes called *estates from period to period,* continue for an *indefinite length of time without a specific expiration date.* They may run for a certain amount of time: month to month, week to week or year to year. The agreement is automatically renewed for similar succeeding periods until one of the parties gives notice to terminate.

A **month-to-month tenancy** is created when a tenant takes possession with no definite termination date and pays rent on a monthly basis.

> **FOUR TYPES OF LEASEHOLD ESTATES:**
>
> 1. Estate for years
> 2. Periodic estate
> 3. Tenancy at will
> 4. Tenancy at sufferance

A New York tenant who remains in possession of leased premises after giving notice of intention to quit the premises **(holdover tenancy)** may be held liable for double rent if he or she stays beyond the date stated in the notice. When the lease term is longer than one month, the landlord may commence proceedings to remove a tenant who has held over. Any later acceptance of rent by the landlord will create a tenancy from month to month.

To *terminate* a periodic estate, either the landlord or the tenant must give *proper notice.* To end a month-to-month tenancy, New York State requires one month's written notice; New York City requires 30 days' notice. Notice must be given at least one day before a date on which rent is due. If rent is due on September 1, the landlord who wants the tenant to vacate by October 1 must give notice no later than August 31.

▼ **Tenancy at Will**

An estate that gives the tenant the right to possess with the *consent of the landlord* and no definite period of time is a **tenancy at will.** It might occur when property has been put on the market and the landlord gives the present tenant (who has no lease) permission to remain until the indefinite time when a sale is closed. The term is indefinite, but the tenancy may be terminated by giving proper notice. Unlike other tenancies, an estate at will is automatically terminated by the death of either landlord or tenant.

▼ **Tenancy at Sufferance**

A **tenancy at sufferance** arises when a tenant continues, after his or her rights have expired, to occupy the premises *without the consent of the landlord.* Examples of estates at sufferance might be when a tenant for years *fails to leave* at the expiration of the lease and when a mortgagor refuses to leave after a foreclosure sale. In New York a tenant may be charged up to double rent for the period while in possession as a tenant at sufferance after notice to quit the premises has been given.

Standard Lease Provisions

The lease may be written, oral or implied, depending on the circumstances. New York State requires a *plain-English* format for residential leases. The requirements for a valid lease are essentially the same as those for any other real estate contract. In New York the eight essentials of a valid lease include the following:

ESSENTIALS OF A VALID LEASE:
• Capacity to contract
• Demising clause
• Description of the premises
• Statement of terms
• Specification of rent
• Lease must be in writing
• Signatures
• Delivery

1. *Capacity to contract:* The parties must be sane adults.
2. A *demising clause:* The lessor agrees to let and the lessee to take the premises.
3. *Description of the premises:* A description of the leased premises should be clearly stated. If the lease covers land, the legal description of the real estate should be used. If the lease is for part of a building, such as office space or an apartment, the space itself should be clearly described.
4. A clear statement of the *term* (duration) of the lease must be provided.
5. *Specification of the rent and how it is to be paid:* In New York, unless the lease states otherwise, rent is considered due in arrears rather than in advance.
6. The *lease must be in writing* if it is to be for more than one year.
7. *Signatures:* A lease should be signed by both parties.
8. *Delivery:* The lease must be delivered by landlord to tenant, with duplicate originals for each.

▼ Use of Premises

A lessor may restrict a lessee's use of premises through provisions included in the lease. This is most important in leases for stores or commercial space. A lease may provide, for example, that the leased premises are to be used *only* as a real estate office. In the absence of such limitations a lessee may use the premises for any lawful purpose.

Disabled tenants are entitled to make any reasonable alterations that are necessary to accommodate their disabilities. These tenants must pay for the alterations themselves and landlords may require that a tenant restore the premises to their former state at the end of the lease term.

▼ Term of Lease

The term of a lease is the period for which it will run, and it should be set out precisely. The date of the beginning of the term and the date of its ending should be stated, together with a statement of the total period of the lease: for example, "for a term of five years beginning June 1, 1995, and ending May 31, 2000."

▼ Security Deposits

Many leases require that a tenant provide a **security deposit** to guarantee payment of rent or safeguard against a tenant's destruction of the premises. Where trade fixtures are to be installed, the landlord may want an extra deposit to ensure that the property will be restored to its original state when they are removed.

Under the *New York General Obligations Law* a landlord must hold all security deposits in trust and *must not commingle* them with his or her own funds because *such deposits continue to belong to the tenants who have advanced them*. If the building contains six or more units, the landlord must notify tenants in writing where security funds are being held in a New York interest-bearing bank account and must turn over to the tenants all but 1 percent of any interest earned. A tenant may choose to receive interest annually or at the end of the lease. Any provisions in a lease requiring a tenant to waive any provisions of this law are void. The rules also apply to mobile home parks.

A landlord who conveys rental property must turn over any security deposits to the new owner within five days of the deed's delivery. The landlord also must notify tenants by registered or certified mail that their deposits have been turned over and must include the new owner's name and address. The new owner is responsible for eventual return of the security deposits to the extent received from the grantor. However, if the building contains six or more dwelling units, the new owner is responsible for *all* security deposits, even if he or she never received them.

With a rent-stabilized apartment no more than one month's rent may be charged for security deposit.

Legal Principles of Leases

New York provides that a lease can be recorded. Memoranda of leases that exceed three years in duration also may be recorded. The recording places the world on notice of the long-term rights of the tenant. Commercial leases are sometimes recorded.

When there is a written nonresidential lease of more than three years, a lien for a commission may be placed on the premises if the brokerage services were performed pursuant to a written contract.

▼ Improvements

The tenant may make improvements with the landlord's permission, but any such alterations generally become the property of the landlord; they become fixtures. A tenant may, however, be given the right to install trade fixtures. It is customary to provide that such trade fixtures may be removed by the tenant before the lease expires, provided the tenant restores the premises to their original condition.

▼ Maintenance of Premises

Every residential New York lease, oral or written, is considered to contain an **implied warranty of habitability.** The landlord guarantees that the leased property is fit for human habitation and that the tenant will not be subjected to any conditions that could endanger life, health or safety. The landlord is required to maintain dwelling units in a habitable condition and to make any necessary repairs to common elements such as hallways, stairs or elevators. The tenant does not have to make any repairs (unless otherwise provided in the lease) but must return the premises in the same condition they were received with allowances for ordinary wear and tear.

▼ Assignment and Subleasing

The tenant may assign or sublease if the lease terms do not prohibit it. A tenant who transfers the entire remaining term of a lease *assigns* the lease. One who transfers less than all of the term but retains some of the rights and obligations **subleases** (see Figure 8.1). The original tenant's interest in the real estate is known as a *sandwich lease.* In most cases the sublease or assignment of a lease does not relieve the original tenant of the obligation to make rental payments unless the landlord agrees to waive such liability.

If the building contains four or more residential units and the landlord unreasonably withholds consent to assignment, the lease may not be assigned but the tenant is released from the lease with 30 days' notice. If the landlord unreasonably withholds consent to a request to sublet, the tenant may nevertheless sublet the unit.

New York's Real Property Law sets guidelines for a detailed written request from the tenant; the landlord's right to ask for additional information within 10 days; and the landlord's written response, including the reasons for any

Figure 8.1 Assignment versus Subletting

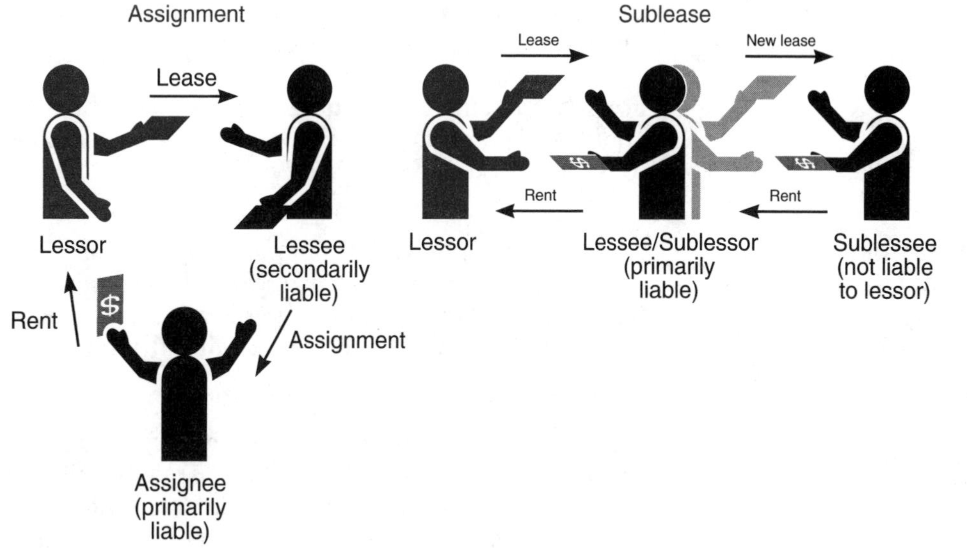

denial, within 30 days. The landlord's failure to respond is considered consent for the sublet.

Special regulations apply to the subletting of rent-stabilized apartments: For a furnished sublet, the original tenant may charge the subtenant as much as 10 percent more than the original rent figure; the landlord may in turn collect an additional 5 percent from the original tenant. The original tenant must establish that the apartment is his or her primary residence and will be reoccupied. A rent-stabilized apartment may not be sublet for more than half of any four-year period. The original tenant, not the subtenant, is entitled to the right of a renewal lease and any right resulting from a co-op conversion.

▼ **Apartment Sharing**

In New York State a lease may not restrict occupancy of an apartment to the named tenant and that tenant's immediate family. (Landlords may, however, limit the total number of occupants to comply with health laws on overcrowding.) The apartment may be shared with one additional occupant and that occupant's dependent children. If the lease names more than one tenant and one of them moves out, that tenant may be replaced with another occupant and that person's dependent children. At least one of the original tenants named in the lease or that person's spouse must continue to occupy the shared apartment as a primary residence.

Tenants must inform their landlords of the name of any occupant within 30 days after the occupant moves into an apartment.

▼ **Renewals**

Sometimes a lease contains a clause stating that it will be *automatically renewed* *unless* the tenant gives *notice* of intent not to renew. No such clause is valid in New York unless the landlord reminds the tenant about the automatic renewal provision 15 to 30 days before the tenant's notice would be due.

On the other hand many leases contain an *option* that grants the lessee (the tenant) the privilege of *renewing* the lease but requires that the lessee give *notice* on or before a specific date of intention to exercise the option. Some leases grant to the lessee the option to purchase the leased premises; the provisions for the option to purchase vary widely. Any option must contain all the essential elements of an offer to purchase.

For any residence constructed before 1978, the tenant must be given a booklet about lead paint hazards before signing a lease. The requirement does not apply to rentals for less than 100 days.

▼ **Termination of Lease**

A written lease for a definite period of time expires at the end of that time period; no separate notice is required to terminate. Oral and written leases that do not specify a definite expiration date (such as a month-to-month or year-to-year tenancy or a tenancy at will) may be terminated by giving proper written notice.

When the conditions of a lease are breached, a landlord may terminate the lease and evict the tenant. This action must be handled through a court proceeding. The landlord who wishes to be rid of a tenant is not allowed to use threats of violence, change locks, discontinue essential services like water or heat or seize the tenant's possessions.

It is possible for the parties to agree to cancel the lease. The tenant may offer to surrender the lease, and acceptance by the landlord will result in termination. A tenant who abandons leased property, however, remains liable for the rent. The terms of the specific lease will usually dictate whether the landlord is obligated to try to rerent the space.

When the property is sold, *the lease does not terminate.* If a landlord conveys leased real estate, the new owner takes the property subject to the rights of the tenant. The lease *survives* the sale and continues as it was.

If a tenant dies, the lease remains in effect; the deceased lessee's heirs are bound by the terms of the lease. New York State provides, however, that the estate may assign the lease or sublet, subject to the landlord's consent. If consent is unreasonably withheld, the lease is terminated.

Any tenant aged 62 or older who has been accepted in an adult care facility, residential health facility or housing unit receiving federal, state or local subsidies for housing senior citizens may break a current lease by giving 30 days' notice and presenting to the current landlord a document of admission to the new facility.

▼ **Breach of Lease**

When a tenant breaches any lease provision, the landlord may sue for a judgment to cover past-due rent, damages to the premises or other defaults. Likewise, when a landlord breaches any lease provision, the tenant is entitled to remedies. The landlord's nonperformance of some obligation under a nonresidential lease, short of eviction, does not, however, affect the tenant's obligation to pay rent.

In New York, grounds for which the landlord can institute proceedings include nonpayment of rent, illegal use of the premises, remaining in possession after expiration of the lease without permission and bankruptcy or insolvency of the tenant.

Suit for possession—actual eviction. When a tenant breaches a lease or improperly retains possession, the landlord may regain possession through a **suit for possession** or *summary proceeding to recover possession of real estate.* This process is known as **actual eviction.** The landlord must serve *notice* on the tenant before commencing the suit. In New York, only a three-day notice must be given before filing a suit for possession based on a default in payment of rent. When a court issues a judgment for possession, the tenant must peaceably leave, or the landlord can have the judgment enforced by a sheriff, constable or marshal, who will *forcibly remove* the tenant and his or her possessions.

Tenants' remedies—constructive eviction. If a landlord breaches any clause of a lease agreement, the tenant has the right to sue, claiming a judgment for damages against the landlord. If an action or omission on the landlord's part results in the leased premises becoming uninhabitable for the purpose intended in the lease, the tenant may have the right to abandon the premises. This action, called **constructive eviction,** terminates the lease if the tenant can prove that the premises have become unusable because of the landlord's neglect. To claim constructive eviction, the tenant must actually move from the premises while the uninhabitable condition exists.

For example, a lease requires that the landlord furnish steam heat; because of the landlord's failure to repair a defective heating plant, the heat is not provided. If this results in the leased premises becoming uninhabitable, the tenant may abandon them. Some leases provide that if the failure to furnish heat is accidental and not the landlord's fault, it is not grounds for constructive eviction.

THREE TYPES OF LEASES:
1. Gross lease
2. Net lease
3. Percentage lease

Pro-Tenant Legislation

In New York State a landlord may not legally retaliate because a tenant joins a tenants' organization. If the landlord fails to furnish heat as stipulated in the lease, tenants in New York may pay a utility company directly and deduct the sum from rent due. In New York City at least one-third of the tenants of a multiple-unit dwelling, acting together, may start a special court proceeding to use their rent money to remedy conditions dangerous to life, health or safety. Retaliatory evictions are illegal.

Types of Leases

Three primary types of leases are outlined in Table 8.2.

▼ Gross Lease

In a **gross lease** the tenant pays a *fixed rental* and the landlord pays all taxes, insurance, mortgage payments, repairs and the like (usually called *property charges*). This type of lease most often is used for residential rentals.

▼ Net Lease

The **net lease** provides that in addition to the rent the *tenant pays some or all of the property charges.* The monthly rental paid is net income for the landlord. Leases for commercial or industrial buildings, ground leases and long-term leases are often net leases. With a *triple-net* lease, the tenant pays taxes, insurance and all other expenses except debt service (mortgage payments).

▼ Percentage Lease

Either a gross lease or a net lease may be a **percentage lease**, normally used for retail business locations.

The percentage lease provides for a minimum fixed rental fee plus a percentage of the tenant's business income that exceeds a stated minimum. For example, a

Table 8.2 Types of Leases

Type of Lease	Tenant Pays	Landlord Pays
Gross Lease Residential (also small commercial)	Basic Rent	Property Charges (taxes, repairs, insurance, etc.)
Net Lease Commercial/Industrial	Basic Rent Plus Most or All Property Charges	Few or No Property Charges Mortgage (if any)
Percentage Lease Commercial/Industrial	Basic Rent Plus Percent of Gross Sales (may pay some or all property costs)	Any Agreed Property Charges

lease might provide for a minimum monthly rental of $1,200 with the further agreement that the tenant pay an additional amount each month equivalent to 5 percent of all gross sales in excess of $30,000. The percentage charged in such leases varies widely with the nature of the business.

▼ **Other Lease Types**

Several types of leases allow for increases in the rent during the lease period. Two of the more common ones are the *graduated lease,* which provides for increases in rent at set future dates, and the *index lease,* which allows rent to be increased or decreased periodically based on changes in the government cost-of-living index.

Ground leases. When a landowner leases land to a tenant who agrees to *erect a building* on it, the lease is referred to as a **ground lease.** It is usually for a long enough term to make it worth the tenant's while to invest in the building. These leases are generally *net leases* that require the lessee to pay rent as well as real estate taxes, insurance, upkeep and repairs. Net ground leases often run for terms of 50 years or longer, and a lease for 99 years is not impossible. Although these leases are considered personal property, leaseholders may have some of the rights and obligations of real property owners.

Oil and gas leases. When oil companies lease land to explore for oil and gas, a special agreement must be negotiated. Usually the landowner receives a cash payment for executing the lease. If no well is drilled within the period stated, the lease expires.

If oil and/or gas is found, the landowner usually receives a fraction of its value as a royalty. In this case the lease will continue for as long as oil or gas is obtained in significant quantities. Oil and gas leases are common across the southern tier and in the western part of New York State. An oil or gas lease constitutes a cloud on title, and a buyer may refuse to purchase unless he or she has specifically agreed to take title subject to such a lease.

Key Terms

actual eviction	month-to-month tenancy
constructive eviction	net lease
estate for years	percentage lease
gross lease	periodic estate
ground lease	security deposit
holdover tenancy	statute of frauds
implied warranty of habitability	sublease
lease	suit for possession
leasehold estate	tenancy at sufferance
lessee/lessor	tenancy at will

Summary

A lease grants someone the right to use the property of another for a certain period in return for consideration.

A leasehold estate that runs for a specific length of time creates an estate for years, whereas one that runs for an indefinite period creates a periodic tenancy (year to year, month to month) or a tenancy at will. A leasehold estate is generally classified as personal property.

The requirements of a valid lease include the capacity to contract, a demising clause, description of premises, statement of terms, rent and signatures. The state statute of frauds requires that any lease for more than a year be in writing. Most leases also include clauses relating to rights and obligations of the landlord and tenant: the use of the premises, subletting, judgments, maintenance of the premises and termination of the lease period.

In New York an oral lease is valid if it is for a period of one year or less. A lease for three years or more, if properly acknowledged, may be entered in the public records. State regulations require that the owner of six or more residential units hold security deposits in an interest-bearing New York bank account with all interest less a 1 percent fee due the tenant. State law gives the tenant in any building with four or more residential units the right to sublet, subject to the landlord's consent, which may not be unreasonably withheld.

Leases may be terminated by the expiration of the lease period, mutual agreement of the parties or a breach of the lease by either landlord or tenant. Neither the death of the tenant nor the landlord's sale of the rental property terminates a lease.

On a tenant's default on any of the lease provisions, a landlord may sue for a money judgment or for actual eviction where a tenant has improperly retained possession of the premises. If the premises have become uninhabitable (whether or not due to the landlord's negligence), the tenant may refuse to pay rent until the problem is remedied.

Basic types of leases include net leases, gross leases and percentage leases, classified according to the method used in determining the rental rate of the property.

1. A lease is considered to be
   a. a freehold estate.
   b. personal property.
   c. a reversionary interest.
   d. real property.

2. Tracy Peters agrees to rent Beverly Ashton her upstairs apartment for the next six months. Beverly has a(n)
   a. estate for years.
   b. periodic estate.
   c. tenancy at will.
   d. tenancy at sufferance.

3. Willie James agrees to rent Dana Gibson her upstairs apartment from month to month. To end the arrangement, Willie must
   a. file a court suit to recover possession.
   b. give at least 60 days' notice from the day the rent is due.
   c. give at least one month's notice from a day before the rent is due.
   d. simply refuse to accept the next month's rent on the day it is due.

4. A tenant's lease has expired, the tenant has neither left nor negotiated a renewal lease and the landlord has said she does not want the tenant to remain. The tenancy is called a(n)
   a. estate for years.
   b. periodic estate.
   c. tenancy at will.
   d. tenancy at sufferance.

5. Mary Withers sells her six-unit apartment building in Queens to George Brown. Now
   a. George may give all the tenants 30 days' notice.
   b. tenants should collect their security deposits from Mary.
   c. George must renegotiate all leases with the tenants.
   d. Mary must turn over security deposits to George.

6. Connie Smith fears that if the building is sold, a new landlord may not honor the year remaining on her apartment lease. Actually, the new owner
   a. would have to give her 90 days' notice to move.
   b. must honor the lease but may charge double rent.
   c. must abide by the terms of her original lease.
   d. can terminate her rental only if he intends to occupy the apartment himself.

7. An automatic renewal clause in a lease
   a. is not allowed on rent-stabilized apartments.
   b. is granted every tenant in a building with four or more units.
   c. is illegal in New York State.
   d. requires notice from the landlord calling the tenants' attention to the clause.

8. Jane Miller's apartment lease agreement states that it will expire on April 30, 1998. When must her landlord give notice that her tenancy is to terminate?
   a. January 31, 1998
   b. February 28, 1998
   c. April 1, 1998
   d. No notice is required.

9. If a tenant falls three months behind in rent payments, a landlord may
   a. turn down the heat.
   b. move out the tenant's possessions, storing them carefully.
   c. start a court suit for possession.
   d. All of the above

10. In Question 9 the landlord who turns down the heat has terminated the lease through
    a. the demising clause.
    b. constructive eviction.
    c. payment in arrears.
    d. assigning the lease.

11. With a triple-net lease, the tenant pays
    a. rent only.
    b. rent plus a share of business profits.
    c. rent plus any increase in property taxes.
    d. everything but the mortgage.

12. A ground lease is usually
    a. terminable with 30 days' notice.
    b. based on percentages.
    c. long term.
    d. a gross lease.

13. Jason has a lease until June on his apartment. The building is sold in February. Jason
    a. must vacate by March 30.
    b. should negotiate a new lease with the new owner.
    c. can stay if he pays an extra month's rent.
    d. can abide by the terms of the original lease.

14. Ms. Doran manufactures knitwear in a small rented building. In addition to monthly rent she pays heat, light and property taxes on the building. She probably has a
    a. net lease.   c. percentage lease.
    b. periodic lease.   d. security lease.

15. In New York a tenant usually may sublet an apartment if the
    a. new tenant is paying a premium over the rent.
    b. building contains four or more living units.
    c. lease is for three years or more.
    d. original tenant has a written lease.

16. Terrence says to Jim, "I'll let you rent my attic apartment for $500 a month until the first of the year." Jim agrees. The agreement
    a. constitutes a binding lease.
    b. is invalid because it is not in writing.
    c. binds the landlord only.
    d. will be enforceable only if it is recorded.

17. A gross lease is most likely to be used for rental of
    a. an apartment.
    b. a factory building.
    c. land under a post office.
    d. a farm.

18. Before entering into an oral or written lease, prospective tenants must be given a lead paint warning if the property
    a. is an office building.
    b. was built before 1978.
    c. contains six or more units.
    d. has asbestos siding.

Real Estate Instruments: Contracts

Laura Secord always meant to take her grandmother's antique chandelier from the dining room after she sold the house. She told the buyers so the day they first saw the place. But when they moved in and found the chandelier missing, they took Laura to small claims court. Laura doesn't know how she can prove she told them about it.

The real estate business makes use of many different types of contracts, including listing agreements, leases and sales contracts. Brokers and salespeople can help prevent misunderstandings among buyers, sellers, landlords and tenants if they understand how contracts work.

Contract Law

A **contract** is a *voluntary agreement between legally competent parties to perform or refrain from performing some legal act, supported by legal consideration.*

Depending on the situation and the nature or language of the agreement, a contract may be

- expressed or implied;
- unilateral or bilateral;
- executory or executed; and
- valid, unenforceable, voidable or void.

▼ Express and Implied Contracts

In an **express contract** the parties state the terms and show their intentions in words. An express contract may be either oral or written. A listing agreement is an *express* contract between seller and broker that names the broker as fiduciary representative (agent) of a seller.

In an **implied contract** the agreement of the parties is demonstrated by their acts and conduct. The patron who orders a meal in a restaurant has implied a promise to pay for the food.

▼ Bilateral and Unilateral Contracts

Contracts also may be classified as either bilateral or unilateral. In a **bilateral contract** both parties promise to do something; one promise is given in exchange for another. A real estate sales contract is a bilateral contract because the seller promises to sell a parcel of real estate to the buyer, who promises to pay a certain sum of money. "I will do this, *and* you will do that." "OK."

A **unilateral contract,** on the other hand, is a one-sided agreement whereby one party makes a promise to be kept only if a second party does something. The second party is not legally obligated to act; however, if the second party does

Table 9.1   Legal Effects of Contracts

Type of Contract	Legal Effect	Example
Valid	Binding and Enforceable on Both Parties	Agreement Complying with Essentials of a Valid Contract
Void	No Legal Effect	Contract for an Illegal Purpose
Voidable	Valid, but May Be Disaffirmed by One Party	Contract with a Minor
Unenforceable	Valid Between the Parties, but Neither May Force Performance	Certain Oral Agreements

comply, the first party must keep the promise. An option is a real estate example of a unilateral contract. "I will sell you the property for $150,000 within two years if you wish." ("I will do this if you do that.") Only the owner is bound by an option; the other party is free either to buy or not to buy.

▼ Executed and Executory Contracts

A contract may be classified as either executed or executory. An **executed contract** is one in which both parties have fulfilled their promises and performed the contract. An **executory contract** exists when something remains to be done. A *real estate sales contract* is executory before final settlement; after the closing it is executed.

▼ Validity of Contracts

A contract can be described as valid, void, voidable or unenforceable (see Table 9.1), depending on the circumstances.

A **valid contract** complies with all the essential elements (which will be discussed later in this chapter) and is binding and enforceable on both parties.

A **void contract** is one that has no legal effect because it does not meet the essential elements of a contract. One of those essential elements is that a contract be for a legal purpose; thus a contract to commit a crime, or to pay interest higher than allowed by usury law, would be void.

A **voidable contract** is one that seems on the surface to be valid but may be voided, or disaffirmed, by one of the parties. For example, a contract entered into with a minor usually is voidable; a minor generally is permitted to disaffirm a real estate contract within a reasonable time after reaching legal age. A voidable contract is considered by the courts to be valid if the party that could disaffirm the agreement does not do so within a reasonable period of time.

An **unenforceable contract** also seems on the surface to be valid; however, neither party can successfully sue the other to force performance. For example, if one party tries to enforce an otherwise valid contract after the statute of limitations has expired, the contract is unenforceable. Unenforceable contracts are said to be "valid as between the parties" because if both desire to go through with it, they can do so.

> **A CONTRACT MAY BE**
>
> - expressed or implied;
> - unilateral or bilateral;
> - executory or executed; and
> - valid, unenforceable, voidable or void.

▼ Elements Essential to a Valid Contract

The five essentials of a valid contract are

1. **Competent parties:** To enter into a binding contract in New York, a person must be at least 18 years old and of sound mind. A married person younger

than 18 is considered an adult for the purposes of buying a principal residence.

2. **Offer and acceptance:** This requirement, also called *mutual assent,* means there must be a meeting of the minds. The contract must express all the agreed-on terms and must be clearly understood by the parties.

3. **Consideration:** The agreement must be based on good or valuable consideration. Consideration is what the parties promise in the agreement to give to or receive from each other. Consideration may consist of legal tender, exchange of value or mutual promises. The price or amount must be stated definitely and payable in exchange for the deed or right received.

4. **Legality of object:** To be valid and enforceable, a contract must not involve a purpose that is illegal or against public policy.

5. **Agreement in writing and signed:** New York's **statute of frauds** requires that certain types of contracts be in writing. These include all contracts for the sale of real estate and for leasing or listing real property for more than one year.

The **parol evidence** rule states that the written contract takes precedence over oral agreements or promises. A promise that is not in the written contract may not be legally binding.

Undue influence and duress. Contracts signed by a person under duress or undue influence are voidable (may be canceled) by such person or by a court. Extreme care should be taken when one or more of the parties to a contract is elderly, sick, in great distress or under the influence of drugs or alcohol. To be valid, every contract must be signed as the free and voluntary act of each party.

▼ **Performance of Contract**

A contract may call for a specific time by which the agreed-on acts must be completely performed. In addition, many contracts provide that **"time is of the essence."** This means that the contract must be performed within the time limit specified. Any party who has not performed on time is guilty of a breach of contract. This powerful phrase is a two-edged sword, and brokers should leave its use to attorneys.

When a contract does not specify a date for performance, the acts it requires should be performed within a reasonable time, depending on the situation. A real estate contract usually names a date and place for closing. If that date comes and goes without settlement, the contract is still valid, and either party has the right to a reasonable adjournment. Either party may later make time of the essence; again, that action should be taken only with a lawyer's advice.

▼ **Assignment and Novation**

Often after a contract has been signed one party wants to withdraw without actually ending the agreement. This may be accomplished through either assignment or novation.

Assignment refers to a transfer of rights and/or duties under a contract. Generally, rights may be assigned to a third party unless the agreement forbids such an assignment. Most contracts include a clause that either permits or forbids assignment.

A contract also may be performed by **novation,** or the substitution of a *new* contract for an existing agreement. The new agreement may retain the same parties or substitute a new party for either (*novation of the parties*). A real estate example might be the assumption of a present mortgage by the new owner of a property, with the lender releasing the original borrower and substituting the new one.

▼ **Discharge of Contract**

A contract may be completely performed, with all terms carried out, or it may be breached (broken) if one of the parties defaults. There are also various other methods by which a contract may be discharged (ended):

- *Partial performance* of the terms along with a written acceptance by the person for whom acts have not been done or to whom money has not been paid.
- *Substantial performance,* in which one party has performed most of the contract but does not complete all details exactly as the contract requires. This may be sufficient to force payment with certain adjustments for any damages suffered by the other party.
- *Impossibility of performance,* in which an act required by the contract cannot be legally accomplished.
- *Mutual agreement* of the parties to cancel.
- *Operation of law,* as in the voiding of a contract by a minor, as a result of fraud, owing to the expiration of the statute of limitations or because of alteration of a contract without written consent of all parties involved.

▼ **Default—Breach of Contract**

A **breach** of contract is a violation of any of the terms or conditions of a contract without legal excuse.

If a seller defaults, the buyer has three alternatives:

- The buyer may *rescind, or cancel, the contract* and recover the earnest money deposit.
- The buyer may file a court suit, known as an action for **specific performance,** to force the seller to perform the contract (*that is, sell the property*).
- The buyer may *sue the seller for compensatory damages.*

If the *buyer defaults,* the seller may pursue one of the following courses:

- The seller may *declare the contract forfeited.* The right to forfeit usually is provided in the terms of the contract, and the seller usually is entitled to retain the earnest money and all payments received from the buyer.
- The seller may *rescind the contract;* that is, he or she may cancel, or terminate, the contract as if it had never been made.
- The seller may *sue for specific performance.* This may require that the seller offer a valid deed to the buyer to show that the seller is ready to meet the contract terms.
- The seller may *sue for compensatory damages.*

Statute of limitations. New York allows a specific time limit of *six years* during which parties to a contract may bring legal suit to enforce their rights. Any party who does not take steps to enforce his or her rights within this **statute of limitations** may lose those rights. The six-year period applies to contracts, foreclosures, mortgages and cases of fraud. Lawsuits to recover real property have a ten-year statute of limitations in New York.

The principal of **laches** is similar to that of the statute of limitations. Laches is an undue delay or failure to assert a claim or right that can result in the loss of that claim or right.

Contracts Used in the Real Estate Business

The written agreements most commonly used by brokers and salespeople are listing agreements, buyers' broker agreements, real estate sales contracts, option agreements, contracts for deed and leases.

▼ Broker's Authority to Prepare Documents

The New York Department of State specifically states that the real estate broker's license does not confer the right to draft legal documents or give legal advice. However, a decision by the New York Appellate Court has stated that a broker has a right to complete a simple contract. No court decisions have yet been made as to what constitutes a "simple" contract.

The preparation of legal documents by a broker may result in the loss of commissions, loss of license or other penalties or damages. In upstate areas many brokers fill in the blanks on forms or simple sales contracts; in the New York City area the seller's attorney usually prepares the sales contract.

The *Duncan and Hill* decision recommended that New York State brokers and salespersons who prepare purchase and sales contracts protect themselves against charges of unauthorized practice of law by making the contracts subject to (effective only after) approval by attorneys for both the buyer and seller. An attorney then may ask for changes to protect the client's interest; any such changes constitute a counteroffer and must be accepted by the other party.

Note that in some cases a buyer who is having second thoughts may simply instruct his or her attorney to disapprove the contract. The Appellate Division of the State Supreme Court ruled in one case that a buyer who did so was acting in bad faith and forfeited the right to attorney's approval. The contract was ruled valid.

Contract forms. *Printed forms* are used for all kinds of contracts because many transactions basically are similar in nature. The use of printed forms raises three problems: (1) what information should be used to *fill in the blanks*, (2) what printed matter is not applicable to a particular sale and can be *ruled out* by drawing lines through the unwanted words and (3) what additional clauses or agreements (called *riders*) are to be *added*. All changes and additions usually are initialed by both parties.

▼ Listing Agreements

Listing agreements are contracts that establish the rights of the broker as agent and of the buyer or seller as principal. Explanations of the types of listing agreements are presented in Chapter 3.

▼ Sales Contracts

A **real estate sales contract** sets forth all details of the agreement between a buyer and a seller for the purchase and sale of a parcel of real estate. Depending on the locality, this agreement may be known as an offer to purchase, a contract of purchase and sale, an earnest money agreement, a binder and deposit receipt or other variations of these titles. New York does not mandate any specific form of listing or sales contract. An example of a real estate contract form used by some brokers appears as Figure 9.1.

In a few localities, notably in and around New York City, brokers prepare a nonbinding **memorandum of sale,** data sheet or terms sheet. This sheet of information states the essential terms of the agreement. The parties agree to have a

Figure 9.1   Purchase and Sale Contract for Residential Property

PURCHASE AND SALE CONTRACT
FOR RESIDENTIAL PROPERTY

Plain English Form published by and only for use of members of the Greater Rochester Association of Realtors, Inc. and the Monroe County Bar Association.
COMMISSIONS OR FEES FOR THE REAL ESTATE SERVICES TO BE PROVIDED ARE NEGOTIABLE BETWEEN REALTOR AND CLIENT.
When Signed, This Document Becomes A Binding Contract. Buyer or Seller May Wish To Consult Their Own Attorney.

TO: _____ (Seller) FROM: _____ (Buyer)

OFFER TO PURCHASE

Buyer offers to purchase the property described below from Seller on the following terms:

1. PROPERTY DESCRIPTION.

Property known as No. _____ in the (Town) (City) (Village) of_____, State of New York, also
known as Tax No. _____ including all buildings and any other improvements and all rights which the Seller has in or with the property.
Approximate Lot Size: _____. (Check if applicable) [ ] As described in more detail in the attached description.

Description of Buildings on Property: _____

2. OTHER ITEMS INCLUDED IN PURCHASE. The following items, if any, now in or on the property are included in this purchase and sale. All heating, plumbing, septic and private water systems, lighting fixtures, flowers, shrubs, trees, window shades and blinds, curtain and traverse rods, storm windows, storm doors, screens, awnings, TV antennae, water softeners, sump pumps, window boxes, mail box, tool shed, fences, underground pet containment fencing with control devices, wall-to-wall carpeting and runners, exhaust fans, hoods, garbage disposal, electric garage door opener and remote control devices, intercom equipment, humidifier, security systems, smoke detectors, all fireplace screens and enclosures, swimming pool and all related equipment and accessories, and the following, if built-in: cabinets, mirrors, stoves, ovens, dishwashers, trash compactors, shelving and air conditioning (except window units). Buyer agrees to accept these items in their present conditions. Other items to be included in the purchase and sale are: _____

[ ] Seller represents to the best of Seller's knowledge that any heating, plumbing, air conditioning, electrical systems and included appliances are presently in good working order, except for

_____

Items not included are:_____

Seller represents that he has good title to all of the above items to be transferred to Buyer, and will deliver a Bill of Sale for the same at closing.

3. PRICE: AMOUNT AND HOW IT WILL BE PAID: The purchase price is _____ Dollars
$ _____, Buyer shall receive credit at closing for any deposit made hereunder. The balance of the purchase price shall be paid as follows: (Check and complete applicable provisions.)

[ ] (a) Seller agrees to pay a loan fee of _____% of the mortgage amount.

[ ] (b) All in cash, or certified check at closing.

[ ] (c) By Buyer assuming and agreeing to pay according to its terms, the principal balance of the mortgage in the approximate amount of $ _____
held by_____, provided that the mortgage is assumable without the holder's approval. Buyer
understands that the mortgage bears interest at the rate of _____% per year and the monthly payments are $ _____ which includes principal,
interest, taxes and insurance (strike out any item not included in payment), with the last payment due on approximately _____ 19/20_____. Buyer agrees to pay the
balance of the purchase price over the amount of the assumed mortgage in cash or certified check at closing. Buyer understands that principal balance may be lower at time of closing because
of monthly payments made after this contract is signed. If the mortgage to be assumed provides for graduated or balloon payments, then a copy of the original bond and mortgage shall be
furnished to Buyer's attorney for approval within ten days after acceptance of this offer.

[ ] (d) By Buyer delivering a purchase money bond and mortgage to Seller at closing. This purchase money bond and mortgage shall be in the amount of $ _____
shall be amortized over a term of _____ years and all due and payable in _____ years from the date of closing, shall bear interest at the rate of _____% per year, and shall
be paid in monthly installments of $ _____, including principal and interest. The mortgage shall contain the statutory clauses as to payment, insurance,
acceleration on default of thirty days, taxes, assessments, and water rates and also shall provide for late charges of 2% of any monthly payment which is not paid within 15 days after it is due
and for recovery of reasonable attorney's fees if the mortgage is foreclosed.

The mortgage shall allow Buyer to prepay all or part of the mortgage without penalty at any time but shall also provide that the mortgage be paid in full if Buyer sells the property, unless Seller
consents in writing to assumption of the mortgage debt. The balance of the purchase price will be paid at closing in cash, or certified check.

4. CONTINGENCIES. Buyer makes this offer subject to the following contingencies. If any of these contingencies is not satisfied by the dates specified, then either Buyer or Seller may cancel
this contract by written notice to the other. (Check and complete applicable provisions.)

[ ] (a) **Mortgage Contingency.** This offer subject to Buyer obtaining and accepting a _____ mortgage loan commitment in an amount not to
exceed _____ at an interest rate not to exceed _____% , for a term of _____ years. Buyer shall immediately apply for this loan and shall
have until _____ to obtain and accept a written mortgage commitment. The conditions of any such mortgage commitment shall not be deemed contingencies of this
contract but shall be the sole responsibility of Buyer. If the loan commitment requires repairs, replacements, or improvements to be made or painting to be done, before closing, then Seller shall
do the work and install the materials and improvements needed or have the same done, at Seller's expense. However, if the cost of doing so exceeds $_____
Seller shall not be obligated to have such work done, and Buyer will be allowed either to receive credit at closing for the amount recited above and incur any necessary expenses to comply with
the loan commitment requirements, or to cancel this contract by written notice to Seller, and any deposit shall be returned to Buyer. Issuance and acceptance by the Buyer of a written mortgage
commitment shall be deemed a waiver and satisfaction of this contingency.

[ ] (b) **Mortgage Assumption Contingency.** This offer is subject to Buyer obtaining permission to assume the existing mortgage loan balance referred to above in (3c) by _____ 19_____.
If the mortgage holder requires that the interest rate be increased for such approval to be given, Buyer agrees to assume the mortgage at such rate as long as it does not exceed _____%
at the time of the commitment. [ ]Buyer agrees to obtain a release of Seller's liability and to pay any assumption or release of liability fees.

Figure 9.1 (continued)

[ ] (c) **Sale Contract Contingency.** This offer is subject to Buyer obtaining a contract for the sale of Buyer's property located at _____ no later than _____, 199_____. Unless and until Buyer has removed this sale contingency in writing, if Seller receives another acceptable purchase offer, Seller may notify Buyer in writing that Seller wants to accept the other offer and Buyer will then have _____ days to remove this sale contingency by written notice to the Seller. If Buyer does not remove this sale contingency after receiving notice from Seller, Buyer's rights under this contract shall end, and Seller shall be free to accept the other purchase offer and Buyer's deposit shall be returned. Buyer may not remove this sale contingency if Buyer's mortgage loan commitment requires the sale and/or transfer of this property as a condition of the mortgage loan funding, unless Buyer has a contract for the sale of this property which is not then subject to any unsatisfied contingencies.

[ ] (d) **Transfer of Title Contingency.** This offer is contingent upon the transfer of title to Buyer's property located at _____ no later than _____, 199_____. [ ] Buyer represents that Buyer has entered into a contract for sale of Buyer's property which is now subject to the following contingencies: [ ] None; [ ] Mortgage; [ ] Assumption of Mortgage; [ ] Sale of Property; [ ] Transfer of Title; [ ] Attorney Approval; and/or [ ] Other_____. Unless and until Buyer has obtained a contract for sale of Buyer's property which is not subject to any unsatisfied contingencies, and has so notified the Seller in writing, if Seller receives another acceptable purchase offer, Seller may notify Buyer in writing that Seller wants to accept the other offer and Buyer will then have _____ days to remove this transfer of title contingency by written notice to the Seller. If Buyer does not remove this transfer of title contingency after receiving notice from Seller, Buyer's rights under this contract shall end, and Seller shall be free to accept the other purchase offer and Buyer's deposit shall be returned. Buyer may not remove this transfer of title contingency if Buyer's mortgage loan commitment requires the sale and transfer of this property as a condition of the mortgage loan funding, unless Buyer has a contract for sale of this property which is not then subject to any unsatisfied contingencies.

[ ] (e) **Attorney Approval.** This contract is subject to the written approval of attorneys for Buyer and Seller within _____ days from date of acceptance (the "Approval Period"). If either attorney makes written objection to the contract within the Approval Period, and such objection is not cured by written approval by both attorneys and all of the parties within the Approval Period, then either Buyer or Seller may cancel this contract by written notice to the other and any deposit shall be returned to the Buyer.

[ ] (f) **Waiver of Attorney Approval.** This offer is not subject to the Buyer's attorney approval.

[ ] (g) **Other Contingencies.** _____

5. Closing Date and Place. Transfer of title shall take place at the _____ County Clerk's Office or at the offices of Buyer's lender on or before _____, 19_____.

6. Buyer's Possession of Property.
[ ] Buyer shall have possession of the property on the day of closing, in broom clean condition, with all keys to the property delivered to Buyer at closing.
[ ] Seller shall have the right to retain possession for_____ days after closing at the cost of $_____ per day, plus utilities. At possession, the property shall be broom clean and all keys shall be delivered to Buyer.

7. Title Documents. Seller shall provide the following documents in connection with the sale:
A. Deed. Seller will deliver to Buyer at closing a properly signed and notarized Warranty Deed with lien covenant (or Executor's Deed, Administrator's Deed or Trustee's Deed, if Seller holds title as such).

GRAR 3/94

B. Abstract, Bankruptcy and Tax Searches, and Instrument Survey Map. Seller will furnish and pay for and deliver to Buyer or Buyer's attorney at least 15 days prior to the date of closing, fully guaranteed tax, title and United States Court Searches dated or redated after the date of this contract with a local tax certificate for Village, or City taxes, if any, and an instrument survey map dated or redated after the date of this contract. Seller will pay for the map or redated map and for continuing such searches to and including the day of closing. Any survey map shall be prepared or redated and certified to meet the standards and requirements of Buyer's mortgage lender and of the Monroe County Bar Association

8. Marketability of Title. The deed and other documents delivered by Seller shall be sufficient to convey good marketable title in fee simple, to the property free and clear of all liens and encumbrances. However, Buyer agrees to accept title to the property subject to restrictive covenants of record common to the tract or subdivision of which the property is a part, provided these restictions have not been violated, or if they have been violated, that the time for anyone to complain of the violations has expired. Buyer also agrees to accept title to the property subject to public utility easements along lot lines as long as those easements do not interfere with any buildings now on the property or with any improvements Buyer may construct in compliance with all present restrictive covenants of record and zoning and building codes applicable to the Property. Seller agrees to furnish a smoke alarm affidavit at closing and to cooperate in executing any documents required by federal or state laws for transfer of title to residential property.

9. Objections to Title. If Buyer raises a valid written objection to Seller's title which means that the title to the property is unmarketable, Seller may cancel this contract by giving prompt written notice of cancellation to Buyer. Buyer's deposit shall be returned immediately, and if Buyer makes a written request for it, Seller shall reimburse Buyer for the reasonable cost of having the title examined. However, if Seller gives notice within 5 days that Seller will cure the problem prior to the closing date, or if the title objection is insurable and Buyer is willing to accept insurable title, then this contract shall continue in force until the closing date, subject to the Seller performing as promised and/or providing insurable title at Seller's expense. If Seller fails to cure the problem within such time, Buyer will not be obligated to purchase the property and Buyer's deposit shall be returned together with reimbursement for the reasonable cost of having the title examined.

10. Recording Costs, Mortgage Tax, Transfer Tax and Closing Adjustments. Seller will pay the real property transfer tax and special additional mortgage recording tax, if applicable. Buyer will pay mortgage assumption charges, if any, and will pay for recording the deed and the mortgage, and for mortgage tax. The following, as applicable, will be prorated and adjusted between Seller and Buyer as of the date of closing: current taxes computed on a fiscal year basis, excluding any delinquent items, interest and penalties; rent payments; fuel oil on the premises; water charges; pure water charges; sewer charges; mortgage interest; current common charges or assessments; prepaid F.H.A. Mortgage Insurance Premium (M.I.P.) of approximately $_____, with the exact amount to be calculated at closing in accordance with F.H.A. formulae. Any F.H.A. insurance premium which is not prepaid, but rather paid monthly, shall be adjusted at closing. If there is a water meter at the property, Seller shall furnish an actual reading to a date not more than thirty (30) days before the closing date set forth in this contract. At closing the water charges and any sewer rent shall be apportioned on the basis of such actual reading.

11. Zoning. Seller represents that the property is in full compliance with all zoning or building ordinances for use as a _____. If applicable laws require it, the Seller will furnish at or before closing, a Certificate of Occupancy for the property, dated within ninety (90) days of the closing, with Seller completing the work and installing the materials and improvements needed to obtain Certificate of Occupancy. However, if the cost of obtaining a Certificate of Occupancy exceeds $_____, Seller shall not be obligated to have such work done, and Buyer will be allowed either to receive credit at closing for the amount recited above, and incur the necessary expenses to obtain the Certificate of Occupancy, or to cancel this contract by written notice to Seller, and any deposit shall be returned to Buyer.

12. Risk of Loss. Risk of loss or damage to the property by fire or other casualty until transfer of title shall be assumed by the Seller. If damage to the property by fire or such other casualty occurs prior to transfer, Buyer may cancel this contract without any further liability to Seller and Buyer's deposit is to be returned. If Buyer does not cancel but elects to close, then Seller shall transfer to Buyer any insurance proceeds, or Seller's claim to insurance proceeds payable for such damage.

13. Condition of Property. Buyer agrees to purchase the property "as is" except as provided in paragraph 2, subject to reasonable use, wear, tear, and natural deterioration between now and the time of closing. However, this paragraph shall not relieve Seller from furnishing a Certificate of Occupancy as called for in paragraph 11, if applicable. Buyer shall have the right, after reasonable notice to Seller, to inspect the property within 48 hours before the time of closing.

14. Services. Seller represents that property is serviced by: _____ Public Water, _____ Public Sewers, _____ Septic System, _____ Private Well.

15. Deposit to Listing Broker. Buyer (has deposited) (will deposit upon acceptance) $_____ in the form of a _____ with _____ (Escrow Agent) at _____ (bank), which deposit is to become part of the purchase price or returned if not accepted or if Buyer's contract thereafter fails to close for any reason not the fault of the Buyer. If Buyer fails to complete Buyer's part of this contract, Seller is allowed to retain the deposit to be applied to Seller's damages, and may also pursue other legal rights Seller has against the Buyer, including a lawsuit for any real estate brokerage commission paid by the Seller.

Figure 9.1 (continued)

16. Real Estate Broker.
[ ] The parties agree that _____ brought about this purchase and sale.
[ ] It is understood and agreed by both Buyer and Seller that no broker secured this contract.

17. Life of Offer. This offer shall expire on_____, 19_____, at _____ .m.

18. Responsibility of Persons Under This Contract; Assignability. If more than one person signs this contract as Buyer, each person and any party who takes over that person's legal position will be responsible for keeping the promises made by Buyer in this contract. If more than one person signs this contract as Seller, each person or any party who takes over that person's legal position, will be fully responsible for keeping the promises made by Seller. However, this contract is personal to the parties and may not be assigned by either without the other's consent.

19. Entire Contract. This contract when signed by both Buyer and Seller will be the record of the complete agreement between the Buyer and Seller concerning the purchase and sale of the property. No verbal agreements or promises will be binding.

20. Notices. All notices under this contract shall be deemed delivered upon receipt. Any notices relating to this contract may be given by the attorneys for the parties.

21. Addenda. The following Addenda are incorporated into this contract:
[ ] All Parties Agreement [ ] Services [ ] Engineer's Inspection [ ] Mediation [ ] Electric Availability [ ] Utility Surcharge [ ] Lead Warning [ ] Other:_____

Dated: _____   BUYER _____

Witness: _____   BUYER _____

[ ] ACCEPTANCE OF OFFER BY SELLER   [ ] COUNTER OFFER BY SELLER

Seller certifies that Seller owns the property and has the power to sell the property. Seller accepts the offer and agrees to sell on the terms and conditions above set forth.

[ ] Waiver of Seller's attorney approval. This offer is not subject to Seller's attorney approval.

Dated: _____   SELLER _____

Witness: _____   SELLER _____

——————————ADMINISTRATIVE INFORMATION——————————

Buyer:_____   Seller:_____

Social Security Number:_____   Social Security Number:_____

Address:_____   GRAR MLS # _____

_____ Zip:_____   Address:_____

Phone: (H) _____(B) _____   _____ Zip:_____

Attorney:_____   Phone:(H) _____(B) _____

Address:_____   Attorney:_____

Phone:(B) _____(FAX) _____   Address:_____

Selling Broker: _____   Phone:(B) _____(FAX) _____

Address:_____   Listing Broker: _____

Phone: _____Broker Code: _____   Address:_____

Selling Agent: _____Phone:(H) _____   Phone: _____Broker Code: _____

Selling Agent I.D. #_____FAX_____   Listing Agent: _____Phone:(H) _____

                                             Listing Agent I.D. #_____FAX_____

formal and complete contract of sale drawn up by an attorney. Throughout the state a preliminary memorandum might be used in any situation where the details of the transaction are too complex for a standard sales contract form.

The contract of sale is the most basic document in the sale of real estate because it sets out in detail the agreement between the buyer and the seller and establishes their legal rights and obligations. *The contract, in effect, dictates the contents of the deed* and is a blueprint for closing the sale.

Offer and acceptance. One of the essential elements of a valid contract of sale is a *meeting of the minds,* whereby the buyer and seller agree on the terms of the sale. This usually is accomplished through the process of offer and acceptance.

A broker lists an owner's real estate for sale at the price and conditions set by the owner. A party who wants to purchase the property at those terms or some other terms is found. Upstate, an offer to purchase is drawn up, signed by the prospective buyer and presented by the broker to the seller. This is an *offer.* If the seller agrees to the offer *exactly as it was made* and signs the contract, the offer has been *accepted,* and the contract is *valid.* The broker then must advise the buyer of the seller's acceptance, obtain lawyers' approval if the contract calls for it and deliver a duplicate original of the contract to each party.

In some downstate areas the broker prepares a precontract agreement, known as a *binder,* which may or may not be legally enforceable but usually contains many of the essential terms that will later be included in a contract. It also may acknowledge receipt of an earnest money deposit. The danger in using a binder is that it may be legally enforceable without containing all the terms needed to protect the parties. In the New York City area purchase offers often are handled by attorneys.

Any attempt by the seller to change the terms proposed by the buyer ("Okay, except that . . .") creates a **counteroffer**. The buyer is no longer bound by the original offer because the seller has, in effect, rejected it. The buyer can accept the seller's counteroffer or reject it or, if desired, make another counteroffer. Any change in the last offer made results in a counteroffer until one party finally agrees completely with the other party's last offer and both parties sign the final contract.

A contract is not considered valid until the person making the offer has been *notified of the other party's acceptance.*

Equitable title. A buyer who signs a contract to purchase real estate does not receive title to the land; only a deed can actually convey title. However, after the contract is signed, the buyer has an interest in the land known as **equitable title**. In New York a buyer under a land contract also acquires equitable title. If the parties decide not to go through with the purchase and sale, they usually enter into a written **release,** freeing each other from any obligation under the contract.

Destruction of premises. New York State has adopted the *Uniform Vendor and Purchaser Risk Act (Section 5-1311 of the General Obligations Law),* which provides that the seller (vendor) bears any loss, most commonly from a fire, that occurs before the title passes or the buyer (vendee) takes possession.

Earnest money deposits. It is customary, but not essential, for a purchaser to provide a cash deposit when making an offer to purchase real estate. This cash deposit, commonly referred to upstate as **earnest money** and downstate as a *down payment* or *contract deposit, gives evidence of the buyer's intention to carry out the terms of the contract.* It is often held by one of the brokers involved in the sale (upstate) or the seller's attorney (New York City area). The state requires that each sales contract name the person holding the deposit and the bank where it is to be held. If the offer is not accepted, the earnest money deposit is returned immediately to the would-be buyer.

The deposit generally should be sufficient to discourage the buyer from defaulting, compensate the seller for taking the property off the market and cover any expenses the seller might incur if the buyer defaults. A purchase offer with no earnest money is, however, valid. Most contracts provide that the deposit and any interest earned on it becomes the seller's property if the buyer defaults. The seller might also claim further damages.

Earnest money must be held by a broker or lawyer in a special *trust,* or *escrow, bank account.* This money cannot be *commingled,* or mixed, with a broker's personal funds. A broker may not use such funds for personal use; this illegal act is known as *conversion.*

A broker need not open a special escrow account for each earnest money deposit received. One account into which all such funds are deposited is sufficient. A broker should maintain full, complete and accurate records of all earnest money deposits.

SIX ELEMENTS REQUIRED FOR A VALID REAL ESTATE CONTRACT:

1. Contract in writing
2. Competent parties
3. Agreement to buy and sell
4. Adequate description of the property
5. Consideration
6. Signatures of the parties

Parts of a sales contract. In New York the six essentials of a valid contract for the sale of real property are

1. contract in writing,
2. competent parties,
3. agreement to buy and sell,
4. adequate description of the property,
5. consideration (price and terms of payment) and
6. signatures of the parties. (The signature of a witness is not essential for a valid contract.)

Important, although not essential, for a valid contract are provisions covering

1. grantor's agreement to convey (should specify type of deed) and
2. place and time of closing.

Further included in most sales contracts are the following:

- Encumbrances to which the deed will be made subject
- Earnest money deposit
- Mortgage financing the buyer plans to obtain and other contingencies
- Possession by the buyer
- Title evidence
- Prorations and adjustments
- Destruction of the premises before closing
- Default by either party
- Miscellaneous provisions

Miscellaneous provisions. In recent years, increasing awareness of consumer's rights has increased the number of disclosures that must be made to a buyer before that person is bound by a purchase contract. Among these are disclosure of agency relationships (discussed in Chapter 3) and disclosures relating to possible problems with lead paint (Chapters 3 and 17), agricultural districts (Chapter 3) and electric service (Chapter 3).

When the purchaser intends to secure an FHA or a VA loan, special clauses provide that the contract may be voided if the property is appraised by the lending institution for less than the sales price. Sometimes provisions are added stipulating that the seller or buyer will furnish satisfactory reports on such matters as termite or insect infestation, quality of a private water supply or condition of plumbing or heating equipment. In some transfers a certificate of occupancy must be obtained from a municipality; the contract should make it clear whose responsibility this will be. The purchaser may want the right to inspect the property shortly before settlement.

Contingencies are happenings without which the contract will not be performed. Among the more common are the buyer's need to secure a specific loan, the purchaser's right to a satisfactory engineer's and environmental report on the property within a specified time period, approval of the contract by a family member or the purchaser's attorney within a short period of time and the buyer's need to sell a present home before buying the next one.

Where the buyer has another home that must be sold first, the seller may insist on an **escape clause,** or kickout. Such a provision allows the seller to look for a more favorable offer, with the original purchaser retaining the right, if challenged, either to firm up the first sales contract (dropping the contingency) or to void the contract.

Liquidated damages are an amount of money, agreed to in advance by buyer and seller, that will serve as total compensation if one party does not live up to the contract. If a sales contract specifies that the earnest money deposit will serve as liquidated damages, the seller will be entitled to only the deposit if the buyer refuses to perform for no good reason. The seller who does agree to accept the deposit as liquidated damages may not sue later for any further damages.

Plain-language requirement (Sullivan Law). New York law requires that certain written agreements for the sale or lease of residential property be written in a clear and coherent manner with words that are common in everyday usage. The copy also must be appropriately divided and captioned in its various sections. The plain-language requirement does not apply to agreements involving amounts over $50,000. Figure 9.1 is an example of a plain-English contract.

Lead-Based Paint Hazard Disclosure. A buyer who purchases almost any residential property built before 1978 must be furnished with a booklet discussing lead-based paint hazards. Any purchase contract involving the sale of pre-1978 residential property must allow the buyer ten days in which to investigate potential lead-based paint hazards, before the contract becomes binding. Buyers and sellers may, however, agree to shorten or waive this time period (this agreement must be included in the purchase contract itself).

▼ Option Agreements

An **option** is a *contract by which an optionor (owner) gives an optionee (prospective purchaser or lessee) the right to buy or lease the owner's property at a fixed price within a stated period of time.* The optionee pays a fee (the agreed-on consideration) for this right and has no other obligation. The optionee is free to decide within the specified time to either buy or lease the property or allow the option to expire. The owner is bound to sell if requested; the optionee is not bound to buy. An option is often used by a tenant, who may then choose either to buy or to remain as a tenant. Options must contain all the terms required for a valid contract of sale.

▼ Land Contracts

A real estate sale can be made under a **land contract**, sometimes called a *contract for deed* or *an installment contract.* Under a typical land contract the seller, also known as the *vendor,* retains ownership, while the buyer, known as the *vendee,* moves in and has an equitable interest in the property. Each land contract is different, but in a common form the buyer agrees to give the seller a down payment and pay regular installments of principal and interest over a number of years. The buyer also agrees to pay real estate taxes, insurance premiums, repairs and upkeep on the property. Although the buyer obtains possession when the contract is signed by both parties, *the seller is not obligated to execute (sign) and deliver a deed to the buyer until the terms of the contract have been satisfied.* Depending on the agreement, this might occur when the buyer can obtain a regular mortgage loan and pay off the balance due on the contract.

Real estate is occasionally sold with the new buyer assuming an existing land contract from the original buyer/vendee. Generally, the seller/vendor must approve the new purchaser.

Land contracts require extensive legal input from lawyers experienced in real estate matters. The broker who negotiates a land contract should consult attorneys for both parties at every step of the way and refrain from specifying any detailed terms in the agreement.

▼ Local Forms

To gain familiarity with the forms used in a local area, the student should go to brokers or real estate companies and ask for copies of the sales contract, listing agreement and other forms they use. More general forms also can be obtained at a title or abstract company and some banks and savings and loan associations, or they may be purchased at local office supply and stationery stores.

▼ Rescission

With contracts for the purchase of some types of personal property, the buyer has three days in which to reconsider and rescind (cancel) the contract. No such right of rescission applies to contracts for the purchase of real estate (with certain exceptions, e.g., when lead-based paint laws apply).

Borrowers who change their minds about a mortgage loan have three days in which to cancel the transaction if the mortgage was for *refinance* of presently owned property. No right of rescission, however, applies to mortgage loans used for the *purchase* of real estate.

Key Terms

agreement in writing and signed	legality of object
assignment	liquidated damages
bilateral contract	memorandum of sale
breach	novation
competent parties	offer and acceptance
consideration	option
contingency	parol evidence
contract	real estate sales contract
counteroffer	release
earnest money	specific performance
equitable title	statute of frauds
escape clause	statute of limitations
executed contract	time is of the essence
executory contract	unenforceable contract
express contract	unilateral contract
implied contract	valid contract
laches	void contract
land contract	voidable contract

Summary

A contract is defined as an agreement made by competent parties with adequate consideration, to take or to refrain from some lawful action.

Contracts may be classified according to whether the parties' intentions are expressed or are implied by their actions. They also may be classified as bilateral, when both parties have obligated themselves to act, or unilateral, when one party is obligated to perform only if the other party does. In addition, contracts may be classified according to their legal enforceability as valid, void, voidable or unenforceable.

An executed contract is one that has been fully performed. An executory contract is one in which some act remains to be performed.

The essentials of a valid contract are (1) competent parties, (2) offer and acceptance, (3) consideration, (4) legality of object and (5) agreement in writing and signed by the parties.

In many types of contracts either party may transfer his or her rights and obligations by assignment of the contract or novation (substitution of a new contract).

A party who has suffered a loss because of the other's default may sue for damages to cover the loss. A party who insists on completing the transaction may sue for specific performance of the terms of the contract; a court may order the other party to comply with the agreement.

A real estate sales contract binds a buyer and a seller to a definite transaction as described in the contract. The buyer is bound to purchase the property for the amount stated in the agreement. The seller is bound to deliver title, free from liens and encumbrances (except those allowed by the contract).

Under an option agreement the optionee purchases from the optioner, for a limited time period, the exclusive right to purchase or lease the optioner's property. A land contract, or installment contract, is a sales/financing agreement under which a buyer purchases a seller's real estate on time. The buyer takes possession of and responsibility for the property but does not receive the deed immediately.

1. Laura Secord told her buyers, when they first looked at her house, that she intended to remove her grandmother's antique chandelier. It was not mentioned in the contract. Now they are suing her. A judge is likely to say that

   a. Laura's oral announcement was enough; she could take the chandelier.
   b. the chandelier should remain because of the rule of parol evidence.
   c. because the chandelier wasn't mentioned in the written contract, it remained personal property.
   d. there was no legal way Laura could have retained the chandelier.

2. Markus Barnes drives into a filling station and tops off his gas tank. He is obligated to pay for the fuel through what kind of contract?

   a. Express
   b. Implied
   c. Oral
   d. Voidable

3. A contract is said to be *bilateral* if

   a. one of the parties is a minor.
   b. the contract has yet to be fully performed.
   c. only one party to the agreement is bound to act.
   d. all parties to the contract are bound to act.

4. A contract for the sale of real estate that does not state the consideration to be paid for the property would be

   a. voidable.
   b. executory.
   c. void.
   d. enforceable.

5. During the period of time after a real estate sales contract is signed but before title actually passes, the status of the contract is

   a. voidable.
   b. executory.
   c. executed.
   d. implied.

6. Derrick Smith, who is 17 years old, signs a contract to buy a home for himself. The contract is

   a. voidable.
   b. optional.
   c. executed.
   d. unilateral.

7. A buyer signed an offer to purchase a property for $10,000 less than the asking price and deposited $5,000 with the broker. The owner cannot be reached to tell him of the signed document. At this point the document is a(n)

   a. voidable contract.
   b. offer.
   c. executory agreement.
   d. implied contract.

8. Consideration offered in exchange for a deed might take the form of

   a. love and affection.
   b. a purchase-money mortgage.
   c. cash.
   d. Any of the above

9. Under the statute of frauds, any contract for the sale of real estate must be

   a. drawn up by a lawyer.
   b. on a preprinted form.
   c. in writing.
   d. accompanied by an earnest money deposit.

10. Broker Snively treated homeowner Arthur to several drinks at the neighborhood bar before obtaining a signed listing contract on Arthur's house. The contract is

    a. valid.
    b. void.
    c. voidable.
    d. illegal.

11. In New York State, who fills in the blanks on purchase contracts?
    a. Seller's attorney
    b. Buyer's attorney
    c. Real estate broker
    d. Any of the above, according to local custom

12. If a real estate sales contract does not state that time is of the essence and the stipulated date of transfer comes and goes without a closing, the contract is then
    a. binding for only 30 more days.
    b. novated.
    c. still valid.
    d. automatically void.

13. Tom has a contract to buy Blackacre but would rather let his friend Mary buy it instead. If the contract allows, Mary can acquire Tom's right to buy by the process known as
    a. assignment.
    b. substantial performance.
    c. subordination.
    d. mutual consent.

14. A suit for specific performance of a real estate contract asks for
    a. money damages.
    b. a new contract.
    c. a deficiency judgment.
    d. a forced sale or purchase.

15. In filling out a sales contract someone crossed out several words and inserted others. To eliminate future arguments, the usual procedure is to
    a. write a letter to each party listing the changes.
    b. have each party write a letter approving the changes.
    c. redraw the entire contract.
    d. have both parties initial or sign in the margin near each change.

16. A broker listed a vacant building for sale at 6 percent commission. Marketing the property proved lengthy and difficult, and advertising costs mounted. Finally the seller accepted an offer brought in by the broker. Before the closing the broker insisted the commission be raised to 10 percent. The seller refused to pay more than 6 percent. At that point the
    a. sale cannot close.
    b. seller need pay only 6 percent.
    c. seller has violated the fiduciary relationship.
    d. broker and seller should compromise on 8 percent.

17. The Foxes offer in writing to purchase a house for $140,000, drapes included, with the offer to expire Saturday at noon. The Wolfs reply in writing on Thursday, accepting $140,000 but excluding the drapes. On Friday while the Foxes are considering this counteroffer, the Wolfs decide to accept the original offer, drapes included, and state that in writing. At this point the Foxes
    a. must buy and have a right to insist on the drapes.
    b. are not bound to buy and can forget the whole thing.
    c. must buy but are not entitled to the drapes.
    d. must buy and can deduct the value of the drapes from the $140,000.

18. In New York State a valid contract for the sale of real estate must include
    a. an earnest money deposit.
    b. an adequate description of the property.
    c. the signatures of witnesses.
    d. All of the above

19. The sales contract says Timothy Jones will purchase only if his wife flies up to New York and approves the sale by the following Saturday. Mrs. Jones's approval is a
    a. contingency.   c. warranty.
    b. reservation.   d. consideration.

20. When the buyer promises to purchase only if he can sell his own present home, the seller gains some protection from an
    a. escrow.   c. equitable title.
    b. option.   d. escape clause.

21. Real estate licensees who fill in the blanks on purchase contracts can protect themselves by making the contracts subject to
    a. operation of law.
    b. novation.
    c. attorney's approval.
    d. specific performance.

22. An option to purchase binds
    a. the buyer only.
    b. the seller only.
    c. neither buyer nor seller.
    d. both buyer and seller.

23. Failure to fulfill one's obligations under a contract is called a
    a. novation.
    b. default.
    c. delinquency.
    d. defect.

24. The purchaser of real estate under an installment contract
    a. generally pays no interest charge.
    b. receives title immediately.
    c. is not required to pay property taxes for the duration of the contract.
    d. is called a *vendee.*

25. The consumer has the right to change his or her mind and rescind the transaction within three days after a
    a. real estate purchase.
    b. firm purchase contract.
    c. refinance mortgage.
    d. lease option.

Title Closing and Costs

When they buy their house next Monday, the O'Briens have been told to bring a cashier's check for the money they will need. But what about the fuel oil the seller put in the tank? The year's taxes the seller already paid? Interest due on the mortgage they are assuming? How will they know how much to bring?

Final closing of a real estate sale (also called *settlement* or *transfer of title*) involves many financial details to be settled between the buyer and seller. Even more important, however, is the buyer's need to receive unchallenged ownership, or clear title.

Public Records and Recording

Before purchasing a parcel of real estate, the prospective buyer wants to be sure that the seller can convey good title to the property. The present owner of the real estate undoubtedly purchased from a previous owner, so the same question has been asked many times in the past.

▼ Recording Acts

Parties interested in real estate may record, or file, documents affecting real estate in the *public records*, to give notice to the world of their interest.

Public records are maintained by the recorder of deeds, registrar, county clerk, county treasurer, city clerk and collector, and clerks of various courts of record. Records involving taxes, special assessments, ordinances, and zoning and building also are open for anyone's inspection.

▼ Necessity for Recording

A *deed or mortgage may not be effective as far as later purchasers are concerned unless it has been recorded.* The public records should reveal the condition of the title, and a purchaser should be able to rely on a search of the records.

In New York, to give subsequent purchasers constructive notice of a person's interest, all deeds, mortgages or other written instruments affecting an interest in real estate must be recorded in the county clerk's office of the county where the real estate is located (or, in four of the New York City counties, the Register's Office). All documents must be properly acknowledged and show proof of payment of the real estate transfer tax on deeds or the mortgage tax on mortgages before the documents will be accepted for recording.

A deed will not be accepted for recording in counties outside the city of New York unless it is accompanied by a *real property transfer report*, which will be used by the New York State Board of Equalization and Assessment. A real estate transfer tax (FORM TP584) **affidavit** (sworn statement) also must be filed. In New York City a deed may not be recorded unless it is accompanied by a *multiple dwelling registration statement,* or an affidavit that no statement is due, an affidavit stating that the property contains a smoke alarm and a New York City Real Property Transfer Tax Form (FORM TP584).

The county clerk's office maintains general indexes of instruments recorded in that office. Documents are also recorded in the Office of the New York City Register in borough offices in Manhattan (New York County), Brooklyn (Kings County), the Bronx and Jamaica (Queens).

▼ **Notice**

Through the legal maxim of **caveat emptor** ("let the buyer beware"), the courts hold prospective real estate buyers or mortgagees (lenders) responsible for inspecting the property and searching the public records to find out the interests of other parties. **Constructive notice** assumes that the information is available, so the buyer or lender could have learned it.

Constructive notice, or what a person can find out, is distinguished from **actual notice,** or what the person *actually knows.* An individual who has searched the public records and inspected the property has actual notice of the information learned.

Unrecorded liens. A special search may be needed for unrecorded liens. Estate taxes and franchise taxes are placed against all real estate owned either by a decedent at the time of death or by a corporation at the time the franchise tax became a lien; these liens also are not recorded.

Recording sales contracts. Occasionally it is desirable to record a real property sales contract. Any document to be recorded must be acknowledged. If neither the buyer nor seller can be reached for an acknowledgment, it will be sufficient if a witness to their signatures appears before a notary.

▼ **Chain of Title**

The **chain of title** shows the record of ownership of the property over a period of time. An **abstract of title** is a condensed history of all the instruments affecting a particular parcel of land.

In New York, chains of title frequently date back to a grant from the king of England or a grant to a Dutch patroon.

Through the chain of title, the sequence of owners can be traced from its origin to its present owner. When this cannot be done, there is a *gap* in the chain. In such cases ownership usually must be established by a court action called a **suit to quiet title,** or an Article 15 proceeding.

Evidence of Title

When dealing with an owner of real estate, a purchaser or lender requires satisfactory proof that the seller or borrower is the owner and has good title to the property. This documentary proof is called **evidence of title.**

Generally four forms of title evidence are used: (1) abstract of title and lawyer's opinion, (2) title insurance policy, (3) Torrens certificate and (4) certificate of title. A deed is not proof of title. It proves the grantee received the property but does not prove the grantor had good title in the first place. The only effective proof is one of the evidences of title, based on an adequate search of the public records.

▼ Abstract of Title and Lawyer's Opinion

An abstract of title is a brief history of the instruments appearing in the county record that affect title to the parcel in question. The abstractor lists and summarizes each instrument in order, along with information about taxes, judgments, special assessments and the like. The abstractor concludes with a certificate indicating which records were examined and when, and then he or she signs the abstract. *An abstractor does not, however, pass judgment on or guarantee the condition of the title.*

The abstract illustrated in Figure 10.1 shows that on June 3, 1947, Ida Hughey mortgaged her property at 47 Rowley Street to Rochester Savings Bank for $5,000. The rubber stamp on the record shows that the mortgage was paid off in 1958. The mortgage document evidently carried two legal descriptions: one by plat of subdivision, the other by metes and bounds.

In 1952 Hughey granted a five-year lease on the property to Michael and Mildred Franco, who recorded the document. The next year the Francos bought the property. This particular abstract later goes on to report a driveway easement the Francos negotiated with their neighbors to the north and then traces the property through several later owners with mortgages placed and paid off along the way.

Where the abstract will be used for proof of title, the seller's attorney usually orders the abstract continued to cover the current date. It is then submitted to the buyer's attorney, who *examines the entire document.* Following a detailed examination, the attorney must evaluate all the material and prepare a written report for the purchaser. This report is called an **attorney's opinion of title.** (Abstracts with attorneys' opinions of title are not customary in New York City.)

Mortgage lenders prefer that the seller's title be proved by the use of title insurance, which is required in all commercial transactions and is required by the secondary market for residential loans that are to be resold.

▼ Title Insurance

A **title insurance policy** protects the policyholder against loss if a defect in the owner's title is challenged by anyone at any time. The policy is paid for only once and is in force for the whole period of ownership.

When a seller, buyer or lender applies for a policy, the title company examines the title records. If it is satisfied, it agrees to insure against certain undiscovered defects, usually those that may be found in the public records and such items as forged documents, documents of incompetent grantors, incorrect marital statements and improperly delivered deeds. Exactly which defects the company will insure against depends on the type of policy; the New York State Insurance Department sets standards. The policy amount is the purchase price in the case of an owner's policy and the loan amount in the case of the lender's policy.

On completing the examination, the title company usually issues a report of title or a commitment to issue a title policy. An owner's policy usually *excludes* coverage against unrecorded documents, unrecorded defects of which the policyholder has knowledge, rights of parties in possession and facts discoverable by survey. The insurance company agrees to defend the title at its own expense and to reimburse the policyholder up to the amount of the policy for damages sustained by reason of any defect not excepted. Title companies in New York must offer a homeowner the right to purchase insurance covering future market value.

Figure 10.1 Portion of an Abstract

ABSTRACT OF TITLE

-TO-

#47 West side Rowley Street, being
Part of Lots #27 and 28 of the
Brooks Tract (N. Part) in the
City of Rochester

Maps: Liber 2 of Maps, page 120 and 138
Liber 3 of Maps, page 45
1935 Hopkins Atlas, Vol. 1, Plate 4

CORRECTLY DISCHARGED OF RECORD
BY MORTGAGEE 12/19/58
BY ASSIGNEE
BY PAYMENT OF RECORD
ABSTRACT TITLE INSURANCE CORPORATION
PER

1 Ida May Hughey — Mortgage to secure $5000.00

-To- Dated June 3, 1947

Ack. same day

Rochester Savings Bank — Rec. same day at 12:30 P. M.
47 Main Street West
Rochester, New York — Liber 1800 of Mortgages, page 344

(A) Conveys land in the City of Rochester, being on the west side of Rowley Street in said City and being part of lots Nos. 27 and 28 in the Brooks Tract as shown on a map of said Tract made by M. D. Rowley, surveyor, May 15, 1869 and filed in Monroe County Clerk's Office and counded and described as follows:

Beginning at a point in the west line of Rowely Street 15 feet northerly from the southeast corner of said lot #27; thence northerly on the west line of Rowley Street, forth (40) feet; thence westerly on a line parallel with the south line of said lot #27, 121 feet; thence southerly on a line parallel with the west line of Rowley Street, 40 feet; thence easterly 121 feet to the place of beginning. (A)

Figure 10.1 (continued)

Being the same premises conveyed to the mortgagor by Liber 2258 of Deeds, page 178.

Subject to any restrictions and public utility easements of record.

- -

2   Ida May Hughey, Landlord   Lease

       -To-   Dated May 23, 1952
                   Ack.   same day
Michael Franco   Rec.   August 4, 1952
Mildred Franco,his wife,
Tenants, 17 Glendale Park, Liber 2769 of Deeds, page 290
Rochester, N.Y.,(Second
parties not certified)

First party leases to second parties premises described as #47 Rowley Street, Rochester, New York, being a 12 room house for a term of 5 years commencing July 16, 1952 and ending July 15, 1957 on certain terms and conditions set forth herein.

Second parties shall have the right of renewal on the same terms and conditions as herein for an additional period of 5 years provided that written notice of intention to renew is served upon Landlord or her assigns at least 30 days prior to end of initial term hereof.

- -

3   Ida May Hughey,   Warranty Deed

       -To-   Dated Oct. 30, 1953
                   Ack. Same day
Michele Franco, Mildred Rec. Same day at 10:50 A.M.
Franco, his wife, as
tenants by the entirety, Liber 2861 of Deeds, page 411
#47 Rowley St., Rochester,
N.Y. (Second parties not
certified).

Conveys same as #1.

Subject to all covenants, easements and restrictions

Title companies issue various forms of policies, the most common of which are the *owner's* title insurance policy (a *fee* policy) and the *mortgage* or *lender* title insurance policy. The owner's policy protects the owner and his heirs or devisees. The mortgage policy protects the lender's interests.

▼ **The Torrens System**

The **Torrens system** is a legal registration system used to verify ownership and encumbrances. Registration in the Torrens system provides evidence of title without the need for an additional search of the public records. Under the Torrens system a written application to register a title to real estate is made with the clerk of the court of the county in which the real estate is located. If the applicant proves that he or she is the owner, the court enters an order to register the real estate, and the registrar of titles issues a certificate of title. At any time the Torrens certificate in the registrar's office reveals the owner of the land and all mortgages, judgments and similar liens. It does not reveal federal or state taxes and some other items. The Torrens system is no longer used in New York.

▼ **Certificate of Title**

With an older system, which still may be used for transfers where no lending institution is involved, a *certificate of title prepared by an attorney* is used, and no abstract is prepared. The attorney examines the public records and issues a certificate of title that expresses his or her opinion of the title's status. It is not, however, a title insurance policy and does not carry the full protection of such a policy. The person who sustains damages by relying on it may look to the lawyer for satisfaction.

▼ **Marketable Title**

Under the terms of the usual real estate sales contract the seller is required to deliver marketable or insurable title to the buyer at the closing. Generally a **marketable title** is one that is so free from significant defects (other than those specified in the sales contract) that the purchaser can be insured against having to defend the title. Proper evidence of title is proof that the title is in fact marketable.

A buyer cannot be forced to accept a conveyance that is materially different from the one bargained for in the sales contract; he or she cannot be forced to buy a problem. Questions of marketable title must be raised by a purchaser (or the purchaser's attorney) before acceptance of the deed. If a buyer accepts a deed with unmarketable title, the only available legal recourse is to sue the seller under the covenants or warranty (if any) contained in the deed.

Closing the Transaction

Although salespeople usually are not burdened with the technicalities of closing, they must clearly understand what takes place. A real estate specialist should be able to assist in preclosing arrangements and advise the parties in estimating expenses and the approximate amounts the buyer will need and the seller will receive at the closing.

Generally the closing of a real estate transaction involves a gathering of interested parties at which the promises made in the *real estate sales contract are kept*, or *executed*; that is, a deed is delivered in exchange for the purchase price. In many sales transactions two closings actually take place at this time: (1) the closing of the buyer's loan and the disbursement of mortgage funds in exchange for the note and mortgage and (2) the closing of the sale.

As discussed in Chapter 9, a sales contract is the blueprint for the completion of a real estate transaction. The buyer must be sure that the seller is delivering good title and that the property is in the promised condition. This involves inspecting the title evidence; the deed the seller will give; any documents representing the removal of undesired liens and encumbrances; and any survey, physical and/or environmental inspection, termite report or leases (if there are tenants on the premises). The seller must be sure that the buyer has obtained financing and has the funds to complete the purchase. Both parties should inspect the closing statement to ensure that all monies involved in the transaction have been properly accounted for. In New York State, the parties usually are represented by attorneys.

When everything is in order, the exchange is made and all pertinent documents then are recorded.

▼ Where Closings Are Held and Who Attends

Closings may be held at a number of locations, including the offices of the title company, the lending institution, the office of one of the parties' attorneys, the broker's office, the office of the county clerk (or other local recording official) or an escrow company. Those attending a closing may include any of the following interested parties: buyer, seller, real estate agent(s), attorney(s) for the seller and/or buyer, representatives for the lending institutions involved and representatives of the title insurance company.

▼ Broker's Role at Closing

Depending on the locality, the broker's role at a closing can vary from simply collecting the commission to conducting the proceedings. Because a real estate broker is not authorized to give legal advice or otherwise engage in the practice of law, a broker's job is essentially over when there has been a meeting of the minds. At that point attorneys take over. Even so, a broker's service generally continues after the contract is signed as he or she advises the parties in practical matters, aids the buyer with a mortgage application and makes sure all details are taken care of so that the closing can proceed smoothly. In this capacity the broker might make arrangements for such items as appraisals, termite inspections and repairs or might suggest sources of these services to the parties.

▼ Lender's Interest in Closing

When a buyer is obtaining a new loan, the lender wants to protect its security interest in the property to make sure that the buyer is getting good, marketable title and that tax and insurance payments are maintained so that there will be no liens with greater priority than the mortgage lien and the insurance will be paid up if the property is damaged or destroyed. For this reason the lender frequently requires the following items: (1) a title insurance policy; (2) a fire and hazard insurance policy with receipt for the premium; (3) additional information such as a survey, a termite or other inspection reports or a certificate of occupancy (for newly constructed buildings, multiple dwellings and, in areas in and around New York City, all buildings); (4) establishment of a reserve, or escrow, account for tax and insurance payments; and (5) representation by its own attorney at the closing.

▼ Homeowners' Insurance

Where mortgaging is involved, the buyer must bring to the closing proof of insurance on the property and, occasionally, proof of flood insurance. The insurance policy or binder usually names the lender as lienholder and copayee in case of loss under the policy.

Although it is possible for a homeowner to obtain individual policies for each type of risk, most residential property owners take out insurance in the form of a packaged homeowner's policy. These standardized policies insure holders against the destruction of their property by fire or windstorm, injury to others that occurs on the property and theft of any personal property on the premises that is owned by the insured or members of his or her family.

The package homeowner's policy also includes **liability coverage** for personal injuries to others resulting from the insured's acts or negligence, voluntary medical payments and funeral expenses for accidents sustained by guests or resident employees on the property of the owner and physical damage to the property of others caused by the insured.

Characteristics of homeowners' packages. There are four major forms of homeowners' policies. The *basic* form, known as *HO-1*, provides property coverage against fire or lightning, glass breakage, windstorm or hail, explosion, riot or civil commotion, damage by aircraft, damage from vehicles, damage from smoke, vandalism and malicious mischief, theft and loss of property removed from the premises when endangered by fire or other perils.

Increased coverage is provided under a *broad* form, known as *HO-2*, that also covers falling objects; weight of ice, snow or sleet; collapse of the building or any part of it; bursting, cracking, burning or bulging of a steam or hot water heating system or of appliances used to heat water; accidental discharge, leakage or overflow of water or steam from within a plumbing, heating or air-conditioning system; freezing of plumbing, heating and air-conditioning systems and domestic appliances; and injury to electrical appliances, devices, fixtures and wiring from short circuits or other accidentally generated currents.

Further coverage is provided by *comprehensive* forms *HO-3*, the most popular form, and *HO-5*. These policies cover all possible perils except flood, earthquake, war and nuclear attack. Other policies include *HO-4*, a form designed specifically for apartment renters, and *HO-6*, a broad-form policy for condominium owners. Apartment and condominium policies generally provide fire and windstorm, theft and public liability coverage for injuries or losses sustained within the unit but usually do not extend to cover losses or damages to the structure. The structure is insured by either the landlord or the condominium owners' association.

Claims. Most homeowners' insurance policies contain a **coinsurance clause.** This provision requires the insured to maintain fire insurance on the property equal to at least 80 percent of the **replacement cost** of the dwelling (not including the price of the land). With such a policy the owner may make a claim for the cost of the repair or replacement of the damaged property without deduction.

In any event, the *total settlement cannot exceed the face value of the policy.* Because of coinsurance clauses, it is important that homeowners review their policies regularly to be certain that the coverage is equal to at least 80 percent of the current replacement cost of their homes. Some policies carry automatic increases in coverage to adjust for inflation.

▼ **Federal Flood Insurance Program**

Property owners in certain areas must obtain flood damage insurance before they can obtain federally related mortgages. Federally related loans include those made by banks, savings and loan associations or other lenders whose deposits are insured by federal agencies (FDIC or FSLIC); those insured by the

FHA or guaranteed by the VA; mortgages administered by the U.S. Department of Housing and Urban Development; and loans intended to be sold by the lender to Fannie Mae, Ginnie Mae or Freddie Mac. An owner may be able to avoid purchasing flood insurance if he or she can furnish a survey showing that the lowest part of the building is above the 100-year flood mark.

▼ **RESPA Requirements**

The federal **Real Estate Settlement Procedures Act (RESPA)** ensures that the buyer in a *residential* real estate transaction has knowledge of all settlement costs. *RESPA requirements apply when the purchase is financed by a federally related mortgage loan.*

RESPA regulations apply to transactions involving new first mortgage loans, refinance loans, second mortgages, home equity loans and lines of credit. When a transaction is covered by RESPA, the following requirements must be met:

- *Special information booklet:* Lenders must give a copy of the HUD booklet *Settlement Costs and You* to every person from whom they receive or for whom they prepare a loan application.
- *Good-faith estimate of settlement costs:* At the time of the loan application or within three business days the lender must provide the borrower with a good-faith estimate of the settlement costs the borrower is likely to incur. A lender who requires use of a particular attorney or title company to conduct the closing must state whether it has any business relationship with that firm and must estimate the charges for this service.
- *Uniform Settlement Statement (HUD Form 1):* Loan closing information must be prepared on a special HUD form, the Uniform Settlement Statement, designed to detail all financial particulars of a transaction (see Figure 10.2). The completed statement must itemize all charges imposed by the lender. Items paid for before the closing must be clearly marked as such on the statement and are omitted from the totals. On the borrower's request the closing agent must permit the borrower to inspect the settlement statement, to the extent that the figures are available, one business day before the closing. Lenders must retain these statements for two years after the date of closing unless the loan (and its servicing) is sold or otherwise disposed of.
- *Prohibition against kickbacks:* RESPA explicitly prohibits the payment of kickbacks, or unearned fees; for example, when an insurance agency pays a kickback to a lender for referring one of the lender's recent customers to the agency. This prohibition does *not* include fee splitting between cooperating brokers or members of multiple-listing services, brokerage referral arrangements or the division of a commission between a broker and his or her salespeople. (RESPA is administered by HUD.)

The Title Procedure

On the date when the sale is actually completed, that is, the date of delivery of the deed, the buyer has a title commitment or an abstract that was issued several days or weeks before the closing. For this reason the title or abstract company is usually required to make a second search of the public records. A last-minute search is often made at the moment of closing.

The title company will ask the seller to sign an *affidavit of title*. This is a sworn statement in which the seller assures the title company that since the date of the title examination there have been no judgments, bankruptcies or divorces involving the seller; no repairs or improvements that have not been paid for; and that he or she is in possession of the premises. Through this affidavit the

Figure 10.2   RESPA Uniform Settlement Statement

A. **Settlement Statement**	U.S. Department of Housing and Urban Development	
		OMB Approval No. 2502-0265

B. Type of Loan

1. ☐ FHA 2. ☐ FmHA 3. ☐ Conv. Unins. 4. ☐ VA 5. ☐ Conv. Ins.	6. File Number	7. Loan Number	8. Mortgage Insurance Case Number

C. Note: This form is furnished to give you a statement of actual settlement costs. Amounts paid to and by the settlement agent are shown. Items marked "(p.o.c.)" were paid outside the closing; they are shown here for informational purposes and are not included in the totals.

D. Name and Address of Borrower	E. Name and Address of Seller	F. Name and Address of Lender
Brook Redemann 22 King Court Riverdale	John and Joanne Iuro 3045 North Racine Avenue Riverdale	Thrift Federal Savings 1100 Fountain Plaza Riverdale

G. Property Location	H. Settlement Agent	
3045 North Racine Avenue Riverdale	Open Door Real Estate Company	
	Place of Settlement Open Door Real Estate Company 720 Main Street, Riverdale	I. Settlement Date June 15

J. Summary of Borrower's Transaction		K. Summary of Seller's Transaction	
100. Gross Amount Due From Borrower		**400. Gross Amount Due To Seller**	
101. Contract sales price	$115,000.00	401. Contract sales price	$115,00.00
102. Personal property		402. Personal property	
103. Settlement charges to borrower (line 1400)	5,075.84	403.	
104.		404.	
105.		405.	
Adjustments for items paid by seller in advance		*Adjustments for items paid by seller in advance*	
106. City/town taxes to		406. City/town taxes to	
107. County taxes to		407. County taxes to	
108. Assessments to		408. Assessments to	
109.		409.	
110.		410.	
111.		411.	
112.		412.	
120. Gross Amount Due From Borrower	$120,075.84	**420. Gross Amount Due To Seller**	$115,000.00
200. Amounts Paid By Or In Behalf Of Borrower		**500. Reductions In Amount Due To Seller**	
201. Deposit or earnest money	23,000.00	501. Excess deposit (see instructions)	
202. Principal amount of new loan(s)	92,000.00	502. Settlement charges to seller (line 1400)	8,080.00
203. Existing loan(s) taken subject to		503. Existing loan(s) taken subject to	
204.		504. Payoff of first mortgage loan	57,964.47
205.		505. Payoff of second mortgage loan	
206.		506.	
207.		507.	
208.		508.	
209.		509.	
Adjustments for items unpaid by seller		*Adjustments for items unpaid by seller*	
210. City/town taxes to		510. City/town taxes to	
211. County taxes 1/1/ to 6/15/	790.63	511. County taxes 1/1/ to 6/15/	790.63
212. Assessments to		512. Assessments to	
213.		513.	
214.		514.	
215.		515.	
216.		516.	
217.		517.	
218.		518.	
219.		519.	
220. Total Paid By/For Borrower	$115,790.63	**520. Total Reduction Amount Due Seller**	$ 66,835.10
300. Cash At Settlement From/To Borrower		**600. Cash At Settlement To/From Seller**	
301. Gross Amount due from borrower (line 120)	120,075.84	601. Gross amount due to seller (line 420)	115,000.00
302. Less amounts paid by/for borrower (line 220)	(115,790.63)	602. Less reductions in amt. due seller (line 520)	(66,835.10)
303. Cash ☐ From ☐ To Borrower	$ 4,285.21	**603. Cash** ☐ To ☐ From Seller	$ 48,164.90

Figure 10.2   (continued)

L. Settlement Charges		Paid From Borrowers Funds at Settlement	Paid From Seller's Funds at Settlement
700. Total Sales/Broker's Commission based on price $ 115,000 @ 6 % = $6,900.00			
Division of Commission (line 700) as follows:			
701. $	to		
702. $	to		
703. Commission paid at Settlement			$ 6,900.00
704.			
800. Items Payable In Connection With Loan			
801. Loan Origination Fee	%	$ 920.00	
802. Loan Discount 2	%	$1,840.00	
803. Appraisal Fee $125.00	to Swift Appraisal	POC	
804. Credit Report $ 60.00	to ACME Credit Bureau	· POC	
805. Lender's Inspection Fee			
806. Mortgage Insurance Application Fee to			
807. Assumption Fee			
808.			
809.			
810.			
811.			
900. Items Required By Lender To Be Paid In Advance			
901. Interest from 6/16 to 6/30 @$ 25.556 /day		383.34	
902. Mortgage Insurance Premium for	months to		
903. Hazard Insurance Premium for 1	years to Hite Ins. Co.	345.00	
904.	years to		
905.			
1000. Reserves Deposited With Lender			
1001. Hazard insurance 3	months@$ 28.75 per month	86.25	
1002. Mortgage insurance	months@$ per month		
1003. City property taxes	months@$ per month		
1004. County property taxes 7	months@$ 143.75 per month	1,006.25	
1005. Annual assessments	months@$ per month		
1006.	months@$ per month		
1007.	months@$ per month		
1008.	months@$ per month		
1100. Title Charges			
1101. Settlement or closing fee	to		
1102. Abstract or title search	to		
1103. Title examination	to		
1104. Title insurance binder	to		
1105. Document preparation	to		10.00
1106. Notary fees	to		
1107. Attorney's fees	to	300.00	400.00
(includes above items numbers:)			
1108. Title insurance	to		540.00
(includes above items numbers:)			
1109. Lender's coverage	$ 395.00		
1110. Owner's coverage	$ 145.00		
1111.			
1112.			
1113.			
1200. Government Recording and Transfer Charges			
1201. Recording fees: Deed $ 10.00 ; Mortgage $ 10.00 ; Releases $ 10.00		20.00	10.00
1202. City/county tax/stamps: Deed $; Mortgage $			
1203. State tax/stamps: Deed $ 460.00 ; Mortgage $			460.00
1204. Record two documents to clear title			20.00
1205.			
1300. Additional Settlement Charges			
1301. Survey to		175.00	
1302. Pest inspection to			85.00
1303.			
1304.			
1305.			
1400. Total Settlement Charges (enter on lines 103, Section J and 502, Section K)		$5,075.84	$8,425.00

Public Reporting Burden for this collection of information is estimated to average 0.25 hours per response, including the time for reviewing instructions, searching existing data sources, gathering and maintaining the data needed, and completing and reviewing the collection of information. Send comments regarding this burden estimate or any other aspect of this collection of information, including suggestions for reducing this burden, to the Reports Management Officer, Office of Information Policies and Systems, U.S. Department of Housing and Urban Development, Washington, D.C. 20410-3600; and to the Office of Management and Budget, Paperwork Reduction Project (2502-0265), Washington, D.C. 20503 title company obtains the right to sue the seller if his or her statements in the affidavit prove incorrect.

▼ Checking the Premises

It is important that the buyer inspect the property to determine the interests of any parties in possession or other interests that cannot be determined from inspecting the public record. A *survey* is frequently required so that the purchaser will know the location, size and legal description of the property. The buyer should also make a last-minute inspection before closing to check that the house remains in the condition originally presented and that the seller is leaving behind any appliances or other personal property stipulated in the written sales contract. This inspection right is often set forth in a clause in the purchase and sale agreement.

▼ Releasing Existing Liens

When the purchaser pays cash or obtains a new mortgage to purchase the property, the seller's existing mortgage usually is paid in full and released in the public record. To know the exact amount required to pay the existing mortgage, the seller secures a current *payoff statement* from the mortgagee. The same procedure is followed for any other liens that must be released before the buyer takes title.

When the buyer is assuming the seller's existing mortgage loan, the buyer needs to know the exact balance of the loan as of the closing date. The buyer receives a **mortgage reduction certificate** (sometimes referred to as an *estoppel certificate*) from the lender, stating the exact balance due and the last interest payment made.

Closing in Escrow

In the western United States most transactions are closed in escrow, but the system is seldom used in New York.

In an **escrow** closing a third party coordinates the closing activities. The escrow agent may be an attorney, a title company, a trust company, an escrow company or the escrow department of a lending institution. Buyer and seller deposit all pertinent documents, money and other items with the escrow agent. When all conditions of the escrow agreement have been met, the agent pays the purchase price to the seller and records the deed and mortgage (if a new mortgage has been executed by the purchaser).

Preparation of Closing Statements

A typical real estate sales transaction involves numerous expenses for both parties in addition to the purchase price. There are a number of property expenses that the seller will have paid in advance or that the buyer will pay in the future. The financial responsibility for these items must be *prorated* (adjusted or divided) between the buyer and seller. In closing a transaction it is customary to account for all these items by preparing a written statement to determine how much money the buyer needs and how much the seller will net after the broker's commission and expenses. There are many different formats of closing, or settlement, statements, but all are designed to achieve the same results.

Closing statements in New York are prepared by the buyer's and seller's attorneys or bank representatives. The broker should, however, be able to give the seller an estimate of sale costs. In addition the buyer must be prepared with the proper amount of money to complete the purchase, and again the broker should be able to assist by making a reasonably accurate estimate.

▼ **How the Closing Statement Works**

The completion of a **closing statement** involves an accounting of the parties' debits and credits. A **debit** is a charge, an amount that the party being debited owes and must pay at the closing. A **credit** is an amount entered in a person's favor: an amount that the party already has paid, an amount that he or she must be reimbursed for or an amount the buyer promises to pay in the form of a loan.

To determine the amount the buyer needs at the closing, the buyer's debits are totaled. Any expenses and prorated amounts for items prepaid by the seller are added to the purchase price. Then the buyer's credits are totaled. These would include the earnest money (already paid), the balance of the loan the buyer is obtaining or assuming and the seller's share of any prorated items that the buyer will pay in the future. Finally the total of the buyer's credits is subtracted from the total amount the buyer owes (debits) to arrive at the actual amount of cash the buyer must bring to the closing. Usually the buyer brings a bank cashier's check or a certified personal check.

A similar procedure is followed to determine how much money the seller actually will receive. The seller's debits and credits are totaled separately. The credits include the purchase price plus the buyer's share of any prorated items that the seller has prepaid. The seller's debits include expenses, the seller's share of prorated items to be paid later by the buyer and the balance of any mortgage loan or other lien that the seller is paying off. Finally the total of the seller's charges is subtracted from the total credits to arrive at the amount the seller will receive.

▼ **Expenses**

In addition to the sales price, taxes, interest and the like, a number of other expenses and charges, including the following items, may be involved in a real estate transaction.

Broker's commission. The broker's commission is usually paid by the seller because the broker is usually the seller's agent. When the buyer has employed the broker, either party may pay the commission, according to agreement.

Attorney's fees. If either party's attorney will be paid from the closing proceeds, that party will be charged with the expense in the closing statement.

Recording expenses. Charges for recording documents vary from one county to another. A county might charge $5.50 for recording a document plus $3.00 per page. Thus a single-page deed would cost $8.50 to record, while the charge for a four-page mortgage would be $17.50.

The seller usually pays recording charges (filing fees) needed to clear all defects and furnish the purchaser with clear title. Items usually charged to the seller include the recording of satisfaction of mortgages, quitclaim deeds, affidavits and satisfaction of mechanic's lien claims. Items usually charged to the purchaser include recording the deed and any new mortgage.

Transfer tax. Any *New York State* conveyance is taxed at a rate of $2 per $500 or fraction thereof of the consideration paid minus the amount of any mortgage being assumed. (Those who inspect old deeds to estimate sales prices should know that before 1983 the rate was $.55 per $500.) The transfer tax must be paid, usually by the seller, when the deed is recorded. Local taxes also may be due. Shares in a cooperative are taxed at the same rate.

New York City levies a transfer tax of 1 percent on sales of less than $500,000 on one- to three-family dwellings. Other transfers require payment of a higher city tax. The tax is paid by the grantor when the deed is recorded.

Personal property transferred with the real estate (drapes, for example) is covered by a bill of sale and is subject not to transfer tax but to state sales tax unless it is included in the sale of the real estate without additional consideration.

The 10 percent New York State capital gains tax on properties sold for more than $1 million was repealed in 1996.

> The closing statement lists sales price, earnest money deposit and all adjustments and prorations between buyer and seller.

State mortgage tax. New York State imposes a tax of $.75 for each $100 or fraction thereof for every mortgage recorded within the state, and in many counties there is an additional $.25 for each $100 or fraction thereof. The first $10,000 of a mortgage for any one- or two-family residence is taxed at a rate of $.50 for each $100. If the mortgage covers property improved by a structure with six or fewer cooking units, the mortgagee must pay a portion of the mortgage tax—$.25 for each $100 or fraction thereof. Private lenders do not pay the $.25 portion; lending institutions do. When a land contract is recorded, mortgage tax is due on the amount borrowed. Local mortgage taxes also may be imposed. In counties that levy additional tax, none is due on the first $10,000 of the loan for a one- or two-family residence.

Title expenses. The responsibility for title expenses varies according to the contract, which usually follows local custom. If the buyer's attorney inspects the evidence or if the buyer purchases title insurance policies, the buyer is charged for these expenses. In some situations the title or abstract company makes two searches of the public records: the first shows the status of the seller's title on the date of the sales contract and the second continues through the date on which the purchaser's deed is recorded. In some areas the seller pays for the initial search and the purchaser pays for the redate charge. Elsewhere the buyer pays for the full search.

Loan fees. When the purchaser is securing a mortgage to finance the purchase, the lender (mortgage company) usually charges a service charge or an origination fee. The fee is a flat charge and is usually paid by the purchaser at the time the transaction is closed. The buyer also may be charged an assumption fee for assuming the seller's financing and in some cases may pay discount points. As discussed in Chapter 11, the seller also may be charged discount points.

Tax reserves and insurance reserves (escrows). A *reserve* is a sum of money set aside to be used later for a particular purpose. The mortgage lender usually requires that the borrower establish and maintain a reserve so that there will be sufficient funds to pay property taxes and renew hazard insurance when these items become due. To set up the reserve, the borrower makes a lump-sum payment to the lender when the mortgage money is paid out (usually at the time of closing). After that the borrower pays into the escrow account an amount equal to one month's portion of the *estimated* general tax and insurance premium as part of the monthly PITI payment to the mortgage company.

Additional fees. An FHA borrower owes a lump sum for prepayment of the mortgage insurance premium if it is not being financed as part of the loan. A VA mortgagor pays a fee directly to the VA at closing. If a conventional loan carries private mortgage insurance, the buyer prepays one year's insurance premium at closing.

Appraisal fees. When the buyer obtains a mortgage, the lender usually requires an appraisal, which the buyer pays for.

Survey fees. A purchaser who obtains new mortgage financing customarily pays the survey fees. In some cases the sales contract may require that the seller furnish a survey.

▼ **Prorations**

Most closings involve the dividing of financial responsibility between the buyer and seller for items such as loan interest, taxes, rents, fuel and utility bills. These allowances are called prorations or adjustments. Prorations are necessary to ensure that expenses are divided fairly between the seller and the buyer. For example, when the coming year's property taxes have been paid in advance, the seller is entitled to partial reimbursement at the closing. If the buyer assumes the seller's existing mortgage, the seller usually owes the buyer a credit for accrued interest through the date of closing.

Accrued items are items to be prorated that are owed by the seller but eventually will be paid by the buyer. The seller therefore gives the buyer credit for these items at closing. Because interest usually is paid in *arrears* (the opposite of in *advance*), each payment covers interest for the preceding month. At a mid-month closing the seller who has not made the current month's payment would owe six weeks' back interest on a mortgage.

Prepaid items are items to be prorated (such as taxes or fuel oil left in the tank) that have been paid for by the seller but not fully earned (not fully used up). They are therefore credits to the seller.

General rules for prorating. The rules or customs governing the computation of prorations for the closing of a real estate sale vary:

- In New York it is generally provided that the buyer owns the property on the closing date. In practice, however, either buyer or seller may be charged with that day's expenses.
- Mortgage interest, real estate taxes, water bills and similar expenses are computed in some areas by using *360 days in a year and 30 days in a month*. In other areas prorations are computed using the actual number of days in the calendar month of closing.
- *Special assessments* for municipal improvements such as sewers, water mains or streets are usually paid in annual installments over several years. Sellers are sometimes required to pay off special assessments entirely. In other cases buyers may agree to assume future installments.
- *Rents* are usually adjusted on the basis of the actual number of days in the month of closing. The buyer often will agree in the contract or by a separate letter to collect any uncollected rents for the current month and remit a share to the seller.

Security deposits generally are transferred by the seller to the buyer; the tenant must be notified of the transfer of deposit.

▼ **Accounting for Credits and Charges**

Items accounted for in the closing statement fall into two general categories: (1) prorations or other amounts due to either the buyer or seller (credit to) and paid for by the other party (debit to) and (2) expenses or items paid by the seller or buyer (debit only).

Items Credited to Buyer (debited to seller)	**Items Credited to Seller (debited to buyer)**
1. buyer's earnest money*	1. sales price*
2. unpaid principal balance of outstanding mortgage being assumed by buyer*	2. fuel oil on hand, usually figured at current market price
3. insurance and tax reserve (if any) when mortgage is being assumed by buyer	3. interest on existing assumed mortgage not yet paid (accrued)
4. portion of current rent collected in advance	4. refund to seller of prepaid water charge or similar expenses
5. purchase-money mortgage	5. portion of general real estate tax paid in advance
6. unpaid water bills	

Items with an asterisk (*) are not prorated; they are entered in full as listed. The *buyer's earnest money*, while credited to the buyer, is *not usually debited to the seller*. The buyer receives a credit because he or she has already paid that amount toward the purchase price. Under the usual sales contract the money is held by the broker or attorney in escrow until the settlement, when it will be included as part of the total amount due the seller. If the seller is paying off an existing loan and the buyer is obtaining a new one, these two items are accounted for with a debit only to the seller for the amount of the payoff and a credit only to the buyer for the amount of the new loan.

Accounting for expenses. Expenses paid out of the closing proceeds are usually debited only to the party making the payment.

The Arithmetic of Proration

There are three basic methods of calculating prorations:

1. The yearly charge is divided by a 360-day year or 12 months of 30 days each.
2. The monthly charge *is divided by the actual number of days in the month of closing* to determine the amount.
3. The yearly charge *is divided by 365* to determine the daily charge. Then the actual number of days in the proration period is determined, and this number is multiplied by the daily charge.

In some cases when a sale is closed on the 15th of the month, the half-month charge is computed simply by dividing the monthly charge by two.

The final proration figure will vary slightly, depending on which computation method is used.

Sample Closing Statements

Figure 10.3 shows a buyer's closing statement, and Figure 10.4 shows a seller's closing statement for the same transaction. The property is being purchased for $89,500, with $49,500 down and the seller taking back a mortgage for $40,000. Closing takes place on August 12.

▼ Prorations

The buyer is taking over a house on which taxes have been paid, in one case until the end of the year. The buyer therefore will reimburse the seller for the time in which the buyer will be living in a tax-paid house. Specifically, the seller has paid city and school taxes of $1,176.35 for the tax year that started July 1 and will receive a large portion of that back as a credit from the buyer. County taxes of $309.06 were paid January 1 for the year ahead, so the buyer will also credit the seller for the four months and 18 days remaining in the year, an adjustment of $118.52.

The buyer owes the seller (total seller's credits) the purchase price plus unearned taxes, for a total of $90,657.68. Toward this sum the buyer receives credit for an earnest money deposit of $500 in a broker's escrow account. (The seller's attorney and the broker will take this sum into consideration later when the commission is paid.) The buyer also receives credit for the $40,000 bond and mortgage given to the seller at closing. The buyer therefore gives the seller cash (or a certified check) for the remaining sum, $50,157.68.

The upper half of the closing statement accounts for the transaction between buyer and seller; the lower part details each one's individual expenses. The buyer pays to record the deed and mortgage, part of the mortgage tax and the buyer's attorney.

The seller's expenses include last-minute payment of the school tax (plus a small late-payment penalty), for which the seller is largely reimbursed. Also paid by the seller is the required lender's share of the mortgage tax (seller/lender happens to be a corporation). The seller pays the real estate commission, legal costs of proving title, transfer tax and incidental out-of-pocket expenses incurred by the seller's attorney, who also deducts his or her own fee and turns over the net proceeds to the seller.

Figure 10.3 Buyer's Closing Statement, Closing on August 12

SELLER'S CREDITS

Sale Price _____ $ 89,500.00

ADJUSTMENT OF TAXES

School Tax 7/1   to 6/30   Amount $ 1176.35   Adj. 10 mos. 18 days $ 1,039.16

City/School Tax 7/1/   to 6/30/   Amount $_____ Adj. ____ mos. ____ days $_____

County Tax 19____   Amount $ 309.06   Adj. 4 mos. 18 days $ 118.52

Village Tax 6/1/   to 5/31/   Amount $_____ Adj. ____ mos. ____ days $_____

City Tax Embellishments   Amount $_____ Adj. ____ mos. ____ days $_____

Total Seller's Credits $ 90,657.68

PURCHASER'S CREDITS

Deposit with ___Nothnagle_____ $ 500.00

(Assumed) (New) Mortgage with Seller $480.07 p/m $ 40,000.00

beg. 9-12   , 12% int., 15 yrs. $_____

_____ $_____

_____ $_____

_____ $_____

_____ $_____

_____ $_____

_____ $_____

Total Purchaser's Credits $ 40,500.00

Cash (Rec'd) (Paid) at Closing $ 50,157.68

EXPENSES OF PURCHASER		EXPENSES OF SELLER	
Mortgage Tax	$ 275.00	Title Search Fee	$_____
Recording Mortgage	$ 11.00	Transfer Tax on Deed	$_____
Recording Deed	$ 12.00	Filing of Gains Tax Affidavit	$_____
		Discharge Recording Fee	$_____
ESCROWS:		Mortgage Tax	$_____
___ mos. insurance $_____		Surveyor's Fees	$_____
___ mos. school tax $_____		Points	$_____
___ mos. county tax $_____		Mortgage Payoff	$_____
___ mos. village tax $_____		Real Estate Commission	$_____
PMI FHA Insurance $_____		Water Escrow	$_____
Total: $_____			$_____
Bank Attorney Fee	$_____		$_____
Points	$_____		$_____
Title Insurance	$_____	Legal Fee	$_____
Interest	$_____	Total	$_____
	$_____		
	$_____	Cash Received:	$
	$_____	Less Seller's Expenses:	$
Legal Fee	$ 500.00	Net Proceeds:	$
Total	$ 798.00		

Cash paid to Seller: $ 50,157.68

Plus Purchaser's Expenses: $ 798.00

Total Disbursed: $ 50,955.68

Figure 10.4 Seller's Closing Statement, Closing on August 12

SELLER'S CREDITS

Sale Price _____ $ 89,500.00

ADJUSTMENT OF TAXES

School Tax 7/1 to 6/30   Amount $ 1176.35 Adj. 10 mos. 18 days $ 1,039.16

City/School Tax 7/1/ to 6/30/   Amount $____ Adj. ____mos.____days $____

County Tax 19____   Amount $ 309.06 Adj. 4 mos. 18 days $ 118.52

Village Tax 6/1/ to 5/31/   Amount $____ Adj. ____mos.____days $____

City Tax Embellishments   Amount $____ Adj. ____mos. ____days $____

Total Seller's Credits $ 90,657.68

PURCHASER'S CREDITS

Deposit with _Nothnagle_ _____ $ 500.00

(Assumed) (New) Mortgage with _seller_ _____ $ 40,000.00

12% interest, 15 years, payments _____ $____

$ 480.07, beginning 9/12 _____ $____

_____ $____

_____ $____

_____ $____

_____ $____

_____ $____

_____ $____

Total Purchaser's Credits $ 40,500.00

Cash (Rec'd) (Paid) at Closing $ 50,157.68

EXPENSES OF PURCHASER		EXPENSES OF SELLER	
Mortgage Tax	$____	Title Search Fee	$ 220.00
Recording Mortgage.	$____	Transfer Tax on Deed	$ 358.00
Recording Deed.	$____	Filing of Gains Tax Affidavit	$ 1.00
		Discharge Recording Fee	$____
ESCROWS:		Mortgage Tax	$ 100.00
____ mos. insurance $____		Surveyor's Fees	$____
____ mos. school tax $____		Points	$____
____ mos. county tax $____		Mortgage Payoff	$____
____ mos. village tax $____		Real Estate Commission	$ 4870.00
PMI/FHA Insurance $____		Water Escrow	$____
Total: $____		school tax	$ 1,182.14
Bank Attorney Fee.	$____	Federal express	$ 14.00
Points.	$____		$____
Title Insurance.	$____		$____
Interest.	$____	Legal Fee.	$ 550.00
	$____	Total.	$ 7,295.14
	$____		
	$____	Cash Received:	$ 50,157.68
Legal Fee.	$____	Less Seller's Expenses:	$ 7,295.14
Total.	$____	Net Proceeds:	$ 42,862.54
Cash paid to Seller.	$		
Plus Purchaser's Expenses:	$		
Total Disbursed:	S		

Key Terms

abstract of title	homeowner's policy
accrued item	liability coverage
actual notice	marketable title
adjustments	mortgage reduction certificate
affidavit	prepaid item
attorney's opinion of title	proration
caveat emptor	public records
chain of title	Real Estate Settlement Procedures
closing statement	Act (RESPA)
coinsurance clause	replacement cost
constructive notice	suit to quiet title
credit	title insurance policy
debit	Torrens system
escrow	Uniform Settlement Statement
evidence of title	

Summary

The public records give constructive notice to the world of different parties' interests in real estate. Possession of real estate gives notice of possible rights of the person in possession. Actual notice is whatever one actually knows; constructive notice is what one could find out by investigating.

Title evidence shows whether a seller is conveying marketable title, one so free from defects that the buyer can be assured title will not be challenged. Four forms of title evidence may used throughout the United States: (1) abstract of title and lawyer's opinion, (2) owner's title insurance policy, (3) Torrens certificate and (3) certificate of title. A deed proves that a previous grantor transferred his or her interest but does not prove the grantor actually had any interest in the property.

At closing a buyer may be required to prove hazard insurance coverage to a lender. A standard homeowner's insurance policy covers fire, theft and liability and can be extended to cover less common risks. Insurance covering personal property is available only to those in apartments and condominiums. For some property located in flood plains, flood insurance is needed to obtain a federally related mortgage loan. Many homeowner's policies contain a coinsurance clause requiring that the policyholder insure for at least 80 percent of the replacement cost of the house. Otherwise the policyholder may not be reimbursed for full repair costs in case of loss.

The federal Real Estate Settlement Procedures Act (RESPA) requires disclosure of all settlement costs when a residential real estate purchase is financed by a federally related loan. RESPA requires that lenders use a Uniform Settlement Statement.

The actual amount paid by the buyer at closing is computed by preparing a closing statement. This lists the sales price, earnest money deposit and all adjustments and prorations between buyer and seller.

1. Public records may be inspected by
   a. anyone.
   b. anyone, but only after obtaining permission under the Freedom of Information Act.
   c. New York attorneys and abstractors only.
   d. attorneys, abstractors and real estate licensees only.

2. An instrument affecting title to a parcel of real estate gives constructive notice to the world when filed with the
   a. county clerk.
   b. city clerk.
   c. secretary of state.
   d. title company.

3. Barbara Barnes checked the public records. She found that the seller was the grantee in the last recorded deed and that no mortgage was on record against the property. She may assume that
   a. all taxes are paid and no judgments are outstanding.
   b. the seller has good title.
   c. the seller did not mortgage the property.
   d. no one else is occupying the property.

4. An abstractor inspects the county records for documents affecting title and then
   a. writes a brief history of the title.
   b. insures the condition of the title.
   c. personally inspects the property.
   d. issues a certificate of title.

5. If the broker holds the buyer's earnest money in a separate trust account, when does the seller usually receive it?
   a. At the time the offer is accepted
   b. After approval by the buyer's and seller's attorneys
   c. When the buyer receives a firm mortgage commitment
   d. When the property is actually transferred

6. Last year Maureen O'Brien gave a house in Watertown, valued at $110,000, to her son Richard. Richard assumed an existing $30,000 mortgage on the property. Transfer tax due on the gift was
   a. $220.   c. $440.
   b. $320.   d. nothing.

7. Ann needs to know how much her parents paid for the Elmira house they bought from a builder in 1954. She finds tax stamps on their old deed totaling $22.55. She can conclude that they paid roughly
   a. $6,000.   c. $22,550.
   b. $20,500.   d. $60,000.

8. Last summer Douglas Maloof sold his home in Schenectady to the Auerbachs for $160,000. The Auerbachs assumed his existing mortgage in the amount of $76,578. State transfer tax on the sale came to approximately
   a. $91.85.   c. $334.
   b. $176.   d. $640.

9. Susan Johnson, a Manhattan resident, purchases farmland in Clinton County as an investment. The deed she receives should
   a. not be recorded.
   b. be recorded in Manhattan.
   c. be recorded in Clinton County.
   d. be recorded in both the borough of Manhattan and Clinton County.

10. The principle of *caveat emptor* states that if the purchaser buys a faulty title, responsibility for the problem lies with the
   a. buyer.   c. broker.
   b. seller.   d. abstractor.

11. Which of the following is *not* acceptable proof of title?
   a. Torrens certificate
   b. Title insurance policy
   c. Abstract with lawyer's opinion
   d. Deed signed by last seller

12. Mortgage title policies protect which parties against loss?
   a. Buyers only
   b. Sellers only
   c. Buyers and sellers only
   d. Lenders only

13. At closing the seller of a single home must give the buyer an affidavit that the house has
   a. hazard insurance.
   b. title insurance.
   c. a working smoke alarm.
   d. insulation.

14. Robert Dunn is selling a two-family dwelling. The buyer's lending institution is likely to require
   a. proof of hazard insurance.
   b. a certificate of occupancy.
   c. title insurance.
   d. All of the above

15. The terms *basic, broad* and *comprehensive* describe types of
   a. title insurance.
   b. mortgage documents.
   c. homeowner's insurance.
   d. attorney's services.

16. A coinsurance clause can penalize the homeowner who does not carry insurance for at least what part of replacement cost?
   a. 50 percent   c. 100 percent
   b. 80 percent   d. 120 percent

17. Flood insurance may be required before mortgaging property if it is
   a. a multiple dwelling.
   b. in a flood-prone area on a special map.
   c. owned by the FHA or the VA.
   d. going to have title insurance.

18. The RESPA Uniform Settlement Statement must be used for
   a. every real estate closing.
   b. transactions financed by FHA and VA only.
   c. residential transactions financed by federally related loans.
   d. all transactions involving commercial property.

19. A mortgage reduction certificate is issued by a(n)
   a. lending institution.
   b. attorney.
   c. abstract company.
   d. grantor.

20. Earnest money left on deposit with the broker or lawyer is a
   a. credit to the seller.
   b. credit to the buyer.
   c. debit to the seller.
   d. debit to the buyer.

21. The buyers are assuming a mortgage loan that had a principal balance of $27,496 as of June 1. Interest is at 12 percent, payable in arrears. The June payment has not been made, and closing is on June 15. Which of the following is true as to the interest adjustment?
   a. Credit buyer $274.96; debit seller $274.95.
   b. Credit buyer $412.44; debit seller $412.44.
   c. Credit seller $137.48; debit buyer $137.48.
   d. No adjustment is necessary.

22. The calendar year's taxes amount to $1,800 and were paid ahead on January 1. If closing is set for June 15, which of the following is true?

    a. Credit seller $825; debit buyer $975.
    b. Credit seller $1,800; debit buyer $825.
    c. Credit buyer $975; debit seller $975.
    d. Credit seller $975; debit buyer $975.

23. Which of the following items is usually not adjusted between buyer and seller?

    a. Recording charges
    b. Property taxes
    c. Rents
    d. Interest on assumed mortgage

24. The seller collected June rent of $800 from the tenant in the upstairs apartment. At the closing on June 15

    a. credit buyer $400; debit seller $400.
    b. credit buyer $400; credit seller $400.
    c. debit buyer $400; credit seller $400.
    d. credit buyer $800; no debit to seller.

25. The O'Briens have been told to bring a cashier's check for the amount they will need to close on the house they're buying. Where can they get an estimate of money needed?

    a. The public records
    b. An abstractor
    c. The broker
    d. Their insurance agent

Real Estate Finance I

Bill and Maria want to buy a home together. They have never purchased a home before, but they read the real estate section of their local newspaper regularly. Even though they have read several articles about home mortgages, they find the many types of loans and rates confusing. The advice they get from relatives and friends is often conflicting and not helpful. What should they do?

Most home buyers report that they received guidance from a broker or salesperson in obtaining their mortgages. Keeping track of the ever-changing mortgage market is one of the biggest challenges for real estate licensees.

MORTGAGE DEFINED

A **mortgage** is a pledge of property given by a borrower as **security** for a loan. Some states recognize the lender as the owner of mortgaged land. These states are called **title theory** states. Connecticut, for example, is a title theory state.

New York, however, interprets a mortgage purely as a lien on real property and is called a **lien theory** state. If a mortgagor (borrower) defaults, the lender can foreclose the lien (generally through a court action), offer the property for sale and apply the funds received from the sale to reduce or pay off the debt.

▼ Loan Instruments

When property is to be mortgaged, the owner must execute, or sign, two separate instruments (sometimes combined into one form):

1. A **note** or **bond,** which is a *personal promise* to repay a loan. It acts as evidence of the promise to repay the debt. The promissory note signed by a borrower (known as the maker or payer) states the amount of the debt, the time and method of payment and the rate of interest. Figure 11.1 is an example of a note commonly used in some areas of New York State.
2. A **mortgage,** which is a pledge of property given by a borrower as **security** for a loan. The mortgage creates a lien as security for the debt. The *mortgagor* is the one who does the mortgaging, pledging real estate as security for a loan. The *mortgagee* accepts, takes and holds the mortgage and gives money in exchange. To help in keeping the terms straight, it is useful to note that *bOrrOwer,* like *mOrtgagOr,* contains two *Os; lEndEr* and *mortgagEE* each contain two *Es.*

   The mortgage document refers to the terms of the note and clearly establishes that the land is security for the debt. It identifies the lender as well as the borrower and includes an accurate legal description of the property. It should be signed by all owners of the property. It also sets forth the obligations of the borrower and the rights of the lender.

Figure 11.1   Note

NOTE

.... April 12 ...., 19 95 .... Albany ...., ... New York ....
                                                    [City]   [State]

.... 222 Kelly Avenue, Albany, New York 12203 ....
[Property Address]

1. BORROWER'S PROMISE TO PAY

In return for a loan that I have received, I promise to pay U.S. $ 79,000.00 .... (this amount is called "principal"), plus interest, to the order of the Lender. The Lender is .. First City Savings and Loan .... Association of Albany, New York .... I understand that the Lender may transfer this Note. The Lender or anyone who takes this Note by transfer and who is entitled to receive payments under this Note is called the "Note Holder."

2. INTEREST

Interest will be charged on unpaid principal until the full amount of principal has been paid. I will pay interest at a yearly rate of .... 9.5 ....%.

The interest rate required by this Section 2 is the rate I will pay both before and after any default described in Section 6(B) of this Note.

3. PAYMENTS

(A) Time and Place of Payments

I will pay principal and interest by making payments every month.

I will make my monthly payments on the .... 1st .. day of each month beginning on ... May 1 ...., 19 .. 95 .. I will make these payments every month until I have paid all of the principal and interest and any other charges described below that I may owe under this Note. My monthly payments will be applied to interest before principal. If, on .... April 1, 2025 ...., I still owe amounts under this Note, I will pay those amounts in full on that date, which is called the "maturity date."

I will make my monthly payments at ..... 130 North LaSalle Street, Albany, New York .... or at a different place if required by the Note Holder.

(B) Amount of Monthly Payments

My monthly payment will be in the amount of U.S. $ .. 664.29 ....

4. BORROWER'S RIGHT TO PREPAY

I have the right to make payments of principal at any time before they are due. A payment of principal only is known as a "prepayment." When I make a prepayment, I will tell the Note Holder in writing that I am doing so.

I may make a full prepayment or partial prepayments without paying any prepayment charge. The Note Holder will use all of my prepayments to reduce the amount of principal that I owe under this Note. If I make a partial

Figure 11.1 (continued)

prepayment, there will be no changes in the due date or in the amount of my monthly payment unless the Note Holder agrees in writing to those changes.

5. LOAN CHARGES

If a law, which applies to this loan and which sets maximum loan charges, is finally interpreted so that the interest or other loan charges collected or to be collected in connection with this loan exceed the permitted limits, then: (i) any such loan charge shall be reduced by the amount necessary to reduce the charge to the permitted limit; and (ii) any sums already collected from me which exceeded permitted limits will be refunded to me. The Note Holder may choose to make this refund by reducing the principal I owe under this Note or by making a direct payment to me. If a refund reduces principal, the reduction will be treated as a partial prepayment.

6. BORROWER'S FAILURE TO PAY AS REQUIRED

(A) Late Charge for Overdue Payments

If the Note Holder has not received the full amount of any monthly payment by the end of ......fifteen.... calendar days after the date it is due, I will pay a late charge to the Note Holder. The amount of the charge will be ....5..% of my overdue payment of principal and interest. I will pay this late charge promptly but only once on each late payment.

(B) Default

If I do not pay the full amount of each monthly payment on the date it is due, I will be in default.

(C) Notice of Default

If I am in default, the Note Holder may send me a written notice telling me that if I do not pay the overdue amount by a certain date, the Note Holder may require me to pay immediately the full amount of principal which has not been paid and all the interest that I owe on that amount. That date must be at least 30 days after the date on which the notice is delivered or mailed to me.

(D) No Waiver By Note Holder

Even if, at a time when I am in default, the Note Holder does not require me to pay immediately in full as described above, the Note Holder will still have the right to do so if I am in default at a later time.

(E) Payment of Note Holder's Costs and Expenses

If the Note Holder has required me to pay immediately in full as described above, the Note Holder will have the right to be paid back by me for all of its costs and expenses in enforcing this Note to the extent not prohibited by applicable law. Those expenses include, for example, reasonable attorneys' fees.

7. GIVING OF NOTICES

Unless applicable law requires a different method, any notice that must be given to me under this Note will be given by delivering it or by mailing it by first class mail to me at the Property Address above or at a different address if I give the Note Holder a notice of my different address.

Any notice that must be given to the Note Holder under this Note will be given by mailing it by first class mail to the Note Holder at the address stated in Section 3(A) above or at a different address if I am given a notice of that different address.

MULTISTATE FIXED RATE NOTE—Single Family—**FNMA/FHLMC UNIFORM INSTRUMENT**   Form 3200 12/83

In some areas of the country, and in certain situations, lenders prefer to use an instrument known as a *trust deed*, or *deed of trust*, rather than a mortgage. A trust deed conveys the real estate as security for the loan to a third party, called the *trustee*. In case of default the lender with a trust deed can gain possession of the property more promptly and more simply than can a lender who forecloses on a mortgage.

▼ **Duties of the Mortgagor**

The borrower's obligations usually include the following:

- Paying the debt as promised in the note
- Paying all real estate taxes on the property
- Maintaining adequate hazard insurance to protect the lender if the property is destroyed or damaged
- Obtaining the lender's authorization before making any major alterations
- Maintaining the property in good repair at all times

Failure to meet any of these obligations can result in a borrower's **default.** When this happens, the mortgage usually provides a grace period (30 days, for example) during which the borrower can meet the obligation and cure the default. If he or she does not do so, the lender has the right to foreclose the mortgage and collect on the note. The most frequent cause of default is the borrower's failure to pay monthly installments.

Most mortgages contain a late-payment clause. For one-family to six-family owner-occupied residences, New York allows a late-payment penalty 15 days after payment is due. An individual may charge a 2 percent penalty; a lending institution may charge 4 percent on government-backed mortgages, 5 percent on conventional loans.

▼ **Provisions for Default**

A mortgage may include an **acceleration clause** to assist the lender in a foreclosure. If a borrower defaults, the lender has the right to accelerate the debt—to declare the *entire* debt due and owing *immediately.*

Other clauses in a mortgage enable the lender to take care of the property in the event of the borrower's negligence or default. If the borrower does not pay taxes or insurance premiums or make necessary repairs on the property, for example, the lender may step in and do so to protect its security. Any money advanced by the lender to cure such defaults is either added to the unpaid debt or declared immediately due and owing from the borrower.

▼ **Foreclosure**

When a borrower defaults in making payments or in fulfilling any of the obligations set forth in the mortgage, the lender can enforce its rights through a **foreclosure,** with the property sold at public auction. The buyer at a foreclosure sale receives the property *free of the mortgage and all junior liens* but subject to any prior liens. (Any unpaid property taxes must be paid out of the proceeds of the sale.)

There are two general types of foreclosure proceedings—judicial and strict foreclosure. *Strict foreclosure,* in which the lender may regain title to the property, is rarely used. *Judicial foreclosure* is the procedure followed in most cases. On a borrower's default the lender may declare the whole debt immediately due and payable and ask the court to order a public sale, which is advertised. The real estate is sold to the highest bidder. The borrower has the right to redeem the property *until the moment of sale* by producing full payment including back interest and costs incurred in the foreclosure proceedings. In New York the defaulting borrower does not have the right to redeem the property after the foreclosure sale. The buyer at a foreclosure sale receives a deed signed by a court-appointed referee.

Deed in lieu of foreclosure. An alternative to foreclosure is for the lender to accept a *deed in lieu of foreclosure* from the borrower. This is sometimes known as a *friendly foreclosure* because it is by agreement rather than by civil action. The major disadvantage is that the mortgagee takes the real estate subject to all junior liens, whereas foreclosure eliminates all such liens. In addition, the IRS considers the amount of debt that was forgiven as taxable income to the borrower.

Deficiency judgment. If a foreclosure sale does not produce sufficient cash to pay the loan balance in full after deducting expenses and unpaid interest, the mortgagee may be entitled to seek a *personal judgment* against the signer of the note for the unpaid balance. Such a judgment is called a **deficiency judgment.** It may be obtained against the original borrower and any later owners of the property who assumed the debt by written agreement. If, on the other hand, there are any surplus proceeds from the foreclosure sale after the debt is paid off and expenses and subordinate liens are deducted, they are paid to the borrower.

▼ **Sale of Property That Is Mortgaged**

Anyone who purchases real estate and takes over the mortgage presently on it may take the property **subject to the mortgage** or may **assume the seller's mortgage** and *agree to pay* the debt. This technical distinction becomes important if the buyer later defaults and the mortgage is foreclosed.

When the property is sold *subject* to the mortgage, the purchaser is not personally obligated to pay the debt in full. The new owner has bought the real estate knowing that he or she should make the loan payments or risk losing the property through a foreclosure sale. If a foreclosure sale did not pay off the entire debt, however, the new owner would not be personally liable for the shortfall.

In contrast, when the new owner not only purchases the property subject to the mortgage but *assumes and agrees to pay* the debt, he or she becomes personally responsible. If the mortgage is foreclosed and the court sale does not bring enough to pay the debt in full, a deficiency judgment against both the assumptor and the original borrower can be obtained for the unpaid balance.

When a mortgage is being assumed or paid off early, the borrower requires a statement from the mortgagee detailing the amount currently due. This **reduction certificate** is often referred to as an *estoppel certificate.*

Alienation clause. Real estate lenders frequently wish to prevent future purchasers of property from assuming the existing loans. For this reason most lenders include an **alienation clause** (also known as a *resale clause* or *due-on-sale clause*) in the note. An alienation clause provides that on the sale of the property, the lender has the choice of either declaring the entire debt immediately due or permitting the buyer to assume the loan.

In New York State any mortgage is assumable unless the document contains a specific alienation clause.

Assignment of the mortgage. *A note or bond may be sold to a third party, or assignee.* (It is a negotiable instrument.) An **estoppel certificate** signed by the borrower will verify the amount owed and interest rate.

▼ **Recording of the Mortgage**

The mortgage document must be recorded in the recorder's office of the county in which the real estate is located. This gives notice to the world of the borrower's obligations and establishes the lien's priority over future mortgages or other liens.

First and second mortgages. Mortgages and other liens normally have priority in the order in which they have been recorded. A mortgage on land that has no prior mortgage lien on it is a *first mortgage.* When the owner of this land later places another mortgage for additional funds, the new mortgage becomes a *second mortgage,* or *junior lien,* when recorded. In recent years, the term home equity loan is used for what are really second mortgages.

The first mortgage has first claim to the value of the land pledged as security. The priority of mortgage liens may be changed by the execution of a *subordination agreement* if the first lender agrees to yield first place to the second lender.

▼ **Satisfaction of the Mortgage Lien**

When all payments have been made and the note paid in full, the mortgagor wants the public record to show that the debt has been paid and the lien satisfied. The lender is required to execute a *release of mortgage,* or **satisfaction of mortgage.**

This satisfaction should be entered in the public records to show that the mortgage lien has been removed from the property. According to New York law, financial institutions must file a satisfaction of mortgage within 45 days of a request to do so and must provide a copy to the mortgagor or the mortgagor's designee. Penalties can be imposed for noncompliance, and after a 90-day period the mortgagor may file an affidavit with the county recording officer that shows that the lien has been satisfied.

Types of Mortgages

Mortgages may be conventional or sponsored by a government agency, such as the Federal Housing Administration (FHA) or the Department of Veterans Affairs (VA). However, for many different types of mortgages, the source of the financing is the same.

▼ **Primary Sources of Real Estate Financing**

Funds used to finance the purchase of real estate come from a variety of sources that make up the **primary mortgage market**—lenders who supply funds directly to real estate borrowers. Some lenders then keep the loans in their own portfolios, whereas others later sell them to other investors in the secondary mortgage market (discussed more fully in Chapter 12).

Institutional lenders. Most of the loans made to finance real estate purchases are obtained from financial institutions designed to hold individuals' savings. Institutional lenders include savings associations, ("thrifts") commercial banks and savings banks.

Credit unions. Credit unions are cooperative organizations whose members place money in savings accounts. In the past most made only short-term consumer and home-improvement loans, but in recent years they have been branching out into mortgage loans for their own members.

Insurance companies. Amassing large sums of money from the premiums paid by policyholders, insurance companies invest much of it in real estate loans, most often large, long-term loans on commercial and industrial properties. They also purchase large blocks of FHA-insured and VA-guaranteed loans on the secondary mortgage market.

Mortgage banking companies. Mortgage bankers are not thrift institutions and offer neither checking nor savings accounts. They are licensed by the New York Banking Department. **Mortgage bankers** make real estate loans that later may be sold to investors (with the mortgage company receiving a fee if it continues to service the loans). Mortgage bankers originate a large percentage of all home loans. They are not mortgage *brokers.* Mortgage bankers must have a net worth of at least $250,000 and an existing line of credit of at least $1 million from a credit facility approved by the Superintendent of Banks. They must file a $50,000 surety bond with the Superintendent of Banks or establish a trust fund in the same amount that can be used to reimburse customers if it is determined that the mortgage banker has charged improper fees.

Mortgage brokers. Residential mortgage brokers act as intermediaries between lenders and borrowers. They are registered with the state banking department. They charge a fee, often of the borrower, for their services. The Superintendent of Banks may require that a mortgage broker obtain a surety bond or establish a trust fund in the amount of $25,000. Mortgage brokers may originate FHA loans.

The State of New York Mortgage Agency. Sonny Mae (SONYMA) provides lower-interest loans for specific purposes in specific locations. Loans with low down payments are made through local lending institutions to first-time home buyers. Income and home price limits vary from one region to another but are usually in the moderate category. In designated target areas, higher income limits apply, and the purchaser need not be a first-time buyer. The program varies from time to time; information is available by mail from SONYMA, 260 Madison Avenue, New York NY 10016, or by phone at 1-800-382-HOME.

The Rural Economic and Community Development Administration. Formerly the Farmer's Home Administration, this federal agency under the Department of Agriculture channels credit to rural residents. Loan programs fall into two categories: (1) guaranteed loans made and serviced by a private lender and guaranteed by the agency and (2) insured loans that are made and serviced directly by the agency. For low-income first-time home buyers in rural areas, mortgage interest may be subsidized and be as low as 1 percent. Only modest residences are eligible. The address of a local office and further information are available from the Rural Economic and Community Development Administration, New York State Office, at 1-315-423-5302.

Payment Plans

Among the most basic words needed to discuss mortgages efficiently are *down payment, loan-to-value ratio, equity, interest, servicing* and *principal.*

The buyer who has only $10,000 to give a seller as a **down payment** on a $100,000 home will have to borrow the rest with a mortgage loan. If $90,000 is being borrowed on property worth $100,000, the loan is said to have a 90 percent **loan-to-value (LTV) ratio** (amount borrowed divided by the property's value). **Loan servicing** is provided by the institution that collects and credits payments, issues monthly or annual reports on the status of the loan to the borrower and handles contact with the borrower.

After the transaction has closed, the buyers will have $10,000 **equity** in the home, *equity* being defined as the amount the owner would receive if the property were sold and all liens against it paid off. In a few years, if the loan has been paid down to $89,000 and the property's value has increased to $110,000, the owner's equity would amount to $21,000 ($110,000 value, minus $89,000 **principal** still owed).

Interest is a charge made by a lender for the use of money. Interest rates charged by lending institutions vary as changes occur in the availability of money to lend.

Low down payments. For years home buyers have received help in obtaining low-down-payment mortgage loans through insurance and guarantees from the FHA, the VA and SONYMA. In addition, private mortgage insurance companies offer programs to help those who need high LTV ratios on conventional (non–government-backed) loans. The various types of loans are discussed in more detail in Chapter 12.

▼ **Types of Amortization**

Most mortgage loans are **amortized loans.** Payments over a term of 15 to 30 years are set high enough to include not only interest due but also a portion of the principal owed. At the end of the term the full amount of the principal will have been paid off. The process is known as *amortization of the debt.*

Most amortized mortgage loans are paid in monthly installments. These payments may be computed based on different mortgage plans.

The most common plan requires that the mortgagor pay the same amount in each payment period, usually each month. The lender credits each payment first to the interest due, and then applies the rest to reduce the amount borrowed (the principal). Each month, as the principal is reduced, not quite as much interest is due, so more of the payment can be used to whittle down the debt. At the end of the **term,** that is, the originally scheduled number of years, the entire debt has been paid off. This is known as a *fully amortized loan.*

A mortgagor may choose a *straight payment plan* that calls for payments of *interest only,* with the principal to be paid in full at the end of the loan term. This is known as a **straight** or **term loan.** Such plans are generally used for home improvement loans or construction loans rather than for residential first mortgage loans.

A combination of the two plans already mentioned is a *partially amortized loan.* Monthly payments may include enough to pay down the debt for a specific number of years. At the end of that period the entire remaining principal is due in a final payment, known as a **balloon payment.**

Adjustable-rate mortgages (ARMs) shift the risk or reward of changing interest rates from the lender to the borrower. As rates rise and fall, changes are made in the monthly payment or (occasionally) in the remaining principal.

In recent years some mortgages have offered combinations of fixed and adjustable rates in ways that may fit certain borrowers' own financial situations and future plans. For example, **biweekly mortgages** involve payments every two weeks instead of monthly. This schedule produces the equivalent of 13 monthly payments a year. Because of the compounding effect of more-frequent principal reduction, a 30-year loan can be paid off in 20 or 21 years. Most biweekly loans involve automatic payment from the borrower's checking or savings account.

▼ **Interest**

A lender charges a certain percentage of the principal as interest each year the debt is outstanding. The amount of interest due on any payment date is calculated by figuring total yearly interest based on the unpaid balance and dividing that figure by the number of payments made each year.

On an amortized loan of $100,000 for 30 years at an annual interest rate of 11 percent, the amount due after the first month's payment has been made can be calculated as follows:

a. $100,000 × 11% = $11,000 annual interest
b. $11,000 ÷ 12 months = $916.67 first month's interest
c. $952.34 monthly payment (will amortize the loan in 30 years)
d. −$916.67 first month's interest due
e. $35.67 first month's principal reduction
f. $100,000 principal due at start of month
g. −$35.67 principal repayment
h. $99,964.33 principal due at end of first month

The following month, because less is now owed, not quite so much interest will be due, and the principal can be reduced by a slightly larger amount. Table 11.1 shows an *amortization schedule* for the first eight months of this 360-payment loan.

Interest is usually due at the end of each payment period (payment in arrears, as opposed to payment in advance). The principal and interest on a 30-year mortgage is shown in Figure 11.2. Amortization formulas are complicated. Most real estate practitioners carry small books of amortization tables or special calculators with built-in tables.

Usury. The maximum rate of interest that may be charged on mortgage loans is set by state law. Charging interest in excess of this rate is called **usury**. New York has a *floating usury rate*. The maximum rate that may be charged is adjusted up or down at specific intervals by the New York State Banking Board.

Sellers taking back **purchase-money mortgages** always have been exempt from usury limits. (Purchase-money mortgages secure promissory notes given by buyers to sellers.) Loans in the amount of $2.5 million or more and loans made to corporations are generally exempt from usury laws, except for New York's criminal usury limit of 25 percent on loans up to $2.5 million. Lending institutions are also exempt up to the criminal usury limit. *Other individuals making mortgage loans, however, are still bound by the New York usury limit.*

Table 11.1 Amortization Table

Loan Amortization Schedule　　　　　　　　　　　　　　　**Simple Interest Loan**

Principal	$100,000
Monthly payment	$ 952.34
Annual interest rate	11.000
Term in months	360

Payment	Old Balance	Interest Payment	Principal Payment	Total Payment	New Balance
1	$100,000.00	$916.67	$35.67	$952.34	$99,964.33
2	99,964.34	916.34	35.99	952.34	99,928.35
3	99,928.35	916.01	36.32	952.34	99,892.03
4	99,892.03	915.68	36.65	952.34	99,855.38
5	99,855.38	915.34	36.99	952.34	99,818.39
6	99,818.39	915.00	37.33	952.34	99,781.06
7	99,781.06	914.66	37.67	952.34	99,743.39
8	99,743.39	914.31	38.02	952.34	99,705.37

Such an individual might be an employer making a mortgage loan to an employee or a real estate broker lending the buyer money to help with a sale (which the broker should not do without the consent of the seller). In those cases, the person making the loan should check with the state banking department to make sure the interest charged is within current limits.

Points. When a new mortgage is placed, the lending institution may ask for a lump-sum payment of extra prepaid interest in the form of up-front **points.** *Each point is 1 percent of the new loan.* On an $80,000 loan each point would be $800; a charge of two points would total $1,600. Payment of points is a one-time affair, usually at the time of closing but occasionally at mortgage application or issuance of a mortgage commitment by the lender. Points may be paid by either the buyer or the seller, depending on the terms of the sales contract.

Annual percentage rate. If a mortgage loan is made at 10 percent but also requires three points in prepaid interest or other service fees, the loan really costs more than 10 percent. The exact rate depends on the length of the proposed mortgage and requires some complicated calculations. The rate, which would total slightly more than 10 percent, is known as the **annual percentage rate (APR).** Federal regulations (Regulation Z of the Truth-in-Lending Law, discussed in Chapter 12) require that the borrower be advised of the APR in advertisements and in writing when a loan is placed. It enables borrowers to compare widely differing mortgage plans.

Buydowns. With some mortgage plans, lending institutions are willing to lower the interest rate in return for payment of extra points. The arrangement is known as a **buydown.** Many buydowns lower the rate for a period of time, for example, by 3 percent the first year of the loan, 2 percent the second year and 1 percent the third year (3-2-1-buydown). Other buydowns last for the whole term of the loan.

Figure 11.2   Level-Payment Amortized Loan

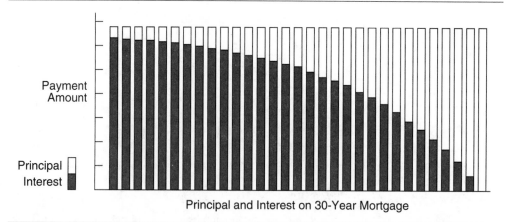

Principal and Interest on 30-Year Mortgage

▼ **Tax-Deductible Interest Payments**

Taxpayers may deduct on income tax returns the interest paid on mortgage loans up to a total of $1 million if borrowed to acquire and/or improve both a first and a second (vacation) residence. Interest on additional borrowing (second mortgages, home equity loans) of up to $100,000 also qualifies for income tax deduction, no matter what the money is used for. Homeowners also may deduct all property taxes, prepaid interest points (whether paid by buyer or seller) and any mortgage prepayment penalties. Somewhat different income tax regulations apply to mortgage loans on investment property and to refinance mortgages.

▼ **Prepayment**

Some mortgage notes charge a **prepayment premium,** or **penalty,** if the loan is paid off before its full term. For a one- to six-family dwelling used as a principal residence, the maximum prepayment premium a lender can charge in New York is 90 days' interest on the unpaid balance if the loan is paid in full during the first year. No penalty can be charged after the loan is a year old. No prepayment penalties may be charged on FHA or VA loans.

▼ **Tax and Insurance Reserves**

Many lenders require that borrowers provide a reserve, or escrow, fund to meet future real estate taxes and insurance premiums. When the mortgage loan is made, the borrower starts the reserve by depositing funds to cover partial payment of the following year's tax bill. The insurance premium reserve is started with the deposit of one-twelfth of the annual tax and insurance premium liability. After that the monthly payments will include principal, interest and escrow for tax and insurance reserves **(PITI).**

To be certain that these important bills are being paid, the lender accumulates the borrower's money in the escrow account. Property tax bills and insurance premium bills are sent directly to the lending institution, which pays them and renders an accounting to the borrower. The borrower is entitled to 2 percent interest on the money thus held. When the mortgage loan is eventually paid off, any money remaining in the escrow account is returned to the borrower.

RESPA, the federal *Real Estate Settlement Procedures Act,* limits the amount of tax and insurance reserves a lender may require. RESPA is discussed in Chapter 10.

Key Terms

acceleration clause	mortgage
adjustable-rate mortgage (ARM)	mortgage bankers
alienation clause	mortgage broker
amortized loan	mortgagee
annual percentage rate (APR)	mortgagor
assuming a mortgage	note
balloon payment	points
biweekly mortgage	prepayment premium (penalty)
bond	primary mortgage market
buydown	principal
default	PITI
deficiency judgment	purchase-money mortgage
down payment	reduction certificate
equity	satisfaction of mortgage
estoppel certificate	Sonny Mae (SONYMA)
foreclosure	straight (term) loan
interest	subject to a mortgage
lien theory	term
loan servicing	title theory
loan-to-value (LTV) ratio	usury

Summary

Mortgage loans involve a borrower, called the mortgagor, and a lender, called the mortgagee.

The borrower is required to execute a note agreeing to repay the debt and a mortgage placing a lien on the real estate to secure the note. The mortgage document is recorded in the public record to give notice to the world of the lender's interest. Payment in full entitles the borrower to a satisfaction, or release, which is recorded to clear the lien from the public records.

Default by the borrower may result in acceleration of payments and a foreclosure sale. If the proceeds fail to clear the debt, the mortgagee may seek a deficiency judgment against the borrower. A subsequent owner who assumes the loan is also personally responsible and liable to a deficiency judgment; one who takes the property subject to the mortgage is not.

The note for most common forms of mortgage loans provides for amortization, the gradual repayment of principal borrowed along with interest. The note also sets the rate of interest the borrower must pay as a charge for borrowing the money.

Charging more than the maximum interest rate allowed by state statute is called usury and is illegal. Sellers taking back mortgages are exempt from usury limits.

1. The Scotts' new home cost $150,000, and they borrowed $135,000 on a mortgage loan, paying $15,000 in cash as a down payment. That $15,000 now represents their
   a. loan-to-value ratio.
   b. equity.
   c. qualifying ratio.
   d. underwriting.

2. A mortgage broker generally
   a. brings borrower and lender together.
   b. makes mortgage loans using investor's funds.
   c. provides credit and appraisal reports.
   d. places packages of loans in the secondary market.

3. A borrower obtains a $76,000 mortgage loan at 11.5 percent interest. If the monthly payments of $772.52 are credited first to interest and then to principal, what will the balance of the principal be after the borrower makes the first payment?
   a. $75,227.48   c. $75,524.56
   b. $75,923.48   d. $75,955.81

4. When Tiny Tim buys his house, Old Scrooge allows monthly mortgage payments to be figured on a 30-year basis so that Tim can handle them. At the end of the fifth year, however, Scrooge wants the whole remaining debt paid off in a
   a. graduated payment.
   b. shared-equity payment.
   c. balloon payment.
   d. blanket payment.

5. With some exceptions a homeowner may take as an income tax deduction the
   a. mortgage insurance premium.
   b. mortgage interest paid.
   c. property insurance premium.
   d. All of the above

6. New York's usury limits do not apply to interest on mortgage loans made by
   a. sellers.
   b. individuals other than sellers.
   c. regular lending institutions.
   d. the Rural Economic and Community Development Administration.

7. John Reilly sells his home for $200,000 and agrees to pay three points to his buyer's lending institution. The buyer is putting 20 percent down on the property. How much will the points cost John?
   a. $900   c. $4,800
   b. $1,600   d. $6,000

8. A lending institution may require that the buyer send in an extra monthly payment to cover future bills for
   a. property taxes and insurance premiums.
   b. major repairs.
   c. possible default in monthly payments.
   d. All of the above

9. The buyer of a $96,000 property is offered a mortgage with 10 percent down and a loan origination fee of 1.5 percent. Disregarding other possible closing costs, how much cash must the buyer produce to complete the transaction?

   a. $1,290
   b. $1,440
   c. $9,600
   d. $10,896

10. Bill and Maria are looking for a mortgage loan. They will be least likely to apply to a

   a. savings and loan association.
   b. mortgage banking company.
   c. insurance company.
   d. credit union.

96,000
9600
――――――
86 400 × 1.5

9600
864
432
――――
10,896

Real Estate Finance II

Bill and Maria want to buy a home together, but they're not married, Bill is self-employed and they have only $10,000 available for a down payment. They assume those are three reasons to be turned down for a mortgage loan. Are they right?

Keeping track of the changing standards for loan qualifications is vital. A real estate agent who does not know how much money his or her customer will be able to borrow does not know how expensive a home that customer can afford to buy.

Types of Loans

▼ Private Mortgages

A borrower and lender can tailor financing to suit the type of transaction and the financial needs of both parties. Especially in times of tight or expensive mortgage money, such creative financing gains prominence.

Imputed interest. A purchase-money mortgage held by the seller is exempt from usury limitations on interest rate. If seller financing is at an artificially low interest rate, however, the IRS will invoke **imputed interest;** that is, it will "impute" a higher rate and tax the recipient accordingly. The seller must charge at least 9 percent or a rate equal to the applicable federal rate (AFR), whichever is lower. The AFR is set monthly by the federal government. A seller who charges less will be taxed as if income were received at the required rate. An exception is made for certain transfers of vacant land within a family.

Reverse annuity loans. A **reverse annuity loan** is one in which regular monthly payments are made to the borrower based on the equity the homeowner has in the home. A reverse mortgage allows senior citizens on fixed incomes to tap the equity buildup in their homes without having to sell. The loan accumulates interest and is eventually paid from the sale of the property or from the mortgagor's estate on his or her death. New York allows such mortgages where the homeowner is at least 60 years old. The American Association of Retired Persons (AARP) has taken an active role in pioneering these loans, and the federal government has backed a reverse mortgage called a *home equity conversion mortgage* (HECM), intended for those 62 or older.

Temporary loans. The homeowner who is selling one residence and buying another may find it necessary to buy the new home before the closing date on the present one. In that situation a temporary loan, variously called a **bridge loan, a swing loan** or **interim financing** may be arranged.

Shared-equity mortgages. Under the **shared-equity mortgage** the purchaser receives help with the down payment, a low interest rate or assistance with monthly payments from a partner. The "partner" may be a lending institution, the seller or a relative. Typically the partner receives a share of the profit when the property is sold.

Package loans. **Package loans** include not only the real estate but also appliances and furniture on the premises. In recent years this kind of loan has been used to finance furnished condominium units.

Open-end mortgages. **Open-end mortgages** (not to be confused with an "open mortgage") are used by borrowers to obtain additional funds to improve property. The borrower "opens" the mortgage to increase the debt after the debt has been reduced by payments over a period of time.

Blanket mortgages. **Blanket mortgages** cover more than one parcel or lot and are often used to finance subdivision developments. When one parcel or lot is sold, the borrower makes a partial payment to release it from the overall mortgage.

Wraparound mortgages. **Wraparound mortgages** frequently are used to refinance or finance a purchase when an existing mortgage is to be retained. The buyer gives a large mortgage to the seller, who will collect payments on the new loan, usually at a higher interest rate, and continue to make payments on the old loan. *Wraparound mortgages, like all unusual arrangements, require careful study by attorneys. The broker who negotiates one should exercise special care not to give legal advice.*

Swing loans. A **swing loan** is a short-term loan that enables the borrower to buy a new property based on the strength of the equity the borrower has in property the borrower is currently selling. The loan "swings" on the equity the borrower has in the existing property.

Purchase-money mortgages. A **purchase-money mortgage** is any mortgage placed when property is bought. This is in contrast to refinancing, further borrowing after the realty is already owned. Strictly speaking, the term *purchase-money mortgage* means a mortgage loan made by the seller to enable the buyer to purchase ("seller take-back financing"). A purchase-money mortgage may be used to cover a portion of the purchase price or may be a first mortgage to finance the entire price.

Construction loans. Also called *building loan agreements,* **construction loans** are made to finance the construction of improvements on real estate. A construction loan can be difficult to secure unless the applicant works through a recognized builder or contractor. Payments are made on a scheduled basis to the general contractor or owner for work that has been completed since the previous payment. The lender usually inspects the work before each payment. This kind of mortgage loan generally bears a higher interest rate because of risks assumed by the lender. It is short term. The borrower arranges for a permanent loan (also known as an *end,* or *take-out, loan*) when the work is completed.

Land contracts. As discussed in Chapter 9, real estate can be purchased under a land contract. Real estate is often sold on contract when mortgage financing is not available or is too expensive or when the purchaser does not have a sufficient down payment.

Sale-and-leaseback arrangements. **Sale-and-leaseback agreements** are sometimes used as a means of financing large commercial or industrial plants. The land and building used by the seller are sold to an investor such as an insurance company. The investor then leases back the real estate to the seller, who continues to conduct business on the property as a tenant. This enables a business firm that has money invested in a plant to free that money for working capital. The buyer benefits from an assured long-term tenant. Real estate brokers should consult legal and tax experts when involved in this type of complex transaction.

Home equity loans. A form of second mortgage, the **home equity loan** has grown in popularity in recent years. Homeowners whose property has appreciated in value may borrow up to new loan-to-value (LTV) ratios or, in one popular version, establish a line of credit that is based on the equity position in their home, borrowing against it as they choose.

Bridge loan. This is a short-term loan used to "bridge" the gap between the termination of one loan (such as a construction loan) and the beginning of another loan (the permanent take-out loan). It also may be used to finance the conversion of an apartment house to a condominium. A bridge loan is sometimes referred to as *gap financing*.

> **MORTGAGE LOANS HAVE SEVERAL CLASSIFICATIONS**
> - Conventional loans
> - Government-backed loans
> - Loans direct from the government
> - Private loans

Methods of Finance

Mortgage loans fall into several classifications:

- Conventional loans are those arranged entirely between borrower and lending institution.
- Government-backed loans include those insured by the FHA or guaranteed by the VA. With both types the actual loan comes from a local lending institution.
- Loans directly from the government include State of New York Mortgage Agency (SONYMA) mortgages and Farmer's Home Administration (FmHA) loans.
- Private loans are those made by individuals, often the seller of the property or a relative of the buyer.

▼ Conventional Loans

In making **conventional loans,** lending institutions set their own standards, governed always by banking regulations. As a result a variety of mortgage plans is often offered, and some flexibility is occasionally available. A conventional loan may be useful where a short processing time is needed or where an unusual house or unusual buyer is involved. Conventional loans are also popular when interest rates for mortgage loans are low. Conventional mortgages may be fixed rate, adjustable rate or a combination of plans.

Most fixed-rate conventional mortgages are not assumable by a subsequent buyer of the property; some adjustable-rate mortgages are assumable, but only when the buyer can prove financial qualification.

Private mortgage insurance. In general, conventional loans call for higher down payments (lower LTV ratio) than government-backed mortgages. Banking theory holds that it risks depositors' money to lend more than 80 percent of the value of real estate. With any down payment below 20 percent, therefore, a conventional loan in New York State must be accompanied by **private mortgage insurance (PMI).** The borrower pays a yearly premium (or, optionally, a lump sum at closing) for insurance that protects the lender in case of loss after a foreclosure. New York State law requires that the lender discontinue collecting PMI premiums when the loan has been paid down to 75 percent of the value of the property.

Adjustable-rate mortgages. Until the early 1980s almost all mortgages were fixed-rate. As interest rates began to skyrocket, lenders found themselves locked into unprofitable long-term commitments with money loaned out at rates like 5, 6 and 7 percent, far below the then-current cost of money. This led to serious problems for lending institutions, and many were reluctant to make any further fixed-interest loans, even at high rates.

Out of a chaotic variety of new mortgage instruments, the adjustable-rate mortgage (ARM) emerged and became a national standard. As interest rates rose, borrowers across the country increasingly chose ARMs. The ARM shifts the risk of rising interest rates to the borrower, who also stands to benefit if rates drop during the period of the loan. When interest rates fall, on the other hand, most new borrowers choose to lock in fixed-rate loans.

The vocabulary of ARMs includes the following:

- *Adjustment period:* The anniversary on which interest rate adjustments may be made. Most borrowers elect one-year adjustments, but they might be made more frequently or only after three or five years.
- *Index:* The interest rate on the loan changes following an increase or decrease in a national indicator, or **index,** of current rates. The most commonly chosen index is the rate paid on one-year U.S. Treasury bills. Next in popularity is a slower-changing index, the 11th District Federal Home Loan Bank Average Cost of Funds.
- *Margin:* The borrower pays a specific percentage above the index. That percentage is known as the **margin.** If Treasury bills were selling at 8 percent interest, for example, the borrower with a 2 percent margin over Treasury bills would be charged 10 percent.
- *Cap:* The loan agreement may set a **cap** of, for example, 2 percent on any upward adjustment. If interest rates (as reflected by the index) went up 3 percent by the time of adjustment, the interest rate could be raised only 2 percent. Depending on the particular mortgage, the extra 1 percent might be treated one of three ways:
  1. It could be saved by the lender to be used at the next adjustment period, even if rates had fallen in the meantime.
  2. It could be absorbed by the lender with no future consequences to the borrower.
  3. It could be added to the amount borrowed so that the principal would increase instead of decreasing (negative amortization).
- *Ceiling:* A **ceiling** (sometimes called a *lifetime cap*) is a maximum allowable interest rate. Typically a mortgage may offer a five-point ceiling. If the interest rate started at 8 percent, it could never go beyond 13 percent, no matter what happened to national rates.

- *Negative amortization:* **Negative amortization** could result from an artificially low initial interest rate. It also could follow a hike in rates larger than a cap allows the lender to impose. Not all mortgage plans include the possibility of negative amortization. Sometimes the lender agrees to absorb any shortfalls. The possibility must always be explored, however, when an ARM is being evaluated.
- *Convertibility:* Some ARMs are **convertible,** that is, the borrower may choose to change to a fixed-rate mortgage at then-current interest levels. With some plans any favorable moment may be chosen. More commonly the option is available on the third, fourth or fifth anniversary of the loan. The borrower may be charged a slightly higher interest rate in return for this option.
- *Initial interest rate:* With many loan plans the rate during the first year, or the first adjustment period, is set artificially low (discounted) to induce the borrower to enter into the agreement ("teaser" rate). Buyers who plan to be in a home for only a few years may be delighted with such arrangements, especially if no adjustment is planned for several years. Other borrowers, however, may end up with negative amortization and payment shock at the first adjustment.
- *Assumability:* Many ARMs are assumable by a financially qualified next owner of the property, with the lender's approval and the payment of service fees.

To help consumers compare different ARMs, lenders must give anyone considering a specific ARM a uniform disclosure statement that lists and explains indexes, history of past interest rate changes and other information. A method for calculating the highest possible payment is included. The disclosures must be furnished before the loan applicant has paid any nonrefundable application fee.

▼ FHA-Insured Loans

The Federal Housing Administration (FHA), which operates under the Department of Housing and Urban Development (HUD), does not lend money itself. Rather it insures mortgage loans made by approved lending institutions. It does not insure the property, but it does insure the lender against loss. The common term **FHA loan,** then, refers to a loan that is not made by the agency but insured by it.

Because the federal government insures the lending institution against loss, borrowers can place FHA mortgages with very low down payments.

FHA 203(b). The most widely used FHA mortgage is known as *203(b)* and may be placed on one- to four-family residences. The following are among the requirements set up by the FHA before it will insure a loan.

Owners/occupants. The loan is available only to an owner/occupant, someone who intends to live in the property as a primary residence. Like many FHA regulations, this requirement has been changed over the years. At one time investors could place FHA loans, and second homes were sometimes eligible.

Mortgage insurance premium. In addition to paying interest, the borrower is charged a lump sum as a **mortgage insurance premium (MIP).** This amount is payable in cash at the closing or may be financed for the term of the loan. If the loan is subsequently paid off within the early years of the loan, some refund of unused premium is due the borrower from HUD.

On FHA loans made since July 1991, borrowers are charged the initial lump-sum premium at closing and also .05 percent MIP (mortgage insurance premium) per month as interest for a number of years, depending on the size of the down payment.

Estimate of value. The real estate must be evaluated by an FHA-approved appraiser. The maximum loan will be a percentage of the appraised value. If the purchase price is higher than the FHA appraisal, the buyer must pay the difference in a higher cash down payment or may decide not to purchase. On Section 203(b) loans, minimum down payment requirements are

- for property appraised at less than $50,000, 3 percent. A house appraised at $40,000 would require $1,200 down with a $38,800 mortgage possible. A 3 percent down payment means a 97 percent LTV ratio.
- for property appraised at more than $50,000, the requirement is 3 percent down on the first $25,000 and 5 percent on amounts between $25,000 and $125,000. The borrower pays 10 percent down on anything above $125,000. A house appraised at $75,000 would require $2,500 down for the first $50,000, and $1,250 (5 percent) for the remaining $25,000, for a total down payment of $3,750.

Note that FHA borrowers are allowed to finance a portion of their closing costs. The amount of the financed closing costs is added to the base loan amount. Therefore, the total amount borrowed may exceed the purchase price of the property in some cases.

The FHA sets top limits on its loans, depending on price levels in different areas. Its loan maximums vary from one county to another within the state. The highest levels within the state are set for areas in and around New York City, in parts of Long Island and in Tioga County. The goal is to keep the top loan within 95 percent of the median sales price in each community, with higher levels set for multiple dwellings. The FHA raises its limits from time to time to meet changing conditions.

Repairs. The FHA may stipulate repair requirements to be completed before it will issue mortgage insurance on a specific property. Certain energy-saving improvements may be financed along with an FHA mortgage.

Assumability. Older FHA loans may be assumed by the next owner of the property with no change in interest rate, no credit check on the buyer and only a small charge for paperwork. The assumptor could be a nonoccupant/investor. The original borrower is not released from liability, however, unless the new borrower is willing to go through a formal assumption, which involves the lender's approval of credit and income.

For FHA loans made after December 15, 1989, the buyer wishing to assume the mortgage must be a prospective owner/occupant and prove financial qualification; the original borrower is then relieved of liability. Optionally, the new borrower may pass a simple credit check and the property a new appraisal, with the original borrower sharing joint liability for five years after the assumption. After that time, if payments are current, the original borrower has no further liability for the debt.

Other FHA programs. Among other FHA programs, which may or may not be handled by a particular local lender at any given time, are ARMs and special plans intended for veterans, for rehabilitation of housing being purchased and for no-down-payment purchase of modest homes. Other FHA programs are sometimes available to finance mobile homes, manufactured housing and condominiums.

The program known as 203(k) allows money to be borrowed to cover both the purchase and rehabilitation of a house in need of substantial repair.

▼ **VA-Guaranteed Loans**

The Department of Veterans Affairs (VA), formerly the Veterans Administration, can guarantee lending institutions against loss on mortgage loans to eligible veterans. Because the VA guarantees part of the loan, no down payment is required (though individual lenders may sometimes ask for a small down payment). Although no top limit is set for the loan, the guarantee is for up to $50,750, which in practice dictates a loan of up to $203,000.

VA mortgages are intended only for owner-occupied property, owned by veterans or veterans and their spouses, and may be placed on one- to four-family residences. While the guarantee comes from the federal government, the loan itself is made by a local lending institution. The veteran pays a funding fee directly to the VA at closing. The amount of the funding fee depends on the size of the down payment.

- No down payment: 1.25 percent
- Down payment between 5 and 10 percent: .75 percent
- 10 percent or more down payment: .50 percent
- Assumptions of VA loans: .50 percent

Eligibility. The right to a VA guarantee does not expire. To qualify, a veteran must have a discharge that is "other than dishonorable" and the required length of service.

- For those in the National Guard or the reserves, six years' service
- For those who enlisted before September 7, 1980, at least 90 days' continuous active service since September 16, 1940 (or 90 days' service during a war)
- For those who first enlisted after September 7, 1980, two years' active duty
- Reservists called up for at least 90 days during the Persian Gulf War, whether or not they went overseas.

The veteran who applies for a VA loan must furnish a certificate of eligibility, which can be obtained by writing to:

VA Regional Office
Federal Building
111 West Huron Street   or
Buffalo, NY 14202
1-800-827-0619

VA Regional Office
252 Seventh Avenue
New York, NY 10001
1-800-827-8954

Veterans who have used some or all of their eligibility to guarantee one loan sometimes can place another VA mortgage. Eligibility may still be available if

- the first loan used only part of the guarantee,
- the original VA loan has been paid off and the home sold or
- the original VA loan was formally assumed by another veteran.

The widow or widower of a veteran who died of a service-connected disability and who has not remarried may use the veteran's eligibility.

Qualified veterans' home loan entitlement will be restored one time only if the veteran has repaid the prior VA loan in full but has not disposed of the property securing that loan. If veterans wish to use their VA entitlement again, they must dispose of all property previously financed with a VA loan, including the property not disposed of under the "one time only" provision.

Assumability. Any VA mortgage loan made before March 1, 1988, may be assumed by the next owner of the property, who need not be a veteran and need not prove qualification to the lender or the VA. For loans made after March 1, 1988, the assumptor (who need not be a veteran) must prove creditworthiness, and the original borrower is free of future liability.

▼ **Government Backing via the Secondary Market**

Earlier, we discussed lenders in the primary mortgage market; they originate loans directly to borrowers. Some keep the loans in their own portfolios, but other primary lenders may sell packages of loans to large investors in the **secondary market.** A lender may wish to sell a number of loans when it needs more money to meet the mortgage demands in its area. The federal government is active in the secondary mortgage market.

A major source of secondary mortgage market activity is a warehousing agency, which purchases mortgage loans and assembles them into large packages of loans for resale to investors such as insurance companies and pension funds. The major warehousing agencies are the Federal National Mortgage Association (FNMA), the Government National Mortgage Association (GNMA) and the Federal Home Loan Mortgage Corporation (FHLMC).

When these three institutions were first created, they were easily distinguishable by the type of mortgages they purchased. Originally, FNMA purchased mortgages from commercial banks, GNMA purchased FHA-insured and VA-guaranteed mortgages and FHLMC purchased mortgages from savings and loan associations. Over time, the different organizations became empowered to purchase a greater variety of mortgage loans, and today FNMA and FHLMC can buy a variety of mortgage loans from a variety of different financial institutions. Generally, however, GNMA still purchases FHA-insured and VA-guaranteed mortgages.

Federal National Mortgage Association. The **FNMA,** often referred to as **Fannie Mae,** is (despite its name) a privately owned corporation. It raises funds to purchase loans by selling government-guaranteed FNMA bonds.

Mortgage bankers are actively involved with FNMA, originating loans and selling them to FNMA while retaining the servicing functions. FNMA is the nation's largest purchaser of mortgages.

When Fannie Mae talks, lenders listen. Because FNMA eventually purchases one mortgage out of every ten, it has great influence on lending policies. When Fannie Mae announces that it will buy a certain type of loan, local lending institutions often change their own regulations to meet the requirements. When lenders are experimenting with new types of loans, a Fannie Mae announcement can standardize the innovative mortgage plans and bring order out of chaos.

Government National Mortgage Association. The common name for **GNMA** is **Ginnie Mae.** The *Ginnie Mae pass-through certificate* lets small investors buy a share in a pool of mortgages that provides for a monthly "pass-through" of principal and interest payments directly to the certificate holder.

Federal Home Loan Mortgage Corporation. **FHLMC** or **Freddie Mac,** also provides a secondary market for mortgage loans. Freddie Mac buys mortgages, pools them and sells bonds with the mortgages as security.

Most lenders use standardized mortgage application and other forms that are accepted by Freddie Mac and Fannie Mae.

Nonconforming Loans. When Fannie Mae and Freddie Mac announce that they will buy loans only up to a certain size (recently at more than $200,000), many local lenders set that as their own limit. Loans higher than Fannie's or Freddie's maximum loan limit are known as **jumbo loans.** The borrower who wants to place one would search for a local lending institution that either sells jumbo mortgages to private investors or makes portfolio loans, lending its own money and taking mortgages it intends to keep and collect without selling them to secondary investors. A jumbo loan usually carries a slightly higher rate of interest.

Nonconforming mortgages do not have to meet uniform underwriting standards, and can be flexible in their guidelines. The borrower with an unusual credit situation or a unique house may need a nonconforming loan. A lending institution may want such loans at one time but not at other times. Following the rapidly changing mortgage market is often the greatest part of a real estate broker's work.

Financing Legislation

The federal government regulates the lending practices of mortgage lenders through the Truth-in-Lending Law, Equal Credit Opportunity Act and Real Estate Settlement Procedures Act.

▼ Regulation Z

The Truth-in-Lending Law, enforced through **Regulation Z,** requires that credit institutions inform borrowers of the true cost of obtaining credit so that the borrower can compare the costs of various lenders and avoid the uninformed use of credit. All real estate transactions made for personal or agricultural purposes are covered. The regulation does not apply to business or commercial loans.

Regulation Z requires that the customer be fully informed of all finance charges, as well as the true annual interest rate, before a transaction is consummated. In the case of a mortgage loan made to finance the purchase of a dwelling, the lender must compute and disclose the annual percentage rate (APR) in a written Truth-in-Lending statement provided to the mortgagor.

Three-day right of rescission. In the case of most consumer credit transactions covered by Regulation Z, the borrower has three days in which to rescind the transaction merely by notifying the lender. This right of rescission does not apply to residential purchase-money first mortgage loans, but does apply to refinances. In an emergency the right to rescind may be waived in writing to prevent a delay in funding.

Advertising. Regulation Z provides strict regulation of real estate advertisements that include mortgage financing terms. General phrases like "liberal terms available" may be used, but if specifics are given they must comply with this act. The APR, which includes all charges, rather than the interest rate alone, must be stated.

Specific credit terms, known as "triggering terms"—such as the down payment, monthly payment, dollar amount of the finance charge or term of the loan—may not be advertised unless the following information is set forth as well: cash price; required down payment; number, amounts and due dates of all payments; and APR. The total of all payments to be made over the term of the mortgage must also be specified unless the advertised credit refers to a first mortgage to finance acquisition of a dwelling.

Penalties. Regulation Z provides substantial penalties for noncompliance, ranging from a fine of $5,000 to $10,000 for each day the misleading advertising continues to a year's imprisonment.

▼ **Federal Equal Credit Opportunity Act**

The federal Equal Credit Opportunity Act **(ECOA)** prohibits lenders and others who grant or arrange credit to consumers from discriminating against credit applicants on the basis of race, color, religion, national origin, sex, marital status, age (provided the applicant is of legal age) or dependence on public assistance. Lenders must inform all rejected credit applicants in writing of the principal reasons why credit was denied or terminated.

The National Affordable Housing Act requires that borrowers be presented with a statement of their rights if their loan servicing is transferred. The borrower must be notified at least 15 days before the date of transfer and provided with a toll-free or collect-call telephone number of the new servicer. Servicers are also required to acknowledge borrowers' inquiries within a certain number of days.

▼ **Real Estate Settlement Procedures Act**

The federal Real Estate Settlement Procedures Act (RESPA) was created to ensure that the buyer and seller in a residential real estate transaction involving a purchase mortgage or refinance loan have knowledge of all settlement costs. This important federal law is discussed in detail in Chapter 10.

Lender's Criteria for Granting a Loan

All mortgage lenders require that prospective borrowers file an application for credit that provides the lender with basic information. A prospective borrower must submit personal information including age, family status, employment, earnings, assets and financial obligations. Details of the real estate that will be the security for the loan also must be provided, including legal description, improvements and taxes. For loans on income property or those made to corporations, additional information is required, such as financial and operating statements, schedules of leases and tenants, and balance sheets. Self-employed applicants will be asked to show two years' income tax returns. Anyone employed by a family member will be asked to show a current pay stub and the most recent tax return.

▼ **Evaluating the Property**

The value of the property is an important element of the lender's underwriting process. The amount of the loan is based on the sales price of the property or appraised value, whichever is less. The lender then applies its LTV ratio to this figure. (LTV ratios are discussed in Chapter 11.) For example, suppose the property's sales price is $150,000, its appraised value is $152,000, and the buyer is applying for a 90 percent loan (which means he or she is making a 10 percent downpayment). To determine the maximum loan amount, the lender would multiply $150,000 (the lesser of the sales price and appraised value) by 90 percent. The maximum loan amount would be $135,000. (The borrower would have to make a $15,000 down payment.)

LENDER'S CRITERIA FOR GRANTING A LOAN:

- Evaluating the property
- Evaluating the borrower
- Qualifying ratios

To determine the appraised value of the property, the lender will order that an appraisal be performed. When valuing the property, the appraiser will take into consideration such elements as the property's location, its size and square footage, the number of bedrooms and bathrooms, the size of the lot and the condition of the property. If the property is a condominium or cooperative unit, the appraiser also will look at the project as a whole and examine the condominium declarations and bylaws filed with the attorney general or the cooperative's proprietary lease and by-laws. Appraisal is discussed in detail in Chapter 23.

The lender is concerned about the value of the property because if the borrower defaults on the loan, the lender will have the property sold through a foreclosure process and use the proceeds of the sale to pay off the mortgage debt.

▼ Evaluating the Potential Borrower

Of course, a lender would much rather have its borrowers pay off their mortgage loans as agreed. Thus, lenders are very careful to examine and evaluate a loan applicant's income and employment history. If the applicant does not make enough money to meet the mortgage payments or if the applicant's continued employment is doubtful, the loan application will be rejected.

Lenders like to see a reasonably stable income history, with at least two years' continuous employment or employment in the same line of work. Bonuses, commissions, and seasonal and part-time income are considered with certain time limits and employer verifications. Dividend and interest income, Social Security income and pension income are included in qualifying the borrower. Projected rental income is accepted in varying amounts (for example, 50 percent on VA applications, 95 percent toward FHA qualification, 75 percent of actual cash flow with conventional loans). Unrelated coborrowers may pool their incomes to qualify, just as a married couple might.

If the borrower's income is marginal, the lender may look at the borrower's education and training to determine whether his or her skills are in demand in the employment marketplace and whether his or her income is likely to increase in the future.

In judging whether a borrower qualifies to carry the requested loan, lenders analyze the present debts, including any with more than six months (VA and FHA) or ten months (conventional) to run. Lenders sometimes consider potential, as well as actual, balances on credit cards.

Borrowers usually must show that they have liquid assets amounting to the cash that will be required at closing without further borrowing. A credit report also will be ordered on the applicant. An applicant who has gone through a bankruptcy may have to wait between one and five years after discharge, depending on the type of loan desired, and show good credit history since.

Through the process known as **underwriting** the lender analyzes the application information. Verification forms are sent to the applicant's employers, financial institutions and lenders. These forms are returned to the lender and examined to make sure the information on the loan application is correct. The lender also studies the credit reports and the appraisal of the property before deciding whether to grant the loan.

The lender's acceptance is written in the form of a loan commitment, which creates a contract to make a loan and sets forth the details. This loan commitment must be signed by the borrower and returned to the lender within a specific time period.

Qualifying ratios. With each mortgage plan offered, the lender has certain qualifying ratios that will be applied to each borrower. A typical ratio for a conventional loan is 28/36; the borrower will be allowed to spend up to 28 percent of gross monthly income for housing expenses (PITI—principal, interest, taxes, and insurance) and up to 36 percent of income for both housing expenses and other payments on long-term debts. The applicant must qualify under both ratios before the loan will be approved.

For example, suppose a prospective buyer earns $3,000 a month. She pays $350 a month on long-term debts, including a car loan and credit card balances. If a lender applies the qualifying ratios to her income, the results will be as follows:

- 28 percent of $3,000 is $840. This is the maximum monthly payment for the loan amount she will qualify for under the *housing* expense-to-income ratio.
- 36 percent of $3,000 is $1,080; $1,080 minus $350 (monthly long-term payments) equals $730. This is the maximum monthly payment for the loan amount she will qualify for under the *total* expenses-to-income ratio.

Because a borrower must qualify under both ratios, the highest monthly loan payment this borrower would qualify for is $730.

Other loan programs can have different ratios. For example, to qualify for an FHA loan, applicants can spend no more than 29 percent of their gross monthly income on housing expenses and no more than 41 percent of their gross monthly income on both housing expenses and payments on long-term debts.

To qualify for a VA loan, applicants must spend no more than 41 percent of their gross income on both housing expenses and long-term debt payments, and must also meet the VA's cash flow guidelines (called residual income requirements). Ratio requirements can be changed from time to time.

Broker's Issues In Real Estate Finance

There are several issues that brokers should become familiar with. These include commercial mortgages, construction loans, sale-leasebacks, and how the economy affects real estate finance.

▼ Commercial Financing

Commercial property includes property that produces income, such as apartment and office buildings, restaurants, shopping centers, hotels and motels, and gas stations. The sources of much of the financing for commercial properties are insurance companies and pension plans, which have large amounts of money to invest in long-term mortgages. Both types of lenders often work through loan correspondents such as mortgage brokers. There are other sources of commercial mortgage funds as well, including commercial banks, savings and loans, sellers, syndicates and industrial revenue bonds.

Commercial lenders tend to have exacting underwriting standards and require low LTV ratios. For instance, when lenders underwrite a commercial loan, they complete a detailed analysis of the project's ability to generate adequate cash flow. The project's cash flow must be adequate to pay for principal and interest payments, property taxes, insurance and maintenance costs. (All of these expenses must be paid before the project can reach a breakeven point.) Lenders examine existing leases and lease pledges to determine cash flow and overall financial health. Because of this, every planned and existing large commercial real estate project includes an ongoing marketing program to secure tenants.

Lenders use the property's rental income to estimate the property's value, then apply a low LTV ratio to determine the loan amount. Most commercial loans have maximum LTV ratios of between 70 percent and 75 percent, depending on the financial rating. For example, on a triple net, A-rated property, one could finance up to 100 percent of the mortgage payments.

There are several types of common commercial real estate loans. Note that many require balloon payments.

Bullet loans (also called *intermediate* or *conduit financing*). A bullet loan has an intermediate term of 3 to 5 years; a conduit loan, 7 to 10 years. It is virtually always a fixed-rate loan. It is partially amortized, so a substantial balloon payment is required at the end of the loan term. In some cases, only the interest is paid in the first years of the loan.

Miniperm loans. A miniperm loan is a variable-rate loan that has an *interest accrual* feature. This type of loan is used by borrowers who want to increase their cash flow in the early years of a project.

Floating rate loans with accrual. These commercial loans are adjustable-rate loans, similar to those available on residential property. The interest rate is based on a standard index and then fluctuates throughout the life of the loan, depending on the movements of the index. However, unlike residential ARMs, the debt service on this loan is a fixed amount. Any deficiency in interest is added to the principal. Loan terms are quite short, usually no longer than five years.

Participation loans. **Participation loans** give lenders the opportunity to enhance their profits by earning extra revenue from an increase in a project's net income and resale value. During periods of high interest rates and tight money, lenders will offer financing at lower-than-market rates in exchange for a percentage of net income and/or increases in value. Participation loans are often available when other types of permanent financing are not.

Land-leaseback. In a *land-leaseback,* the investor buys the land, then leases it back to the developer under a long-term lease. The developer then constructs a building on the land. This type of transaction reduces the equity the developer needs to fund a project. Land-leasebacks are related to sale-lease-backs, discussed later.

Joint ventures. Traditionally, when a lender or investor and borrower decide on a joint venture, the lender or investor puts up 100 percent of the funds and the developer does all the work. Ownership may be divided between the two 50/50, or any other split (75/25, 90/10, etc.) that equitably reflects the work and risk involved. The lender or investor generally has the first claim to any income generated from the project up to an amount that equals an agreed-on return on the original investment (a safety-first position). The rest of the income is divided between the partners according to a previously agreed-on formula.

▼ Construction Loans

Construction loans (also called **interim loans**) finance the construction of improvements on real estate. A construction loan is temporary; when the construction is completed the loan is replaced with permanent financing. One of the unique features of this loan is the fact that the building that is used as security for the loan does not exist when the loan is made. Because only the land exists at the time the loan is made, construction lenders use various methods to protect their security interest. These methods include strict underwriting procedures and unique ways of disbursing the loan funds.

Loan application. Constructions loans vary in size from one small enough to finance the construction of a home to one large enough to finance the construction of a shopping center or a multistory office building. However, the application process is essentially the same regardless of the size of the loan. The first step the borrower takes when applying for a construction loan is to submit plans and specifications for the proposed building. Typically, the borrower already owns the lot on which the building will be constructed. Some lenders insist that the lot be owned lien-free, so that the construction lender will have the security of a first-lien position. Other lenders allow the lot to be encumbered with a mortgage loan, as long as the mortgage contains a subordination clause that gives the construction loan first priority over the previously existing mortgage.

The construction loan amount is based on the total value of the land and the future building. The LTV ratio rarely exceeds 75 percent. For instance, a borrower owns a $40,000 lot and wants to construct a $150,000 house on it. The total value of the property after the house is constructed will be $190,000. Seventy-five percent of the combined value of the lot and home is $142,500. That is the maximum loan amount the lender will agree to. Construction loans are usually large enough to cover all or most of the costs of the construction, with the owner's equity being represented by ownership of the lot.

Disbursement of funds. Construction loan funds are virtually never disbursed in one lump sum when the application process is completed. Disbursing all the funds at once would be too risky; it would be too easy for the borrower to squander the loan funds on cost overrides, on last-minute changes or by mismanagement, leaving the lender with an incomplete building as security for the loan. Instead, the loan funds are disbursed according to a prearranged plan. One of the most common plans is that of a series of draws as construction is completed. For instance, the lender may utilize a five-stage plan, whereby 20 percent of the loan funds are distributed each time another one-fifth of the construction is completed. The last 20 percent is typically held by the lender until all labor and materials have been paid for (i.e., lien waivers have been received from contractors and subcontractors and certificates of completion and approval for occupancy have been issued by a building inspector) and the period for filing a mechanic's lien has passed.

Another method of disbursing construction funds requires that the borrower submit the construction bills to the lender, who pays the bills as they arrive. The benefit of this method is that it gives the lender greater control over the possibility that mechanic's liens will be filed.

Note that interest is charged on the funds only after they have been disbursed. Both lenders and borrower must keep careful records showing when each disbursement was made.

Paying off construction loans. Construction loans are short-term loans. Terms may range from six months for a house to three years for a commercial project. Construction loans are set up so that the lender will be paid in full—including all accrued interest—at the end of this short loan term. Typically, the construction loan is paid off (replaced) with a permanent **takeout loan.** Often the borrower makes arrangements for permanent financing before the construction loan is even applied for. This kind of arrangement is called a **standby loan commitment.** Naturally, permanent lenders impose conditions on their standby loan commitments. For instance, when completed, the building must meet all building codes and conform to the plans and specification that were submitted at the time of the loan application. Some lenders refuse to fund the permanent loan until the project has been leased up to its **breakeven point.**

▼ **Sale-Leasebacks**

Sale-leasebacks are used to finance larger projects, nearly always commercial. The property owner sells it to an investor and then immediately leases it back. The lease is usually a full net long-term lease. The sale of the property frees up the original owner's equity in the property, and the lease is for a long enough period for the investor to recover the sale funds plus make a fair profit on the investment.

As a method of financing, sale-leasebacks offer a number of advantages. For the seller-lessee, the benefits include staying in possession of the property while receiving cash from the sale and getting a tax deduction for the full amount of the rental payments. Many sellers-lessees use the cash from the sale to expand or remodel their facilities.

The primary advantage of this arrangement for the buyer-lessor is the receipt of the rental payments. The rental payments usually include a fair profit on the investment and the return of the investment capital itself.

Sometimes a sale-leaseback includes an option for the tenant to repurchase the property at the end of the lease term. This type of arrangement is called a *sale-leaseback-buyback.* At the time of the original sale, the parties will generally set the repurchase price. If the repurchase price is the same as the original sales price, the parties may run into problems with the Internal Revenue Service. Special tax and legal advice should be sought in sale-leaseback and sale-lease-back-buyback transactions.

▼ **The Economy and Real Estate Cycles**

Brokers should understand the basic ways in which our economy as a whole affects the real estate market. The two are closely tied together: when interest rates and unemployment are high, real estate sales and financing activities are low, and vice versa. The general economy has some obvious impacts on real estate finance. *Stock market activity, employment rates, inflation rates,* and *income levels* all affect real estate values and the ability of potential home buyers to purchase real estate. For example, when unemployment rates are high, interest rates are high and income levels are low, fewer potential buyers will be able to obtain or afford the financing necessary to purchase a home. On the other hand, when the economy is healthy and interest rates and inflation are low, more people feel confident enough to apply for mortgage loans, and more applicants will qualify for those loans.

Economic influences. There are several economic factors that affect real estate cycles, including supply and demand, population characteristics, social attitudes and property value fluctuations.

The influence of supply and demand encompasses two different commodities: real property and mortgage funds. A demand for property will encourage building and cause prices to increase. For instance, in an area with a healthy economy, employment levels are high and incomes are steady. As a result of these factors, the demand for housing increases. (More people can afford to buy homes—the supply of property cannot keep pace with the demand.) This demand spurs building and causes the prices of already built homes to increase.

At the same time, the demand for mortgage funds is also increasing. As more people are able to purchase homes, more people also will want to finance those homes. Thus, there needs to be a healthy supply of money to lend for a strong housing market to continue. If money is tight and interest rates are too high, fewer people will be able to qualify for mortgages and the demand for housing will decrease. Supply will outstrip demand, and housing prices will decrease.

Money may become tight because of the actions of those forces that compete for mortgage funds. The two largest competitors for mortgage funds are the federal government and industry. Both are heavy borrowers: the federal government to cover the enormous federal deficit and industry because it usually takes large sums of money to expand operations.

Economic indicators help the broker stay abreast of economic changes. Rates of *inflation* (an increase in the amount or money or credit in relation to available goods or services) and *stagflation* (persistent inflation combined with stagnant consumer demand and high unemployment rates) are important gauges of the relative health of the economy. And to judge future opportunities in real estate markets, brokers must keep aware of the possibility of *recessions* (period of low general economic activity) or, in extremely rare cases, *depressions* (periods of low general economic activity marked by rising levels of unemployment).

The influence of individuals. The behavior of the population has a dramatic impact on real estate cycles. Demographic trends include the rate of homeownership and what kinds of homes are desired. The savings habits of individuals also affect real estate cycles. For example, when individuals invest their funds in stocks, bonds or mutual funds instead of in savings accounts, lenders no longer have as much money to lend, and real estate loans become harder to get. This phenomenon is known as **disintermediation.**

The influence of the federal government. The actions of the federal government also have a significant impact on real estate cycles. The federal government, through the Federal Reserve, tries to lessen the likelihood of economic downturns (recessions, depressions and inflation) and decrease the impact of those downturns should they occur. The secondary mortgage market also helps lessen the impact of local real estate cycles by creating a national market for real estate mortgages.

Tax laws also affect real estate cycles. For example, the Tax Reform Act of 1986 eliminated many tax benefits once enjoyed by real estate owners and investors. With limited exceptions, losses from property investments can no longer shelter other income. Depreciation time periods were increased significantly (making the yearly tax deduction much smaller).

Federal Reserve System. The role of the Federal Reserve System (also known as the "Fed") is to maintain sound credit conditions, help counteract inflationary and deflationary trends and create a favorable economic climate. The Federal Reserve System divides the country into 12 federal reserve districts, each served by a federal reserve bank. All nationally chartered banks must join the Federal Reserve and purchase stock in its district reserve banks.

The Federal Reserve regulates the flow of money and interest rates in the marketplace indirectly, through its member banks, by controlling their reserve requirements and discount rates.

The Federal Reserve requires that each member bank keep a certain amount of its assets on hand as reserve funds unavailable for loans or any other use. This requirement was intended primarily to protect customer deposits, but more important, it provides a means of manipulating the flow of cash in the money market.

By increasing its **reserve requirements** the Federal Reserve in effect limits the amount of money that member banks can use to make loans, thus causing interest rates to rise. In this manner, the government can slow down an overactive economy by limiting the number of loans that would have been directed toward major purchases of goods and services. The opposite is also true: by decreasing the reserve requirements the Federal Reserve can allow more loans to be made, thus increasing the amount of money circulated in the marketplace and causing interest rates to drop.

Federal Reserve member banks are permitted to borrow money from the district reserve banks to expand their lending operations. The interest rate that the district banks charge for the use of this money is called the **discount rate.** This rate is the basis on which the banks determine the percentage rate of interest that they, in turn, charge their loan customers. Theoretically, when the Federal Reserve discount rate is high, bank interest rates are high; therefore, fewer loans will be made and less money will circulate in the marketplace. Conversely, a lower discount rate results in lower interest rates, more bank loans and more money in circulation.

Influence of lending policies. As mentioned earlier, the availability of mortgage money influences real estate cycles. When interest rates are high or money is tight, real estate sales decrease. Other ways lenders influence the real estate market include how stringent their lending criteria are (who can qualify for a mortgage), documentation requirements, the time frame for loan approval and LTV ratios. For example, in the 1980s 95 percent loans were made readily available. This meant that people could purchase a home with a modest 5 percent down payment. Those who would have been unable to come up with a 10 percent or 20 percent down payment were now able to purchase homes. A few years later, however, 95 percent loans were discovered to have extremely high default rates. Now 95 percent loans are extremely rare, which means fewer people can afford to purchase homes.

Publications. To keep up with all the elements that influence real estate cycles, real estate brokers should read various publications, including the *Wall Street Journal,* local or regional newspapers and professional publications. All of these publications are excellent sources for various economic indicators, such as the discount rate, unemployment rate, inflation rate, interest rates and housing starts.

Key Terms

bridge loan	mortgage insurance premium (MIP)
bullet loan	negative amortization
cap	nonconforming mortgage
ceiling	open-end mortgage
construction loan	package loan
conventional loan	participation loan
convertibility	private mortgage insurance (PMI)
disintermediation	purchase money mortgage
ECOA	Regulation Z
FHA loan	reverse annuity loan
FHLMC (Freddie Mac)	sale-and-leaseback agreement
FNMA (Fannie Mae)	secondary market
GNMA (Ginnie Mae)	shared-equity mortgage
home equity loan	swing loan
imputed interest	takeout loan
index	underwriting
interim financing	VA mortgage
joint venture	wraparound mortgage
jumbo loan	
margin	

Summary

Mortgage loans include conventional loans, those insured by the FHA or an independent mortgage insurance company, those guaranteed by the VA and loans from private lenders. The federal government sets interest rates on VA loans. Lenders may charge discount points; each point is 1 percent of the new mortgage. FHA and VA mortgages are generally assumable, with some exceptions and regulations.

Other types of real estate financing include purchase-money mortgages, buydowns, graduated-payment loans, shared-equity loans, reverse annuity mortgages, blanket mortgages, package mortgages, open-end mortgages, wraparound mortgages, construction loans, sale-and-leaseback agreements, land contracts and investment group financing.

Adjustable-rate mortgages are those under which the interest rate is changed each adjustment period to a stipulated margin above a national index of current mortgage rates. A cap may limit the size of possible adjustments, and a ceiling may limit the adjustment over the life of the loan. In instances where monthly payments do not cover the interest due, negative amortization is possible, with the total debt increasing instead of decreasing as it does with normal amortization.

The federal government affects real estate financing by participating in the secondary mortgage market. The secondary market is composed of investors who purchase and hold the loans as investments. Fannie Mae (Federal National Mortgage Association), Ginnie Mae (Government National Mortgage Association) and Freddie Mac (Federal Home Loan Mortgage Corporation) take an active role in creating a secondary market by regularly purchasing mortgage loans from originators and retaining, or warehousing, them until investment purchasers are available.

Regulation Z, the federal Truth-in-Lending Law, requires that institutional lenders inform borrowers of all finance charges involved. Severe penalties are imposed for noncompliance. The federal Equal Credit Opportunity Act prohibits creditors from discriminating against credit applicants on the basis of race, color, religion, national origin, sex, marital status, age or dependence on public assistance. The Real Estate Settlement Procedures Act (RESPA) requires that lenders inform both buyers and sellers in advance of all fees for the settlement of a residential mortgage loan.

A lender underwrites a loan by examining the borrower's income, employment history, credit history and net worth and the value of the property. The lender is concerned about the borrower's income and employment history because the lender wants to make sure that the borrower is likely to repay the mortgage debt as agreed. The lender is concerned about the value of the property because if the borrower does default, the property will be sold at a foreclosure sale and the proceeds used to repay the mortgage debt.

When evaluating the borrower's income, lenders typically use two ratios: the borrower may not spend more than a certain amount (for example, 28 percent) of his or her gross monthly income on housing expenses or more than a certain amount (for example, 36 percent) of his or her gross monthly income on both housing expenses and other long-term debt payments.

1. Private mortgage insurance (PMI) is required whenever the
   a. loan is to be placed with the FHA.
   b. property covers more than 2.5 acres.
   c. loan exceeds $67,500.
   d. conventional LTV ratio exceeds 80 percent.

2. The Department of Housing and Urban Development insures mortgage loans made through
   a. the FHA.   c. Fannie Mae.
   b. the VA.   d. Freddie Mac.

3. Bill and Maria want to buy a home together. A mortgage application is likely to fail, though, if
   a. they are not married.
   b. they are self-employed.
   c. Bill declared bankruptcy eight months ago.
   d. they have less than 10 percent down payment.

4. The terms index, margin and cap are used in evaluating what type of mortgage?
   a. Package   c. Conventional
   b. Blanket   d. Adjustable-rate

5. Negative amortization refers to a situation in which the
   a. debt is gradually reduced through monthly payments.
   b. debt grows larger instead of smaller each month.
   c. regular adjustments reduce the interest rate.
   d. interest rate may rise or fall according to an index.

6. The Williamses are purchasing a lakefront summer home in a new resort development. The house is completely equipped and furnished, and the Williamses have obtained a loan that covers all the personal as well as the real property. This kind of financing is called a(n)
   a. wraparound mortgage.
   b. package mortgage.
   c. blanket mortgage.
   d. unconventional loan.

7. A developer obtains one mortgage for a whole subdivision. As he sells each lot, he obtains a release of one parcel from the
   a. package mortgage.
   b. reverse mortgage.
   c. balloon mortgage.
   d. blanket mortgage.

8. Martin Tones buys a local factory from a company that intends to remain and rent it from him. Martin has put together a
   a. participation transaction.
   b. sale and leaseback.
   c. secondary market.
   d. reserve for escrow.

9. A savings and loan institution offers a mortgage plan with an 80 percent LTV ratio. On the purchase of a property appraised at $150,000, how much downpayment will be required?
   a. $12,000   c. $30,000
   b. $20,000   d. $120,000

10. Fannie Mae's purpose is to
    a. insure loans.   c. make loans.
    b. buy loans.   d. service loans.

11. Regulation Z protects the consumer from
    a. misleading advertising.
    b. fraudulent mortgage plans.
    c. discrimination in lending.
    d. substandard housing.

12. Fannie Mae is
    a. the leading purchaser of mortgages on the secondary market.
    b. a lender for homes in rural areas.
    c. a government agency that regulates interest rates.
    d. a government agency that regulates commercial banks.

13. Bill and Maria are applying for a home loan. They are not married, Bill is self-employed and they have $10,000 for a down payment. Which of the following is *not* true?
    a. Unrelated borrowers may pool their income to qualify for a home loan.
    b. Self-employed applicants can never qualify for a home loan.
    c. $10,000 could be enough money for a down payment; it would depend on the value of the property and the amount of the loan.
    d. Bill and Maria may want to look into an FHA loan program because it may be more attractive to them than a conventional loan.

CHAPTER 13

Land-Use Regulations

L. J. Blake owns a house containing eight studio apartments, but it is in an area zoned for one-family to four-family residences. He thinks it has been used that way since the turn of the century. Now he is ready to sell the property and worries about whether another owner can continue using it for studios.

To serve buyers and sellers properly, the real estate licensee needs to understand government regulations as they affect an owner's use of real property.

Planning for the Future

While private property owners generally own the complete bundle of rights—that is, the rights to use, sell, lease and improve their property—governments on all levels also have an interest in private property. It is in the government's interest to make sure that property owners do not use their property in such as way as to harm the public at large. For instance, a property owner may not use his or her property to unduly pollute the air or water, to create a nuisance for neighbors or to substantially decrease the value of a neighbor's property (such as by operating a factory within a residential neighborhood). The government protects its interest in the use of private property through broad land-use regulations, which range from zoning to environmental protection laws.

All types of land-use regulations have become increasingly important in recent years, as rapidly growing populations crowd cities and rural areas alike, as the increasing demand for products and services calls for more productive industry and as the increasing awareness of environmental concerns causes friction between various interest groups. It has become the government's difficult task to balance the needs of the public at large with the needs of individual property owners in all of these areas and more.

Private Land-Use Controls

The government is not the only entity that can regulate land use. Individual property owners and subdivision developers can restrict the uses to which land can be put. An individual seller or donor can set **deed restrictions**, such as giving property to a grandchild, for example, with the restriction that no intoxicating liquors ever be served on the premises. The restriction would be binding on future owners as well. The restriction is set by including a *restrictive covenant* in the deed. In the past, deed restrictions might have forbidden any future sale of the property to a member of a particular religious or ethnic group. Today such restrictions are in violation of human rights laws and are not enforceable. Neither are restrictions that forbid owners from selling or mortgaging in the future.

A subdivider may establish restrictions on the right to *use* land through a *covenant* in a deed or by a separate recorded declaration. These restrictions are usually considered valid if they are reasonable and for the benefit of neighboring owners. They are binding on all future buyers in that subdivision. Such restrictions usually relate to type of building, use to which the land may be put, type of construction, height, setbacks, square footage and cost. "No dwelling of less than 2,000 square feet ever to be constructed in this subdivision" is an example. Some restrictions have a *time limitation,* for example, "effective for a period of 25 years from this date."

Where a deed restriction and a zoning provision cover the same subject, the more limiting restriction will prevail. If deed restrictions say lots in a subdivision must measure at least two acres but the town allows half-acre lots, the two-acre restriction can be enforced by neighbors.

▼ **Enforcement of Deed Restrictions**

Each lot owner has the right to apply to the court for an injunction to prevent a neighboring owner from violating the recorded restrictions. If granted, the court *injunction* will direct the violator to stop the violation or be in contempt of court. If adjoining lot owners stand idly by while a violation is being committed, they can *lose the right* through *laches,* that is, loss of a right through undue delay or failure to assert it. In New York, neighboring owners have a two-year statute of limitations on objections to violations of the general plan (type of building, height, setbacks) and ten years in which to object to violations of conditions mentioned in the deed.

Government Powers

Although an individual has maximum rights in the land owned, these rights are subject to certain powers held by federal, state and local governments. Because they are for the general welfare of the community, these limitations have priority over the rights of the owner. Government rights include the following:

GOVERNMENT POWERS OVER LAND INCLUDE

- taxation,
- police power,
- eminent domain and
- escheat.

- Taxation: Taxation is a charge on real estate to raise funds to pay for government services.
- Police power: This is the government's power to preserve order, protect the public health and safety and promote the general welfare. The use and enjoyment of property is subject to restrictions including both environmental protection laws and zoning and building ordinances regulating the use, occupancy, size, location, construction and rental of real estate.
- Eminent domain: Through a **condemnation suit** a government may exercise this right to acquire privately owned real estate for public use. Three conditions must be met:
  1. The proposed use must be declared by the court to be a public use.
  2. Just compensation must be paid to the owner.
  3. The rights of the owner must be protected by due process of law.
     Condemnation proceedings are instituted only when the owner's consent cannot be obtained. Otherwise public agencies acquire real property through negotiation and purchase from the owner.
- Escheat: State laws provide for ownership of real estate to revert, or escheat, to the state when an owner dies leaving no natural heirs and no will disposing of real property.

▼ **Taxation**

Ad valorem taxes are charged against each parcel according to the **assessed value** placed on land and improvements by a public official known as an *assessor.* Tax rates are set to raise whatever sum is needed for the public budget. A rate might be quoted as, for example, $26 per $1,000 of assessed valuation. The same rate, in a different community, might be expressed as $2.60 per $100, or

26 mills (a mill being one-tenth of a cent) per $1 of assessed value. At that rate a house assessed at $100,000 would have a property tax bill of $2,600. Municipalities frequently assess real property at less than 100 percent of its full value.

Special assessments are additional taxes that run for a few years to enable certain neighborhoods to pay for particular improvements. Property on one street might be subject to special assessment property taxes, for example, to install sidewalks or streetlights on that particular street.

Protesting assessments. Taxpayers who feel their assessment is unfair can research tax records to see how their valuation compares with that of their neighbors. Obtaining solid data on comparative parcels is of prime importance in protesting an assessment. Recent nearby sales are particularly relevant.

Some assessors will visit the property and discuss the matter. If no agreement results, the next step is to present a grievance to the local assessment board of review. The taxpayer who wants to take matters beyond that point may go to court or take advantage of New York State's simple small claims procedure intended for review of grievances on residential property.

A property owner may bring a court action called a **certiorari proceeding.** This is a proceeding used to obtain a judicial review by a higher court of a case or proceeding by an inferior court, board or tribunal. It is commonly used by property owners to challenge their tax assessments when other actions have failed.

In New York partial reduction of some property taxes may be available to qualified veterans, religious organizations and homeowners aged 65 or older who have limited income.

Property taxes have first priority as liens. Foreclosure of a tax lien is often *in rem*, against the property and not against the delinquent taxpayer personally. Property taxes are discussed at greater length in Chapter 22.

Government Land-Use Controls

The government controls and regulates land use through (1) public land-use controls and (2) public ownership of land, including parks, schools and expressways, by the federal, state and local governments.

Public Land-Use Controls

The increasing demands placed on our limited natural resources have made it necessary for cities, towns and villages to increase their limitations on the private use of real estate. We now have controls over noise, air and water pollution as well as population density. Regulations governing use of privately owned real estate include planning; zoning; subdivision regulations; codes that regulate building construction, safety and public health; and environmental protection legislation (see Figure 13.1). Note that subdivision regulations and the real estate agents' duties regarding subdivisions are discussed in Chapter 21.

▼ The Master Plan

A local government recognizes development goals through a comprehensive **master plan,** also referred to as a *general plan.* Cities and counties develop master plans to ensure that social and economic needs are balanced against environmental and aesthetic concerns. Economic and physical surveys are essential in preparing a master plan. Countywide plans must coordinate numerous civic plans to ensure orderly growth. City plans are put into effect by zoning ordinances.

Figure 13.1   Environmental Protection Legislation

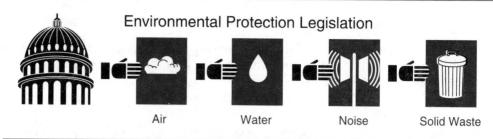

Environmental Protection Legislation

Air   Water   Noise   Solid Waste

▼ Zoning

Zoning ordinances are laws of local government authorities that control the use of land and structures within designated districts. Zoning regulates such things as use of the land, lot sizes, types of structures permitted, building heights, setbacks (the minimum distance from streets or sidewalks that structures may be built) and density (the number of units that can be built in an area). Often the purpose of zoning is to implement a local master plan.

In New York State, zoning powers are given to municipal governments; there are no statewide zoning ordinances. These local authorities enact zoning ordinances, grant any zoning variations, hold planning meetings and listen to zoning appeals.

Zoning ordinances generally divide land use into residential, commercial, industrial, vacant, agricultural, open space, institutional and recreational classifications. Now many communities include *cluster zoning* and *multiple-use zoning,* which permit unusual planned unit developments. Zoning classifications found in a typical New York State community might include R-1, one-family residential; R-2, multifamily residential; C-1, commercial-retail; C-2, heavy commercial; and I-1, industrial.

Residential areas may be subdivided to provide for detached single-family dwellings, semidetached structures containing not more than four dwelling units, walk-up apartments, high-rise apartments and so forth. Variations exist among municipalities, and some may have as many as 15 classifications. In some cases the use of land located *within one to three miles* of an incorporated area must receive approval and consent even though the property is not next to the village, town or city.

Tests commonly applied to determine if zoning violates the rights of individuals require that the

- power be exercised in a reasonable manner;
- provisions be clear and specific;
- ordinance be free from discrimination;
- ordinance promote public health, safety and general welfare under the police power concept; and
- ordinance apply to all property in a similar manner.

Zoning laws are enforced through local requirements that building permits be obtained before property owners build on their land. A permit will not be issued unless a proposed structure conforms to the permitted zoning, among other requirements.

Accessory building/use. An **accessory building** is one used for a purpose other than that of the principal building on the same lot. For example, a garage, pool house or a storage shed would be considered an accessory building.

An **accessory use** is a use other than that normally allowed on the property that is in conjunction with a principal use. An example of an accessory use would be an apartment allowed by special permit and under prescribed conditions in a single-family residence (a mother-in-law apartment).

Nonconforming use. A frequent problem is a building that does not conform to the zoning use because it was used that way since before the enactment of the zoning law. Such a **nonconforming use** is allowed to continue. If the building is destroyed or torn down, however, any new structure must comply with the current zoning ordinance. Local laws may say that the right to a nonconforming use is lost if it is discontinued for a certain period, usually one year.

Zoning boards of appeal have been established in most communities to hear complaints about the effects of zoning ordinances on specific parcels of property. Petitions may be presented to the appeal board for exceptions to the zoning law. Determinations can be challenged in state courts through an "Article 78" proceeding. (An *Article 78 proceeding* is a court proceeding by which a party can seek several types of relief, including a court review of administrative agency decisions [such as a real estate license revocation hearing], an order requiring another person or entity to perform a specific act or an order prohibiting a judicial or quasi-judicial officer from acting outside his or her authority.)

Spot zoning affects only a small area. If it is not in harmony with the neighborhood (a chemical plant in a residential area, for example), it is illegal in New York.

Zoning variations. Each time a plan is created or a zoning ordinance enacted, some owners are inconvenienced to the point of hardship. To alleviate some of the problems caused by zoning ordinances, two zoning variations are provided.

A **special-use permit** may be granted to allow a use of property that is in the public interest. For example, a restaurant may be built in an industrially zoned area if it is necessary to provide meal services for area workers, or a church might be allowed in a residential area. Also, a property owner who has suffered hardship as a result of a zoning ordinance may seek a variance. For example, if an owner's lot is level next to a road but slopes steeply 50 feet back from the road, the zoning board may be willing to allow a variance so the owner can build closer to the road than normally would be allowed.

A *use variance* requires "unnecessary hardship." The property owner must show that

- he or she is deprived of all economic use or benefit;
- the hardship is unique, not universal to the area or neighborhood;
- the variance will not change the essential character of the neighborhood; and
- the alleged hardship is not self-created.

An *area variance* requires "practical difficulty," affecting the health, safety or welfare of the community. The property owner must show that

- the variance will not cause an undesirable change or detriment to neighboring properties,
- the benefit sought by the person seeking the variance could not be achieved through other means,
- the variance would not have an adverse effect on environmental or physical conditions in the neighborhood or district,
- the difficulty suffered by the property owner was not self-created (does not preclude granting) and
- the requested variance is not substantial.

▼ **Building Codes**

Most cities and towns have enacted ordinances to specify *construction standards* that must be met during building construction or repair. These are called **building codes,** and they set requirements for kinds of materials, sanitary equipment, electrical wiring, fire prevention standards and the like. New York has a state-wide building code that applies where no local code exists or where local codes are less restrictive.

Most communities require the issuance of a **building permit** by a building department or another authority before anyone can build a structure or alter an existing building. Officials can verify compliance with building codes and zoning ordinances by examining the plans and inspecting the work. After the new construction is found satisfactory, the inspector issues a **certificate of occupancy (C of O)** or, for an altered building, a certificate of compliance. The certificate of occupancy is also required for some transfers of existing buildings. If the construction violated a private deed restriction (discussed earlier in this chapter), a building permit still might be issued. A building permit is merely evidence of the applicant's compliance with municipal regulations.

▼ **Subdivision Regulations**

Article 9-A of the real property law governs subdivided lands. This law is discussed in detail in Chapter 21.

Most communities have adopted subdivision regulations, often as a part of a master plan. Subdivision regulations usually provide for

- location, grading, alignment, surfacing and widths of streets, highways and other rights-of-way;
- installation of sewers and water mains;
- minimum dimensions of lots;
- building and setback lines;
- areas to be reserved for public use, such as parks or schools; and
- easements for public utilities.

▼ **Environmental Protection Legislation**

Federal and state legislators have passed a number of environmental protection laws in an attempt to respond to public concern over preservation of America's natural resources. Of particular importance are the New York Environmental Conservation Law and the federal Comprehensive and Environmental Response, Cleanup, and Liability Act of 1980 **(CERCLA),** discussed at greater length in Chapter 17. CERCLA places responsibility for cleanup of environmental disasters on the original offenders and also on future owners of the property, including lending institutions that might acquire the property through foreclosure.

In 1986 the Superfund Amendments and Reauthorization Act **(SARA)** further defined responsibility for cleanup caused by past activities. The "innocent" buyer is given an opportunity to defend against liability for previous owners' actions, provided there is proper diligent investigation of possible contamination before the purchase. Proof of an environmental audit before purchase would be a good defense.

The New York State Navigation Law, originally intended to cover liability for oil spills, includes an Environmental Lien Amendment under which the state can hold any property owner accountable for environmental cleanup.

Many of these laws were triggered by the 1978 Love Canal disaster, in which a toxic waste dump started leaking and contaminated a residential area and school, which had to be abandoned (although the government later claimed that the dangerous conditions were overstated).

Even when the federal and state officials declared part of the neighborhood cleaned up and safe, banks were unwilling to offer would-be buyers any mortgage loans on the boarded-up houses, fearing liability if future problems arose. Lawsuits to determine who was liable for the cleanup involved Hooker Chemical and Plastics Corp., which originally buried the chemicals; Occidental Chemical Corp., which bought the Hooker company in 1968; and the school board and city of Niagara Falls, which built a grade school and roads on the site.

Wetlands. In 1976 the New York legislature passed a law to protect designated wetlands, those areas designated by the state as having groundwater on or near the surface of the land. Improvements may be constructed only with a state permit; most agricultural uses are exempt from the law. The federal government's Clean Waters Act also requires a permit from the Army Corps of Engineers and EPA approval for building on designated wetlands. Cities and counties also frequently pass environmental legislation of their own.

Real estate practitioners must be alert to possible environmental problems so that sellers and prospective buyers will be fully informed about potential liabilities. The subject is discussed more fully in Chapter 17.

▼ Landmark Preservation

In New York State, local governments may enact regulations intended to preserve individual buildings and areas of historic or architectural significance. Regulations setting up local historic areas or landmark preservation districts may restrict owners' rights to alter the exteriors of certain old buildings. Interior remodeling is typically free from regulation. Individual buildings located outside a historic area also may be designated as landmarks.

Direct Public Ownership

A certain amount of land is owned by the government for such uses as municipal buildings, state legislature houses, schools and military stations. **Direct public ownership** is a means of land control.

Publicly owned streets and highways serve a necessary function for the entire population. In addition, public land is often used for such recreational purposes as parks. National and state parks and forest preserves create areas for public use and recreation and at the same time help to conserve our natural resources. At present the federal government owns approximately 775 million acres of land. Much of that is in Alaska.

Key Terms

ad valorem	escheat
accessory buildings/uses	master plan
assessed value	nonconforming use
building codes	police power
building permit	SARA
CERCLA	special assessments
certificate of occupancy (C of O)	special-use permit
certiorari proceeding	spot zoning
condemnation suit	taxation
deed restriction	variance
direct public ownership	zoning boards of appeal
eminent domain	zoning ordinances

Summary

Private land use controls are exercised by owners, often subdividers, who control use of subdivision lots through deed restrictions that apply to all lot owners. The usual recorded restrictions may be enforced by adjoining lot owners' obtaining a court injunction to stop a violator.

Government powers limiting private rights in land include taxation, eminent domain, police power and escheat. The control of land use is exercised through public controls, private (or nongovernment) controls and public ownership.

Public controls are ordinances based on the states' police power to protect the public health, safety and welfare. Cities and municipalities enact master plans and zoning ordinances.

Zoning ordinances segregate residential areas from business and industrial zones and control not only land use but also height and bulk of buildings and density of population. Zoning boards of appeal can grant special-use permits and variances and recognize nonconforming uses. Subdivision regulations maintain control of development.

Building codes control construction by specifying standards for plumbing, sewers, electrical wiring and equipment. A building inspector may issue a certificate of occupancy when a completed building meets standards.

In addition to land-use control on the local level, the state and federal governments have intervened to preserve natural resources through environmental legislation. Important are CERCLA and SARA, which placed responsibility on landowners for environmental cleanups, and wetlands legislation that limits building on designated lands.

Public ownership provides land for such public purposes as parks, highways, schools and municipal buildings.

1. In New York State the most effective way to protest a high property tax assessment is to
   a. show that neighboring similar property is assessed at lower figures.
   b. produce proof of the cost basis of the property, purchase price plus improvements.
   c. place the property on the market and see how much is offered for it.
   d. offer to sell to the assessor for the assessed value.

2. A homeowner who is dissatisfied with assessed valuation can take a complaint to
   a. the assessor personally.
   b. a board of review.
   c. a small claims hearing.
   d. Any of the above

3. When the Thruway was constructed, the route ran through the Adams farm. Mr. Adams refused to sell the necessary land. The state then used its right of eminent domain through a court proceeding known as
   a. escheat.   c. condemnation.
   b. variance.   d. downzoning.

4. The right of escheat allows New York State to acquire land
   a. through a developer's dedication of property.
   b. when someone dies without leaving a will or heirs.
   c. through a gift from a donor.
   d. when property taxes are not paid as due.

5. L. J. Blake's house contains eight studio apartments, four more than zoning laws allow on his street. To receive a permit for a nonconforming use, Blake must prove that the
   a. present use is in the public interest because the neighborhood is short of rental units.
   b. house has been used that way every year since before the zoning ordinance was adopted.
   c. deed he received specifically lists eight apartments in the building.
   d. zoning ordinance is unreasonably restrictive.

6. Doctor Spock goes before her local zoning board asking for permission to open an office in her residential neighborhood because the area has no medical facilities. She is asking for a
   a. variance.
   b. nonconforming use.
   c. special-use permit.
   d. restriction.

7. Dan Hill asks the zoning board to allow him to build a fence to keep his children safe on a busy corner, though he does not have room for the required ten-foot setback. He is asking for a
   a. variance.
   b. nonconforming use.
   c. special-use permit.
   d. restriction.

8. Public land-use controls include all but which of the following?
   a. Subdivision regulations
   b. Deed restrictions
   c. Environmental protection laws
   d. Master plan specifications

9. The building inspector who is satisfied that construction is satisfactory may issue a

   a. certificate of occupancy.
   b. subdivision regulation.
   c. restrictive covenant.
   d. conditional-use permit.

10. The purpose of a building permit is to

    a. override a deed restriction.
    b. maintain municipal control over the volume of building.
    c. provide evidence of compliance with municipal regulations.
    d. regulate area and bulk of buildings.

11. The New York State Navigation Law is concerned with

    a. riparian rights.
    b. environmental cleanups.
    c. the Barge Canal system.
    d. Niagara Falls.

12. CERCLA and SARA are federal laws establishing

    a. restrictions on wetlands development.
    b. national building code standards.
    c. liability for past environmental contamination.
    d. regulations for environmental safety in the workplace.

13. Miss Muffet's Greek Revival home is located in a historic preservation district. She probably can't change

    a. the number of bathrooms in the building.
    b. the exterior of the building.
    c. the interior of the building.
    d. either the exterior or the interior.

14. The term *laches* refers to

    a. loss of a right if it isn't exercised in time.
    b. responsibility for environmental cleanup.
    c. land set aside for recreational use in a master plan.
    d. the process of downzoning.

15. The grantor of real estate may place effective deed restrictions forbidding

    a. any future sale of the property.
    b. rental of the property to a member of a particular ethnic group.
    c. division of the parcel into small building lots.
    d. Any of the above

16. A deed restriction requires 250 feet of road frontage per lot. The town building code requires only 100 feet, and a builder constructs two houses on his 250-foot lot. The neighbors can

    a. ask the court to order one house torn down.
    b. act only before he has obtained certificates of occupancy.
    c. do nothing because he complied with all town regulations.
    d. enforce their rights by calling the police.

Construction I

The Mortensons' house was brand-new when they bought it seven years ago. Over the years they've had a host of problems. Now they've realized that the shingles the builder used were defective, the heating system was improperly installed and that the foundation is settling. They're wondering if it's too late to sue their builder for any or all of these problems.

Buyers and sellers often consult real estate brokers for advice on renovations and repairs. The agent who has a knowledge of basic construction is often able to judge quality and spot problems. It's also important, though, to know when outside expertise is needed, and to advise hiring a professional building inspector and/or engineer.

Site Preparation

In real estate practice, the term *site* is used to refer to a parcel of land that has been prepared for construction of some sort of an improvement. Site preparation involves clearing the land and grading it to provide drainage and a building location. Access and utilities also must be provided for. In locations that are not served by public utilities, an on-site well and/or sanitary waste (septic) system may need to be installed. On-site wells and septic systems must meet standards established by the state Department of Health and enforced by county Departments of Health.

Regulation of Residential Construction

Building construction begins with the construction documents: the plans and specifications. Plans are scale drawings of the building and its various components, including floor plans, elevations, sections and construction details. Separate plans are often drawn to show the locations and features of electrical, plumbing, HVAC (heating, ventilation and air-conditioning) and sewage-disposal systems. Specifications are written text; they tell the builder what materials to use and what construction techniques to follow, which have a great impact on construction costs.

With construction documents in hand, the builder or owner's next step is to obtain a building permit from the local permitting agency. This process involves payment of a permit fee, and the agency then will review the plans to ensure that the building meets all the requirements of the building codes that are in effect in the locality. Separate permits may be required from agencies regulating construction, electrical systems, plumbing systems and other aspects of the construction. Approval from environmental protection agencies often is required as well.

As construction progresses, the permitting agency or agencies will perform inspections of the building in progress. If construction has progressed in accordance with the approved plans and specifications, the inspector(s) will issue the necessary approvals. The final approval results in a *certificate of occupancy*, which means the building has been approved for human habitation.

New York State has a minimum standards building code, but local municipalities may *add* to it or *impose tighter* restrictions. Examples of local codes in various New York communities: requiring sprinkler systems, underground wiring or sump pumps in all new residential construction; banning the use of polyvinyl chloride for plumbing; requiring that plumbers, electricians, carpenters or builders be licensed. New York's Board of Fire Underwriters must approve all electrical installations, independent of local approval.

Wood-Frame Construction

Most houses in New York State are built with underlying wood-frame construction covered with an exterior of brick, stone, wood or vinyl siding. Wood-frame houses are preferred because they are less expensive than other kinds of construction, they can be built rapidly, they are easy to insulate and they allow flexibility of design.

Throughout this chapter, certain terms are followed by a bold number in brackets that refers to the numbered terms in *the house diagram* in Figure 14.1.

▼ Architectural Styles

Although details of construction are rigidly specified by building codes, architectural styles may vary greatly. Some popular styles include colonial, Georgian, ranch, Cape Cod, contemporary, split-level, Dutch colonial, French provincial and Spanish. Examples of several typical architectural styles are shown in Figure 14.2.

▼ Foundations

The term **foundation** includes footings, foundation walls, columns, pilasters, slab and all other parts that provide support for the house. Foundations are constructed of cut stone, stone and brick, concrete block, poured concrete and even specially treated wood. Poured concrete and concrete block are the most common foundation materials because of their strength and resistance to moisture. In recent years Styrofoam has been used to insulate foundation walls. The two major types of foundations are concrete slab and pier and beam.

Concrete slab. A **concrete slab foundation** is supported around the perimeter and in the center by concrete beams sunk into the earth. It is made of poured concrete reinforced with steel rods. It rests directly on the earth, with only a waterproofing membrane between the concrete and the ground. Foundations formed by a single pouring of concrete are called monolithic, whereas those in which the footings and the slab are poured separately are referred to as **floating slab foundations.**

Pier and beam. In a **pier and beam foundation**, shown in Figure 14.3, the foundation slab rests on a series of isolated columns, called piers, that extend above ground level. The space between the ground and the foundations is called the *crawlspace*. Each support of a pier and beam foundation consists of a *pier* [55], or column, resting on a *footing* [1], or base. The pier, in turn, supports the *sill* [8], which is attached to the pier by an *anchor bolt* [7]. The *floor joists* [10] that

Figure 14.1 House Diagram

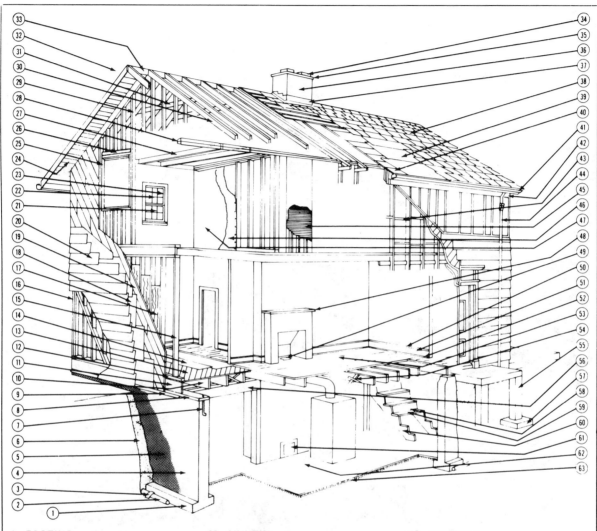

1. FOOTING	22. MUNTIN	43. FIRESTOP
2. FOUNDATION DRAIN TILE	23. WINDOW SASH	44. DOWNSPOUT
3. FELT JOINT COVER	24. EAVE (ROOF PROJECTION)	45. LATHS
4. FOUNDATION WALL	25. WINDOW JAMB TRIM	46. PLASTER BOARD
5. DAMPPROOFING OR WEATHERPROOFING	26. DOUBLE WINDOW HEADER	47. PLASTER FINISH
	27. CEILING JOIST	48. MANTEL
6. BACKFILL	28. DOUBLE PLATE	49. ASH DUMP
7. ANCHOR BOLT	29. STUD	50. BASE TOP MOULDING
8. SILL	30. RAFTERS	51. BASEBOARD
9. TERMITE SHIELD	31. COLLAR BEAM	52. SHOE MOULDING
10. FLOOR JOIST	32. GABLE END OF ROOF	53. FINISH MOULDING
11. BAND OR BOX SILL	33. RIDGE BOARD	54. BRIDGING
12. PLATE	34. CHIMNEY POTS	55. PIER
13. SUBFLOORING	35. CHIMNEY CAP	56. GIRDER
14. BUILDING PAPER	36. CHIMNEY	57. FOOTING
15. WALL STUD	37. CHIMNEY FLASHING	58. RISER
16. DOUBLE CORNER STUD	38. ROOFING SHINGLES	59. TREAD
17. INSULATION	39. ROOFING FELTS	60. STRINGER
18. BUILDING PAPER	40. ROOF SHEATHING	61. CLEANOUT DOOR
19. WALL SHEATHING	41. EVE TROUGH OR GUTTER	62. CONCRETE BASEMENT FLOOR
20. SIDING	42. FRIEZE BOARD	63. GRAVEL FILL
21. MULLION		

Figure 14.2 Architectural Styles

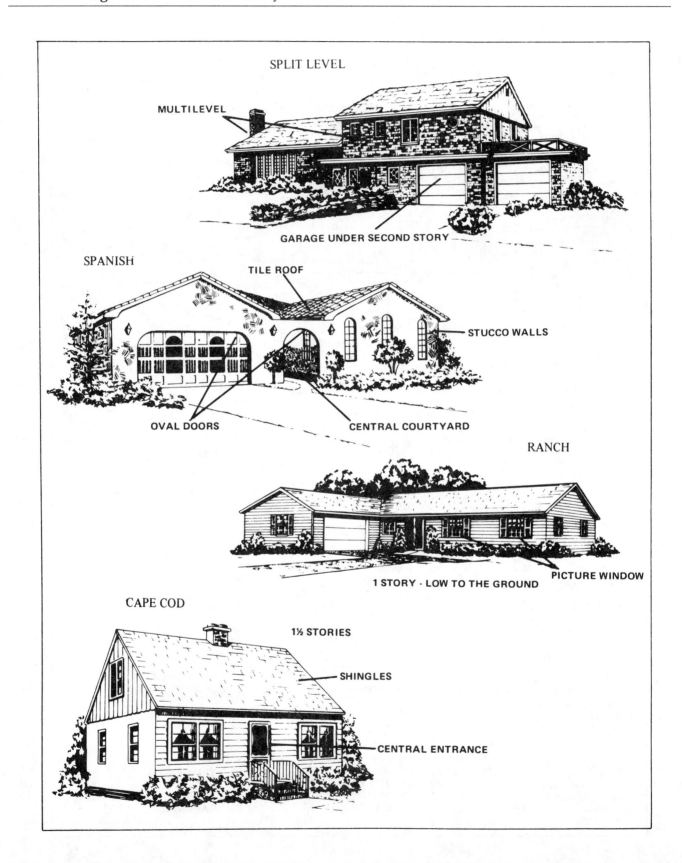

Figure 14.2 (continued)

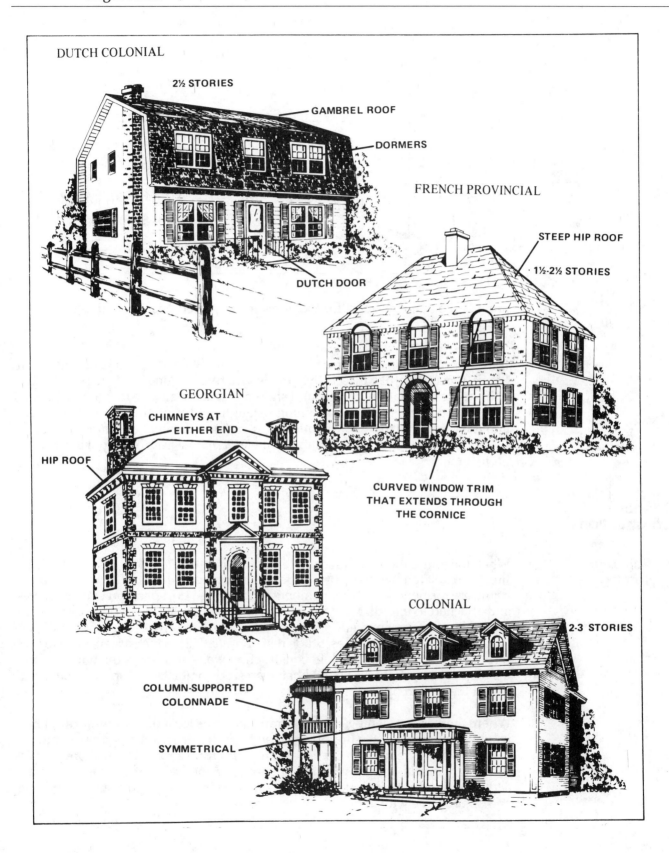

DUTCH COLONIAL

2½ STORIES

GAMBREL ROOF

DORMERS

DUTCH DOOR

FRENCH PROVINCIAL

STEEP HIP ROOF

1½-2½ STORIES

CURVED WINDOW TRIM
THAT EXTENDS THROUGH
THE CORNICE

GEORGIAN

CHIMNEYS AT
EITHER END

HIP ROOF

COLONIAL

2-3 STORIES

COLUMN-SUPPORTED
COLONNADE

SYMMETRICAL

Figure 14.3   Pier and Beam Foundation

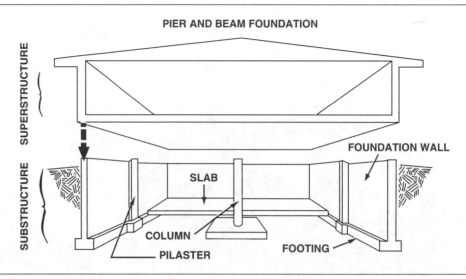

provide the major support for the flooring are placed perpendicular to and on top of the sills.

Termite protection. In some areas of New York State the earth is infested with termites, active antlike insects that are destructive to wood. Prior to pouring the slab for the foundation, the ground should be chemically treated to poison termites and prevent them from coming through or around the foundation and into the wooden structure. Chemical or pressure treatment of lumber used for sills and beams and the installation of metal *termite shields* [9] also will provide protection.

Exterior Construction

▼ Walls and Framing

When the foundation is in place, exterior walls are erected. The first step is **framing.** The skeleton members of a building are called its frame. The walls of a frame are formed by vertical members called *studs* [15], spaced at even intervals and attached to the sill. Many building codes require that for a one-story house the stud spacing not exceed 24 inches on centers. For a two-story house the spacing may not exceed 16 inches. Studs rest on *plates* [12], which are secured to and rest on the *foundation wall* [4]. In constructing walls and floors the builder will install *firestops* [43], blocks nailed between studs or joists to stop drafts and retard the spread of fire.

Where there is an opening in a wall frame, such as for a door or window, a horizontal *header* is used to support the weight of the structure over the opening. Wider openings require larger headers for structural support. In masonry walls, the weight over a door or window opening may be supported by an *arch* or by a *lintel.* A lintel is a piece of stone, steel or wood that is used to span the opening and support the wall above.

In framing, many builders are moving away from the traditional 2 × 4s placed 16 inches on center, using 2 × 6s instead. This allows a deeper wall for more extensive insulation.

Three basic types of wood-frame construction— *platform, balloon* and *post and beam*—are shown in Figure 14.4.

Platform frame construction. The most common type of wall framing for both one-story and two-story residential structures is **platform framing construction,** also known as *western frame construction.* Only one floor is built at a time, and each floor serves as a platform for the next story. Wall studs are attached to the upper and lower plates, and the entire assemblage is then raised into place and anchored to the sill.

Balloon frame construction. This type of construction differs from the platform method in that the studs extend continuously to the ceiling of the second floor. The second-floor joists rest on *ledger boards* or *ribbon boards* set into the interior edge of the studs. The *balloon* method gives a smooth, unbroken wall surface on each floor level, thus alleviating the unevenness that sometimes results from settling when the platform method is used. The balloon method is usually employed when the exterior finish will be brick, stone veneer or stucco.

Post-and-beam frame construction. With this method the ceiling planks are supported on beams that rest on posts placed at intervals inside the house. Because the posts provide some of the ceiling support, rooms can be built with larger spans of space between the supporting side walls. In some houses the beams are left exposed and the posts and beams are stained to serve as part of the decor.

Lumber. Lumber used in residential construction is graded according to moisture content and structural quality as established by the 1970 National Grade Rule. Grading rules require that dimension lumber (2″ × 4″, 2″, 2″ × 6″) that is classified as *dry* have a moisture content of 19 percent or less. Lumber that has a higher moisture content is classified as *green.* All species and grades are assigned stress ratings to indicate their strength when used in spanning distances between two supports. Actual dimensions of lumber differ from nominal measurements. A 2″ × 4″ actually measures 1¾″ × 3¾″.

Exterior walls. After the skeleton is constructed, the exterior wall surface must be built and *sheathing* [19] and *siding* [20] applied. Sheathing is nailed directly to the *wall studs* [15] to form the base for siding. Sheathing is generally hardboard, insulated board or chipboard. If the house is to have a masonry veneer, the sheathing may be gypsum board. Fabricated sheathings are available in both strip and sheet material. Sheathing is wrapped in tar paper or, more recently, in Tyvek plastic.

The final exterior layer, called *siding,* may be vinyl, wood, aluminum, stone, brick or other material.

▼ **Insulation**

To ensure adequate protection, *insulation* [17] should be placed in exterior walls and upper-floor ceilings. *Band insulation* of fiberglass is placed with a sill sealer above the foundation walls. The New York code requires varying amounts of

Figure 14.4 Frame Construction

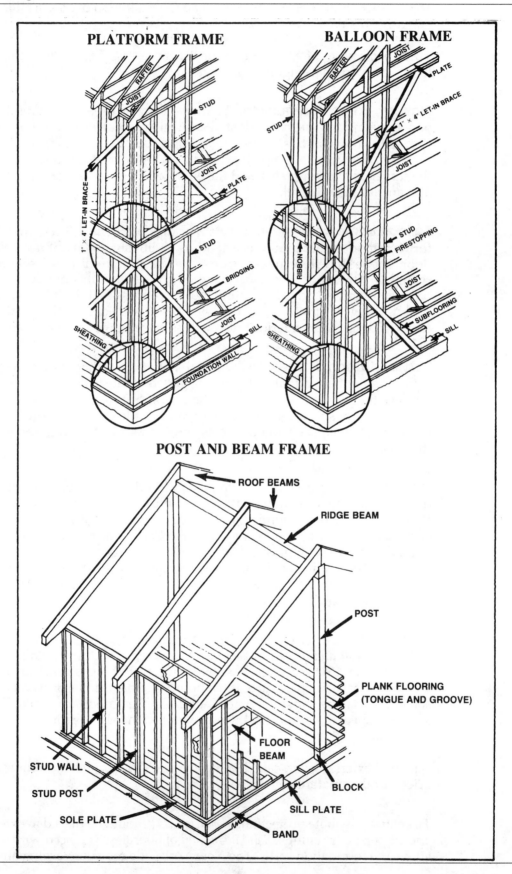

insulation in different regions of the state, as well as storm windows and doors. For conversion of existing units to gas or electric heat, **cap insulation** (under the attic floor) is required and storm windows or insulated glass where single-glazing had been used.

Insulation is rated according to its **R-value,** which indicates its resistance to heat transfer. The higher the R-value, the better the insulation. The most commonly used insulation material is fiberglass, which comes in either Kraft (paper) or foil-faced batts that can be placed between the studs. Other materials used are rigid Styrofoam, cellulose fiber (usually blown into existing structures) or rock wool. Proper insulation will contribute to the efficiency of both heating and air-conditioning systems.

Each set of building plans must be certified by a licensed architect or engineer, who puts the appropriate energy code on the plan. Different styles and designs and different regions have varying code requirements. For example, the manufacturer of a log house may certify that no insulation is necessary (because the logs do the job and the windows are small), whereas a contemporary-style home with vast areas of glass could require a great deal of insulation.

Urea formaldehyde foam insulation (UFFI) was used in some construction and remodeling in the 1970s. This type of insulation was banned in 1982, because of the potential health hazard from formaldehyde gas that leaks out of the insulation. UFFI is relatively uncommon in single-family houses.

▼ **Window and Door Units**

After the foundation exterior walls are completed, the next step is installation of exterior window and door units. Windows may be either side-hinged or vertically hinged (*casement*) or may slide up and down (*sash*). Basic window styles include the following:

- **Single-hung window:** A sash window with only one movable sash, usually the bottom one.
- **Double-hung window:** A sash window with two vertically sliding sashes; both single-hung and double-hung window sashes are controlled and held in place by springs or weights.
- **Slider window:** A sash window that opens by moving horizontally.
- **Casement window:** A window hinged like a door that opens or closes by the action of a gear handle.
- **Jalousie window:** A window formed by horizontal slats of glass that open or close horizontally by the action of a gear.

Many modern windows can be removed from the inside for easy cleaning. Window frames are most commonly vinyl, wood, steel or aluminum. The quality of a window depends on its construction, additional security and insulating factors. State code requires either double-glazing (two panes of sealed glass with insulating airspace between) or storm windows.

The thickness of an interior door is usually 1⅜ inches; an exterior door is usually 1¾ inches. Most are made of mahogany, birch, walnut or oak. Glass doors, screen doors with aluminum or steel frames and insulated metal doors are primarily exterior doors used for patios, porches or garden areas. Energy considerations dictate *triple-glazing* for many windows in recent years.

▼ Roof Framing and Coverings

The construction of the skeleton framing for the roofing material is the next step in building. Residential roofs are made in several styles, including gabled, shed, salt box and flat. Roof construction includes the *rafters* [30], *sheathing* [39] and *exterior trimming* [42]. Skeleton framings are classified as either conventional or truss (see Figures 14.5 and 14.6).

Joist and rafter roof framing. A **joist and rafter roof** consists of *rafters* [30], *collar beams* [31], *ceiling joists* [27] and *ridge board* [33]. Rafters are the sloping timbers that support the weight of the roof and establish the roof's pitch, or slant. Collar beams give rigidity to the rafters, and the ridge board aligns and receives the rafters.

Truss roof framing. A **truss roof** has four parts. It has *lower chords, upper chords,* *"W" diagonals* and *gusset plates.* The lower chords are similar to ceiling joists, and the upper chords are the equivalent of rafters in a joist and rafter roof. The "W" diagonals are the equivalent of the collar beams. Gusset plates are solid pieces of metal or wood that add rigidity to the roof. All integral parts are assembled and held in place by gusset plates, bolt connections or nails. A truss roof is generally prefabricated at a mill and set in place in sections by a crane, while a joist and rafter roof is assembled piece by piece on the site. Truss roof framing is the strongest type of roof framing.

Exposed rafter and roof framing. *Exposed,* or *sloping, rafter roofs* are often used with post-and-beam frame construction. The rafters are supported by central support posts and by the exterior walls. There are no ceiling joists or lower chords to provide additional support. The rafters in this type of roof are often left exposed for decorative purposes.

Exterior trim. The overhang of a pitched roof that extends beyond the exterior walls of the house is called the *eaves* [41], or *cornice.* The cornice is composed of the *soffit, frieze board, fascia board* and *extended rafters.* The *frieze board* [42] is the exterior wood trim board used to finish the exterior wall between the top of the siding and eaves, or overhang, of the roof framing. The *fascia board* is exterior trim used along the line of the butt end of the rafters where the roof overhangs the structural walls. The overhang of the cornice provides a decorative touch to the exterior of a house as well as some protection from sun and rain (see Figure 14.7).

Roof sheathing and roofing. With the skeleton roof in place, the rafters are covered with sheathing. The type of sheathing to be used depends on the choice of outside roofing material. Shingles are commonly of *fiberglass* or *asphalt* and are laid over plywood covered with tar paper. If wood shingles are used, spaced sheathing of 1" × 4" boards may be used to provide airspace to allow the shingles to dry after rain.

Interior Construction

▼ Walls and Finishing

Interior walls are usually covered with *drywall* (also called *plasterboard* or *wall-board*) [46], although *lath* [45] and *plaster* [47] may be used. Drywall is finished by a process known as *taping and floating.* Taping covers the joints between the

Figure 14.5   Roof Construction

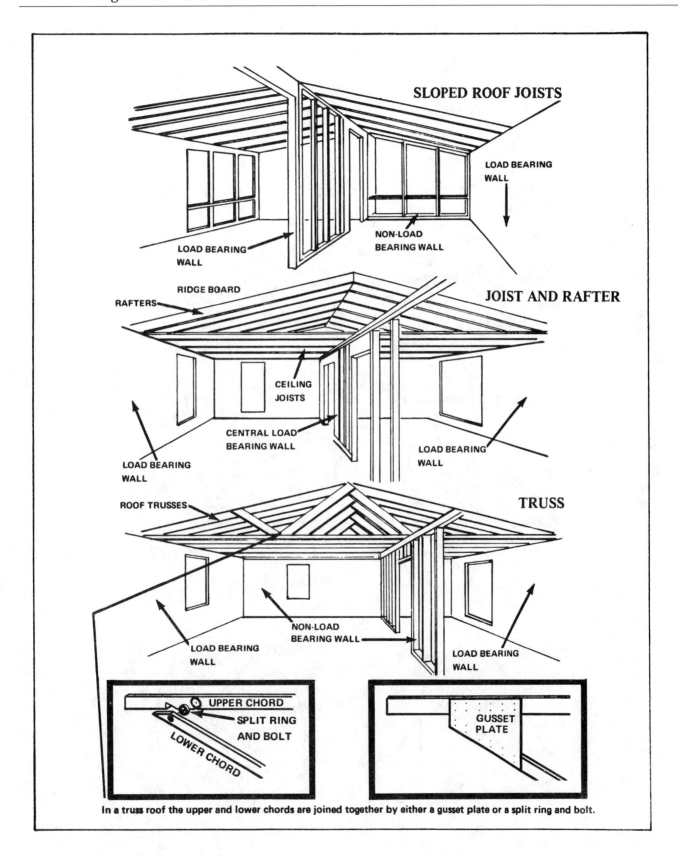

In a truss roof the upper and lower chords are joined together by either a gusset plate or a split ring and bolt.

Figure 14.6 Roof Styles

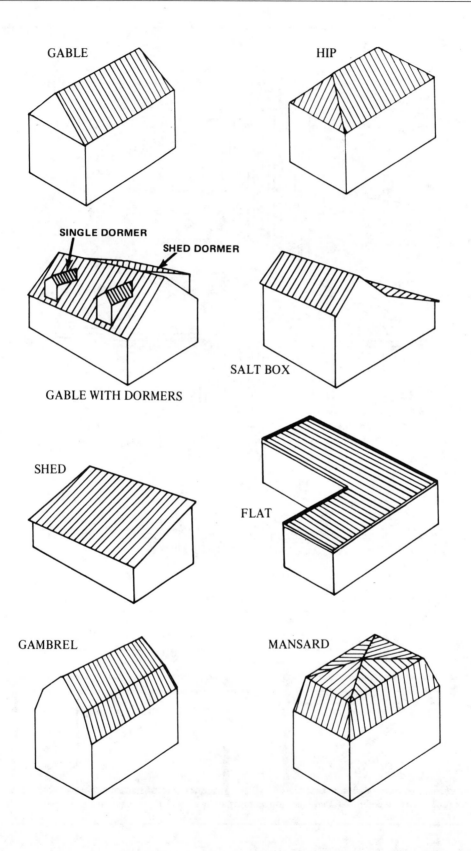

GABLE

HIP

SINGLE DORMER

SHED DORMER

GABLE WITH DORMERS

SALT BOX

SHED

FLAT

GAMBREL

MANSARD

Figure 14.7   Eave or Cornice

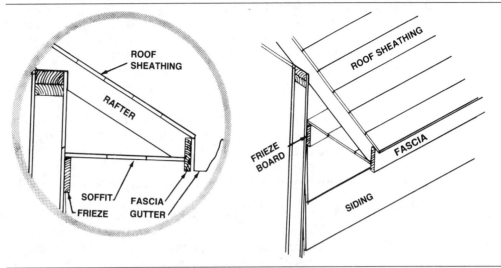

sheets of drywall. Floating is the smoothing out of the walls over the joints and the rough edges where nails attach drywall to the studs. Texturing may be applied with a roller prior to painting, wood paneling or wallpapering.

Final features added include (1) *floor covering*, (2) *trim*, (3) *cabinet work* and (4) *wall finishings* of paint, wallpaper or paneling. Floor coverings of vinyl, asphalt tile, wood (either in strips or blocks), carpet, brick, stone or ceramic tile are applied over the wood or concrete subflooring. Trim masks the joints between the walls and ceiling and gives a finished touch to the room. Cabinet work in the home may be either built in on the job or prefabricated in the mill.

▼ **Plumbing**

Plumbing must be installed subject to strict inspections and in accordance with local building codes that dictate materials and the method of installation. Sewer pipes are of cast iron, concrete or plastic, whereas water pipes are of copper, plastic or (in older homes) galvanized iron. Recently, plastic has been used more frequently for waste lines because it eliminates piping joints in the foundation slab.

All drain pipes must be connected to vents leading out of the building to operate properly. Water supply pipes must be sized adequately to provide sufficient flow of water to faucets or fixtures. The main water lines in a home are usually 1 inch or ¾ inch diameter, while the branch lines running to individual outlets are ½ inch diameter.

Domestic hot water may be supplied directly from a coil in the heating system or by a separate hot-water heater. If a separate unit is used, the water is heated by electricity, gas or oil. Well-water supplies may require water softeners.

Lead-tin solder, used widely for copper plumbing, has been under scrutiny by the Environmental Protection Agency, which limits lead content to 8 percent and recommends the use of tin-antimony solder instead.

Bathtubs, toilets and sinks are made of cast iron or pressed steel coated with enamel, plastic or artificial marble. Fiberglass is gaining in popularity.

▼ **Heating and Air-conditioning**

Warm-air heating systems and hot-water baseboards are the most common heating systems in use today. Steam heat is found in some older homes. In recent years some areas of northern New York have seen increasing dependence on wood as a fuel. A forced-warm-air system consists of a furnace, warm-air distributing ducts and ducts for the return of cool air. Combination heating-cooling systems are common in new homes; the most common is the conventional warm-air heating system with a cooling unit attached.

Heating systems can be powered by electricity, oil or natural gas. Oil-fired systems use oil from a storage tank located on the property, either above ground (AST) or buried underground (UST). (Note that should USTs leak, costly cleanup procedures will be required.) Natural gas may be supplied through a utility pipeline or from a separate pressurized gas tank on the property.

Each furnace has a capacity rated in **British thermal units (BTUs).** The number of BTUs given represents the furnace's heat output from gas, oil or electric firing. A heating and cooling engineer can determine the cubic area of the building as well as its construction, insulation and window and door sizes and from these data compute the furnace capacity required in the coldest possible weather and the cooling capacity needed for air-conditioning. Air-conditioning units are rated either in BTUs or in tons. Twelve thousand BTUs is equivalent to a one-ton capacity.

All gas pipes for heating and cooking are made of black iron. Gas pipes are installed in the walls or run overhead in the attic, where adequate ventilation is possible. They are never placed in the slab.

Solar heating. One of the most promising sources of heat for residential buildings is **solar energy.** Most solar heating units suitable for residential use operate by gathering the heat from the sun's rays with one or more *solar collectors.* Water or air is forced through a series of pipes in the solar collector to be heated by the sun's rays. The hot air or water is then stored in a heavily insulated storage tank until it is needed to heat the house or for use as a hot-water heater.

More immediately practical in the New York State area is *passive solar heating.* Without any additional special equipment, a house may be built or remodeled to take advantage of the sun's rays. Large areas of glass on a southern exposure and few windows on the north side of a building are typical of passive solar arrangements. Substantial savings in fuel may be obtained.

Heat pumps, which utilize heat from outside air in a form of reverse air-conditioning, are often used in conjunction with backup heating units of more conventional design. Where electricity is expensive, use of a heat pump may bring down costs. The heat pump also serves in summer for air-conditioning. Geothermal systems utilize the constant temperature underground to aid in heating and cooling. At depths of four to six feet and greater, the earth maintains about the same temperature year-round, approximately 52°F in New York State.

Ventilation. Ventilation in a home is important for several reasons: to provide fresh air for the occupants to breathe, to prevent the accumulation of moisture that could damage the structure and to eliminate harmful or offensive gases and odors. Enclosed unheated spaces such as attics and crawlspaces must be ventilated by screened openings in the structure. Bathrooms and kitchens are normally ventilated by means of fans that connect to ducts leading out of the building. Exhaust fumes from oil- or gas-fired equipment also must be vented to the outside through ducts.

▼ **Electrical Services**

Electrical power lines can be run underground or strung from power poles. Electrical services are brought into the home through a transformer and meter into a distribution panel (**circuit breaker box** or *fuse box*). The utility company owns and maintains the parts of the system up to and including the meter. The rest of the system, including the distribution panel and interior circuits, is the responsibility of the homeowner.

Electricity is measured in terms of volts, amperes (amps) and watts. Voltage indicates the strength of the electrical charge. Amperage indicates the amount of current that is flowing in response to the voltage. *Wattage* is equal to volts times amps; a 100-watt light bulb operating at 100 volts would draw a current of one amp. Wattage measures the amount of electric power that is being delivered and used. One thousand watts of power, used for one hour, is called a kilowatt hour.

Most residential circuits operate at approximately 110 volts and are rated to carry 15 or 20 amps of current. Larger appliances require 220-volt circuits and may draw 30 to 60 amps. The amount of amperage a circuit can carry is limited by the size (rating) of the fuse or circuit breaker that controls the circuit: **110-volt circuits** have two wires, one hot and one neutral, and they may also have a separate ground wire; **220-volt circuits** have two hot wires and one neutral wire, and may have a separate ground wire as well.

Electrical wiring is rated by its gauge or thickness. A lower gauge indicates a larger diameter of wire. The gauge determines how much current (amperage) the wire can safely carry. For example, 15-amp circuits require 14-gauge wire, while 20-amp circuits call for 12-gauge wire. Most residential wiring is made of copper, although aluminum wiring is sometimes used. Aluminum wiring requires the use of specially designed receptacles that are approved for use with this type of wire.

Modern construction uses cable known as Romex, which has two or three insulated wires and a bare ground wire covered with a plastic sheathing. Exposed cable or wiring must be run through metal conduit to provide protection from physical damage. Conduit can be either rigid metal or plastic tubes or flexible metal tubing. Flexible conduit is sometimes called *Greenfield*.

The circuit breaker box is the distribution panel for the many electrical circuits in the house. In case of a power overload the heat generated by the additional flow of electricity will cause the circuit to open, thus reducing the possibility of electrical fires. All electrical installations are inspected by the New York Board of Fire Underwriters. New York State standards require at least 100-ampere service and, for new home construction, a 110-volt smoke detector and a ground fault interrupter on each water hazard circuit (kitchen, baths, exterior outlets). The ground fault interrupter is a supersensitive form of circuit breaker.

Residential wiring circuits are rated by the voltage they are designed to carry. In the past most residences were wired only for 110-volt capacity. Today, because of the many built-in appliances in use, 220-volt service is standard.

New York Laws

▼ **Home Improvement Law**

New York State requires that the sale of home improvement goods and services costing more than $500 to homeowners, co-op owners or tenants conform to certain regulations.

A copy of a written plain-English contract must be given to the customer before any work is done. It must contain the contractor's name, address and telephone number; approximate start and completion dates; specifics of the work and materials (brands, model number, price); and a notice that the customer has an unconditional right to cancel the contract in writing within three days after it is signed. Any contractor's waiver of the right to file a mechanic's lien, of the sort formerly included in some construction contracts, is void in New York State.

Contractors are required to put into a trust (escrow) account in a New York State bank any contract payments by a customer, to be withdrawn only under a reasonable payment schedule agreed to by contractor and customer or on substantial completion of the job. If the customer violates the contract, funds may be withdrawn only to the amount of the contractor's reasonable costs. As an alternative to the escrow account, the contractor may deliver to the customer, within ten days of receiving the funds, a bond guaranteeing that the customer's money will be properly used or returned.

Where the contractor fails to adequately secure customers' deposits, to provide a written contract or otherwise violates the law, penalties include fines of up to 10 percent of the contract price, with a maximum of $1,000 for a first offense, $2,500 for a second one and $5,000 for a third or succeeding violation.

▼ **New Home Warranty**

New York requires that the buyer of a new home receive the following warranties: one year's protection against faulty workmanship and defective materials; two years' protection against defective installation of plumbing, electrical, heating, cooling and ventilation systems; and six years' protection against major structural defects (a foundation that settles, a roof that sags, a wall that bows).

Some builders carry warranty insurance at a cost of several hundred dollars per house.

Warranty law allows builders a reasonable time to make repairs and does not cover construction done by the buyer that is beyond the builder's control.

Notice of problems must be given to the builder within 30 days after expiration of the warranty. Lawsuits must be filed within four years for the one-year and two-year warranties and within seven years for the six-year warranty. If the home is sold within the warranty period, the new owner is covered as the original owner was.

Key Terms

British thermal unit (BTU)	joist and rafter roof
casement window	110-volt circuit
circuit breaker box	pier and beam foundation
concrete slab foundation	platform framing construction
double-hung window	R-value
floating slab foundation	single-hung window
foundation	slider window
framing	solar energy
heat pump	truss roof
insulation	220-volt circuit
jalousie window	

Summary

State and local building codes set standards for health and safety in construction. Working drawings and written specifications establish the quality of materials and workmanship needed.

Foundations include footings, foundation walls and slabs. The two major types of foundations are concrete slab and pier-and-beam.

Wood-frame construction is the type most frequently used in building single-family houses in New York State. The three basic types of exterior wall framing are platform, balloon and post-and-beam. Multilevel balloon construction differs from the platform method in that the studs extend continuously to the ceiling of the second floor, whereas with the platform method only one floor is built at a time. Post- and-beam construction utilizes interior posts to support the roof.

Windows may be sash windows, which are single-hung, double-hung or sliders; casement windows, side-hinged or vertically hinged; or jalousie windows, which are formed of horizontal slats of glass. Door styles include panel, slab, and hollow or solid core.

Skeleton roof framing may be joist and rafter, exposed rafter or truss. The skeleton roof rafters or upper chords are covered with sheathing, generally plywood, and then with fiberglass, wood or asphalt shingles.

Interior walls are generally covered with drywall and finished with paint or wallpaper. Final interior features include wall finishings, trim, floor covering and cabinet work. Plumbing, heating, air-conditioning and electrical wiring require careful installation to adhere to building codes.

New York State requires that the sale of home improvement goods and services costing more than $500 to homeowners, co-op owners or tenants conform to certain regulations. New York requires that the buyer of a new home receive certain warranties.

1. Most building codes emphasize
   a. safety.
   b. sanitation.
   c. structural strength.
   d. All of the above

2. Which is described as a 1½ story house?
   a. Split-level   c. Colonial
   b. Ranch   d. Cape Cod

3. A gambrel roof is found on what type of house?
   a. Dutch colonial
   b. French provincial
   c. Georgian
   d. Spanish

4. Which is a type of foundation?
   a. Balloon   c. Floating slab
   b. Post-and-beam   d. Chord

5. The components of a pier-and-beam foundation include
   a. the footings.   c. the anchor bolts.
   b. the sill or beam. d. All of the above

6. Which of the following are installed in horizontal position?
   a. Joists   c. Rafters
   b. Studs   d. Posts

7. Blocks nailed between studs and joists are called
   a. trusses.   c. bolts.
   b. firestops.   d. sills.

8. In a frame or wooden skeleton, studs rest on
   a. plates.   c. joists.
   b. balloons.   d. ridges.

9. Which of the following characteristics is considered when grading lumber?
   a. Age   c. Fragrance
   b. Color   d. Moisture content

10. Sheathing is found on the outside
    a. walls.   c. foundation.
    b. windows.   d. doors.

11. Cap insulation, which has the greatest payback in lowered fuel bills, is found
    a. under the attic floor.
    b. on the basement ceiling.
    c. in sidewalls.
    d. just under the roof.

12. Roof framing constructed on the site, with sloping rafters supported by ceiling joists, is called
    a. truss.   c. exposed rafter.
    b. joist and rafter. d. platform.

13. Drywall is also known as
    a. plasterboard.   c. sheathing.
    b. siding.   d. paneling.

14. Heat from outside air is utilized through a
    a. reverse conditioner.
    b. passive solar system.
    c. heat pump.
    d. cold air return.

15. A contractor must give the customer a written contract in advance of any work when home improvement goods and services will cost more than
    a. $100.   c. $500.
    b. $250.   d. $750.

16. A new-home buyer receives a warranty of six years' protection against
    a. defective materials.
    b. structural defects.
    c. defective installation of heating systems.
    d. All of the above

17. The Mortensens are worried about possible problems with the Victorian home they have fallen in love with. Before their purchase contract becomes firm, they may want to consult a
    a. building inspection engineer,
    b. soil engineer.
    c. framer.
    d. firestop specialist.

Dr. and Mrs. Goodhue have been trying to sell their home for many months and reject their broker's advice to drop the price, because, they say, "It's already below market value." Their broker claims it's impossible for real estate to remain unsold if it's priced below market value. That sounds like nonsense to the Goodhues.

If the owner prices property too high, no one comes to see it. Price it too low, and the seller loses out. The listing agent who understands valuation techniques can offer solid *advice* on pricing when property is put on the market.

Characteristics of Real Estate

Unlike other commodities, real estate has unique characteristics that affect its value. These fall into two categories: (1) economic characteristics and (2) physical characteristics.

▼ Economic Characteristics

The basic *economic* characteristics of land that influence its value are relative scarcity, improvements, permanence of investment and area preference.

Relative scarcity. The total supply of land is fixed; no matter how many people want land, there is only so much available.

> **BASIC ECONOMIC CHARACTERISTICS INFLUENCING VALUE:**
> - Relative scarcity
> - Improvements
> - Permanence of investment
> - Area preference

Improvements. The building of an improvement on one parcel of land has an effect on the value of neighboring parcels or on whole communities. For example, the construction of a shopping mall or the selection of a site for a landfill can influence values in a large area.

Permanence of investment. Even if older buildings are torn down, improvements such as drainage, electricity, water and sewerage remain.

Area preference. This economic characteristic, often called **situs,** refers to people's choices and preferences for a given area. It is what makes one house sell for twice as much as an almost identical one on the other side of town. Area preference is the most important economic characteristic of land. (As the old joke goes, the three most important factors in determining the value of real estate are location, location and location.)

▼ Physical Chararcteristics

The basic *physical* characteristics of land are immobility, indestructibility and nonhomogeneity.

BASIC PHYSICAL CHARACTERISTICS OF LAND:
• Immobility
• Indestructibility
• Nonhomogeneity

Immobility. Land is immobile. Even if soil is removed, that part of Earth's surface always remains. The geographic location can never be changed. Because land is immobile, *real estate laws and markets tend to be local in character.*

Indestructibility. Just as land is immobile, it is *durable and indestructible.* This permanence, not only of land but also of the improvements (including the buildings) placed on it, has tended to stabilize investments in land.

Nonhomogeneity. No two parcels of land are ever exactly the same. Although there may be substantial similarity, *all parcels differ geographically* because each has its own location.

Real Estate—The Business of Value

Value is not the same as price, nor is it the same as cost. Value can be defined as *the amount of goods or services that will be offered in the marketplace in exchange for any given product.* It also has been described as the *present worth of future benefits.*

In real estate the concept of *cost* generally relates to the past, *price* to the present and *value* to the future.

Supply and Demand

The forces of supply and demand continually interact in the market to establish price levels. Usually when supply goes up, prices drop; when demand increases, prices rise (see Figure 15.1).

Supply can be defined as the amount of goods offered for sale within the market at a given price during a given time period.

Demand can be defined as *the number of people willing and able to accept the available goods at a given price during a given time period.*

Supply and demand in the real estate market. Because real estate is fixed (immobile), the real estate market is relatively slow to adjust to changes in supply and demand. The product cannot be removed from the market or transferred elsewhere, so an oversupply usually results in lower price levels. But because development of and construction on real estate take considerable time from conception to completion, increases in demand may not be met immediately. Thus when demand is high, prices rise.

▼ Factors Affecting Supply

Labor supply and construction costs. A shortage of labor in the skilled building trades, an increase in the cost of building materials or a scarcity of materials will tend to lower the amount of housing built. High interest rates or scarce loans also reduce construction.

Government controls and financial policies. The government can influence the amount of money available for real estate investment through its monetary policies. At the local level, policies on taxation of real estate can have either positive or negative effects. Community amenities such as churches, schools and parks and efficient governmental policies all affect the real estate market.

▼ Factors Affecting Demand

Population. Because shelter (whether in the form of owned or rented property) is a basic human and family need, the general need for housing will grow as the

Figure 15.1 Supply and Demand

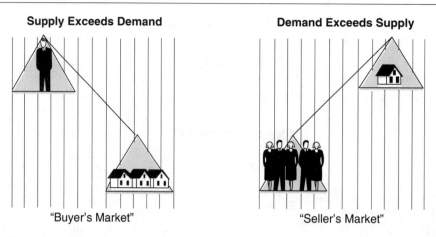

population grows. At any given time some areas are gaining population while others are losing.

In a consideration of the impact of population on the real estate market, the makeup of the population, or *demographics,* also must be taken into account. In recent years, for example, an increasing number of homes have been bought by single persons or one-parent families.

Employment and wage levels. Employment opportunities and wage levels in a small community can be affected drastically in a short time by decisions made by major employers in the area.

Vacancy levels. Vacancy levels in a community provide a good indication of the demand for housing. A growing shortage of housing will result in increasing rents. On the other hand, because real estate is a fixed commodity and cannot be removed from the market, an increase in vacancies will force rents down (see Figure 15.2).

Appraisal

An appraisal is an estimate or opinion of value. An *appraisal* is sometimes defined as an *unbiased estimate* of the nature, quality, value or utility of an interest in or aspect of identified real estate and related personal property. *Valuation* may be defined as the *process of estimating* the value of an identified interest in specific property as of a given date.

In the real estate business the highest level of appraisal activity is conducted by professional real estate appraisers who are recognized for their knowledge, training, skill and integrity in this field and who are licensed or certified by New York State. Formal appraisal reports are relied on in important decisions made by mortgage lenders, investors, public utilities, government agencies, businesses and individuals.

Not all estimates of value are made by professional appraisers. Often the real estate licensee must help a seller arrive at a market value for his or her property without the aid of a formal appraisal report.

Figure 15.2   Factors Affecting Supply and Demand

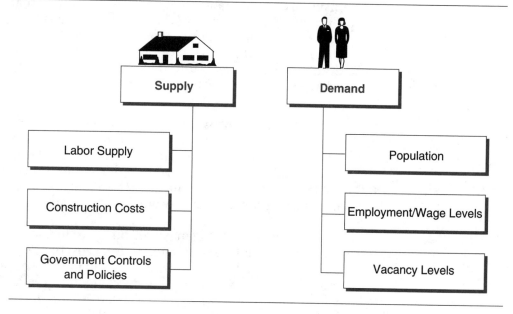

Types of Value

An appraiser may be asked to estimate one of several different types of value, including market value, investment value, insurable value or some other defined type of value (value in use, for example). The most frequently estimated type of value is market value.

▼ Market Value

Market value is an important concept defined as *the probable price a property will bring in a competitive and open market, offered by an informed seller and allowing a reasonable time to find a purchaser who buys the property with knowledge of all the uses to which it is adapted, neither buyer nor seller being under duress.*

In other words, market value is the most likely price obtainable in a free, open and informed market. The concept of market value also supposes an **arm's-length transaction,** defined as one between relative strangers, each trying to do the best for himself or herself. A sale between mother and son, for example, is not likely to be an arm's-length transaction and may not yield full market value for the property.

Market value should not be confused with cost or even with selling price. In an ideal market each parcel would sell for its exact value, but outside factors may cause a sale to be made below market value and sometimes above market value.

Included in the definition of market value are the following key points:

- Market value is the most probable price a property will bring.
- Payment must be made in cash or its equivalent.
- Both buyer and seller must act *without* undue pressure.
- A reasonable length of time must be allowed for the property to be exposed in the open market.
- Both buyer and seller must be well informed about the property's assets, defects and potential.
- Market value presupposes an arm's-length transaction, one between relative strangers, each of whom is trying to do the best for himself or herself.

Market value versus market price. *Market value* is an estimate based on an analysis of comparable sales and other pertinent market data. *Market price*, on the other hand, is what a property actually sells for—its selling price. Theoretically the ideal market price would be the same as the market value. There are circumstances under which a property may be sold below market value, however, as when a seller is forced to sell quickly or when a sale is arranged between relatives.

Market value versus cost. It is important also to distinguish between market value and cost. (*Cost* includes *direct costs,* such as labor and materials, and *indirect costs,* such as architectural and engineering fees.)One of the most common errors made in valuing property is the assumption that cost represents market value. Cost and market value may be equal and often are when the improvements on a property are new and represent the highest and best use of the land.

However, market value may well be lower than cost. For example, suppose a house was built two years ago at a total cost of $125,000. Six months ago, a new airport was opened two miles away from the house. Because of the loss of value due to the nearby airport (a loss in value that is called *external obsolescence*), the value of the property is now $95,000, substantially less than its cost.

Sometimes market value is higher than cost alone. Location makes the greatest difference, and so do *amenities*—features that add to owner satisfaction, such as a fine view, a nearby park or excellent public transportation.

▼ Approaches to Appraisal

Real estate is usually appraised using one of three different approaches: *cost approach, income capitalization approach* or *direct sales comparison approach.*Each is appropriate for different types of real estate. Some appraisals study the *subject property* (the parcel being evaluated) through all three methods, *reconciling* the results for a final estimate of value.

> **REAL ESTATE IS APPRAISED USING ONE OF THREE DIFFERENT APPROACHES:**
>
> 1. Cost approach
> 2. Income capitalization
> 3. Direct sales comparison approach

The **cost approach** estimates the amount needed to reproduce or replace the property being studied.This approach is most appropriate for non-income-producing buildings that cannot easily be compared with others: hospitals, schools, churches, fire stations. It also is used for insurance purposes.

The cost approach considers not only the cost of reconstructing buildings but also the amount of **depreciation** that already has subtracted value from the property. Depreciation falls into three categories: **physical deterioration, functional obsolescence** (undesirable or outmoded features) and **external (economic or locational) obsolescence** (undesirable factors located beyond the property lines).

The **income capitalization approach** to appraisal estimates value by analyzing the income generated by the property being considered.It is appropriate for valuation of rental property.

> **THREE CATEGORIES OF DEPRECIATION:**
>
> 1. Physical deterioration
> 2. Functional obsolescence
> 3. External obsolescence

Vital to the appraisal of investment or income property is the concept of the **present value of money.** It considers the question, "Would you rather have $1 today or $1 a year from now?" Obviously today's dollar is more valuable. The next question is, "Would you rather have $.95 today or $1 a year from now?" Depending on current interest rates and investment opportunities, one might even prefer $.90 today. That figure would be the *present value* of next year's dollar. More complex calculations are used to determine the present value of, for example, rental income or a stream of mortgage payments over a period of many years.

The **direct sales comparison** (market data) **approach** to appraisal evaluates property through careful study of similar parcels recently sold. The process is based on research and study of data. It is most appropriate for single residences. Chapter 23 contains a detailed discussion of appraisal.

Comparative Market Analysis

"Real estate properly priced is half sold." Even though it is the responsibility of the broker or salesperson to advise and assist, it is the *seller* who must determine a listing price for the property. Because the average seller usually does not have the background to make an informed decision about a fair market price, the real estate agent must be prepared to offer knowledge, information and expertise in this area.

A broker or salesperson can help the seller determine a listing price for the property through a **comparative market analysis (CMA).** This study compares the prices of recently sold homes that are similar in location, style and condition to the home being put on the market.

Although it has some resemblance to a direct sales comparison approach appraisal (discussed in Chapter 23), a CMA differs from an appraisal in several important ways. It is usually offered as a free service by a salesperson or broker, contrasting with the paid appraisal rendered by a fee appraiser. Both studies analyze recent sales of similar properties, but the CMA does so in a more superficial manner. The CMA includes material not usually considered in regular appraisals: information on nearby properties that failed to sell, for example, and a list of competing properties currently on the market. It also includes significant DOM (days on market before the sale) information. Broker ethics dictate that a CMA is never called a "free appraisal."

Information needed for comparative market analysis. When preparing a comparative market analysis, the broker must obtain as much information as possible on the parcel of real estate, including the following (where appropriate):

- Names and addresses of owners
- Adequate description of the property
- Size of lot (frontage and depth)
- Number and size of rooms and total square footage
- Construction and age of the building
- Information relative to the neighborhood (schools, churches, transportation)
- Current taxes
- Amount of existing financing
- Utilities and average payments
- Appliances to be included in the transaction
- Zoning classification (especially important for vacant land)
- Detailed list of exactly what personal property and fixtures will or will not be included in the sales price
- Environmental hazards

Among factors that should *not* determine listing price are the original cost, assessed value, replacement cost and amount the seller needs to realize from the property.

Once the broker has all the pertinent information on the subject property, he or she must select properties with the same general characteristics from the neighborhood (or a similar neighborhood) that have sold recently, that are listed or that have recently expired listings. The same types of information are gathered for these properties. The broker then uses the information about these similar properties to arrive at an informal estimate of value of the subject property.

The broker generally uses a comparative market analysis form, similar to the one illustrated in Figure 15.3, to prepare a written CMA to present to the property owner. A well-researched and well-prepared CMA will help the broker explain to the seller that the eventual selling price is set by the buying public through the operation of supply and demand in the open market. The CMA gives the seller an effective way to gauge the supply and demand in the market objectively and choose a reasonable listing price.

When the broker presents a CMA to the property owner, it is imperative that he or she explain how the similar properties were chosen and why. It is important for the owner to understand that location is a primary factor of value, and that the similar properties must be chosen from the same or a similar neighborhood. The broker should point out the features of both the subject property and the similar properties that are considered assets and drawbacks to the average buyer. Does the subject property have more or less appeal than the similar properties? Is the buyer offering more or less favorable financing terms? Are the market conditions in the area more or less favorable now? The answers to these questions and more are important pieces of information the owner will use to arrive at his or her final listing price.

It is often particularly helpful to point out the properties that did not sell during their listing period. Generally, a property does not sell because it is overpriced. Therefore, the prices of those properties must necessarily represent the upper ceiling of a listing price. While a property owner may feel, because of emotional reasons, that his or her property is worth more than similar properties that have recently sold, looking at the prices of homes that failed to sell will often inject a necessary measure of reality. Discussing these properties helps the broker explain to the seller that the eventual selling price is set by the buying public through the operation of *supply and demand* in the open market.

The Real Estate Agent's Role

In valuing property and presenting the owner with a CMA, the real estate agent must be careful to act competently and with due diligence. The agent should keep a copy of the CMA presented to the owner and also copies of any documentation used to complete the CMA. Most important, the agent must communicate value information accurately and completely. All agents should make sure that owners understand the estimates of value, how those estimates were determined and what they mean to the owner.

Figure 15.3 Comparative Market Analysis

Date: ______ Comparative Market Analysis for ______

Sugg. list price $______

Address	Style	Const	Age	No. of Rms	No. of Bdrms	No. of Baths	Gar	Fplc	Pool	C/A	Size Prop	Assess Value	Taxes	Comments & Extras	Fair Market Value

1. SIMILAR HOMES RECENTLY SOLD: These tell us what people are willing to pay . . . for this kind of home . . . in this area . . . at this time

Address	Style	Const	Age	No. of Rms	No. of Bdrms	No. of Baths	Gar	Fplc	Pool	C/A	Size Prop	Assess Value	Taxes	Comments & Extras	Closed Price	Date	Adjustd Price

2. SIMILAR HOMES FOR SALE NOW: These tell us what we are competing against. Buyers will compare your home against these homes.

Address	Style	Const	Age	No. of Rms	No. of Bdrms	No. of Baths	Gar	Fplc	Pool	C/A	Size Prop	Assess Value	Taxes	Comments & Extras	Askg Price	Days On Mkt.

3. EXPIRED LISTINGS – SIMILAR HOMES UNSOLD FOR 90 DAYS OR MORE: These illustrate the problems of over pricing.

Address	Style	Const	Age	No. of Rms	No. of Bdrms	No. of Baths	Gar	Fplc	Pool	C/A	Size Prop	Assess Value	Taxes	Comments & Extras		

PROBLEMS OF OVERPRICING:

A. HARD to get salespeople excited.
B. HARD to get people to make an offer.
C. HARD to get good buyers to look.
D. HARD to get financing.

Source: John E. Cyr and Joan m. Sobeck, Real Estate Brokerage: A Success Guide, 3rd Ed. (Chicago: Real Estate Education Company, 1992), p. 244.

Key Terms

arm's-length transaction	functional obsolescence
comparative market analysis (CMA)	income capitalization approach
	locational obsolescence
cost approach	market value
demand	physical deterioration
depreciation	present value of money
direct sales comparison approach	situs
economic obsolescence	supply
external obsolescence	value

Summary

The economic characteristics of land include scarcity, improvements, permanence of investment and area preferences (situs). The physical characteristics are immobility, nonhomogeneity and indestructibility.

A property's value is the present worth of its future benefits. Value is not the same as price; price is determined in the marketplace.

Because of its unique characteristics, real estate is relatively slow to adjust to the forces of supply and demand. Supply is the amount of goods available. Demand is the number of people willing to accept those goods at a given price.

The supply of and demand for real estate are affected by population changes, wage and employment levels, percentage of unoccupied space, construction costs and availability of labor, and governmental monetary policy and controls.

Real estate is appraised through the use of three different methods. The cost approach estimates the money needed to reconstruct the building and subtracts any loss in value due to depreciation. Depreciation may be physical (wear and tear), functional (outmoded features) or external (locational due to features beyond the property boundaries).

The income capitalization approach calculates value based on income generated by the subject property.

The direct sales comparison (market data) approach evaluates property by analyzing similar nearby properties recently sold.

Market value is defined as the probable price a property will bring in a competitive and open market, offered by an informed seller and allowing a reasonable time to find a purchaser who buys the property with knowledge of all the uses to which it is adaptable, neither buyer nor seller being under duress.

The comparative market analysis is a rudimentary form of direct sales comparison appraisal.

1. The Goodhues will not drop the asking price on their house because "it's already priced below market value." Their agent needs to explain that
   a. if nobody comes forward to offer that sum, by definition it can't be market value.
   b. market value is an ideal figure seldom actually reached in today's real estate climate.
   c. they can expect to get market value only if they happen upon a buyer who is under pressure.
   d. if they wanted to get market value, they should not have put their house into a widespread multiple-listing system.

2. The single most important factor in estimating the value of real property is its
   a. quality of construction.
   b. size.
   c. location.
   d. original cost.

3. Any two parcels of real estate
   a. can never be the same.
   b. can be the same only with identical tract houses.
   c. are considered the same if they have identical sales prices.
   d. are identical because of situs.

4. If six houses are offered for sale on the same street, sales prices probably will
   a. be identical.
   b. be disappointingly low.
   c. set new highs for that neighborhood.
   d. None of the above

5. Real estate markets tend to be
   a. similar across the country.
   b. statewide in their characteristics.
   c. stable despite economic changes.
   d. local in character.

6. Tom Wills is asked to estimate the market value of a church. He will give most emphasis to which appraisal approach?
   a. Cost
   b. Income
   c. Competitive analysis
   d. Direct sales comparison

7. The income approach to appraisal is most appropriate for a(n)
   a. tract ranch house.
   b. library.
   c. apartment house.
   d. vacant lot.

8. The direct sales comparison approach to appraisal utilizes
   a. asking prices for property on the market.
   b. building costs in the area.
   c. analysis of functional obsolescence.
   d. recent sales prices of similar parcels.

9. An example of external obsolescence might be a
   a. faulty heating system.
   b. poor floor plan.
   c. tenant who will not pay rent.
   d. used-car lot next door.

10. The highest price that would be paid by an informed buyer when property is widely exposed on the market is known as
    a. cost.   c. sales price.
    b. listing price. d. market value.

11. In the final analysis selling price for real estate is set by
    a. the seller.
    b. the broker.
    c. comparative market analysis.
    d. the buying public.

12. The actual listing price for property is based on
    a. its tax assessment figure.
    b. an appraisal.
    c. the seller's decision.
    d. a comparative market analysis.

16 Human Rights and Fair Housing

Mrs. Townsend has the upstairs apartment in her Albany home to rent out. She would prefer renting to a woman, and second-hand cigarette smoke makes her ill. She would like to advertise for a "nonsmoker, woman," but wonders if that would violate human rights laws.

Besides damaging society, unfair housing practices can land property owners and real estate licensees in serious trouble, with ruinous consequences. Understanding the complex laws and regulations concerning human rights is the first step toward fair treatment of all parties.

Equal Opportunity in Housing

Federal, state and local laws about human rights and fair housing affect rentals, sales and every phase of the real estate sales process from listing to closing.

The goal of these equal opportunity laws and regulations is to create a single, unbiased housing market, one in which every home seeker has the opportunity to buy any home in the area he or she chooses and can afford. The student of real estate must be aware of undesirable and illegal housing practices so as to avoid them. Failure to comply with fair housing practices is not only grounds for loss of license but also an unlawful act.

Federal Fair Housing Laws

The efforts of the federal government to guarantee equal housing opportunities to all U.S. citizens began soon after the Civil War with the **Civil Rights Act of 1866.** This law, an outgrowth of the Civil War, prohibits any type of discrimination based on *race or color*. All citizens of the United States shall have the same right in every state and territory as is enjoyed by white citizens thereof to inherit, purchase, lease, sell, hold, and convey real and personal property." A summary of fair housing laws appears in Table 16.1.

▼ Federal Fair Housing Act of 1968

In 1968 a major event greatly encouraged the progress of fair housing: the passage of the **federal Fair Housing Act of 1968,** which is contained in *Title VIII of the Civil Rights Act of 1968.* This law originally provided that it is unlawful to discriminate on the basis of *race, religion* or *national origin* when selling or leasing residential property.

In 1974 an amendment added *sex* (gender) as a **protected class,** and in 1988 two new classes were added: those with mental or physical *handicaps* and *familial status* (presence of children in the family). Protection of the handicapped extends to those with hearing, mobility and visual impairments; chronic alcoholics; AIDS; and mental retardation. Anyone currently using illegal drugs is not

Table 16.1   Fair Housing Laws Summary

Law	Protected Classes
Civil Rights Act of 1866	Prohibits discrimination in housing based on race or color (without exception)
Title VII of the Civil Rights Act of 1968 (Federal Fair Housing Act)	Prohibits discrimination in housing based on race, color, religion or national origin (with certain exceptions)
Housing and Community Development Act of 1974	Extends prohibitions to discrimination in housing based on sex (gender)
Fair Housing Amendments Act of 1988	Extends protection to cover handicaps and families with children (with exceptions)
New York Executive Law	Covers race, creed, color, national origin, sex, disability, age and marital status (some exceptions)
New York Real Property Law	Prohibits discrimination based on presence of children in a family or pregnancy
Americans with Disabilities Act	Prohibits discrimination based on disabilities

protected as handicapped, nor are those who pose a threat to the health or safety of others.

Landlords must make *reasonable accommodations for the disabled,* for example, allowing a guide dog in a no pets building or setting aside easy-access parking for a handicapped tenant. The tenant who needs to make reasonable modifications to an apartment must be allowed to do so if he or she agrees to restore the property to its original condition when the rental is over. Newly constructed multifamily buildings with four or more units must provide for wheelchair access to all ground floor units and to all upper floor units in buildings with elevators.

Housing developments intended for *older persons* may exclude children if such developments are occupied solely by persons 62 and older or if 80 percent of the units are occupied by at least one person 55 or older and there are policies and procedures published and adhered to demonstrating an intent to provide housing for persons 55 or older.

Prohibited acts. The Federal Fair Housing Act specifically prohibits the following acts, where they are based on prospective tenants' or buyers' membership in a protected group:

- Refusing to sell, rent or negotiate with any person, or otherwise making a dwelling unavailable to any person

    Example: Broker Bill is negotiating a listing with Seller Sue. Sue informs Bill that she will not sell her property to anyone who is not a "god-fearing Christian." Because refusing to sell on the basis of religion is a forbidden practice, Bill should refuse to accept the listing.

- Changing terms, conditions or services for different individuals as a means of discrimination

Example: The Sky Towers Apartments has a policy of collecting a $500 security deposit from its tenants. However, in the case of families with children, Sky Towers requires a security deposit of $1,000. This variation in the terms of the apartment leases on the basis of family status is a violation of fair housing laws.

- Practicing discrimination through any statement or advertisement that restricts the sale or rental of residential property

   Example: Jones Realty advertises its listings in the classified section of the local newspaper. The ads include the slogan "Jones Realty—specializing in homes for Asian immigrants." The ad's implication that certain housing is more suitable to persons of a particular race, color or national origin is a clear violation of fair housing requirements. (This is known as **steering**.)

- Representing to any person, as a means of discrimination, that a dwelling is not available for sale or rental

   Example: When George applies to rent an apartment, the manager takes his application but informs him that there are no units currently available. While it is true that all the units are currently occupied, one of the tenants is due to move out in three days. The manager simply prefers to rent the unit to a woman, since she believes they make better tenants. This is a case of unlawful housing discrimination on the basis of sex.

- Making a profit by inducing owners of housing to sell or rent because of the prospective entry into the neighborhood of persons of a particular race, color, religion, national origin, handicap or familial status

   Example: Acme Real Estate Company is running a direct mail campaign attempting to solicit listings from the predominantly white Alderbrook neighborhood. Included in the direct mail package are the results of a demographic study that projects that the population of Alderwood will become increasingly nonwhite in the next few years. Use of such "scare tactics" to generate profit through increased listings puts Acme in violation of fair housing laws. (This is known as **blockbusting**.)

- Altering the terms or conditions for a home loan to any person who wishes to purchase or repair a dwelling or otherwise denying such a loan as a means of discrimination

   Example: Citywide Mortgage company has a policy of refusing to make loans for properties located in the Valley View neighborhood, claiming that borrowers from Valley View have historically been at higher risk of default. Since this policy does not consider the creditworthiness of individual borrowers from Valley View, it is more than likely intended to discriminate against such borrowers on the basis of some other characteristic, such as race or national origin. (This is known as **redlining**.)

- Denying people membership or limiting their participation in any multiple-listing service, real estate brokers' organization or other facility related to the sale or rental of dwellings, as a means of discrimination

   Example: A multiple-listing service cannot lawfully exclude brokers from participation on the basis of their race, color, sex, religion, age, national origin, family status or handicap.

In New York, real estate advertising is often monitored by state and federal government agencies to detect evidence of discriminatory practices. There has been

Figure 16.1   HUD's Advertising Guidelines

CATEGORY	RULE	PERMITTED	NOT PERMITTED
Race Color National Origin	No discriminatory limitation/ preference may be expressed	"master bedroom" "good neighborhood"	"white neighborhood" "no French"
Religion	No religious preference/ limitation	"chapel on premises" "kosher meals available" "Merry Christmas"	"no Muslims" "nice Christian family" "near great Catholic school"
Sex	No explicit preference based on sex	"mother-in-law suite" "master bedroom" "female roommate sought"	"great house for a man" "wife's dream kitchen"
Handicap	No exclusions or limitations based on handicap	"wheelchair ramp" "walk to shopping"	"no wheelchairs" "able-bodied tenants only"
Familial Status	No preference or limitation based on family size or nature	"two-bedroom" "family room" "quiet neighborhood"	"married couple only" "no more than two children" "retiree's dream house"
Photographs or Illustrations of People	People should be clearly representative and nonexlusive	Illustrations showing ethnic races, family groups, singles, etc.	Illustrations showing only singles, African-American families, elderly white adults, etc.

much confusion about what types of property descriptions are and are not appropriate or legal to use in an ad. In an effort to clarify federal regulations regarding real estate advertising, HUD issued the following policy guidelines in January 1995 (also see Figure 16.1):

- *Race, color, national origin.* Real estate advertisements should state no discriminatory preference or limitation on account of race, color or national origin. Use of words describing the housing, the current or potential residents or the neighbors or neighborhood in racial or ethnic terms (i.e., white family home, no Irish) will create liability under this section.

  However, advertisements that are facially neutral will not create liability. Thus, complaints over use of phrases such as master bedroom, rare find or desirable neighborhood *should not be filed.*
- *Religion.* Advertisements should not contain an explicit preference, limitation or discrimination on account of religion (i.e., no Jews, Christian home). Advertisements that use the legal name of an entity that contains a religious reference (for example, Roselawn Catholic Home) or those that contain a religious symbol (such as a cross) standing alone, may indicate a religious preference. However, if such an advertisement includes a disclaimer (such as

the statement, "This home does not discriminate on the basis of race, color, religion, national origin, sex, handicap or familial status"), it will not violate the act. Advertisements containing descriptions of properties (apartment complex with chapel) or services (kosher meals available) *do not* on their face state a preference for persons likely to make use of those facilities and are not violations of the act.

- The use of secularized terms or symbols relating to holidays, such as Santa Claus or the Easter Bunny, or St. Valentine's Day images, or phrases such as "Merry Christmas," "Happy Easter" or the like *does not* constitute a violation of the act.
- *Sex.* Advertisements for single-family dwellings or separate units in a multi-family dwelling should contain no explicit preference, limitation or discrimination based on sex. Use of the term master bedroom *does not* constitute a violation of either the sex discrimination provisions or the race discrimination provisions. Terms such as "mother-in-law suite" and "bachelor apartment" are commonly used as physical descriptions of housing units and do not violate the act.
- *Handicap.* Real estate advertisements should not contain explicit exclusions, limitations or other indications of discrimination based on handicap (i.e., no wheelchairs). Advertisements containing descriptions of properties (great view, fourth-floor walk-up, walk-in closets), services or facilities (jogging trails) or neighborhoods (walk to bus stop) do not violate the act. Advertisements describing the conduct required of residents ("nonsmoking", "sober") do not violate the act. Advertisements containing descriptions of accessibility features are lawful (wheelchair ramp).
- *Familial status.* Advertisements may not state an explicit preference, limitation or discrimination based on familial status. Advertisements may not contain limitations on the number or ages of children or state a preference for adults, couples or singles. Advertisements describing the properties (two-bedroom, cozy, family room), services and facilities (no bicycles allowed) or neighborhoods (quiet streets) *are not* facially discriminatory and do not violate the act.

Exceptions. The following exemptions to the Federal Fair Housing Act are provided:

> Protected classes under the New York Executive Law for Fair Housing cover race, creed, color, national origin, sex, disability, age and marital status (some exceptions).

- The sale or rental of a single-family home is exempted when the home is owned by an individual who does not own more than three such homes at one time and when the following conditions exist: (a) *a broker, salesperson or agent is not used* and (b) *discriminatory advertising is not used.* If the owner is not living in the dwelling at the time of the transaction or was not the most recent occupant, only one such sale by an individual is exempt from the law within any 24-month period.
- The rental of units is exempted in an *owner-occupied one- to four-family dwelling* (but again, discriminatory advertising may not be used).
- Dwelling units owned by *religious organizations* may be restricted to people of the same religion if membership in the organization is not restricted on the basis of race, color, national origin, handicap or familial status.
- A *private club* that is not in fact open to the public may restrict to its members the rental or occupancy of lodgings that it owns as long as the lodgings are not operated commercially.

▼ **Jones v. Mayer**

The second significant fair housing development of 1968 was the Supreme Court decision in the case of *Jones v. Alfred H. Mayer Company.* In its ruling the Court held that the Civil Rights Act of 1866 "prohibits all racial discrimination, private or public, in the sale and rental of property."

This decision is important because although the 1968 federal law exempts individual homeowners and certain groups, the 1866 law *prohibits all racial discrimination without exception.* So despite any exemptions in the 1968 law, an offended person may seek a remedy for racial discrimination under the 1866 law against any homeowner, regardless of whether the owner employed a real estate broker and/or advertised the property. *Where race or color is involved, no exceptions apply.* (Note that in 1987, U.S. Supreme Court decisions implied that the 1866 law, to which there are no exceptions, extended to ethnic and/or religious groups as well.)

▼ **Equal Housing Poster**

An equal housing opportunity poster (illustrated in Figure 16.2) can be obtained from HUD. Displayed in a broker's office, it informs the public about fair housing laws and shows the firm's intention to comply. When HUD investigates a broker for discriminatory practices, it considers failure to display the poster evidence of discrimination. The poster should be prominently displayed in any location where the broker conducts business, including model homes.

▼ **Blockbusting and Steering**

Blockbusting and steering are undesirable housing practices frequently discussed in connection with fair housing. They are prohibited by federal and New York State law.

Blockbusting means inducing homeowners to sell by using scare tactics about the entry of a certain group into the neighborhood. The blockbuster frightens homeowners into selling and makes a profit by buying the homes cheaply, then selling them at considerably higher prices to minority persons.

Steering is *the channeling of home seekers to particular areas on the basis of race, religion, country of origin or other protected class.* Steering is often difficult to detect, because the steering tactics can be so subtle that home seekers are unaware that their choices have been limited. Steering may be done unintentionally by agents who are not aware of their own unconscious assumptions. An increasingly common means of detecting steering is the use of testers, which is described in more detail later in this chapter.

▼ **Redlining**

Denying applications for mortgage loans or insurance policies in specific areas without regard to the economic qualifications of the applicant is known as *redlining.* This practice, which often contributes to the deterioration of older, transitional neighborhoods, is frequently based on race rather than on any supportable objections to the applicant.

Enforcement. A person who believes illegal discrimination has occurred has up to one year after the alleged act to file a charge with the **Department of Housing and Urban Development (HUD)** or may bring a federal suit within two years.

Figure 16.2 Equal Housing Opportunity Poster

U.S. Department of Housing and Urban Development

EQUAL HOUSING OPPORTUNITY

We Do Business in Accordance With the Federal Fair Housing Law
(The Fair Housing Amendments Act of 1988)

It is Illegal to Discriminate Against Any Person Because of Race, Color, Religion, Sex, Handicap, Familial Status, or National Origin

■ In the sale or rental of housing or residential lots

■ In advertising the sale or rental of housing

■ In the financing of housing

■ In the provision of real estate brokerage services

■ In the appraisal of housing

■ Blockbusting is also illegal

Anyone who feels he or she has been discriminated against may file a complaint of housing discrimination:
    1-800-669-9777 (Toll Free)
    1-800-927-9275 (TDD)

**U.S. Department of Housing and Urban Development
Assistant Secretary for Fair Housing and Equal Opportunity
Washington, D.C. 20410**

Previous editions are obsolete   *U.S. Government Printing Office: 1991—521-598   form **HUD-928.1** (3-89)

For those who think their rights may have been violated, HUD maintains toll-free hot lines: 1-800-669-9777 (Voice) and 1-800-927-9275 (TTD). Complaints may also be made by mail to

Fair Housing and Equal Opportunity
HUD Regional Office
26 Federal Plaza
New York, NY 10278-0068

HUD will investigate, and if the department believes a discriminatory act has occurred or is about to occur, it may issue a charge. Any party involved (or HUD) may choose to have the charge heard in a federal district court. If no one requests the court procedure, the charge will be heard by an administrative law judge within HUD itself.

The administrative judge has the authority to issue an *injunction* (court order). This would order the offender to do something (rent to the complaining party, for example) or to refrain from doing something. In addition, penalties can be imposed, ranging from $10,000 for a first violation to $25,000 for a second violation within five years and $50,000 for further violations within seven years. If the case is heard in federal court, an injunction and actual and punitive damages are possible, with no dollar limit. The Department of Justice may also on its own sue anyone who seems to show a *pattern of illegal discrimination*. Dollar limits on penalties in such cases start at $50,000, with a possible $100,000 penalty for repeat violations.

The guilty party may be required to pay the other side's legal fees and court costs, which can add up to substantial amounts.

Complaints brought under the Civil Rights Act of 1866 must be taken directly to a federal court. The only time limit for action is three years, which is New York's statute of limitations for *torts*, that is, *injuries done by one individual to another*. There is no dollar limit on damages.

▼ **Threats or Acts of Violence**

The federal Fair Housing Act of 1968 contains provisions protecting the rights of those who seek the benefits of the open housing law as well as rights of owners, brokers or salespersons who assist them. Threats and intimidation should be reported immediately to the local police and to the nearest office of the Federal Bureau of Investigation (FBI).

▼ **Americans with Disabilities Act of 1992**

The **Americans with Disabilities Act (ADA)** of 1992, a federal antidiscrimination law, was enacted primarily to protect disabled persons from discrimination in public accommodations and commercial facilities. It also provides protection from discrimination and mandates easy access in new multifamily housing with at least four units.

In the event a tenant wishes to make alterations at his or her own expense in order to make an existing dwelling unit more accessible, the tenant may do so. The landlord may require that the tenant restore the premises, as necessary, to their original state when vacating.

New York Human Rights Law

Blockbusting, forbidden under federal statutes, is specifically mentioned in the **New York Human Rights Law** (Article 15, Executive Law) and also is prohibited by a New York Department of State (DOS) regulation. The DOS has, in the past, responded to complaints by the public by issuing **cease and desist orders** that prohibit canvassing for listings to certain homeowners.

A person charging discrimination may initiate a private lawsuit (with no dollar limit mentioned under state law) and also lodge a complaint with the DOS if the offender is licensed. A complaint also may be filed with the **New York State Division of Human Rights within a one-year period.**

Under sections of the Executive Law, New York statutes broaden the nondiscrimination rules to cover commercial real estate. They also add several other categories in which discrimination is prohibited, including age and marital status. The age provisions apply only to those 18 and older.

The **Real Property Law** forbids denial of rental housing because of children or an eviction because of a tenant's pregnancy or new child. The rules extend to mobile homes.

Various exceptions are made to the New York State rules, but these exceptions will not apply where the discrimination is racially based, because the federal Civil Rights Act of 1866, which covers race, permits no exceptions. With that in mind, New York State excepts

- public housing that may be aimed at one specific age group;
- restriction of all rooms rented to members of the same sex;
- rental of a room in one's own home; and
- restriction of rentals to persons 55 years of age or older.

Although an owner sometimes may discriminate under these exemptions, *a licensee may not participate in the transaction*, either through ownership or employment. In general the New York statutes cover renting, selling, leasing and advertising. Public accommodations also are included. The law further forbids any real estate board to discriminate in its membership because of any of the listed categories, which in this case include age. New York regulations are generally more restrictive than federal laws. Table 16.2 summarizes the categories covered by the various federal and New York State laws.

▼ Local Regulations

Local governments may add other groups to the list of protected categories. New York City, Syracuse and Albany have prohibited housing discrimination based on *sexual orientation*. The New York City Human Rights Commission has adopted the standard of *domestic partner* (an unmarried adult person who can prove emotional and financial commitment and interdependence) for gay or lesbian couples who deal with co-op boards. The definition also has been used in disputes over rights to rent-controlled and rent-stabilized apartments. The city also prohibits discrimination on the basis of *lawful occupation* or *citizenship* and allows no exceptions to fair housing laws for the rental of an owner-occupied two-family house.

Code for Equal Opportunity

The National Association of REALTORS® has adopted a **Code for Equal Opportunity**. The code sets forth suggested standards of conduct for Realtors so that they may comply with fair housing laws.

Table 16.2   Protected Classes

	Civil Rights Act of 1866	Fair Housing Act of 1968	New York Law
Race	Yes	Yes	Yes
Color	Yes	Yes	Yes
Religion		Yes	Yes ("creed")
National origin		Yes	Yes
Sex		Yes (1974)	Yes
Age			Yes (over 18)
Handicap		Yes (1988)	Yes
Marital Status			Yes
Children in family (Familial Status)		Yes (1988)	Yes
Exceptions	No	Yes	Yes

▼ Voluntary

In November of 1996, the National Association of REALTORS® entered into a new voluntary cooperative agreement with HUD. This agreement, called the Fair Housing Partnership Agreement, stipulates that HUD and NAR® will work together to identify Fair Housing issues, concerns and solutions.

Implications for Brokers and Salespersons

To a large extent the laws place the burden of responsibility for effecting and maintaining fair housing on real estate licensees, the brokers and salespeople. *A complainant does not have to prove specific intent, but only the fact that discrimination occurred. In addition, brokers are liable for the discriminatory behavior of their salespeople and employees, even if they have nondiscrimination policies in effect and are not aware of the illegal activities.*

There are a number of steps that a broker can take to ensure compliance with fair housing laws.

- Include the fair housing logo and/or slogan in all display ads and all classified ads of six column inches or more.
- Prominently display the fair housing logo and/or slogan in all brochures, circulars, billboards, signs and direct mail advertising, as well as any other forms of marketing.
- When using human models in an advertisement, select the models in such a way as to indicate that the housing is available to all persons without regard to race, color, religion, sex, national origin, family status or handicap.
- Prominently display the fair housing poster at all real estate offices, model homes or other locations where properties are offered for sale or rent.
- Make fair housing information readily available to salespeople and employees, and encourage them to become familiar with it and to attend fair housing education programs.
- Directly inform salespeople and employees of their responsibilities under the fair housing laws through in-house or other training.
- Establish and monitor office procedures to ensure compliance with fair housing regulations and objectives. At a minimum, such procedures should ensure that prospective buyers and renters are made aware of all available properties within their price range and areas of interest and are provided with complete and accurate information.

- Use the "Equal Employment Opportunity" slogan in all employment advertising and take appropriate steps to ensure a broad range of potential recruits.
- Require that salespeople educate sellers regarding their fair housing obligations by providing them with fair housing brochures and other information, and refuse to accept listings from sellers who do not agree to abide by fair housing requirements.

In addition, the National Association of REALTORS® suggests a sign stating that it is against company policy as well as state and federal laws to offer any information on the *racial, ethnic or religious composition of a neighborhood* or to place restrictions on listing, showing or providing information on the availability of homes for any of these reasons.

If a prospect still expresses a locational preference for housing based on race, the association's guidelines suggest the following response: "I cannot give you that kind of advice. I will show you several homes that meet your specifications. You will have to decide which one you want."

A broker's responsibility for the discriminatory behavior of his or her salespeople presents unique problems. Although brokers may wish to limit their control of salespeople to protect the salesperson's independent contractor status, effective control of behavior in the area of fair housing is essential to protect the broker from liability under civil rights laws. Brokers should have formal office policies regarding discriminatory behavior, and they should require that salespeople acknowledge in writing that they understand those policies and that they have received adequate training to be aware of the requirements of the fair housing laws.

In addition, brokers must have some system for monitoring the activities of salespeople in regard to fair housing compliance. One way to do this is through a record-keeping system that requires that salespeople keep a record of all prospects, including the prospects' qualifying information, the properties that were identified for the prospects and the prospects' reactions to each individual property. Periodic review of such records by the broker will help identify any instances where a salesperson may be in violation of fair housing standards.

Discrimination involves a sensitive area, human emotions. The broker or salesperson who complies with the law still has to deal with a general public whose attitudes cannot be altered by legislation alone. Therefore, a licensee who wishes to comply with the fair housing laws and also succeed in the real estate business must work to educate the public.

In recent years brokers sometimes have been caught in the middle when local governments enacted well-meaning **reverse discrimination** regulations. Intended to preserve racial balance in given areas, local laws sometimes run counter to federal and state rules, posing a real problem for the conscientious licensee.

From time to time real estate offices are visited by **testers** or *checkers*, undercover investigators who want to see whether all customers and clients are being treated with the same cordiality and are being offered the same free choice within a given price range. For example, two testers—one black and one white—with similar qualifications and interests may separately visit a real estate office to inquire about properties. If the two testers are treated differently by the office or are shown a different range of properties, it may be an indication of unlawful discriminatory behavior by the office. It is legal for testers to use "entrapment"; courts have held that such practice is permissible as the only way to test compliance with the fair housing laws that are of such importance to American society.

When a real estate broker is charged with discrimination, it is *no defense* that the offense was unintentional or that the broker did not know about the law. Citing past service to or with members of the same minority group is of little value. The agent's best course is to study fair housing law, develop sensitivity on the subject and follow routine practices designed to reduce the danger of unintentionally hurting any member of the public.

These practices include careful record keeping for each customer: financial analysis, properties suggested, houses shown, check-back phone calls. Using a standard form for all qualifying interviews is essential. Special care should be taken to be on time for appointments and to follow through on returning all phone calls. Besides helping to avoid human rights violations, these practices are simply good business and should result in increased sales.

Key Terms

affirmative marketing agreement (NAR)
Americans with Disabilities Act (ADA)
blockbusting
cease and desist order
Civil Rights Act of 1866
Code for Equal Opportunity
Department of Housing and Urban Development (HUD)
Executive Law

federal Fair Housing Act of 1968
New York Human Rights Law
New York State Division of Human Rights
protected classes
Real Property Law
redlining
reverse discrimination
steering
testers

Summary

Federal regulations regarding equal opportunity in housing are principally contained in two laws. The Civil Rights Act of 1866 prohibits all racial discrimination, and the federal Fair Housing Act (Title VIII of the Civil Rights Act of 1968) prohibits discrimination on the basis of race, color, religion, sex, national origin, handicap or the presence of children in a family in the sale or rental of residential property. Discriminatory actions include refusing to deal with an individual or a specific group, changing any terms of a real estate or loan transaction, changing the services offered for any individual or group, making statements or advertisements that indicate discriminatory restrictions or otherwise attempting to make a dwelling unavailable to any person or group because of membership in a protected class. Some exceptions apply to owners but none to brokers and none when the discriminatory act is based on race. Complaints under the federal Fair Housing Act may be reported to and investigated by the Department of Housing and Urban Development and may be taken to a U.S. district court. Complaints under the Civil Rights Act of 1866 must be taken to a federal court.

New York's Executive Law (Human Rights Law) adds age and marital status to the grounds on which discrimination is forbidden.

The National Association of REALTORS® Code for Equal Opportunity suggests a set of standards for all licensees to follow.

1. Mrs. Townsend is advertising for a tenant for the other half of her home. Which of these ads would violate human rights law?

   a. No pets
   b. Nonsmoker preferred
   c. No children
   d. No Republicans need apply

2. Salesperson Davis was listing the Johnsons' house. Mr. Johnson informed Davis that he would not sell to a member of a particular religious sect. Davis should *not*

   a. accept the listing.
   b. explain to Johnson why he should change his mind.
   c. discuss the situation with his broker.
   d. refer Johnson to another real estate company.

3. Which of the following acts is permitted under the federal Fair Housing Act?

   a. Advertising property for sale only to a special group
   b. Altering the terms of a loan for a member of a minority group
   c. Refusing to sell a home to an individual because of a poor credit history
   d. Telling nervous owners in a changing neighborhood to sell before their homes lose value

4. The Civil Rights Act of 1866 is unique because it

   a. generally covers only the area of race.
   b. provides no exceptions.
   c. requires a federal court suit by the complainant.
   d. All of the above

5. "I hear they're moving in; there goes the neighborhood. Better sell to me today!" is an example of

   a. steering.   c. redlining.
   b. blockbusting.   d. testing.

6. The broker who suggests only predominantly white areas to a white couple when there are others in their price range is guilty of

   a. blockbusting.
   b. redlining.
   c. steering.
   d. nothing; this is permitted under the Fair Housing Act of 1968.

7. Which would *not* be permitted under the Federal Fair Housing Act?

   a. The Harvard Club in New York will rent rooms only to graduates of Harvard who belong to the club.
   b. The owner of a 20-unit apartment building rents to women only.
   c. A convent refuses to furnish housing for a Jewish man.
   d. All of the above

8. Under federal law, families with children may be refused rental or purchase in buildings where occupancy is reserved exclusively for those aged at least

   a. 55.   c. 62.
   b. 60.   d. 65.

9. A lending institution may not refuse to make a residential real estate loan simply because of the
   a. questionable financial situation of the applicant.
   b. location of the property.
   c. applicant's not being of legal age.
   d. deteriorated condition of the building.

10. Under federal law, no exceptions apply when the discrimination is based on
    a. race.
    b. gender.
    c. handicap.
    d. country of origin.

11. A Utica landlord refused to rent to anyone on public assistance and thereby violated
    a. no law.
    b. the New York Executive Law.
    c. the Fair Housing Act of 1968.
    d. the Civil Rights Act of 1866.

12. The Ithaca housewife who refuses to rent rooms to any students is in violation of
    a. no law.
    b. the New York Executive Law.
    c. the Fair Housing Act of 1968.
    d. the Civil Rights Act of 1866.

13. Refusing an apartment to a couple because they are unmarried violates
    a. no law.
    b. New York Executive Law.
    c. the Fair Housing Act of 1968.
    d. the Civil Rights Act of 1866.

14. The Fly-by-Night Mortgage Company makes it a practice not to lend money on any inner-city property. This practice is known as
    a. redlining.
    b. blockbusting.
    c. steering.
    d. qualifying.

15. A court found Debbie Barnes guilty of illegal discrimination and ordered her to rent her next available apartment to the person who was unfairly hurt. The court order is an example of
    a. punitive damages.
    b. actual damages.
    c. an injunction.
    d. a monetary penalty.

16. The seller who requests prohibited discrimination in the showing of a home should be told
    a. "As your agent I have a duty to warn you that such discrimination could land you in real trouble."
    b. "I am not allowed to obey such instructions."
    c. "If you persist, I'll have to refuse to list your property."
    d. All of the above

17. A good precaution against even unconscious discrimination is
    a. detailed record keeping on each customer.
    b. use of a standard financial interview form.
    c. routine follow-up phone calls.
    d. All of the above

18. The federal Fair Housing Amendments of 1988 added which of the following as new protected classes?
    a. Handicap and familial status
    b. Occupation and source of income
    c. Political affiliation and country of origin
    d. Prison record and marital status

19. The fine for a first violation of the Federal Fair Housing Act could be as much as
    a. $500.
    b. $1,000.
    c. $5,000.
    d. $10,000.

20. The only defense against an accusation of illegal discrimination is proof that it
    a. was unintentional.
    b. didn't cause financial loss to anyone.
    c. arose because the agent was ignorant of the law.
    d. didn't occur.

21. Undercover investigation to see whether fair housing practices are being followed is sometimes made by
    a. testers.
    b. evaluators.
    c. operatives.
    d. conciliators.

CHAPTER 17

Environmental Issues

The Bensons were interested in purchasing a duck and potato farm on eastern Long Island. They were concerned about possible hazardous substances on the farm. How can the Bensons ease their fears about hazardous substances?

Pollution and Environmental Risks in Real Estate Transactions

Environmental concern has come to the forefront of contemporary issues. Both actual and perceived pollution problems have the ability to stir anger, fear and other feelings. Indeed, perhaps no other modern issue has a greater ability to elicit strong emotions. The increasing public awareness of and concern about pollution problems and their health and economic effects have had *significant consequences on real estate sales and values.*

Economically the actual dollar value of real property can be affected significantly by both real and perceived pollution. The desirability and salability of land and buildings may change drastically. Also, the cost of cleaning up and removing pollution may be much greater than the dollar value of the property before pollution.

The National Association of REALTORS® and the National Association of Environmental Risk Auditors report that in some areas of the United States mortgage and title insurance approval in many cases depends on inspection of the property for **hazardous substances** and proof of their absence.

For all of these reasons real estate professionals should be alert to the possibility of pollution and hazardous substances on property being sold. Knowledgeable real estate professionals should ask property owners about the possibility of hazardous substances associated with a property. In addition, licensees can expect increasing numbers of questions from customers concerned about pollution. Licensees should consider the consequences of potential liability in real estate transactions where hazardous substances may be involved.

Pollution is an impurity in the environment that was not there originally. The simple act of throwing a piece of paper on the ground creates an unsightly, minor form of pollution. Major pollution problems can result from hazardous substances associated with industrial and other activities, such as farming. Real estate licensees often, however, do not have the technical expertise required to determine if a hazardous material is present on or near the property. Government agencies and private consulting firms may be contacted for information, guidance and detailed study. Brokers and salespersons must be scrupulous in considering environmental issues and must exercise a *high degree of care* in all real estate transactions.

Long-Standing Issues

▼ Water

Water contamination exists in every state in the United States; what varies is the degree of contamination. Contaminants that can endanger health include *bacteria, viruses, protozoa, nitrates, metals such as lead or mercury, fertilizers, pesticides* and *radon*. There are other contaminants that can affect the taste and odor of water. The sources of these contaminants include industrial discharges, runoff from urban areas (such as landfills), septic systems that are improperly located and maintained, and pesticides and fertilizers from agricultural areas.

Contaminated water can cause a variety of physical symptoms, from mild stomach aches and intestinal cramping to severe nausea and diarrhea, kidney and liver damage, and death. Some adverse effects, even if nonfatal, last for one or two weeks, others last for months or years. There is recent evidence that water contaminants (particularly nitrates and radon) cause cancer.

The quality of drinking water can be tested by a local health authority or water supplier. Typically, test results are compared with national water standards, although some states have imposed stricter standards. Federal regulations (the **Safe Drinking Water Act**) require that public water suppliers test the drinking water for contamination periodically. If your water comes from a well, it can be tested by health authorities or private laboratories. Anyone who uses a well should make sure the well is properly designed and maintained. Some experts advise testing private water supplies at least once a year.

If water contamination is suspected, alternate sources of water should be used until it is determined that the water is safe.

Groundwater contamination. The term **groundwater** is sometimes confusing to the general public. It consists not only of the runoff at ground level but also includes the underground water systems that are used as sources of wells for both private and public facilities. Underground streams are formed in the rocks, crevices and caves under the ground and flow just as dramatically as do rivers above the ground. This underground water table can be as shallow as two or three feet below the surface or range all the way down to several hundred feet.

Contamination of this water supply is a serious health threat. Many experts believe that water someday will become an extremely valuable asset, because this general contamination will make pure, clean water a scarce commodity.

Water can be contaminated from a number of sources, including waste disposal sites and underground storage tanks. It also is contaminated by the use of pesticides and herbicides that are typically found in farming communities. Heavy regulation in these areas is about the only protection the general public has against water contamination. Once contamination has been identified, its source can be eliminated, but such a process is often time-consuming and extremely expensive. Many times freshwater wells must be relocated to provide water for residents and commercial establishments.

▼ Waste Disposal Sites

The American culture has become increasingly a *throwaway* society. Landfill operations have been the main receptacle for this type of garbage. A **landfill** is a specific site that has been excavated and lined with either a clay or a synthetic liner to prevent leakage of waste material into the local water system. Garbage is then laid at the bottom of the excavation and a layer of topsoil is compacted onto the garbage. The procedure is used again and again until the excavation has been filled. Although there is no height limitation for the garbage, it is usually *capped* when it reaches several hundred feet. Capping a landfill means to layer from two to four feet of topsoil onto the very top and then plant some type of vegetation. Completed landfills have been used for such purposes as parks and golf courses.

The construction and maintenance of a landfill operation is heavily regulated by state and federal authorities. Well-run landfill operations do not have to be a source of pollution. However, landfills at improper locations and improperly managed sites have been a source of major problems. Landfills constructed on the wrong type of soil will leak waste into nearby wells, causing major damage. Federal, state and local authorities and private industry have set up test wells around such landfill operations to monitor the water in the local areas constantly.

Radioactive waste is material that has accumulated as waste from nuclear energy power plants and from various uses of radioactive material in medicine and scientific research. Emissions from such waste can be extremely harmful, sometimes causing cancer or even death.

Radioactive material can have a life expectancy of thousands of years. Much is still to be learned about disposal techniques, and in most cases the only alternative is to put the material in some type of containment facility. The container is then either buried or dropped in the sea. The obvious problem is that sometimes these containers can leak or be damaged in transit.

Although waste disposal is heavily regulated, no one is interested in living next to a hazardous waste dump. Real estate professionals must be aware of such facilities within their area and take the appropriate action when dealing with potential buyers or sellers.

▼ Septic Systems

It is estimated that about 25 percent of American homes use *septic systems* for the disposal of household wastewater. Household wastewater is made up of water from toilets, washing machines, dishwashers, sinks, bathtubs and showers. The average family of four produces about 300 gallons of wastewater every day. A **septic system** is an individual treatment and disposal system that is usually built underground. A septic system consists of a large storage tank (septic tank), in which the wastewater is partially broken down by bacteria, and an absorption (leach) field, which receives and filters the wastewater. Solid material settles out of the wastewater, remains at the bottom of the septic tank and must be pumped out periodically (at least once every three to five years).

Before a septic tank can be installed, the property owner must have the soil tested to determine how much wastewater the soil can process (**percolation test**). The septic tank also must be the correct size for the number of occupants, and the proper size is determined by the number of bedrooms in the house.

When the septic tank is property installed and maintained, a septic system is generally adequate for wastewater disposal and treatment. However, if the system is not working properly, there may be serious consequences, including contamination of ground water and wells; contamination of nearby streams, rivers and lakes; and the pooling of wastewater above the surface.

There are various signs that a septic system is malfunctioning, including wastewater odors inside or outside the home, lush grass and spongy soil over the absorption field, pooled "gray" water over the absorption field and sluggish or backed-up drains.

If the septic system has failed, pumping the septic tank may solve the problem. More serious malfunctions may require the installation of a new septic system, new fields, new pumps or distribution boxes or the installation of a sewer system.

▼ Termites

Termites are antlike insects that live in the earth. In some New York regions termites are a common problem for homeowners because these insects are so destructive to wood. It is vital that when a home or other structure is built, no untreated wood touches the soil. The ground often is treated before laying the foundation, to keep termites from coming up through the foundation. Metal termite shields also may be used to prevent termite infestation.

Termite damage, which typically occurs in homes that are more than five or ten years old, is often hard to detect. Termite inspectors must probe the foundation and base wood structure of a house with a tool similar to an ice pick. If the pick sinks down into the wood, it has probably been eaten away inside (although rot may also be the culprit). Termites may also leave tunnellike trails as evidence of their presence.

When termite damage or infestation is present, a thorough extermination is required, and the termite damage must be repaired.

▼ Asbestos

Asbestos is a mineral that has been used for many years as insulation on plumbing pipes and heat ducts and as general insulation because it is a poor conductor of heat. It also has been used in floor tile and in roofing material.

Due to its heat-containing property and the fact that it is relatively inexpensive, asbestos has been used in the insulation of almost all types of buildings, especially public buildings such as libraries, schools and government buildings. Although it remains relatively harmless if not disturbed, it can become life-threatening when removed because of the accompanying dust.

Contemporary environmental concerns affecting real estate include asbestos, lead, radon gas, indoor air quality and PCBs.

Exposure to the dust can come in several ways. One is when the asbestos material gets old and starts to disintegrate. Remodeling projects that include the removal of asbestos shingles, roof tile or insulation can cause the dust to form in the air and expose people in the area to the health hazard.

Once a building has been determined to have an asbestos problem, the owner can take several approaches to eliminating the problem. One is to leave well enough alone. Asbestos roofing, floor tile and insulation, if undisturbed, do not expose humans to asbestos. The alternative is to remove any asbestos material. Public laws have been passed that require that all school buildings and other buildings used by the general public eliminate all asbestos insulation. Removal can be accomplished only by professionals experienced and knowledgeable in this field.

The third approach is to encapsulate the material; in other words, if the exposure comes because of the dust in the air, it is possible to contain the dust by enclosing the insulation with a plastic or paint that does not allow the dust to reach the air. Again, such procedures should be carried out by professionals.

▼ **Lead Poisoning**

Lead is a substance that has been used for centuries because of its pliability and its ability to block water flow. It has been used as an ingredient in paint to protect wood from damage by water and also has been used in the installation of water pipes. It becomes a health hazard when ingested. Once in the body, it can impair physical and mental development in young children and aggravate high blood pressure in adults.

Lead poisoning comes from two main sources. The first is peeling or flaking paint that small children sometimes put into their mouths. The second is the plumbing system. Sometimes lead in connecting water pipes or in insulation for hot-water heaters contaminates the water that flows through them. Concentrated amounts of lead can lead to serious health effects.

Lead was used in many oil-based paints until 1978. Once various health problems were linked to lead poisoning, lead was immediately banned as an ingredient of any paint material. Other limitations have been imposed on all materials that contain lead to keep the lead away from all materials that may be ingested. However, one can still be exposed to lead in many older homes.

In the early 1990s, the FHA and VA started requiring that every buyer of a home built before 1978 be furnished with information about possible lead paint contamination before signing a purchase offer. The federal government then extended the requirement to all rentals and sales. Currently, both sellers and landlords must disclose information regarding lead-based paint to buyers and renters of pre-1978 residential properties. Sellers and landlords must

- disclose the location of any lead-based paint that they are aware of,
- provide a copy of any report concerning lead-based paint in the property to buyers or tenants,
- give buyers or tenants a copy of a pamphlet on lead-based paint prepared by the government and
- offer buyers or tenants a 10-day period in which to have the home tested for lead-based paint.

Note that sellers and landlords are not required to actually test for lead-based paint or make any repairs. (See Figure 3.1 on page 54.)

▼ **Radon Gas**

Radon gas is an odorless, radioactive gas produced by the decay of other radioactive materials in rocks under the surface of the earth. As radon is released from the rocks, it finds its way to the surface and is usually released into the general atmosphere. In some cases it is trapped in buildings and increases in concentration. Radon enters a house through cracks in the foundation or through floor drains. It can become concentrated in crawl spaces or in basements. Long-term exposure to radon gas is said to cause lung cancer.

Radon was identified as being a hazardous problem in homes in 1984. Since that time the U.S. Environmental Protection Agency has established levels of radon gas that are felt to be unsafe. Testing techniques also have been developed that allow homeowners to determine the exact quantity of radon gas in their homes. The level of radon that necessitates remediation is 4 picocuries (pci). However, if a level of radon lower than 4 pci can be simply and inexpensively lowered, it would be wise to do so. Note that there is a synergistic effect when radon is combined with smoking.

Generally the elimination of radon gas from a home is a relatively simple matter. Radon is a potential health threat only if found in concentrated amounts. Therefore, proper ventilation systems or small exhaust fans can move the radon gas from the area of concentration into the general atmosphere.

If a home has been determined to have radon gas, the seller is obligated to find a way to eliminate such a hazard, regardless of whether the danger is actual or only perceived. The value of the property can be reduced dramatically under such conditions. Typically it would be reduced by the amount necessary to eliminate the problem.

New York State's radon information line is 1-800-458-1158.

▼ **Indoor Air Quality**

Indoor air quality has become increasingly significant as two results of poor air quality have become more readily diagnosed. These are *sick building syndrome* and *building related illness.*

Sick building syndrome (SBS) is the name for a wide range of symptoms suffered by building occupants that are present only when the occupants are in the building and subside when the occupants leave the building. These symptoms include headaches, dizziness, drowsiness, memory loss, coughing, asthma, hoarseness, stinging skin, runny noses and watery eyes.

Building-related illness (BRI), caused by toxic substances or pathogens, continues to affect the building occupant even after he or she has left the building. BRI symptoms include hypersensitivity, pneumonitis, asthma and certain allergic reactions.

The major sources of interior air contamination include *volatile inorganic compounds* (chemical emissions from products such as paints, adhesives, cleaners, pesticides, fixtures and furnishings), *microorganisms* (fungi, bacteria, viruses, pollen and mites) and *particulates* (dust and dander).

▼ **Polychlorinated Biphenyls (PCBs)**

Polychlorinated biphenyls (PCBs) are found mostly in electrical equipment. For example, transformers found in electrical vaults within basements of buildings may contain PCBs. Although this type of electrical equipment is slowly being replaced by other equipment, transformers and other electrical equipment should be inspected by the local electric utility experts and replaced if they are found to contain PCBs.

Future Concerns

▼ Underground Storage Tanks

Underground storage tanks have been used in both residential and commercial settings for many years. One estimate is that there are from 3 million to 5 million underground storage tanks in the United States that contain hazardous substances, including gasoline. The risk comes when such containers become old, rust and start to leak. The toxic material then can enter the groundwater to contaminate wells and can pollute the soil.

The most obvious source of such pollution is the millions of gas stations scattered around the United States. Older stations sometimes have steel tanks that have developed leaks through oxidation (rusting). Another major source is the underground containers that were used to hold fuel oil for older homes. Many times the homeowner has converted the heating system to natural gas and has abandoned the use of the old oil tank. This, again, raises the risk of leakage and pollution of the general area.

Recent federal legislation has called for the removal of such tanks and all the polluted soil around them. The tank and the soil are then disposed of in a hazardous waste facility. Such a program is extremely expensive, sometimes costing hundreds of thousands of dollars to revamp a gas station, for instance. Legislation regarding underground storage tanks is discussed in more detail later in this chapter.

▼ Electromagnetic Fields

Electromagnetic fields are generated by the presence and movement of electrical charges, that is, electric current. Electromagnetic fields are generally associated with the use of electric power. Common sources of electromagnetic fields (aside from those generated by the earth's magnetic field) include high tension (or high voltage) transmission lines; primary and secondary distribution lines; and electric appliances inside homes, such as televisions, computers, microwave ovens, conventional electric ovens, electric blankets, even electric clocks.

Currently, there is controversy over exactly what, if any, damage is caused by electromagnetic fields. There is some evidence to suggest that exposure to electromagnetic fields may cause cancer, hormonal changes and changes in behavior.

Reducing exposure to electromagnetic fields ranges from the simple to the impossible. For example, if a home is built near primary or secondary transmission lines, there is little the occupants can do to reduce their exposure except move. On the other hand, exposure to electromagnetic fields generated by electrical appliances can be reduced by sitting or standing farther away from them—it is generally assumed that standing a distance of two to three feet away from low-voltage electrical appliances is safe.

▼ Chlorofluorocarbons

Chlorofluorocarbons (CFCs) are considered to be a significant cause of the depletion of the ozone layer around the earth. CFCs are gases produced by the propellants used in older aerosol containers and by a refrigerant called *Freon*. (When used in its liquid form, Freon removes, or absorbs, heat; when released, it becomes a gas.) CFCs are no longer legal in aerosol cans, and the use of Freon is no longer allowed. However, old-model refrigerators, automobile air conditioners, residential air conditioners, freezers and heat pumps may present potential leakage problems. The removal of Freon from older appliances is required by law.

Environmental Assessments

Whenever environmental concerns are present, a *Phase I Environmental Assessment* (or *audit*) should be performed. A Phase I Environmental Assessment is an investigation conducted by an environmental professional to determine whether hazardous substances are present on or being released from the property.

A Phase I assessment consists of reviewing the previous ownership and uses of the property by examining all deeds, easements, leases, restrictions and covenants for a period of 50 years; aerial photographs; any recorded environmental cleanup liens; federal, state and local government records of sites or facilities where there has been a release of hazardous substances; and a visual site inspection of the property and all its improvements.

If the Phase I Assessment discloses the presence or release of hazardous substances on the property, further action may be necessary to confirm the contamination. If confirmation is necessary, a Phase II Environmental Assessment will be performed, which consists of sample testing and evaluation. The Phase II assessment must be conducted by a qualified environmental engineer.

Phase III includes remedying the contamination, if any is confirmed, and Phase IV includes management of the environmental hazards.

Legal Considerations

The majority of legislation dealing with environmental problems has been enacted within the past two decades. Although the **Environmental Protection Agency (EPA)** was created at the federal level to oversee such problems, there are several other federal agencies whose areas of concern generally overlap. The federal laws also were created in such a way as to encourage state and local governments to prepare legislation affecting their own jurisdiction. All of the legislation lies on a background of common law being established by the court systems that creates liability for the seller, the buyer, the listing broker, the selling broker, the appraiser, lenders and anyone involved in the real estate business.

> An environmental assessment consists of investigating, testing and confirming, remedying and managing the contamination.

Federal environmental law is administered by such agencies as the U.S. Department of Transportation under the Hazardous Material Transportation Act; the Occupational Safety and Health Administration (OSHA) and the U.S. Department of Labor, which administer the standards for all employees working in the manufacturing sector; and the EPA, which administers such laws as the Toxic Substance Control Act, the federal Clean Water Act and the Resource Conservation and Recovery Act.

The following discussion is designed to give a broad overview of and a historical background to those laws that affect real estate. Increases in technology and public awareness of the problem mean that this is a dynamic area of the law with many areas of liability still being defined.

▼ Statutory Law

The need for federal legislation was recognized after the Love Canal situation developed in New York. A hazardous waste leak created untold problems from both a physical health and a property standpoint. The Resource Conservation

Figure 17.1   Environmental Issues

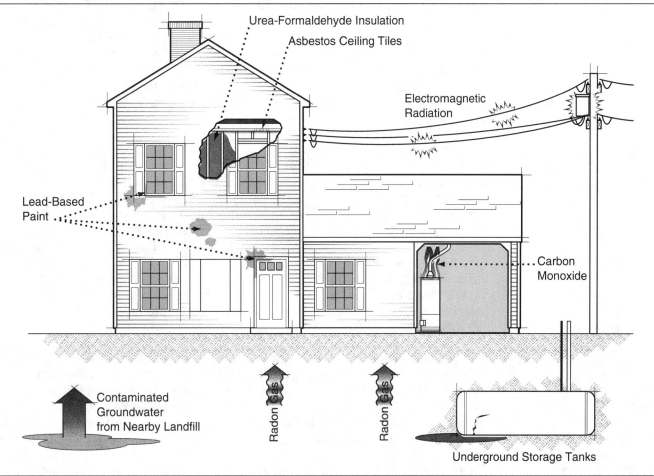

and Recovery Act (RCRA) of 1976 consequently was created to regulate the generation, transportation, storage, use, treatment, disposal and cleanup of hazardous waste. However, it quickly became apparent that the legislation was not sufficiently comprehensive to cover all the situations that were quickly becoming a matter of concern.

The *Comprehensive Environmental Response, Compensation, and Liability Act (CERCLA)* was created in 1980. It established a fund of $9 billion, called the *Superfund*, to clean up uncontrolled hazardous waste dumps and to respond to spills. It created a process for identifying liable parties and ordering them to take responsibility for the cleanup action. A landowner may become liable under this act when there has been a release or is a threat of release of a hazardous substance. Regardless of whether the contamination is the result of the landowner's actions or those of others, the owner could be held responsible for cleaning up any resulting contamination. The liability includes the cleanup of the landowner's property and any neighboring property that has been contaminated. A landowner who is not responsible for the contamination can seek recovery reimbursement for the cleanup cost from previous landowners, any other responsible party or the Superfund.

If the EPA determines that there has been a release of hazardous material into the environment, the agency is given the authority to begin remedial action. It will initially attempt to determine the responsible parties for the leak and approach these **potentially responsible parties (PRPs)** to see if they will voluntarily cooperate in the cleanup. For a given site the PRPs may include hundreds of industrial generators of waste, previous landowners and transporters. The PRPs must then decide whether and on what terms they can fund the cleanup. If this is not done, EPA will begin work through its own contractors and charge the responsible parties for this cost. If a court determines liability after the cleanup and the refusal to pay, the responsible parties could be required to pay triple damages.

Liability under the Superfund is considered to be *strict, joint and several*, and *retroactive*. *Strict liability* means that the owner is responsible to the injured party without excuse. *Joint and several liability* means that each of the individual owners is personally responsible for the damages in whole. If only one of the owners is financially able to handle the total damage, then that owner will have to pay all and collect the proportionate share from the rest of the owners whenever possible. *Retroactive liability* means that the liability is not limited to the person who currently owns the property but is shared by people who have owned the site in the past. Basically, the liability provision means that *all owners and transporters of hazardous waste are liable for the resulting cleanup cost without regard to fault*. Therefore, the EPA need not prove wrongdoing to complete the cleanup or obtain recovery costs.

The *New York Environmental Protection Act of 1993* establishes a funding mechanism and procedures to enhance state and local efforts to preserve natural resources. The law provides assistance to state agencies, municipalities and other organizations for the purposes of open space preservation, waterfront revitalization, coastal rehabilitation, landfill closure and municipal waste reduction and recycling programs.

The law provides local governments with veto power over land acquisition proposals not contained in the state *master plan*, and requires that all land purchases be approved by the state legislature in the annual budget.

The *Adirondack Park Commission* and the *Long Island Pine Barrens Advisory Committee* are examples of regional land use management.

Underground Storage Tanks. Underground chemical or petroleum storage tanks have been regulated under a 1984 amendment to the Resource Conservation and Recovery Act. A program called **Leaking Underground Storage Tanks (LUST)** was established that governs for the first time on a nationwide scale *installation, maintenance, monitoring and failure of underground storage tanks*. The focus of LUST regulation is to protect groundwater in the United States through release prevention, detection and correction.

The basic provisions of the program require that owners of commercial underground storage tanks and pipes register the present tanks, meet standards for installation, make the tanks leakproof for their entire lives, install leak detection systems, keep the required records and install no bare steel tanks in soils that will cause rust (otherwise the tanks must be corrosion-proof). Owners also must correct leaks and have funds available to cover potential damage from leaks.

The federal law generally *exempts* farm and residential tanks holding fewer than 1,100 gallons of motor fuel that is used for noncommercial purposes, tanks storing heating oil at the premises where it is consumed and septic tanks. An important legal point is that LUST places the financial responsibility on the tank owner.

Currently, fuel storage tanks with a capacity of 1,100 gallons or more also are regulated under *New York's Underground Storage Tank Act*. However, owners of small residential tanks are liable for cleanup costs under the state's Environmental Response Act if there is a leak or spill from their tanks. Because of this liability, it is sometimes difficult to sell property that has an underground tank.

Contamination problems are caused by rusting tanks, leaky piping and spills or overfills during fuel delivery. A recommended practice is that homeowners replace tanks every 15 years, routinely inspect tank fittings and monitor fuel levels with a dipstick during summer months to detect any unwarranted fuel losses. Homeowners should use above-ground tanks, if possible, and purchase quality equipment to minimize the risk of any significant contamination problem.

Superfund Amendments and Reauthorization Act (SARA). In 1986 the United States Congress reauthorized the Superfund. The amended statute contains stronger cleanup standards for contaminated sites and provides five times the funding of the original Superfund, which expired in September 1985.

The amended act also seeks to clarify the obligation of lenders. As previously mentioned, liability under the Superfund Act extends to both the present and all previous owners of the contaminated site. Real estate lenders found themselves either as the present owner or somewhere in the chain of ownership through foreclosure proceedings.

The amendments created a concept called *innocent landowner immunity*. It was recognized that in certain cases a landowner in the chain of ownership had been completely innocent of all wrongdoing and therefore should not be held liable. The innocent landowner immunity clause establishes the criteria by which to judge whether a person or business can be exempted from that liability. Among the criteria are stipulations that the pollution must have been caused by a third party, that the property was acquired after the fact, that the landowner did not have actual or constructive knowledge of the damage, that *due care* was exercised when the property was purchased (the landowner made a reasonable search to determine that there was no damage to the property) and that reasonable precautions were taken in the exercise of ownership rights.

▼ **Common Law**   **Common law,** which is created by past court decisions, provides a backup for federal, state and local statutes to govern situations that do not specifically fall within the law. Common law offers an important remedy for personal injuries or property damages that are not covered under legislation.

A good example of this is the concept of *negligence,* a field of law that defines the duty that members of the public owe to each other to take reasonable care to avoid foreseeable harm. Negligence can be defined as *the failure to use such care as a reasonably prudent and careful person would use to avoid harm to others that is foreseeable.* This doctrine can be used against all owners, whether public or private, of sites and facilities who make mistakes resulting in hazardous waste being released into the environment. Negligent acts that result in the release of chemicals into the environment are sometimes called *toxic torts.* Such torts are said to carry strict liability.

Implications of Environmental Law

The real estate professional must be aware of the exposure of all parties involved. The real estate broker, for instance, is often the central player in a real estate transaction. The other players in the transaction have little if any knowledge of environmental law, let alone the type of exposure that they might be subjected to.

Sellers, as mentioned earlier, often carry the majority of the liability. Innocent landowners may be held responsible even though they did not know that the property had been exposed to environmental pollution.

It is also necessary to advise the buyer of the potential for risk posed by neighboring properties. If the broker represents a seller whose property abuts a gas station, the broker must be aware of the possibility of a leak and make the appropriate disclosures. The trend of the legal system is such that all possible risk must be disclosed to the buyer in any situation in which there might be an environmental problem. Although the preceding example is rather blatant, sellers might also be vulnerable to possible litigation in terms of exposure to radon, asbestos and lead.

The entity from which the majority of lawsuits originate is the buyer. The days of "caveat emptor" (let the buyer beware) are dwindling. Both the statutes and the courts are taking steps to protect the innocent buyer whenever possible. The real estate professional has no other choice but to help protect the buyer in all situations.

▼ Liability of Real Estate Professionals

Additional liability is created for the auxiliary functions to the transaction. For instance, the real estate appraiser must mention and make the proper adjustments in the estimate of market value. Most of the environmental problems associated with residential units can be cleaned up, and the adjustment to market value typically reflects the cost of that cleanup plus a factor of the *concern* that exists in the current market. Although the sales price can be affected dramatically, it is possible that the underlying market value would remain relatively equal to others in the neighborhood.

The real estate appraiser is at the forefront of liability with regard to the lender. Proper diagnosis by the appraiser or proper diagnosis coupled with the lender's determination to make the mortgage anyway can create specific liability for the lender. Again, the lender is protected under certain conditions through the 1986 amendments to the Superfund Act. But in any event the lender must be notified of any potential problems existing with the property.

The last and certainly not the least member of the group that might be affected by the transaction is the insurance carrier. The mortgage insurance companies will protect the lender's investment in the mortgage and may be required to carry part of the ultimate responsibility in case of a loss. More important, the hazard insurance carrier may be deemed directly responsible for the damages if such coverage was included in the initial policy.

Environmental law is a relatively new phenomenon. Although the statutes have defined many of the liabilities involved, common law is still used to make definitive points. The real estate professional and all associated with the real estate transaction must be aware of both actual and potential liability.

All parties to the real estate transaction should be certain to ascertain that "due diligence" has been conducted on the property by having an *environmental screening* done before the purchase of the property. The environmental screening can take the form of a report or become a complete environmental audit with complete engineering and scientific tests being conducted.

Modern computer technology now allows the various environmental databases to be used to effectively "screen" properties for potential problems based on the "footprint" of information regarding the subject property. Nationally, one such system, VISTA Environmental profiles, is an example of a screening system that can be used by real estate professionals to prevent any environmental surprises from occurring. This system, when used by qualified individuals, can provide a key element in the environmental assessment of a property in a matter of minutes. Techniques such as this will enable real estate professionals to become more knowledgeable regarding environmental factors relating to subject properties and also will prevent large amounts of time and capital from being expended on marketing only to find that an environmental problem became a *deal killer* in the final stages of negotiation.

Key Terms

asbestos	percolation test
building-related illness (BRI)	pollution
chlorofluorocarbons (CFCs)	polychlorinated biphenyls (PCBs)
common law	potentially responsible
electromagnetic field	parties (PRPs)
Environmental Protection Agency	radioactive waste
(EPA)	radon gas
groundwater	Safe Drinking Water Act
hazardous substances	septic system
landfill	sick building syndrome (SBS)
lead poisoning	termites
Leaking Underground Storage	underground storage tanks
Tanks (LUST)	

Summary

In today's marketplace, environmental concerns have significant effects on real estate values. The desirability of property is affected by the presence of pollution, and the cost of cleaning up and removing the sources of pollution may be greater than the value of the land itself.

Several long-standing concerns include water pollution (including groundwater pollution), waste disposal sites, contamination caused by septic systems and damage caused by termites. Some of the more contemporary issues include asbestos, lead poisoning, radon gas, indoor air quality, PCBs. Some environmental issues that are becoming more important include underground storage tanks, electromagnetic fields and CFCs.

There are four phases of environmental assessments: Phase I, an investigation to determine where hazardous substances may be present; Phase II, an investigation to confirm the presence of contaminants; Phase III, which includes remedying the contamination; and Phase IV, which includes managing environmental hazards on an ongoing basis.

One of the most important environmental laws that directly affect property owners is the Comprehensive Environmental Response, Compensation, and Liability Act (CERCLA), which established a Superfund to clean up uncontrolled hazardous waste and to respond to spills. It also imposes liability on property owners for the costs of cleaning up contaminants.

Underground storage tanks are regulated by both federal and state law: the Resource Conservation and Recovery Act, and the New York Underground Storage Tank Act. These laws regulate larger tanks, those with capacities greater than 1,100 gallons and 1,000 gallons, respectively.

1. Which of the following is *not* a potential polluter of drinking water?
   - a. Viruses
   - c. Bacteria
   - b. Pesticides
   - d. Radio

2. Which federal regulations require periodic testing of public water supplies?
   - a. CERCLA
   - b. SARA
   - c. Safe Drinking Water Act
   - d. LUST

3. Asbestos is rarely used for
   - a. insulation.
   - c. wallboard.
   - b. floor tile.
   - d. roofing.

4. Which of the following is a hazardous gas?
   - a. Radon
   - c. Asbestos
   - b. Lead
   - d. Mercury

5. Eliminating radon from a house is generally
   - a. a fairly simple matter.
   - b. a difficult matter.
   - c. an impossibility.
   - d. hazardous.

6. Sick building syndrome (SBS)
   - a. affects the building occupant even after he or she leaves the building.
   - b. occurs only while an occupant is in a building.
   - c. causes hypersensitivity.
   - d. causes pneumonitis.

7. Building-related illness (BRI)
   - a. affects the building occupant even after he or she leaves the building.
   - b. occurs only while an occupant is in the building.
   - c. causes runny noses.
   - d. causes memory loss.

8. Asbestos should be removed only by a
   - a. seller.
   - b. buyer.
   - c. handyman.
   - d. certified professional.

9. New York's Underground Storage Tank Act regulates fuel storage tanks with a capacity of
   - a. 550 gallons or larger.
   - b. 1,750 gallons or larger.
   - c. 1,000 gallons or larger.
   - d. 2,000 gallons or larger.

10. A Phase I environmental assessment is common before purchasing a
    - a. ranch.
    - b. commercial property.
    - c. condominium.
    - d. residential lot.

11. Liability under Superfund is *not* considered to be
    - a. strict.
    - b. based only on negligence.
    - c. joint and several.
    - d. retroactive.

12. CERCLA established
    a. the EPA.
    b. the Landfill Act.
    c. Superfund.
    d. OSHA.

13. Prospective purchasers who are worried about possible contamination of the property they are interested in should ask the seller for a
    a. petition to the Environmental Protection Agency.
    b. Phase I environmental assessment.
    c. percolation test.
    d. lead paint disclosure statement.

18 ▶ Real Estate Investment

The Agostinos are being transferred out of town and can't decide what to do about their home. If they rent it out, they can clear about $400 a month over their mortgage payment, which would help with payments on their new home. If they sell it, they will have about $60,000 after paying off their present loan. They have asked a real estate broker whether they would be wise to keep the house as an investment.

Often customers want a real estate broker or salesperson to act as an investment counselor. The licensee should understand the fundamentals of income property, but should also recommend that a potential real estate investor consult a tax accountant, attorney or investment specialist who can give expert advice regarding the investor's needs.

The Nature of Real Estate Investment

Investing in real estate usually means buying property and holding it for the production of income. Real estate has been called the best way to build an estate.

Real estate investment, though, takes a constant investment of effort. One can buy shares of stock and then limit further effort to checking the quotations every week in the Sunday paper. Not so with a duplex three blocks from home. The owner must be ready for a 6 a.m. phone call about a burst water heater and have a prompt replacement delivered and arrange for someone to meet the plumber that very day. For small properties it is very difficult to be an absentee landlord.

In addition, real estate investment is not liquid. Money can be taken out of the stock market with a simple phone call to a stockbroker. Investors in real estate, however, should not count on taking out their capital within perhaps six months. When local unemployment is high, investors may not be able to take out their money until the economic cycle changes.

Preparing To Be an Investor

An investor faces two challenges: finding and buying the right property, then managing it. The beginning investor needs

- a lawyer who specializes in real estate,
- an accountant and
- a real estate broker familiar with investment real estate.

All three should be lined up before the first purchase so they can assist in locating and analyzing the proposed investment. Meanwhile, the new investor should get information about the market by reading the papers and visiting open houses and develop the expertise needed to recognize a bargain.

Starting small. Investors would be wise to start small for the first few transactions so they do not risk too much capital or take on too much liability while learning. A one- to six-unit building, located reasonably close to the investor's own home, is often best. Out-of-town property that cannot be monitored or controlled can be disappointing.

Avoiding vacant land. Building lots in resort areas and vacant land held in anticipation of development are not for the beginning investor. Land would have to appreciate markedly before it would pay off, because it produces no income, ties up money, cannot be depreciated and requires property tax payments. Judging which areas will be in demand in years to come takes skill and expertise, and even experienced investors can be burned.

▼ **Leverage**

Pyramiding. Traditionally real estate investors have used **leverage** (other people's money) to **pyramid** a small amount of capital. If, for example, an investor had $100,000 and bought one property that went up in value by 5 percent in the next year, the investor would make $5,000 in appreciation. To use leverage, one might search for ten such parcels, putting $10,000 down on each and getting sellers to take back $90,000 mortgages. If each went up by 5 percent, the investor would have appreciation totaling $50,000 in one year and would control $1 million worth of real estate.

This technique runs into problems, however, where local conditions change, employment drops and finding tenants who will pay enough to cover those ten mortgage payments becomes difficult. The investors who delighted in *owning* $1 million worth of real estate now find themselves *owing* on $1 million worth, which is a different matter.

▼ **Risk and Reward**

The purpose of investing is to generate a **return,** or profit. An investor expects both a return *of* capital (recovery of the invested funds) and a return *on* capital (profit or reward). The rate of return that an investor expects is directly related to the degree of risk in the investment. Real estate investments must offer the promise of higher returns to attract capital away from other, safer investments.

> The purpose of investing is to generate a return or profit. An investor expects both a return of capital and a return on capital.

One of the most important risks for a real estate investment is the possibility that the property will decline in value during the investment holding period. On the other hand, an increase in property value can be a significant component of an investment's profit. For this reason, real estate investors must give considerable attention to the trends that affect real estate values. Statistical data from government agencies and private research groups are an important source of information in this regard. Such data can help to identify economic and social trends that will affect property values over time.

Analyzing Property Income

A key factor in any investment is the amount of income that can be expected. In the case of income-producing real estate, an investor is concerned with the amount of rent that the property can generate and also with the amount of expenses that are necessary to maintain the property. A property's income and expenses are typically recorded in the form of operating statements.

▼ **Operating Statements**

An operating statement is basically a list of revenues and expenses associated with a property for a given time period, such as one month or one year. The different categories of revenue (rent, parking fees, etc.) are listed at the top,

Figure 18.1 Operating Statement

15-Nov-94	ANNUAL PROPERTY OPERATING DATA		9:27 AM

Owner: XYZ APARTMENTS
Location: 621 DALE ROAD
City, St: NORTH LAUDERALE, FL 33068
Type: APARTMENT
Size: 100
Purpose: Owner's Statement

PREPARED BY:
R. BARRY DEICKLER,CRB,EMS
DEICKLER REAL ESTATE
40 WEST MAIN STREET
MT. KISCO, NY
Financing:

PRICE: 3,750,000
LOANS:
EQUITY: 3,750,000
FEE:

Assessed/Appraised: Value Value %
Land
Improvements
Personal Property
TOTAL
Adjusted Cost Basis:
Net Rentable Sq. Ft.:

Existing: Amount Int. Rate Due Mo. Pymt. Annual Pymt.
1st Loan
2nd Loan
3rd Loan
Potential:
1st Loan
2nd Loan

	ANNUAL INCOME/EXPENSES	$SQ.FT.	GSI %	EXPENSES	INCOME	
1	GROSS SCHEDULED INCOME		100.00%		721,560	THE FIGURES AND DATA HEREIN 1
2	Less Vac. & Cr. Losses		2.99%		21,560	ARE NOT GUARANTEED, BUT 2
3	EFFECTIVE RENTAL INCOME		97.01%		700,000	ARE BELIEVED TO BE RELIABLE. 3
4	Plus: Other Income					PLEASE GET ADVICE FROM 4
5	GROSS OPERATING INCOME		97.01%		700,000	YOUR CPA and ATTORNEY 5
6	OPERATING EXPENSES					COMMENTS / FOOTNOTES 6
7	Accounting & Legal		1.00%	7,000		7
8	Advertising		0.71%	5,000		8
9	Insurance		1.57%	11,000		9
10	Maintenance & Repair		3.57%	25,000		10
11	Management		3.57%	25,000		11
12	Payroll		4.57%	31,980		12
13	Payroll Taxes		0.36%	2,500		13
14	Postage					14
15	Real Estate Taxes		9.687%	67,808		15
16	Telephone					16
17	Other					17
18	Gas					18
19	Electric		2.87%	20,090		19
20	Water/Sewer		2.31%	16,200		20
21	Rubbish		2.48%	17,348		21
22	Reserves		2.14%	15,000		22
23	Leasing Commissions					23
24	Licences & Permits					24
25	Supplies					25
26	Miscellaneous		0.71%	5,000		26
27	Contract Services					27
28	Lawn/Snow Removal		0.19%	1,345		28
29	Pool		0.71%	5,000		29
30	Janitorial					30
31	TOTAL EXPENSES		36.47%	255,271		31
32	NET OPERATING INCOME				444,729	CAP RATE 11.86% 32
33	Less: Annual Debt Service	Debt Cov. Ratio ERR				LTV RATIO 33
34	CASH FLOW BEFORE TAXES				444,729	CASH ON CASH 11.86% 34

along with their amounts, and the amounts are totaled. Next come the various expenses associated with the property, which are also totaled. At the bottom of the statement, total expenses are subtracted from total revenues and the resulting *net operating income (NOI)* is noted. Net operating income (the "bottom line") is a critical factor in investment analysis. Figure 18.1 is an example of a completed operating statement.

▼ **Current Rent Roll**

An operating statement for a property will show the total amount of rent generated for the period of the statement, but it does not go into the details. This information is found in a rent roll or rent schedule, which lists the current rent for each tenant of the property. This information is important to investment analysis for several reasons. It indicates the level of vacancies in the property, and it also shows the rates at which various units are currently leased. It would be a disadvantage to the investor, for example, if units were subject to long-term leases at below market rental rates.

▼ **Pro Forma Statements**

While the owner's operating statements and rent roll are important sources of information for investment analysis, they do not predict what the property will earn in the future. And *future earnings* are precisely what investors are concerned with. Consequently, investment analysis makes use of **pro forma statements,** which are hypothetical future operating statements for a property.

Pro forma statements differ from regular operating statements in several key features. First of all, as just noted, pro forma statements list *potential* future revenues and expenses, while operating statements show actual past revenues and expenses. Second, in a pro forma statement the amount of rent is based on current market rates, as opposed to the currently scheduled rents for the property, unless the scheduled rents are locked in by long-term lease agreements. A pro forma statement shows the total amount of rent that the property is *capable of generating,* and then records a separate deduction for anticipated vacancies and collection losses. A regular operating statement simply shows the amount of rent that was actually collected.

Expense items also may be listed *differently* on a pro forma statement. Two critical items are *depreciation* and *mortgage debt service.* **Depreciation** is an expense item that is listed on operating statements for income tax purposes. The amount of depreciation expense is related to the owner's *tax basis* in the property and also to the relevant tax code provisions. The current owner's depreciation expense is irrelevant to investment analysis, so it is not included in a pro forma. In its place, a line item expense is shown for replacement reserves, the anticipated costs for replacing parts of the property (such as a roof or heating equipment) as they wear out.

Mortgage debt service refers to the *payments of principal and interest that must be made on loans that are secured by a property.* Here again, the current owner's debt service is essentially irrelevant to investment analysis, since the new investor will need to obtain new financing. In any case, *debt service is never considered to be a component of net operating income in investment analysis.* Net operating income is calculated independently, and then any debt service (current or pro forma) is deducted to determine the investment's *cash flow* (pretax cash flow). Like net operating income, *pretax cash flow* is a key figure in investment analysis.

A typical pro forma statement would first list the investment's *potential* **gross rental income.** Market rate rental figures may be used, unless the present rentals are locked in with long-term leases, which would survive a sale.

From potential gross rents, the following items would then be subtracted:

- An estimated allowance for vacancies and uncollected rents (normally 5 percent or so of gross rental income)
- Utilities paid by the landlord including, if applicable, electric power, fuel for heating and cooling, water, sewer, trash collection and so forth
- Property taxes
- Hazard and liability insurance premiums
- Estimate for repairs
- Maintenance services such as janitor service, snow removal, lawn care and the like
- Property management salaries or fees, if applicable
- A reserve for future large improvements such as a new roof or furnace, with the estimated amount based on the building's present condition and perhaps running to 2 percent of the value of the property

Projected expenses subtracted from gross rental yields annual **net operating income.** Next subtracted is **debt service** (mortgage payments). The resulting figure shows **cash flow**--actual dollars one can expect to take out of the property each year. If the figure is a minus, the investment is likely to yield **negative cash flow,** requiring a contribution from the investor's pocket each year.

Investment Ownership Structure

Ownership structure refers to the type of entity that will make the investment. For example, an individual may wish to purchase property through a corporation, either to limit personal liability exposure or for tax or accounting purposes. Ownership also may be structured in the form of a real estate syndicate or other specialized investment group.

A **real estate investment syndicate** is a form of business venture in which a group of people pool their resources to own and/or develop a particular piece of property. In this manner people with only modest capital can invest in large-scale, high-profit operations, such as highrise apartment buildings and shopping centers. A certain amount of profit is realized from rents collected on the investment, but the main return usually comes when the syndicate sells the property.

Syndicate participation can take many different legal forms, from tenancy in common and joint tenancy to various kinds of partnerships, corporations and trusts.

In 1994, the *New York Limited Liability Company Law* was enacted, which allows the formation of **limited liability companies (LLCs)** and **limited liability partnerships (LLPs).** Both LLCs and LLPs allow investors to take advantage of the federal tax benefits and flexibility of a partnership and the limited liability of a corporation. It is anticipated that LLCs will become a popular form of business organization.

Private syndication, **which** generally involves a small group of closely associated and/or widely experienced investors, **is distinguished from** *public syndication,* **which** generally involves a much larger group of investors who may or may not be knowledgeable about real estate as an investment. Any pooling of individuals' funds raises questions of registration of securities under federal securities laws and state securities laws, commonly referred to as *blue-sky laws.*

Securities laws control and regulate the offering and sale of securities to protect members of the public who are not sophisticated investors but may be solicited to participate. Real estate securities must be registered with state officials and/or with the federal Securities and Exchange Commission (SEC) *when they meet the defined conditions of a public offering.* The number of prospects solicited, the total number of investors or participants, the financial background and sophistication of the investors and the value or price per unit of investment are pertinent facts. Salespeople of such real estate securities may be required to obtain special licenses and register with the state's attorney general and the federal Securities and Exchange Commission.

▼ Forms of Syndicates

A **general partnership** is organized so that *all members of the group share equally in the managerial decisions, profits and losses.* A certain member (or members) of the syndicate is designated to act as trustee for the group, holding title to the property and maintaining it in the syndicate's name.

Under a **limited partnership** agreement *one party* (or parties), usually a property developer or real estate broker, organizes, operates and is responsible for the entire syndicate. This person is called the *general partner.* The other members of the partnership are merely investors; they have no voice in the organization and direction of the operation. These passive investors are called *limited partners* (and may also be called *silent partners*).

The limited partners share in the profits and compensate the general partner out of such profits. The limited partners stand to lose only as much as they invest, nothing more. The general partner(s) is (are) totally responsible for any excess losses incurred by the investment. The sale of a limited partnership interest involves the sale of an *investment security,* as defined by the SEC. Therefore, such sales are subject to state and federal laws concerning the sale of securities. Unless exempt, the securities must be registered with the federal Securities and Exchange Commission and the appropriate state authorities.

▼ Real Estate Investment Trusts

By directing their funds into **real estate investment trusts (REITs),** real estate investors can take advantage of the same tax benefits as mutual fund investors. A real estate investment trust does not have to pay corporate income tax as long as 95 percent of its income is distributed to its shareholders and certain other conditions are met. There are three types of investment trusts: equity trusts, mortgage trusts and combination trusts. To qualify as a REIT, at least 75 percent of the trust's income must come from real estate.

Equity trusts. Much like mutual fund operations, equity REITs pool an assortment of large-scale income properties and sell shares to investors. This is in contrast to a real estate syndicate, through which several investors pool their funds to purchase one particular property. An equity trust also differs from a syndicate in that the trust realizes and directs its main profits through the income derived from the various properties it owns rather than from the sale of those properties.

Mortgage trusts. Mortgage trusts operate similarly to equity trusts, except that the mortgage trusts buy and sell real estate mortgages (usually short-term, junior instruments) rather than real property. A mortgage trust's major sources of income are mortgage interest and origination fees. Mortgage trusts also may make construction loans and finance land acquisitions.

Combination trusts. Combination trusts invest shareholders' funds in both real estate assets and mortgage loans. It has been predicted that these types of trusts will be best able to withstand economic slumps because they can balance their investments and liabilities more efficiently than can the other types of trusts.

▼ Real Estate Mortgage Investment Conduits

The **real estate mortgage investment conduit (REMIC),** which issues securities backed by a pool of mortgages, has complex qualification, transfer and liquidation rules. Qualifications include the "asset test" (substantially all assets after a start-up period must consist of qualified mortgages and permitted investments) and the requirement that investors' interests consist of one or more classes of regular interests and a single class of residual interests. Holders of regular interests receive interest or similar payments based on either a fixed rate or a variable rate. Holders of residual interests receive distributions (if any) on a pro rata basis.

Holding Period and Disposition

One of the key considerations in an investment strategy is the question of when to get out of the investment, when to sell. This is especially true of real estate investments, due to the relative illiquidity of real estate. Choosing to sell at the wrong time can more than wipe out any gains that were realized during the ownership of a property. For this reason, real estate investment strategy must focus on both the *holding period* of the investment and the *timing of its disposition*.

The **holding period** is the length of time between the date the investor purchases the property and the date the investor resells the property. During this period, investment strategy is focused on the property's income and cash flow. Will the property generate enough income to cover the investor's financing costs and the expenses of maintaining the property? Does the investor have the resources to handle any periods of negative cash flow that may arise? Is the projected rate of return sufficient to compensate for the degree of investment risk posed by the property?

The strategy of **disposition** is *interrelated* with the strategy of the holding period. An anticipated gain or loss from the sale of the property will obviously affect the overall rate of return on the investment, which must be commensurate with the risk. The investor must balance the anticipated income during the holding period against the likelihood of a change in property value. A lower rate of income during the holding period may be acceptable if there is a strong probability of appreciation in value, whereas market uncertainty may demand a high rate of holding period income.

Financing considerations also come into play in the *investor's timing strategy.* Loan rates are dependent on the term of the loan, with lower rates often available for shorter term financing. An investor might be able to obtain a more favorable rate on a five-year balloon loan, for example, but then assumes the risk of needing to refinance on less desirable terms if market conditions preclude a profitable resale of the property after five years.

Types of Investment Properties

There are several types of properties investors are interested in, including the following:

- *Retail.* Retail properties include freestanding buildings and traditional shopping centers (which range from strip centers to superregional malls).
- *Office.* Office properties can be small properties with one or two tenants, highrise complexes or office parks. They may be situated in downtown urban areas or in suburban developments.
- *Apartment.* Multifamily housing is a popular type of investment property. Apartment buildings can range from five or six units to highrise complexes.
- *Mixed Developments.* Mixed developments are increasing in popularity. These developments combine several types of property uses, such as residential (apartments), office space and retail space.
- *Hotels/Motels.* Hotels and motels are a very specialized type of property and require expert management. While the failure rate for hotels and motels is quite high, they can be a good investment if the properties are in a good location and are well managed.

Investment Analysis Techniques

To a certain extent, investment analysis is a subjective operation, because it depends on the *goals* and the *situation* of the particular investor. One investor may have $50,000 to invest, and another may wish to invest $500,000. Some investors are naturally conservative, while others thrive on risky ventures. Often an investor has definite ideas about the type(s) of properties he or she is interested in. Although these subjective factors will affect any given investment analysis, certain techniques are widely used by a broad spectrum of real estate investors. The broker counseling a potential investor must have knowledge and expertise in the analysis of many types of investments.

▼ Discounted Cash-Flow Analysis

Discounting is a mathematical technique for calculating the present value of a future amount. In discounting, the value of $1 that will be received at some future date depends on two factors: the length of *time* until the money is paid and the *rate* at which the payment is discounted. In general, a shorter repayment term or a lower discount rate means a higher present value.

Selecting the discount rate is a critical part of discounted cash flow analysis. This rate corresponds to the investor's expected rate of return on the investment. The **discount rate** must take into account *the time value of money, anticipated inflation or deflation and the particular risks associated with the future cash flows.* For example, a discount rate of 12 percent may be based on a "safe" rate of 5 percent, anticipated inflation of 3 percent, and an additional 4 percent to account for investment risk.

Although discounted cash flow analysis often is used to analyze a series of regular annual cash flows, it also can be applied to *individual cash flows that vary from year to year.* Different discount rates may be used for different payments, to reflect differences in risk. Assume, for example, that a property is subject to a long-term lease with a highly reputable tenant. Because the income from lease payments is at relatively low risk in this case, it may be discounted at a lower rate than the income that will come from resale of the property at the conclusion of the investment.

Net present value. **Net present value (NPV)** is sometimes used as a measure of *investment performance*. NPV is simply the difference between the present value of all positive cash flows and the present value of all capital outlays (negative cash flows). For example, assume that the present value of the positive cash flows from an investment is $110,000 and that the only capital outlay for the investment is its initial purchase price of $100,000. In this case the NPV is $10,000. (The $100,000 price does not need to be discounted in this case, because it represents a current amount.)

Analysis of NPV still requires that the investor select appropriate discount rates for the various cash flows. In addition, the investor must consider separately the total amount of capital outlays involved in the investment, because two investments with the same NPV can have vastly different amounts of capital outlays.

Internal rate of return. **Internal rate of return (IRR)** is related to NPV. It is the single discount rate that when applied to all positive and negative cash flows from an investment, results in an NPV of zero. In this sense, IRR represents a sort of absolute measure of investment performance. It is important to note, however, that IRR analysis does not allow for the possibility of different discount rates for individual cash flows and that investments with comparable internal rates of return do not necessarily involve comparable risks. Also, as in the case of NPV, IRR does not reflect the total amount of capital outlay that is associated with an investment.

Sensitivity Analysis. **Discounted cash flow analysis** is essentially a mathematical model of an investment. Even simple investments involve a number of variables, such as discount rates, cash flow amounts and cash flow timing. **Sensitivity analysis** *is designed to discover which of the variables are most critical for a particular investment* and therefore represent the greatest risk factors. In essence, this technique involves changing a single variable in the mathematical model for the investment (a discount rate, cash flow amount or time period) and looking at the effect on the outcome. When a small change in a variable results in a large change in calculated investment value, then that variable is a sensitive risk factor.

Income Tax Considerations

▼ Depreciation

Depreciation allows an investor to recover the cost of an income-producing asset by way of tax deductions over the period of the asset's useful life. *Land cannot be depreciated*—technically, it never wears out or becomes obsolete. If depreciation is taken in equal amounts over an asset's useful life, the method used is called *straight-line depreciation.* For certain property purchased before 1987, it is also possible to use an *accelerated cost recovery system* (ACRS) to claim greater deductions in the early years of ownership.

In past years, tax rules allowed depreciation over as little as 15 years, allowing deduction of one-fifteenth of the cost of real property each year. For property placed in service after January 1, 1987, the Tax Reform Act of 1986 increased the recovery period for residential rental property to 27.5 years and for nonresidential property to 31.5 years. Just as important, only straight-line depreciation is allowed. After the act investors began to judge income property more on its own merits and less on its tax benefits.

Subtracting depreciation from net operating income yields the profit or loss the investor can declare on an income tax return. An accountant can determine whether any loss can be taken as a loss against other sources of income. The rules are complex. If total income is less than $100,000, the investor who actively manages the property may be able to claim up to $25,000 in losses against other types of income, such as salary or dividends. (An owner actively manages property when he or she is involved in management decisions, such as setting rental rates.) With total income up to $150,000, part of a loss may be deducted. Otherwise a paper loss can be taken only against other **passive income** (the category into which all rental income now falls for tax purposes). In the early 1990s real estate brokers and investors campaigned strenuously for Congress to change these passive loss tax rules. Income tax considerations are calculated at the investor's **marginal tax rate** (highest applicable tax bracket).

▼ **Capital Gains**

Capital gain is defined as the difference between the adjusted basis of property and its net selling price. At various times tax law has excluded a portion of capital gains from income tax, ranging from 0 to 50 percent.

Basis. The **basis** of property is the investor's initial cost for the real estate, plus the cost of any subsequent capital improvements. Any depreciation claimed as a tax deduction is then subtracted to arrive at the property's **adjusted basis.** Sales price is also adjusted, with commissions and legal costs of selling deducted. When the property is sold, adjusted sales price minus adjusted cost basis equals the capital gain taxable as income.

For example, an investor purchased a small one-family dwelling for use as a rental property. Purchase price was $45,000. The investor is now selling the property for $100,000. The investor made $3,000 worth of capital improvements to the house. Depreciation of $10,000 has been taken during the investor's ownership. The investor will pay a broker's commission of 7 percent of the sales price and also will pay closing costs of $600. The investor's capital gain is computed as follows:

Selling price:		$100,000
Less:		
7% commission	$ 7,000	
closing costs	+600	
	$ 7,600	−$7,600
Net sales price:		$92,400
Basis:		
original cost	$45,000	
improvements	+3,000	
	$48,000	
Less:		
depreciation	−10,000	
Adjusted basis:	$38,000	−$38,000
Total capital gain:		$54,400

▼ Exchanges

Real estate investors can postpone taxation of capital gains by arranging what is known as a **Section 1031 property exchange.** To qualify as a tax-deferred exchange, the properties involved must be of *like kind* and be investment property or a property used in trade or business (as defined by the IRS). For example, vacant land held as an investment may be exchanged for a shopping center, or an apartment building may be exchanged for water rights to a stream in Colorado. State law determines what qualifies as real estate. For example, a cooperative in New York and in 17 other states is considered real estate for the purpose of exchanging. Any additional capital or personal property included to even out the exchange is considered **boot,** and the party receiving boot is taxed on it at the time of the exchange.

Suppose investor Brown owns an apartment building with an adjusted basis of $225,000 and a market value of $375,000. Brown exchanges the building plus $75,000 cash for another apartment building having a market value of $450,000. That building, owned by investor Grey, has an adjusted basis of $175,000. Brown's basis in the new building will be $300,000 (the $225,000 basis of the building exchanged plus the $75,000 cash boot paid), and Brown has no tax liability on the exchange. Grey must pay tax on the $75,000 boot received and has a basis of $175,000 (the same as the previous building) in the building now owned. In a 1031 exchange, the investor's basis is transferred to the new property.

Brown	Exhanges with	Grey
$375,000	Price	$450,000
$225,000	Basis	$175,000
$ 75,000	Boot	

Amount necessary to exchange: $375,000 + $75,000 cash = $450,000

The $75,000 cash/boot is taxable to Grey

Brown's new basis = $300,000 ($225,000 + $75,000)

Grey's basis = $175,000

Section 1031 exchanges involve strict time limitations and require complicated paperwork. The guidance of a broker, attorney and/or accountant familiar with the procedure is essential.

▼ Tax Credits

A **tax credit** is a direct reduction in tax due, rather than a deduction from income before tax is computed. A tax credit is therefore of far greater value.

Investors in older building renovations and low-income housing projects may use designated tax credits to offset tax on up to $25,000 of other income. This is a major exception to the rule requiring active participation in the project. Even passive investors can take advantage of the tax credits. The maximum income level at which the credits can be taken is also higher. Investors with adjusted gross income of up to $200,000 are entitled to the full $25,000 offset, which is reduced by $.50 for every additional dollar of income and eliminated entirely for incomes above $250,000.

Tax credits of up to 20 percent of money spent are available for taxpayers who renovate historic property. Historic property is property so designated by the Department of the Interior and listed in the *National Register of Historic Land-marks* or property of historic significance located in a state or locally certified *historic district.* The property can be depreciated, but the full amount of the tax credit must be subtracted from the basis derived by adding purchase cost and renovation expenses.

The work must be accomplished in accordance with federal historic property guidelines and must be certified by the Department of the Interior or other state, county or local entity. After renovation, the property must be used as a place of business or rented; it cannot be used as the personal residence of the person taking the tax credit.

There is also a credit of 10 percent of rehabilitation costs for nonhistoric buildings placed in service before 1936. Nonhistoric buildings must be nonresidential property.

Also available are tax credits ranging from 4 percent to 9 percent each year over a ten-year period for expenditures on new construction or renovation of certain low-income housing.

▼ Installment Sales

A taxpayer who sells real property and receives payment on an *installment basis* may report and pay taxes on any profit on the transaction year by year as it is collected. Any *accelerated depreciation* previously taken, however, must be *recaptured* immediately. There are many complex provisions regarding installment sales.

Key Terms

adjusted basis	limited partnership
basis	marginal tax rate
boot	mortgage debt service
capital gain	negative cash flow
cash flow	net operating income
debt service	net present value (NPV)
depreciation	passive income
discount rate	pro forma statement
discounted cash flow analysis	pyramid
discounting	real estate investment syndicate
disposition	real estate investment trust (REIT)
general partnership	real estate mortgage investment
gross rental income	conduit (REMIC)
holding period	return
internal rate of return (IRR)	Section 1031 property exchange
leverage	sensitivity analysis
limited liability company (LLC)	tax credit
limited liability partnership (LLP)	

Summary

Traditionally real estate investment has offered a high rate of return while at the same time acting as an effective inflation hedge and allowing an investor to make use of other people's money to make investments through leverage. There may also be tax advantages to owning real estate. On the other hand, real estate is not a highly liquid investment and often carries with it a high degree of risk. Also, it is difficult to invest in real estate without expert advice, and a certain amount of involvement is usually required to establish and maintain the investment.

Net operating income on an investment is calculated by subtracting expenses (including vacancies and reserve for expected improvements) from gross rental income. Subtracting debt service (mortgage payments) then yields the figure representing actual cash flow. Total return is composed of cash flow plus mortgage amortization plus appreciation and tax benefits. A property's operating statements indicate its historical performance, while future performance must be estimated through the use of pro forma statements.

An investor hoping to use maximum leverage in financing an investment will make a small down payment, pay low interest rates and spread mortgage payments over as long a period as possible. By holding and refinancing properties, known as pyramiding, an investor may substantially increase investment holdings without contributing additional capital. The process can run into trouble if vacancy rates rise and rental income falls.

Individuals may invest in real estate through an investment syndicate; these include general and limited partnerships. Other forms of real estate investment are the real estate investment trust (REIT) and the real estate mortgage investment conduit (REMIC).

The holding period of an investment and its eventual resale are important factors in investment analysis. Discounted cash flow analysis is commonly used to evaluate investments, along with net present value, internal rate of return and sensitivity analysis.

Depreciation allows an investor to recover in tax deductions the basis of an asset over the period of its useful life. Only costs of improvements to land may be recovered, not costs for the land itself. The Tax Reform Act of 1986 greatly limited the potential for investment losses to shelter other income, but tax credits are still allowed for projects involving low-income housing and older buildings.

Capital gain represents the taxable profit when property is sold, calculated by subtracting adjusted cost basis from adjusted sales price. Adjusted cost basis represents original cost plus improvements, minus depreciation claimed.

By exchanging one property for another with an equal or greater selling value, an investor can defer paying tax on the gain realized until a sale is made. Any extra cash or property received in the exchange is called boot and is taxed.

An investor may defer federal income taxes on gain realized from the sale of an investment property through an installment sale of property.

The real estate licensee should be familiar with the rudimentary tax implications of real property ownership, but should refer clients to competent tax advisers for answers to questions to specific matters.

1. Many experts advise that a first real estate investment be
   a. within a short drive of the investor's own home.
   b. in a popular resort area.
   c. located only where professional management is available.
   d. handyman special property in need of upgrading.

2. The beginning investor should first consult an accountant when
   a. preparing the present year's income tax return.
   b. establishing cost basis for depreciation.
   c. analyzing a prospective purchase.
   d. researching fair market rentals.

3. Among the disadvantages of real estate investment is
   a. leverage.
   b. the need for physical and mental effort.
   c. tax shelter.
   d. equity buildup.

4. Jim's property has a gross rental income of $12,000 a year and total expenses, including debt service, of $13,000. Jim is experiencing
   a. leverage.
   b. negative cash flow.
   c. recapture.
   d. deflation.

5. A small multifamily property generates $50,000 in rental income with expenses of $45,000 annually, including $35,000 in debt service. The property appreciates about $15,000 a year. The owner realizes another $5,000 through income tax savings. On this property, the cash flow is
   a. $5,000.   c. $20,000.
   b. $15,000.   d. $35,000.

6. In question 5, the owner's return is
   a. $5,000.   c. $25,000.
   b. $15,000.   d. $35,000.

7. Leverage involves the extensive use of
   a. cost recovery.
   b. borrowed money.
   c. government subsidies.
   d. alternative taxes.

8. Property that has a net operating income of $28,000 with annual depreciation of $10,000 and debt service of $18,000, which includes $17,000 interest, has taxable income of
   a. $38,000.   c. $10,000.
   b. $28,000.   d. $1,000.

9. The primary source of tax shelter in real estate investments comes from the accounting concept known as
   a. recapture.
   b. boot.
   c. depreciation.
   d. net operating income.

10. For tax purposes the initial cost of an investment property plus the cost of any subsequent improvements to the property, less depreciation, represents the investment's
    a. adjusted basis.
    b. capital gain.
    c. basis.
    d. salvage value.

11. The money left in an investor's pocket after expenses, including debt service, have been paid is known as
    a. net operating income.
    b. gross income.
    c. cash flow.
    d. internal rate of return.

12. The concept of depreciation of income property is of most value to the taxpayer in
    a. the top income bracket.
    b. a marginal income tax bracket.
    c. the lowest income tax bracket.
    d. any tax bracket.

13. Julia Kinder is exchanging her apartment building for an apartment building of greater market value and must include a $10,000 boot to even out the exchange. Which of the following may she use as a boot?
    a. $10,000 cash
    b. Emeralds with a current market value of $10,000
    c. A parcel of raw land with a current market value of $10,000
    d. Any of the above if acceptable to the exchangers

14. In question 13, which of the following is true?
    a. Julia may owe income tax on $10,000.
    b. Each may owe tax on $10,000.
    c. The other investor *may* owe tax on $10,000.
    d. No one owes any tax at this time.

15. An investment syndicate in which all members share equally in the managerial decisions, profits and losses involved in the venture would be an example of which of the following?
    a. Real estate investment trust
    b. Limited partnership
    c. Real estate mortgage trust
    d. General partnership

16. The term *debt service* refers to
    a. total operating expenses.
    b. real estate and income taxes only.
    c. principal and interest on mortgage loans.
    d. interest payments only.

17. In an installment sale of real estate, taxable gain is usually received and reported as income by the seller
    a. in the year the sale is initiated.
    b. in the year the final installment payment is made.
    c. in each year that installment payments are received.
    d. at any one time during the period installment payments are received.

18. Depreciation allows the investor to charge as an expense on each year's tax return part of the
    a. purchase price minus land value.
    b. down payment.
    c. mortgage indebtedness.
    d. equity.

19. A separate license and/or registration is required for the sale of
    a. all investment property.
    b. real estate securities.
    c. installment property.
    d. boots.

20. An investor bears unlimited liability for a share of possible losses in a
    a. general partnership.
    b. limited partnership.
    c. real estate investment trust.
    d. corporation.

21. Harvey, a limited partner in a partnership that is renovating an historic waterfront property, is entitled to offset up to $25,000 in tax credits against
    a. no more than the amount he has at risk.
    b. income up to $100,000.
    c. income up to $200,000.
    d. income up to $250,000.

22. Helen has purchased a dilapidated town house that is 40 years old and of no particular historic value. Helen intends to renovate the town house and live in it. For her renovation expenditures Helen will be entitled to tax credits of
    a. $25,000.
    b. $0.
    c. $12,500.
    d. 25 percent.

23. Jim exchanged his office building, purchased for $475,000 and valued at $650,000, for an office building valued at $750,000. Jim also paid $100,000 cash to the owner of the other building. Jim
    a. received $100,000 "boot."
    b. must report $100,000 as income.
    c. must reduce his adjusted basis by $100,000.
    d. now has a property basis of $575,000.

24. A new tax entity that issues securities backed by a pool of mortgages is a
    a. REIT.
    b. REMIC.
    c. TRA.
    d. general partnership.

25. The Agostinos are being transferred out of town. They decide to keep their current home as an investment property. They ask a real estate broker to manage the property for them. In the first year, they end up losing $1,500 on the investment property, due to a combination of depreciation and a three-month vacancy. For income tax purposes, they can deduct this loss
    a. against passive income.
    b. against salary, as long as they make less than $200,000.
    c. against a 1031 exchange.
    d. under no circumstances.

Property Management

Broker Larry has managed a small ten-unit apartment house for years and never faced a quandary like this one. A prospective tenant, who is handicapped, has good credit and Larry would like to rent to her. He does not want to discriminate against the handicapped, but the property owner has told Larry that he should not accept as a tenant someone who intends to widen doorways and add grab bars in the bathroom. What should Larry do?

Tenant protection regulations are among the important matters to be mastered by property managers, who administer rentals either on their own properties or as the hired agents of investors.

Property Management

In recent years the increased size of buildings; the technical complexities of construction, maintenance and repair; and the trend toward absentee ownership by individual investors and investment groups have led to the expanded use of professional property managers for both residential and commercial properties.

Property management has become so important that some brokerage firms maintain separate management departments. Many corporations that own real estate have also established property management departments. Many real estate investors still will manage their own property, however, and must acquire the knowledge and skills of a property manager. In some instances property managers must hold real estate licenses.

Property managers may look to corporate owners, apartment and condominium associations, homeowners' associations, investment syndicates, trusts and absentee owners as possible sources of management business.

The Property Manager

A **property manager** does more than just find tenants and collect rents. A property manager's job is to maximize income while maintaining the value of the property. Thus the property manager is closely involved in a variety of activities related to generating income, including budgeting, market analysis, advertising and negotiating leases. Because it is important that the value of the property be maintained or enhanced as well, the manager is also involved in property maintenance, security supervision and insurance evaluation.

A property manager may be an individual, a part of a property management firm, or a member of a real estate firm. He or she also may be in charge of managing corporate-owned property or work for a trust.

Types of Property That Are Managed

Property can be divided into four major categories for management purposes:

1. Residential property (including condominiums, cooperatives, and subsidized housing)
2. Office space
3. Retail property
4. Industrial property

▼ Residential Property

Residential property includes any type of property that is used for dwelling space. Both single-family homes and multifamily residences can be managed by a professional property manager, although the management of multifamily properties is more common. Multifamily residences include garden apartments, walkup buildings, highrise complexes, cooperatives and condominiums.

▼ Office Space

Office properties include lowrise buildings, highrise complexes and office or business parks. The ownership and occupancy of office property varies widely, from one owner-occupant to a multitude of individual tenants with a single, nonoccupant owner. Some office properties attract certain types of tenants, such as medical professionals, financial consultants and so forth. Office properties can be found in both downtown urban areas and suburban areas.

▼ Retail Property

Retail properties come in a wide range, from free-standing buildings to traditional shopping centers. Shopping centers come in many different sizes, including strip centers, neighborhood centers, community centers, regional shopping centers and superregional malls. Discount and factory outlet shopping centers also are becoming increasingly common.

▼ Industrial Property

Industrial property is defined as all land and facilities used for manufacturing and the storage and shipment of goods. Industrial property may be a large, individually owned and occupied property or a large industrial park with several tenants.

The Management Agreement

The first step in taking over the management of any property is to enter into a **management agreement** with the owner. This agreement creates an agency relationship between the owner and the property manager. A property manager usually is considered a *general agent*, whereas a real estate broker usually is considered a *special agent*. As agent the property manager is charged with the usual fiduciary duties.

The management agreement should be in writing and should cover the following points:

- *Identification of the parties.* The name of the owner of the property should appear in the agreement just as it does on the deed to the property. If the owner is a partnership, each partner should sign the contract. If the owner is a corporation, a duly authorized officer of the corporation must sign the contract.
- *Description of the property.* Typically, the street address of the property is sufficient, but it is always wise to use a legal description in real estate documents. It is important that the contract be clear on the extent of the property to be managed. For instance, if an office building is the subject of the manage-

ment agreement but the building contains a coffee shop that is to be managed separately, that exclusion should be carefully noted.

- *Time period the agreement will be in force.* The length of the term is purely a matter of negotiation between the parties. Property owners generally want a shorter time period, to allow them to seek other management if they are not satisfied with the current arrangements. On the other hand, property managers usually insist on a contract term that is long enough to make all the extra work required during the initial start-up period worthwhile. One year is usually the minimum time period. It is also a good idea to include provisions for canceling or renewing the agreement on proper notice.
- *Definition of management's responsibilities.* All duties should be stated, and exceptions should be noted. The manager's responsibilities include preparing monthly earnings statements (itemizing income and expenses) and making the necessary disbursements to keep the property operating smoothly. It is important to detail what will happen if the property's account does not contain enough funds to cover the required disbursements.
- *Extent of manager's authority as an agent.* This provision should state what authority the manager is to have in such matters as hiring, firing and supervising employees; fixing rental rates for space; making expenditures; and authorizing repairs within certain limits.
- *Owner's responsibilities.* The owner's responsibilities need to be as clearly defined as the manager's. For instance, is the owner responsible for maintaining proper insurance? The owner also should be responsible for providing the manager with a list of monthly payments, including debt service, taxes and special assessments.
- *Reporting.* Frequent detailed reports allow the owner to monitor the manager's work and serve as a basis for planning policy.
- *Management fee.* The fee can be based on a percentage of gross or net income, a commission on new rentals, a fixed fee or a combination of these. A fixed fee is often to the manager's disadvantage, because he or she has to negotiate a new fee with the owner before the fee is increased, no matter how much work the manager is completing. A percentage fee will increase if the manager is effective in generating income from the property and decrease if the property's income decreases. A minimum guaranteed fee plus a percentage guarantees the manager at least a certain amount per unit to reimburse the manager for spending time on jobs that do not necessarily increase revenues immediately.
- *Allocation of costs.* The agreement should state which of the property management expenses, such as custodial and other help, advertising, supplies and repairs, are to be paid by the owner.

Functions of the Property Manager

A property manager preserves the value of an investment property while generating income as an agent for the owners. A property manager is expected to merchandise the property and control operating expenses to maximize income. A manager should maintain and modernize the property to preserve and enhance the owner's capital investment. The manager carries out these objectives by securing suitable tenants, collecting rents, caring for the premises, budgeting and controlling expenses, hiring and supervising employees, keeping proper accounts and making periodic reports to the owner.

Planning and Budgeting

One of the first things a property manager does when a property management agreement is signed (and sometimes even before a property management agreement is signed) is to develop a management plan. A management plan includes, at the minimum, a market analysis, an operating budget, financing proposals and recommendations as to how the property should be managed.

▼ **Market Analysis**

The **market analysis** includes a regional analysis, a neighborhood analysis and a property analysis. The purpose of the market analysis is to give the manager information about the local economic conditions, the supply of and demand for similar properties in the neighborhood and the competitiveness of other properties that are similar to the property to be managed.

Regional analysis. A **regional analysis** includes economic and demographic information about the regional or metropolitan area in which the property is located. For example, the regional analysis may include figures on local wage levels, employment levels, major employers, population trends and the availability of transportation and government services. All of these separate pieces of information are used to derive a clear picture of the local economy. Essentially, the property manager is seeking the answer to the question, "Is there a healthy demand for this type of property in this regional or metropolitan area?"

Neighborhood analysis. A **neighborhood analysis** is similar to the regional analysis in its focus on economic factors, government services, demographics and transportation. However, a neighborhood analysis focuses on the local, rather than on the regional, level.

Generally speaking, property management activities take place on a local, or neighborhood, level, so it is important to be familiar with neighborhood trends. A neighborhood usually is defined as an area whose limits are defined by some natural or artificial boundaries, such as major arterial thoroughfares, a body of water or a type of land use. Sometimes a neighborhood is only a few square blocks, sometimes it may be a few square miles.

The health of a neighborhood's economy can be measured by several factors: the number and type of businesses in the area, growth trends, wage levels and current rental and occupancy rates. Obviously, areas that contain well-diversified businesses, have low occupancy rates and high rents and are experiencing growth are more economically healthy than neighborhoods that are experiencing the opposite trends. A property manager generally will have an easier time finding and keeping tenants in economically prosperous neighborhoods.

The presence of government and utility services also is important. Adequate fire and police protection; well-maintained roads; and the easy availability of electricity, gas, water and a sewage disposal system are all necessary to attract both residential and office tenants. Transportation is also important. A neighborhood that is served by good arterial roads, highways or freeways; bus or train travel; or other means of transportation tends to be valued more highly by tenants. Good transportation makes commuting to and from work and places of entertainment easier for residential tenants, makes the transportation of goods and services easier for industrial and office tenants and makes shopping access easier for retail tenants.

Especially for residential tenants, extra amenities that can be found in the neighborhood also are important. For example, convenient access to parks, schools, restaurants, playgrounds, theaters and places of worship are all important to potential tenants.

A MANAGEMENT PLAN INCLUDES

- a market analysis,
- an operating budget,
- financing proposals and
- recommendations for managing a property.

Special attention should be paid to vacancy rates for similar properties in the neighborhood. Not only do vacancy (or occupancy) rates indicate the economic climate in the neighborhood, they also reflect the supply of and demand for similar properties in the neighborhood. Supply and demand has a tremendous impact on the rental levels that can be charged for the subject property. For example, an oversupply of rental space means a high vacancy rate and probably a demand for lower rates. On the other hand, an undersupply of rental space usually translates into low vacancy rates and rent increases.

Property analysis. Examining the region and the neighborhood gives the property manager a good idea of the economic climate and the supply of and demand for similar types of properties. From the information gathered, the property manager also should be able to tell what the optimum rental rates are for competitive space in the neighborhood.

At this point, the property manager needs to turn his or her attention to the subject property itself. The property manager must determine how the subject property compares with competitive properties. Is the subject property in a stronger or a weaker position than competing properties to attract tenants?

In the **property analysis,** the property manager examines the terms of each tenant's existing lease, the quantity and quality of the rentable space and the physical condition of the property itself.

As the property manager studies the existing leases, he or she is gauging the amount and durability of the rental income. The manager also examines the lease renewal rate for the building (tenant turnover), vacancy rate and bad debt rate. These elements help determine whether tenant relations are managed wisely and whether the rental rate is right for the current market.

Curb appeal—the building's overall appearance—is one of the more important elements the manager studies. Curb appeal includes the building's age, design and condition. The manager also checks the interior space, including measuring the total amount of usable space or number of units, the layout and the hardware and fixtures (such as carpeting and plumbing). The physical condition of all aspects of the property is inspected in light of housekeeping and maintenance requirements.

Part of the property analysis includes studying the features of comparable properties in the neighborhood to determine how the subject property measures up. If the subject property has less curb appeal and higher tenant turnover than competing properties, this may mean that maintenance has been ignored in the past, that current rental rates are too high or that tenant services are lacking.

Owner objectives. After the property manager has analyzed the region, neighborhood, and subject property, he or she then must analyze the *goals of the owner*. Those goals may vary from maximizing income or cash flow to increasing the value of the property. It is the manager's job to put the owner's goals into concrete terms so that the management plan can reflect those goals (and the manager can more easily achieve them).

▼ **Budgeting**

An important part of the planning stage includes preparing a *detailed operating budget*. A property manager should develop an operating budget based on anticipated revenues and expenses and reflecting the long-term goals of the owner. The manager begins by allocating money for such continuous fixed expenses as employees' salaries, real estate taxes, property taxes and insurance premiums. Next the manager establishes a *cash reserve fund* for such variable expenses as repairs, decorating and supplies. The amount allocated for the reserve fund can be computed from the previous yearly costs of variable expenses.

If an owner and a property manager decide that modernization or renovation of the property will enhance its value, the manager should budget money to cover the costs of remodeling, which are called capital expenditures. The manager should be thoroughly familiar with the principle of contribution (an improvement is only worth the additional value it adds to the property, not its cost) or seek expert advice when estimating any increase in value expected from an improvement. In the case of large-scale construction, the expenses charged against the property's income should be spread over several years. Although budgets should be as accurate an estimate of cost as possible, adjustments may sometimes be necessary, especially in the case of new properties.

Marketing

One of the first steps a property manager must take when beginning to manage a new property is to develop a marketing plan. Unless a property is effectively marketed, well-qualified tenants will be difficult to find, and existing tenants will fail to renew their leases.

Marketing plans will vary widely, depending on the type of property that is being managed. Obviously, a property manager will develop an entirely different marketing plan for residential property than for industrial property. However, there are some marketing principles that apply to any type of property. First, a property manager must be thoroughly acquainted with the property he or she is trying to market. The property's features, as well as the property's layout, should be known and noted. The manager must be familiar with the property's strengths as well as its weaknesses. And the manager should make sure the property is "prepared" for the marketing effort--that is, that the space is clean and in good condition.

Another marketing principle property managers should be aware of is that satisfied tenants are the best, most cost-effective way to market the property. Happy tenants give good referrals and can often supply names of other prospective tenants.

▼ Marketing Activities

A successful marketing plan includes both advertising and promotional efforts and person-to-person selling. A property manager must be able to effectively engage in all three types of activities.

Advertising. The way in which a property manager advertises property depends a great deal on the type of property. Residential, commercial and industrial properties draw tenants from different sectors of the public. Furthermore, new properties are often advertised in a different manner than established concerns are. For example, a newly completed large apartment complex needs to find hundreds of new tenants at the same time, whereas an existing apartment complex needs to find only "replacement" tenants on an ongoing basis.

Several media can be effectively used to market rental space, including

- signs,
- newspaper advertising,
- periodicals,
- radio and television and
- direct mail.

Most advertising plans combine one or more of these media.

Signs that identify the management firm for the building and the contact person should be placed outside residential, office and retail properties. When space is currently available, "For Rent" signs describing the type of space can be posted outside the building or in vacant store windows. Billboards are sometimes used for large industrial or commercial properties.

Newspaper advertising is perhaps the most commonly used medium. Classified advertisements are used for residential properties, and the larger display ads are used for large residential complexes and sometimes retail or office space. Regional periodicals and other publications are used to advertise large residential and retail properties.

Radio advertising sometimes is used for large residential, commercial and industrial properties. Its major disadvantage is that radio audiences cannot be targeted very effectively; there are likely to be few potential tenants among the listeners. The same is true for television, with the added disadvantage that television advertising is very costly.

Direct mail can be used effectively for some industrial and commercial properties. Well-tailored mailing lists often can be obtained for likely prospects, so direct marketing can be targeted to an appreciative audience. Of course, the direct mail pieces must look professional. Brochures often are developed for large residential, commercial and industrial properties and are given to prospects who actually inquire about available space.

Promotions. *Promotional efforts* include any activities that serve to improve the reputation of the building and increase its desirability to tenants. For example, the property manager may speak in front of various interest groups, offer to share professional expertise, prepare press releases and send them to various local publications and send news releases to real estate sections of newspapers or real estate journals. Promotional activities generally translate into free advertising, which is why they can be so valuable to a property manager.

Personal selling activities. This aspect of marketing involves the responses of the property manager or management staff to a prospective tenant. The manager or employee needs expert selling skills to deal effectively with qualifying the prospect, creating interest, dealing with objections and negotiating and closing the agreement.

Qualifying the prospect includes determining the prospective tenant's space needs, price range, parking needs and required improvements. In selecting commercial or industrial tenants, a manager should be sure that each tenant will "fit the space." The manager should be certain that (1) the size of the space meets the tenant's requirements, (2) the tenant will have the ability to pay for the space for which it contracts, (3) the tenant's business will be compatible with the building and the other tenants and (4) if the tenant is likely to expand in the future, expansion space will be available. After a prospect becomes a tenant, the manager must be sure that the tenant remains satisfied.

If the tenant's needs coincide with the available space, the manager can move to the next step, creating interest and desire on the tenant's part. Note that it is a waste of time and money to try to interest a tenant in available space when it will not suit that tenant's needs. The tenant either will reject the space or will sign a lease but vacate the premises before the end of the lease term.

In selecting tenants, the property manager must comply with all federal and local fair housing laws. Tenants with handicaps must be allowed to make appropriate modifications at their own expense if they agree to return the property to its original state when they leave.

Creating interest and desire is largely a matter of describing the property's special features and benefits while showing the prospect the building. Taking a tour of both the exterior and interior of the building and of both the rentable space and the common areas is virtually always advisable. Any questions the prospect may have about the space should be answered promptly, and objections should be dealt with persuasively. Once all answers have been given and objections resolved, the manager then moves to the negotiation and closing stage of marketing. Getting the tenant to sign on the dotted line is, naturally, the prime objective of marketing.

Managing Leases and Tenant Relations

The manager who has moved through the marketing stages and found rental prospects then must attend to managing leases and tenant relations.

▼ Renting the Property

The role of the manager in managing a property should not be confused with that of a broker acting as a leasing agent and solely concerned with renting space. The property manager may use the services of a leasing agent, but that agent does not undertake the full responsibility of maintaining and managing the property.

For low-income or moderate-income residential rentals, managers and owners may want to consider participating in the FHA's **Section 8** program. Qualified tenants pay no more than 30 percent of their income in rent, with HUD carrying the rest.

Setting rental rates. A basic concern in establishing rental rates is that income from the rentable space must cover the fixed charges and operating expenses and also provide a fair return on the investment. Consideration also must be given to prevailing rates in comparable buildings and the current level of vacancy in the property to be rented—supply and demand. Following a detailed survey of the competitive space available in the neighborhood, prices should be adjusted for differences between neighboring properties and the property being managed. Annual rent adjustments are often warranted.

Office and commercial space rentals are usually quoted according to either annual or monthly rate per square foot of space.

If a high level of vacancy exists, an immediate effort should be made to determine why. *A high level of vacancy does not necessarily indicate that rents are too high.* The trouble may be inept management or defects in the property. Conversely, *a high percentage of occupancy may appear to indicate an effective rental program, but it could also mean that rental rates are too low.* With an apartment house or office building, whenever the occupancy level exceeds 95 percent, serious consideration should be given to raising rents.

▼ **Negotiating Leases**

A lease is a contract and like any other contract, it must satisfy certain requirements to be valid. These requirements include competent parties, consideration, offer and acceptance and a lawful purpose. Many leases also must be in writing, according to the provisions of the statute of frauds.

Leases also must contain a description of the property, the amount of rent and when it is due, the term of the lease, the use of the premises and the rights and obligations of each party.

Typically, the tenant's main obligation is the prompt payment of rent. The lease usually provides for a late penalty if the rental payment is paid after a certain date and termination of the lease if the rent remains unpaid after proper notice by the landlord.

Security deposits usually are required. Security deposits protect the landlord from tenant default. They are available to the landlord should the tenant fail to pay accrued rent or should the tenant damage the property (beyond normal wear and tear). Security deposits should be in a separate account, and the tenant is entitled to all but 1 percent of the interest earned on the deposit. The 1 percent may be retained by the owner as compensation for managing the account.

Tenants usually also are required to comply with local laws and regulations (such as land-use laws and health and safety codes), seek permission before altering or improving the property and remove personal property on vacating the premises.

Landlords generally are required to maintain the common areas and guarantee the tenant's "quiet enjoyment" of the premises. That is, the tenant has exclusive possession of the premises, and the landlord can gain entrance only for certain purposes with the proper notice or in emergency situations.

Other lease provisions may address such items as

- possession of the premises,
- rental rate adjustments,
- tax and insurance requirements,
- condemnation,
- assignment and subletting and
- fire and casualty damage.

One of the most important elements involved with managing leases is negotiating tenant alterations and tenant concessions. The property manager must maintain a proper balance between flexibility and practicality. While the manager wants to offer the tenant the proper incentives to enter into the lease, he or she also must keep the "bottom line" in mind and not enter into a transaction that is not in the ultimate best interests of the property owner. Some concessions commonly made to tenants are rental rebates, expansion options (guaranteeing the tenant the option to lease additional space) and reimbursement of moving expenses.

▼ **Collecting rents**

Once the tenant has signed the lease and moved onto the premises, a major responsibility of the manager becomes rent collection. The best way to minimize problems with rent collection is to make a *careful selection* of tenants in the first place. A desire for a high level of occupancy should not override good judgment. A property manager should investigate financial references, local credit bureaus and, when possible, the prospective tenant's former landlord.

The terms of rental payment should be spelled out in detail in the lease agreement. A *firm and consistent collection plan* with a sufficient system of notices and records should be established. In cases of delinquency every attempt must be made to make collections without resorting to legal action. When it is required, a property manager must be prepared to initiate and follow through with legal counsel.

▼ **Tenants' Rights**

New York's Multiple Dwelling Law, in effect in New York City and Buffalo, sets the following requirements for buildings with three or more living units: automatic self-closing and self-locking doors, two-way voice buzzers (for buildings with eight or more units), mirrors in each self-service elevator and peepholes and chain door-guards on the entrance door of each apartment. Tenants may install their own additional locks but must provide the landlord with a duplicate key on request. Heat must be provided from October 1 to May 31. Additional regulations apply in various communities.

Postal regulations require that landlords of buildings with three or more units provide secure mailboxes. *Smoke detectors* always are required. In New York City, tenants with children under 11 years of age must receive *window guards* on request. Protective guards also must be installed on all public hall windows.

Throughout the state the landlord of a building with three or more apartments is specifically required to keep apartments and public areas in good repair and to maintain electrical, plumbing, sanitary, heating and ventilation systems in good working order. Landlords also must maintain appliances that are furnished to tenants. Landlords have a legal duty to keep buildings free of vermin, dirt and garbage. Landlords also have the duty to inform their tenants of hazards posed by lead-based paint. Lead-based paint disclosure requirements are discussed in Chapter 17.

A landlord may enter the tenant's apartment only with reasonable prior notice, to provide repairs or service in accordance with the lease or to show the apartment to prospective tenants or purchasers. The landlord may enter without prior permission only in an *emergency*.

A tenant who is disabled has the right to make alterations to improve accessibility at his or her own expense. The landlord may not charge this tenant more rent or a larger security deposit, but may require that the tenant post a bond to ensure that the property is restored as much as is necessary upon vacating.

Mobile home park tenants must be offered at least a one-year written lease. If they do not have leases, they are entitled to 90 days' written notice before rent increases. Rules must not be changed without 30 days' written notice. Rules must be posted conspicuously or a copy given to each tenant who moves in. Late rent payment charges are limited to 5 percent after a ten-day grace period. Mobile home park tenants, whether they own or rent the home itself, are governed by the same rules as any other tenants with regard to security deposits, subleasing, sharing space, eviction and related matters. (In New York, a mobile home is not considered real property unless it is permanently affixed to the land on a foundation.)

Owners may not discriminate against mobile home tenants with children and may not charge extra for children. Owners have the right to sell their homes within the park with the consent of the park owner, which consent may not be unreasonably withheld. Park owners cannot require any fee or commission in connection with the sale of a mobile home unless they act as sales agent pursuant to a written contract. Owners may not foster park monopolies.

Owners of mobile home parks with more than two units must register with the New York Division of Housing and Community Renewal, which enforces the rights of mobile home tenants in the state.

Maintaining the Property

One of the most important functions of a property manager is the supervision of **property maintenance**. A manager must learn to balance services and costs to satisfy the tenants' needs while minimizing operating expenses. *Maintenance* covers several types of activities. First, the manager must *protect the physical integrity* of the property to ensure that the building and grounds stay in good condition over the long term. Repainting the exterior or replacing the heating system will help keep the building functional and decrease routine maintenance costs.

A property manager also must *supervise routine cleaning and repairs* of the building, including cleaning of common areas; minor carpentry and plumbing; and regularly scheduled upkeep of heating, air-conditioning and landscaping.

In addition, especially when dealing with commercial or industrial space, a property manager will be called on to make tenant improvement alterations to the interior of the building to meet the functional demands of the tenant. These alterations can range from repainting to completely gutting the interior and redesigning the space. Tenant improvements are especially important when renting new buildings, because the interior is usually left incomplete so that it can be adapted to the needs of individual tenants ("make-ready").

Supervising the modernization or renovation of buildings that have become functionally obsolete and thus unsuited to today's building needs is also important (see Chapter 23 for a definition of *functional obsolescence*). The renovation of a building often increases the building's marketability and thus its possible income.

▼ Hiring Employees versus Contracting for Services

One of the major decisions a property manager faces is whether to contract for maintenance services from an outside firm or hire on-site employees to perform such tasks. This decision should be based on a number of factors, including size of the building, complexity of tenants' requirements and availability of suitable labor.

Owner Relations, Reports and Insurance

A property manager is an agent of the property owner, and thus must act in a fiduciary capacity. The manager must act in the best interests of the owner and owes the owner the duties of loyalty and good faith.

▼ Owner Relations

When a property manager first takes over managing a property, he or she should begin building a good foundation for effective owner/manager relations immediately. In the planning process, the manager should have learned the owner's goals and developed the management plan accordingly. The manager should have obtained all the necessary vital information about the owner, including the owner's name, address, telephone number, social security number, state employment number and information on the owner's accountant, attorney and insurance broker. Information about the owner's property financing is also vital. If the property is already operational, current tenant security deposits must be accounted for and long-term accounting procedures established. It also may be necessary for the manager to have the owner set up a working capital fund for operating expenses.

Once the relationship has been established, the manager should go about setting up a procedure for *regular owner contact.* Typically, the major form of communication between the manager and owner is a *monthly earnings report.* This report includes information on receipts, expenses and cash flow. The report should be accompanied by a personal letter from the manager, enumerating any special concerns or other information that the manager feels the owner should know.

The property manager should quickly get to know how involved each owner wishes to be in the management of his or her property. Some owners want to be very involved, and expect frequent communication from the manager.

▼ Insurance Coverage

One of the most important responsibilities of a property manager is to protect the property owner against all major insurable risks. In some cases a property manager or a member of the management firm may be a licensed insurance broker. To avoid charges of *self-dealing,* the owner should be made aware of the situation and consent to it.

In any case a competent, reliable insurance agent who is well versed in all areas of insurance pertaining to property should be selected to survey the property and make recommendations. Final decisions, however, must be made by the property owner. *An insurance broker must have passed a state examination to secure a special license to sell insurance.*

Many kinds of insurance coverage are available to income property owners and managers. Some of the more common types include the following:

- **Fire and hazard:** Fire insurance policies provide coverage against direct loss or damage to property from a fire on the premises. Standard fire coverage can be extended to cover hazards such as windstorm, hail, smoke damage or civil insurrection. Most popular today is the all-risks or special form.
- **Business interruption:** Most hazard policies insure against the actual loss of property but do not cover loss of revenues from income property. Interruption insurance covers the loss of income that occurs if the property cannot be used to produce income.

- **Contents and personal property:** Inland marine insurance covers building contents and personal property during periods when they are not actually located on the business premises.
- **Liability:** Public liability insurance covers the risks an owner assumes when the public enters the building. Medical expenses are paid for a person injured in the building as a result of landlord negligence. Another liability risk is that of medical or hospital payments for injuries sustained by building employees in the course of their employment. These claims are covered by state laws known as **workers' compensation acts.** These laws require that a building owner who is an employer obtain a workers' compensation policy from a private insurance company.
- **Casualty:** Casualty insurance policies include coverage against theft, burglary, vandalism and machinery damage as well as health and accident insurance. Casualty policies usually are written on specific risks such as theft, rather than being all-inclusive.
- **Surety bonds:** Surety bonds cover an owner against financial losses that result from an employee's criminal acts or negligence while carrying out his or her duties. A blanket crime policy is most often chosen.
- **Boiler and machinery coverage:** This covers repair and replacement of heating plants, central air-conditioning units and other major equipment.

Lower premiums may be offered on property that qualifies as a *highly protected risk (HPR),* based on the quality of water supply, sprinklers, alarms, security personnel and loss control programs. Many insurance companies offer **multiperil policies** for apartment and business buildings. These include standard types of commercial coverage: fire, hazard, public liability and casualty.

Claims.   When a claim is made under a policy insuring a building or other physical object, either of two methods can determine the amount of the claim. One is the depreciated, or actual, cash value of the damaged property; the other is replacement cost. If a 30-year-old building is damaged, the timbers and materials are 30 years old and therefore do not have the same value as new material. Thus in determining the amount of the loss under what is called *actual cash value,* the cost of new material would be reduced by the estimated depreciation, based on the time the item had been in the building.

The alternate method is to cover **replacement cost.** This represents the actual amount a builder would charge to replace the damaged property at the time of the loss, including materials. When purchasing insurance, a manager must assess whether the property should be insured at full replacement cost or at a depreciated cost. As with the homeowners' policies discussed in Chapter 10, commercial policies usually carry *coinsurance* clauses that require coverage up to 80 percent of the building's replacement value.

Many property managers, faced with filing an insurance claim, call on professional *private adjusters,* who are skilled in representing owners in negotiations with insurers.

Skills Required of a Property Manager

As is evident from the detailed description of a property manager's functions, a wide variety of skills are required of a property manager. During his or her career, a property manager will "wear many hats" and be called on to display expertise in a number of areas.

The property manager needs to be a *human relations expert,* because he or she handles owner–tenant relations. *Research and planning skills* are required to prepare a marketing plan and perform market analyses. The manager needs excellent *accounting skills* to prepare budgets and monthly reports and to help ensure that the owner's income goals are reached. *Marketing skills,* such as advertising, promotional activities, and person-to-person selling skills, are a must to maintain a high occupancy rate. *Negotiating skills* are required for entering into lease agreements. And of course the property must be *well-maintained,* so the manager must know enough about physical operations to see to it that both the exterior and interior of a building are kept in good condition.

The Management Field

For those interested in pursuing a career in property management, most large cities have local associations of building and property owners and managers that are affiliates of regional and national associations. The Institute of Real Estate Management is associated with the National Association of REALTORS®. Members may earn the designation **Certified Property Manager (CPM).** The Building Owners and Managers Association International (BOMA International) is a federation of local associations of owners and managers, primarily of office buildings. Participation in groups like these allows property managers to gain valuable professional knowledge and to discuss their problems with other managers facing similar issues. Management designation also is offered by the National Association of Home Builders, the New York Association of Building Owners and the International Council of Shopping Centers.

A growing field is management of cooperatives and condominiums. The manager hired by a homeowners' organization must develop different techniques because owners and tenants are one and the same. The Community Associations Institute (CAI) is a nonprofit organization founded in 1974 to research and distribute information on association living and offers training and designation for specialized management.

Rent Regulations

Rent regulation in New York State is administered by the Office of Rent Administration of the New York State **Division of Housing and Community Renewal (DHCR).** It includes two programs: *rent control* and *rent stabilization.*

▼ Rent Control

Rent control dates back to the housing shortage that followed World War II and generally covers property containing three or more units constructed before February 1947 and located in one of the 64 municipalities where the system is in effect. These include New York City, Albany and Buffalo and parts of Albany, Erie, Nassau, Rensselaer, Schenectady and Westchester counties. Also covered are tenants who have been in continuous residence since May 1, 1953, in one- or two-family dwellings in the participating communities.

For buildings with three or more units, the regulations apply to an apartment continuously occupied by the present tenant since July 1, 1971 (with some exceptions in Nassau County). When such an apartment is vacated, it moves to rent stabilization status or is removed from regulation, depending on the municipality.

Rents in controlled apartments initially were based on rentals in effect when rent control was first imposed in 1943. Outside New York City the DHCR determines maximum allowable rates of rent increases, which are available to landlords every two years. Within New York City a **maximum base rent (MBR)** is established for each apartment and is adjusted every two years. Landlords may raise rents by 7.5 percent each year until they reach the maximum base rental figure. Tenants may challenge proposed increases if the building has been cited for violations or the owner's expenses do not warrant an increase.

Under rent control, rent may be increased (1) if the landlord increases services, (2) if the landlord installs a major capital improvement, (3) in cases of hardship and (4) to cover high labor and fuel costs. Rents will be reduced if the landlord fails to correct violations or reduces essential services. The law prohibits harassment of rent-controlled tenants or retaliatory eviction of tenants who exercise their right to complain to a government agency about violations of health or safety laws. In 1992, 155,000 units in New York City remained under rent control, with another 840,000 under the later arrangement known as rent stabilization.

▼ **Rent Stabilization**

In New York City **rent stabilization** applies to apartments in buildings of six or more units constructed between February 1, 1947, and January 1, 1974. Tenants in older buildings are covered if they moved in before January 1, 1971. Buildings with three or more units that were constructed or extensively renovated since 1974 with special tax benefits are also subject to rent stabilization while the tax benefits continue.

Outside New York City rent stabilization applies in those communities that have adopted the Emergency Tenant Protection Act (ETPA). Each community sets a limit on the size of buildings to be covered; in no case is the program applied to property with fewer than six living units.

Where rent stabilization applies, maximum allowable rent increases are set annually by local rent stabilization boards. Tenants may choose one-year or two-year renewal leases.

The DHCR has set up a special unit to assist the owners of buildings with fewer than 50 rental units in filling out registration forms and with record keeping and bookkeeping. The department's main office is located in the World Trade Center.

Key Terms

boiler and machinery coverage	neighborhood analysis
business interruption insurance	office property
casualty insurance	property analysis
Certified Property Manager (CPM)	property maintenance
contents and personal property insurance	property manager
	regional analysis
Division of Housing and Community Renewal (DHCR)	rent control
	rent stabilization
fire and hazard insurance	replacement cost
industrial property	residential property
liability insurance	retail property
management agreement	Section 8
market analysis	security deposit
maximum base rent (MBR)	surety bond
multiperil policies	workers' compensation acts

Summary

Property management is a specialized service to owners of income-producing properties in which a manager, as agent of the owner, becomes administrator of the property.

A management agreement must be prepared carefully to define and authorize the manager's duties and responsibilities.

The manager draws up a budget of estimated variable and fixed expenses. The budget also should allow for any proposed expenditures for major renovations or modernizations. These projected expenses, combined with the manager's analysis of the condition of the building and the rent patterns in the neighborhood, will form the basis on which rental rates for property are determined.

The property manager is responsible for soliciting tenants whose needs are suited to the space and who are capable of meeting the proposed rents. The manager usually collects rents, maintains the building, hires employees, pays taxes for the building and deals with tenant problems.

One of the manager's primary responsibilities is supervising maintenance, which includes safeguarding the physical integrity of the property and performing routine cleaning and repairs as well as adapting interior space and design to suit tenants' needs.

In addition the manager is expected to secure adequate insurance coverage for the premises. The basic types of coverage applicable to commercial structures include fire and hazard insurance on the property and fixtures; business interruption insurance to protect the owner against income losses; and casualty insurance to provide coverage against such losses as theft, vandalism and destruction of machinery. The manager also should secure public liability insurance to insure the owner against claims made by people injured on the premises and workers' compensation policies to cover the claims of employees injured on the job. The Multiple Dwelling Law in New York City and Buffalo sets health and safety standards for apartment buildings. Local communities have additional regulations. The state also regulates mobile home parks.

The Institute of Real Estate Management, a branch of the National Association of Realtors, awards the most widely recognized designation in the field, the CPM, Certified Property Manager.

1. Must a manager allow modifications of the premises to accommodate a handicapped tenant who offers to pay for the work?
   a. Yes, and the landlord must pay for the adaptations.
   b. No, if more suitable accommodations are for rent within a reasonable distance.
   c. No, unless the apartment is located in a rent-controlled building.
   d. Yes, but the tenant must return the premises to its original condition on leaving.

2. An operating budget for income property usually is prepared on what basis?
   a. Daily   c. Monthly
   b. Weekly   d. Annually

3. In the absence of rent regulations the amount of rent charged is determined by the
   a. management agreement.
   b. principle of supply and demand.
   c. operating budget.
   d. local apartment owners' association.

4. Office rentals usually are figured by the
   a. front foot.
   b. amount of desk space.
   c. number of rooms.
   d. square foot.

5. From a management point of view, apartment building occupancy that reaches as high as 98 percent would tend to indicate that
   a. the building is poorly managed.
   b. the building is run-down.
   c. the building is a desirable place to live.
   d. rents should be raised.

6. Which of the following should not be a consideration in selecting a tenant?
   a. The size of the space versus the tenant's requirements
   b. The tenant's ability to pay
   c. The racial and ethnic backgrounds of the tenant
   d. The compatibility of the tenant's business with other tenants' businesses

7. A property manager may be reimbursed with
   a. a percentage of rentals.
   b. rebates from suppliers.
   c. key money.
   d. Any of the above

8. In some situations, municipal or state law may require a landlord to install
   a. elevator mirrors.
   b. window guards.
   c. intercoms and buzzers.
   d. All of the above

9. While her tenants are at work, Laura Landlady may enter their apartment
   a. to leave them a note.
   b. to check on their housekeeping.
   c. in case of fire.
   d. All of the above

10. Which insurance insures the property owner against the claims of employees injured on the job?
    a. Business interruption
    b. Workers' compensation
    c. Casualty
    d. Surety bond

11. A delivery man slips on a defective stair in an apartment building and is hospitalized. A claim against the building owner for medical expenses will be made under which of the following policies held by the owner?
    a. Workers' compensation
    b. Casualty
    c. Liability
    d. Fire and hazard

12. Property manager Frieda Jacobs hires Albert Weston as the full-time janitor for one of the buildings she manages. While repairing a faucet in one of the apartments, Weston steals a television set. Jacobs could protect the owner against liability for this type of loss by purchasing
    a. liability insurance.
    b. workers' compensation insurance.
    c. a surety bond.
    d. casualty insurance.

13. The initials CPM stand for
    a. chargeback percentage mortgage.
    b. contract priority maintenance.
    c. Certified Property Manager.
    d. cardiopulmonary manipulation.

14. Rent regulations in New York are administered by
    a. the New York City Housing Bureau.
    b. the Department of State.
    c. HUD.
    d. the New York Department of Housing and Community Renewal.

15. Rent control regulations are found mainly around the
    a. Adirondacks.
    b. southern tier.
    c. Finger Lakes.
    d. New York City area.

16. When the original tenant dies or moves out, a rent-controlled apartment may become eligible for
    a. rent control.
    b. rent stabilization.
    c. comparative hardship.
    d. freeze.

17. The rent stabilization program is known outside New York City as
    a. ETPA.   c. CPR.
    b. DHCR.   d. HPR.

18. The DHCR's special unit for helping owners with registration, bookkeeping and record keeping is aimed at apartment buildings with fewer than
    a. 3 units.   c. 50 units.
    b. 8 units.   d. 100 units.

CHAPTER 20

Conveyance of Real Property

Every year since Henry can remember, his father planted a vegetable garden in the extra lot attached to their house. After his father died last year, Henry planted a garden himself. Last week he looked over the lot size on his property tax bill and discovered he is not being taxed for the extra land. He investigated and found out the lot really belonged to someone who moved to Alaska and later died. How can Henry gain title to that extra lot? Or does he already own it?

A parcel of real estate may be transferred from one owner to another (alienated) in a number of different ways. It may be given voluntarily by sale, devise or gift or it may be taken involuntarily by operation of law. In a way, the process of alienation is the central point of all of a real estate broker's activity.

Title

Title to real estate means the right to or ownership of the land; in addition it represents the *evidence* of ownership. The term *title* has two functions. It represents the "bundle of rights" the owner possesses in the real estate and denotes the facts that, if proved, would enable a person to recover or retain ownership or possession of a parcel of real estate.

Title to real estate in New York may be transferred during an owner's lifetime by *voluntary alienation* or *involuntary alienation,* and after an owner's death by *will* or by *descent.*

Voluntary Alienation

There are four forms of **voluntary alienation:** *sales, gifts, dedications* and *grants.* In a sale, property is transferred from a seller to a buyer in exchange for something of value, known as *consideration.* A transfer without something of value in return (without consideration) is a gift. To sell property or give it to someone, the owner uses a deed of conveyance.

FOUR FORMS OF VOLUNTARY ALIENATION:
1. Sale
2. Gift
3. Dedication
4. Grant

The word *dedication* is used for a gift from a landowner to the government. A developer passes ownership of subdivision lands earmarked for streets and roads to a city, town or village by dedicating the streets. **Dedications** are often required as a condition of subdivision approval. They benefit the subdivider by allowing development of public access and utilities for the subdivision and relieving the subdivider of responsibility for maintenance, and they benefit the local government by providing lands for these purposes at no cost to taxpayers.

In contrast to dedication, land owned by the government may be transferred to individuals through *public grant,* as when public land (still available in Alaska, for example) is transferred to persons who have created homesteads on it.

Involuntary Alienation

Title to property can be transferred during the owner's lifetime by **involuntary alienation,** without the owner's consent. Land may be taken for public use (condemnation) or it may be sold at foreclosure of an unpaid lien (mortgage, judgment, property taxes). Natural processes such as *erosion* and *accretion* can result in the gain or loss of title to land, and title may also transfer involuntarily by partition or adverse possession.

▼ Condemnation

Federal, state and local governments; school boards; some government agencies; and certain public and quasi-public corporations and utilities (railroads and gas and electric companies) have the power of *eminent domain.* Private property may be taken for public use through a *suit for* **condemnation.** Eminent domain may be exercised only when a court determines that the use is for the benefit of the public and that equitable compensation, as set by the court, will be paid to the owner. Whenever private property is taken in New York, the owner is given the opportunity to challenge in court the amount of money offered. Former property owners are entitled to a 90-day grace period when they continue to occupy the property for residential purposes after state acquisition.

▼ Foreclosure

Land also may be transferred without an owner's consent to satisfy debts contracted by the owner. In such cases the debt is foreclosed, the property is sold and the proceeds of the sale are applied to pay off the debt. Debts that could be foreclosed include mortgage loans, real estate taxes, mechanics' liens or general judgments against the property owner.

▼ Natural Processes

> Involuntary alienation can occur by condemnation, foreclosure, natural processes, partition or adverse possession.

In addition to the involuntary transfer of land by legal processes, land may be transferred by natural forces. Owners of land bordering on rivers, lakes and other bodies of water may acquire additional land through the process of *accretion,* the slow accumulation of soil, rock or other matter deposited by the movement of water on an owner's property. The opposite of accretion is *erosion,* the gradual wearing away of land by the action of water and wind. In addition, property may be lost through *avulsion,* the sudden tearing away of land by natural means such as earthquakes or tidal waves.

▼ Partition

A partition is a legal proceeding used to divide a property that is jointly owned by two or more persons, such as in a joint tenancy or tenancy in common. If cotenants cannot agree on the use or disposition of the property, one of them may start a *partition proceeding* in court. If possible, the court will attempt to physically divide the property among the co-owners, but if this is not possible the court may order the property to be sold and the proceeds of sale to be distributed among the co-owners in proportion to their shares of ownership.

▼ Adverse Possession

Adverse possession is another means of involuntary transfer. An owner who does not use his or her land or does not inspect it for a number of years may lose title to another person who has some claim to the land, takes possession and, most important, uses the land. In New York a person may acquire title by adverse possession to land owned by another by the continuous, open, notorious, hostile and exclusive occupation of the property for *ten years.* After that time the user may perfect the claim of title to land by adverse possession by bringing a court suit to quiet title.

Through a process known as *tacking,* continuous periods of adverse possession may be combined by successive users, thus enabling a person who had not been in possession for the entire ten years to establish a claim of adverse possession. The process is not automatic; legal action is necessary to *perfect* the claim. This is known as an *action to quiet title,* which is used in cases where the ownership of land is in dispute. The original owner may defend title by proving that he or she objected to the unauthorized use of the land or on the other hand specifically gave permission for the use. Adverse possession of publicly owned property is not possible.

Transfer of a Deceased Person's Property

Even the person who dies (the decedent) transfers property in one of two ways: either voluntarily (through a will) or involuntarily (through descent or escheat). Every state has a law known as the *statute of descent and distribution.* When a person dies **intestate** (without a will), the decedent's real estate and personal property pass to the spouse or *natural* **heirs** according to this statute. In effect the state makes a will for such decedents. In contrast a person who dies **testate** has prepared a will indicating the way his or her property will be disposed of after death.

Legally, when a person dies, title to his or her real estate immediately passes either to the heirs by **descent** or to the persons named in the will. Before the heirs can take possession of the property, however, the estate must be probated and all claims against it satisfied.

▼ Probate Proceedings

Probate or administration is a legal process by which a court determines who will inherit the property of a deceased person and what the assets of the estate are. Surrogate court proceedings must take place in the county where the deceased person lived. In the case of a person who has died testate, the court also rules on the validity of the will. If the will is upheld, the property is distributed according to its provisions.

If a person has died without a will, the court determines who inherits by reviewing a *proof of heirship.* This statement, usually prepared by an attorney, gives personal information regarding the decedent's spouse, children and relatives. From this document the court decides which parties will receive what portion of the estate.

To initiate probate or administration proceedings, the custodian of the will, an heir or another interested party must petition the court. The court then holds a hearing to determine the validity of the will and/or the order of descent, should no valid will exist. If for any reason a will is declared invalid by the court, any property owned by the decedent will pass by the laws of descent. The court will appoint an executor, usually named in the will, or an administrator to oversee the administration and distribution of the estate.

▼ Transfer of Title by Will

A **last will and testament** is an instrument made by an owner to convey title to the owner's property after death. A will takes effect only after the death of the decedent; until that time, devisees named in the will have no claim to the property.

A party who makes a will is known as a **testator** or **testatrix** (female); the gift of real property by will is known as a **devise,** and a person who receives real property by will is known as a *devisee*. A gift of personal property is a *legacy* or *bequest;* the person receiving the personal property is a *legatee.*

In New York, children can be disinherited, but a surviving spouse is entitled to at least one-third of the estate, or $50,000 plus one-half of the remainder of the estate, whichever is greater. In a case where a will does not provide the minimum statutory inheritance, the surviving spouse may inform the court that he or she will claim the minimum rather than the lesser share provided in the will. This practice, called a *right of election*, is a right reserved only for a surviving spouse.

A will differs from a deed in that a deed conveys a present interest in real estate during the lifetime of the grantor, while a will conveys no interest in the property until after the death of the testator. To be valid a deed must be delivered during the lifetime of the grantor. The parties named in a will have no rights or interests as long as the party who has made the will is still alive; they acquire interest or title only after the owner's death.

Legal requirements for making a will. A person must be of *legal age* and of *sound mind* when he or she executes the will. Usually the courts hold that to make a valid will the testator must have sufficient mental capacity to understand the nature and effect of his or her acts and to dispose of the property according to some plan. The courts also hold that the drawing of a will must be a voluntary act, free of any undue influence by other people.

New York provides that any person of sound mind who is 18 years of age or older can make a will devising his or her real property. All wills must be in writing and signed by the testator in the presence of at least two witnesses. A holographic will is one that is written entirely in the testator's own handwriting and is not properly attested in the manner just described. Such a document will be enforced by New York courts only under limited circumstances.

▼ **Transfer of Title by Descent**

Title to real estate and personal property of a person who dies intestate passes to what the law regards as natural heirs. Under the descent statutes the primary heirs of the deceased are his or her spouse and close blood relatives. When children have been legally adopted, New York treats them as natural children. In most states illegitimate children inherit from the mother but not from the father unless he has admitted parentage in writing or parentage has been established legally. Such a child who is legally adopted, however, will inherit.

Intestate property will be distributed according to the laws of the state in which the property is located. The New York law of descent and distribution provides that real property belonging to an individual who has died intestate is distributed in the following order. This law and the estate discussed apply only to what remains of the estate after payment of all debts. If a decedent is survived by

- a spouse and children or grandchildren, the spouse receives money or personal property not to exceed $50,000 in value and one-half of what remains of the estate, and the balance of the estate passes to the children or grandchildren.
- a spouse and parents only, the spouse receives the entire estate.
- a spouse only, the spouse receives the entire estate.
- children only, the children receive the entire estate.
- parent or parents only, the parents receive the entire estate.

- siblings only or their children, they receive the entire estate.

If there are no heirs, the decedent's property **escheats** to the state of New York.

Key Terms

adverse possession	intestate
condemnation	involuntary alienation
dedication	last will and testament
descent	probate
devise	testate
escheat	testator/testatrix
executor	voluntary alienation
heir	

Summary

Title to real estate is the right to and evidence of ownership of the land. It is transferred by (1) voluntary alienation, (2) involuntary alienation, (3) will and (4) descent.

Title may be conveyed voluntarily by gift or sale during the owner's lifetime. It may be transferred without the owner's permission by a court action such as a foreclosure or judgment sale, a tax sale, condemnation under the power of eminent domain, adverse possession or escheat. Land also may be transferred by the natural forces of water and wind, which either increase property by accretion or decrease it through erosion or avulsion.

Adverse possession allows someone to claim title to someone else's land that has been used for at least ten years without protest by the owner.

The real estate of an owner who makes a valid will (who dies testate) passes to the devisees through the probating of the will. Generally an heir or a devisee does not receive a deed, because title passes by the law or the will. The title of an owner who dies without a will (intestate) passes according to the provisions of the laws of descent of the state in which the real estate is located.

1. Title to real estate may be transferred during a person's lifetime by
   a. devise.
   b. descent.
   c. involuntary alienation.
   d. escheat.

2. Title to an owner's real estate can be transferred at the death of the owner by which of the following documents?
   a. Warranty deed
   b. Quitclaim deed
   c. Referee's deed
   d. Last will and testament

3. Matilda Fairbanks bought acreage in a distant county, never went to see the acreage and did not use the ground. Harold Sampson moved his mobile home onto the land, had a water well drilled and lived there for 12 years. Sampson may become the owner of the land if he has complied with the state law regarding
   a. requirements for a valid conveyance.
   b. adverse possession.
   c. avulsion.
   d. voluntary alienation.

4. Which of the following is *not* one of the ways in which title to real estate may be transferred by involuntary alienation?
   a. Eminent domain
   b. Escheat
   c. Erosion
   d. Seisin

5. A person who has died leaving a valid will is called a(n)
   a. devisee.   c. legatee.
   b. testator.   d. intestate.

6. Claude Johnson, a bachelor, died owning real estate that he devised by his will to his niece, Annette. In essence, at what point does title pass to his niece?
   a. Immediately on Johnson's death
   b. After his will has been probated
   c. After Annette has paid all inheritance taxes
   d. When Annette executes a new deed to the property

7. An owner of real estate who was adjudged legally incompetent made a will during his stay at a nursing home. He later died and was survived by a wife and three children. His real estate will pass
   a. to his wife.
   b. to the heirs mentioned in his will.
   c. according to the state laws of descent.
   d. to the state.

8. Henry inherited his father's house last year and continued the garden his father had planted on a side lot for decades. Henry recently discovered his father never owned the lot. Which of the following is true?
   a. Henry has no claim because he himself used the land for only one year.
   b. Henry automatically owns the land under the doctrine of adverse possession.
   c. Henry might succeed with a suit to quiet title and declare the land his.
   d. No suit will succeed unless Henry makes bona fide efforts to locate the owner and offer to pay rent.

9. The acquisition of land through deposit of soil or sand washed up by water is called
   a. accretion.
   b. avulsion.
   c. erosion.
   d. condemnation.

10. The person whose land is taken for public use in New York State may
    a. or may not receive compensation.
    b. refuse to give up the property.
    c. still devise it by will.
    d. challenge a money award in court.

CHAPTER 21

Subdivision and Development

Farmer Jensen's widow has been offered a substantial amount for their land, which includes half a mile of road frontage. She has calculated how many lots a subdivider could get from the acreage and how much those lots would sell for. Why not just sell off lots herself, she wonders, and end up with much more money? How hard can it be?

Subdivision and development is a complex branch of real estate involving specialized knowledge, some financial risk and compliance with ever increasing state, federal and local regulation.

Subdivision

Subdivision refers to the process of dividing a single tract of land into smaller parcels. Land in large tracts must receive special attention before it can be converted into sites for homes, stores or other uses. A **subdivider** buys undeveloped acreage and divides it into smaller lots for sale to individuals or developers or for the subdivider's own use. A **developer** (who may also be a subdivider) builds homes or other buildings on the lots and sells them. Developing is generally a much more extensive activity than subdividing. A developer may have a sales staff or may use the services of local real estate brokerage firms.

▼ Restrictions on Land Uses

No uniform city planning and land development legislation affects the entire country. Most laws governing subdividing and land planning are controlled by state and local government bodies. New York State sets standards for villages, cities and towns. Local governments may adopt more restrictive policies. *Article 9-A* of New York's Real Property Law governs subdivision. (A summary of Article 9-A can be found at the end of the chapter.)

A subdivision development plan must comply with any overall local master plan adopted by the county, city, village or town. The developer must consider zoning laws and land-use restrictions adopted for health and safety purposes. Basic city plan and zoning requirements are not inflexible, but long, expensive and frequently complicated hearings are usually required before alterations can be authorized.

Most villages, cities and other areas incorporated under state laws have **planning boards** and/or *planning commissioners.* Communities establish strict criteria before approving new subdivisions. Frequently required are *dedication* of land for streets, schools, parks; assurance by *bonding* that sewer and street costs will be paid; and *compliance* with zoning ordinances governing use and lot size, along with fire and safety ordinances.

Zoning ordinances that systematically exclude certain groups or classes of people from certain areas are *exclusionary* and can be considered discriminatory as well as a violation of a person's right to travel interstate, as provided by the U.S. Constitution.

Local authorities usually require that land planners submit information on how they intend to satisfy sewage disposal and water supply requirements. Development with septic tank installation may first require a *percolation test* of the soil's absorption and drainage capacities. A planner will usually have to submit an *environmental impact report*.

Regulatory taking occurs when rules, regulations or ordinances essentially deprive a property owner of the use or the fair return on the value of the owner's property. In these circumstances, the rules, regulations or ordinances can be considered confiscatory and therefore unlawful or unreasonable.

▼ Environmental Regulations

The Environmental Protection Agency (EPA) has identified 403 chemicals as highly toxic, and innocent future purchasers of land can be held liable. Previous use of land being considered for development should be carefully investigated at the outset. Chemical companies, dry cleaners, old farms with trash dumps or underground gas tanks, airports, warehouses, gas stations and factories of all sorts may have produced potentially dangerous chemical wastes.

Problems faced by unaware future owners could include liability for cleanup, liability for health problems, unfavorable publicity and restrictions on future use of the land. More and more, developers are turning to specialists trained in environmental compliance and documentation.

In the early 1990s New York directed each county clerk or recording officer to compile an index of past and present owners and operators of sites listed on the Inactive Hazardous Waste Registry.

The New York State Environmental Quality Act is commonly referred to as SEQR. Every application to a planning board or a zoning board of appeals must be viewed in light of its environmental impact. Classifications of proposed actions are

- Type I—An *environmental impact statement* (EIS) is required unless the applicant demonstrates conclusively that one is not needed. The next step is to fill out a Preliminary Environmental Review Form (PERF).
- Type II or Exempt Action—No environmental impact statement is needed.
- Unlisted Action—Pending analysis of further information, an environmental impact statement may be required. An environmental assessment form must be prepared.

Most applications to a zoning board of appeals are considered Type II or exempt. Most applicants for subdivision or development before a planning board are required to prepare at least a short form. Larger projects require an EIS and could include hydrologic studies, traffic impact, population density and even light pollution.

In some instances construction requires a permit from the New York **Department of Environmental Conservation (DEC).** Permits are necessary for work in a protected wetland or the 100-foot buffer zone around a wetland. Depending on the circumstances, permits may be needed for work that disturbs the banks of streams, for using some water supplies, for sewage discharges and for sewer extensions. The sale of more than 1,000 tons of fill dirt or gravel per year requires a DEC mining permit. **Environmental impact studies** of varying complexity may be required when the parcel is ruled environmentally sensitive: large projects or those located on floodplains, wetlands, steep slopes, or other environmentally fragile areas.

Environmental impact studies. A *Phase I environmental audit* includes a comprehensive visual site analysis and research of a subject property and surrounding property to determine whether potential environmental risks exist and if additional testing is warranted. A Phase I assessment generally consists of a historical review, an agency file check, a physical inspection and a written report of the findings.

The historical review obtains and analyzes information about past facilities and operations on the site. The agency file check investigates the property's record of regulatory compliance and environmental problems. The site visit is an inspection for characteristics usually associated with environmental problems. The written report provides an overview of the collected information and draws conclusions from it.

A *Phase II environmental audit* involves collection and analysis of suspect materials on or near the subject property to identify and quantify the materials and to establish environmental assessment relevance and relationship to the property. Further investigatory research is also conducted.

Phase III remediation is the legally acceptable cleanup and abatement of otherwise unacceptable environmental characteristics if a Phase II revealed positively identified contamination. (Phase I and Phase II assessments also are discussed in Chapter 17.)

A **wetland survey** is based on the EPA and DEC statutes and is coordinated by the U.S. Army Corps of Engineers. A wetlands survey examines everything from types of plant and animal life to soil composition. Based on the findings, a parcel of land may or may not be classified as wetlands, with severe restrictions on development.

▼ Value of Land for Subdivision

The value of a given tract of land for subdivision purposes depends on many factors. Government land-use restrictions such as minimum lot size requirements, use restrictions and building standards limit the type of development that is possible for a given tract of land. The nature of the land itself is also a factor, particularly if significant portions of the tract are unbuildable owing to soil conditions, wetlands, slopes or other considerations.

> Value for subdivision depends on land-use restrictions, nature and location of the land, availability of services and access.

Location is always a prime consideration in determining real estate value as well. Land will be more valuable for subdivision purposes if it is in a desirable location in an area with strong economic growth and an increasing population. The availability of utility services and access roads is another factor that has a major impact on the cost and practicality of development.

The Process of Subdivision

The process of subdivision involves three distinct stages of development: *initial planning, final planning* and *disposition* or *start-up.*

During the *initial planning stage* the subdivider seeks raw land in a suitable area. The property is analyzed for *highest and best use,* and preliminary subdivision plans are drawn up. Close contact starts with local planning officials. If the project requires zoning variances, negotiation begins along these lines. The subdivider also locates financial backers and initiates marketing strategies.

In the *final planning stage,* plans are prepared, approval of the **plat of subdivision** is sought from local (and, if necessary, state and federal) officials, financing is actually obtained, the land is purchased, final budgets are prepared and marketing programs are designed.

Once final approvals are granted by all the various government agencies, the subdivider may then become the developer (or contractor), sell to a developer, or enter into a joint venture with a contractor.

The *disposition,* or *start-up,* carries the subdividing process to a conclusion. Subdivision plans are recorded with local officials, and streets, sewers and utilities are installed. Buildings, open parks and recreational areas are constructed and landscaped if they are part of the subdivision plan. Marketing programs then are initiated, and title to the individual parcels of subdivided land is transferred as the lots or buildings are sold or leased.

Costs and Financing

Subdivision development involves a range of different costs. In addition to the direct costs of acquiring the land and making improvements such as clearing, grading, roads and utilities, there are indirect costs for subdivision and development permit fees and professional fees for engineers, attorneys and marketing specialists. A large development also may be charged **impact fees,** intended to help a community cope with increased demand for schools, roads and other services. If approval of the subdivision is contingent on the subdivider's making public improvements such as roads or sewers, there is usually a requirement to obtain a bond guaranteeing completion of these improvements.

With all of the costs involved, it is common for subdivision developers to rely on borrowed funds to help finance a project. Development financing is secured by a mortgage lien against the entire project. When a new lot or unit is first sold, the buyer needs to be sure that it is no longer covered by any blanket mortgage lien that applied to the overall project. Blanket mortgage liens commonly have lot release provisions that allow clear title to be passed to a buyer in these situations.

Restrictive Covenants

Often a subdivider creates and records deed restrictions as a means of *controlling and maintaining the desirable quality and character of the subdivision.* Deed restrictions can be set forth in a separate document, which is recorded later, or they can be included in the subdivision plat. When a separate document is used, that document is generally called a *declaration of restrictions.*

Sometimes a deed restriction and a zoning provision cover the same subject. When this happens, the more limiting restriction prevails. For example, if deed restrictions require that subdivision lots be used only for single-family residences but local zoning ordinances allow duplexes, the single-family restriction found in the declaration of restrictions will govern the situation and can be enforced by subdivision residents.

Figure 21.1 Street Patterns

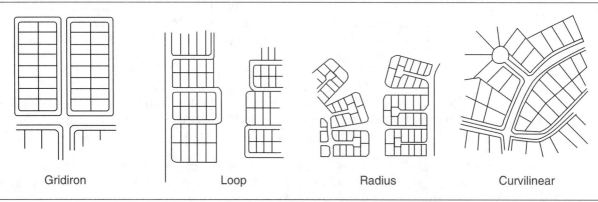

Gridiron   Loop   Radius   Curvilinear

To be valid, a deed restriction must be both reasonable and for the benefit of neighboring owners. Deed restrictions are binding on all future property owners in that subdivision. Common types of deed restrictions include the use to which the land may be put, the type of construction, height, setbacks, square footage and cost, and parking limitations. "No off-road or recreational vehicle may be parked on the subdivision streets" is an example. Some restrictions have a time limitation for example, "effective for a period of 25 years from this date."

▼ **Enforcement of Deed Restrictions**

Each lot owner has the right to apply to the court for an injunction to prevent a neighboring owner from violating the recorded restrictions. If granted, the court injunction will direct the violator to stop the violation or be in contempt of court.

If adjoining lot owners stand idly by while a violation is being committed, they can lose the right to object through *laches,* that is, loss of a right through undue delay or failure to assert it. In New York, neighboring owners have a two-year statute of limitations on objections to violations of the general plan (type of building, height, setbacks) and ten years in which to object to violations of conditions mentioned in the deed.

▼ **Types of Subdivisions and Subdivision Density**

Zoning ordinances often include population density requirements as well as minimum lot sizes. A zoning restriction, for example, may set the minimum lot area on which a subdivider can build a single-family housing unit at 10,000 square feet. The developer would be able to build four houses per acre. Many zoning authorities now establish special density zoning standards for certain subdivisions. **Density zoning** ordinances restrict the average maximum number of houses per acre that may be built within a particular subdivision. If the area is density-zoned at an average maximum of four houses per acre, for example, by clustering building lots the developer is free to achieve an open effect.

Street patterns. By varying street patterns and clustering housing units, a subdivider can dramatically increase the amount of open and recreational space in a development. Some of these patterns are illustrated in Figure 21.1.

The **gridiron pattern** evolved out of the government rectangular survey system. Featuring large lots, wide streets and limited-use service alleys, the system works reasonably well. It can result in busy streets and monotonous neighborhoods, however, and sometimes provides little or no open, park or recreational

Figure 21.2 Clustered Subdivision Plan

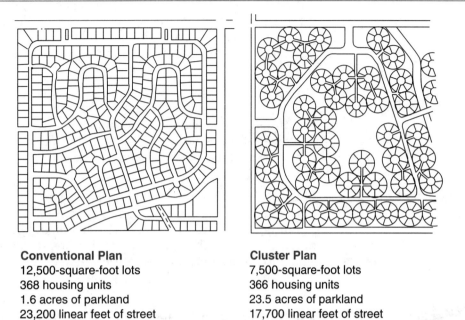

Conventional Plan	Cluster Plan
12,500-square-foot lots	7,500-square-foot lots
368 housing units	366 housing units
1.6 acres of parkland	23.5 acres of parkland
23,200 linear feet of street	17,700 linear feet of street

space. The **curvilinear system** integrates major arteries of travel with smaller secondary and cul-de-sac streets carrying minor traffic. In addition, small open parks are often provided at intersections. The *loop* features serpentine streets that wind through the development and the *radius* pattern is built on a series of cul-de-sacs that radiate from the main street.

Clustering for open space. By slightly reducing lot sizes and clustering them around varying street patterns, a developer can house as many people in the same area as could be done using traditional subdividing plans, but with substantially increased tracts of open space.

For example, the first illustration in Figure 21.2 is a plan for a conventionally designed subdivision containing 368 housing units. It leaves only 1.6 acres open for park areas. Contrast this with the second subdivision pictured. Both subdivisions are equal in size and terrain. But when lots are minimally reduced in size and clustered around limited-access, cul-de-sac streets, the number of housing units remains nearly the same (366), with less street area and drastically increased open space (23.5 acres). In addition, with modern building designs this clustered plan could be modified to accommodate 550 patio homes or 1,100 town houses. Cluster housing may take the form of a **planned unit development (PUD),** with some or all of an entire community's land use established by the developer's original plan.

Land-Use Regulations

Local governments pass zoning ordinances to control the use of land and building within designated districts. Zoning regulates such things as use of the land, lot sizes, types of structures permitted, building heights, setbacks (the minimum distance from streets or sidewalks that structures may be built) and density (the number of units that can be built in an area). An important purpose of zoning is to implement a local master plan.

Zoning ordinances generally divide land use into residential, commercial, industrial, vacant, agricultural, open space, institutional and recreational classifications. Now many communities include cluster zoning and multiple-use zoning, which permit unusual planned unit developments. Zoning and other land-use regulations are discussed in more depth in Chapter 13.

Nonconforming use. When zoning laws are changed, there are usually already-existing buildings that do not conform to the new zoning laws. These buildings are referred to as *nonconforming uses,* and are allowed to continue. However, if the building is destroyed or torn down, any new structure must comply with the current zoning ordinance.

▼ **Building Codes**

Most cities and towns have enacted ordinances to specify construction standards that must be met during building construction or repair. These are called building codes, and they set requirements for kinds of materials, sanitary equipment, electrical wiring, fire prevention standards and the like. New York has a statewide building code that applies where no local code exists or where local codes are less restrictive.

▼ **Interstate Land Sales Full Disclosure Act**

The **Interstate Land Sales Full Disclosure Act** requires those engaged in the interstate sale or leasing of 25 or more lots to file a statement of record and register the details of the land with HUD.

The seller also is required to furnish prospective buyers with a property report containing all essential information about the property, such as distance over paved roads to nearby communities, number of homes currently occupied, soil conditions affecting foundations and septic systems, type of title a buyer will receive and existence of liens. The property report must be given to a prospective purchaser at least three business days before any sales contract is signed.

If a buyer does not receive a property report, the purchaser can cancel such a contract without further liability within two years. Any buyer of land covered by this act has the right to rescind a contract within seven days after signing. If the seller misrepresents the property in any sales promotion, a buyer induced by such a promotion is entitled to sue the seller for civil damages. Failure to comply with the law also may subject a seller to imprisonment and fines.

▼ **New York State Subdivided Land Sales Law**

New York considers land to be covered by subdivision regulations as soon as a fifth lot is carved from the original parcel. Land sold within New York State on the installment plan by a subdivider and out-of-state land offered for sale in New York in any manner may not be offered for sale until at least two documents have been filed with the Department of State. The first covers the identity and address of the offerer, the names of owners of the land, a statement on the subdivider's previous experience with vacant land, any criminal activity, a description of the land complete with maps, a title statement including any encumbrances or liens and the terms on which the land will be sold, with a copy of the contract to be used.

The second document is a copy of the offering statement to be furnished to each buyer with a full financial statement of the assets and liabilities of the subdivider; a description of the subdivision and each lot; information on existing liens and encumbrances, existing or proposed utilities and area, community and

Figure 21.3   Condominium Ownership

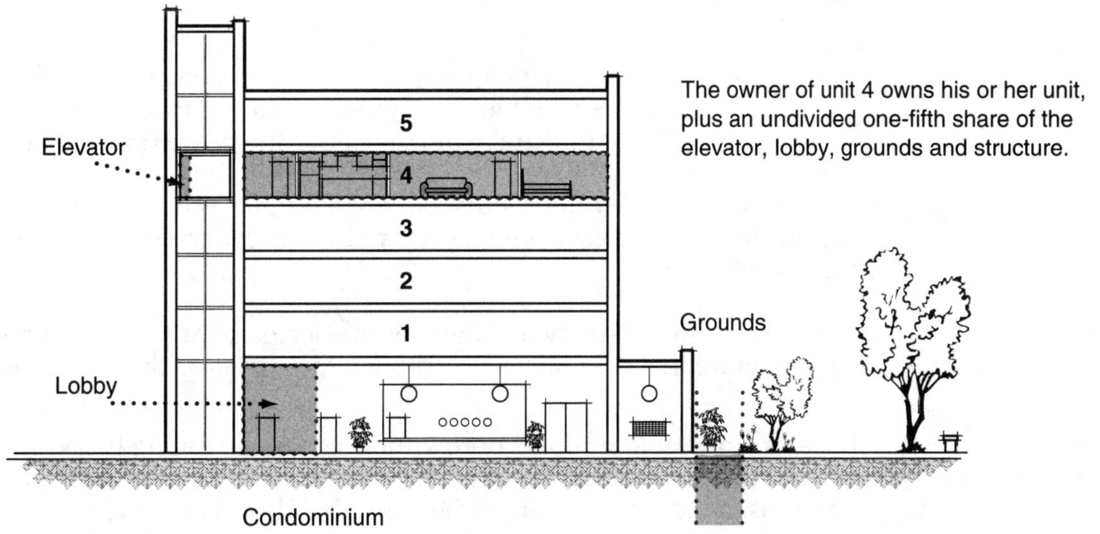

The owner of unit 4 owns his or her unit, plus an undivided one-fifth share of the elevator, lobby, grounds and structure.

Elevator

Lobby

Condominium

Grounds

recreational facilities; and even the weather conditions of the area, as well as the terms of sale.

A copy of any advertising to be used must be filed with the Department of State. The state allows any purchaser who is not represented by an attorney to cancel a contract within ten days.

In addition, New York's Public Health Laws require that any subdivider offering for sale or rent five or more residential building lots file a map of the proposed subdivision with the Department of Health, showing adequate water supply and sewerage facilities. The department must approve the plan before it can be filed. A development of 50 lots or more must have a central municipal water supply rather than individual wells. (These rules are found in Article 9-A.)

Condominiums

The buyer of a condominium receives a *deed* conveying *fee simple ownership* of the unit and an undivided interest in the **common elements** (see Figure 21.3). The unit itself usually consists of little more than airspace bounded by the innermost layers of construction, often interior drywall.

Chief among the common elements are the land and the exteriors of the buildings. Also common property are foyers; hallways; main walls; basements; elevators; stairwells; heating, plumbing and electrical systems; and in suburban locations, driveways, private roads, sidewalks, lawns, landscaping and recreational facilities.

In most respects the law regards a residential condominium owner as it would the owner of a single detached house. The unit receives an individual tax account number and tax bill and may be mortgaged as a house would be. The owner places a separate insurance policy on the living space. Income tax advantages are identical to those for single homes. Owners are free to sell the property, lease it, give it away or leave it to heirs. Each unit is financially independent, and if an adjoining unit is foreclosed, no obligation is incurred by the other owners.

Owners are, however, bound by the **bylaws** of an *owners' association* to which all belong. Monthly fees are levied for the maintenance, insurance and management of common elements. If unpaid, these *common charges* become a lien against the individual unit and even may be enforced by foreclosure. The bylaws also set up **covenants, conditions and restrictions (CC&Rs)** that, for example, may prohibit the display of For Sale signs or the painting of a front door bright red. Owners even may adopt bylaws that restrict leasing of the apartments.

A condominium is usually managed by an elected **board of managers.** When there are more than 25 units, a board often hires professional management.

▼ **Selling Condominiums**

The selling of condominiums or townhouses is now among the activities covered by a broker's or a salesperson's license. The broker who deals in such properties must be concerned with some items that do not apply to the marketing of single homes. The buyer of a condominium must receive detailed statements about the property, should read the CC&Rs and must be alerted to any unpaid common charges against the unit. Prospective buyers should also examine the **reserves,** funds set aside to accumulate for large expenses like new roofs or heating units. The sale of a condominium is arranged on a special form of contract.

Although it is most widely used for residential property, condominium ownership is growing for professional buildings, office buildings and shopping malls.

Cooperative Ownership

Cooperative ownership is common in the New York City metropolitan area and in some resort areas. Under the usual *cooperative* arrangement, title to land and building is held by a *corporation.* Each purchaser of an apartment in the building receives stock in the corporation and a **proprietary lease** for his or her apartment.

Real estate taxes are paid on the whole building by the corporation. A single mortgage, known as the *underlying* or *overlying mortgage,* covers the entire building. Taxes, mortgage interest and principal, and operating and maintenance expenses on the property are shared by the tenants/shareholders as monthly *maintenance charges.* Proprietary leaseholders may individually finance their apartments with a cooperative loan. Most proprietary leases provide that they cannot be assigned, transferred or sublet without the consent of the **board of directors.**

Although cooperative tenants/owners do not actually own an interest in real estate (they own stock, which is *personal property*), they do control the property through their *board of directors.*

One disadvantage of cooperative ownership became particularly evident during the Great Depression and still must be considered. If enough owner/occupants become unable to make prompt payment of their monthly assessments, the corporation may be forced to allow mortgage and tax payments to go unpaid. The entire property could be sold by court order in a foreclosure suit. Such a sale would destroy the interests of all occupant/shareholders, even those who paid their assessments. Accumulation of a substantial reserve fund offers some protection to the cooperative as a whole.

The tenant/owner, not owning actual real estate, may not place a regular mortgage against the unit. Instead shares are pledged against a personal loan. Boards of directors, sensitive to the financial dependence of one tenant on the others, sometimes set down payment requirements that are more stringent than those asked by lending institutions. In some cases they may even refuse prospective tenants unless the purchase is to be made for all cash.

The Internal Revenue Service, however, offers the owner of a cooperative apartment the same income tax treatment as the owner of a condominium or a single home if the cooperative corporation meets the requirements of Section 216 of the Internal Revenue Code. That portion of maintenance charges that covers property taxes and mortgage interest may be taken as a deduction as long as no more than 20 percent of the cooperative's income comes from nonshareholder sources like rental of commercial space and washing machine concessions. Interest paid on the individual's own loan is treated as mortgage interest would be.

Condominium/ Cooperative Construction and Conversion

Many condominium and cooperative projects, particularly in the New York City area, are **conversions** from rental properties. The sale of any form of shared housing is considered a **public offering** and falls under the jurisdiction of the New York attorney general's office. If the proposal is for a condominium, a **declaration,** together with floor plans for each unit, must be filed with the county clerk. The declaration contains a complete description of the land, building and individual units. Common elements are described, and the percentage of ownership for each unit is stated. Bylaws also are included.

Whether for new construction or a conversion, the developer or **sponsor** must file a **disclosure statement** (or offering plan) with the attorney general's office. The statement includes an architect's or engineer's report of the physical condition of the building, a statement of past and projected expenses, prices for each unit and expected amount of tax deductions, management arrangements, a description of the corporation (if a cooperative) and a sample unit deed (for a condominium). The declaration is forwarded along with the disclosure statement. If the offering is for a cooperative, the disclosure statement will include the form of the proprietary lease.

After it has been reviewed by the attorney general's office, the **preliminary prospectus** for a conversion, or **red herring,** is available for inspection by present tenants. At this point it is subject to modification. When a plan is accepted for filing by the attorney general's office (usually within four to six months in the case of a conversion and 30 days in the case of new construction), it is issued as a black book to potential buyers.

▼ Conversion Restrictions

If the property is occupied, special regulations safeguarding the rights of tenants are in effect in New York City and in parts of Westchester, Nassau and Rockland counties. Under a **noneviction plan** in Westchester, Nassau and Rockland counties, unless at least 15 percent of present tenants agree to purchase their units, the property may not be converted to condominium or cooperative ownership. In New York City the property may be converted under a noneviction plan if purchase agreements are signed for 15 percent of the apartments (whether by tenants or outsiders). If the sponsor intends to evict present tenants (eviction plan) at the expiration of their leases, the requirement is that at least 51 percent of the tenants must evince their intention to purchase. Other communities across the state are eligible to adopt the regulations if they choose. Disabled persons and those older then 62 are exempt from eviction. To encourage tenant participation, the sponsor may offer discounts that frequently average one-third off the list price.

Nonpurchasers may have three-year protection from eviction under an **eviction plan** and tenants in occupancy have a 90-day exclusive right to purchase and other benefits. If the sponsor elects the noneviction (15 percent) route, all those tenants who do not wish to purchase may remain as tenants under whatever rent regulations may be in effect. The sponsor's inside sales staff, working as employees, do not require any real estate license.

Town Houses, PUDs and Time-Sharing

The term **town house,** as it refers to shared housing, describes a type of ownership rather than an architectural style. Although the organization, similar to a *planned unit development*, often takes the form of town houses (attached row houses), it also may refer to attached ranch homes or even to small single dwellings in close proximity to each other.

A town house owner has title to the land beneath the individual unit and owns a share in the common elements, most often in the form of shares in a corporation.

A relatively new form of ownership known as **time-sharing** or *vacation ownership* has become popular in resort and vacation areas. The buyer of a time-share receives a fraction of a year's ownership of property, which might be a condominium, town house, single-family detached home, campground or even a motel. Although the concept is most popular in resort areas such as the Caribbean, Colorado, Vermont and Florida, it has been used in Long Island, the Catskills and a few other areas of New York State.

In New York, time-sharing is regulated under the blue-sky securities statute administered by the Department of Law and the Department of State. Sellers must file a public offering statement, and buyers have a ten-day rescission period in which to withdraw from a contract. Real estate licenses are required of those handling such sales.

SUMMARY OF ARTICLE 9-A
OF THE REAL PROPERTY LAW

Subdivided lands. No real estate broker or real estate salesperson should be involved in any way, in the State of New York, with the sale or lease of subdivided lands located within or outside the state, unless the subdivider offering the property for sale or lease has complied with the provisions of Article 9-A of the Real Property Law.

Article 9-A of the Real Property law is designed to protect the residents of New York State in the purchase or lease of subdivided lands located within the State of New York where sold on an installment plan and located outside the State of New York, whether offered on the installment or any other plan, terms and conditions of sale or lease.

Safeguards are inserted into the law to prevent fraud or fraudulent practices that might be employed to include the purchase or lease of vacant subdivided lands. Among such safeguards is the requirement that the subdividers file with the Department of State a statement with substantiating documentation including a certified copy of a map of the subdivided lands, a search of the title to the land reciting in detail all the liens, encumbrances and clouds on the title that may or may not render the title unmarketable.

A subdivider, in addition to the statement required under the law, must file an Offering Statement with the Department of State. The Offering Statement must contain, among other facts, detailed information about the subdivision, including a description of the land, existence of utilities, area, community and recreational facilities, restriction, weather conditions and financial statement of the subdivider. The Offering Statement must be revised yearly. It must clearly indicate that the Department of State has not passed on the merits of the offering.

No sale or lease of subdivided lands shall be made without prior delivery of an Offering Statement to the prospective customer. Any offer to sell or lease subdivided lands prior to

filing both the Offering Statement and the statement constitutes a felony.

Where the land is affected by mortgages or other encumbrances, it is unlawful for the subdivider to sell such vacant lands in the subdivision unless appropriate provisions in the mortgage or lien enable the subdivider to convey valid title to each parcel free of such mortgage or encumbrance. A mortgage on an entire subdivision will usually provide for a release of individual lots from that mortgage on payment of a specified amount of money. If the land is being sold on an installment plan, the law provides that where the amount paid to the subdivider by the purchaser reaches the point where the balance owing is the amount required to release that lot from the mortgage, all monies thereafter received by the seller from the purchaser must be deemed trust funds, be kept in a separate account, and applied only toward clearance of title from the lien of the mortgage.

If, after investigation, the Secretary of State believes that the subdivider is guilty of fraud or that certain sales methods may constitute a fraud on the public, court proceedings to stop these practices may be instituted. The Secretary of State may also withdraw the acceptance previously granted and may order that all sales and advertising in New York State stop.

The law, as amended, also makes it mandatory that all advertising prior to publication be submitted to the Department for acceptance for filing. Misrepresentations in the sale or lease of subdivided lands constitute a misdemeanor.

The law now also provides that in every contract of sale or lease of subdivided lands, if the purchaser or lessee is not represented by an attorney, he or she has a 10-day cancellation privilege.

Sales may not be made based on the representation that the purchase of the property is a good investment, that the purchaser will or may make money on the transaction or that the property can be readily sold. Nothing may be promised that is not contained in the written contract and offering Statement.

Key Terms

board of directors	Interstate Land Sales Full
board of managers	Disclosure Act
bylaws	noneviction plan
common elements	planned unit development (PUD)
conversions	planning board
covenants, conditions and	plat of subdivision
restrictions (CC&Rs)	preliminary prospectus
curvilinear system	proprietary lease
declaration	public offering
density zoning	red herring
Department of Environmental	reserves
Conservation (DEC)	sponsor
developer	subdivider
disclosure statement	subdivision
environmental impact studies	time-sharing
eviction plan	town house
gridiron pattern	wetland survey
impact fees	

Summary

A subdivider buys undeveloped acreage, divides it into smaller parcels and sells it. A land developer builds homes or other improvements on the lots and sells them, either through an in-house sales organization or through local real estate brokerage firms. City planners and land developers, working together, plan whole communities that are later incorporated into cities, towns or villages.

Land development must generally comply with master land plans adopted by counties, cities, villages or towns. This may entail approval of land-use plans by local planning boards or commissioners.

Environmental impact studies are generally required and for sensitive areas may involve increasingly detailed environmental audits.

The process of subdivision includes dividing the tract of land into lots and blocks and providing for utility easements, as well as laying out street patterns and widths. A subdivider generally must record a completed plat of subdivision with all necessary approvals of public officials in the county where the land is located. Subdividers usually place restrictions on the use of all lots in a subdivision as a general plan for the benefit of all lot owners.

By varying street patterns and housing density and clustering housing units, a subdivider can dramatically increase the amount of open and recreational space within a development.

Subdivided land sales are regulated on the federal level by the Interstate Land Sales Full Disclosure Act. This law requires that developers engaged in interstate land sales or the leasing of 25 or more units register the details of the land with HUD. Developers must provide prospective purchasers with a property report containing all essential information about the property at least three business days before any sales contract is signed.

Subdivided land sales also are regulated by New York laws. For the sale of subdivided land on an installment basis, and for sale of any out-of-state land offered in New York, documents must be filed in advance with the Department of State and an offering statement furnished to buyers. The sale of any subdivision of five or more lots requires approval of a water and sewerage plan by the Department of Health, and 500 or more lots requires a central municipal water system.

Condominium and cooperative arrangements for home owning are becoming more frequent due to scarcity of land, the need for economy of construction and operation, and changing lifestyles. Both terms refer to forms of ownership and not to the type of buildings involved.

Condominiums provide fee simple ownership of real property: the living unit and an undivided interest in common elements. Owners may mortgage their units, and they receive individual tax bills and arrange homeowner's insurance. Owners bear no direct financial liability for adjoining units. Management of common elements is administered by a homeowners' association, which levies monthly fees. Bylaws provide regulations binding all owners in the form of covenants, conditions and restrictions.

The owner of a cooperative apartment receives personal property: shares in a corporation that owns the entire building and a proprietary lease to an apartment. Financing is arranged through a single mortgage on the entire property; individual financing comes through personal loans. Each owner shares responsibility for the debts of the corporation. The corporation usually has the right to reject prospective buyers.

Plans for construction or conversion of a condominium or cooperative must be filed with the county recorder and reviewed by the attorney general's office. In the New York City area at least 15 percent of present tenants must agree to buy their apartments before conversion may take place. Regulations in some communities may differ. Certain disabled persons and senior citizens are exempt from eviction in any case.

A town house development involves fee simple ownership of the living unit and the land beneath it. All other land and common elements are owned by a homeowners' association, in which owners are members. Time-sharing involves the purchase of a resort or vacation property for a portion of the year.

Subdivision regulations are complex and require a good deal of expertise. Any property owner who wishes to subdivide and/or develop his or her land must be aware of these regulations and comply with all of them. In many cases, it is a safer course of action to sell the property to an experienced developer.

1. Lila Hurwitz buys farmland near the city and turns it into usable building lots. She is a
   a. site planner.
   b. developer.
   c. surveyor.
   d. subdivider.

2. Overall subdivision guidelines are set by
   a. the federal government.
   b. New York State.
   c. the Department of Health.
   d. the Department of Environmental Conservation.

3. Local governments often regulate subdivision through their
   a. planning boards.
   b. conservationists.
   c. site planners.
   d. building inspectors.

4. A particular subdivision plan may require the services of a(n)
   a. surveyor.
   b. site planner.
   c. engineer.
   d. All of the above

5. A map illustrating the sizes and locations of streets and lots in a subdivision is called a
   a. gridiron pattern.
   b. survey.
   c. plat of subdivision.
   d. property report.

6. Which of the following are *not* usually designated on the plat for a new subdivision?
   a. Easements for sewer and water mains
   b. Land to be used for streets, schools and civic facilities
   c. Numbered lots and blocks
   d. Prices of residential and commercial lots

7. A subdivider turns over streets to public ownership through
   a. development
   b. eminent domain.
   c. dedication.
   d. condemnation.

8. Deed restrictions are usually placed on an entire subdivision by the
   a. building inspector.
   b. state government.
   c. planning board.
   d. subdivider.

9. Which of the following would *not* be a part of the development cost of land?
   a. Curbs and gutters
   b. Installation of telephone lines
   c. Raw land cost
   d. Developer's overhead

10. Gross density refers to which of the following?
    a. The maximum number of residents that may, by law, occupy a subdivision
    b. The average maximum number of houses per acre that may, by law, be built in a subdivision
    c. The maximum size lot that may, by law, be built on in a subdivision
    d. The minimum number of houses that may, by law, be built in a subdivision

11. A street pattern based on the rectangular survey system is called a
    a. block plan.
    b. gridiron system.
    c. loop streets plan.
    d. cul-de-sac system.

12. A street pattern featuring housing units grouped into large cul-de-sac blocks is generally called a
    a. cluster plan.
    b. curvilinear system.
    c. loop street system.
    d. gridiron system.

13. Which of the following kinds of information need not be included in a property report given to a land buyer in compliance with the Interstate Land Sales Full Disclosure Act?
    a. Soil conditions affecting foundations
    b. Financial condition of the seller
    c. Number of homes currently occupied
    d. Existence of liens

14. The Marshes received a property report and consulted a lawyer before they signed a contract to buy a lot in a retirement community in Florida covered by the Interstate Land Sales Full Disclosure Act. They may change their minds and cancel the contract within
    a. seven days.
    b. ten days.
    c. two years.
    d. zero days; they may not cancel.

15. Condominium living provides
    a. economy of construction and operation.
    b. increased square footage per occupant.
    c. accelerated cost recovery.
    d. inexpensive vacations.

16. A separate tax account number, insurance policy and mortgage are available to the owner of
    a. a cooperative apartment.
    b. a condominium.
    c. Both a and b
    d. Neither a nor b

17. Common elements can include
    a. stairwells.
    b. a swimming pool.
    c. foyers.
    d. All of the above

18. The owner of a cooperative apartment receives
    a. a deed.
    b. a property tax bill.
    c. a life estate.
    d. shares in a corporation.

19. The land immediately under the unit is owned individually in a
    a. condominium.   c. town house.
    b. cooperative.   d. time-share.

20. The changing of a rental building into shared ownership is called
    a. conversion.   c. disclosure.
    b. declaration.   d. offering.

CHAPTER 22

Taxes and Assessments

Broker Edwina Abbott is listing a house owned by an elderly minister who does not have much money. Even though the house is modest and in need of repair, the property tax figure mentioned by the owner seems low to Edwina, who asks to see a bill. Sure enough, though, the owner had the right amount. How could this be?

The listing broker who gives the buying public information about the property taxes on a parcel of real estate must exercise great care that the figures are accurate. It helps to understand how taxes are levied and what special provisions apply.

Tax Liens

State and local governments impose *taxes* on real estate to support their services. Because the location of real estate is permanently fixed and ownership cannot be hidden, the government can levy taxes with a high degree of certainty that they will be collected. Liens for property taxes, which usually have priority over other previously recorded liens, may be enforced by the court-ordered sale of the real estate.

Real estate taxes can be divided into two types: *general real estate tax*, or *ad valorem tax*, and *special assessment tax*, or *improvement tax*. Both are levied against specific parcels of property and automatically become liens on those properties.

▼ General Tax (Ad Valorem Tax)

The general real estate tax is made up of taxes levied by the state, cities, towns, villages and counties. Other taxing bodies are school districts, park districts, lighting districts, drainage districts, water districts and sanitary districts. Municipal authorities operating recreational preserves such as forest preserves and parks also may be authorized by the legislature to levy real estate taxes.

General real estate taxes are known as **ad valorem** (to the value) **taxes** because the amount of the tax is determined by the value of the property being taxed.

▼ Special Assessments (Improvement Taxes)

Special assessments are levied only on the parcels of real estate that will benefit from improvements in a limited area. They may be levied, for example, to pay for sidewalks, curbs or street lights in a particular neighborhood.

Property owners may request the improvements, or the local government may propose them. Hearings are held and notices given to owners of the property affected. An *ordinance* may be adopted that sets out the nature of the improvement, its cost and a description of the area to be assessed. The assessment is then spread over the various parcels of real estate that will benefit. The assessment often varies from parcel to parcel, because not all will benefit equally from the improvement.

▼ **Exemptions**

Most property owned by cities, various municipal organizations (schools, parks and playgrounds), the state and federal governments, religious corporations, hospitals or educational institutions is tax-exempt. The property must be used for tax-exempt purposes; if not, it is subject to tax.

New York also allows special exemptions to reduce real estate tax bills for certain property owners or land uses. Homeowners aged 65 or older on limited incomes and veterans may be eligible for reductions in some property taxes. Real estate tax reductions are sometimes granted to attract industries or to encourage construction of multifamily housing. In specific agricultural districts New York may offer reductions for agricultural land to encourage the continuation of agricultural uses. Farmers may claim exemption from school taxes for some or all of their acreage.

Elderly exemption. The state allows local governments (towns, counties and school districts) to offer partial exemption from property taxes on a primary residence to certain homeowners aged 65 or older with modest incomes. Exemptions can range from 10 percent to 50 percent, depending on income levels, which in the late 1990s reached a limit of approximately $25,000 including Social Security payments. Application is made through the local village, town or city hall assessor's office and must be renewed each year.

Applicants who do not understand how early in the year their local tax rolls are closed are often disappointed to find that they must wait up to two years before receiving any benefit. This special tax treatment is known officially by the inelegant title **aged exemption,** and is only an option that the towns, counties and school districts may adopt.

Veterans exemption. Qualified veterans who served during a conflict may receive partial property tax exemption of 15 percent of the value of a primary residence (co-op apartments are not eligible). Those who served in combat are eligible for an additional 10 percent. The exemption, which cannot total more than $5,000, is calculated differently for older veterans discharged before newer regulations took effect. The tax abatement is partial, applying to general municipal taxes but not to school tax. It renews automatically each year.

The real estate broker taking the listing of a parcel of real estate should be alert to the possibility of exemptions and exercise diligence in ascertaining the **true tax** figure.

The Taxation Process

▼ **Assessment**

Assessments in New York are made by municipal officials known as *assessors.* Assessments are made by towns, villages, cities and, in a few cases, counties. The **assessment roll,** open to public inspection, contains assessments for all lands and buildings within the area.

In 1788 New York law mandated **full-value assessment.** The requirement was largely ignored, with most municipalities assessing at less than full value. In 1975 the court of appeals ordered the state either to enforce the law or to change it. More than 400 communities then went to full-value assessment voluntarily or under court order. In 1982 the legislature repealed the 200-year-old requirement. Under the regulations that went into force at that time, Upstate communities were simply required to assess all property at a *"uniform* percentage of value," while New York City and Long Island were allowed to divide real property into four different classes for tax purposes. The question of full-value assessment remains controversial and hotly debated, with court challenges occurring frequently.

Protesting assessments. Property owners who claim that errors were made in determining the assessed value of their property may present their objections and request adjustments. Those who investigate records in the assessor's office may be able to show that the description on file for their property lists more lot size, floor space or amenities than they actually have. Also persuasive are comparisons with neighboring parcels that indicate the protester's assessment is unreasonably high. Documentation to back up the claims can be compiled from the public records.

Problems should be discussed first with the local assessor; it is not necessary to wait for an official *grievance day.* The next step is to apply for a hearing by the local tax appeals board. At the next level a simple and inexpensive small claims procedure is available in New York State for owner-occupied one- to four-family dwellings if the property has an equalized value of less than $150,000 or if the reduction being sought is less than 25 percent. Protests also can be taken to the regular court system in a certiorari proceeding. (See Chapter 13.)

Equalization. Uniformity among districts that may assess at different rates is achieved through use of an **equalization factor.** The New York State Board of Equalization and Assessment receives reports on sales prices and calculates an equalization rate for each municipality. This factor is intended to equalize the assessments in every taxing jurisdiction across the state. No equalization factor applies where full-value assessment is used.

The assessed value of each property is multiplied by the equalization factor, and the tax rate then is applied to the equalized assessment. For example, the assessments in one district are determined to be 20 percent lower than average assessments throughout the rest of the state. This underassessment can be corrected by applying an equalization factor of 125 percent to each assessment in that district. Thus a parcel of land assessed for tax purposes at $98,000 would be taxed on an equalized value of $122,500 ($98,000 × 1.25 = $122,500).

Tax rates. The process of arriving at a real estate tax rate begins with the *adoption of a budget* by each county, city, school board or other taxing district. The budget covers financial requirements for the coming fiscal year, which may be the January through December calendar year or some other 12-month period. The budget must include an estimate of all expenditures for the year and indicate the amount of income expected from all fees, revenue sharing and other sources. The net amount remaining to be raised from real estate taxes is then determined from these figures.

▼ **Appropriation**

The next step is *appropriation,* the action that authorizes the expenditure of funds and provides for the sources of the money. Appropriation involves the adoption of an ordinance or the passage of a law setting forth the specifics of the proposed taxation.

The amount to be raised from the general real estate tax then is imposed on property owners through a tax levy, the formal action taken to impose the tax.

The tax rate for each individual taxing body is computed separately. To arrive at a tax rate, the total monies needed for the coming fiscal year are divided by the total assessments of all real estate located within the jurisdiction of the taxing body. For example, a taxing district's budget indicates that $300,000 must be raised from real estate tax revenues, and the assessment roll (assessor's record) of all taxable real estate within this district equals $10 million. The tax rate is computed thus:

$$\$300,000 \div \$10,000,000 = .03 \; or \; 3\%$$

The tax rate may be stated in a number of different ways. In many areas it is expressed in mills. A **mill** is *1/1,000 of a dollar or $.001.* The tax rate may be expressed as a mill ratio, in dollars per hundred or in dollars per thousand. The tax rate computed in the foregoing example could be expressed as

30 mills (per $1 of assessed value) or $3 per $100 of assessed value
or $30 per $1,000 of assessed value

Tax bills. A property owner's tax bill is computed by applying the tax rate to the assessed valuation of the property. For example, on property assessed for tax purposes at $90,000, at a tax rate of 3 percent, or 30 mills, the tax will be $2,700 ($90,000 × .030 = $2,700). If an *equalization factor* is used, the computation on a property with an assessed value of $120,000 and a tax rate of 4 percent with an equalization factor of 120 percent would be as follows:

$$\$120,000 \; \times \; 1.20 \; = \; \$144,000$$
$$\$144,000 \; \times \; .04 \; = \; \$ \quad 5,760 \; tax$$

Penalties in the form of monthly interest charges are added to all taxes that are not paid when due. The due date also is called the *penalty date.* (Where a lending institution maintains an escrow account to meet a mortgagor's taxes, tax bills may be sent directly to the lender. After the taxes are paid, the receipted bills are forwarded to the property owner.)

New York cities, towns, villages and school districts generally send out their own tax bills, which may include the county tax levy. Improvement district charges are usually included in the town tax bill; benefit charges are often billed separately. State, town and county taxes run from January to December and are payable in advance. Villages may begin their tax year either in March or, more commonly, in June. School taxes are levied from July 1 through June 30, but the tax may not be payable until September or October in some areas and may be payable in installments. School taxes, therefore, are paid in arrears for several months. City taxes frequently are payable in two or four installments during the year.

▼ Enforcement of Tax Liens

To be enforceable, real estate taxes must be valid, which means they must be levied properly, used for a legal purpose and applied equitably to all affected property. Real estate taxes that have remained delinquent for the period of time specified by state law can be collected through either **tax foreclosure** (similar to mortgage foreclosure) or **tax sale.** Many cities and villages enforce their own **tax liens** through tax sales; in most cases towns do not. Some foreclosures are **in rem,** against the property on which taxes are delinquent, without proceeding against the individual owner. When a lienholder, often a municipality, decides to go to court for an in rem foreclosure and subsequently takes title to the property, the lienholder becomes the owner, and the owner and the former owner lose any right or claim to the property. The lienholder (new owner) may then keep the property or dispose of it by sale.

Tax sales are held after a published notice and often are conducted by the tax collector as an annual public sale. The purchaser of the lien must pay at least the amount of delinquent tax and penalty owing. The delinquent taxpayer can redeem the property at any time before the tax sale by paying the delinquent taxes plus interest and charges (any court costs or attorney's fees); this is known as an *equitable right of redemption.* State laws also grant a period of redemption *after the tax sale* during which the defaulted owner or lienholders (creditors of the defaulted owner) may redeem the property by paying the amount paid at the tax sale plus interest and charges. This is known as the *statutory right of redemption.* During the **statutory redemption period** the property owner and other parties who have an interest in the property, including a mortgagee, can redeem the property by paying the back taxes together with penalties and interest.

Counties, cities and villages have different statutory redemption periods. New York City, for example, allows at least four months after taxes are foreclosed, and the period sometimes is extended.

County tax sales. The owner of the property encumbered by the delinquent tax lien is entitled to redeem the property from the tax lien (as sold) within one year following the date of the tax sale. If the property is actually occupied (not vacant land) or if the property is mortgaged, the period for redemption is extended for an additional two years (three years total, following the date of the tax sale). This period may be shortened by a procedure involving service on the owner of a notice to redeem.

Village tax sales. The owner of the property encumbered by the delinquent tax lien is entitled to redeem the property from the tax lien (as sold) within two years following the date of the tax sale.

In most cases the purchasers of tax titles in New York secure title insurance or bring actions to quiet any outstanding claims against the property and do not rely only on the tax deed issued by the municipality. The buyer at a tax foreclosure takes the property free of any junior liens, which is why lending institutions require escrow accounts to give them some control over tax payments.

Key Terms

ad valorem tax	mill
aged exemption	statutory redemption period
assessment roll	tax foreclosure
assessments	tax lien
equalization factor	tax sale
full-value assessment	true tax
in rem	

Summary

Real estate taxes are levied by local authorities. Tax liens generally are given priority over other liens. Payments are required before stated dates, after which penalties accrue. Special assessments are levied to spread the cost of improvements such as new sidewalks, curbs or paving to the particular parcels of real estate that benefit from them.

Partial exemption from property taxes is granted to certain senior citizens on modest incomes (aged exemption), to some veterans and to others for various reasons.

The appraisal process begins with assessment of the taxable value of each parcel. New York mandates either equitable or full-value assessment with variations from one jurisdiction to another adjusted through the use of equalization rates. The money to be raised through taxation is then divided by the total assessment roll to arrive at the tax rate. The tax bill for each parcel is determined by multiplying the tax rate by assessed valuation.

Various taxing authorities send tax bills at different times of the year. Unpaid taxes become a lien against property, usually taking precedence over other liens, and may be enforced through tax foreclosure or sale.

An owner may lose title to property for nonpayment of taxes if the real estate is sold at a tax sale. New York allows a time period during which a defaulted owner can redeem his or her real estate from a tax sale.

1. The broker seeking a property's true tax figure should watch for exemptions granted to certain

   a. veterans.
   b. senior citizens.
   c. religious organizations.
   d. Any of the above

2. Which of the following taxes is used to distribute the cost of civic services among all real estate owners?

   a. Personal property tax
   b. Inheritance tax
   c. Ad valorem tax
   d. Sales tax

3. Sidewalk repairs in one area of the town of Brighton will be paid for through a(n)

   a. mechanic's lien.
   b. special assessment.
   c. ad valorem tax.
   d. utility lien.

4. Which of the following steps is usually required before a special assessment becomes a lien against a specific parcel of real estate?

   a. The State of New York must verify the need.
   b. An ordinance is passed.
   c. The improvement is completed.
   d. A majority of affected property owners must approve.

5. New York statutes require that property be assessed for taxes at which percentage of its value?

   a. 33⅓
   b. 50
   c. Any uniform percentage
   d. 100

6. When real estate is assessed for tax purposes

   a. the homeowner may appeal to a local board of review.
   b. a protest must take the form of a personal suit against the assessor.
   c. the appeal process must start in state court.
   d. no appeal is possible.

7. A specific parcel of real estate has a market value of $180,000 and is assessed for tax purposes at 25 percent of market value. The tax rate for the county in which the property is located is 30 mills. The tax will be

   a. $180.   c. $1,350.
   b. $450.   d. $5,400.

8. What is the annual real estate tax on a property that is valued at $135,000 and assessed for tax purposes at $47,250 with an equalization factor of 125 percent, when the tax rate is 25 mills?

   a. $1,417.50   c. $4,050.00
   b. $1,476.56   d. None of the above

9. An in rem foreclosure proceeds against
   a. the property.
   b. the owner of the property.
   c. the mortgagee of the property, if any.
   d. All of the above

10. During the statutory period of redemption, New York property sold for delinquent taxes may
    a. be redeemed by paying back taxes, penalties and interest.
    b. be redeemed by paying four times the delinquent taxes.
    c. be redeemed only through a court proceeding.
    d. not be redeemed.

CHAPTER

23 ▶ Appraisal

Salesperson Linda O'Brien receives a call from a friend whose father recently died. The estate wants to sell his home and would like an estimate of its value. Linda is asked to furnish it. Linda has never completed a paid appraisal and wonders if she is qualified or legally allowed to do so without special certification.

Even the simplest practice of real estate brokerage involves estimates of value. To deal properly with sellers, buyers and lending institutions, every licensee needs a firm grasp of the fundamental principles of appraising.

Appraising

An **appraisal** is an estimate or opinion of value. In the real estate business the highest level of appraisal activity is conducted by professional real estate appraisers who are recognized for their knowledge, training, skill and integrity in this field and who are licensed or certified by New York State. Formal appraisal reports are relied on in important decisions made by mortgage lenders, investors, public utilities, governmental agencies, businesses and individuals.

Not all estimates of value are made by professional appraisers, however. Often the real estate licensee must help a seller arrive at a market value for his or her property without the aid of a formal appraisal report. Appraisals may be required in a number of situations:

- *Estate purposes*, to establish taxable value or facilitate fair division among heirs
- *Divorce proceedings*, where real estate forms part of property to be shared
- *Financing*, when the amount to be lent depends on the value of the property
- *Taxation*, to furnish documentation for a taxpayer's protest of assessment figures
- *Relocation*, establishing the amount to be guaranteed to a transferred employee
- *Condemnation*, arriving at fair compensation for property taken by government
- *Insurance*, estimating possible replacement expense in cases of loss
- *Damage loss*, used to support income tax deductions
- *Feasibility*, to study possible consequences of a particular use for property

A **fee appraiser** works as an independent contractor, offering services to a number of different clients. A **staff appraiser** is an in-house employee of an organization such as the FHA, a lending institution or a large corporation. A fee appraiser's fees are generally based on time and expenses; fees are never based on a percentage of the appraised value.

Figure 23.1 Kinds of Value

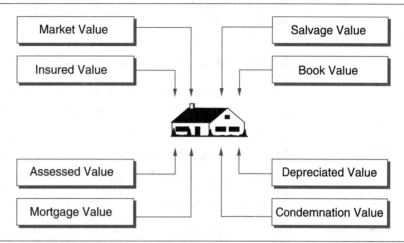

Value

In real estate appraisal *value* may be described as the *present worth of future benefits arising from the ownership of real property.* For a property to have value in the real estate market it must have four characteristics:

1. *Utility:* the capacity to satisfy human needs and desires
2. *Scarcity:* a limited supply
3. *Demand:* the need or desire for possession or ownership backed up by the financial means to satisfy that need
4. *Transferability:* the ability to transfer ownership rights from one person to another with relative ease

▼ Market Value

While a given parcel of real estate may have many different kinds of value at the same time (see Figure 23.1), generally the goal of an appraiser is an estimate of market value (see also Chapter 15). The **market value** of real estate is the most probable price that a property will bring in a competitive and open market, allowing reasonable time to find a purchaser to buy the property with knowledge of all the uses to which it is adapted and for which it is capable of being used, with neither buyer nor seller under duress.

> THE FOUR CHARACTERISTICS OF VALUE IN REAL ESTATE ARE:
>
> 1. utility
> 2. scarcity
> 3. demand
> 4. transferability

Included in the definition of market value are the following key points:

- Market value is the most *probable price* a property will bring.
- Payment must be made in *cash* or its equivalent.
- Both buyer and seller must act without *undue pressure.*
- A *reasonable length of time* must be allowed for the property to be exposed in the open market.
- Both buyer and seller must be *well informed* of the property's assets, defects and potential.
- Market value presupposes an *arm's-length transaction,* one between relative strangers, each of whom is trying to do the best for himself or herself.

Market value versus market price. *Market value* is an estimate based on an analysis of comparable sales and other pertinent market data. *Market price,* on the other hand, is what a property *actually* sells for—its selling price. Theoretically, the ideal market price would be the same as the market value. There are circumstances under which a property may be sold below market value, however, as when a seller is forced to sell quickly or when a sale is arranged between relatives.

Market value versus cost.   It is important also to distinguish between market value and *cost*. One of the most common errors made in valuing property is the assumption that cost represents market value. Cost and market value *may* be equal and often are when the improvements on a property are new and represent the highest and best use of the land.

More often, though, market value differs from cost. Location makes the greatest difference, and almost as important are **amenities**—features that add to owner satisfaction, such as a fine view, nearby park or excellent public transportation.

▼ **Basic Principles of Value**

A number of economic principles affect the value of real estate. The most important are defined in the following paragraphs.

Highest and best use.   The most profitable use to which the property is adapted and for which it is needed or the use that is most likely to be in demand in the reasonably near future is its **highest and best use.** For example, a highest-and-best-use study may show that a parking lot in a busy downtown area should, in fact, be replaced by an office building. An appraisal will estimate highest and best use of the subject property, whether that is the present use or not.

Substitution.   The principle of **substitution** states that the maximum value of a property tends to be set by the cost of purchasing an equally desirable and valuable substitute property. For example, of two similar houses for sale in an area, the one with the lower asking price normally is purchased first.

Supply and demand.   This principle states that the value of a property will increase if the supply decreases and the demand either increases or remains constant and vice versa. For example, the last lot to be sold in a desirable residential area will probably be worth more than the first lot sold in that area.

Conformity.   Maximum value is realized if the use of land conforms to existing neighborhood standards and a reasonable degree of social and economic conformity exists as well. In residential areas of single-family houses, for example, buildings should be similar in design, construction, size and age, and they usually house families of similar social and economic status. Subdivision restrictions rely on the principle of conformity to protect maximum future value.

Anticipation.   This principle holds that value can increase or decrease in anticipation of some future benefit or detriment affecting the property. For example, the value of a house may be affected by rumors that an adjacent parcel may be converted to commercial use in the near future.

Increasing and diminishing returns.   At a certain point adding improvements to land and structures will no longer affect property values. As long as money spent on improvements produces an increase in income or value, the *law of increasing returns* is applicable. But when additional improvements no longer produce a proportionate increase in income or value, the *law of diminishing returns* applies.

Regression and progression. The principle that between dissimilar properties the worth of the better property is adversely affected by the presence of the lesser-quality property is known as **regression.** Thus, in a neighborhood of modest homes, a structure that is larger, better maintained and/or more luxurious will tend to be valued in the same range as the others. Conversely, the principle of **progression** states that the worth of a lesser property tends to increase if it is located among better properties.

Plottage. The principle of **plottage** holds that the merging or consolidation of adjacent lots held by separate land owners into one larger lot may produce a higher total land value than the sum of the two sites valued separately. For example, if two adjacent lots are valued at $35,000 each, their total value if consolidated into one larger lot under a single use might be $90,000. The process of merging the two lots under one owner is known as **assemblage**.

Contribution. The value of any component of a property is what its addition contributes to or its absence detracts from the value of the whole. For example, the cost of installing an air-conditioning system and remodeling an older office building may be greater than would be justified by the increase in market value (a function of expected rent increases).

Competition. This principle states that excess profits tend to attract competition. For example, the outstanding success of one fast-food outlet may attract investors to open others in the area. This tends to mean less profit for all concerned unless the purchasing power in the area increases substantially.

Change. No physical or economic condition remains constant. Real estate is subject to natural phenomena such as tornadoes, fires and routine wear and tear of the elements. Also, like any business, the real estate business is subject to the demands of its market. It is an appraiser's job to be knowledgeable about the past and, therefore, perhaps predictable future effects of natural phenomena and the behavior of the marketplace.

The Three Approaches to Value

To arrive at an accurate estimate of value, three basic approaches, or techniques, are traditionally used by appraisers: the direct sales comparison approach, the cost approach and the income approach. Each method serves as a check against the others and narrows the range within which the final estimate of value will fall. Each method is generally considered most reliable for certain types of property.

▼ The Direct Sales Comparison Approach

In the *direct sales comparison approach,* an estimate of value is obtained by comparing the **subject property** (the property under appraisal) with recently sold **comparable properties.** (Comparable properties are often called "comparables" or "comps" and are properties that are similar to the subject property.) This approach is most often used by brokers and salespeople when helping a seller to set a price for residential real estate in an active market. Because no two parcels of real estate are exactly alike, each comparable property must be compared with the subject property, and the sales prices must be adjusted for any dissimilar features. The principal factors for which adjustments must be made fall into four basic categories:

1. *Date of sale:* An adjustment must be made if economic changes occur between the date of sale of the comparable property and the date of the appraisal.
2. *Location:* An adjustment may be necessary to compensate for locational differences. For example, similar properties might differ in price from neighborhood to neighborhood or even in more desirable locations within the same neighborhood.
3. *Physical features:* Physical features that may require adjustments include age of building, size of lot, landscaping, construction, number of rooms, square feet of living space, interior and exterior condition, presence or absence of a garage, fireplace or air-conditioner and so forth.
4. *Terms and conditions of sale:* This consideration becomes important if a sale is not financed by a standard mortgage procedure.

After a careful analysis of the differences between comparable properties and the subject property, the appraiser assigns a dollar value to each of these differences. On the basis of their knowledge and experience, appraisers estimate dollar adjustments that reflect actual values assigned in the marketplace. The value of a feature present in the subject property but not in the comparable property is *added* to the sales price actually received for the comparable. This presumes that, all other features being equal, a property having a feature (such as a fireplace or wet bar) not present in the comparable property would tend to have a higher market value because of this feature. (The feature need not be a physical amenity; it could be a locational or aesthetic feature.) Likewise, the value of a feature present in the comparable but not in the subject property is *subtracted*.

The terms **CPA** and **CBS** are useful guides—"Comparable Poorer: Add" and "Comparable Better: Subtract." The adjusted sales price represents the probable value range of the subject property. From this range a single market value estimate can be calculated using a weighted average to emphasize those properties most closely comparable. An example is shown in Table 23.1.

The sales comparison approach is essential in almost every appraisal of real estate. It is considered the most reliable of the three approaches in appraising residential property, where the *amenities* (*intangible benefits*) are so difficult to measure.

▼ The Cost Approach

The *cost approach* to value is based on the principle of substitution and assumes that no one will pay more than the price for which the same item could be constructed. The cost approach is sometimes called *appraisal by summation*. It consists of five steps:

1. Estimate the value of the land as if it were vacant and available to be put to its highest and best use.
2. Estimate the current cost of constructing the building(s) and site improvements.
3. Estimate the amount of accrued depreciation resulting from physical deterioration, functional obsolescence and/or external (locational) obsolescence.
4. Deduct accrued depreciation from the estimated construction cost of new building(s) and site improvements.

Table 23.1   Direct Sales Comparison Approach to Value

	Subject Property	Comparables				
		A	B	C	D	E
Sales price		$118,000	$112,000	$121,000	$116,000	$110,000
Location	good	same	poorer +4,500	same	same	same
Age	6 years	same	same	same	same	same
Size of lot	60′ × 135′	same	same	larger –5,000	same	larger –5,000
Landscaping	good	same	same	same	same	same
Construction	brick	same	same	same	same	same
Style	ranch	same	same	same	same	same
No. of rooms	6	same	same	same	same	same
No. of bedrooms	3	same	same	same	same	same
No. of baths	1½	same	same	same	same	same
Sq. ft. of living space	1,500	same	same	same	same	same
Other space (basement)	full basement	same	same	same	same	same
Condition—exterior	average	better –1,500	poorer +1,000	better –1,500	same	poorer +2,000
Condition—interior	good	same	same	better –500	same	same
Garage	2-car attached	same	same	same	same	poorer +5,000
Other improvements						
Financing Date of sale		current	1 yr. ago +3,500	current	current	current
Net adjustments		–1,500	+9,000	–7,000	–0–	+2,000
Adjusted value		$116,500	$121,000	$114,000	$116,500	$112,000

Note: Because the value range of the properties in the comparison chart (excluding comparable B) is close, and comparable D required no adjustment, an appraiser would conclude that the indicated market value of the subject is $116,500.

5. Add the estimated land value to the depreciated cost of the building(s) and site improvements to arrive at the total property value.

Land value (step 1) is estimated by using the sales comparison approach; that is, the location and improvements of the subject site are compared with those of similar nearby sites, and adjustments are made for significant differences.

There are two ways to look at the construction cost of a building for appraisal purposes (step 2): reproduction cost and replacement cost. **Reproduction cost** is the dollar amount required to construct an exact duplicate of the subject building at current prices. **Replacement cost** of the subject property is the construction cost at current prices of a property that is not necessarily an exact duplicate but serves the same purpose or function as the original. Replacement cost is more often used in appraising because it eliminates obsolete features and takes advantage of current construction materials and techniques. An example of the cost approach to value is shown in Table 23.2.

Table 23.2 Cost Approach to Value

Land Valuation: Size 60' × 135' @ $450 per front foot		= $27,000
Plus site improvements: driveway, walks, landscaping, etc.		= 8,000
Total Land Valuation		$35,000
Building Valuation: Replacement Cost		
1,500 sq. ft. @ $65 per sq. ft.	= $97,500	
Less Depreciation:		
Physical depreciation,		
curable		
(items of deferred maintenance)		
exterior painting	$4,000	
incurable (structural deterioration)		9,750
Functional obsolescence	2,000	
External obsolescence	-0-	
Total Depreciation		−15,750
Depreciated Value of Building		81,750
Indicated Value of Cost Approach		$116,750

Determining reproduction or replacement cost. An appraiser using the cost approach computes the reproduction or replacement cost of a building using one of the following four methods:

1. *Square-foot method:* The cost per square foot of a recently built comparable structure is multiplied by the number of square feet in the subject building; this is the most common method of cost estimation. The example in Table 23.2 uses the square-foot method.

    For some property, the cost per *cubic* foot of a recently built comparable structure is multiplied by the number of cubic feet in the subject structure.
2. *Unit-in-place method:* The replacement cost of a structure is estimated based on the construction cost per unit of measure of individual building components, including material, labor, overhead and builder's profit. Most components are measured in units per square foot, although items like plumbing fixtures are estimated by unit cost.
3. *Quantity-survey method:* An estimate is made of the quantities, prices and installation costs of raw materials (lumber, plaster, brick and so on) needed to replace the subject structure. These factors are added to indirect costs (building permit, survey, payroll taxes, builder's profit) to arrive at the total replacement cost of the structure.
4. *Index method:* A factor representing the percentage increase in construction costs up to the present time is applied to the original cost of the subject property.

Depreciation. In a real estate appraisal, *depreciation* refers to any condition that adversely affects the value of an improvement to real property. Land usually does not depreciate, except in such rare cases as misused farmland, downzoned urban parcels or improperly developed land. For appraisal purposes (as opposed to depreciation for tax purposes, which is discussed in Chapter 18), depreciation is divided into three classes according to its cause:

1. *Physical deterioration—curable:* Repairs that are economically feasible and would result in an increase in appraised value equal to or exceeding their cost. Routine maintenance, such as painting, falls in this category.

    Physical deterioration—incurable: Repairs to the separate structural components of a building, which deteriorate at different rates. Roof, electrical system and plumbing fall into this category.

2. *Functional obsolescence—curable:* Physical or design features that are no longer considered desirable by property buyers but could be replaced or redesigned at low cost. Outmoded fixtures, such as plumbing, are usually easily replaced. Room function might be redefined at no cost if the basic room layout allows for it. A bedroom adjacent to a kitchen, for instance, may be converted to a family room.

    Functional obsolescence—incurable: Currently undesirable physical or design features that could not be easily remedied. Many older multistory industrial buildings are considered less suitable than one-story buildings. An office building that cannot be air-conditioned suffers from functional obsolescence.

3. *External* ("locational" or "economic") *obsolescence—incurable only:* Caused by factors not on the subject property, so that this type of obsolescence usually cannot be considered curable. Proximity to a nuisance, such as a polluting factory, is an unchangeable factor that could not be expected to be cured by the owner of the subject property.

THREE CLASSES OF DEPRECIATION:

1. Physical deterioration
2. Functional obsolescence
3. External obsolescence

The *cost approach* is most helpful in the appraisal of **special-purpose buildings** such as schools, churches and public buildings. Such properties are difficult to appraise using other methods because there are seldom many local sales to use as comparables, and the properties do not ordinarily generate income.

▼ The Income Capitalization Approach

The *income capitalization approach* to value is based on the present worth of the future rights to income. It assumes that the income derived from a property will control the value of that property. The income approach is used for valuation of apartment buildings, office buildings, shopping centers and the like. In using the income approach to estimate value, an appraiser goes through the following five steps:

1. Estimate annual potential *gross rental income,* including income from sources like concessions and vending machines.
2. Based on market experience, deduct an appropriate allowance for vacancy and rent collection losses, to arrive at *effective gross income.*
3. Deduct the annual *operating expenses* of the real estate from the effective gross income to arrive at the *annual net operating income.* Management costs are always included as operating expenses even if the current owner also manages the property. Mortgage payments, however (including principal and interest), are **debt service** and *not* considered operating expenses.
4. Estimate the price a typical investor would pay for the income produced by this particular type and class of property. This is done by estimating the rate of return (or yield) that an investor will demand for the investment of capital in this type of building. This rate of return is called the **capitalization** (or "cap") **rate** and is determined by comparing the relationship of net operating income to the sales price of similar properties that have sold in the current market. For example, a comparable property that is producing an annual net income of $15,000 is sold for $187,500. The capitalization rate is $15,000 $187,500, or 8 percent. If other comparable properties sold at prices

that yield substantially the same rate, it may be assumed that 8 percent is the rate that the appraiser should apply to the subject property.

5. Finally, the capitalization rate is applied to the property's annual net income, resulting in the appraiser's estimate of the property value.

With the appropriate capitalization rate and the projected annual net operating income, the appraiser can obtain an indication of value by the income approach in the following manner:

$$\text{Net Operating Income} \div \text{Capitalization Rate} = \text{Value}$$

$$\text{Example: } \$18,000 \text{ income} \div 9\% \text{ cap rate} = \$200,000 \text{ value}$$

This formula and its variations are important in dealing with income property.

$$\frac{\text{Income}}{\text{Rate}} = \text{Value} \qquad \frac{\text{Income}}{\text{Value}} = \text{Rate} \qquad \text{Value} \times \text{Rate} = \text{Income}$$

A simplified version of the computations used in applying the income approach is illustrated in Table 23.3.

The most difficult step in the income approach to value is determining the appropriate capitalization rate for the property. This rate must be selected to recapture the original investment over the building's economic life, give the owner an acceptable rate of return on investment and provide for the repayment of borrowed capital. An income property that carries with it a great deal of risk as an investment generally requires a higher rate of return than would a property considered a safe investment.

Gross rent or income multipliers.   Certain properties such as single-family homes or two-flat buildings are not purchased primarily for income. As a substitute for a more elaborate income analysis, the **gross rent multiplier** (GRM) method is often used in appraising such properties. The GRM relates the sales price of a property to its rental income. (Gross *monthly* income is used for residential property; gross annual income is used for commercial and industrial property.) The formula is as follows:

$$\frac{\text{Sales Price}}{\text{Rental Income}} = \text{Gross Rent Multiplier}$$

For example, if a home recently sold for $82,000 and its monthly rental income was $650, the GRM for the property is computed thus:

$$\frac{\$82,000}{\$650} = 126.2 \text{ GRM}$$

To establish an accurate GRM, an appraiser should have recent sales and rental data from at least four properties similar to the subject property. The most appropriate GRM then can be applied to the estimated fair market rental of the subject property to arrive at its market value. The formula then is

$$\text{Rental Income GRM} = \text{Estimated Market Value}$$

Table 23.3 Income Approach to Value

Gross Annual Rental Income Estimate		$60,000
Less vacancy and collection losses (estimated) @ 6%		− 3,600
		$56,400
Income from other sources		+ 600
Effective Gross Income		$57,000
Expenses:		
Real estate taxes	$ 9,000	
Insurance	1,000	
Heat	2,800	
Maintenance	6,400	
Utilities, electricity, water, gas	800	
Repairs	1,200	
Decorating	1,400	
Replacements of equipment	800	
Legal and accounting	600	
Management	3,000	
Total Expenses		$27,000
Annual Net Operating Income		$30,000

Capitalization Rate = 10%

Capitalization of annual net income: $\dfrac{\$30,000}{.10}$

Indicated Value by Income Approach = $300,000

Table 23.4 shows some examples of GRM comparisons.

If a property's income also comes from nonrental sources (such as sales concessions), a **gross income multiplier** (GIM) is used similarly.

Using multipliers is not a very accurate method because they fail to consider many factors. For example, does the landlord furnish heat or not? Much skill is required to use multipliers, because there is no fixed multiplier for all areas or all types of properties. Many appraisers view the technique simply as a quick, informal way to double-check a value obtained by one of the other methods.

▼ **Reconciliation**

If more than one of the three approaches to value are applied to the same property, they normally will produce as many separate indications of value. **Reconciliation** is the art of analyzing and effectively weighing the findings from the different approaches used.

Although each approach may serve as an independent guide to value, whenever possible all three approaches should be used as a check on the final estimate of value. The process of reconciliation is more complicated than simply taking the

Table 23.4   Gross Rent Multiplier

Comparable No.	Sales Price	Monthly Rent	GRM
1	$93,600	$650	144
2	78,500	450	174
3	95,500	675	141
4	82,000	565	145
Subject	?	625	?

Note: Based on an analysis of these comparisons, a GRM of 145 seems reasonable for homes in this area. In the opinion of an appraiser, then, the estimated value of the subject property would be $625 × 145 or $90,625.

average of the derived value estimates. An average implies that the data and logic applied in each of the approaches are equally valid and reliable. In fact, however, as discussed also in Chapter 15, each approach is more valid and reliable with certain kinds of properties than with others.

For example, in appraising a single-family residence the income approach is rarely used, and the cost approach is of limited value unless the home is relatively new; therefore, the direct sales comparison approach is usually given greatest weight. In appraising income or investment property, the income approach is normally given the greatest weight. In appraising churches, libraries, museums, schools and otherspecial-use properties where there is little or no income or sales revenue, the cost approach is usually assigned the greatest weight. From this analysis, or reconciliation, a single estimate of market value is produced.

The Appraisal Process

The key to an accurate appraisal lies in the methodical collection of data. The appraisal process is an orderly set of procedures used to collect and analyze data to arrive at an ultimate value conclusion. The data are divided into two basic classes:

1. *Specific data,* covering details of the subject property as well as comparative data relating to prices, income and expenses of properties similar to and competitive with the subject property.
2. *General data,* covering the nation, region, city and neighborhood. Of particular importance is the neighborhood, where an appraiser finds the physical, economic, social and political influences that directly affect the value and potential of the subject property.

Figure 23.2 outlines the eight steps an appraiser takes in carrying out an appraisal assignment.

1. *State the problem:* The kind of value to be estimated must be specified, and the valuation approach(es) most valid and reliable for the kind of property under appraisal must be selected.
2. *List the data needed and the sources:* Based on the approach(es) the appraiser will be using, the types of data needed and the sources to be consulted are listed.

Figure 23.2   The Appraisal Process

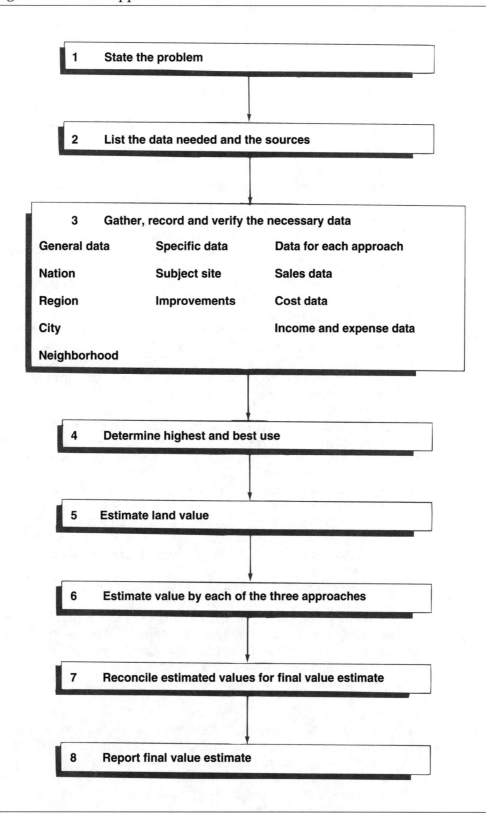

| 1 | State the problem |

| 2 | List the data needed and the sources |

| 3 | Gather, record and verify the necessary data |

General data	Specific data	Data for each approach
Nation	Subject site	Sales data
Region	Improvements	Cost data
City		Income and expense data
Neighborhood		

| 4 | Determine highest and best use |

| 5 | Estimate land value |

| 6 | Estimate value by each of the three approaches |

| 7 | Reconcile estimated values for final value estimate |

| 8 | Report final value estimate |

3. *Gather, record and verify the necessary data.* Detailed information must be obtained concerning the economic, political and social conditions of the nation, region, city and neighborhood, and comments on the effects of these data on the subject property also must be obtained. Specific data about the subject site and improvements must be collected and verified. Depending on the approach(es) used, comparative information relating to sales, income and expenses, as well as construction costs of comparable properties, must be collected. All data should be verified, usually by checking the same information against two different sources. In the case of sales data, one source should be a person directly involved in the transaction.

4. *Determine highest and best use.* The appraiser analyzes market forces such as competition and current versus potential uses to determine the reasonableness of the property's present use in terms of profitability.

5. *Estimate land value.* The features and sales prices of comparable sites are compared to the subject to determine the value of the land alone.

6. *Estimate value by each of the three approaches.* The sales comparison, cost and income capitalization approaches are used to estimate the value of the subject property.

7. *Reconcile estimated values for final value estimate:* The appraiser makes a definite statement of conclusions reached, usually in the form of a value estimate of the property.

8. *Report final value estimate:* After the three approaches have been reconciled and an opinion of value has been reached, the appraiser prepares a *formal written report* for the client. The statement may be a completed *form*, a *letter* or a lengthy written *narrative*. The most complete appraisal report would contain the following information:
   - The estimate of value and the date to which it applies
   - The purpose for which the appraisal was made
   - A description of the neighborhood and the subject property
   - Factual data covering costs, sales, and income and expenses of similar, recently sold properties
   - An analysis and interpretation of the data collected
   - A presentation of one or more of the three approaches to value in enough detail to support the appraiser's final value conclusion
   - Any qualifying conditions
   - Supportive material, such as charts, maps, photographs, floor plans, leases and contracts
   - The certification and signature of the appraiser

Some institutions in the secondary mortgage market require floor plans of the subject property and photographs of both subject property and comparables. Figure 23.3 shows the uniform residential appraisal form widely used for mortgage financing. Even in such a brief report, detailed descriptions of the neighborhood and property being appraised are required.

The Profession of Appraising

Although appraising has existed since the origin of the concept of property, the huge number of foreclosures during the depression of the 1930s gave rise to appraisal as an organized profession. Courses have been established in universities and colleges; books, journals and other publications have been devoted to various aspects of appraising. Appraising has now become one of the most specialized branches of real estate.

Until the early 1990s, when the federal government directed each state to license and certify appraisers, professional designation was made through membership

Figure 23.3   Residential Appraisal Report

X X

Property Description

UNIFORM RESIDENTIAL APPRAISAL REPORT   File No.

SUBJECT			
Property Address	City	State	Zip Code
Legal Description		County	
Assessor's Parcel No.	Tax Year	R.E. Taxes $	Special Assessments $
Borrower	Current Owner	Occupant ☐ Owner ☐ Tenant ☐ Vacant	
Property rights appraised ☐ Fee Simple ☐ Leasehold	Project Type ☐ PUD ☐ Condominium (HUD/VA only)	HOA$	/Mo.
Neighborhood or Project Name	Map Reference	Census Tract	
Sales Price $	Date of Sale	Description and $ amount of loan charges/concessions to be paid by seller	
Lender/Client	Address		
Appraiser	Address		

NEIGHBORHOOD

Location	☐ Urban	☐ Suburban	☐ Rural	**Predominant occupancy**	**Single family housing** PRICE $ (000) AGE (yrs)	**Present land use %**	**Land use change**
Built up	☐ Over 75%	☐ 25-75%	☐ Under 25%			One family ____	☐ Not likely ☐ Likely
Growth rate	☐ Rapid	☐ Stable	☐ Slow	☐ Owner	Low	2-4 family ____	☐ In process
Property values	☐ Increasing	☐ Stable	☐ Declining	☐ Tenant	High	Multi-family ____	To: ____
Demand/supply	☐ Shortage	☐ In balance	☐ Over supply	☐ Vacant (0-5%)	‖‖‖‖ Predominant ‖‖‖‖	Commercial ____	
Marketing time	☐ Under 3 mos.	☐ 3-6 mos.	☐ Over 6 mos.	☐ Vacant (over 5%)		( )	

Note: Race and the racial composition of the neighborhood are not appraisal factors.

Neighborhood boundaries and characteristics: _____

Factors that affect the marketability of the properties in the neighborhood (proximity to employment and amenities, employment stability, appeal to market, etc.):

_____
_____
_____
_____

Market conditions in the subject neighborhood (including support for the above conclusions related to the trend of property values, demand/supply, and marketing time - - such as data on competitive properties for sale in the neighborhood, description of the prevalence of sales and financing concessions, etc.):

_____
_____
_____
_____

PUD

Project Information for PUDs (If applicable) - - Is the developer/builder in control of the Home Owners' Association (HOA)?   ☐ Yes   ☐ No

Approximate total number of units in the subject project _____ . Approximate total number of units for sale in the subject project _____ .

Describe common elements and recreational facilities: _____

SITE

Dimensions _____		Topography _____
Site area _____	Corner Lot ☐ Yes ☐ No	Size _____
Specific zoning classification and description _____		Shape _____
Zoning compliance ☐ Legal ☐ Legal nonconforming (Grandfathered use) ☐ Illegal ☐ No zoning		Drainage _____
Highest & best use as improved ☐ Present use ☐ Other use (explain)		View _____

Utilities	Public	Other	Off-site Improvements	Type	Public	Private	
Electricity	☐		Street	____	☐	☐	Landscaping _____
Gas	☐		Curb/gutter	____	☐	☐	Driveway Surface _____
Water	☐		Sidewalk	____	☐	☐	Apparent easements _____
Sanitary sewer	☐		Street lights	____	☐	☐	FEMA Special Flood Hazard Area ☐ Yes ☐ No
Storm sewer	☐		Alley	____	☐	☐	FEMA Zone ____ Map Date ____
							FEMA Map No. _____

Comments (apparent adverse easements, encroachments, special assessments, slide areas, illegal or legal nonconforming zoning use, etc.): _____

DESCRIPTION OF

GENERAL DESCRIPTION	EXTERIOR DESCRIPTION	FOUNDATION	BASEMENT	INSULATION
No. of Units ____	Foundation ____	Slab ____	Area Sq. Ft. ____	Roof ☐
No. of Stories ____	Exterior Walls ____	Crawl Space ____	% Finished ____	Ceiling ☐
Type (Det./Att.) ____	Roof Surface ____	Basement ____	Ceiling ____	Walls ☐
Design (Style) ____	Gutters & Dwnspts. ____	Sump Pump ____	Walls ____	Floor ☐
Existing/Proposed ____	Window Type ____	Dampness ____	Floor ____	None ☐
Age (Yrs.) ____	Storm/Screens ____	Settlement ____	Outside Entry ____	Unknown ☐
Effective Age (Yrs.) ____	Manufactured House ____	Infestation ____		

ROOMS	Foyer	Living	Dining	Kitchen	Den	Family Rm.	Rec. Rm.	Bedrooms	# Baths	Laundry	Other	Area Sq. Ft.
Basement												
Level 1												
Level 2												

Figure 23.3   (continued)

I M P R O V E M E N T S	Finished area **above** grade contains:		Rooms;		Bedroom(s);		Bath(s);	Square Feet of Gross Living Area

INTERIOR	Materials/Condition	HEATING		KITCHEN EQUIP.		ATTIC		AMENITIES		CAR STORAGE:	
Floors		Type		Refrigerator	☐	None	☐	Fireplace(s) #	☐	None	☐
Walls		Fuel		Range/Oven	☐	Stairs	☐	Patio	☐	Garage	# of cars
Trim/Finish		Condition		Disposal	☐	Drop Stair	☐	Deck	☐	Attached	
Bath Floor		COOLING		Dishwasher	☐	Scuttle	☐	Porch	☐	Detached	
Bath Wainscot		Central		Fan/Hood	☐	Floor	☐	Fence	☐	Built-In	
Doors		Other		Microwave	☐	Heated	☐	Pool	☐	Carport	
		Condition		Washer/Dryer	☐	Finished	☐			Driveway	

COMMENTS

Additional features (special energy efficient items, etc.): _____

Condition of the improvements, depreciation (physical, functional, and external), repairs needed, quality of construction, remodeling/additions, etc.: _____

Adverse environmental conditions (such as, but not limited to, hazardous wastes, toxic substances, etc.) present in the improvements, on the site, or in the immediate vicinity of the subject property: _____

Freddie Mac Form 70   6–93   10 CH.   PAGE 1 OF 2   Fannie Mae Form 1004   6–93

Page of 2 of 2

UNIFORM RESIDENTIAL APPRAISAL REPORT   File No.

Valuation Section

COST APPROACH

ESTIMATED SITE VALUE. = $ _____

ESTIMATED REPRODUCTION COST-NEW OF IMPROVEMENTS:

Dwelling _____ Sq. Ft @ $ _____ = $ _____

_____ Sq. Ft @ $ _____ = _____

_____ = _____

Garage/Carport _____ Sq. Ft @ $ _____ = _____

Total Estimated Cost-New . . . . = $ _____

Less   Physical | Functional | External

Depreciation _____ = $ _____

Depreciated Value of Improvements . . . . = $ _____

"As-is" Value of Site Improvements . . . . = $ _____

INDICATED VALUE BY COST APPROACH . . . . = $ _____

Comments on Cost Approach (such as, source of cost estimate, site value, square foot calculation and, for HUD, VA and FmHA, the estimated remaining economic life of the property): _____

ITEM	SUBJECT	COMPARABLE NO. 1	COMPARABLE NO. 2	COMPARABLE NO. 3
Address				
Proximity to Subject				
Sales Price	$	$	$	$
Price/Gross Liv. Area	$ ☑	$ ☑	$ ☑	$ ☑
Data and/or Verification Sources				

VALUE ADJUSTMENTS	DESCRIPTION	DESCRIPTION	+ (–) $ Adjustment	DESCRIPTION	+ (–) $ Adjustment	DESCRIPTION	+ (–) $ Adjustment
Sales or Financing Concessions							
Date of Sale/Time							
Location							
Leasehold/Fee Simple							
Site							
View							

Figure 23.3 (continued)

SALES COMPARISON ANALYSIS		SUBJECT	COMPARABLE NO. 1	COMPARABLE NO. 2	COMPARABLE NO. 3
	Design and Appeal				
	Quality of Construction				
	Age				
	Condition				
	Above Grade	Total Bdrms Baths	Total Bdrms Baths	Total Bdrms Baths	Total Bdrms Baths
	Room Count				
	Gross Living Area	Sq. Ft.	Sq. Ft.	Sq. Ft.	Sq. Ft.
	Basement & Finished Rooms Below Grade				
	Functional Utility				
	Heating/Cooling				
	Energy Efficient Items				
	Garage/Carport				
	Porch, Patio, Deck, Fireplace(s), etc.				
	Fence, Pool, etc.				
	Net Adj. (total)		☐ + ☐ – $	☐ + ☐ – $	☐ + ☐ – $
	Adjusted Sales Price of Comparable		$	$	$

Comments on Sales Comparison (including the subject property's compatibility to the neighborhood, etc.): _____

ITEM	SUBJECT	COMPARABLE NO. 1	COMPARABLE NO. 2	COMPARABLE NO. 3
Date, Price and Data Source for prior sales within year of appraisal				

Analysis of any current agreement of sale, option, or listing of the subject property and analysis of any prior sales of subject and comparables within one year of the date of appraisal:

INDICATED VALUE BY SALES COMPARISON APPROACH . . . . $ _____

INDICATED VALUE BY INCOME APPROACH (If Applicable) Estimated Market Rent $_____ /Mo. x Gross Rent Multiplier _____ = $ _____

This appraisal is made ☐ "as is" ☐ subject to the repairs, alterations, inspections, or conditions listed below ☐ subject to completion per plans and specifications.

Conditions of Appraisal: _____

Final Reconciliation: _____

The purpose of this appraisal is to estimate the market value of the real property that is the subject of this report, based on the above conditions and the certification, contingent and limiting conditions, and market value definition that are stated in the attached Freddie Mac Form 439/Fannie Mae Form 1004B (Revised _____).

I (WE) ESTIMATE THE MARKET VALUE, AS DEFINED, OF THE REAL PROPERTY THAT IS THE SUBJECT OF THIS REPORT, AS OF _____

(WHICH IS THE DATE OF INSPECTION AND THE EFFECTIVE DATE OF THIS REPORT) TO BE $ _____ .

APPRAISER: **SUPERVISORY APPRAISER (ONLY IF REQUIRED):**

Signature _____	Signature _____	☐ Did ☐ Did Not
Name _____	Name _____	Inspect Property
Date Report Signed _____	Date Report Signed _____	
State Certification # _____ State	State Certification # _____ State	
Or State License # _____ State	Or State License # _____ State	

in appraisal societies. Different designations require varying levels of education, specific courses in appraisal, examinations, demonstration appraisals, experience and continuing education. The **Appraisal Institute,** the largest private society, offers the prestigious designations MAI (Member, Appraisal Institute) and SRA (Senior Residential Appraiser).

Some professional appraisers belong to more than one society. Those along the Niagara frontier, for example, may join an international society, FIABCI. Where expert testimony is provided for court proceedings or before a public body such as a zoning board, specific credentials (MAI, SRA or the equivalent) may be required.

In the late 1980s, the leading appraisal societies founded an overall Appraisal Foundation, with one of its primary objectives being the establishment of standards and guidelines for state and federal legislation regulating appraisers.

▼ **Licensing and Certification**

Federal and state governments suggest licensing or certification for all appraisals, but *require* it only for federally related appraisal assignments with a transaction value of at least $250,000. (An appraisal is federally related if there is any federal government tie-in, such as the fact that the appraisal is used for lending purposes and the lender is a federally chartered bank or savings and loan.)

New York's appraisal licensing and certification process provides for four types of appraiser licenses or certifications:

1. *Appraiser Assistant License.* An appraiser assistant must work under the supervision of a state licensed or certified appraiser, who must cosign all the appraisal reports. An appraiser assistant license is good for two years and may be renewed once.
2. *Licensed Real Estate Appraiser.* A licensed real estate appraiser may appraise noncomplex one- to four-unit residential real property with a transaction value of less than $250,000.
3. *Certified Residential Appraiser.* A certified residential appraiser may appraise any residential property up to four units.
4. *Certified General Appraiser.* A certified general appraiser may appraise any real property.

Education requirements. Various appraisal courses must be completed, depending on the type of license or certification the applicant is seeking. The designated courses include:

Course Number	Course Name	Hours
R-1	Introduction to Real Estate Appraisal	30
R-2	Valuation Principles and Procedures	30
R-3	Applied Residential Property Valuation Case Studies	30
R-4	Elementary Income Capitalization Methods and Techniques	15
G-1	Introduction to Income Property	30
G-2	Principles of Income Property Appraising	30
G-3	Applied Income Property Valuation	30
	Ethics and Standards of Professional Practice	15

To become a licensed appraiser assistant, the applicant must complete courses R-1 and R-2 (60 classroom hours). To become a licensed real estate appraiser, the applicant must complete R-1 and R-2 (60 classroom hours). To become a certified residential appraiser, the applicant must complete R-1, R-2, R-3 and R-4 (105 classroom hours). To become a certified general appraiser, the applicant must complete R-1, R-2, G-1, G-2 and G-3 (150 classroom hours). In addition to these requirements, each applicant also must complete a 15-hour course in Ethics and Standards of Professional Practice.

Experience requirements. Licensure and certification requires a minimum of two years' full-time appraisal experience and at least 240 points, as explained below. The only exception is the entry-level appraiser assistant license, which requires no experience.

The point system assigns credit for each appraisal completed, ranging from one point for appraising a single-family residence to ten points for appraising a commercial/industrial multitenant property. Complex rules govern review appraisals and those where the applicant performs only part of the work. No credit is given for comparative market analyses.

To become a certified general appraiser, at least 180 points must come from appraisals of general property; for all other types of licenses, at least 180 points must come from residential appraisals.

Application. License and certification applications may be obtained by writing to

Customer Service Unit
NYS Department of State
Division of Licensing Services
162 Washington Avenue, 2nd Floor
Albany, NY 12231

Each application form that is sent out is number-coded. A $250 nonrefundable fee must accompany completed applications. If the application is in order, the applicant will receive an admission card to a scheduled walk-in examination (there is a $50 exam fee). The applicant must score 75 percent or higher on the exam to qualify for the license or certificate.

Key Terms

amenities	highest and best use
appraisal	plottage
Appraisal Institute	progression
assemblage	reconciliation
capitalization rate	regression
CBS	replacement cost
comparable property	reproduction cost
CPA	special-purpose buildings
debt service	staff appraiser
fee appraiser	subject property
gross income multiplier	substitution
gross rent multiplier	

Summary

To appraise real estate is to estimate its value. Although there are many types of value, the most common objective of an appraisal is to estimate market value—the most probable sales price of the subject property.

Value is an estimate of future benefits, cost represents a measure of past expenditures and price the actual amount of money paid for a property. Basic to appraising are certain underlying economic principles, such as highest and best use, substitution, supply and demand, conformity, anticipation, increasing and diminishing returns, regression, plottage, contribution, competition and change. A professional appraiser analyzes property through three approaches to value. In the sales comparison approach the subject property is compared with similar nearby properties that have sold recently. Adjustments are made to account for any differences. With the cost approach an appraiser calculates the cost of building a similar structure on a similar site. Then he or she subtracts depreciation (losses in value), which reflects the differences between new property of this type and the present condition of the subject property. The income approach is based on the relationship between the rate of return an investor requires and the net income the property produces.

A special version of the income approach called the gross rent multiplier (GRM) is computed by dividing the sales price of a property by its gross monthly rent.

The application of the three approaches normally results in three different estimates of value. In the process of reconciliation the validity and reliability of each approach are weighed objectively to arrive at the single best and most supportable conclusion of value.

New York State's appraisal licensing and certification process provides for licensure or certification in four categories, requiring various courses and experience. These four categories include licensed appraiser assistant, licensed real estate appraiser, certified residential appraiser, and certified general appraiser.

1. Bert Evans is a fully qualified appraiser. As such he
   a. discovers value.
   b. ensures value.
   c. estimates value.
   d. establishes value.

2. The appraiser who works for a number of different clients is known as a(n)
   a. fee appraiser.
   b. freelance appraiser.
   c. staff appraiser.
   d. in-house appraiser.

3. A house should bring $100,000 but is sold for $90,000 by a hard-pressed seller in a hurry, is then mortgaged for $80,000 and insured for $95,000. Its market value is
   a. $80,000.   c. $95,000.
   b. $90,000.   d. $100,000.

4. Market value is best defined as the
   a. gross rental income of the property.
   b. cash flow after debt service.
   c. most likely price obtainable on the open market.
   d. highest and best use of the subject property.

5. An example of an arm's-length transaction is one between
   a. father and daughter.
   b. employer and employee.
   c. broker and salesperson.
   d. two strangers.

6. Market value and cost are often equal when property
   a. remains in the family a long time.
   b. was recently constructed.
   c. is sold in an arm's-length transaction.
   d. receives a weighted appraisal.

7. Highest and best use of real estate is defined as the use that produces the most
   a. benefit to the community.
   b. conformity.
   c. progression.
   d. money.

8. "Why should I pay more when I can buy almost the same house new for less?" is an example of the principle of
   a. substitution.   c. anticipation.
   b. conformity.   d. change.

9. Houses are likely to reach their maximum value when
   a. a wide range of price levels is represented.
   b. neighbors hold a mix of executive, blue-collar and white-collar jobs.
   c. each house is unique.
   d. demand is high and supply is limited.

10. The principle of value that states that two adjacent parcels of land combined into one larger parcel may have a greater value than the two parcels' value separately is called
    a. substitution.
    b. plottage.
    c. highest and best use.
    d. contribution.

11. Henry has his dream house constructed for $250,000 in an area where most homes would typically sell for $200,000. The value of his house would be affected by the principle of
    a. progression.
    c. change.
    b. assemblage.
    d. regression.

12. You are appraising the house at 23 Oak. The house recently sold at 54 Oak is similar but has a fireplace. What use do you make of the value of the fireplace?
    a. Subtract it.
    c. Ignore it.
    b. Add it.
    d. Reconcile it.

13. The cost approach is most useful for
    a. a library.
    b. insurance purposes.
    c. new construction.
    d. All of the above

14. From the reproduction or replacement cost of the building, an appraiser deducts depreciation, which represents
    a. the remaining useful economic life of the building.
    b. remodeling costs to increase rentals.
    c. loss of value due to any cause.
    d. costs to modernize the building.

15. The difference between reproduction cost and replacement cost involves
    a. functional obsolescence.
    b. estimated land value.
    c. modern versus obsolete methods and materials.
    d. effective gross income.

16. The appraised value of a residence with five bedrooms and one bathroom would probably be reduced because of
    a. locational obsolescence.
    b. functional obsolescence.
    c. physical deterioration—curable.
    d. physical deterioration—incurable.

17. The term external obsolescence refers to
    a. poor landscaping.
    b. a faulty floor plan.
    c. wear and tear.
    d. problems beyond the property line.

18. If a property's annual net income is $37,500 and it is valued at $300,000, what is its capitalization rate?
    a. 12.5 percent
    c. 15 percent
    b. 10.5 percent
    d. 18 percent

19. Certain data must be determined by an appraiser before value can be computed by the income approach. Which of the following is *not* required for this process?
    a. Annual net income
    b. Proper capitalization rate
    c. Accrued depreciation
    d. Annual gross income

20. Which of the following factors would *not* be important in comparing properties under the sales comparison approach to value?
    a. Difference in dates of sale
    b. Difference in real estate taxes
    c. Difference in appearance and condition
    d. Differences in original cost

21. The first step in making an appraisal is to
    a. write the appraisal report.
    b. collect the data.
    c. determine the fee.
    d. define the problem.

22. Reconciliation refers to which of the following?
    a. Loss of value owing to any cause
    b. Separating the value of the land from the total value of the property to compute depreciation
    c. Analyzing the results obtained by the three approaches to value to determine a final estimate of value
    d. The process by which an appraiser determines the highest and best use for a parcel of land

23. Some of the country's foremost appraisers have earned the designation
    a. MAI.
    c. SRE.
    b. REA.
    d. ARE.

24. Salesperson Linda O'Brien is asked by a friend's family to appraise a single home for estate tax purposes. She has never done a paid appraisal and has no special training beyond her license-qualifying courses and several years' sales experience. Linda's best course is to

    a. refuse the work and explain that she is not certified.
    b. offer a free appraisal.
    c. accept the assignment and charge a normal fee.
    d. do the appraisal under her broker's guidance.

25. The New York State certification that allows appraisal of any real estate is

    a. Licensed Appraiser.
    b. Certified Residential Appraiser.
    c. Certified General Appraiser.
    d. Federally Related Certified Appraiser.

CHAPTER 24

Construction II

Broker Brown's salesperson is showing a new listing to a prospective customer. The customer asks if the basement is dry. The salesperson answers, "Of course it is!" The customer buys the house. Four and a half months after the closing, Broker Brown receives a call from the new owner threatening a lawsuit. He said that the basement had flooded, ruining his new washer, dryer, freezer and the rugs and furniture in his newly finished playroom. Is Broker Brown responsible for the salesperson's response?

Even though real estate agents are not engineers or home inspectors, they have certain responsibilities to their clients and customers regarding any misrepresentations that they may make about the condition of any property.

Construction Standards

All real estate agents should be aware of the various sources of construction standards. These standards are established at many levels of government and by a variety of agencies.

▼ Federal Agencies

The *Department of Housing and Urban Development* **(HUD)** establishes construction standards for homes that in some way are funded through HUD programs; for instance, homes that are financed with FHA funds.

The **Army Corps of Engineers** regulates certain waterways and drainage into them. These regulations affect building sites and the manner in which homes may be constructed.

> Federal regulatory agencies include HUD, the Army Corps of Engineers and the Environmental Protection Agency.

The *Environmental Protection Agency* has established standards for the protection of the environment. One of the major effects of these standards is to increase the time and money required to plan and get the necessary approvals for new developments.

▼ State Agencies

New York State regulates **minimum building standards** and requires that various codes and regulations be followed, including building codes, fire codes, sanitary regulations and environmental requirements. The state also has different code requirements for special types of construction, such as schools. (For example, a state inspector must inspect schools for compliance each year.)

The various state codes and other regulations are *minimum standards.* Local counties and municipalities may require stricter standards. For instance, a particular county code may require sprinkler systems in all new residential construction, even though the state code does not. The enforcement of the state codes is largely carried out on a local basis (by county or municipal inspectors), but the state agency also may get involved in enforcement.

The New York State **Board of Fire Underwriters** sets standards for electrical service systems in all buildings. District inspectors enforce the Board's electrical code.

The New York State **Department of Transportation** regulates traffic and must authorize any curb cuts onto a state highway. Naturally, transportation, ingress onto and egress from state highways is an important consideration for any type of development, especially commercial and large residential developments.

The New York State Department of State (DOS) is responsible for the Coastal **Zone Management Program.** Any project on the coast, navigable rivers, lakes or islands such as those in Long Island Sound must have DOS approval.

DOS also is responsible for the **Local Waterfront Revitalization Program (LWRP).** The DOS Office for Local Government Services oversees this program and is a resource for local officials.

▼ **Regional Agencies**

The counties of Nassau, Putnam, Suffolk, Rockland and Westchester, plus the city of New York are under some regulation from the **Metropolitan Transportation Authority (MTA).** The MTA has taxing powers and controls air rights as well as land rights to all properties within these counties.

> **Example:** The owner of an office building wanted to build a pedestrian bridge over the adjacent railroad tracks to provide more convenient access to his building from the parking lot for his tenants. To do so, he had to acquire air rights over the tracks and install a prefabricated pedestrian bridge, to MTA specifications, in a certain number of hours, and with the supervision of MTA personnel. He also had to get approvals from Penn Central (the landowner), from the local Planning Board and from the Zoning Board of Appeals.

New York City. The **New York City Department of Environmental Protection (DEP)** has regulatory powers over New York City's water supply system, from upstate down through the aqueducts and reservoirs and the extensive drainage basins. Land in several counties is included in New York City's watershed. The New York City DEP actually stopped the construction of a modest subdivision that had already received all final approvals from the county board of health and the local planning board, based on its effect on the water supply system (Somers, N.Y.)

Counties. **County boards of health** have jurisdiction over sanitary systems and facilities, local water supplies (water potability), food purveyors or suppliers and so forth.

County planning boards are largely advisory but can establish certain reporting requirements and intermunicipal standards. In more-rural counties, they exercise more authority.

Local municipalities. Most municipalities have a building department that is responsible for ensuring that minimum standards of construction are met. The building department issues a **Certificate of Occupancy** (C of O) when the construction is completed to its satisfaction. Lenders often require a C of O on resale properties as well as on new construction. In some jurisdictions a **Certificate of**

Compliance (C of C) is issued to indicate that the structure meets certain standards, particularly those regarding safety.

Before a building inspector can issue a C of O on a newly constructed building, the inspector must have proof that all other required permits have been issued, such as permits from the Board of Health, from the Board of Fire Underwriters and for highway curb cuts, blasting, excavation, tree cutting and so on. Wetlands review boards, conservation review boards, environmental review boards, architectural review boards or historical district commissions may also need to inspect and approve a project.

Minimum construction standards offer a consumer some assurance of safety and quality. However, building inspectors are not expert on all matters, and their inspections only assure the consumer that *minimum* standards have been met, not that *higher* standards of quality have been met.

All the various permit processes, including any required inspections, necessarily increase the cost of construction. In some areas the preconstruction permit process for even a small subdivision can take up to ten years, and may include exorbitant costs for all kinds of specialists, such as engineers and architects, who must review and alter the plans to meet the demands of local and state agencies. The permit process poses a financial drain on the developer, who must continue to pay the property taxes as well as the other expenses of the permit process while receiving no return on his or her investment. In turn, these expenses drive up the final purchase cost to the home buyer.

Property Faults and Uncommon Conditions

The *primary responsibility* for dealing with and/or correcting faults and problems with a property lie with the builder, if the project is new construction, or with the owner, if the project is a renovation.

> **Examples:** 1. Builder Daley starts site preparation for a duplex and has the foundation dug out. He discovers a natural spring in the center of the proposed basement floor. After studying the course of the water, he creates a drainage system to channel the water away from the area. Thirty-five years later, the basement is still bone dry.
>
> 2. Builder Smith discovers that a stream flowing through her property to a New York City water supply reservoir is full of trash and debris. In the process of making improvements on the property, she digs up an old lawnmower and accompanying oil and gasoline residue. She cleans up the stream according to the specifications of the New York City DEP and removes the lawnmower and the contaminated soil from the site according to the specifications of the EPA.

In both of the above examples, had the builders not exercised **due diligence,** they would have been liable for any resulting property damage or cleanup costs, even after the property had been sold. This liability still may exist years later, if it takes that long to discover the problems.

▼ Legal Exposure

If a septic system fails a short time after the purchase of a new house, to whom does the owner go to remedy the problem? This is a Board of Health matter, but there is the engineer who designed the system, the contractor who installed it and the building department that was to check to make sure the Board of Health had granted final approval of the septic system.

> **Example:** A small subdivision was built adjacent to a New York City reservoir. After about three years, the owners started to have problems with their septic systems. The first owner to hire a company to fix the system found that there was no septic system, only a cesspool (a deep pit filled with gravel). The owners were unable to gain any satisfaction from the builder. The County Board of Health was responsible and, fortunately, was able to exact corrective measures from the original builder.

The Role of the Real Estate Agent. Real estate agents must be knowledgeable about their products; that is, the property and its surrounding area, including any geographic and topographic peculiarities. When listing a property, *due diligence* must be exercised when inspecting the premises. In addition to calculating the square footage and describing the style, acreage, and location of the property, the agent should take note of its general condition, including the condition of the roof, interior and exterior siding, cracks in any masonry (chimney, foundation, porches), broken windows, the type and condition of heating and cooling systems, septic or sewer systems and water supply (whether well, municipal or private). Some of this information is readily obtained by a visible inspection; some must be obtained from the owner.

An astute agent will use a checklist in addition to the listing form, and can even include the names of suppliers and service people. The more information available to the agent, the smoother the sales transaction.

> **Example:** A 32-year-old house was sold by the original owner to a local person who knew the area and understood the types of construction typical to the area (including heating systems, septic systems and the like). This new owner in turn sold the house to an out-of-state couple. The out-of-state buyers panicked when they learned of the underground oil tank, used to store heating oil. In the buyers' own area, the most common type of heating was natural gas. Fortunately, the agent had taken note of the address and phone number of the original owner during the listing process. The original owner was able to show that the oil tank was only four years old, had been purchased and installed by a local firm and met all the current specifications for underground oil tanks.

As of 1997, there was no New York law or regulation that requires sellers to make a written disclosure of the condition of their property. New York is still a "caveat emptor" (let the buyer beware) state. If, however, the property lies in an agricultural district, this fact *must be disclosed.* Also, the *lack of available utilities must be disclosed:* purchasers or their agents must be given written notice when a property is offered for sale for which no utility services are available. A similar notice is required if there is a surcharge for utility services, and the notice must include the type and amount of the surcharge. A seller must furnish, on request, information on utility bills and must sign a statement that there is a smoke alarm.

In many other states, sellers are required to provide a written property condition disclosure statement. The statement is required for the protection of all the parties, the seller, the buyer and the real estate agent.

Example: A seller in California was sued by the buyer of his former home when the basement flooded. In court, the seller produced the seller's property condition disclosure form, which he had signed and the buyer had acknowledged receiving. On the form, the seller had indicated occasional flooding in the basement. On the basis of the disclosure form, the seller (and the broker, who also was sued) was cleared of any wrongdoing.

In New York, many firms routinely use their own property condition disclosure forms (see Figure 24.1).

Building Inspections

Various building inspections are required for new construction, including inspections of the

- footing forms,
- foundation,
- framing,
- roof,
- insulation,
- sheetrock,
- electrical system,
- plumbing system and
- all hook-ups including water and sewer.

Table 24.1 is a sample schedule of procedures to be followed when construction of a new house is undertaken.

Professional home inspections performed for potential buyers or for sellers generally include

- systems: heating, air conditioning, septic or sewer, electric and plumbing;
- water: potability and occasionally other (radon, lead);
- storm windows and screens;
- general condition;
- radon, lead, asbestos;
- insulation; and termites, dry rot.

A seller would be wise to have a professional inspection performed before marketing the property. Any defects that might kill the sale or cause a last-minute problem for closing can be corrected in advance. The sale price and marketability of the property are directly affected by its condition.

A buyer always should have a professional inspection done before committing to a purchase, even for new construction. Serious defects affect the marketability and value of the property.

Example: Mr. and Mrs. Homeowner were retiring and had already purchased a retirement home in the Midwest. Broker Bob was asked to come and list the house for sale. The house was a 35-year-old ranch-style home, concrete block and built on a slab. The heating system was a combination of radiant and forced air heat built into the slab. The ½-acre lot was on a glacial ridge that was very wet. The Homeowners had taken only minimal care of the house, opting to fix things themselves or not at all. They had recently added a deck themselves. One room was crammed full of books, and was impassable. The general condition of the house was poor: it needed a thorough cleaning and

Figure 24.1   Property Condition Disclosure Form

Westchester County Board of Realtors, Inc./WMLS Inc.
OWNER'S ACKNOWLEDGMENT AND REPRESENTATION TO AGENT

Owner acknowledges that Owner has examined the Exclusive Agreement and the Listing Input Form which sets forth the terms of the transaction between Owner and Agent and the details regarding the physical aspects of the property which is the subject of the Agreement. Owner Warrants and represents that to the best of Owner's knowledge and belief, there are no significant defects, malfunctions or reports required to any of the physical aspects of the property set forth in the Listing Input Form except

_____

_____

Are you, the Owner, aware of the following:	Yes	No
1. Features of property shared in common with adjoining land owners such as walls, fences, wells, septic systems, and driveways whose use or responsibility for maintenance may have an effect on the subject property?	( ) ( )	( ) ( )
2. Any encroachments, easements or similar matters that may affect your interest in the subject property?	( )	( )
3. Room additions, structural modifications or other alterations or repairs made without necessary permits or which require the issuance of a Certificate of Occupancy?	( )	( )
4. Room additions, structural modifications or other alterations or repairs which are not in full compliance with all applicable building codes?	( )	( )
5. Landfill, compacted or otherwise or on the property or any portion thereof?	( )	( )
6. Any settling from any cause of slippage, sliding or soil problems?	( )	( )
7. Flooding, drainage or grading problems?	( )	( )
8. Have you had any water accumulation in any portion of the house during the past ten years?	( )	( )
9. Major damage to the property or any of the structures from fire, earthquake, floods or landslides?	( )	( )
10. Any zoning violations, non-conforming uses, violations of setback requirements, etc.?	( )	( )
11. Neighborhood noise problems or other nuisances?	( )	( )
12. Covenants, conditions or other restrictions or other Deed restrictions or obligations affecting the property?	( )	( )
13. Homeowners (or other) Association which has any authority over the subject property?	( )	( )
14. Any common area facilities such as pools, tennis courts, walkways or other areas co-owned in an undivided interest with others?	( )	( )
15. Any notices of abatement or citation against the property?	( )	( )
16. Any lawsuits, bankruptcy or foreclosure proceedings, liens or other claims against you or the property, current or pending?	( )	( )
17. Any toxic wastes or dumping sites located on or in proximity to the property which may have an effect on soil conditions, water supply or any polluting factor with respect to the property?	( )	( )
18. Any asbestos in the property or the structures appertinent thereto?	( )	( )
19. Is your property in a legally designated flood zone?	( )	( )
20. Any radon gas or any unusual pollutants within the structure or structures on this property?	( )	( )
21. Have you had a chemical analysis of the water made with respect to these premises at any time during the past five years?	( )	( )
If applicable, was such analysis abnormal?	( )	( )
22. Has the property been treated for termites or wood destroying insects during the past five years and if so, is there a guarantee of any kind which is transferrable?	( )	( )

If the answer to any of the above questions is "Yes", please explain:

_____

_____

Owner hereby certifies that the information herein is true and correct to the best of Seller's(s') knowledge as of the date signed by the Seller

Dated: _____   Owner: _____   Owner: _____

_____

Source: Model form prepared for Westchester County Board of REALTORS®, Inc., for optional use by members.

Table 24.1 New Home Construction Schedule

Preliminary work: Site engineering, evaluation, preliminary plan, environmental review, etc., county and local agency reviews, signatures and filing of plan. Obtain financing. Site development.

Construction schedule:

Building and other permits

Surveyor stakes out lot and house

Excavator digs basement

Plumber installs sanitary sewer/water service

Building inspector inspects sewer or County Board of Health inspects septic system

Excavator backfills sewer/water trench and digs trench for footings

Mason forms the footings and pours concrete footings; lays up concrete block walls or pours concrete foundation

Framer sets steel beams and columns

Framer frames house

Roofing

Rough HVAC

Rough plumbing and heating

Rough electric, security, cable TV, phone

Backfill basement walls after framing

Building inspector reviews framing, plumbing and heating

Electric inspection, rough wiring

Simultaneous with other work:

    Concrete block wall dampproofing

    Box out driveway and spread gravel

    Mason builds fireplace

    Mason lays up exterior brick or stone

    Set windows, do exterior siding

    Exterior painting/staining

    Gutters, leaders, garage doors

Insulation

Drywall, hanging and finishing

Mason pours concrete floors

Interior trim

Interior painting

Kitchen cabinets and vanities

Ceramic tile walls and floors

Finish flooring—hardwood, vinyl

Finish plumbing, set fixtures

Finish heating

Finish electrical, fixtures, switches

Electrical inspection—final

Mirror/shower doors

Storms and screens

Blacktop

Landscaping

Appliances

Cleanup

Certificate of Occupancy inspection

Surveyor prepares instrument survey "as built"

Building department issues Certificate of Occupancy

Buyer reviews and does a final inspection prior to closing and prepares a punch list if necessary

Close on title

---

redecorating; broken tiles in the shower had allowed water damage to occur and the plumbing leaked throughout the house.

Despite the poor overall condition, the Homeowners claimed that all was working well. Broker Bob asked if there was a permit for the deck. He was told that "everything was okay." The Homeowners refused to have a professional house inspection, but did agree to have someone come in to clean after they moved out.

Broker Bob checked with the building department and found that the Homeowners had not obtained a permit for their deck and that, in fact, the deck violated the setback requirements. The Homeowners appeared before the Zoning Board of Appeals for a variance for the deck, but were denied the variance. The deck had to be removed.

Ultimately, it took two and a half years to sell the house. Each potential buyer had the house inspected and found it wanting until all the major repairs were completed. In the meantime, the Homeowners paid the taxes, heating costs, had the lawn mowed and the snow shoveled. Had the Homeowners been willing to accept their broker's advice and had the property professionally inspected, they could have saved a great deal of time and money.

▼ **Prefabricated Housing**

Housing or portions of houses that are manufactured in a climate controlled environment (a factory) are known as prefabricated housing. *Mobile homes* are prefabricated trailer-type housing units that are semipermanently attached to land, either the fee owned land of the owner or on leased land, such as in a mobile home park. *Modular homes* are produced in a factory and trucked to the prepared site to be installed on a foundation. The home may already be assembled or may be in large sections. *Panelized housing* is created by installing and joining together small segments of a house on a prepared site. The segments can be as small as roof trusses or as large as whole sections of walls.

Key Terms

Army Corps of Engineers	HUD
Board of Fire Underwriters	Local Waterfront Revitalization
certificate of compliance	Program (LWRP)
certificate of occupancy	Metropolitan Transport Authority
Coastal Zone Management	(MTA)
Program	minimum building standards
county boards of health	New York City Department of
county planning boards	Environmental Protection
Department of Transportation	(DEP)
due diligence	professional home inspections

Summary

Standards for construction are established at many levels of government and by a variety of different agencies.

The local building department is the first and most important source of information on the building process.

Primary responsibility for faults or defects with a building lies with the builder or the owner. This would include ensuring proper site preparation and correcting any problems according to legal specifications.

Real estate agents are not engineers or professional inspectors, but they should exercise due diligence when viewing and inspecting a property for a listing. While a seller's property condition disclosure form is not required in New York, one is commonly used by many firms to help avoid potential conflicts. Disclosure is required in New York if the property is in an agricultural district or when the availability of utilities is in question.

1. In New York State, building plans must be signed by a
   a. fire underwriter.
   b. licensed architect or engineer.
   c. site planner.
   d. primary contractor.

2. The Blooms have fallen in love with a wonderful old farmhouse. They are concerned about possible structural problems, so they consult a
   a. framer.
   b. firestop specialist.
   c. soil engineer.
   d. professional inspector.

3. Sarah Salesperson volunteers information about the condition of a house to customer Bob. After Bob purchases the house and moves in, he discovers that Sarah had given him incorrect data. Bob can
   a. bill the former owner for repairs.
   b. sue only Sarah for misrepresentation.
   c. sue only Sarah's broker for misrepresentation.
   d. sue both Sarah and Sarah's broker for misrepresentation.

4. When a residence is built with FHA financing, the government agency that establishes minimum construction standards is the
   a. Department of Heath and Welfare.
   b. Department of Housing and Urban Development (HUD).
   c. Department of State.
   d. Department of Law.

5. Joe Builder is constructing a new single-family residence. The local building inspector must inspect and certify
   a. all electrical systems.
   b. all general construction.
   c. the septic system.
   d. the financing.

6. The New York State Board of Fire Underwriters inspects and certifies
   a. all electrical systems.
   b. all general construction.
   c. the septic system.
   d. the financing.

7. Which of the following would not benefit from a professional house inspection?
   a. The buyer
   b. The seller
   c. The broker
   d. The Department of State

8. New York State law requires
   a. minimum building and electrical standards.
   b. written and signed property condition disclosures.
   c. professional property inspections.
   d. that new houses have underground wiring.

9. The state agency responsible for approving proposed construction on an island in Long Island Sound is the
   a. DOL.   c. DOS.
   b. DOE.   d. DOT.

10. Broker Brown is showing his new listing to a prospective buyer who asks if the basement is dry. Brown answers, "Of course it is, look at how dry it is!" Shortly after this buyer moves into this house the basement floods, ruining some new furniture and appliances. Broker Brown can be sued for
    a. misapprehension.
    b. misconstruing.
    c. misrepresentation.
    d. misunderstanding.

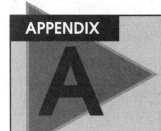

Real Estate Mathematics

The Sterns receive two offers for their property at the same time. The Avilas offer $95,000 in cash. The Browns offer $100,000 subject to obtaining a conventional mortgage loan with a 20 percent down payment if the Sterns will pay three points to the bank. Which offer should the Sterns accept?

This review is designed to familiarize students with basic mathematical formulas frequently used in day-to-day real estate transactions and computations required on state licensing examinations. Those who need additional help may want to order the textbook *Mastering Real Estate Mathematics*, Sixth Edition, by Ventolo, Allaway and Irby. The order form at the back of this book includes this self-instructional text.

Percentages

Many real estate computations are based on the calculation of percentages. A percentage expresses a portion of a whole. For example, 50 percent means 50 parts of the possible 100 parts. Percentages greater than 100 percent contain more than one whole unit. Thus 163 percent is one whole and 63 parts of another whole. A whole is always expressed as 100 percent.

Unless a calculator with a percent key is being used, the *percentage must be converted either to a decimal or to a fraction.* To convert a percentage to a decimal, move the decimal two places to the left and drop the percent sign. Thus

$$60\% = .6 \qquad 7\% = .07 \qquad 175\% = 1.75$$

To change a percentage to a fraction, place the percentage over 100. For example:

$$50\% = \frac{50}{100} \qquad 115\% = \frac{115}{100}$$

These fractions then may be *reduced* to make it easier to work the problem. To reduce a fraction, determine the largest number by which both numerator and denominator can be divided evenly. For example:

$$\frac{25}{100} = \frac{1}{4} \text{ (both numbers divided by 25)}$$

$$\frac{49}{63} = \frac{7}{9} \text{ (both numbers divided by 7)}$$

Percentage problems contain three elements: *percentage, total* and *part*. To determine a specific percentage of a whole, multiply the percentage by the whole:

$$\textbf{percent} \times \textbf{whole} = \textbf{part}$$

$$5\% \times 200 = 10$$

For example: A broker is to receive a 7 percent commission on the sale of a $150,000 house. What will the broker's commission be?

$$.07 \times \$150,000 = \$10,500 \text{ broker's commission}$$

This formula is used in calculating mortgage loan interest, brokers' commissions, loan origination fees, discount points, amount of earnest money deposits and income on capital investments.

A variation, or inversion, of the percentage formula is used to find the total amount when the part and percentage are known:

$$\textbf{whole} = \frac{\textbf{part}}{\textbf{percent}}$$

For example: The Masterson Realty Company received a $9,600 commission for the sale of a house. The broker's commission was 6 percent of the total sales price. What was the total sales price of this house?

$$\frac{\$9,600}{.06} = \$160,000 \text{ total sales price}$$

This formula is used in computing the total mortgage loan principal still due if the monthly payment and interest rate are known. It is also used to calculate the total sales price when the amount and percentage of commission are known and the market value of property when the assessed value and the ratio (percentage) of assessed value to market value are known.

The formula may be used by a real estate salesperson thus: Bertha Buyer has $29,500 available for a down payment, and she must make a 25 percent down payment. How expensive a home can she purchase? The question is $29,500 is 25 percent of what figure?

$$\frac{\$29,500}{.25} = \$118,000$$

Such a problem also may be solved by the use of ratios. Thus, $29,500 is to what number as 25 percent is to 100 percent?

$$\frac{\$29,500}{?} = \frac{25}{100}$$

One type of percentage problem may take several forms. For example, Joe Brown sold property for $90,000. This represents a 20 percent loss from his original cost. What was his cost?

In this problem the student must resist the impulse to multiply everything in sight. Taking 20 percent of $90,000 yields nothing significant. The $90,000 figure represents 80 percent of the original cost, and the question resolves itself into $90,000 is 80 percent of what figure?

$$\frac{\$90,000}{.80} = \$112,500$$

Again: Hester Peters clears $88,200 from the sale of her property after paying a 10 percent commission. How much did the property sell for? Taking 10 percent of $88,200 is an incorrect approach to the problem because the commission was based not on the seller's net but on the full, unknown sales figure; $88,200 represents 90 percent of the sales price.

$$\frac{\$88,200}{.90} = \$98,000$$

To determine the percentage when the amounts of the part and the whole are known:

$$\text{percent} = \frac{\text{part}}{\text{whole}}$$

This formula may be used to find the tax rate when taxes and assessed value are known or the commission rate when sales price and commission amount are known.

The IRV formula, which should be memorized, is basic to investment problems.

$$\text{Income} = \text{Rate} \times \text{Value}$$

Rates

Property taxes, transfer taxes and insurance premiums are usually expressed as rates. A rate is the cost expressed as the amount of cost per unit. For example, tax might be computed at the rate of $5 per $100 assessed value in a certain county. The formula for computing rates is

$$\frac{\text{value}}{\text{unit}} \times \text{rate per unit} = \text{total}$$

For example: A house has been assessed at $90,000 and is taxed at an annual rate of $25 per $1,000 assessed valuation. What is the yearly tax?

$$\frac{\$90,000}{1,000} \times \$25 = \text{total annual tax}$$

$$\$90,000 \div \$1,000 = 90 \text{ (increments of \$100)}$$

$$90 \times \$25 = \$2,250 \text{ total annual tax}$$

Areas and Volumes

To compute the area of a square or rectangular parcel, use the formula

$$\text{area} = \text{width} \times \text{depth}$$

The area of a rectangular lot that measures 100 feet wide by 200 feet deep would be

$$100' \times 200' = 20{,}000 \text{ square feet}$$

The first figure given always represents front feet; a lot described as "80' x 150'" is 80 feet across and 150 feet deep. Area is always expressed in square units.

To compute the amount of surface in a triangular area, use the formula

area = ½ (base × height)

The base of a triangle is the bottom, on which the triangle rests. The height is an imaginary straight line extending from the point of the uppermost angle straight down to the base:

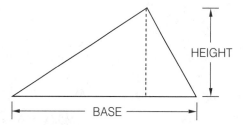

Example: A triangle's base is 50 feet, and its height is 30 feet. What is its area?

$$\tfrac{1}{2}\,(50' \times 30') = \text{area in square feet}$$

$$\tfrac{1}{2}\,(1{,}500) = 750 \text{ square feet}$$

To compute the area of an irregular room or parcel of land, divide the shape into regular rectangles, squares or triangles. Next, compute the area of each regular figure and add the areas together to obtain the total area.

Example: Compute the area of the hallway shown below:

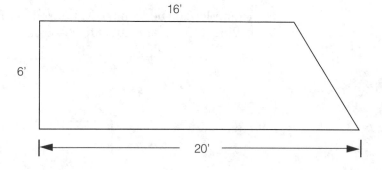

Make a rectangle and a triangle by drawing a single line through the figure:

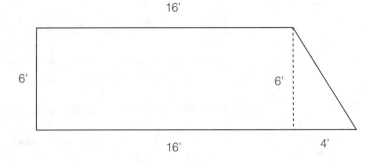

Compute the area of the rectangle:

$$\text{area} = \text{length} \times \text{width}$$

$$16' \times 6' = 96 \text{ square feet}$$

Compute the area of the triangle:

$$\text{area} = \tfrac{1}{2}\,(\text{base} \times \text{height})$$

$$\tfrac{1}{2}\,(4' \times 6') = \tfrac{1}{2}\,(24) = 12 \text{ square feet}$$

Total the two areas:

$$96' + 12' = 108 \text{ square feet in total area}$$

The cubic capacity of an enclosed space is expressed as volume, which is used to describe the amount of space in any three-dimensional area, such as the interior airspace of a room, measured to determine what capacity heating unit is required. The formula for computing cubic or rectangular volume is

$$\textbf{volume} = \textbf{length} \times \textbf{width} \times \textbf{height}$$

Volume is always expressed in cubic units.

For example: The bedroom of a house is 12 feet long, 8 feet wide, 8 feet high to the ceiling. How many cubic feet does the room enclose?

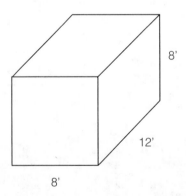

$$8' \times 12' \times 8' = 768 \text{ cubic feet}$$

To compute the volume of a triangular space, such as the airspace in an A-frame house, use the formula

volume = ½ (length × height × width)

For example: What is the volume of airspace in the house shown below?

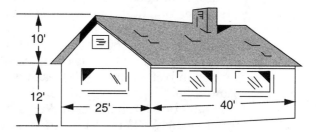

First, divide the house into two shapes, rectangular and triangular, as shown:

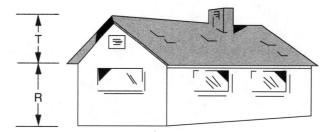

Find the volume of T:

volume = ½ (length × height × width)

½ (25′ × 10′ × 40′) = ½ (10,000) = 5,000 cubic feet

Find the volume of R:

25′ × 40′ × 12′ = 12,000 cubic feet

Total volumes T and R:

5,000′ + 12,000′ = 17,000 cubic feet of airspace in the house

Cubic measurements of volume are used to compute the construction costs per cubic foot of a building, the amount of airspace being sold in a condominium unit or the heating and cooling requirements for a building. When either area or volume is computed, all dimensions used must be given in the same unit of measure. For example, one may not multiply two feet by six inches to get the area; two feet must be multiplied by one-half foot. Thus it is important to remember that

1 yard = 3 feet,

1 square yard = 3′ × 3′ = 9 square feet and

1 cubic yard = 3′ × 3′ × 3′ = 27 cubic feet.

Land Units and Measurements

Some commonly used land units and measurements follow:

- A *rod* is 16½ feet.
- A *chain* is 66 feet, or 100 links.
- A *mile* is 5,280 feet.
- An *acre* contains 43,560 square feet. *Memorize this one.*
- A *section* of land is one square mile and contains 640 acres; a *quarter section* contains 160 acres; a *quarter of a quarter section* contains 40 acres.
- A *circle* contains 360 degrees; a *half segment* of a circle contains 180 degrees; a *quarter segment* of a circle contains 90 degrees. One *degree* (1°) can be subdivided into 60 minutes (60′), each of which contains 60 seconds (60″). One-and-a-half degrees would be written 1°30′.
- A *mill* is one-tenth of a cent, $.001. When a property tax is quoted as 23 mills, that means $.023 per $1 of assessed value, the same rate as $23 per $1,000.

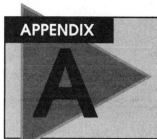
1. A rectangular lot measures 60 feet wide and has an area of 1,200 square yards. What is the depth of the lot?
   - a. 20 feet
   - b. 180 feet
   - c. 20 yards
   - d. 90 yards

2. A buyer is applying for an FHA mortgage on a house priced at $68,000. The minimum down payment required is 3 percent of the first $25,000 of the purchase price and 5 percent of the remaining purchase price. What is the minimum down payment?
   - a. $2,040
   - b. $3,400
   - c. $1,790
   - d. $2,900

3. Ebenezer Scrooge intends to put up a fence between his lot and his neighbor's. The fencing comes in six-foot sections. For a fence 120 feet long, how many fence posts will be required?
   - a. 19
   - b. 20
   - c. 21
   - d. 22

4. A house is valued at $198,000. It is to be insured for 80 percent of its cost. Insurance will cost $6 per $1,000. What is the annual insurance premium?
   - a. $95.40
   - b. $119.80
   - c. $950.40
   - d. $1,198.00

5. John Walton received a net amount of $74,000 from the sale of his house after paying $1,200 in legal and other fees and 6 percent sales commission. What was the selling price of the house?
   - a. $80,000
   - b. $78,440
   - c. $79,640
   - d. $79,000

6. A lending institution will allow its borrowers to spend 28 percent of their income for housing expense. What will be the maximum monthly payment allowed for a family with annual income of $57,000 and no other debts?
   - a. $399
   - b. $1,330
   - c. $1,596
   - d. None of the above

7. Sally Sellright works on a 50/50 commission split with her broker. If she lists a house at $156,000 for 6 percent commission and sells it for $154,000, how much will Sally receive?
   - a. $4,620
   - b. $4,680
   - c. $9,220
   - d. $9,360

8. Dudley Donnelly's monthly mortgage payment for principal and interest is $628.12. His property taxes are $1,800 a year, and his annual insurance premium is $365. What is his total monthly payment for PITI (principal, interest, taxes and insurance)?
   - a. $808.54
   - b. $1,921.24
   - c. $778.12
   - d. None of the above

9. A lot measuring 120' x 200' is selling for $300 a front foot. What is its price?
   - a. $720,000
   - b. $60,000
   - c. $36,000
   - d. $800,000

10. A five-acre lot has front footage of 300 feet. How deep is it?
    - a. 145.2 feet
    - b. 726 feet
    - c. 88 feet
    - d. 160 feet

11. Broker Sally Smith of Happy Valley Realty recently sold Jack and Jill Hawkins's home for $79,500. Smith charged the Hawkinses 6½ percent commission and will pay 30 percent of that amount to the listing salesperson and 25 percent to the selling salesperson. What amount of commission will the listing salesperson receive from the Hawkins sale?

    a. $5,167.50   c. $3,617.25
    b. $1,550.25   d. $1,291.87

12. Susan Silber signed an agreement to purchase a condominium apartment from Perry and Marie Morris. The contract stipulated that the Morrises replace the damaged bedroom carpet. The carpet Silber has chosen costs $16.95 per square yard plus $2.50 per square yard for installation. If the bedroom dimensions are as illustrated, how much will the Morrises have to pay for the job?

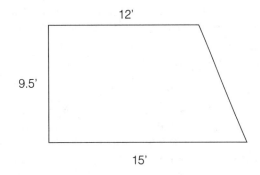

    a. $241.54   c. $277.16
    b. $189.20   d. $2,494.46

13. Hal, Olive, Ron and Marvin pooled their savings and purchased a vacation home for $125,000. If Hal invested $30,000 and Olive and Ron each contributed $35,000, what percentage of ownership was left for Marvin?

    a. 20 percent   c. 28 percent
    b. 24 percent   d. 30 percent

14. Harold Barlow is curious to know how much money his son and daughter-in-law still owe on their mortgage loan. Barlow knows that the interest portion of their last monthly payment was $391.42. If the Barlows are paying interest at the rate of 11½ percent, what was the outstanding balance of their loan before that last payment was made?

    a. $43,713.00   c. $36,427.50
    b. $40,843.83   d. $34,284.70

15. Nick and Olga Stravinski bought their home on Sabre Lane a year ago for $98,500. Property in their neighborhood is said to be increasing in value at a rate of 5 percent annually. If this is true, what is the current market value of the Stravinskis' real estate?

    a. $103,425
    b. $93,575
    c. $104,410
    d. None of the above is within $50.

16. The DeHavilands' home on Dove Street is valued at $95,000. Property in their area is assessed at 60 percent of its value, and the local tax rate is $28.50 per thousand. What is the amount of the DeHavilands' monthly taxes?

    a. $1,625.50   c. $270.75
    b. $570.00   d. $135.38

17. The Fitzpatricks are planning to construct a patio in their backyard. An illustration of the surface area to be paved appears here. If the cement is to be poured as a six-inch slab, how many cubic feet of cement will be poured into this patio?

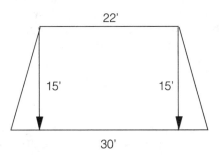

    a. 660 cubic feet   c. 330 cubic feet
    b. 450 cubic feet   d. 195 cubic feet

18. Happy Morgan receives a monthly salary of $500 plus 3 percent commission on all of his listings that sell and 2.5 percent on all his sales. None of the listings that Morgan took sold last month, but he received $3,675 in salary and commission. What was the value of the property Morgan sold?

    a. $147,000   c. $122,500
    b. $127,000   d. $105,833

19. The Salvatinis' residence has proved difficult to sell. Salesperson Martha Kelley suggests it might sell faster if they enclose a portion of the backyard with a privacy fence. If the area to be enclosed is as illustrated, how much would the fence cost at $6.95 per linear foot?

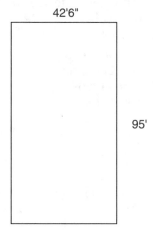

42'6"

95'

HOUSE

   a. $1,911.25   c. $1,615.88
   b. $1,654.10   d. $955.63

20. Andrew McTavish leases the 12 apartments in the Overton Arms for a total monthly rental of $4,500. If this figure represents an 8 percent annual return on McTavish's investment, what was the original cost of the property?

   a. $675,000   c. $54,000
   c. $450,000   d. $56,250

21. A 100-acre farm is divided into house lots. The streets require one-eighth of the whole farm, and there are 140 lots. How many square feet are there in each lot?

   a. 35,004   c. 27,225
   b. 31,114   d. 43,560

22. In a sale of residential property, real estate taxes for the current year amounted to $975 and have already been paid by the seller. The sale is to be closed on October 26; what is the amount of real estate proration to be credited the seller?

   a. $173.33   c. $798.96
   b. $162.50   d. $83.96

23. The buyer is assuming the seller's mortgage. The unpaid balance after the most recent payment (the first of the month) was $61,550. Interest is paid in arrears each month at 13 percent per annum. The sale is to be closed on September 22; what is the amount of mortgage interest proration to be credited to the buyer at the closing?

   a. $666.97   c. $177.82
   b. $488.97   d. $689.01

24. Riley's commission on a sale was $14,100, which was 6 percent of the sales price. What was the sales price?

   a. $235,000.00   c. $846,000.00
   b. $154,255.31   d. $234,500.00

25. A 30-year fixed-rate amortized mortgage for $100,000 at 11 percent interest requires monthly payments of $952.34 for principal and interest. What is the total amount of interest paid on this loan during the life of the mortgage?

   a. $114,280.00   c. $314,272.60
   b. $242,842.40   d. $330,000.00

26. The Duffys are buying a house for $120,000 and seek a fixed-rate loan of $90,000 for 25 years. One lender offers them a 10 percent loan with no points, with monthly payments of $817.85. A second lender requires two points for a 9.5 percent loan, with monthly payments of $786.35. If the Duffys decide to pay the points and take the lower-interest loan, how long will it take before the savings on their lower payments have made up for that extra cost at closing?

    a. Two years, eight months
    b. Three years, two months
    c. Four years, nine months
    d. Seven years, four months

27. The Sterns receive two offers for their property at the same time. The Avilas offer $95,000 in cash. The Browns offer $100,000 subject to obtaining a conventional mortgage loan with 20 percent down payment and ask the Sterns to pay three points to their lending institution. The Sterns decide to accept the all-cash offer. If they had accepted the Browns' offer instead, they would have received

    a. $2,000 more at closing.
    b. $2,400 less at closing.
    c. $2,600 more at closing.
    d. $3,000 less at closing.

NAR Code of Ethics and Standards of Practice

Code of Ethics and Standards of Practice of the NATIONAL ASSOCIATION OF REALTORS®
Effective January 1, 1997

Where the word REALTORS® is used in this Code and Preamble, it shall be deemed to include REALTOR-ASSOCIATE®s.

While the Code of Ethics establishes obligations that may be higher than those mandated by law, in any instance where the Code of Ethics and the law conflict, the obligations of the law must take precedence.

Preamble...

Under all is the land. Upon its wise utilization and widely allocated ownership depend the survival and growth of free institutions and of our civilization. REALTORS® should recognize that the interests of the nation and its citizens require the highest and best use of the land and the widest distribution of land ownership. They require the creation of adequate housing, the building of functioning cities, the development of productive industries and farms, and the preservation of a healthful environment.

Such interests impose obligations beyond those of ordinary commerce. They impose grave social responsibility and a patriotic duty to which REALTORS® should dedicate themselves, and for which they should be diligent in preparing themselves. REALTORS®, therefore, are zealous to maintain and improve the standards of their calling and share with their fellow REALTORS® a common responsibility for its integrity and honor.

In recognition and appreciation of their obligations to clients, customers, the public, and each other, REALTORS® continuously strive to become and remain informed on issues affecting real estate and, as knowledgeable professionals, they willingly share the fruit of their experience and study with others. They identify and take steps, through enforcement of this Code of Ethics and by assisting appropriate regulatory bodies, to eliminate practices which may damage the public or which might discredit or bring dishonor to the real estate profession.

Realizing that cooperation with other real estate professionals promotes the best interests of those who utilize their services, REALTORS® urge exclusive representation of clients; do not attempt to gain any unfair advantage over their competitors; and they refrain from making unsolicited comments about other practitioners. In instances where their opinion is sought, or where REALTORS® believe that comment is necessary, their opinion is offered in an objective, professional manner, uninfluenced by any personal motivation or potential advantage or gain.

The term REALTOR® has come to connote competency, fairness, and high integrity resulting from adherence to a lofty ideal of moral conduct in business relations. No inducement of profit and no instruction from clients ever can justify departure from this ideal.

In the interpretation of this obligation, REALTORS® can take no safer guide than that which has been handed down through the centuries, embodied in the Golden Rule, "Whatsoever ye would that others should do to you, do ye even so to them."

Accepting this standard as their own, REALTORS® pledge to observe its spirit in all of their activities and to conduct their business in accordance with the tenets set forth below.

Duties to Clients and Customers

Article 1

When representing a buyer, seller, landlord, tenant, or other client as an agent, REALTORS® pledge themselves to protect and promote the interests of their client. This obligation of absolute fidelity to the client's interests is primary, but it does not relieve REALTORS® of their obligation to treat all parties honestly. When serving a buyer, seller, landlord, tenant or other party in a non-agency capacity, REALTORS® remain obligated to treat all parties honestly. *(Amended 1/93)*

- **Standard of Practice 1-1**
  REALTORS®, when acting as principals in a real estate transaction, remain obligated by the duties imposed by the Code of Ethics. *(Amended 1/93)*

- **Standard of Practice 1-2**
  The duties the Code of Ethics imposes on agents/representatives are applicable to REALTORS® acting as agents, transaction brokers, facilitators, or in any other recognized capacity except for any duty specifically exempted by law or regulation. *(Adopted 1/95)*

- **Standard of Practice 1-3**
  REALTORS®, in attempting to secure a listing, shall not deliberately mislead the owner as to market value.

- **Standard of Practice 1-4**
  REALTORS®, when seeking to become a buyer/tenant representative, shall not mislead buyers or tenants as to savings or other benefits that might be realized through use of the REALTOR®'s services. *(Amended 1/93)*

- **Standard of Practice 1-5**
  REALTORS® may represent the seller/landlord and buyer/tenant in the same transaction only after full disclosure to and with informed consent of both parties. *(Adopted 1/93)*

- **Standard of Practice 1-6**
  REALTORS® shall submit offers and counter-offers objectively and as quickly as possible. *(Adopted 1/93, Amended 1/95)*

- **Standard of Practice 1-7**
  When acting as listing brokers, REALTORS® shall continue to submit to the seller/landlord all offers and counter-offers until closing or execution of a lease unless the seller/landlord has waived this obligation in writing. REALTORS® shall not be obligated to continue to market the property after an offer has been accepted by the seller/landlord. REALTORS® shall recommend that sellers/landlords obtain the advice of legal counsel prior to acceptance of a subsequent offer except where the acceptance is contingent on the termination of the pre-existing purchase contract or lease. *(Amended 1/93)*

- **Standard of Practice 1-8**
  REALTORS® acting as agents of buyers/tenants shall submit to buyers/tenants all offers and counter-offers until acceptance but have no obligation to continue to show properties to their clients after an offer has been accepted unless otherwise agreed in writing. REALTORS® acting as agents of buyers/tenants shall recommend that buyers/tenants obtain the advice of legal counsel if there is a question as to whether a pre-existing contract has been terminated. *(Adopted 1/93)*

- **Standard of Practice 1-9**
  The obligation of REALTORS® to preserve confidential information provided by their clients continues after the termination of the agency relationship. REALTORS® shall not knowingly, during or following the termination of a professional relationship with their client:
  1) reveal confidential information of the client; or
  2) use confidential information of the client to the disadvantage of the client; or
  3) use confidential information of the client for the REALTOR®'s advantage or the advantage of a third party unless:
     a) the client consents after full disclosure; or
     b) the REALTOR® is required by court order; or
     c) it is the intention of the client to commit a crime and the information is necesary to prevent the crime; or
     d) it is necessary to defend the REALTOR® or the REALTOR®'s employees or associates against an accusation of wrongful conduct. *(Adopted 1/93, Amended 1/97)*

- **Standard of Practice 1-10**
  REALTORS® shall, consistent with the terms and conditions of their property management agreement, competently manage the property of clients with due regard for the rights, responsibilities, benefits, safety and health of tenants and others lawfully on the premises. *(Adopted 1/95)*

- **Standard of Practice 1-11**
  REALTORS® who are employed to maintain or manage a client's property shall exercise due diligence and make reasonable efforts to protect it against reasonably foreseeable contingencies and losses. *(Adopted 1/95)*

Article 2

REALTORS® shall avoid exaggeration, misrepresentation, or concealment of pertinent facts relating to the property or the transaction. REALTORS® shall not, however, be obligated to discover latent defects in the property, to advise on matters outside the scope of their real estate license, or to disclose facts which are confidential under the scope of agency duties owed to their clients. *(Amended 1/93)*

- **Standard of Practice 2-1**
  REALTORS® shall only be obligated to discover and disclose adverse factors reasonably apparent to someone with expertise in those areas required by their real estate licensing authority. Article 2 does not impose upon the REALTOR® the obligation of expertise in other professional or technical disciplines. *(Amended 1/96)*

- **Standard of Practice 2-2**
  When entering into listing contracts, REALTORS® must advise sellers/landlords of:
  1) the REALTOR®'s general company policies regarding cooperation with subagents, buyer/tenant agents, or both;
  2) the fact that buyer/tenant agents, even if compensated by the listing broker, or by the seller/landlord will represent the interests of buyers/tenants; and
  3) any potential for the listing broker to act as a disclosed dual agent, e.g. buyer/tenant agent. *(Adopted 1/93)*

- **Standard of Practice 2-3**
  When entering into contracts to represent buyers/tenants, REALTORS® must advise potential clients of:
  1) the REALTOR®'s general company policies regarding cooperation with other firms; and
  2) any potential for the buyer/tenant representative to act as a disclosed dual agent, e.g. listing broker, subagent, landlord's agent, etc. *(Adopted 1/93)*

- **Standard of Practice 2-4**
  REALTORS® shall not be parties to the naming of a false consideration in any document, unless it be the naming of an obviously nominal consideration.

- **Standard of Practice 2-5**
Factors defined as "non-material" by law or regulation or which are expressly referenced in law or regulation as not being subject to disclosure are considered not "pertinent" for purposes of Article 2. *(Adopted 1/93)*

Article 3

REALTORS® shall cooperate with other brokers except when cooperation is not in the client's best interest. The obligation to cooperate does not include the obligation to share commissions, fees, or to otherwise compensate another broker. *(Amended 1/95)*

- **Standard of Practice 3-1**
REALTORS®, acting as exclusive agents of sellers/landlords, establish the terms and conditions of offers to cooperate. Unless expressly indicated in offers to cooperate, cooperating brokers may not assume that the offer of cooperation includes an offer of compensation. Terms of compensation, if any, shall be ascertained by cooperating brokers before beginning efforts to accept the offer of cooperation. *(Amended 1/94)*

- **Standard of Practice 3-2**
REALTORS® shall, with respect to offers of compensation to another REALTOR®, timely communicate any change of compensation for cooperative services to the other REALTOR® prior to the time such REALTOR® produces an offer to purchase/lease the property. *(Amended 1/94)*

- **Standard of Practice 3-3**
Standard of Practice 3-2 does not preclude the listing broker and cooperating broker from entering into an agreement to change cooperative compensation. *(Adopted 1/94)*

- **Standard of Practice 3-4**
REALTORS®, acting as listing brokers, have an affirmative obligation to disclose the existence of dual or variable rate commission arrangements (i.e., listings where one amount of commission is payable if the listing broker's firm is the procuring cause of sale/lease and a different amount of commission is payable if the sale/lease results through the efforts of the seller/landlord or a cooperating broker). The listing broker shall, as soon as practical, disclose the existence of such arrangements to potential cooperating brokers and shall, in response to inquiries from cooperating brokers, disclose the differential that would result in a cooperative transaction or in a sale/lease that results through the efforts of the seller/landlord. If the cooperating broker is a buyer/tenant representative, the buyer/tenant representative must disclose such information to their client. *(Amended 1/94)*

- **Standard of Practice 3-5**
It is the obligation of subagents to promptly disclose all pertinent facts to the principal's agent prior to as well as after a purchase or lease agreement is executed. *(Amended 1/93)*

- **Standard of Practice 3-6**
REALTORS® shall disclose the existence of an accepted offer to any broker seeking cooperation. *(Adopted 5/86)*

- **Standard of Practice 3-7**
When seeking information from another REALTOR® concerning property under a management or listing agreement, REALTORS® shall disclose their REALTOR® status and whether their interest is personal or on behalf of a client and, if on behalf of a client, their representational status. *(Amended 1/95)*

- **Standard of Practice 3-8**
REALTORS® shall not misrepresent the availability of access to show or inspect a listed property. *(Amended 11/87)*

Article 4

REALTORS® shall not acquire an interest in or buy or present offers from themselves, any member of their immediate families, their firms or any member thereof, or any entities in which they have any ownership interest, any real property without making their true position known to the owner or the owner's agent. In selling property they own, or in which they have any interest, REALTORS® shall reveal their ownership or interest in writing to the purchaser or the purchaser's representative. *(Amended 1/91)*

- **Standard of Practice 4-1**
For the protection of all parties, the disclosures required by Article 4 shall be in writing and provided by REALTORS® prior to the signing of any contract. *(Adopted 2/86)*

Article 5

REALTORS® shall not undertake to provide professional services concerning a property or its value where they have a present or contemplated interest unless such interest is specifically disclosed to all affected parties.

Article 6

When acting as agents, REALTORS® shall not accept any commission, rebate, or profit on expenditures made for their principal, without the principal's knowledge and consent. *(Amended 1/92)*

- **Standard of Practice 6-1**
REALTORS® shall not recommend or suggest to a client or a customer the use of services of another organization or business entity in which they have a direct interest without

disclosing such interest at the time of the recommendation or suggestion. *(Amended 5/88)*

- **Standard of Practice 6-2**

  When acting as agents or subagents, REALTORS® shall disclose to a client or customer if there is any financial benefit or fee the REALTOR® or the REALTOR®'s firm may receive as a direct result of having recommended real estate products or services (e.g., homeowner's insurance, warranty programs, mortgage financing, title insurance, etc.) other than real estate referral fees. *(Adopted 5/88)*

Article 7

In a transaction, REALTORS® shall not accept compensation from more than one party, even if permitted by law, without disclosure to all parties and the informed consent of the REALTOR®'s client or clients. *(Amended 1/93)*

Article 8

REALTORS® shall keep in a special account in an appropriate financial institution, separated from their own funds, monies coming into their possession in trust for other persons, such as escrows, trust funds, clients' monies, and other like items.

Article 9

REALTORS®, for the protection of all parties, shall assure whenever possible that agreements shall be in writing, and shall be in clear and understandable language expressing the specific terms, conditions, obligations and commitments of the parties. A copy of each agreement shall be furnished to each party upon their signing or initialing. *(Amended 1/95)*

- **Standard of Practice 9-1**

  For the protection of all parties, REALTORS® shall use reasonable care to ensure that documents pertaining to the purchase, sale, or lease of real estate are kept current through the use of written extensions or amendments. *(Amended 1/93)*

Duties to the Public

Article 10

REALTORS® shall not deny equal professional services to any person for reasons of race, color, religion, sex, handicap, familial status, or national origin. REALTORS® shall not be parties to any plan or agreement to discriminate against a person or persons on the basis of race, color, religion, sex, handicap, familial status, or national origin. *(Amended 1/90)*

- **Standard of Practice 10-1**

  REALTORS® shall not volunteer information regarding the racial, religious or ethnic composition of any neighborhood and shall not engage in any activity which may result in panic selling. REALTORS® shall not print, display or circulate any statement or advertisement with respect to the selling or renting of a property that indicates any preference, limitations or discrimination based on race, color, religion, sex, handicap, familial status or national origin. *(Adopted 1/94)*

Article 11

The services which REALTORS® provide to their clients and customers shall conform to the standards of practice and competence which are reasonably expected in the specific real estate disciplines in which they engage; specifically, residential real estate brokerage, real property management, commercial and industrial real estate brokerage, real estate appraisal, real estate counseling, real estate syndication, real estate auction, and international real estate.

REALTORS® shall not undertake to provide specialized professional services concerning a type of property or service that is outside their field of competence unless they engage the assistance of one who is competent on such types of property or service, or unless the facts are fully disclosed to the client. Any persons engaged to provide such assistance shall be so identified to the client and their contribution to the assignment should be set forth. *(Amended 1/95)*

- **Standard of Practice 11-1**

  The obligations of the Code of Ethics shall be supplemented by and construed in a manner consistent with the Uniform Standards of Professional Appraisal Practice (USPAP) promulgated by the Appraisal Standards Board of the Appraisal Foundation.

  The obligations of the Code of Ethics shall not be supplemented by the USPAP where an opinion or recommendation of price or pricing is provided in pursuit of a listing, to assist a potential purchaser in formulating a purchase offer, or to provide a broker's price opinion, whether for a fee or not. *(Amended 1/96)*

- **Standard of Practice 11-2**

  The obligations of the Code of Ethics in respect of real estate disciplines other than appraisal shall be interpreted and applied in accordance with the standards of competence and practice which clients and the public reasonably require to protect their rights and interests considering the complexity of the transaction, the availability of expert assistance, and, where the REALTOR® is an agent or subagent, the obligations of a fiduciary. *(Adopted 1/95)*

- **Standard of Practice 11-3**

  When REALTORS® provide consultive services to clients which involve advice or counsel for a fee (not a commission), such advice shall be rendered in an objective manner and the fee shall not be contingent on the substance of the advice or counsel given. If brokerage or transaction services are to be provided in addition to consultive services, a separate compensation may be paid with prior agreement between the client and REALTOR®. *(Adopted 1/96)*

Article 12

REALTORS® shall be careful at all times to present a true picture in their advertising and representations to the public. REALTORS® shall also ensure that their professional status (e.g., broker, appraiser, property manager, etc.) or status as REALTORS® is clearly identifiable in any such advertising. *(Amended 1/93)*

- **Standard of Practice 12-1**
  REALTORS® may use the term "free" and similar terms in their advertising and in other representations provided that all terms governing availability of the offered product or service are clearly disclosed at the same time. *(Amended 1/97)*

- **Standard of Practice 12-2**
  REALTORS® may represent their services as "free" or without cost even if they expect to receive compensation from a source other than their client provided that the potential for the REALTOR® to obtain a benefit from a third party is clearly disclosed at the same time. *(Amended 1/97)*

- **Standard of Practice 12-3**
  The offering of premiums, prizes, merchandise discounts or other inducements to list, sell, purchase, or lease is not, in itself, unethical even if receipt of the benefit is contingent on listing, selling, purchasing, or leasing through the REALTOR® making the offer. However, REALTORS® must exercise care and candor in any such advertising or other public or private representations so that any party interested in receiving or otherwise benefiting from the REALTOR®'s offer will have clear, thorough, advance understanding of all the terms and conditions of the offer. The offering of any inducements to do business is subject to the limitations and restrictions of state law and the ethical obligations established by any applicable Standard of Practice. *(Amended 1/95)*

- **Standard of Practice 12-4**
  REALTORS® shall not offer for sale/lease or advertise property without authority. When acting as listing brokers or as subagents, REALTORS® shall not quote a price different from that agreed upon with the seller/landlord. *(Amended 1/93)*

- **Standard of Practice 12-5**
  REALTORS® shall not advertise nor permit any person employed by or affiliated with them to advertise listed property without disclosing the name of the firm. *(Adopted 11/86)*

- **Standard of Practice 12-6**
  REALTORS®, when advertising unlisted real property for sale/lease in which they have an ownership interest, shall disclose their status as both owners/landlords and as REALTORS® or real estate licensees. *(Amended 1/93)*

- **Standard of Practice 12-7**
  Only REALTORS® who participated in the transaction as the listing broker or cooperating broker (selling broker) may claim to have "sold" the property. Prior to closing, a cooperating broker may post a "sold" sign only with the consent of the listing broker. *(Amended 1/96)*

Article 13

REALTORS® shall not engage in activities that constitute the unauthorized practice of law and shall recommend that legal counsel be obtained when the interest of any party to the transaction requires it.

Article 14

If charged with unethical practice or asked to present evidence or to cooperate in any other way, in any disciplinary proceeding or investigation, REALTORS® shall place all pertinent facts before the proper tribunals of the Member Board or affiliated institute, society, or council in which membership is held and shall take no action to disrupt or obstruct such processes. *(Amended 1/90)*

- **Standard of Practice 14-1**
  REALTORS® shall not be subject to disciplinary proceedings in more than one Board of REALTORS® or affiliated institute, society or council in which they hold membership with respect to alleged violations of the Code of Ethics relating to the same transaction or event. *(Amended 1/95)*

- **Standard of Practice 14-2**
  REALTORS® shall not make any unauthorized disclosure or dissemination of the allegations, findings, or decision developed in connection with an ethics hearing or appeal or in connection with an arbitration hearing or procedural review. *(Amended 1/92)*

- **Standard of Practice 14-3**
  REALTORS® shall not obstruct the Board's investigative or disciplinary proceedings by instituting or threatening to institute actions for libel, slander or defamation against any party to a professional standards proceeding or their witnesses. *(Adopted 11/87)*

- **Standard of Practice 14-4**
  REALTORS® shall not intentionally impede the Board's investigative or disciplinary proceedings by filing multiple ethics complaints based on the same event or transaction. *(Adopted 11/88)*

Duties to REALTORS®

Article 15

REALTORS® shall not knowingly or recklessly make false or misleading statements about competitors, their businesses, or their business practices. *(Amended 1/92)*

Article 16

REALTORS® shall not engage in any practice or take any action inconsistent with the agency of other REALTORS®.

- **Standard of Practice 16-1**

  Article 16 is not intended to prohibit aggressive or innovative business practices which are otherwise ethical and does not prohibit disagreements with other REALTORS® involving commission, fees, compensation or other forms of payment or expenses. *(Adopted 1/93, Amended 1/95)*

- **Standard of Practice 16-2**

  Article 16 does not preclude REALTORS® from making general announcements to prospective clients describing their services and the terms of their availability even though some recipients may have entered into agency agreements with another REALTOR®. A general telephone canvass, general mailing or distribution addressed to all prospective clients in a given geographical area or in a given profession, business, club, or organization, or other classification or group is deemed "general" for purposes of this standard.

  Article 16 is intended to recognize as unethical two basic types of solicitations:

  First, telephone or personal solicitations of property owners who have been identified by a real estate sign, multiple listing compilation, or other information service as having exclusively listed their property with another REALTOR®; and

  Second, mail or other forms of written solicitations of prospective clients whose properties are exclusively listed with another REALTOR® when such solicitations are not part of a general mailing but are directed specifically to property owners identified through compilations of current listings, "for sale" or "for rent" signs, or other sources of information required by Article 3 and Multiple Listing Service rules to be made available to other REALTORS® under offers of subagency or cooperation. *(Amended 1/93)*

- **Standard of Practice 16-3**

  Article 16 does not preclude REALTORS® from contacting the client of another broker for the purpose of offering to provide, or entering into a contract to provide, a different type of real estate service unrelated to the type of service currently being provided (e.g., property management as opposed to brokerage). However, information received through a Multiple Listing Service or any other offer of cooperation may not be used to target clients of other REALTORS® to whom such offers to provide services may be made. *(Amended 1/93)*

- **Standard of Practice 16-4**

  REALTORS® shall not solicit a listing which is currently listed exclusively with another broker. However, if the listing broker, when asked by the REALTOR®, refuses to disclose the expiration date and nature of such listing; i.e., an exclusive right to sell, an exclusive agency, open listing, or other form of contractual agreement between the listing broker and the client, the REALTOR® may contact the owner to secure such information and may discuss the terms upon which the REALTOR® might take a future listing or, alternatively, may take a listing to become effective upon expiration of any existing exclusive listing. *(Amended 1/94)*

- **Standard of Practice 16-5**

  REALTORS® shall not solicit buyer/tenant agency agreements from buyers/tenants who are subject to exclusive buyer/tenant agency agreements. However, if a buyer/tenant agent, when asked by a REALTOR®, refuses to disclose the expiration date of the exclusive buyer/tenant agency agreement, the REALTOR® may contact the buyer/tenant to secure such information and may discuss the terms upon which the REALTOR® might enter into a future buyer/tenant agency agreement or, alternatively, may enter into a buyer/tenant agency agreement to become effective upon the expiration of any existing exclusive buyer/tenant agency agreement. *(Adopted 1/94)*

- **Standard of Practice 16-6**

  When REALTORS® are contacted by the client of another REALTOR® regarding the creation of an agency relationship to provide the same type of service, and REALTORS® have not directly or indirectly initiated such discussions, they may discuss the terms upon which they might enter into a future agency agreement or, alternatively, may enter into an agency agreement which becomes effective upon expiration of any existing exclusive agreement. *(Amended 1/93)*

- **Standard of Practice 16-7**

  The fact that a client has retained a REALTOR® as an agent in one or more past transactions does not preclude other REALTORS® from seeking such former client's future business. *(Amended 1/93)*

- **Standard of Practice 16-8**

  The fact that an agency agreement has been entered into with a REALTOR® shall not preclude or inhibit any other REALTOR® from entering into a similar agreement after the expiration of the prior agreement. *(Amended 1/93)*

- **Standard of Practice 16-9**

  REALTORS®, prior to entering into an agency agreement, have an affirmative obligation to make reasonable efforts to determine whether the client is subject to a current, valid exclusive agreement to provide the same type of real estate service. *(Amended 1/93)*

- **Standard of Practice 16-10**

  REALTORS®, acting as agents of buyers or tenants, shall disclose that relationship to the seller/landlord's agent at first contact and shall provide written confirmation of that disclosure to the seller/landlord's agent not later than execution of a purchase agreement or lease. *(Amended 1/93)*

- **Standard of Practice 16-11**

  On unlisted property, REALTORS® acting as buyer/tenant agents shall disclose that relationship to the seller/landlord at first contact for that client and shall provide written confirmation of such disclosure to the seller/landlord not later than execution of any purchase or lease agreement.

  REALTORS® shall make any request for anticipated compensation from the seller/landlord at first contact. *(Amended 1/93)*

- **Standard of Practice 16-12**

  REALTORS®, acting as agents of sellers/landlords or as subagents of listing brokers, shall disclose that relationship to buyers/tenants as soon as practicable and shall provide written confirmation of such disclosure to buyers/tenants not later than execution of any purchase or lease agreement. *(Amended 1/93)*

- **Standard of Practice 16-13**

  All dealings concerning property exclusively listed, or with buyer/tenants who are exclusively represented shall be carried on with the client's agent, and not with the client, except with the consent of the client's agent or except where such dealings are initiated by the client. *(Adopted 1/93, Amended 1/97)*

- **Standard of Practice 16-14**

  REALTORS® are free to enter into contractual relationships or to negotiate with sellers/landlords, buyers/tenants or others who are not represented by an exclusive agent but shall not knowingly obligate them to pay more than one commission except with their informed consent. *(Amended 1/94)*

- **Standard of Practice 16-15**

  In cooperative transactions REALTORS® shall compensate cooperating REALTORS® (principal brokers) and shall not compensate nor offer to compensate, directly or indirectly, any of the sales licensees employed by or affiliated with other REALTORS® without the prior express knowledge and consent of the cooperating broker.

- **Standard of Practice 16-16**

  REALTORS®, acting as subagents or buyer/tenant agents, shall not use the terms of an offer to purchase/lease to attempt to modify the listing broker's offer of compensation to subagents or buyer's agents nor make the submission of an executed offer to purchase/lease contingent on the listing broker's agreement to modify the offer of compensation. *(Amended 1/93)*

- **Standard of Practice 16-17**

  REALTORS® acting as subagents or as buyer/tenant agents, shall not attempt to extend a listing broker's offer of cooperation and/or compensation to other brokers without the consent of the listing broker. *(Amended 1/93)*

- **Standard of Practice 16-18**

  REALTORS® shall not use information obtained by them from the listing broker, through offers to cooperate received through Multiple Listing Services or other sources authorized by the listing broker, for the purpose of creating a referral prospect to a third broker, or for creating a buyer/tenant prospect unless such use is authorized by the listing broker. *(Amended 1/93)*

- **Standard of Practice 16-19**

  Signs giving notice of property for sale, rent, lease, or exchange shall not be placed on property without consent of the seller/landlord. *(Amended 1/93)*

Article 17

In the event of contractual disputes or specific non-contractual disputes as defined in Standard of Practice 17-4 between REALTORS® associated with different firms, arising out of their relationship as REALTORS®, the REALTORS® shall submit the dispute to arbitration in accordance with the regulations of their Board or Boards rather than litigate the matter.

In the event clients of REALTORS® wish to arbitrate contractual disputes arising out of real estate transactions, REALTORS® shall arbitrate those disputes in accordance with the regulations of their Board, provided the clients agree to be bound by the decision. *(Amended 1/97)*

- **Standard of Practice 17-1**

  The filing of litigation and refusal to withdraw from it by REALTORS® in an arbitrable matter constitutes a refusal to arbitrate. *(Adopted 2/86)*

- **Standard of Practice 17-2**

  Article 17 does not require REALTORS® to arbitrate in those circumstances when all parties to the dispute advise the Board in writing that they choose not to arbitrate before the Board. *(Amended 1/93)*

- **Standard of Practice 17-3**

  REALTORS®, when acting solely as principals in a real estate transaction, are not obligated to arbitrate disputes with other REALTORS® absent a specific written agreement to the contrary. *(Adopted 1/96)*

- **Standard of Practice 17-4**

  Specific non-contractual disputes that are subject to arbitration pursuant to Article 17 are:

  1) Where a listing broker has compensated a cooperating broker and another cooperating broker subsequently claims to be the procuring cause of the sale or lease. In such cases the complainant may name the first cooperating broker as respondent and arbitration may proceed without the listing broker being named as a respondent. Alternatively, if the complaint is brought against the listing broker, the listing broker may name the first cooperating broker as a third-party respondent. In either instance the decision of the hearing panel as to procuring cause shall be conclusive with respect to all current or subsequent claims of the parties for compensation arising out of the underlying cooperative transaction. *(Adopted 1/97)*

  2) Where a buyer or tenant representative is compensated by the seller or landlord, and not by the listing broker, and the listing broker, as a result, reduces the commission owed by the seller or landlord and, subsequent to such actions, another cooperating broker claims to be the procuring cause of sale or lease. In such cases the complainant may name the first cooperating broker as respondent and arbitration may proceed without the listing broker being named as a respondent. Alternatively, if the complaint is brought against the listing broker, the listing broker may name the first cooperating broker as a third-party respondent. In either instance the decision of the hearing panel as to procuring cause shall be conclusive with respect to all current or subsequent claims of the parties for compensation arising out of the underlying cooperative transaction. *(Adopted 1/97)*

  3) Where a buyer or tenant representative is compensated by the buyer or tenant and, as a result, the listing broker reduces the commission owed by the seller or landlord and, subsequent to such actions, another cooperating broker claims to be the procuring cause of sale or lease.

In such cases the complainant may name the first cooperating broker as respondent and arbitration may proceed without the listing broker being named as a respondent. Alternatively, if the complaint is brought against the listing broker, the listing broker may name the first cooperating broker as a third-party respondent. In either instance the decision of the hearing panel as to procuring cause shall be conclusive with respect to all current or subsequent claims of the parties for compensation arising out of the underlying cooperative transaction. *(Adopted 1/97)*

4) Where two or more listing brokers claim entitlement to compensation pursuant to open listings with a seller or landlord who agrees to participate in arbitration (or who requests arbitration) and who agrees to be bound by the decision. In cases where one of the listing brokers has been compensated by the seller or landlord, the other listing broker, as complainant, may name the first listing broker as respondent and arbitration may proceed between the brokers. *(Adopted 1/97)*

The Code of Ethics was adopted in 1913. Amended at the Annual Convention in 1924, 1928, 1950, 1951, 1952, 1955, 1956, 1961, 1962, 1974, 1982, 1986, 1987, 1989, 1990, 1991, 1992, 1993, 1994, 1995 and 1996.

Explanatory Notes

The reader should be aware of the following policies which have been approved by the Board of Directors of the National Association:

In filing a charge of an alleged violation of the Code of Ethics by a REALTOR®, the charge must read as an alleged violation of one or more Articles of the Code. Standards of Practice may be cited in support of the charge.

The Standards of Practice serve to clarify the ethical obligations imposed by the various Articles and supplement, and do not substitute for, the Case Interpretations in *Interpretations of the Code of Ethics.*

Modifications to existing Standards of Practice and additional new Standards of Practice are approved from time to time. Readers are cautioned to ensure that the most recent publications are utilized.

NATIONAL ASSOCIATION OF REALTORS®
430 North Michigan Avenue
Chicago, Illinois 60611

Salesperson's Review Examination

1. A broker legitimately may pay all or part of a real estate commission to
   a. the seller.
   b. the salesperson.
   c. the buyer.
   d. a friend who provided a listing lead.

2. The minimum age for a New York real estate broker's license is
   a. 19.   c. 20.
   b. 18.   d. 21.

3. Which of the following acts would require a real estate license in New York?
   a. Sale of one's own property
   b. Sale by the owner's lawyer
   c. Sale of land by an auctioneer
   d. Foreclosure sale by court order

4. An associate broker may
   a. sponsor a person for a salesperson's license.
   b. collect his or her own real estate fees.
   c. act as a principal broker for another broker.
   d. work as a salesperson for a principal broker.

5. Violation of the license law is a misdemeanor, punishable by up to a year in jail and a fine of up to
   a. $500.   c. $1,000.
   b. $2,000.   d. $1,500.

6. Jane and Joe Sigmund have acquired an apartment information vendor's license and are maintaining a $5,000 interest-bearing escrow account. They can renew their license annually if they pay a fee of
   a. $250.   c. $500.
   b. $400.   d. $1,000.

7. Lucy Latimer decided to change real estate offices from LMN Realty to PDQ Land Company.
   I. LMN Realty must notify the DOS of the termination and submit a $10 fee.
   II. PDQ Land Company must notify the DOS of the affiliation and submit a $10 fee.
   a. I only   c. Both I and II
   b. II only   d. Neither I nor II

8. When does offering a client's business for sale require a real estate license?
   a. Never
   b. Always
   c. When the business includes any real estate
   d. When more than half the value is in real estate

9. Broker Bobbs had received a commission of $4,225 for a transaction for which she later was found to be in violation of license law. In addition to having her license suspended, she could be held liable for up to
   a. three times $4,225.
   b. two times $4,225.
   c. five times $4,225.
   d. four times $4,225.

10. When a license is revoked, how long must a licensee wait before applying to have the license reinstated?
    a. 18 months   c. 6 months
    b. 1 year   d. 2 years

11. The form of listing whereby an owner lists property for sale with a number of brokers is known as a(n)
    a. exclusive agency.
    b. open listing.
    c. exclusive right to sell.
    d. net listing.

12. To avoid possible liability for the actions of cooperating members of a multiple listing system, the owner who lists property for sale may decline to offer
    a. commission to the selling agent.
    b. subagency.
    c. cooperation with other firms.
    d. vicarious responsibility.

13. In New York all of the following must be in writing **except:**
    a. the listing agreement.
    b. the deed.
    c. the mortgage.
    d. the option to purchase.

14. Jan Lipson gave Sun City Realty an exclusive agency listing on her property. If she sells the property herself without involving Sun City, she will owe Sun City
    a. half of the commission.
    b. all of the commission.
    c. no commission.
    d. only reimbursement for Sun City's expenses.

15. When selling a property in New York, the licensee is required to disclose to a potential buyer that
    a. there is a group home ⅛ mile away.
    b. the property lies in an agricultural district.
    c. there is a fundamentalist church 3 blocks away.
    d. the former owners were divorced.

16. The commission to be paid in a written listing agreement is the
    a. rate set by law.
    b. amount of money over the net listing amount.
    c. customary rate in the area.
    d. percentage of the sales price as negotiated and agreed or a flat fee.

17. The relationship between an agent and his or her principal is
    a. fiduciary.   c. allodial.
    b. alluvial.   d. executory.

18. If you are selling a house in New York, it is necessary to disclose that
    a. there is a utility surcharge.
    b. the former owner committed suicide.
    c. the train station is 8 miles away.
    d. a shopping center in the nearby town is closing.

19. When selling a parcel of land in New York, you must disclose that
    a. a mental hospital is buing built in the county.
    b. there is a parochial school 10 blocks away.
    c. your broker is a REALTOR®.
    d. there is no utility service to the property.

20. To create an agency relationship, all that is necessary is
    a. the principal's delegation of authority.
    b. the agent's consent to act.
    c. Only a
    d. Both a and b

21. Which of the following occurrences would *not* cause the termination of an open listing agreement?
    a. Death or insanity of either party
    b. Bankruptcy of either party
    c. A kitchen fire
    d. Sale by another broker

22. A listing agreement that is illegal in New York State is a(n)
    a. net listing.
    b. exclusive agency.
    c. exclusive right to sell.
    d. open listing.

23. Which of the following terms would *not* be essential to effect a meeting of the minds?
    a. Price and amount of cash
    b. Closing the title
    c. Amortization
    d. Mortgage terms and interest

24. Penalties for violating an agent's fiduciary duties include all of the following **except:**
    a. loss of agent's fee.
    b. an adverse judgment in a civil court.
    c. 390 days in jail.
    d. loss of agent's license plus fines and penalties.

25. A broker is generally entitled to a commission in the event that the transaction does not close if the _____ defaults.
    a. seller   c. bank
    b. buyer   d. title company

26. Big Apple Realty is concerned that its commission on a sale will not be paid. Big Apple Realty may
    a. file a lis pendens.
    b. request a de minimis gift.
    c. file an affidavit of entitlement.
    d. file a mechanic's lien.

27. A real estate salesperson's compensation is set by
    a. the local realty association.
    b. the Department of State, Division of Licensing Services
    c. agreement between broker and salesperson.
    d. the cooperating broker in a transaction.

28. The *Duncan Hill* decision cautioned real estate licensees against
    a. misrepresentation.
    b. consumer fraud.
    c. the unauthorized practice of law.
    d. undisclosed dual agency.

29. In a typical real estate transaction, all the following may be considered a subagent, **except:**
    a. the salesperson who worked for the listing broker.
    b. the buyer's agent.
    c. a cooperating MLS broker.
    d. a licensee working for the seller.

30. A selling broker may be any of the following, **except** a(n):
    a. buyer's agent.   c. MLS agent.
    b. broker's agent.   d. subagent.

31. If a selling broker is not acting as the seller's agent, he or she owes the seller which of the following duties?
    a. Fair and honest business dealing
    b. Loyalty
    c. Confidentiality
    d. Disclosure

32. The acknowledgment of the parties to the contract in the NYS disclosure form need not be signed if
    a. the real estate agent had the rest of the form signed.
    b. the title company forgets to ask to have it signed.
    c. the seller has already moved to Virginia.
    d. both seller and buyer are represented by attorneys throughout.

33. Agency relationships in an in-house sale require
    a. no notice to the principal broker.
    b. full discussion and disclosure in writing to all parties.
    c. notice to the title company.
    d. notice to the MLS.

34. In a buyer agency relationship the broker owes the seller
    a. care.
    b. accounting.
    c. obedience.
    d. fair and honest dealing.

35. Which of the following statements is true regarding buyer agency in New York?
    a. Buyer agency creates the risk that an agent will waste time with a buyer who eventually buys from another agent.
    b. Buyer agency does not limit the broker's liability exposure for a seller's misrepresentation.
    c. A problem with buyer agency is that it does not help ensure a buyer's loyalty and cooperation.
    d. Buyer agency does not violate any fiduciary or professional duties to sellers.

36. In a real estate transaction, a broker had a written representation agreement with the buyer, but was paid six percent of the selling price at the closing by the seller. Under these facts, whose agent was this broker?
    a. The seller's
    b. The buyer's
    c. The broker is a dual agent
    d. The broker has violated New York's real estate license laws, and may have his or her license suspended or revoked.

37. A broker signed a listing agreement with the Ghents to market their luxury downtown condominium. A few days later, the broker signed a buyer representation agrreement with the Smiths, who were looking for a modest suburgan single-family home. If the buyers decide they're in the market for a luxury downtown condominium instead, and want to see the Ghent's property, what should the broker do?
    a. Say nothing, and collect a commission from the sellers and a fee from the buyers.
    b. Disclose the unintended dual agency, and obtain both parties' written consent.
    c. Withdraw from representing one of the parties, to avoid any appearance of self-dealing.
    d. Nothing: as long as the broker accepts compensation from only one of the parties, there is no undisclosed dual agency issue.

38. DOS regulation 175.7: "A real estate broker shall make it clear for which party he is acting . . . ." applies to
    a. the sale or lease of one to four unit residential properties.
    b. only condominiums and cooperatives.
    c. the sale or lease of commercial space.
    d. all types of transactions, not just residential.

39. A seller signs a six-month listing agreement with a broker in May. In June, the seller dies. The seller's heirs claim the broker is now their agent, and threaten to sue if she removes the "For Sale" sign from the yard. Under these facts, which of the following statements is true?
    a. The broker must leave the sign where it is until the agreement expires, because an agency relationship is not necessarily terminated by the death of only one party.
    b. The broker must leave the sign where it is until the agreement expires, because an agency relationship may be terminated by the death of the agent, but not of the principal.
    c. The broker may remove the sign, because an agency relationship is terminated by the death of either party.
    d. The broker may remove the sign, because the purpose for which this agency relationship was formed has been completed.

40. In which clause in a deed would you find metes and bounds and monuments?
    a. Demising   c. Description
    b. Defeasance   d. Habendum

41. If Mr. Jones owns his home free and clear of encumbrances and can will it to his daughter, this type of ownership is a(n)
    a. life estate.   c. estate at will.
    b. fee simple.   d. leasehold.

42. The Goodmans purchased a cottage bounding on a stream. They have rights to the stream known as
    a. reversionary.   c. laches.
    b. littoral.   d. riparian.

43. Which of the following would *not* be considered chattel?
    a. A tractor   c. The draperies
    b. The barn   d. A trade fixture

44. The most complete type of ownership in real estate is
    a. fee on condition. c. qualified fee.
    b. life estate.   d. fee simple.

45. Deed restrictions can be established only by the
    a. grantor.
    b. local government.
    c. zoning board of appeals.
    d. grantee.

46. When an owner creates a deed restriction, he or she may limit any of the following **except:**
    a. the free transfer of the property.
    b. the minimum acreage per lot.
    c. further subdivision.
    d. the total number of lots in a subdivision.

47. Any right to or interest in the land interfering with its use or transfer is called an
    a. encumbrance.   c. easement.
    b. encroachment.   d. appurtenance.

48. A deed is valid when it is
    a. delivered.   c. signed.
    b. recorded.   d. notarized.

49. Which type of deed is used to convey title to a parcel of land through a foreclosure proceeding?
    a. Bargain and sale
    b. Quitclaim
    c. Referee's
    d. Warranty

50. An instrument in writing duly executed and delivered that conveys title to real property is a
    a. contract.   c. lease.
    b. lien.   d. deed.

51. Daniel paid Robert $2,000 for the right, if he chooses, to lease a store within 60 days at a specified annual rental. The agreement was a(n)
    a. lease-option.   c. implied contract.
    b. open lease.   d. option.

52. The tenant who pays property taxes and heating bills for the store he or she rents probably has what type of lease?
    a. Net   c. Percentage
    b. Participation d. Gross

53. A contract transferring the transfer of rights to possession of real property for a specified term is known as a
    a. lis pendens.   c. lease.
    b. lien.   d. laches.

54. Under the New York General Obligations Law, security deposits by a tenant
    a. become the property of the landlord.
    b. are held in trust by the landlord.
    c. may be commingled with the landlord's funds.
    d. can be retained by the landlord after he or she sells the property.

55. A tenant learns that her building has been sold to a new landlord. Based on these facts, which of the following statements is true regarding the tenant's lease?
    a. The sale of the property automatically terminates all pre-existing leases, and the tenant will need to negotiate a new lease with the new landlord.
    b. Under New York's tenant protection law, the sale of the property automatically renews the lease for an additional term, although the tenant has the option of declining the renewal.
    c. The lease survives the sale of the property, and the tenant must make timely rent payments to the new owner.
    d. While the sale of the property terminates the lease, the tenant is entitled to a legal holdover tenancy for the remainder of the stated lease term.

56. A legally enforceable agreement between competent parties in which each party acquires a right is called a
    a. certiorari.   c. contract.
    b. consideration.   d. clause.

57. The usual listing agreement between a seller and a real estate agent is a(n)
    a. implied contract.
    b. breach of contract.
    c. express contract.
    d. discharge of contract.

58. When the agreement of the parties is demonstrated by their acts and conduct, this is known as a(n) _____ contract.
    a. express
    b. voidable
    c. implied
    d. unilateral

59. When a new contract is substituted for an existing agreement, this is called a(n)
    a. novation.
    b. innovation.
    c. assignment.
    d. default.

60. Any conveyance in New York State is taxed at _____ minus the amount of any mortgage being assumed.
    a. $.55 per $500 or fraction thereof of the consideration paid
    b. 1 percent on a sale of less than $500,000
    c. 10 percent where the consideration is more than $1 million
    d. $2 per $500 or fraction thereof of the consideration paid

61. Which of the following items would be credited to the buyer at closing?
    a. sales price
    b. prepaid insurance
    c. unpaid water bills
    d. fuel oil on hand

62. The Flintstones sold their house to the Simpsons and are to close on July 1, 1998. The Flintstones paid their annual town taxes in April 1998. At the closing the Simpsons will reimburse the Flintstones for
    a. the tax for the balance of the year.
    b. the tax due in November.
    c. nothing.
    d. the tax due in January.

63. RESPA explicitly prohibits the payment of kickbacks or unearned fees. This does not prohibit a
    a. referral fee from an insurance agent.
    b. fee to a furniture supplier.
    c. brokerage referral fee.
    d. fee to a moving company.

64. An instrument in writing that is the security for a debt with specific property as a pledge is a
    a. bond.
    b. mortgage.
    c. deed.
    d. lease.

65. A Department of Veterans Affairs mortgage is
    a. insured.
    b. guaranteed.
    c. conventional.
    d. prepaid.

66. When a house purchase is financed by a federally related mortgage loan, RESPA requires that loan closing information be prepared on the
    a. Uniform Settlement Statement.
    b. Fannie Mae form.
    c. Mortgage Reduction Certificate.
    d. Affidavit of Title.

67. A mortgage with a final payment larger than the preceding ones is known as a(n)
    a. blanket mortgage.
    b. balloon mortgage.
    c. open mortgage.
    d. variable-rate mortgage.

68. Discount charges imposed by a lender to raise the yield on a loan are called
    a. negative amortization.
    b. points.
    c. laches.
    d. lis pendens.

69. Margo and Clarence Stilton have applied for an FHA insured loan. The insurance is
    I. backed by the full faith and credit of the U.S. Government.
    II. backed by the insurance fund set up by the Federal Housing Administration.
    a. I only
    b. II only
    c. Both I and II
    d. Neither I nor II

70. U Kan Tu Realty negotiated a sale at $172,000. The buyers need a mortgage of $142,000. The lender will approve only an 80 percent LTV mortgage. U Kan Tu prepares a second set of agreements with a purchase price of $177,500, has the sellers and the buyers sign them and presents them to the lender.
    I. U Kan Tu Realty is liable for a criminal act.
    II. The sellers and the buyers are liable for a criminal act.
    a. I only
    b. II only
    c. Both I and II
    d. Neither I nor II

71. A mortgage loan in which the interest rate may be higher or lower at specified intervals, keyed to an economic indicator, is a(n) _____ mortgage.
    a. pledged account
    b. shared equity
    c. growing equity
    d. adjustable rate

72. Extra prepaid interest that a bank may charge up front, based on a percentage of the loan, is called
    a. floating interest.
    b. points.
    c. prepayment.
    d. usury.

73. When a lender is willing to lower the interest rate in return for extra payments of points up front, this is called
    a. a buydown.
    b. prepayment.
    c. points.
    d. usury.

74. Each of the following is a basic zoning classification **except:**
    a. commercial.
    b. residential.
    c. industrial.
    d. municipal.

75. In a community, rezoning is the responsibility of the
    a. planning board.
    b. town or village board.
    c. environmental conservation board.
    d. zoning board of appeals.

76. Which of the following is *not* considered a valid reason for the granting of a zoning variance?
    a. The convenience of the owner
    b. Hardship or practical difficulty
    c. An addition to a building that does not increase an existing nonconforming area setback
    d. Formal approval of a preexisting land use defect

77. Land use is controlled or regulated through all of the following **except:**
    a. public land-use controls.
    b. the local assessor's authority.
    c. private land-use controls.
    d. public ownership of land.

78. A village rezoned a one-acre parcel located in a single-family ½ acre residential zone to permit the construction of a gas station. In New York this is considered
    a. a good idea to create the convenience of a gas station.
    b. good land-use planning.
    c. spot zoning and illegal.
    d. as of right zoning.

79. Which of the following is always required for a building certificate of occupancy?
    a. Board of Fire Underwriters Certificate
    b. Variance from the Zoning Board of Appeals
    c. Approval by an Architectural Review Board
    d. Approval by the Department of State

80. Each of the following is a type of heating or cooling system **except:**
    a. oil-fired hot water baseboard.
    b. electric hot air.
    c. gas-fired steam.
    d. earth berm.

81. Which of the following is *not* an architectural style?
    a. Split level
    b. Post and beam
    c. Colonial
    d. Ranch

82. The most common foundation materials in New York are

    a. poured concrete and concrete block.
    b. Styrofoam.
    c. concrete slab.
    d. pier and beam.

83. The most commonly used insulation material is

    a. rock wool.
    b. cellulose fiber.
    c. urea formaldehyde foam.
    d. fiberglass.

84. Value of real property is best defined as

    a. cost.
    b. price.
    c. present worth of future benefits.
    d. attractiveness and location.

85. When a comparative market analysis is done, which approach to real estate evaluation is being used?

    a. Income approach
    b. Direct sales comparison
    c. Cost approach
    d. Guesstimate

86. All of the following are elements used to determine market value, **except:**

    a. buyers and sellers acting without undue pressure.
    b. property exposed to the market a reasonable amount of time.
    c. the presumption of an arm's length transaction.
    d. the cost of labor and material for construction.

87. A factor that helps to determine a listing price includes

    a. original cost of construction.
    b. current sale prices of similar properties.
    c. assessed value.
    d. replacement cost.

88. Federal civil rights legislation forbids housing discrimination based on

    a. political affiliation.
    b. source of income.
    c. country of origin.
    d. prison record.

89. The Civil Rights Act of 1866

    a. prohibits any type of discrimination based on race.
    b. prohibits discrimination in federally funded housing.
    c. allows an exception for an owner-occupied two-family house.
    d. does not apply to nonlicensed persons.

90. Redlining is defined as

    a. steering home seekers to a particular neighborhood.
    b. drawing red lines on a local map indicating what areas to look in for listings.
    c. denying or restricting loans in a certain area by a lending institution.
    d. a zoning procedure.

91. New York State law goes beyond federal human rights law when it forbids discrimination based on

    a. race.
    b. marital status.
    c. religion.
    d. children in a family.

92. PDQ Realty advertises that it specializes in homes for European immigrants. This is a fair housing violation called

    a. redlining.   c. blockbusting.
    b. steering.   d. sexual bias.

93. Using "scare tactics" regarding the possible change in the demographics of a neighborhood when soliciting listings is a violation called

    a. redlining.   c. blockbusting.
    b. steering.   d. harassment.

94. Although a property owner may be exempted sometimes from discrimination laws, a real estate licensee

    a. is exempt as an owner.
    b. can list the property for sale noting the exemption.
    c. can advertise the noted exemption.
    d. may not participate in the transaction in any way.

95. New York Human Rights statutes do *not* cover
    a. renting or leasing.
    b. selling.
    c. out-of-state sales.
    d. advertising.

96. The Underground Storage Tank Act in New York regulates underground fuel storage of tanks that are
    a. 2,000 gallons or larger.
    b. 550 gallons or larger.
    c. 1,000 gallons or larger.
    d. 750 gallons or larger.

97. A certified professional need not be hired for the removal of
    a. radon.   c. lead.
    b. asbestos.   d. UFFI.

98. Signs that a septic system is not working properly do not necessarily include
    a. sluggish or backed-up drains.
    b. pooled "gray" water over the absorption field.
    c. one stopped sink drain.
    d. lush grass and spongy soil over the absorption field.

99. A solution to eliminating an asbestos problem would *not* be to
    a. have a professional remove any asbestos material.
    b. have a professional encapsulate the material.
    c. leave it alone.
    d. have the owner remove it and throw it in the trash.

100. Household electrical appliances are a source of
    a. EMF's.   c. CFC's.
    b. PCB's.   d. EPA's.

Broker's Practice Examination

1. Samantha Shore's first listing was of a house that the owner described as having asbestos and drainage problems. If Sally does not mention this to potential buyers or other brokers, she will be
   a. guilty of fraudulent misrepresentation.
   b. assisting the seller to make a quicker and easier sale.
   c. getting a better price for the seller.
   d. guilty of innocent misrepresentation.

2. Broker Bob Brown and Broker Sally Shore together purchased a property at a very low price from a distressed owner. Bob and Sally did not tell the owner that they were brokers. They then proceeded to sell the property, making a profit of 125 percent. This was a(n)
   a. fair business transaction.
   b. unethical and illegal business practice.
   c. violation of Fair Housing laws.
   d. example of cooperative brokerage.

3. In a real estate business formed as a sole proprietorship, which of the following is *not* true?
   a. The broker may draw a regular salary or take profits as income.
   b. The broker's salary is taxed twice.
   c. The broker would enjoy the best tax advantages for a small office.
   d. The broker has unlimited financial liability.

4. A real estate business formed as a limited liability company
   a. does not avoid the tax disadvantages of a regular corporation.
   b. is illegal in New York.
   c. offers unlimited financial liability.
   d. offers some limited financial liability.

5. Errors and omissions insurance covers
   a. intentional acts of a broker to deceive.
   b. punitive damages.
   c. the defense of "nuisance cases."
   d. negligence when buying or selling for one's own account.

6. The mixing of clients' or customers' funds with an agent's personal funds is known as
   a. commingling.   c. collateral.
   b. consideration.   d. codicil.

7. The Internal Revenue Service will challenge "independent contractor" status if the sales associate
   a. is licensed as a real estate broker or salesperson.
   b. receives health and life insurance as an employment benefit.
   c. has income based on sales output, subject to fluctuation.
   d. performs services pursuant to a written contract specifying independent contractor status.

8. Operating a real estate office in restraint of trade violates the
   a. General Obligations Law.
   b. Sherman Antitrust Act.
   c. Civil Rights Act.
   d. statute of frauds.

9. A salesperson who is an independent contractor
   a. has income tax and Social Security withheld from wages.
   b. has health and life insurance supplied as a benefit.
   c. can be told what to do but not how to do it.
   d. must keep hours as assigned by the broker.

10. It is *not* considered fraudulent when a broker
    a. conceals or doesn't disclose important facts about a property.
    b. makes false statements about a property.
    c. makes a misstatement based on information supplied to him or her by the owner.
    d. attempts to close a transaction by not mentioning to the buyer that an amusement park is to be built on the next lot.

11. A real estate broker is most generally a(n)
    a. universal agent. c. special agent.
    b. general agent.   d. ostensible agent.

12. ABC Realty may place a **For Sale** sign on a property only
    a. if the owner is in China and will not be aware of the sign.
    b. if it is an open listing.
    c. with the owner's consent.
    d. if it is an exclusive right to sell.

13. In real estate advertising which of the following is correct?
    a. The listing salesperson's name must appear in the ad.
    b. The advertisement must indicate that the advertiser is a broker.
    c. A property may be listed as being "in the vicinity of" without stating the exact location.
    d. The ad may indicate only the rate of interest on available financing.

14. A principal broker is responsible for
    a. getting listing leads for sales associates.
    b. training sales associates.
    c. sales associates' clothing allowance.
    d. salespersons' business calls placed from their home phones.

15. Several brokerage firms may legitimately get together to
    a. collaborate to establish reasonable fees for services rendered.
    b. cooperate to divide up various market areas so as to limit the competition between them.
    c. work together to prevent a "discount broker" from getting business or cobrokerage.
    d. cooperate to enhance the ethical practices in their area.

16. An associate broker may
    a. sponsor an applicant for a salesperson's license.
    b. work as a salesperson under the name and supervision of another principal broker.
    c. collect his or her own real estate fees.
    d. act as a principal broker.

17. When handling funds for others, a broker must
    a. place all monies in his or her own business account.
    b. use the interest to take care of the expenses he or she incurs.
    c. maintain a separate special bank account exclusively for deposit of monies of his or her principals.
    d. not give a full account of the funds to a principal.

18. When a broker is recruiting new salespersons, which of the following laws does *not* apply to the recruiting process?
    a. Title VII of the Civil Rights Act of 1964
    b. Article 9-A of the Real Property Law
    c. The Age Discrimination in Employment Act
    d. The Americans with Disabilities Act

19. "Triggering terms" for Regulation Z do *not* include
    a. term or period of repayment.
    b. amount of any payment.
    c. amount of any finance charge.
    d. annual percentage rate.

20. A legal proceeding through which a debtor may seek relief from overwhelming financial problems and have a chance at a fresh start is called
    a. certiorari.
    b. bankruptcy.
    c. capital recapture.
    d. dispossess proceedings.

21. A clause in a mortgage instrument that states that in the event of the default of the mortgagor the entire debt is due and payable is called the
    a. habendum clause.
    b. acceleration clause.
    c. demising clause.
    d. granting clause.

22. The document in which a borrower (mortgagor) certifies the amount owed on a mortgage loan and the rate of interest is called a(n)
    a. mortgage reduction certificate.
    b. estoppel certificate.
    c. mortgage statement.
    d. covenant.

23. An FHA (Federal Housing Administration) loan is always
    a. conventional.   c. insured.
    b. guaranteed.   d. prepaid.

24. The amount of a mortgage loan in relation to the value of a house is called
    a. percentage.
    b. the loan-to-value ratio.
    c. negative amortization.
    d. an equity loan.

25. Discount charges imposed by lenders to raise the yields on their loans are called
    a. negative amortizations.
    b. points.
    c. laches.
    d. lis pendens.

26. RESPA requirements do not apply when the
    a. sale of property is paid in cash and in full.
    b. loan is made by a federally insured lender.
    c. loan is insured by FHA or guaranteed by VA.
    d. loan is administered by the U.S. Department of Housing and Urban Development.

27. Stockholders of a corporation are liable
    a. only to the extent of their investment in the firm.
    b. personally for debts and losses.
    c. for the debts of another shareholder.
    d. for the entire debt of the corporation.

28. A Real Estate Investment Trust (REIT)
    a. usually pays out of cash flow.
    b. has a general partner running a project as a fiduciary.
    c. can stay in the business indefinitely by investing in further projects.
    d. passes cash and tax losses to partners.

29. A real estate limited partnership
    a. is often traded on stock exchanges.
    b. is managed by a board of directors.
    c. has a reinvestment plan.
    d. usually liquidates one project in five to seven years.

30. Which of the following is *not* a form of business entity that could own real property?
    a. Partnership   c. Corporation
    b. Syndicate   d. Ratification

31. A transaction in which an owner sells his or her improved property and, as part of the same transaction, signs a long-term lease to remain in possession of the property is called a(n)
    a. equity of redemption.
    b. land contract.
    c. sale and leaseback.
    d. conditional contract of sale.

32. A statutory accounting concept in real estate investments known as *depreciation* is also called
    - a. cost recovery.
    - b. appreciation.
    - c. substantiation.
    - d. rehabilitation.

33. An investor sells residential property that was depreciated using an accelerated recovery method. The portion of the gain in excess of what would have been earned using straight-line recovery will be taxed as ordinary income rather than as capital gains. This is known as
    - a. depreciation.
    - b. appreciation.
    - c. recapture.
    - d. basis.

34. A clause found in the lease whereby the landlord (lessor) leases and the tenant (lessee) takes the property is called a
    - a. demising clause.
    - b. habendum clause.
    - c. subletting clause.
    - d. defeasance clause.

35. In a residential lease in New York, which would *not* apply under the implied warrant of habitability?
    - a. The landlord must paint the interior every three years.
    - b. The leased property must be fit for human habitation.
    - c. The common elements must be maintained in good repair.
    - d. The tenant cannot be subjected to conditions that could endanger life, health or safety.

36. Which of the following is *not* true of an apartment information vendor's license?
    - a. The fee is $400 for each office, main or branch.
    - b. The holder must maintain interest-bearing escrow accounts of $5,000 for the main office and $2,500 for each branch office.
    - c. The license is issued for and renewable for one year.
    - d. The holder may retain all advance fees if the client does not rent the apartment to which he or she was referred.

37. The Emergency Tenant Protection Act (ETPA) of 1974 was *not* designed to
    - a. prevent excessive rent increases in the decontrolled sector of the rental housing market.
    - b. be a local option to communities with escalating rents.
    - c. increase the housing stock.
    - d. help tenants faced with extraordinary rental increases.

38. Each of the following are included in the more common types of insurance a property manager would utilize **except:**
    - a. life insurance.
    - b. fire and hazard insurance.
    - c. liability insurance.
    - d. casualty insurance.

39. Ideally, a property manager would *not*
    - a. merchandise the property.
    - b. control operating expenses.
    - c. maintain and modernize the property.
    - d. cut corners on maintenance to temporarily increase profits.

40. If a tenant is actually removed from possession of a premises either by force or by process of law, it is known as
    - a. partial eviction.
    - b. actual eviction.
    - c. constructive eviction.
    - d. tentative eviction.

41. Mr. Landlord allows Ms. Tenant to occupy an apartment without any agreement as to the amount of rent or term of occupancy. This is known as a tenancy
    - a. at sufferance.
    - b. at will.
    - c. by the entirety.
    - d. for life.

42. Because of the complexity of the laws that affect properties, a property manager should be familiar with all of the following **except:**
    - a. environmental hazards.
    - b. accessible construction.
    - c. nondiscriminatory practices.
    - d. investment securities laws.

43. Which of the following is illegal for a New York landlord?
    a. Ejectment
    b. Retaliatory eviction
    c. Constructive eviction
    d. Actual eviction

44. Which of the following is *not* known as a negotiable instrument?
    a. A promissory note
    b. A check
    c. A stock certificate
    d. A certificate of deposit

45. If one agent in a firm lists a house and another is working as buyer's agent for someone who wants to see that house, the fiduciary problem is sometimes avoided by making them
    a. dual agents.
    b. express agents.
    c. non-agents.
    d. desginated agents.

46. A written agreement between two or more parties providing that a certain property will be placed with a third party and will be delivered to a designated person on the performance of some act or condition is called an
    a. estate.   c. equity.
    b. escrow.   d. egress.

47. Under the Uniform Vendor and Purchaser Risk Act in New York, the party who bears any loss to property that occurs before the title passes or the buyer takes possession is the
    a. seller.   c. bank.
    b. buyer.   d. title company.

48. Fred Freeman and Apple Annie together own 20 acres. Each has an undivided interest in severalty, without right of survivorship. This form of ownership is known as
    a. tenancy by sufferance.
    b. tenancy by the entirety.
    c. tenancy in common.
    d. joint tenancy.

49. A history of conveyances and encumbrances affecting a title as far back as records are available is known as a(n)
    a. color of title.
    b. marketable title.
    c. chain of title.
    d. abstract of title.

50. In every contract for sale or lease of subdivided lands, if the purchaser or lessee is not represented by an attorney, he or she has
    a. a 30-day cancellation privilege.
    b. a 90-day cancellation privilege.
    c. a 10-day cancellation privilege.
    d. no cancellation privilege.

51. An offer to sell or lease subdivided lands before the filing of both the offering statement and the statement of documentation constitutes
    a. a misdemeanor.   c. escheat.
    b. a felony.   d. insubordination.

52. The sale or lease of subdivided lands in New York is primarily governed by
    a. Article 9-A of the Real Property Law.
    b. the statute of limitations.
    c. the Uniform Commercial Code.
    d. the Civil Rights Act of 1866.

53. Misrepresentation in the sale or lease of subdivided lands constitutes
    a. a misdemeanor.   c. escheat.
    b. a felony.   d. insubordination.

54. The absolute ownership of an apartment or a housing unit plus an undivided interest in the ownership of the common elements that are jointly owned is called a
    a. leasehold.   c. condominium.
    b. cooperative.   d. dominant tenement.

55. A residential multiunit building with title held by a trust or corporation that is owned and operated for the benefit of persons living within the building, each of whom has a proprietary lease, is called a
    a. leasehold.   c. condominium.
    b. cooperative.   d. dominant tenement.

56. State laws regarding subdivision apply to land offerings when a
    a. third lot is carved from a parcel.
    b. fourth lot is carved from a parcel.
    c. fifth lot is carved from a parcel.
    d. sixth lot is carved from a parcel.

57. To compute the taxes on a property when you know the value, the assessment rate and the tax rate, the calculation is
    a. value × tax rate × assessed rate = taxes.
    b. assessed value ÷ tax rate = taxes.
    c. tax rate × value ÷ assessed rate = taxes.
    d. value × assessment rate − assessed value × tax rate = taxes.

58. In New York, a special exemption to reduce a real estate tax bill does not exist for some
    a. senior citizens.
    b. agricultural uses of land.
    c. veterans.
    d. parents of children enrolled in private schools.

59. Special taxes levied on real estate to pay for street lights or sewers are
    a. ad valorem taxes.
    b. in rem.
    c. special assessments.
    d. the true tax.

60. A legal proceeding against the realty directly, as distinguished from a proceeding against a person, is called
    a. a tax lien.   c. a mill.
    b. in rem.   d. ad valorem tax.

61. The tax rate expressed in mills is
    a. 1/100 of a dollar or $.001.
    b. 1/100 of a dollar or $.01.
    c. $1 per $400 of assessed value.
    d. $4 per $100 of assessed value.

62. At the closing the seller is usually required to pay all of the following **except:**
    a. the mortgage tax.
    b. the title search fee.
    c. the real estate commission.
    d. the transfer tax.

63. The transfer tax in New York State is
    a. 1 percent on a sale of less than $500,000.
    b. 10 percent on any sale of over $1 million.
    c. $2 per $500 or any fraction thereof.
    d. $.55 per thousand or any fraction thereof.

64. Private mortgage insurance is required on conventional loans in New York State when
    a. the down payment is less than 20 percent.
    b. there is a 5 percent down payment on an FHA loan.
    c. the down payment is more than 20 percent.
    d. there is a VA mortgage.

65. A buyer puts $20,000 down on a $200,000 house and will finance the rest with a mortgage of $180,000. In this example 90 percent represents
    a. the buyer's equity
    b. the loan-to-value ratio.
    c. a deficiency judgment.
    d. the amortization of the mortgage.

66. In terms of real estate appraisal, *the present worth of future benefits arising from the ownership of real property* is the definition of
    a. cost.   c. price.
    b. value.   d. amenities.

67. Which of the following is *not* a basic approach or technique employed by an appraiser to arrive at an accurate estimate of value?
    a. Market data   c. Quantity survey
    b. Cost   d. Income

68. To find the value of a property when you know the income and the capitalization rate, you
    a. divide the cap rate by the income.
    b. divide the income by the cap rate.
    c. multiply the cap rate by the income.
    d. add the income to the cap rate.

69. The art of analyzing and effectively weighing the findings of value on a property when all the basic approaches to appraisal are used is called
    a. repudiation.   c. calculation.
    b. amortization.   d. reconciliation.

70. Which is *not* a physical characteristic of land?
    a. Scarcity
    b. Immobility
    c. Nonhomogeneity
    d. Indestructibility

71. Which of the following should be included in the calculation of square feet of living area in a house?
    a. Front porch
    b. Bathrooms
    c. Garage
    d. Below-grade family room

72. The level of government that is responsible for the standards and policing of water supply and sewage disposal is
    a. local.
    b. county.
    c. state.
    d. federal.

73. In New York, building plans must be signed by the
    a. builder.
    b. developer.
    c. architect.
    d. land planner.

74. A house that is completely factory built, delivered to the site by truck, already joined and with systems hooked up is called a
    a. bi-level.
    b. rambler.
    c. mobile home.
    d. modular home.

75. The merging of two or more adjacent lots under one owner is
    a. contribution.
    b. competition.
    c. assemblage.
    d. anticipation.

76. To find the cubic yards of space in a warehouse you
    a. multiply the height and length.
    b. multiply the length and width.
    c. divide the height by the length and width.
    d. multiply the height, length and width.

77. The most commonly used insulation material is
    a. Styrofoam.
    b. fiberglass.
    c. cellulose fiber.
    d. rock wool.

78. The Wallaces are worried about possible problems with the Victorian house they plan to buy. Before the contract is firm, they should consult a
    a. building inspection engineer.
    b. soil engineer.
    c. framer.
    d. firestop specialist.

79. The Environmental Protection Agency considers solder materials dangerous when they contain more than 8 percent
    a. copper.
    b. lead.
    c. tin.
    d. antimony.

80. Federal law requires that a landlord modify an older building at the request of a handicapped tenant who
    a. qualifies for a handicap parking certificate.
    b. produces a doctor's letter.
    c. agrees to a rent increase.
    d. is willing to pay for the modifications.

81. The most common type of wood frame construction for one- and two-story residential structures is
    a. platform-frame.
    b. balloon frame.
    c. post-and-beam.
    d. pier and beam.

82. Primary responsibility for dealing with and/or correcting problems with a new structure lies with the
    a. County Board of Health.
    b. Building Inspector.
    c. Board of Fire Underwriters.
    d. builder/contractor.

83. If a property is located in an agricultural district or if there is a lack of available utilities, a purchaser must
    a. ask the seller about it.
    b. be given written notice.
    c. ask the building inspector.
    d. sue the agent.

84. The federal law that prohibits any type of discrimination based on race, with no exception, is the
    a. Civil Rights Act of 1964.
    b. Civil Rights Act of 1866.
    c. Fair Housing Act of 1968.
    d. Executive Order No. 11063.

85. Failure to display the equal housing opportunity poster is considered by HUD to be
    a. evidence of discrimination.
    b. illegal.
    c. redlining.
    d. blockbusting.

86. The exemptions to the Federal Fair Housing Act of 1968 do *not* include
    a. private clubs not open to the public, restricting the rental of rooms to members, but not operating commercially.
    b. dwelling units owned by religious institutions, restricted to members of the religion if membership is not discriminatory.
    c. rentals of rooms in owner-occupied two-family houses based on national origin.
    d. changing terms or conditions for different persons.

87. An individual who visits real estate offices to check on compliance with fair housing laws is
    a. always a HUD employee.
    b. usually a disgruntled customer.
    c. a tester.
    d. always a welfare recipient.

88. A way of imposing conditions on permitted zoning uses in a municipality is through
    a. an area variance.
    b. a use variance.
    c. spot zoning.
    d. a special-use permit.

89. To be granted a use variance by a zoning board of appeals, the applicant must prove
    a. convenience.   c. permanence.
    b. hardship.   d. practical difficulty.

90. A lien on real estate
    a. binds only the current owner.
    b. runs with the land.
    c. prevents the sale of the property.
    d. binds the owner's heirs.

91. Which type of lien generally holds priority over all others?
    a. Mechanic's   c. Real estate taxes
    b. Mortgage   d. Vendor's

92. The easement granted to New York State Electric and Gas to put electric service across another's property is a(n)
    a. easement appurtenant.
    b. easement in gross.
    c. dominant easement.
    d. servient easement.

93. Anything given to induce entering into a contract, such as money or personal services, is called
    a. consideration.   c. conversion.
    b. condemnation.   d. caveat emptor.

94. Nancy and Chris sign a contract under which Nancy will convey Blackacre to Chris. Nancy changes her mind, and Chris sues for specific performance. What is Chris seeking in this lawsuit?
    a. A forced sale of the property
    b. Money damages
    c. A new contract
    d. A deficiency judgment

95. An example of a unilateral contract is
    a. a land contract.
    b. a contract on a house sale.
    c. the offer of a reward.
    d. a contract to sell a car.

96. A person who delays taking steps to enforce a contractual right within the statute of limitations may lose that right through
    a. lis pendens.   c. litigation.
    b. laches.   d. lien.

97. Agreements written into deeds that promise performance or nonperformance of certain acts or stipulate certain uses or nonuses of the property are known as
    a. covenants.   c. commissions.
    b. considerations.   d. certioraris.

98. The legal description of a property always should include
    a. an exact description.
    b. metes and bounds.
    c. monuments.
    d. government survey data.

99. To be valid, a warranty deed need *not* include
    a. words of conveyance.
    b. a habendum clause.
    c. the full price paid.
    d. an adequate description.

100. The deed that provides the grantee with the least protection of any deed is the
    a. bargain and sale deed.
    b. referee's deed.
    c. warranty deed.
    d. quitclaim deed.

Glossary

abstract of title The condensed history of the title to a particular parcel of real estate.

abstract of title with lawyer's opinion An abstract of title that a lawyer has examined and has certified to be, in his or her opinion, an accurate statement of fact.

acceleration clause The clause in a note or mortgage that can be enforced to make the entire debt due immediately if the mortgagor defaults.

accretion The increase or addition of land by the deposit of sand or soil washed up naturally from a river, lake or sea.

accrued items On a closing statement, items of expense that have been incurred but are not yet payable, such as interest on a mortgage loan.

acknowledgment A formal declaration made before a duly authorized officer, usually a notary public, by a person who has signed a document.

acre A measure of land equal to 43,560 square feet, 4,840 square yards, 4,047 square meters, 160 square rods or 0.4047 hectare.

actual eviction Action whereby a defaulted tenant is physically ousted from rented property pursuant to a court order. (*See also* eviction.)

actual notice That which is known; actual knowledge.

adjacent Lying near to but not necessarily in actual contact with.

adjoining Contiguous; attaching, in actual contact with.

adjustable-rate mortgage (ARM) A mortgage loan in which the interest rate may increase or decrease to specific intervals, following an economic indicator.

adjusted basis Basis minus depreciation.

adjustments Divisions of financial responsibility between a buyer and seller (also called *prorations*).

administrator A person appointed by court to administer the estate of a deceased person who left no will, i.e., who died intestate.

ad valorem tax A tax levied according to value; generally used to refer to real estate tax. Also called the *general tax.*

adverse possession The actual, visible, hostile, notorious, exclusive and continuous possession of another's land under a claim of title. Possession for ten years may be a means of acquiring title.

affidavit A written statement sworn to before an officer who is authorized to administer an oath or affirmation.

affirmative marketing Program to inform all buyers in a minority community about housing opportunities available, without discrimination.

agency That relationship wherein an agent is employed by a principal to do certain acts on the principal's behalf.

agency coupled with an interest An agency relationship in which the agent has an interest in the property.

agent One who undertakes to transact some business or to manage some affair for another by authority of the latter.

agricultural real estate Farms, timberland, pasture land and orchards.

air rights The right to use the open space above a property, generally allowing the surface to be used for another purpose.

alienation The act of transferring property to another.

alienation clause The clause in a mortgage stating that the balance of the secured debt becomes immediately due and payable at the mortgagee's option if the property is sold.

Americans with Disabilities Act (ADA) Federal law requiring reasonable accommodations and accessibility to goods and services for persons with disabilities.

amenities Elements of a property or its surroundings that contribute to its attractiveness to potential buyers and to owner satisfaction.

amortized loan A loan in which the principal as well as the interest is payable in monthly or other periodic installments over the term of the loan.

annual percentage rate (APR) Rate of interest charged on a loan, calculated to take into account up-front loan fees and points. Usually higher than the *contract interest rate.*

antitrust laws Laws designed to preserve the free enterprise of the open marketplace by making illegal certain private conspiracies and combinations formed to minimize competition.

appeals Complaints made to a higher court requesting the correction of errors in law made by lower courts.

appellate division Courts of appeal.

apportionments Adjustment of the income, expenses or carrying charges of real estate usually computed to the date of closing of title so that the seller pays all expenses to that date.

appraisal An estimate of a property's valuation by an appraiser who is usually presumed to be expert in this work.

Appraisal Institute Largest private organization for professional appraisers.

appreciation An increase in the worth or value of a property due to economic or related causes.

appurtenances Those rights, privileges and improvements that belong to and pass with the transfer of real property but are not necessarily a part of the property, such as rights-of-way, easements and property improvements.

APR *See* annual percentage rate.

ARM *See* adjustable-rate mortgage.

arm's-length transaction A transaction between relative strangers, each trying to do the best for himself or herself.

Army Corps of Engineers Federal body responsible for regulating waterways and drainage.

Article 9A The section of New York State's Real Property Law relating to subdivision.

Article 12A The section of New York State's Real Property Law relating to real estate licenses.

asbestos Commonly-used insulating mineral that becomes toxic when it is exposed and fibers and dust are released into the air.

assemblage The merging of two separate parcels under one owner.

assessed valuation A valuation placed on property by a public officer or a board as a basis for taxation.

assessment The imposition of a tax, charge or levy, usually according to established rates.

assessment roll Public record listing assessed value for all real property in a village, town, city or county.

assignment The transfer in writing of interest in a bond, mortgage, lease or other instrument.

associate broker A broker who chooses to work as a salesperson under the name and supervision of another broker.

assumption of mortgage Acquiring title to property on which there is an existing mortgage and agreeing to be personally liable for the terms and conditions of the mortgage, including payments.

attorney-in-fact A person who has been given a power of attorney on behalf of a grantor. The power must be recorded, and ends on the death of the grantor.

attorney's opinion of title Report in which a lawyer examines and evaluates an abstract of title.

avulsion The removal of land from one owner to another when a stream suddenly changes its channel.

balloon payment The final payment of a mortgage loan that is considerably larger than the required periodic payments because the loan amount was not fully amortized.

bargain and sale deed A deed that carries with it no warranties against liens or other encumbrances but that does imply that the grantor has the right to convey title.

bargain and sale deed with covenant A deed in which the grantor warrants or guarantees the title against defects arising during the period of his or her tenure and ownership of the property but not against defects existing before that time.

basis The cost that the Internal Revenue Service attributes to an owner of an investment property for the purpose of determining annual depreciation and gain or loss on the sale of the asset.

benchmark A permanent reference mark or point established for use by surveyors in measuring differences in elevation. *See* datum.

beneficiary The person who receives or is to receive benefits resulting from certain acts.

bequeath To give or hand down by will; to leave by will.

bequest That which is given by the terms of a will.

bilateral contract A contract in which both parties promise to do something; an exchange of promises.

bill of sale A written instrument given to pass title of personal property from vendor to vendee.

binder An agreement that may accompany an earnest money deposit for the purchase of real property as evidence of the purchaser's good faith and intent to complete the transaction.

biweekly mortgage A loan that is paid in 26 half-month (biweekly) payments each year, resulting in an earlier payoff and lower interest costs over the life of the loan.

black book Offering plan for a cooperative or condominium as accepted for filing by the attorney general and used for marketing.

blanket mortgage A mortgage covering more than one parcel of real estate.

blanket unilateral offer of cooperation A seller's option to agree to a commission split with the selling broker without subagency.

blanket unilateral offer of subagency Traditionally, a seller's automatic consent to subagency by submitting a listing to a MLS.

blockbusting The illegal practice of inducing homeowners to sell their property by making representations regarding the entry or prospective entry of minority persons into the neighborhood.

blue-sky laws Common name for those state and federal laws that regulate the registration and sale of investment securities.

board of directors Elected managing body of a corporation, specifically of a cooperative apartment building.

Board of Fire Underwriters New York state agency responsible for oversight of electrical systems and for enforcing its electrical code.

board of managers Elected managing body of a condominium.

boiler and machinery coverage Insurance policy covering repair and replacement of major equipment and systems such as central air-conditioners and heating plants.

bond The evidence of a personal debt that is secured by a mortgage or other lien on real estate.

boot Money or property given to make up any difference in value or equity between two properties in an *exchange*.

branch office A secondary place of business apart from the principal or main office from which real estate business is conducted.

breach of contract Violation of any terms or conditions in a contract without legal excuse; for example, failure to make a payment when it is due.

bridge loan A short-term loan designed to cover a gap between the sale of one property and the purchase of another (also called a *swing loan, temporary loan* or *interim financing*).

British thermal unit (BTU) A unit of measure of heat that is used to rate air-conditioning and heating equipment capacity. One BTU raises one pound of water one degree Fahrenheit.

broker One who buys and sells for another for a fee. *See also* real estate broker.

broker's agent A broker who assists the listing broker in marketing a property under a formal agency agreement.

brokerage The business of buying and selling for another for a fee.

building codes Regulations established by state and local governments fully stating the structural requirements for building.

building line A line fixed at a certain distance from the front and/or sides of a lot, beyond which no building can project.

building loan agreement An agreement whereby the lender advances money to an owner with partial payments at certain stages of construction.

building permit Written permission from the local government to build or alter a structure.

building-related illness (BRI) Symptoms such as hypersensitivity, asthma and allergic reactions caused by toxic substances and pathogens in a building that remain with the affected individual even when he or she is away from the building. *See* sick building syndrome.

bullet loan A short- or intermediate-term (3 to 5 years) interest-only loan with a balloon payment at the end of the term (also called an *intermediate loan* or *conduit financing*).

bundle of legal rights The concept of land ownership that includes ownership of all legal rights to the land—for example, possession, control within the law and enjoyment.

business interruption insurance Insurance policy coverage against a financial loss resulting from a property's inability to generate income.

buydown A financing technique used to reduce the monthly payments for the first few years of a loan. Funds in the form of discount points are given to the lender by the builder or seller to buy down or lower the effective interest rate paid by the buyer, thus reducing the monthly payments for a set time.

buyer agency An agency relationship in which the broker/agent represents the interests of the buyer.

buyer's broker A broker who has entered into an agreement to represent a buyer (the broker's principal and client) in finding a suitable property.

bylaws Rules and regulations adopted by an association.

cap With an adjustable-rate mortgage, a limit, usually in percentage points, on how much the interest rate or payment might be raised in each adjustment period. For *lifetime cap, see* ceiling.

capital gains Profits realized from the sale of assets such as real estate.

capitalization A mathematical process for estimating the value of a property using a proper rate of return on the investment and the annual net income expected to be produced by the property.

capitalization rate The rate of return a property will produce on the owner's investment.

cash flow The net spendable income from an investment.

casualty insurance Insurance policy coverage against theft, burglary, vandalism, physical damage to systems and health and accident coverage on a specific-risk basis.

caveat emptor A Latin phrase meaning "Let the buyer beware."

CC&Rs Covenants, conditions and restrictions of a condominium or cooperative development.

ceiling With an adjustable-rate mortgage, a limit, usually in percentage points, beyond which the interest rates or monthly payment on a loan may never rise. Sometimes known as a *lifetime cap*.

certificate of compliance (C of C) Verification that a construction project meets certain standards, primarily safety-related.

certificate of occupancy (C of O) Document issued by a municipal authority stating that a building complies with building, health and safety codes and may be occupied.

certificate of title A statement of opinion of title status on a parcel of real property based on an examination of specified public records.

Certified Property Manager (CPM) A real property manager who has completed specific educational requirements, demonstration reports and qualified for the CPM designation, which is granted by the Institute of Real Estate Management of the National Association of REALTORS®.

certiorari proceeding A judicial proceeding seeking higher court review of a lower court's decision in a case or proceeding.

chain of title The conveyance of real property to one owner from another, reaching back to the original grantor.

Chapter 7, Chapter 11, Chapter 13 Different forms of bankruptcy.

chattel Personal property such as household goods or fixtures.

chattel mortgage A mortgage on personal property.

checkers *See* testers.

chlorofluorocarbons (CFCs) Gases produced by propellants once used in aerosol sprays and the common coolant, freon. CFCs are linked to depletion of the earth's ozone layer.

client The principal.

Civil Rights Act of 1866 Federal law that prohibits racial discrimination in the sale and rental of property.

closing date The date on which the buyer takes title to the property.

closing statement A detailed cash accounting of a real estate transaction showing all cash received, all charges and credits made and all cash paid out in the transaction.

cloud on the title An outstanding claim or encumbrance that, if valid, would affect or impair the owner's title.

clustering The grouping of home sites within a subdivision on smaller lots than normal with the remaining land used as common areas.

CMA *See* comparative market analysis.

C of C *See* certificate of compliance.

C of O *See* certificate of occupancy.

Code for Equal Opportunity Professional standard of conduct for fair housing compliance, promulgated by the National Association of REALTORS® (NAR).

coinsurance clause A clause in insurance policies covering real property that requires that the policyholder maintain fire insurance coverage generally equal to at least 80 percent of the property's actual replacement cost.

commercial real estate Business property, including offices, shopping malls, theaters, hotels and parking facilities.

commingling The illegal act of a real estate broker who mixes other people's money with his or her own.

commission Payment to a broker for services rendered, such as in the sale or purchase of real property; usually a percentage of the selling price.

common elements Parts of a property normally in common use by all of the condominium residents.

common law The body of law based on custom, usage and court decisions.

community property A system of property ownership not in effect in New York.

company dollar A broker's net commission income after cooperating brokers and the firm's own salespersons have been paid.

comparables Properties listed in an appraisal report that are substantially equivalent to the subject property. Also called *comps.*

comparative market analysis (CMA) A study, intended to assist an owner in establishing listing price, of recent comparable sales, properties that failed to sell and parcels presently on the market.

competent parties Those recognized by law as being able to contract with others; usually those of legal age and sound mind.

Comprehensive Environmental Response, Compensation, and Liability Act (CERCLA) Enacted in 1980 and reauthorized by the Superfund Amendments and Reauthorization Act of 1986 (SARA), this federal law imposes liability on lenders, occupants, operators and owners for correcting environmental problems discovered on a property.

concrete slab foundation Foundation made of poured concrete and steel rod reinforcement, resting on a waterproof sheet directly on the ground; supported by sunken concrete beams (footings).

condemnation A judicial or administrative proceeding to exercise the power of eminent domain through which a government agency takes private property for public use and compensates the owner.

condominium The absolute ownership of an apartment or a unit (generally in a multiunit building) plus an undivided interest in the ownership of the common elements, which are owned jointly with the other condominium unit owners.

consideration (1) That received by the grantor in exchange for a deed. (2) Something of value that induces a person to enter into a contract. Consideration may be *valuable* (money) or *good* (love and affection).

construction loan *See* interim financing.

constructive eviction Landlord actions that so materially disturb or impair the tenant's enjoyment of the leased premises that the tenant is effectively forced to move out and terminate the lease without liability for any further rent.

constructive notice Notice given to the world by recorded documents. Possession of property is also considered constructive notice.

contents and personal property insurance Coverage of personal property and other building contents when they are not on the insured premises.

contingency A provision in a contract that requires that a certain act be done or a certain event occur before the contract becomes binding.

contract An agreement entered into by two or more legally competent parties by the terms of which one or more of the parties, for a consideration, undertakes to do or refrain from doing some legal act or acts.

contract for deed A contract for the sale of real estate wherein the purchase price is paid in periodic installments by the purchaser, who is in possession of the property even though title is retained by the seller until final payment. Also called an *installment contract* or *land contract.*

conventional loan A loan not insured or guaranteed by a government.

conversions Process by which an existing residential property is changed into a cooperative or condominium.

convertibility An adjustable rate mortgage in which the borrower may elect to change to a fixed-rate mortgage, either whenever current rates are favorable, or at specific set conversion dates.

conveyance The transfer of title of land from one to another. The means or medium by which title to real estate is transferred.

cooperating broker A broker other than the listing broker who is involved in a real estate transaction. In an MLS transaction, a subagent of the seller, unless a declared agent of the buyer.

cooperative A residential multiunit building whose title is held by a corporation owned by and operated for the benefit of persons living within the building, who are the stockholders of the corporation, each possessing a proprietary lease.

co-ownership Ownership by two or more persons.

corporation An entity or organization created by operation of law whose rights of doing business are essentially the same as those of an individual.

corporation franchise tax Tax levied on corporations as a condition of allowing them to do business in New York State.

cost approach The process of estimating the value of property by adding to the estimated land value the appraiser's estimate of the reproduction or replacement cost of the building, less depreciation.

cost basis *See* basis.

counteroffer A new offer made as a reply to an offer received.

county boards of health County-level boards with authority over public health issues, such as sanitary systems, water supplies and food standards.

county planning boards Primarily advisory county agencies that promulgate reporting requirements and standards; county planning boards have greater authority in rural counties.

covenants Agreements written into deeds and other instruments promising performance or nonperformance of certain acts.

covenants, conditions and restructions (CC&Rs) Provision in condominium by-laws restricting the owners' usage of the property.

CPM Certified Property Manager, a designation awarded by the Institute of Real Estate Management.

credit On a closing statement, an amount entered in a person's favor.

criminal law That branch of law defining crimes and providing punishment.

cubic-foot method A technique for estimating building costs per cubic foot.

curvilinear system Street pattern system that integrates major arteries with smaller winding streets and cul-de-sacs.

customer A potential buyer of real estate; should not be confused with a property seller (i.e., listing broker's client).

damages The indemnity recoverable by a person who has sustained an injury, either to person, property or rights, through the act or default of another.

datum Point from which elevations are measured. Mean sea level in New York harbor, or local datums.

DBA "Doing business as"; an assumed business name.

dealer An IRS classification for a person whose business is buying and selling real estate on his or her own account.

debit On a closing statement, a charge or amount a party owes and must pay at the closing.

debt service Mortgage payments, including principal and interest on an amortized loan.

DEC The New York Department of Environmental Conservation.

decedent A person who has died.

declaration A formal statement of intention to establish a condominium.

dedication The voluntary transfer of private property by its owner to the public for some public use such as for streets or schools.

deed A written instrument that, when executed and delivered, conveys title to or an interest in real estate.

deed restriction An imposed restriction in a deed for the purpose of limiting the use of the land by future owners.

default The nonperformance of a duty, whether arising under a contract or otherwise; failure to meet an obligation when due.

deficiency judgment A personal judgment levied against the mortgagor when a foreclosure sale does not produce sufficient funds to pay the mortgage debt in full.

delinquent taxes Unpaid past-due taxes.

delivery and acceptance The transfer of the possession of a thing from one person to another.

demising clause A clause in a lease whereby the landlord (lessor) leases and the tenant (lessee) takes the property.

density zoning Local ordinances that limit the number of housing units that may be built per acre within a subdivision.

Department of Environmental Conservation (DEC) Agency that issues permits for developments in or around a protected wetland or other environmentally-sensitive area.

Department of Housing and Community Renewal The New York State department charged with administering rent regulations.

Department of Housing and Urban Development (HUD) Federal agency that administers the Fair Housing Act of 1968.

Department of Transportation State agency with oversight of New York's highway system.

deposition Sworn testimony that may be used as evidence in a suit or trial.

depreciation In appraisal, a loss of value in property due to any cause, including physical deterioration, functional obsolescence and external (locational) obsolescence.

descent Acquisition of an estate by inheritance in which an heir succeeds to the property by operation of law.

designation An indication of special training and expertise, awarded by various real estate organizations.

determinable fee estate A fee simple estate in which the property automatically reverts to the grantor on the occurrence of a specified event or condition.

developer One who improves land with buildings, usually on a large scale, and sells to homeowners and/or investors.

devise A gift of real property by will; the act of leaving real property by will.

devisee One who receives a bequest of real estate made by will.

devisor One who bequeaths real estate by will.

direct public ownership Land-use control method through which land is owned by the government for such public uses as municipal buildings, parks, schools and roads.

direct sales comparison approach An appraisal method in which a subject property is evaluated in comparison with similar recently sold properties; most useful for single residential properties.

disclosure A broker is responsible for keeping a principal fully informed of all facts that could affect a transaction. If a broker fails to disclose such information, he or she may be liable for any damages that result.

disclosure statement Document that must be filed by the developer of a new or converted condominium or cooperative project, including an architect's or engineer's evaluation of the structure, an expense statement, prices per unit and other financial and administrative information.

discounted cash flow analysis Mathematical model of variables inherent in an investment.

discounting Method for mathematically calculating present value of money, based on time and the discount rate.

discount points An added loan fee charged by a lender to make the yield on a lower-than-market-value loan competitive with higher-interest loans.

discount rate Rate of return needed to compensate an investor for risk; the Federal Reserve's loan rate for eligible banks.

disintermediation A tight-money real estate lending market (in which real estate loans are more difficult to obtain) that results when investors choose to invest in stocks, bonds and mutual funds rather than savings accounts, limiting the funds available to lenders.

disposition Investment strategy for reconciling anticipated gain or loss with the risk involved.

Division of Housing and Community Renewal (DHCR) New York agency that administers rent control and stabilization programs.

documentary evidence Evidence in the form of written or printed papers.

dominant estate A property that includes in its ownership the right to use an easement over another person's property for a specific purpose.

DOS New York Department of State; administers license law.

down payment The amount of cash that a purchaser will pay at closing.

dual agency Representing both parties to a trans action.

due diligence A fair and responsible degree of care.

due-on-sale *See* alienation clause.

duress Unlawful constraint or action exercised on a person who is forced to perform an act against his or her will.

earnest money deposit Money deposited by a buyer under the terms of a contract, to be applied to the purchase price if the sale is closed.

easement A right to use the land of another for a specific purpose, as for a right-of-way or utilities; an incorporeal interest in land. An easement appurtenant passes with the land when conveyed.

easement appurtenant An easement involving adjacent parcels that runs with the land (is permanently attached), so that subsequent owners are bound by it, and it passes with the land when conveyed.

easement by necessity An easement allowed by law as necessary for the full enjoyment of a parcel of real estate; for example, a right of ingress and egress over a grantor's land.

easement by prescription An easement acquired by continuous, open, uninterrupted, exclusive and adverse use of the property for the period of time prescribed by state law.

easement in gross An easement that is not created for the benefit of any *land* owned by the owner of the easement but that attaches *personally to the easement owner.*

economic obsolescence *See* external obsolescence.

electromagnetic field (EMF) Invisible energy fields created by the movement of electrical currents in high tension wires and electrical appliances. EMFs may be responsible for occurrences of cancer, hormonal changes and behavioral disorders.

emblements Growing crops, such as grapes and corn, that are produced annually through labor and industry; also called *fructus industriales.*

eminent domain The right of a government or quasi-public body to acquire property for public use through a court action called *condemnation.*

encroachment A building or some portion of it—a wall or fence, for instance—that extends beyond the land of the owner and illegally intrudes on some land of an adjoining owner or a street or alley.

encumbrance Any claim by another—such as a mortgage, a tax or judgment lien, an easement, an encroachment, or a deed restriction on the use of the land—that may diminish the value of a property.

endorsement An act of signing one's name on the back of a check or note with or without further qualifications.

environmental impact study Report detailing the effect of a proposed development on the existing environment, including possible alternative measures to remedy or repair environmental damage.

Environmental Protection Agency (EPA) A federal agency involved with the problems of air and water pollution, noise, pesticides, radiation and solid-waste management. EPA sets standards, enforces environmental laws, conducts research, allocates funds for sewage-treatment facilities and provides technical, financial and managerial assistance for municipal, regional and state pollution control agencies.

Equal Credit Opportunity Act (ECOA) The federal law that prohibits discrimination in the extension of credit because of race, color, religion, national origin, sex, age or marital status.

equalization The raising or lowering of assessed values for tax purposes in a particular county or taxing district to make them equal to assessments in other counties or districts.

equitable title The interest held by a vendee under a land contract or an installment contract; the equitable right to obtain absolute ownership to property when legal title is held in another's name.

equity The interest or value that an owner has in property over and above any mortgage indebtedness and other liens.

equity of redemption A right of the owner to reclaim property before it is sold through foreclosure by the payment of the debt, interest and costs.

erosion The gradual wearing away of land by water, wind and general weather conditions; the diminishing of property caused by the elements.

errors and omissions insurance A form of malpractice insurance for real estate brokers.

escape clause A provision in a contract that allows one party to unilaterally void the contract with out penalty; for instance, a seller may be allowed to look for a more favorable offer, while the purchaser retains the right to drop all contingencies or void the contract if another offer is received.

escheat The reversion of property to the state or county, as provided by state law, in cases where a person dies intestate without heirs capable of inheriting or when the property is abandoned.

escrow The closing of a transaction through a third party called an *escrow agent*. Also can refer to earnest money deposits or to a mortgagee's trust account for insurance and tax payments.

estate The degree, quantity, nature and extent of interest that a person has in real property.

estate at will The occupation of lands and tenements by a tenant for an indefinite period, terminable by one or both parties at will.

estate for years An interest for a certain, exact period of time in property leased for a specified consideration.

estate in land The degree, quantity, nature and extent of interest a person has in real property.

estate tax Federal tax levied on property transferred upon death.

estoppel certificate A document in which a borrower certifies the amount he or she owes on a mortgage loan and the rate of interest. Often used for *reduction certificate*.

eviction A legal process to oust a person from possession of real estate.

eviction plan Method of converting a rental property into a condominium or cooperative, in which existing tenants will be evicted when their leases expire.

evidence of title Proof of ownership of property; commonly a certificate of title, a title insurance policy, an abstract of title with lawyer's opinion or a Torrens registration certificate.

exchange A transaction in which all or part of the consideration for the purchase of real property is the transfer of *like-kind* property (that is, real estate for real estate).

exclusive-agency listing A listing contract under which the owner appoints a real estate broker as his or her exclusive agent. The owner reserves the right to sell without paying anyone a commission.

exclusive right to sell A listing contract under which the owner appoints a real estate broker as his or her exclusive agent and agrees to pay the broker a commission when the property is sold, whether by the broker, the owner or another broker.

exclusive right to represent The most common form of buyer agency agreement.

executed contract A contract in which all parties have fulfilled their promises and thus performed the contract.

execution The signing and delivery of an instrument. Also, a legal order directing an official to enforce a judgment against the property of a debtor.

Executive Law New York State Human Rights Law.

executor A male person, corporate entity or any other type of organization designated in a will to carry out its provisions.

executory contract A contract under which something remains to be done by one or more of the parties.

executrix A woman appointed to perform the duties of an executor.

express contract An oral or written contract in which the parties state the contract's terms and express their intentions in words.

external obsolescence Reduction in a property's value caused by factors outside the subject property, such as social or environmental forces or objectionable neighboring property.

fair employment laws Laws designed to prevent employers from making their hiring and firing decisions on factors unrelated to job performance.

Fair Housing Amendment Act of 1988 Effective March 12, 1989, this amendment to the federal Fair Housing Act added two more classes protected from discrimination: those physically and mentally handicapped, and those with children under age 18.

Fair Housing Partnership Agreement Voluntary agreement between NAR and HUD to cooperate in identifying fair housing problems, issues and solutions.

Fannie Mae *See* Federal National Mortgage Association (FNMA).

Federal Fair Housing Act of 1968 The federal law that prohibits discrimination in housing based on race, color, religion, sex, handicap, familial status or national origin. Amended in 1988 to include persons with physical and mental disabilities, and those with children under 18.

Federal Home Loan Mortgage Corporation (FHLMC) A corporation established to purchase primarily conventional mortgage loans in the secondary mortgage market.

Federal National Mortgage Association (FNMA) A quasi-government agency established to purchase any kind of mortgage loans in the secondary mortgage market from the primary lenders.

fee appraiser An appraiser who works as an independent contractor, performing appraisal services for various clients.

fee simple estate The maximum possible estate or right of ownership of real property, continuing forever. Sometimes called a *fee* or *fee simple absolute.*

FHA loan A loan insured by the Federal Housing Administration and made by an approved lender in accordance with the FHA's regulations.

fiduciary One in whom trust and confidence is placed; a reference to a broker employed under the terms of a listing contract or buyer agency agreement.

fiduciary relationship A relationship of trust and confidence as between trustee and beneficiary, attorney and client or principal and agent.

financing statement *See* Uniform Commercial Code.

fire and hazard insurance Policy providing coverage for direct loss of or damage to property resulting from fire, storms, hail, smoke or riot.

first substantive contact The point at which agents must disclose and obtain signed acknowlegments of their agency relationships.

fixture An item of personal property that has been converted to real property by being permanently affixed to the realty.

floating slab foundation Type of concrete slab foundation in which the footings and slab are poured separately.

foreclosure A procedure whereby property pledged as security for a debt is sold to pay the debt in the event of default in payments or terms.

franchise An organization that leases a standardized trade name, operating procedures, supplies and referral service to member real estate brokerages.

fraud Deception that causes a person to give up property or a lawful right.

Freddie Mac *See* Federal Home Loan Mortgage Corporation (FHLMC).

freehold estate An estate in land in which ownership is for an indeterminate length of time, in contrast to a leasehold estate.

front foot A standard measurement, one foot wide, of the width of land, applied at the frontage on its street line.

full covenant and warranty deed A deed that provides the greatest protection, in which the grantor makes five legal promises (covenants of seisin, quiet enjoyment, further asurances, warranty forever, against encumbrances) that the grantee's ownership will be unchallenged.

full-value assessment Practice of assessing property at its full value, rather than by a percentage of full value.

functional obsolescence A loss of value to an improvement to real estate due to functional problems, often caused by age or poor design.

future interest A person's present right to an interest in real property that will not result in possession or enjoyment until some time in the future.

gap A defect in the chain of title of a particular parcel of real estate; a missing document or conveyance that raises doubt as to present ownership.

general agent One authorized to act for the principal in a specific range of matters.

general contractor A construction specialist who enters into a formal contract with a landowner or lessee to construct a building or project.

general lien The right of a creditor to have all of a debtor's property—both real and personal—sold to satisfy a debt.

general partnership *See* partnership.

general tax *See* ad valorem tax.

Ginnie Mae *See* Government National Mortgage Association (GNMA).

Government National Mortgage Association (GNMA) A government agency that plays an important role in the secondary mortgage market. It sells mortgage-backed securities that are backed by pools of FHA and VA loans.

grace period Additional time allowed to perform an act or make a payment before a default occurs.

graduated lease A lease that provides for a graduated change at stated intervals in the amount of the rent to be paid; used largely in long-term leases.

grant A sale or gift of real property.

grantee A person who receives a conveyance of real property from the grantor.

granting clause Words in a deed of conveyance that state the grantor's intention to convey the property. This clause is generally worded as "convey and warrant," "grant," "grant, bargain and sell" or the like.

grantor The person transferring title to or an interest in real property to a grantee.

GRI (Graduate, REALTORS® Institute) A professional designation earned by any member of a state-affiliated Board of REALTORS® who completes specific courses approved by the board.

gridiron pattern Street pattern systems that evolved out of the government rectangular survey, featuring a regular grid of straight-line streets and alleys.

gross income Total income from property before any expenses are deducted.

gross income multiplier The figure used as a multiplier of the gross annual income of a property to produce an estimate of the property's value.

gross lease A lease of property under which a landlord pays all property charges regularly incurred through ownership, such as repairs, taxes and insurance.

gross rent multiplier (GRM) A figure used as a multiplier of the gross rental income of a property to produce an estimate of the property's value.

ground lease A lease of land only, on which the tenant usually owns a building or is required to build as specified in the lease. Such leases are usually long-term net leases; the tenant's rights and obligations continue until the lease expires or is terminated through default.

groundwater Surface runoff and underground water systems.

group boycott An agreement among members of a trade to exclude other members from fair participation in the activities of the trade.

habendum clause That part of a deed beginning with the words "to have and to hold" following the granting clause and defining the extent of ownership the grantor is conveying.

hazardous substances Materials such as chemicals, industrial and residential byproducts, biological waste and other pollutants that pose an actual or suspected threat to human health, quality of life and the environment.

heat pump Mechanism that uses heat from outside air to reduce heating and air-conditioning costs.

heir One who might inherit or succeed to an interest in land under the state law of descent when the owner dies without leaving a valid will.

highest and best use That possible use of land that would produce the greatest net income and thereby develop the highest land value.

holding period The time an investment or asset is possessed.

holdover tenancy A tenancy whereby a lessee retains possession of leased property after his or her lease has expired and the landlord, by continuing to accept rent, agrees to the tenant's continued occupancy.

holographic will A will that is written, dated and signed in the testator's handwriting but is not witnessed.

home equity loan A loan (sometimes called a line of credit) under which a property owner uses his or her residence as collateral and can then draw funds up to a prearranged amount against the property.

homeowners' association A nonprofit group of homeowners in a condominium, cooperative or PUD that administers common elements and enforces covenants, conditions and restrictions.

homeowner's insurance policy A standardized package insurance policy that covers a residential real estate owner against financial loss from fire, theft, public liability and other commercial risks.

homestead Land that is owned and occupied as the family home. The right to protect a portion of the value of this land from unsecured judgments for debts.

impact fees Charges levied by a local government to help the community absorb the public costs involved in the development of a new subdivision.

implied contract A contract under which the agreement of the parties is demonstrated by their acts and conduct.

implied creation of a subagency The unintended creation of a fiduciary relationship through an informal cooperation arrangement between brokers.

implied warranty of habitability A theory in landlord/tenant law in which the landlord renting residential property implies that the property is habitable and fit for its intended use.

improvement Any structure erected on a site to enhance the value of the property—buildings, fences, driveways, curbs, sidewalks or sewers.

imputed interest An IRS concept that treats some concessionary low-interest loans as if they had been paid and collected at a statutory rate.

income approach The process of estimating the value of an income-producing property by capitalization of the annual net income expected to be produced by the property during its remaining useful life.

incompetent A person who is unable to manage his or her own affairs by reason of insanity, imbecility or feeblemindedness.

independent contractor Someone retained to perform a certain act but subject to the control and direction of another only as to the end result and not as to the way in which he or she performs the act; contrasted with employee.

index With an adjustable-rate mortgage, a measure of current interest rates, used as a basis for calculating the new rate at the time of adjustment.

industrial real estate Warehouses, factories, land in industrial districts and research facilites (sometimes referred to as *manufacturing property*).

informed consent Agreement to an act based on the full and fair disclosure of all the facts a reasonable person would need in order to make a rational decision.

inheritance tax New York State tax levied on those who inherit property located in the state.

injunction An order issued by a court to restrain one party from doing an act deemed to be unjust to the rights of some other party.

in rem A proceeding against the realty directly as distinguished from a proceeding against a person.

installment contact *See* land contract.

installment sale A method of reporting income received from the sale of real estate when the sales price is paid in two or more installments over two or more years.

instrument A written legal document created to effect the rights of the parties.

interest A charge made by a lender for the use of money.

interest rate The percentage of a sum of money charged for its use.

interim financing A short-term loan usually made during the construction phase of a building project (in this case often referred to as a *construction loan*).

internal rate of return (IRR) Discount rate that, when applied to both positive and negative cash flows, results in zero net present value.

Interstate Land Sales Full Disclosure Act A federal law that regulates the sale of certain real estate in interstate commerce.

intestate The condition of a property owner who dies without leaving a valid will.

involuntary alienation Transfer of real estate without the owner's initiative, as in foreclosure or condemnation.

involuntary bankruptcy A bankruptcy proceeding initiated by one or more of the debtor's creditors.

involuntary lien A lien imposed against property without consent of the owners, i.e., taxes, special assessments.

irrevocable consent An agreement filed by an out-of-state broker stating that suits and actions may be brought against the broker in the state where a license is sought.

joint tenancy Ownership of real estate between two or more parties who have been named in one conveyance as joint tenants. On the death of a joint tenant, his or her interest passes to the surviving joint tenant or tenants.

joint venture The joining of two or more people to conduct a specific business enterprise.

joist and rafter roof Roofing system that relies on sloping timbers supported by a ridge board and made rigid by interconnecting joists.

judgment The formal decision of a court regarding the respective claims of the parties to an action.

jumbo loan A loan that exceeds FNMA and FHLMC maximum loan limit.

junior lien An obligation such as a second mortgage that is subordinate in priority to an existing lien on the same realty.

kickbacks The return of part of the commission as gifts or money to buyers or sellers.

laches Loss of a legal right through undue delay in asserting it.

land The earth's surface, extending downward to the center of the earth and upward infinitely into space.

land contract *See* contract for deed.

landfill A site for the burial, layering and permanent storage of waste material, consisting of alternating layers of waste and topsoil.

landlord One who rents property to another.

last will and testament An instrument executed by an owner to convey the owner's property to specific persons after the owner's death.

latent defects A hidden defect that is not discoverable by ordinary inspection.

law of agency The law that governs the relationships and duties of agents, clients and customers. *See* agent.

lead poisoning Illness, including the impairment of physical and mental development in children and aggravated blood pressure in adults, resulting from the ingestion of lead toxins, primarily in paint or plumbing.

Leaking Underground Storage Tanks (LUST) Federal environmental protection program to protect the nation's groundwater by identifying underground tanks and preventing or correcting leakage of hazardous materials.

lease A written or oral contract between a landlord (the lessor) and a tenant (the lessee) that transfers the right to exclusive possession and use of the landlord's real property to the lessee for a specified period of time and for a stated consideration (rent).

leasehold estate A tenant's right to occupy real estate during the term of a lease; generally considered personal property.

legacy A disposition of money or personal property by will.

legal description A description of a specific parcel of real estate complete enough for an independent surveyor to locate and identify it.

legality of object The requirement that a valid and enforceable contract may not involve an illegal purpose or one that is against public policy.

lessee Tenant.

lessor Landlord.

leverage The use of borrowed money to finance the bulk of an investment.

liability insurance Standard package homeowner's insurance policy coverage for personal injuries to others resulting from the insured's acts or negligence, voluntary medical payments and funeral expenses for accidents sustained by guests or resident employees on the property and physical damage to other's property.

license (1) A privilege or right granted to a person by a state to operate as a real estate broker or salesperson. (2) The revocable permission for a temporary use of land.

lien A right given by law to certain creditors to have their debt paid out of the property of a defaulting debtor, usually by means of a court sale.

lien theory Some states interpret a mortgage as being purely a lien on real property. The mortgagee thus has no right of possession but must foreclose the lien and sell the property if the mortgagor defaults.

life estate An interest in real or personal property that is limited in duration to the lifetime of its owner or some other designated person.

life tenant A person in possession of a life estate.

like-kind property *See* exchange.

limited partnership *See* partnership.

limited liability company (LLC) A hybrid business entity that combines the managerial freedom of partnerships with the limited liability for owner and avoidance of income taxes offered by corporations.

liquidated damages An amount of money, agreed to in advance, that will serve as the total compensation due to the injured party if the other does not comply with the contract's terms.

liquidity The ability to sell an asset and convert it into cash at a price close to its true value in a short period of time.

lis pendens A recorded legal document giving constructive notice that an action affecting a particular property has been filed in court.

listing agreement A contract between a landowner (as principal) and a licensed real estate broker (as agent) by which the broker is employed as agent to sell real estate on the owner's terms within a given time, for which service the landowner agrees to pay a commission or fee.

listing agent The broker with whom a seller enters into a valid listing agreement for the sale of his or her real estate.

littoral rights (1) A landowner's claim to use water in large navigable lakes and oceans adjacent to his or her property. (2) The ownership rights to land bordering these bodies of water up to the high-water mark.

loan servicing The lender's duties in administering a loan, such as collecting payments, accounting and bookkeeping, maintaining records and issuing loan status reports to the borrower.

loan-to-value (LTV) ratio The relationship between the amount of the mortgage loan and the value of the real estate being pledged as collateral.

locational obsolescence *See* external obsolescence.

management agreement Employment contract between property owner and manager, under which the manager assumes the responsibility for administering and maintaining the property as the owner's general agent.

margin With an adjustable-rate mortgage, the number of points over an *index* at which the interest rate is set.

marginal tax rate Percentage at which the last dollar of income is taxed; top tax bracket.

marketable title Good or clear title reasonably free from the risk of litigation over possible defects.

market allocation An agreement among members of a trade to refrain from competition in specific areas.

market analysis Study undertaken by a property manager of the local and regional market, as well as the underlying property itself, to provide information about the economic conditions, supply, demand and similar competing properties.

market data approach *See* direct sales comparison approach.

market price The actual selling price of a property.

market value The probable price a ready, willing, able and informed buyer would pay and a ready, willing, able and informed seller would accept, neither being under any pressure to act.

master plan A comprehensive plan to guide the long-term physical development of a particular area.

maximum base rent (MBR) Under rent control, the maximum rent allowable for an individual unit.

mechanic's lien A statutory lien created in favor of contractors, laborers and material suppliers who have performed work or furnished materials in the erection or repair of a building.

meeting of the minds *See* offer and acceptance.

memorandum of sale A nonbinding information sheet prepared by brokers in some New York localities that states the essential terms of the agreement; the final contract is later drawn up by an attorney.

metes-and-bounds description A legal description of a parcel of land that begins at a well-marked point and follows the boundaries, using direction and distances around the tract, back to the place of beginning.

Metropolitan Transport Authority (MTA) Regional agency with taxing power and jurisdiction over certain air and land rights.

mill One-tenth of one cent. A tax rate of 52 mills would be $.052 tax for each dollar of assessed valuation of a property.

minimum building standards Degree of quality and care mandated by the state; local codes and regulations may require adherence to a higher standard.

minor A person under 18 years of age.

MIP Mortgage insurance premium.

misrepresentation A false statement or concealment of a material fact made with the intent of causing another party to act.

month-to-month tenancy A periodic tenancy; that is, the tenant rents for one period at a time. In the absence of a rental agreement (oral or written), a tenancy is generally considered to be month to month.

monument A fixed natural or artificial object used to establish real estate boundaries for a metes-and-bounds description.

mortgage A conditional transfer or pledge of real estate as security for the payment of a debt. Also, the document creating a mortgage lien.

mortgage bankers Companies that are licensed to make real estate loans that are sold to investors.

mortgage broker An individual who acts as an intermediary between lenders and borrowers for a fee.

mortgagee A lender in a mortgage loan transaction.

mortgage insurance premium (MIP) Lump sum premium for mortgage insurance coverage, payable either in cash at closing or financed over the mortgage term.

mortgage lien A lien or charge on the property of a mortgagor that secures the underlying debt obligations.

mortgage reduction certificate An instrument executed by the mortgagee setting forth the present status and the balance due on the mortgage as of the date of the execution of the instrument.

mortgagor A borrower who conveys his or her property as security for a loan.

multiperil policies Insurance policies offering protection from a range of potential perils, such as fire, hazard, public liability and casualty, in a single policy.

multiple listing service A marketing organization composed of member brokers who agree to share their listings with one another in the hope of procuring ready, willing and able buyers more quickly and efficiently.

negative amortization Gradual building up of a large mortgage debt when payments are not sufficient to cover interest due and reduce the principal.

negative cash flow Negative figure resulting when expenditures on an investment exceed the income it produces.

negligence An unintentional tort caused by failure to exercise reasonable care.

negotiable instrument A signed promise to pay a sum of money.

net lease A lease requiring that the tenant pay not only rent but also some or all costs of maintaining the property, including taxes, insurance, utilities and repairs.

net listing A listing based on the net price the seller will receive if the property is sold. Under a net listing the broker is free to offer the property for sale at any price to increase the commission. Outlawed in New York.

net operating income (NOI) The income projected for an income-producing property after deducting losses for vacancy and collection and operating expenses.

net present value (NPV) Difference between the present value of all positive and negative cash flows.

New York City Department of Environmental Protection (DEP) Local agency with authority over the city's water supply (from its source to local reservoirs), and which ensures that construction projects do not interfere with the watershed.

New York State Division of Human Rights Agency with which a complaint of housing discrimination may file a complaint within one year of the alleged act.

New York Human Rights Law State law prohibiting discrimination in housing.

nonconforming mortgage Flexible loan that does not meet standard uniform underwriting requirements, usually structured for borrowers who have unique credit situations or who wish to purchase an unusual property.

nonconforming use A use of property that is permitted to continue after a zoning ordinance prohibiting it has been established for the area.

noneviction plan Method of converting a rental property into a condominium or cooperative.

nonhomogeneity A lack of uniformity; dissimilarity. Because no two parcels of land are exactly alike, real estate is said to be nonhomogeneous.

notary public A public officer who is authorized to take acknowledgments to certain classes of documents such as deeds, contracts and mortgages and before whom affidavits may be sworn.

note An instrument of credit given to attest a debt.

novation Substituting a new obligation for an old one or substituting new parties to an existing obligation.

nuisance An act that disturbs another's peaceful enjoyment of property.

NYSAR New York State Association of REALTORS®.

obsolescence *See* external obsolescence; functional obsolescence.

offer and acceptance Two essential components of a valid contract; a "meeting of the minds," when all parties agree to the exact terms.

office property Any type of structure (lowrise, highrise, complex or campus) used by such non-manufacturing, non-retail tenants as medical, legal and financial professionals.

open-end mortgage A mortgage loan that is expandable to a maximum dollar amount, the loan being secured by the same original mortgage.

open listing A listing contract under which the broker's commission is contingent on the broker's producing a ready, willing and able buyer before the property is sold by the owner or another broker.

option An agreement to keep open for a set period an offer to sell or purchase property.

package loan A real estate loan used to finance the purchase of both real property and personal property, such as the purchase of a new home that includes carpeting, window coverings and major appliances.

package mortgage A method of financing in which the loan that finances the purchase of a home also finances the purchase of items of personal property such as appliances.

parcel A specific piece of real estate.

parol evidence rule A rule of evidence providing that a written agreement is the final expression of the agreement of the parties, not to be varied or contradicted by prior or contemporaneous oral or written negotiations.

participation financing A mortgage in which the lender participates in the income of the mortgaged venture.

partition The division of real property made between those who own it in undivided shares.

partnership An association of two or more individuals who carry on a continuing business for profit as co-owners. A *general partnership* is a typical form of joint venture in which each general partner shares in the administration, profits and losses of the operations. A *limited partnership* is administered by one or more general partners and funded by limited or silent partners who are by law responsible for losses only to the extent of their investments.

party wall A wall that is located on or at a boundary line between two adjoining parcels of land and is used by the owners of both properties.

passive income Income derived from an investment activity in which the investor does not take an active management or participatory role.

percentage lease A lease commonly used for commercial property whose rental is based on the tenant's gross sales at the premises.

percolation Test of soil's ability to process waste water prior to installing a septic system.

periodic estate An interest in leased property that continues from period to period—week to week, month to month or year to year.

personal property Items, called *chattels*, that do not fit into the definition of real property; movable objects.

personal representative The administrator or executor appointed to handle the estate of a decedent.

physical deterioration Loss of value due to wear and tear or action of the elements.

PITI Principal, interest, taxes and insurance: components of a regular mortgage payment.

pier and beam foundation Foundation style in which partly-submerged columns (piers) support the foundation slab, with an air pocket (crawlspace) between the slab and the ground.

planned unit development (PUD) A planned combination of diverse land uses such as housing, recreation and shopping in one contained development or subdivision.

planning board Municipal body overseeing orderly development of real estate.

plat A map of a town, section or subdivision indicating the location and boundaries of individual properties.

platform framing construction Common form of construction for one- and two-story residential buildings; one floor is built at a time, with the lower floor providing a platform on which the upper floor is built.

plottage The increase in value or utility resulting from the consolidation (assemblage) of two or more adjacent lots into one larger lot.

PMI Private mortgage insurance.

point A unit of measurement used for various loan charges; one point equals 1 percent of the amount of the loan. *See also* discount points.

point of beginning In a metes-and-bounds legal description, the starting point of the survey, situated in one corner of the parcel. Also called *place of beginning.*

police power The government's right to impose laws, statutes and ordinances, including zoning ordinances and building codes, to protect the public health, safety and welfare.

policy and procedures guide A broker's compilation of guidelines for the conduct of the firm's business.

pollution Artificially-created environmental impurity.

polychlorinated biphenyls (PCBs) Potentially hazardous chemical used in electrical equipment, principally transformers.

potentially responsible parties (PRPs) Under Superfund, the landowners suspected of contaminating a property.

power of attorney A written instrument authorizing a person, the *attorney-in-fact,* to act as agent on behalf of another person.

precedent A court decision that serves as authority for later cases.

preliminary prospectus Description of new or converted condominium or cooperative property, subject to change, available for inspection by present tenants after review by the attorney general (also referred to as a red herring).

premises Lands and tenements; an estate; the subject matter of a conveyance.

prepayment clause A clause in a mortgage that gives the mortgagor the privilege of paying the mortgage indebtedness before it becomes due.

prepayment penalty A charge imposed on a borrower who pays off the loan principal early.

present value of money Money's value changes over time: For example, the present value of $1 receivable in one year is $1 minus the lost potential interest on the dollar. If the interest rate is 7 percent, then the present value of $1 to be received in one year is 93¢ today.

price-fixing An agreement between members of a trade to artificially maintain prices at a set level.

primary mortgage market Lenders who make loans directly to real estate borrowers.

principal (1) A sum lent or employed as a fund or an investment as distinguished from its income or profits. (2) The original amount (as in a loan) of the total due and payable at a certain date. (3) A main party of a transaction; the person for whom the agent works.

principal broker *See* supervising broker.

priority The order of position or time.

private mortgage insurance (PMI) Insurance that limits a lender's potential loss in a mortgage default, issued by a private company rather than by the FHA.

probate To establish the will of a deceased person.

procuring cause The effort that brings about the desired result. Under an open listing the broker who is the procuring cause of the sale receives the commission.

professional home inspections Examination of a property's structure and systems performed by a trained professional for either prospective buyers, lenders or home owners.

progression Economic principle that a lower-quality property's worth will be enhanced by its proximity to higher-quality properties.

property manager Someone who manages real estate for another person for compensation.

proprietary lease A written lease in a cooperative apartment building, held by the tenant/shareholder, giving the right to occupy a particular unit.

prorations Expenses, either prepaid or paid in arrears, that are divided or distributed between buyer and seller at the closing.

prospectus A printed statement disclosing all material aspects of a real estate project.

protected classes Groups of individuals who have been found to be in need of protection by federal, state or local laws and regulations against discriminatory actions or conditions.

public offering A transaction falling under the jurisdiction of the New York attorney general's office, requiring certain specific transactional and financial disclosures. The sale of any form of shared housing in New York is a public offering.

PUD *See* planned unit development.

puffing Exaggerated or superlative comments or opinions not made as representations of fact and thus not grounds for misrepresentation.

pur autre vie For the life of another. A life estate pur autre vie is a life estate that is measured by the life of a person other than the grantee.

purchase-money mortgage (PMM) A note secured by a mortgage or deed of trust given by a buyer, as borrower, to a seller, as lender, as part of the purchase price of the real estate.

pyramid Investment strategy of refinancing existing properties and using the borrowed money.

quiet enjoyment The right of an owner or a person legally in possession to the use of property without interference of possession.

quiet title suit *See* suit to quiet title.

quitclaim deed A conveyance by which the grantor transfers whatever interest he or she has in the real estate, if any, without warranties or obligations.

radioactive waste Hazardous by-product of uses of radioactive materials in energy production, medicine and scientific research.

radon gas Odorless, naturally-occurring radioactive gas that becomes hazardous when trapped and accumulated in unventilated areas of buildings. Long-term exposure to radon is suspected of causing lung cancer.

ratification Method of creating an agency relationship in which the principal accepts the conduct of someone who acted without prior authorization as the principal's agent.

ready, willing and able buyer One who is prepared to buy property on the seller's terms and is ready to take positive steps to consummate the transaction.

release The act or writing by which some claim or interest is surrendered to another.

real estate A portion of the earth's surface extending downward to the center of the earth and upward infinitely into space including all things permanently attached thereto, whether by nature or by a person.

real estate broker Any person, partnership, association or corporation that sells (or offers to sell), buys (or offers to buy) or negotiates the purchase, sale or exchange of real estate, or that leases (or offers to lease) or rents (or offers to rent) any real estate or the improvements thereon for others and for a compensation or valuable consideration.

real estate investment syndicate Business organization in which individuals combine their resources to invest in, manage or develop a particular property.

real estate investment trust (REIT) Trust ownership of real estate by a group of individuals who purchase certificates of ownership in the trust.

real estate mortgage investment conduit (REMIC) A tax vehicle created by the Tax Reform Act of 1986 that permits certain entities that deal in pools of mortgages to pass income through to investors.

real estate sales contract A contract for the sale of real estate, in which the purchaser promises to pay the agreed purchase price, and the seller agrees to deliver title to the property.

Real Estate Settlement Procedures Act (RESPA) The federal law that requires certain disclosures to consumers about mortgage loan settlements. The law also prohibits the payment or receipt of kickbacks and certain kinds of referral fees.

real property Real estate plus all the interests, benefits and rights inherent in ownership. Often referred to as *real estate.*

Real Property Law New York law governing the real estate profession, including prohibitions against discrimination in housing.

REALTORS® A registered trademark term reserved for the sole use of active members of local REALTOR® boards affiliated with the National Association of REALTORS®.

reconciliation The final step in the appraisal process, in which the appraiser reconciles the estimates of value received from the direct sales comparison, cost and income approaches to arrive at a final estimate of value for the subject property.

recording The act of entering or recording documents affecting or conveying interests in real estate in the recorder's office established in each county.

rectangular survey system A system established in 1785 by the federal government providing for surveying and describing land outside the 13 original colonies by reference to principal meridians and base lines.

redemption period A period of time established by state law during which a property owner has the right to redeem his or her real estate from a tax sale by paying the sales price, interest and costs.

red herring Preliminary offering plan for a cooperative or condominium project submitted to the attorney general and to tenants and subject to modification.

redlining The illegal practice of a lending institution denying loans or restricting their number for certain areas of a community.

reduction certificate A statement from the lender detailing the amount remaining and currently due on a mortgage, usually sought when a mortgage is being assumed or prepaid (also referred to as an *estoppel certificate*).

regional analysis Study of the economic and demographic character of the larger regional or metropolitan area in which a property is located.

regression Economic principle that the worth of a higher-quality property will be diminished by its proximity to lower-quality properties.

Regulation Z Law requiring credit institutions and advertisers to inform borrowers of the true cost of obtaining credit; commonly called the *Truth-in-Lending Law.*

release The act or writing by which some claim or interest is surrendered to another.

remainder The remnant of an estate that has been conveyed to take effect and be enjoyed after the termination of a prior estate, as when an owner conveys a life estate to one party and the remainder to another.

remainder interest The remnant of an estate that has been conveyed to take effect and be enjoyed after the termination of a prior estate, such as when an owner conveys a life estate to one party and the remainder to another.

remainderman The person who is to receive the property after the death of a life tenant.

rent A fixed, periodic payment made by a tenant of a property to the owner for possession and use, usually by prior agreement of the parties.

rent control State or local regulations restricting the amount of rent that may be charged for particular properties.

rent stabilization Local regulations that stem from the adoption of the Emergency Tenant Protection Act, and which limit maximum allowable rent increases.

replacement cost The construction cost at current prices of a property that is not necessarily an exact duplicate of the subject property but serves the same purpose or function as the original.

reproduction cost The construction cost at current prices of an exact duplicate of the subject property.

reserves Money set aside to accumulate for future expenses.

residential real estate All property used for housing, from acreage to small city lots, both single-family and multifamily, in urban, suburban and rural areas.

restraint of trade The unreasonable restriction of business activities as the result of the cooperation or conspiracy of members of the trade.

restriction A limitation on the use of real property, generally originated by the owner or subdivider in a deed.

retail property Any type of property used for commercial retail purposes, including storefronts, shopping centers and enclosed malls.

return The income from a real estate investment, calculated as a percentage of cash invested.

reverse-annuity mortgage (RAM) A loan under which the homeowner receives monthly payments based on his or her accumulated equity rather than a lump sum. The loan must be repaid at a prearranged date or upon the death of the owner or the sale of the property.

reverse discrimination *(benign discrimination)* Housing discrimination, usually based on quotas, designed by a municipality to achieve a racial balance perceived as desirable.

reversion The remnant of an estate that the grantor holds after he or she has granted a life estate to another person, if the estate will return, or revert, to the grantor; also called a *reverter*.

reversionary right The return of the rights of possession and quiet enjoyment to the lessor at the expiration of a lease.

reversionary interest The remnant of an estate that the grantor holds after he or she has granted a life estate to another person, if the estate will return, or revert, to the grantor; also called a *reverter*.

revocation An act of recalling a power of authority conferred, such as the revocation of a power of attorney, a license or an agency.

right of survivorship *See* joint tenancy.

right-of-way The right to pass over another's land more or less frequently according to the nature of the easement.

riparian rights An owner's rights in land that borders on or includes a stream, river, lake or sea. These rights include access to and use of the water.

R-value Numerical measurement of insulating material's resistance to heat transfer; a higher R-value indicates superior insulation.

Safe Drinking Water Act Federal law requiring local public water suppliers to periodically test the quality of drinking water.

sale and leaseback A transaction in which an owner sells his or her improved property and, as part of the same transaction, signs a long-term lease to remain in possession of the premises.

sales comparison approach The process of estimating the value of a property by examining and comparing actual sales of comparable properties.

sales contract A contract containing the complete terms of the agreement between buyer and seller for the sale of a particular parcel of real estate.

salesperson A person who performs real estate activities while employed by or associated with a licensed real estate broker.

satisfaction piece A document acknowledging the payment of a debt. Also called *satisfaction of mortgage.*

S corporation A form of corporation taxed as a partnership.

secondary mortgage market A market for the purchase and sale of existing mortgages, designed to provide greater liquidity of mortgages.

section A portion of a township under the rectangular survey (government survey) system. A section is a square with mile-long sides and an area of one square mile, or 640 acres.

Section 8 Federal housing assistance program administered by the FHA, in which low- and moderate-income tenants pay a fixed portion of their income in rent, with HUD paying the remainder.

Section 1031 property exchange A tax-deferred exchange of like-kind investment or commercial property.

security deposit A payment by a tenant, held by the landlord during the lease term and kept (wholly or partially) on default or destruction of the premises by the tenant.

seisin The possession of land by one who claims to own at least an estate for life therein.

self-dealing The act of a broker who lists property and then buys it and collects the agreed-on commission.

selling broker The broker who successfully finds a ready, willing and able buyer for a property (may or may not be the listing broker).

septic system Wastewater treatment and disposal system used by individual households.

servient tenement Land on which an easement exists in favor of an adjacent property (called a *dominant estate*); also called *servient estate.*

setback The amount of space local zoning regulations require between a lot line and a building line.

severalty Ownership of real property by one person only; also called *sole ownership.*

shared-appreciation mortgage A mortgage loan in which the lender, in exchange for a loan with a favorable interest rate, participates in the profits (if any) when the property is eventually sold.

sick building syndrome (SBS) Range of symptoms, such as asthma, coughing and hoarseness, that are related to the individual's presence in the affected building, but that disappear when he or she is not exposed to the building's environment. *See* building-related illness.

single agency An agency relationship in which the agent represents a single party.

situs The location of a property.

small claims court A special local court for settling disputes without the need for attorneys or expensive court costs.

solar energy Use of solar collectors to convert heat from the sun into usable heat and energy for a building.

sole proprietorship A business owned by one individual.

Sonny Mae (SONYMA) The state of New York Mortgage Agency.

special agent One authorized by a principal to perform a single act or transaction.

special assessment A tax or levy customarily imposed against only those specific parcels of real estate that will benefit from a proposed public improvement like a street or sewer.

special purpose real estate Religious institutions, schools, cemeteries, hospitals and government-held land.

special-use permit Permission granted by a local government to allow a use of property that, although in conflict with zoning regulations, is nonetheless in the public interest (a house of worship in a residential neighborhood, for instance, or a restaurant in an industrial zone).

special warranty deed A deed in which the grantor warrants, or guarantees, the title only against defects arising during the period of his or her tenure and ownership of the property and not against defects existing before that time, generally using the language "by, through or under the grantor but not otherwise."

specific lien A lien affecting or attaching only to a certain specific parcel of land or piece of property.

specific performance suit A legal action brought in a court of equity in special cases to compel a party to carry out the terms of a contract.

sponsor The developer or owner organizing and offering for sale a condominium or cooperative development.

spot zoning Special zoning actions that affect only a small area. Uses that are not in harmony with the surrounding uses are illegal in New York.

staff appraiser A professional appraiser employed in-house to perform appraisals solely for the employer.

statute of frauds The part of state law requiring that certain instruments, such as deeds, real estate sales contracts and certain leases, be in writing to be legally enforceable.

statute of limitations That law pertaining to the period of time within which certain actions must be brought to court; in New York, six years for contracts.

statutory lien A lien imposed on property by statute—a tax lien, for example—in contrast to a voluntary lien such as a mortgage lien that an owner places on his or her own real estate.

statutory redemption The right of a defaulted property owner to recover the property after its sale by paying the appropriate fees and charges.

steering The illegal practice of channeling home seekers to particular areas for discriminatory ends.

straight-line method A method of calculating cost recovery for tax purposes, computed by dividing the adjusted basis of a property by the number of years chosen.

straight (term) loan A loan in which only interest is paid during the term of the loan, with the entire principal amount due with the final interest payment.

subagency An agency relationship in which the broker's sales associate, or a cooperating broker, assumes a fiduciary duty to the principal who has designated the broker as an agent.

subagent A broker's sales associate in relation to the principal who has designated the broker as an agent.

subchapter S corporation *See* S corporation.

subcontractor *See* general contractor.

subdivision A tract of land divided by the owner, known as the *subdivider,* into blocks, building lots and streets according to a recorded subdivision plat.

subject property The property being appraised.

subject to a mortgage When a property is taken "subject to" a mortgage, the purchaser is not personally liable to the mortgagee for satisfaction of the pre-existing debt (unless he or she agrees to be held liable).

sublease *See* subletting.

subletting The leasing of premises by a tenant to a third party for part of the tenant's remaining term. *See also* assignment.

subordination agreement Relegation to a lesser position, usually in respect to a right or security.

subrogation The substitution of one creditor for another with the substituted person succeeding to the legal rights and claims of the original claimant.

subscribing witness One who writes his or her name as witness to the execution of an instrument.

substitution An appraisal principle stating that the maximum value of a property tends to be set by the cost of purchasing an equally desirable and valuable substitute property.

subsurface rights Ownership rights in a parcel of real estate of any water, minerals, gas, oil and so forth that lie beneath the surface of the property.

suit for possession A court suit initiated by a landlord to evict a tenant from leased premises after the tenant has breached one of the terms of the lease or has held possession of the property after the lease's expiration.

suit to quiet title A court action intended to establish or settle the title to a particular property, especially when there is a cloud on the title.

Superfund Amendments and Reauthorization Act (SARA) Federal law defining landowner responsibility for cleanup of environmental contamination resulting from past activities. Establishes innocent landowner defense against liability for contamination caused by prior owners.

supervising broker The one broker registered with the Department of State as in charge of a real estate office, responsible for the actions of salespersons and associate brokers.

surety bond Bond covering an owner against financial losses resulting from the criminal acts or negligence of an employee in the course of performing his or her job.

surface rights Ownership rights in a parcel of real estate that are limited to the surface of the property and do not include the air above it (air rights) or the minerals below the surface (subsurface rights).

surrender The cancellation of a lease by mutual consent of the lessor and the lessee.

surrogate's court (probate court) A court having jurisdiction over the proof of wills, the settling of estates and adoptions.

survey The process by which a parcel of land is measured and its area ascertained; also, the map showing the measurements, boundaries and area.

suspension or revocation The action of punishing violations of the license law by recalling a license temporarily (*suspension*) or permanently (*revocation*).

swing loan A short term loan similar to a bridge loan that uses the strength of the borrower's equity in the property he or she is selling, to purchase a new property.

syndicate A combination of people or firms formed to accomplish a joint venture of mutual interest.

tacking Adding or combining successive periods of continuous occupation of real property by several different adverse possessors.

takeout loan A loan commitment obtained prior to a lender extending a construction loan, under the terms of which the takeout lender will pay off the construction loan once the work is finished. Provides assurance for the construction lender that the initial short-term loan will be satisfied.

taxation The process by which a government or municipal quasi-public body raises monies to fund its operation.

tax credit A direct reduction in tax payable, as opposed to a deduciton from income.

tax deed An instrument, similar to a certificate of sale, given to a purchaser at a tax sale.

tax foreclosure Legal proceeding (comparable to a private mortgage foreclosure) brought by a taxing body against the property itself (*in rem*); former owner loses all rights and claims.

tax lien A charge against property created by operation of law. Tax liens and assessments take priority over all other liens.

tax rate The rate at which real property is taxed in a tax district or county. For example, real property may be taxed at a rate of .056 cents per dollar of assessed valuation (56 mills).

tax sale A court-ordered sale of real property to raise money to cover delinquent taxes.

tenancy at will An estate that gives the lessee the right to possession until the estate is terminated by either party; the term of this estate is indefinite.

tenancy by the entirety The joint ownership acquired by husband and wife during marriage. Upon the death of one spouse, the survivor becomes the owner of the property.

tenancy in common A form of co-ownership by which each owner holds an undivided interest in real property as if he or she were sole owner. Each individual owner has the right to partition. Tenants in common have no right of survivorship.

tenant One who holds or possesses lands or tenements by any kind of right or title.

tenant at sufferance One who comes into possession of land by lawful title and keeps it afterward without any title at all.

term The originally scheduled period of time over which a loan is to be paid.

termites Wood-boring insects whose presence causes structural damage.

testate Having made and left a valid will.

testator The (male) maker of a valid will.

testatrix The (female) maker of a valid will.

testers Members of civil rights and neighborhood organizations, often volunteers, who observe real estate offices to assess compliance with fair housing laws.

tie-in arrangement An arrangement by which provision of certain products or services is made contingent on the purchase of other, unrelated products or services.

time is of the essence A phrase in a contract that requires the performance of a certain act within a stated period of time.

time-sharing Undivided ownership of real estate for only a portion of the year.

title Evidence that the owner of land is in lawful possession thereof; evidence of ownership.

title insurance A policy insuring the owner or mortgagee against loss by reason of defects in the title to a parcel of real estate, other than the encumbrances, defects and matters specifically excluded by the policy.

title search An examination of the public records to determine the ownership and encumbrances affecting real property.

title theory Some states interpret a mortgage to mean that the lender is the owner of mortgaged land. Upon full payment of the mortgage debt the borrower becomes the landowner.

Torrens system A method of evidencing title by registration with the proper public authority, generally called the *registrar*.

tort A civil wrong done by one person against another.

town house A hybrid form of real estate ownership in which the owner has fee simple title to the living unit and land below it, plus a fractional interest in common elements.

township The principal unit of the rectangular survey (government survey) system, a square with six-mile sides and an area of 36 square miles.

trade fixtures Articles installed by a tenant under the terms of a lease and removable by the tenant before the lease expires.

transfer tax Tax stamps required to be affixed to a deed by state and/or local law.

trespass An unlawful intrusion on another's property.

true tax Actual taxes payable for a property after all exemptions and reductions for which the property or its owner is qualified.

truss roof Particularly strong roofing system composed of chords, diagonals and gusset plates, pre-assembled at a mill.

trust A fiduciary arrangement whereby property is conveyed to a person or an institution, called a *trustee*, to be held and administered on behalf of another person, called a *beneficiary*.

trust account Escrow account for money belonging to another.

trust deed An instrument used to create a mortgage lien by which the mortgagor conveys his or her title to a trustee, who holds it as security for the benefit of the note holder (the lender); also called a *deed of trust*.

trustee *See* trust.

trustor The individual who establishes a trust.

umbrella policy An insurance policy that covers additional risk beyond several underlying policies.

underground storage tanks Buried containers used for storage or disposal of chemicals, fuel and gas that pose an actual or potential environmental hazard in the event of a leak.

underwriting The process by which a lender evaluates a prospective borrower's application through verification of employment and financial information and analysis of credit and appraisal reports.

undisclosed dual agency Representation of both principal parties in the same transaction without full written disclosure to and approval of all parties.

undivided interest *See* tenancy in common.

unenforceable contract A contract that seems on the surface to be valid, yet neither party can sue the other to force performance of it.

Uniform Commercial Code A codification of commercial law, adopted in most states, that attempts to make uniform all laws relating to commercial transactions, including chattel mortgages and bulk transfers.

Uniform Settlement Statement (HUD Form 1) A special form designed to detail all financial particulars of a transaction.

unilateral contract A one-sided contract wherein one party makes a promise so as to induce a second party to do something. The second party is not legally bound to perform; however, if the second party does comply, the first party is obligated to keep the promise.

unity of ownership The four unities traditionally needed to create a joint tenancy: unity of title, time, interest and possession.

universal agent One empowered by a principal to represent him or her in all matters that can be delegated.

usury Charging interest at a rate higher than the maximum established by law.

valid contract A contract that complies with all the essentials of a contract and is binding and enforceable on all parties to it.

VA loan A mortgage loan on approved property made to a qualified veteran by an authorized lender and guaranteed by the Department of Veterans Affairs to limit the lender's possible loss.

valuation Estimated worth or price. The act of valuing by appraisal.

value The power of a good or service to command other goods in exchange for the present worth of future rights to its income or amenities.

variance Permission obtained from zoning authorities to build a structure or conduct a use that is expressly prohibited by the current zoning laws; an exception from the zoning ordinances.

vendee A buyer under a land contract or contract of sale.

vendor A seller under a land contract or contract of sale.

vicarious liability Liability that is created not because of a person's actions but because of the relationship between the liable person and other parties.

voidable contract A contract that seems to be valid on the surface but that may be rejected or disaffirmed by one of the parties.

void contract A contract that has no legal force or effect because it does not meet the essential elements of a contract.

voluntary alienation Transfer of title by gift or sale according to the owner's wishes.

voluntary lien A lien created by the owner's voluntary action, such as a mortgage.

waiver The renunciation, abandonment or surrender of some claim, right or privilege.

warranty deed A deed in which the grantor fully warrants good clear title to the premises.

waste An improper use or an abuse of a property by a possessor who holds less than fee ownership, such as a tenant, life tenant, mortgagor or vendee.

wetland survey An intensive examination of property, coordinated by the U.S. Army Corps of Engineers, to determine whether or not it should be classified and protected as a wetland.

will A written document, properly witnessed, providing for the transfer of title to property owned by the deceased, called the *testator*.

without recourse Words used in endorsing a note or bill to denote that the future holder is not to look to the endorser in case of nonpayment.

wraparound loan A method of refinancing in which the new mortgage is placed in a secondary, or subordinate, position; the new mortgage includes both the unpaid principal balance of the first mortgage and whatever additional sums are advanced by the lender. In essence it is an additional mortgage in which another lender refinances a borrower by lending an amount over the existing first mortgage amount without disturbing the existence of the first mortgage.

wraparound mortgage An additional mortgage in which another lender refinances a borrower by lending an amount including the existing first mortgage amount without disturbing the existence of the first mortgage.

year-to-year tenancy A periodic tenancy in which rent is collected from year to year.

zone An area set off by the proper authorities for specific use subject to certain restrictions or restraints.

zoning boards of appeal Official local government bodies established to hear complaints about the impact of zoning ordinances on individual properties, and to consider variances and special-use permits.

zoning ordinances An exercise of police power by a municipality to regulate and control the character and use of property.

Answer Key

▼ CHAPTER 1
License Law

1. c
2. d
3. c
4. c
5. b
6. d
7. c
8. b
9. d
10. c
11. b
12. d
13. a
14. b
15. c
16. a
17. b
18. c
19. b
20. d
21. b
22. a

▼ CHAPTER 2
Law of Agency

1. a
2. b
3. b
4. b
5. c
6. c
7. c
8. c
9. d
10. d
11. b
12. c
13. c

14. c
15. a
16. d

▼ CHAPTER 3
Types of Agency

1. d
2. b
3. c
4. a
5. b
6. d
7. d
8. c
9. c
10. d
11. d
12. a
13. a
14. c

▼ CHAPTER 4
Business of Real Estate Brokerage

1. d
2. c
3. b
4. a
5. c
6. b
7. c
8. d
9. d
10. a
11. d
12. c
13. c
14. d

▼ CHAPTER 5
Estates and Interests

1. b
2. d
3. b
4. b
5. c
6. c
7. a
8. c
9. c
10. c
11. a
12. b
13. d
14. b
15. a
16. b
17. b
18. a
19. b
20. b
21. b
22. b
23. b
24. b
25. a

▼ CHAPTER 6
Liens and Easements

1. b
2. b
3. b
4. a
5. c
6. a
7. d
8. d
9. a

10. b
11. d
12. d
13. b
14. d
15. b
16. a
17. d
18. a
19. a
20. a
21. a

▼ CHAPTER 7
Real Estate Instruments: Deeds

1. a
2. c
3. d
4. d
5. c
6. a
7. c
8. b
9. b
10. b
11. b
12. b
13. a

▼ CHAPTER 8
Real Estate Instruments: Leases

1. b
2. a
3. c
4. d
5. d
6. c

7. d
8. d
9. c
10. b
11. d
12. c
13. d
14. a
15. b
16. a
17. a
18. b

▼ **CHAPTER 9**
Real Estate
Instruments:
Contracts

1. b
2. b
3. d
4. c
5. b
6. a
7. b
8. d
9. c
10. c
11. d
12. c
13. a
14. d
15. d
16. b
17. b
18. b
19. a
20. d
21. c
22. b
23. b
24. d
25. c

▼ **CHAPTER 10**
Title Closings
and Costs

1. a
2. a
3. c
4. a
5. d
6. d
7. b

8. c
9. c
10. a
11. d
12. d
13. c
14. d
15. c
16. b
17. b
18. c
19. a
20. b
21. b
22. d
23. a
24. a
25. c

▼ **CHAPTER 11**
Real Estate Finance I

1. b
2. a
3. d
4. c
5. b
6. a
7. c
8. a
9. d
10. c

▼ **CHAPTER 12**
Real Estate
Finance II

1. d
2. a
3. c
4. d
5. b
6. b
7. d
8. b
9. c
10. b
11. a
12. a
13. b

▼ **CHAPTER 13**
Land-Use
Regulations

1. a
2. d
3. c
4. b
5. b
6. c
7. a
8. b
9. a
10. c
11. b
12. c
13. b
14. a
15. c
16. a

▼ **CHAPTER 14**
Construction I

1. d
2. d
3. a
4. c
5. d
6. a
7. b
8. a
9. d
10. a
11. a
12. b
13. a
14. c
15. c
16. b
17. a

▼ **CHAPTER 15**
Valuation

1. a
2. c
3. a
4. b
5. d
6. a
7. c
8. d
9. d
10. d

11. d
12. c

▼ **CHAPTER 16**
Human Rights
and Fair Housing

1. c
2. a
3. c
4. d
5. b
6. c
7. b
8. c
9. b
10. a
11. a
12. a
13. b
14. a
15. c
16. d
17. d
18. a
19. d
20. d
21. a

▼ **CHAPTER 17**
Environmental
Issues

1. d
2. c
3. c
4. a
5. a
6. b
7. a
8. d
9. c
10. b
11. b
12. c
13. b

▼ **CHAPTER 18**
Real Estate
Investment

1. a
2. c
3. b
4. b

5. a
6. c
7. b
8. d
9. c
10. a
11. c
12. a
13. d
14. c
15. d
16. c
17. c
18. a
19. b
20. a
21. c
22. b
23. d
24. b
25. a

▼ CHAPTER 19
Property Management

1. d
2. d
3. b
4. d
5. d
6. c
7. a
8. d
9. c
10. b

11. c
12. c
13. c
14. d
15. d
16. b
17. a
18. c

▼ CHAPTER 20
Conveyance of Real Property

1. c
2. d
3. b
4. d
5. b
6. a
7. c
8. c
9. a
10. d

▼ CHAPTER 21
Subdivision and Development

1. d
2. b
3. a
4. d
5. c
6. d
7. c
8. d

9. b
10. b
11. b
12. a
13. b
14. a
15. a
16. b
17. d
18. d
19. c
20. a

▼ CHAPTER 22
Taxes and Assessment

1. d
2. c
3. b
4. b
5. c
6. a
7. c
8. b
9. a
10. a

▼ CHAPTER 23
Appraisal

1. c
2. a
3. d
4. c
5. d

6. b
7. d
8. a
9. d
10. b
11. d
12. a
13. d
14. c
15. c
16. b
17. d
18. a
19. c
20. d
21. d
22. c
23. a
24. d
25. c

▼ CHAPTER 24
Construction II

1. b
2. d
3. d
4. b
5. b
6. a
7. d
8. a
9. c
10. c

▼ **APPENDIX A**
Real Estate Mathematics

1. **b. 180 feet**
   1,200 square yards × 9 = 10,800 square feet

   area = length × width
   10,800 = length × 60
   10,800 ÷ 60 = 180 feet

2. **d. $2,900**
   $25,000 × 3% = $25,000 × .03 = $750

   $68,000 − $25,000 = $43,000 remaining
   purchase price
   $43,000 × 5% = $43,000 × .05 = $2,150
   $750 + $2,150 = $2,900 total down payment

3. **c. 21**
   120 feet ÷ 6 feet per section = 20 sections
   One fence post must be added to anchor the
   other end

   20 + 1 = 21 fence posts

4. **c. $950.40**
   $198,000 × 80% = $198,000 × .80 = $158,400
   insured value

   $158,400 ÷ 1,000 = 158.4 thousands
   158.4 × $6 per thousand = $950.40

5. **a. $80,000**
   $74,000 + $1,200 = $75,200 sales price less
   commission

   $75,200 = 94% of sales price
   $75,200 ÷ .94 = $80,000 sales price

6. **b. $1,330**
   $57,000 ÷ 12 = $4,750 monthly income

   $4,750 × .28 = $1,330 permissible mortgage
   payment

7. **a. $4,620**
   $154,000 × .06 = $9,240 total commission

   $9,240 × .50 = $4,620 Sally's share

8. **a. $808.54**
   $1,800 ÷ 12 = $150 monthly property taxes

   $365 ÷ 12 = $30.42 monthly ins. premium
   $150 + $30.42 + $628.12 = $808.54 total monthly
   payment

9. **c. $36,000**
   120 front feet × $300 = $36,000 sales price

10. **b. 726 feet**
    43,560 feet per acre × 5 = 217,800 square feet

    217,800 ÷ 300 = 726 feet depth

11. **b. $1,550.25**
    $79,500 sales price × 6½% commission =

    $79,500 × .065 = $5,167.50 Happy Valley's
    commission
    $5,167.50 × 30% or $5,167.50 × .30 = $1,550.25
    listing salesperson's commission

12. **c. $277.16**
    12′ × 9.5′ = 114 square feet, area of rectangle

    ½ (3′ × 9.5′) = ½ (28.5) = 14.25 square feet, area
    of triangle
    114 + 14.25 = 128.25 square feet

To convert square feet to square yards divide by 9:

    128.25 ÷ 9 = 14.25 square yards
    $16.95 carpet + $2.50 installation = $19.45 cost
    per square yard
    $19.45 × 14.25 square yards = $277.1625
    rounded to $277.16

13. **a. 20%**
    $30,000 Hal + $35,000 Olive + $35,000 Ron =
    $100,000

    $125,000 − $100,000 = $25,000 Marvin's
    contribution
    part ÷ whole = percent
    $25,000 ÷ $125,000 = .20, or 20%

14. **b. $40,843.83**
    391.42 × 12 = $4,697.04, annual interest

    part ÷ whole = percent
    $4,697.04 ÷ 11½% or $4,697.04 ÷ .115 =
    $40,843.826

15. **a. $103,425**
    $98,500 × 5% = $98,500 × .05 = $4,925, annual
    increase in value

    $98,500 + $4,925 = $103,425, current market
    value

16. **d. $135.38**
    $95,000 × 60% or $95,000 × .60 = $57,000, assessed value

    divided by 1,000 because tax rate is stated per thousand dollars
    $57,000 ÷ 1,000 = 57
    57 × $28.50 = $1,624.50, annual taxes
    divide by 12 to get monthly taxes
    $1,624.50 ÷ 12 = $135.375

17. **d. 195 cubic feet**
    22′ × 15′ = 330 square feet, area of rectangle

    ½ (4′ × 15′) = ½ (60) = 30 square feet, area of each triangle
    30 × 2 = 60 square feet, area of two triangles
    330 + 60 = 390 square feet, surface area to be paved
    6′ deep = ½ foot
    390 × ½ = 195 cubic feet, cement needed for patio

18. **b. $127,000**
    $3,675 − $500 salary = $3,175 commission on sales

    $3,175 ÷ 2.5% = $3,175 ÷ .025 = $127,000, value of property sold

19. **c. $1,615.88**
    two sides of 95′ plus one side of 42′6″

    95′ × 2 = 190 feet
    42′6″ = 42.5 feet
    190 + 42.5 = 232.5 linear feet
    232.5 × $6.95 = $1,615.875

20. **a. $675,000**
    $4,500 × 12 = $54,000 annual rental

    $54,000 ÷ 8% or $54,000 ÷ .08 = $675,000, original cost of property

21. **c. 27,225 square feet**
    100 acres × 43,560 square feet per acre = 4,356,000 total square feet

    4,356,000 × ⅞ available for lots = 3,811,500 square feet
    3,811,500 ÷ 140 lots = 27,225 square feet per lot

22. **a. $173.33**
    $975 ÷ 12 months = $81.25/month's property tax

    $81.25 ÷ 30 days = $2.708 day's property tax
    $81.25 × 2 months = $162.50
    $2.708 × 4 days = $10.832
    $162.50 + $10.832 = $173.332 rounded to $173.33, prepaid unused tax

23. **b. $488.97**
    $61,550 × 13% = $61,550 × .13 = 58,001.50 annual interest

    $8,001.50 ÷ 12 months = $666.792/month's interest
    $666.792 ÷ 30 days = $22.226/day's interest
    $22.226 × 22 days = $488.972 rounded to $488.97 unpaid back interest

24. **a. $235,000**
    $14,100 commission ÷ 6% commission rate = $14,100 ÷ .06 = $235,000 sales price

25. **b. $242,842.40**
    30 years × 12 months = 360 payments

    360 payments × $952.34 = $342,842.40 total payments for principal and interest
    $342,842.40 total payments − $100,000 principal
    repayment = $242,842.40 total interest paid

26. **c. four years, nine months**
    Two points on a $90,000 loan = $90,000 × .02 or 2 percent = $1,800 paid in points

    $817.85 − $786.35 = $31.50 saved each month with lower payment
    $1,800 ÷ $31.50 = 57.14 months to recoup the payment of points
    57.14 months = 4 years, 9 months

27. **c. $2,600 more at closing**
    $80,000 × 3 percent or .03 = $2,400 payment for points

    $100,000 − $95,000 = $5,000 received with the higher offer
    $5,000 − $2,400 payment for points = $2,600 realized with the higher offer after payment of points

▼ SALESPERSON'S REVIEW EXAMINATION

The subject and chapter reference precedes each block of questions for easy reference.

License Law and Regulations, Chapter 1

1. b
2. a
3. c
4. d
5. c
6. b
7. c
8. d
9. d
10. b

Law of Agency, Chapters 2, 3 and 4

11. b
12. b
13. a
14. c
15. b
16. d
17. a
18. a
19. d
20. d
21. c
22. a
23. b
24. c
25. a
26. c
27. c
28. c
29. b
30. c
31. a
32. d
33. b
34. d
35. d
36. b
37. b
38. d
39. c

Estates and Interests, Chapters 5

40. c
41. b
42. d
43. b
44. d

Liens and Easements, Chapter 6

45. a
46. a
47. a

Deeds, Chapter 7

48. a
49. c
50. d

Leases, Chapter 8

51. d
52. a
53. c
54. b
55. c

Contracts, Chapter 9

56. c
57. c
58. c
59. a

Title Closing and Costs, Chapter 10

60. d
61. c
62. a
63. c

Financing, Chapters 11 and 12

64. b
65. b
66. a
67. b
68. b

69. b
70. c
71. d
72. b
73. a

Land-Use Regulations, Chapter 13

74. d
75. b
76. a
77. b
78. c

Construction I, Chapter 14

79. a
80. d
81. b
82. a
83. d

Valuation, Chapter 15

84. c
85. b
86. d
87. b

Human Rights and Fair Housing, Chapter 16

88. c
89. a
90. c
91. b
92. b
93. c
94. d
95. c

Environmental Issues, Chapter 17

96. c
97. a
98. c
99. d
100. a

▼ **BROKER'S PRACTICE EXAMINATION**

1. a Broker's license law
2. b Broker's agency
3. b Broker's agency
4. d Broker's agency
5. c Broker's agency
6. a Broker's license law
7. b Broker's agency
8. b Broker's agency
9. c Broker's agency
10. c Broker's license law
11. c Broker's agency
12. c Broker's license law
13. b Broker's license law
14. b Broker's license law
15. d Broker's agency
16. b Broker's license law
17. c Broker's license law
18. b Broker's agency/license law
19. d Financing/advertising
20. b Financing/advertising
21. b Financing
22. b Financing
23. c Financing
24. b Financing
25. b Financing
26. a Financing
27. a Investments
28. c Investments
29. d Investments
30. d Investments
31. c Investments
32. a Investments
33. c Investments
34. a Leases
35. a Leases
36. d Property management/license law
37. c Property management
38. a Property management
39. d Property management
40. b Property management/estates and interests
41. b Property management/leases
42. d Property management
43. b Property management
44. c Conveyance of real property
45. d Conveyance of real property
46. b Conveyance of real property
47. a Conveyance of real property
48. c Conveyance of real property
49. d Conveyance of real property
50. c Subdivision and development
51. b Subdivision and development
52. a Subdivision and development
53. a Subdivision and development
54. c Subdivision and development
55. b Subdivision and development
56. c Subdivision and development
57. d Taxes and assessments
58. d Taxes and assessments
59. c Taxes and assessments
60. b Taxes and assessments
61. a Taxes and assessments
62. b Closings and closing costs
63. c Closings and closing costs
64. a Closings/taxes
65. b Closings/financing
66. b Appraisal
67. c Appraisal
68. b Appraisal
69. d Appraisal
70. a Appraisal
71. b Appraisal
72. b Construction/land use
73. c Construction/land use
74. d Construction
75. c Construction/subdivisions
76. d Construction/investments
77. b Construction
78. a Construction
79. b Construction/environmental
80. d Construction/fair housing/property management
81. a Construction
82. d Construction
83. b Construction/agency
84. b Fair housing
85. a Fair housing
86. d Fair housing
87. c Fair housing
88. d Land use
89. b Land use
90. b Liens and easements
91. c Liens and easements
92. b Liens and easements
93. a Contracts
94. a Contracts
95. c Contracts
96. b Contracts
97. a Deeds
98. a Deeds
99. c Deeds
100. d Deeds

Index

New York State Commercial Association of
 REALTORS®, Inc., 86
New York State Society of Real Estate
 Appraisers, 86
Niagara Falls, 229
Nonconforming loan, 210
Nonconforming mortgage, 210
Nonconforming use, 227, 340
Noneviction plan, 343
Nonhomogeneity, 253
Nonresident license, 14
Note, 188–91
Notice, 166
 of eviction, 143
 of pendency, 112, 115
 renewal clause, 141–42
Novation, contract, 150–51

O

Obedience, 30
Occidental Chemical Corp., 229
Occupational Safety and Health
 Administration (OSHA), 284
Offer, 12, 43
Offer and acceptance, 150, 156
Offering statement, 340–41
Office exclusive, 60
Office property, 300, 310
Oil lease, 144
110-volt circuits, 247
Open buyer agency agreement, 61
Open-end mortgage, 203
Open listing, 52–53
Operating expenses, 36, 365
Operating statement, 294–96
Operation of law, 151
Opinion, 33–34
Option
 agreement, 159
 renewal, 141–42
Ordinance, 350
Ordinary life estate, 98
Outsourcing, 319
Owner
 objectives, 313
 -occupant, 206
 relations, 320
Ownership
 estates in land, 96–99
 forms of, 99–102
 rights, 91
 unity of, 100

P

Package loan, 203
Panelized housing, 387
Parcel, 92
Parol evidence, 150
Partially amortized loan, 195
Partial performance, 151
Participation loan, 214
Partition, 101, 104, 328
Partnership, 82, 103
Party wall, 117
Passive income, 302
Payment plans, 194–95
Penalties, license, 16, 198
Penalty date, 353
Percentage fee, 51
Percentage lease, 143–44
Percentages, 390–92
Percolation test, 279, 335

Periodic estate, 97, 138
Permanence of investment, 252
Personal property, 97, 342
 real vs., 94–96
 stock as, 103
Personal selling activities, 315–16
Phase I-IV Environmental Assessments
 (audit), 284
Physical characteristics, 252–53
Physical deterioration, 256, 365
Pier, 234
Pier and beam foundation, 234, 238
PITI, 198, 213
Plain-language requirement, 158
Planned unit development (PUD), 339, 344
Planning, 311–14
Planning board, 334
Planning commissioners, 334
Plaster, 242
Plasterboard, 242
Plates, 238
Platform framing construction, 239, 240
Plattsburgh, 5
Plat of subdivision, 124, 126, 337
Plottage, 361
Plumbing, 245
Point (place) of beginning (POB), 122
Points, 197
Police power, 224
Policy and procedures guide, 84–85
Pollution, 277
 septic systems, 279–80
 waste disposal sites, 278–79
 water, 278
Polychlorinated biphenyls (PCBs), 282
Population, 253–54
Possession, 91
Post-and-beam frame construction, 239, 240
Potentially responsible parties (PRBs), 286
Preclusive agreement, 36–37
Prefabricated housing, 387
Preliminary prospectus, 343
Premises
 checking, 176
 description of, 139
 destruction of, 142, 156–57
 maintenance of, 140
 use of, 139
Prepaid items, 179
Prepayment premium, 198
Present value of money, 256–57
Price-fixing, 74–75
Primary mortgage market, 193–94
Principal, 22, 25, 195, 198
 agency duties to, 28–32
 buyer as, 25
 seller as, 25
Principal-agent relationship, 23
Principal-subagent relationship, 44–45
Printed forms, 152
Priority, 112–13
Private adjuster, 321
Private mortgage, 202–4
Private mortgage insurance, 205
Private syndication, 297–98
Probate, 329
Procuring cause of sale, 37
Professional home inspections, 384, 386–87
Professional organizations, 85–87
Profit, 294
Pro forma statement, 296–97
Progression, 361
Promotions, 315

Property
 analysis, 313
 charges, 143
 condition, 36
 deficiencies, 32
 evaluating, 211–12
 faults, 382–84
 income analysis, 294–97
 maintenance, 319
Property Condition Disclosure Statement, 34,
 385
Property management, 309
 agreement, 310–11
 insurance coverage, 320–21
 leases, tenant relations, 316–19
 marketing, 314–16
 owner relations, 320
 planning and budgeting, 311–14
 types of, 310
Property manager, 309
 functions of, 311
 skills of, 321–22
Property value, 32
Proration, 179–81
Protected class, 263
Public health law, 341
Public land-use controls
 building codes, 228
 environmental protection, 226
 environmental protection legislation, 226,
  228
 landmark preservation, 229
 master plan, 225
 subdivision regulations, 228
 zoning, 226–28
Public offering, 298, 343
Public records, 165–66
Public syndication, 297–98
Publications, 218
Puffing, 33
Pur autre vie life estate, 98
Purchase, offers to, 12
Purchase-money mortgage, 196–97, 203
Putnam, 381
Pyramid, 294

Q

Qualified fee estate, 97
Qualifying course, 4
Qualifying ratio, 213
Quantity-survey method, 364
Quiet enjoyment covenant, 129
Quitclaim deed, 131

R

Radioactive waste, 279
Radio advertising, 315
Radon gas, 281–82
Rafter, 242
Rafter roofs, 242
Ranch home, 236
Rates, 392
Ratification, 24
Ready, willing and able buyer, 36
Real estate, 92, 93, 97
 characteristics, 252–53
 cycles, 216–18
 description, 128
 investment syndicate, 297
 license laws, 1–4
  exceptions, 3–4
  qualifications for, 4, 5